D1598549

The French Campaign in Portugal, 1810–1811

An Account by Jean Jacques Pelet

Published
with assistance from
the Roger E. Joseph Memorial Fund
for greater understanding
of public affairs, a cause in which
Roger Joseph believed

THE FRENCH CAMPAIGN IN PORTUGAL, 1810-1811

An Account by Jean Jacques Pelet

Edited,
Annotated, and Translated
by
Donald D. Horward

UNIVERSITY OF MINNESOTA PRESS
MINNEAPOLIS

Printed in the United States of America at
the University of Minnesota Printing Department, Minneapolis
Published in the United Kingdom and India by the Oxford University
Press, London and Delhi, and in Canada
by the Copp Clark Publishing Co. Limited, Toronto

Library of Congress Catalog Card Number: 72-79098

ISBN 0-8166-0658-7

To Annabel Lee

PREFACE

During the summer of 1967, while working in the Archives de la Guerre at Vincennes, France, I came across a 1,178-page handwritten manuscript entitled "Campagne de Portugal."[1] This manuscript, composed by Jean Jacques Germain Pelet-Clozeau, was based on his experiences as first aide-de-camp to Marshal André Masséna during the invasion of Portugal in 1810–1811. The document presented a new and strikingly original view of the campaign which became pivotal in the outcome of the Peninsular War. Although English participants published a significant number of journals, diaries, and correspondence, the French were less anxious to recall the heroic but disastrous efforts of their Army of Portugal. Pelet's manuscript is thus unique for its accurate description and analysis of the campaign from the point of view of Masséna and his staff; in fact, it is the first contemporary French account of the campaign to appear in almost seventy years.

Chef de bataillon Pelet based his account on the daily Journal and letter registries that he kept during the campaign.[2] The accuracy with

1. The manuscript is in the general collection, "Mémoires historiques," bound up in volumes 920^{1-2} and 921^{1-2}. Although it totals 1,178 handwritten pages, there is a discrepancy of 100 pages in the pagination from pp. 699 to 800; thus the last numbered page is 1,278. In addition to the version of the manuscript in the 920–921 series of volumes, there is a rough draft in 917^{1-2}.

2. According to Pelet's service record at the Archives de la Guerre, he held the rank of *chef de bataillon* during the Portuguese campaign; this is usually equated

which he recalled conversations and small incidents attests to his extraordinary memory for details as well as to his industry in entering copious notes in his Journal. Between 1816 and 1818 Pelet utilized information from these sources to compile his "Campagne de Portugal."[3] Its value is enhanced by the author's habit of copying verbatim extensive extracts from his Journal without altering the original impressions that he formed in 1810–1811.[4]

Pelet did not consider publishing any information on the Portuguese campaign until the appearance in 1820 of the twentieth volume of an ambitious series entitled *Victoires, conquêtes, désastres, revers et guerres civiles des français de 1792 à 1815.* Two chapters of that volume contained numerous misconceptions and errors in fact concerning Masséna's invasion, and Pelet therefore prepared a thirty-page rebuttal entitled "Notes sur la campagne de Portugal en 1810 et 1811," which appeared in 1820 as an appendix to the twenty-first volume of the series. In 1827 *Le Spectateur militaire* carried his article "Coup d'oeil militaire sur le Portugal," a short descriptive study of topographical conditions at the time of the invasion.

However, Pelet refused to publish any additional information on the campaign. He was willing and even anxious to bring out studies of the other military operations in which he had participated between 1805 and 1815, but he could not bring himself to share his highly personal observations on the Portuguese invasion with the reading public. Thus the "Campagne de Portugal," though listed in a general inventory of

with the rank of major. However, Masséna's letters to Pelet always addressed him as *Colonel,* and in a letter to Berthier dated January 20, 1811, Masséna requested Pelet's promotion from *lieutenant colonel* to *adjudant commandant.* To further complicate matters, General Marbot, who served during the Empire, writes that the formal rank of *lieutenant colonel* did not exist in the French army in 1810. In all probability Masséna's use of such terms reflects his years of service in the Republican armies prior to the Napoleonic reorganization.

3. In 1841 Commandant Fririon published his father's journal of the campaign in Portugal in *Le Spectateur militaire.* When Pelet read the installments, he complained to the *Spectateur*'s director, "I cannot blame the susceptibility of a son who defends the *souvenirs* of his father, but he must permit me to retrace mine which are supported by a Journal of 1,100 pages written at the time, by a great number of documents, and by a history of the Campaign in Portugal drawn up five years after the events." Hence Pelet's "Campagne de Portugal" was started in 1816 and must have been completed by 1818; these dates are further verified by the fact that he does not cite any works published after 1817.

4. At numerous points in the manuscript, Pelet indicates that he is incorporating lengthy segments of his Journal directly into the "Campagne de Portugal."

manuscripts in the Archives de la Guerre in 1912,[5] remained virtually forgotten at Vincennes for more than one hundred and fifty years.

In a variety of ways Pelet's account adds new dimensions to our understanding of Masséna's invasion of Portugal, designed by Napoleon "to drive the English leopard into the sea." The detailed and colorful narrative describes both the complex operations of the *état major* and the author's personal activities during the campaign. More than five hundred manuscript pages are devoted to the five-month sojourn of the French army before the Lines of Torres Vedras, a period about which little has been previously known. Pelet discusses at length the problems, dissensions, and suffering in the army, as well as Masséna's personal relationships with his subordinates. The author's analysis of the abilities, contributions, and personal conflicts of divisional and corps commanders provides a fresh view of such men as Reynier, Éblé, Montbrun, Loison, and particularly Foy; comments on Marshal Ney both augment and modify previously accepted details of the controversy with Masséna which culminated in Ney's recall to France. In addition the manuscript includes valuable tactical and logistical observations on the maintenance of an army, and specifically a French army, in a hostile country.

Pelet also presents a new interpretation of Masséna. Instead of the distrustful, vindictive, and licentious old condottiere who brought wanton destruction to Portugal, we are shown a brave but compassionate soldier who struggled to maintain discipline and support within his army. The manuscript describes Masséna's concern about the hostages of Coimbra and the garrison of Ciudad Rodrigo, as well as his attempts to curtail the brutality of his soldiers, the excesses of the pillagers, and the exactions and reprisals of his officers. Documents in the Correspondance: Armée de Portugal at Vincennes and the Archives de Masséna now in the possession of André Masséna, the sixth Prince d'Essling, corroborate most of Pelet's assertions and indicate that Masséna was unfairly treated by his enemies at home and abroad for his activities in Portugal. Nevertheless, Pelet did not hesitate to criticize the Marshal when he disagreed with his decisions (though he maintained a discreet silence on the subject of Masséna's relations with his

5. Pelet's manuscript is cited in *Catalogue général des manuscrits des bibliothèques publiques de France: Archives de la guerre* compiled by Louis Tuetey in 1912.

mistress, Henriette Leberton). Indeed, on occasion Pelet became involved in bitter controversies with his commander and only deferred to Masséna's judgment for the good of the service. As an experienced tactician who had taken part in fifteen campaigns, Pelet was similarly critical of many of Wellington's actions and judgments. He presents a detailed analysis of the British maneuvers and strategy, as well as of the overall designs for the defense of Portugal. Although often justifiably skeptical of Wellington's tactics, Pelet acknowledged his notable achievements in mobilizing Portugal; he could not, however, accept Wellington's methods, which he regarded as dishonorable.

The manuscript also provides a valuable refutation of the criticism that has been directed against Pelet himself and his role in the campaign. The vain General Jean-Baptiste Marbot complained in his *Mémoires* (1891) that Pelet was an inadequate replacement for Masséna's former aide-de-camp, Charles Sainte-Croix, whose promotion to the rank of general he termed a "misfortune for Masséna . . . at a moment when, already old and left to his own resources, he had to oppose an enemy such as the Duke of Wellington." Marbot believed that despite his good service in the Austrian campaign of 1809 Pelet lacked "practice in the art of war. . . . Yet Pelet became Masséna's chief adviser; he alone was consulted," while the advice of Ney, Reynier, Junot, the divisional generals, and the chief of staff was almost never sought. "Masséna," said Marbot, "in yielding, by habit, to the inspiration of his first aide-de-camp, disaffected his lieutenants and produced the disobedience which led us into reverses." Masséna's chief of staff, François Nicolas Fririon, also criticized Pelet in his *Journal historique de la campagne de Portugal* (1841), but unlike Marbot he minimized Pelet's role in the campaign. Charles Oman similarly expressed a low opinion of Masséna's aide in the third volume of his *History of the Peninsular War* (1908), where he commented that "Pelet's writings give a poor impression of his brain-power and his love of exact truth."[6] The "Campagne de Portugal," substantiated by documents in the army correspondence and Masséna's archives, as well as by the

6. In a recent biography of Masséna, the author, relying on Marbot, writes, "The Marshal followed Pelet's advice on almost every occasion. Pelet, an officer of the corps of engineer-topographers, was an able mathematician and map-surveyor, but without experience of staff duties with troops. Masséna's reliance on Pelet's counsels gave constant umbrage to his Corps Commanders." See James Marshall-Cornwall, *Marshal Massena* (London, 1965), p. 189.

various eyewitness accounts, proves that these opinions were for the most part unjustified and inaccurate.

Pelet's observations about historical figures, literature, the arts, and language suggest that he was a well-educated man. His manuscript is sprinkled with Latin phrases from such writers as Horace and Vergil; his knowledge of history extended from the time of the ancient Greeks to his own century; his familiarity with works of art, especially paintings, seems extensive; and his understanding of the Portuguese people, history, and culture provided him with excellent background information during the invasion. Pelet was also greatly interested in nature. He spent much of his free time surveying the scenery of the Portuguese countryside, and the manuscript frequently digresses from tactical and logistical considerations to describe a waterfall, a pine forest, or the details of a quaint village. The author's vivid descriptions of Portugal represent more than the professional interest of a topographic officer; they depict a man keenly sensitive to the beauties of nature.

The manuscript reveals Pelet as an unusual young man in a period of great men. Only thirty-three years old at the time of the invasion, he demonstrated a mature grasp of strategy and an excellent understanding of the Peninsular struggle and its ramifications. He was one of the few writers of his century to see Masséna's invasion as the key to the entire Peninsular War. In view of his capacity for work, his powers of analysis and eye for detail, his courage, determination, and loyalty, his detachment, and his unobtrusive personality, it is not surprising that he was indispensable to Masséna, who trusted him implicitly. When Masséna absented himself from headquarters, he delegated the command to Pelet rather than to the old generals. Indeed, the campaign in Portugal was influenced more by Pelet than by any other man in the army, with the exception of Masséna himself. As a lowly *Chef de bataillon* who advised Masséna on all matters (though often without success) and planned detailed maneuvers as well as overall strategy, Pelet often found himself resented and ostracized by influential senior officers and staff members. He nevertheless persisted in his duties, confident of Masséna's support and convinced that his efforts and sacrifices would contribute to the glory of France, his commander, and himself.

Eleven years old when the French Revolution began, Pelet had grown to manhood indoctrinated with the revolutionary principles of *liberté, egalité, et fraternité.* He was a republican and a passionate nationalist committed to the ideas of the Revolution and the Enlightenment, but he apparently had little difficulty accommodating himself to the principles of the Empire. To him France and Napoleon were synonymous and he served them unhesitatingly. There was, however, something incongruous in his psychological makeup. Though he was an ambitious and loyal soldier of the French Empire, he never lost his individuality nor his moral commitment to humanity. As he observed at Coimbra, "How horrible war is when it is shown without the varnish of glory and generosity which hide its awful truth." No doubt he was impressed by the splendor and glory of military life, but he was never able to accustom himself to the necessity of suffering and death. As a participant in a war he detested, Pelet generally found justification for his role in the opportunity it gave him to spread the ideas of the Revolution and, more immediately, to mitigate the horrors of warfare — something he tried to do throughout his military career.

In the translation and editing of this manuscript, I have made a number of editorial revisions, especially in verb forms and punctuation, to make the text more readable. Since some of Pelet's sentences run more than twenty lines in length with only an isolated pronoun, while others are highly compressed expressions of his thought, editorial changes have been necessary to maintain clarity and continuity. Nevertheless, every effort has been made to retain Pelet's meaning and style. Although the manuscript is highly descriptive and includes material that might be considered extraneous, I have omitted only a few illegible phrases and a single paragraph, because Pelet's detailed accounts of locations and sites contain a wealth of information on Portugal as it existed in 1810–1811. In fact, Pelet's descriptions of various locations can no longer be approximated in any printed or archival sources.

At several points Pelet elaborated upon his text in explanatory footnotes; these comments have been incorporated into my own footnotes or, where appropriate, integrated directly into the text. Because of the inadequate maps at his disposal, Pelet was occasionally unable to provide the name of a village; such omissions have been indicated by a long dash (———). However, whenever possible the correct name has been supplied within brackets. In addition, I have eliminated the numerous short Latin phrases scattered through the text, supplied chapter titles, and silently corrected a few inaccuracies. Pelet, for example, refers to the English unit analogous to the French corps as a British corps; I have replaced this term with the appropriate designation, the division. Similarly, errors made in assigning ranks to the various line and staff officers have been rectified.

A great difficulty in editing the manuscript was the determination of the correct spelling of the towns, villages, rivers, and mountains named and often written phonetically by Pelet. With the exception of locations marked with an asterisk (*) at their first appearance in the text, all the many hundreds of sites mentioned have been located on at least one of a number of maps published between 1779 and 1962.[7] Modern spellings of place names have been taken primarily from the gazetteers published by the United States Board on Geographic Names except for major locations that were spelled consistently in most contemporary sources. "Ponte de Murcella," for example, has been retained although the present spelling is "Mucela." Geographic locations retain their national spelling — the Douro River in Portugal is the Duero in Spain.

The names of persons, also occasionally spelled phonetically, have similarly been corrected. The asterisk (*) has again been used at first reference to indicate names of officers that could not be verified in the various lists of the Army of Portugal or the service records at Vincennes. Finally, an Appendix detailing the complement of the French and Allied armies and a Glossary of technical military terms have been included for the reader's convenience.

D. D. H.

Tallahassee, Florida, August 7, 1970

7. Among the most useful maps were "Atlas Geográfico de Espagñe que comprehende de mapa general del Reyno, y los particulares de sus Provincias," by Don Tomas Lopez, 1779; *Maps and Plans of the Principal Movements, Battles, and Sieges in which the British Army was engaged during the War from 1808 to 1814 in the Spanish Peninsula and the South of France,* published by James Wyld, London, 1841; "Carte des lignes de Torres Vedras, elevées par l'armée Anglo-Portugaise pour couvrir Lisbonne en 1810," in *Mémoire sur les Lignes de Torrès Védras . . .* by John T. Jones, trans. M. Gosselin (Paris, 1832); "Western Europe," Army Maps Service, Corps of Engineers, U.S. Army (Washington, D.C., 1953–54), from "Carta Militar de Portugal, Serviços Cartográficos do Exército," 1933–50, etc.; *Portugal and the Cape Verde Islands* and *Spain and Andorra,* Gazetteers No. 50, 51, United States Board on Geographic Names (Washington, D.C. 1961); and *Guia de Portugal,* "Beira Litoral," published by the Fundação Calouste Gulbenkian (Lisbon, 1945). In addition, a number of contemporary road maps distributed by Firestone, Michelin, Hallwag, and Automóvel Club de Portugal were used.

Acknowledgments

The translation and editing of this manuscript of more than a quarter of a million words could not have been undertaken without the aid and support of many people. I would like to acknowledge the financial assistance of the Calouste Gulbenkian Foundation of Lisbon, Portugal. The support, encouragement, and kindness of the former director and assistant director of the foundation's International Department, Drs. Pedro Theotónio Pereira and Jorge Braga de Oliveira, and of its current director, Guilherme de Ayala Monteiro, made possible my research in Paris, Lisbon, and London. I am also indebted to D. António Pereira Forjaz, director of the Academia de Ciências; to the late Colonel João Carlos de Sé Nogueira and his aide, Lieutenant Júlio Emilio Conçalves Louro of the Arquivo Historico Militar; and to the director of the Biblioteca Nacional for their many courtesies, as well as to Miss Maria Tereza Pimenta, who acted as my research assistant in Portugal.

My research in Paris could not have been completed without the cooperation of the former and present directors of the Service historique de l'armée, General Charles de Cossé-Brissac and General Jean Fournier. The aid of their staff — archivist M. Jean-Claude Devos, Lieutenant Colonel Guillaume Mabille du Chesne, chief of the Section ancienne of the Service historique, Mme Hélène Servais, Mme Marguerite Rogaume, and my friend of many years, M. Bernard Farve — was invaluable in completing my research at Vincennes. I am also delighted to acknowledge the assistance of the Sixth Prince and Princess d'Essling and their son Victor André; they permitted me to use their vast archives, and their kind hospitality and helpful comments gave me a better understanding of Masséna and a point of reference for his relationship with Pelet.

I would like to thank the Keeper of the Public Record Office and the Trustees of the British Museum for their cooperation in facilitating my research. I must also express my appreciation to Dean Robert M. Johnson and Dean Thomas R. Lewis for their financial support, and to Dr. Earl R. Beck for listening to me ramble on about Pelet. I have incurred a particular debt of gratitude to Dr. Raoul Vinson, originally of Mauritius and a doctoral candidate in French at Florida State University in 1968 when he worked with me, word by word, through two of my many revisions in the translation. My thanks are also due to a former student, Dr. Jeanne A. Ojala of the University of Utah, and to William R. Johnston for proofreading the manuscript and making valuable suggestions, and to my cartographers William E. Angelus and Richard T. Roche.

Obtaining a picture of Pelet presented serious difficulties; the portrait hanging in the dark stairwell of the Pavillon des Armes at Vincennes has deteriorated badly and defied all attempts at photographic reproduction. However, with the aid of a number of slides taken of the painting at Vincennes, Mrs. Claribel T. Jett has painted an extraordinarily faithful oil portrait of Pelet which has been photographed for inclusion in this book.

I would also like to express my appreciation for the helpful suggestions and advice of the staff of the University of Minnesota Press, whose expertise and judgment improved the style and readability of the manuscript and gave indispensable aid at each phase of the writing. Finally, I must pay homage to the indomitable warrior who made this volume possible — Jean Jacques Pelet. May he rest in peace, confident that those who read his account of the Portuguese campaign will gain new respect for the men who served in the armies of France and followed the Imperial eagles throughout Europe.

CONTENTS

Maps

The French Campaign in Portugal, 1810–1811

An Account by Jean Jacques Pelet

PROLOGUE

Jean Jacques Germain Pelet-Clozeau was born in Toulouse, France, on July 15, 1777. After studying at the College of Science and Arts at Toulouse, he enlisted in the army at the age of twenty-two. Young Pelet became a sergeant in an auxiliary battalion of Haute Garonne in 1800, but in line with his interests and training he was soon reassigned to a unit of engineers in the Army of Italy. The following year Pelet was promoted to second lieutenant and employed as a geographic engineer. He accompanied Marshal Jean Baptiste Jourdan on his reconnaissance of the Tyrolian mountains and continued to work in the topographic section of the army until 1805 when Marshal Masséna, the commander of the Army of Italy, asked him to serve in his *état major*. Within a month, Pelet was one of Masséna's aides-de-camp, and he was to serve in this capacity for the next six years.

Fighting at Caldiero on October 28–30, 1805, Pelet was wounded by a gunshot in the head; he nevertheless accompanied Masséna to Naples in January 1806. After serving with distinction in the Calabrian campaign, Pelet was promoted to the rank of captain. He was in Poland with Masséna in 1807 but did not see further action until 1809 when Austria and England had formed the Fifth Coalition against France. During the advance along the Danube into Austria, Pelet was wounded in the bitter fighting at the bridge of Ebersberg on May 3; twelve days later he was made a *chef de bataillon*. He was in the thick of the battle at Essling and his occupation of the vital Island of Moulin on July 2 guaranteed the passage of the Danube. Ten days later he fought at Znäim where an armistice was signed, culminating in the Treaty of Schönbrunn of October 14, 1809.[1]

When Pelet returned to Paris after the victorious Austrian campaign, he remained attached to Masséna's staff. The fall and winter of 1809–1810 were peaceful and as he regained his strength he looked forward to new campaigns. The exhausted Masséna, suffering from injuries received in a fall before the battle of Wagram and a serious respiratory illness, had retired to his estate at Rueil to recuperate. In the early spring of 1810 rumors began to circulate that Masséna, recently created Prince d'Essling, would receive a new assignment, but it was not until he attended Napoleon's marriage ceremony in April 1810 that the Emperor indicated his intentions with the words, "My cousin, I intend to give you an important command." On April 16 Masséna received a dispatch from the minister of war, General Henri Clarke, declaring that "His Majesty the Emperor has decided the Prince d'Essling will command the army of Portugal."[2] Masséna's primary assignment was to invade Portugal and drive the English into the sea. The next day an imperial decree announced the creation of the Army of Portugal, composed of the 2nd, 6th, and 8th Corps of the Army of Spain.[3]

Masséna was not happy about his appointment and when he visited Napoleon's Major General, Marshal Alexandre Berthier, Prince de Neufchâtel, on April 18, he expressed his apprehension about reassuming command of an army before he had fully recovered from his injuries. He also expressed serious reservations about the personal qualities and limitations of his subordinates, Ney and Junot.

Dissatisfied with Berthier's unsympathetic attitude, Masséna resolved to appeal directly to Napoleon for relief from his unwelcome assignment. When he reached the Emperor's quarters, he found that Napoleon was determined to send him to Portugal in spite of his misgivings. Napoleon accused Masséna of creating imaginary problems

1. Biographical details are based on Jean Jacques Pelet, *Mémoires sur la guerre de 1809, en Allemagne* (Paris, 1824–26).

2. Édouard Gachot, "Masséna en Portugal, 1810–1811," *Revue de la société des amis du musée de l'armée* (Paris, 1958), LXI, 19.

3. *Correspondance de Napoléon Ier publiée par ordre de l'Empereur Napoléon III* (Paris, 1858–69), No. 16385, Imperial Decree, April 17, 1810, XX, 338.

and isolating himself in a world of pessimism. The Emperor promised, "You will lack nothing in resources. In Portugal you will be absolute master and you will make all your own preparations for opening the campaign. Do not speak to me of insufficient means." Dismissing Masséna's objections as insignificant, Napoleon asked, "Who will I send to Portugal to restore my affairs, which have been compromised by incompetency? Am I able to leave Paris now? I can send you in my place, but you refuse me with futile and imaginary pretexts that you fear the insubordination of the generals under your command." Napoleon admitted that Ney and Junot were "impetuous and passionate" but asked, "Do you suppose they will defy your orders with impunity and dare to incur my disgrace?"[4] Masséna had very little opportunity to present his views during this one-sided interview.[5] After leaving the Emperor's quarters, he had no choice but to begin preparations to assume command of the Army of Portugal.

In the meantime Pelet was informed of Masséna's new appointment and notified that he had been named as the Prince's first aide-de-camp, replacing Charles Escorches de Sainte-Croix, who had been promoted and given a brigade of dragoons in Junot's 8th Corps. Pelet collected his belongings, said farewell to family and friends, and set off to join the Prince. Meanwhile Masséna, accompanied by his son, his secretary Vacherat, his mistress Henriette Leberton, and a small entourage, left Rueil on the morning of April 26 for his last campaign. Pelet eagerly anticipated the forthcoming operations, confident that French arms would repeat the heroic deeds he had witnessed on the banks of the Danube in 1809. Masséna, however, did not share his young aide's optimism. He was well aware that many of his fellow marshals had marched their corps into the Peninsula during the previous two and one half years only to become sunk in a quagmire of insoluble problems.

In 1807, while Masséna was still in Eastern Europe, Napoleon's first

4. When Ney learned of Masséna's appointment, he wrote to Berthier on May 7, 1810, "Although it is difficult for me always to be in a subordinate position, I am at least obliged to recognize with satisfaction in these circumstances that the abilities and experience of the Prince d'Essling justify the choice." See Henri Bonnal, *La vie militaire du maréchal Ney, duc d'Elchingen, prince de la Moskowa* (Paris, 1910–14), III, 316.

5. Jean Baptiste Koch, *Mémoires de Masséna rédigés d'après les documents qu'il a laissés et sur ceux du dépot de la guerre et du dépot des fortifications* (Paris, 1848–50), VII, 20–21.

army unit, the *Ier Corps d'observation de la Gironde,* commanded by General Junot, the future Duc d'Abrantès, had crossed the Bidassoa River into Spain and marched toward Portugal. After extreme hardships in western Spain and on the mountainous frontier of Portugal, Junot's advance guard staggered into Lisbon on November 30. Within a month the French had solidified their control in Portugal: the major fortresses were occupied, the Portuguese army disbanded with the exception of some 10,000 elite troops sent to France, and the population partially disarmed. The Regent of Portugal, John, had fled into exile in Brazil, and Portugal seemed firmly in the hands of the French.

While Portugal was being subdued Napoleon sent more than a hundred thousand troops into Spain, deposed the incompetent Bourbons, and installed his brother Joseph as king in Madrid. However, from Galicia to Catalonia the Spanish, led by the local clergy and minor officials, took up arms in defense of their king and country. England, always anxious to support any country that defied Napoleon, began negotiations to send supplies and financial support to the Spanish. The insurrection spread to Portugal during the summer of 1808, and in August Sir Arthur Wellesley landed in central Portugal with an expeditionary force of more than 14,500 men. Wellesley inflicted defeats on Junot at Roliça and Vimeiro, and the French general, decisively outnumbered and isolated from the other French corps in Spain, was forced to sign the Convention of Sintra and evacuate Portugal.

Simultaneously resistance in Spain reached a climax in July 1808 when General Pierre Dupont de l'Étang was defeated and forced to surrender at Baylen. As a result of this battle, a counteroffensive by the Spanish armies, and the determined resistance of several Spanish towns, King Joseph was forced to retire behind the Ebro River with the remnants of his armies and await Napoleon's aid.

The Emperor was exasperated by the disasters in Spain. Hoping to recoup the French losses, crush the Spanish armies, drive the English into the sea, and pacify the entire Peninsula, Napoleon invaded Spain with 100,000 men. Within a month, he had dispersed the Spanish armies and entered Madrid. He had only to march down the Tagus valley, defeat the English army, and occupy Lisbon to ensure his control of the Peninsula. But before Napoleon could implement these plans, he was diverted toward Corunna by a British army of some 30,000 men under the command of Lieutenant General John Moore. Although the Emperor pursued Moore as far as Astorga, he was forced to return to Paris and leave the pursuit to Soult. Moore's army was finally caught at Corunna and after an indecisive battle forced to embark for England.

Before leaving Spain for Paris Napoleon, still concerned about Portugal and its vital position in the Peninsula, ordered Soult to invade Portugal from the north while Marshal Claude Victor advanced westward from Spain. Although Soult successfully occupied Oporto at the end of March, he was subsequently forced from the city by Wellesley and driven out of Portugal in May 1809.

When Napoleon learned of the failure of this second invasion, he decided to launch another expedition against Portugal as soon as possible. He ordered Soult to form an army composed of his own corps and those of Ney and Mortier. "These three corps," he wrote, "are to maneuver together, march upon the English . . . and drive them into the sea."[6] But before Soult could execute the new orders, his forces were directed to aid King Joseph, whose capital was threatened by Wellesley's drive on Talavera. By the time Madrid's safety was assured, Napoleon had changed his plans. At the end of July he wrote to General Clarke, "No attack is to be made on Portugal during the month of August (it is too hot), but they are to make preparations for the expedition in February."[7] Thus the Portuguese remained unconquered and defiant, and operations and counter-operations continued in the Peninsula through the last half of 1809 without predictable end.

When Napoleon returned to Paris in the fall of 1809 after the Austrian campaign, he contemplated another expedition to the Peninsula. He was determined to end the Peninsular War, the "bleeding sore" which dragged on interminably and sapped the strength of the Empire. Portugal no longer affected his economic strategy against England, but it served as a base of operations for the ever-increasing

6. *Correspondance de Napoléon Ier*, No. 15340, Napoleon to Clarke, June 12, 1809, XIX, 116–17.

7. *Ibid.*, No. 15594, Napoleon to Clarke, July 29, 1809, XIX, 338.

British forces and a direct menace to imperial control in the Peninsula. As long as the English remained in Portugal, supported by its citizens and its government, they were a constant threat to isolated French units as well as a source of moral, economic, and military strength to all those opposing French domination.

Despite Napoleon's intentions to return to the Peninsula himself, the pressure of domestic and foreign problems forced him to remain in Paris. He therefore began to search for a general with the ability and experience to counter the victorious Wellington, as well as the determination and perseverance to drive the English to the banks of the Tagus. As we have seen, he selected André Masséna, *l'enfant chéri de la victoire.* The choice was a logical one since Masséna had had as much experience leading French troops as the Emperor himself. He had commanded the vital right wing of Napoleon's army during the first Italian campaign, and while Bonaparte was pursuing his destinies in Egypt Masséna achieved his greatest victory by turning back the Russian armies of Suvórov at Zurich and saving France from imminent invasion. His two-month defense of Genoa in 1800 was instrumental in Napoleon's victory at Marengo; as a result, he was awarded command of the Army of Italy. Masséna held various independent commands in Italy until 1807, when he was given a corps of the Grand Army. He commanded the right flank of this army in the Austrian campaign of 1809 and played a major role in the bloody battle of Aspern-Essling. Indeed, throughout his military career, Masséna had demonstrated those qualities which Napoleon felt were necessary for the success of French arms in the Peninsula. And so it was that Masséna found himself on the route to Spain, unhappy and apprehensive about his appointment but unable to alter the Emperor's decision.

Nevertheless the situation in the Peninsula looked promising. The armies of the Spanish insurgents and the hostile resistance of the population seemed on the verge of collapse. At the beginning of 1810 Soult had invaded Andalusia with 70,000 men and subdued the entire region except for Cadiz in less than two weeks. The corps of Suchet and Augereau dominated the plains of Aragon and Catalonia, and other detached units occupied scattered cities throughout Spain. Indeed, with 370,000 French troops in the Peninsula, 100,000 of which were nominally under his command, and with the Emperor's personal guarantee of all the necessary men and supplies, Masséna could look forward to a successful campaign culminating in the capture of Lisbon and the expulsion of the English.

Chapter One

PRELIMINARY OPERATIONS IN SPAIN THE ARRIVAL OF MASSÉNA

I have always considered the War of the Revolution [1792–1815] to be a continuation of the old rivalry existing between France and England—an endless struggle between a continental and a maritime power. Initiated by an avaricious desire to seize our disorganized provinces, rather than by a need to protect or avenge the throne, this war was later carried on to contain the ideals of the Revolution. The conflict no longer had any actual object after the exhausted and often dissident powers saw a stable government established in France. However, England recognized that her eternal rival was growing considerably more powerful as a result of the prodigious activity that follows all revolutions. In her future she could foresee the loss of her maritime preponderance, her [economic] monopoly, and with them her complete ruin. From that time on, she decided to fight until the death, prepared to employ without hesitation all the schemes at her disposal.

I have also regarded all the wars that have taken place on the Continent since the revolutionary period as episodic actions in this greater struggle between land and sea and as diversions created against us by English gold and intrigues. Usually, France has been attacked or has been obliged to occupy strategic positions in the interest of the system of war in which she found herself. Thus in 1805, at the moment when France was prepared to strike a fatal blow to

England and when the actual embarkation for England was about to take place, Austria attacked our unprotected frontiers without any declaration of war. Moreover, the campaigns of 1806 and 1807 were the result of British negotiations, interrupted momentarily by the battle of Austerlitz. The northern aggression, as violent as it was unexpected, ended twice—at Jena and at Friedland. The Treaty of Tilsit, aimed against England alone, indicated clearly enough that she was the soul of this fallen coalition, just as the Diet of the Kings at Erfurt proved how little she wanted peace. Therefore the British government was declared the enemy of all Europe. A means for combating her power was then agreed upon.[1]

The occupation of Spain seemed to be acknowledged as necessary, and it was legitimatized by all the sovereigns who recognized its new king [Joseph]. Spain was invaded by fresh troops sent to reinforce our weak detachments, which had been forced to evacuate Madrid. An auxiliary English army, waging war on Spain, immediately appeared. Before the end of December 1808, this army was pursued and forced to seek refuge aboard its vessels. All the Spanish troops were dispersed and the authority of the weak Joseph was ultimately confirmed; the British cabinet, however, had already found auxiliaries for its vanquished army. Austria was again preparing aggression, and Bavaria was invaded without cause or previous notification. There was also a mass uprising of all the Germans, though this disturbance did not have time to become effective. Thus Napoleon was forced to leave his affairs in Spain as quickly as possible. The battles of Eckmühl and Wagram once more avenged the double violation of the treaties of Lunéville and Pressburg.[2]

It is said that the British oligarchy, after testing its strength by imposing conditions on the Prince of Wales's regency,[3] united all the

1. By the treaties of Tilsit, signed in 1807 after the collapse of the Fourth Coalition, all the European nations except Portugal and Sweden joined the Continental System against England.

2. The battles of Eckmühl (April 22, 1809) and Wagram (July 5–6, 1809) were major encounters in the defeat of Austria and the Fifth Coalition. The Treaty of Lunéville terminated Austria's role in the Second Coalition, while the Treaty of Pressburg forced Austria from the Third Coalition.

3. George IV, then Prince of Wales, was approached in 1788 when George III lapsed into insanity. Pitt and the cabinet proposed a regency under the terms of which the queen would retain custody of the king and his household and the prince regent would be unable to create new peerages, dispose of the king's property, or grant office pensions. George III recovered sufficiently to reassume the

old ministerial nobility of Europe, who were frightened by the direct threats of Napoleon and the advancement of his popular system. It appears that the true interests of the sovereigns and states, still part of our alliance, were sacrificed in many instances to the private interests of this monstrous league. At first the nations of the north [Prussia and Russia] were called upon to help the southern countries until the latter were able to support the invasion of the north. The Russian war became a turning point of this terrible drama, and in two or three days the fate of Europe was decided. As soon as England's league discovered that the French army was no longer invincible, they united everyone against us. They were forced into a heterogeneous coalition, secretly organized and directed by the ministerial oligarchy. Napoleon, pressed by all of Europe, winning where he could fight in person and losing where he could not be present, suffered one reverse after another. With his defeat the long struggle ended. England believes she has triumphed, but indeed she has formed a force that will demand an accounting for her invasion and domination of the seas.

If the Spanish War was only one act of this huge European war, the campaign in Portugal becomes only an episodic scene, but a scene of the highest interest. The two greatest European powers, fighting hand to hand, were about to decide the fate of Portugal and Spain. Tired of resistance without success, of the destruction brought about by its defenders as well as by its enemy, Spain would have been pacified and easily subjugated with the English army's departure. If this campaign is not comparable to some of those catastrophes to which we have since become accustomed, it has nevertheless retained much brilliance because of the great reputations of the generals who commanded the opposing armies, as well as the famous warriors who were there. It offers to the world a unique opportunity to examine closely and judge those two great captains who fought as though in a tilt-field. One came and ended a career that had been made illustrious by many triumphs. The other found a celebrity that filled all Europe with memories of him.

powers of the crown before the Prince of Wales could be declared regent. In 1811 George III became irremediably mad; the Prince of Wales then undertook the responsibilities of the realm although fettered by a number of ministerial regulations.

My memoirs of this campaign will offer to military men a rigorous examination of projects and movements, a continuous application of military principles to carefully selected strategic points of action, an evaluation of the immediate and the far-reaching consequences of errors, a description of the continuing administrative work, a general consideration of principal operations, and finally a kind of theoretical and practical picture of the war. The reader will find subjects for reflection and instruction in this memoir.

There are many analogies between the last Spanish war [1808–1813] and that of 1701.[4] The events of 1701 might have furnished excellent lessons in terms both of mistakes to be avoided and of good examples to be followed. In fact the situation then was similar to what it is now: a changing dynasty; a prince who first left his capital and then reconquered it by taking up arms against insurrections that were stimulated by foreign powers and sustained by their armies. One should note, however, in the more recent period the appearance of terrible insurrectionary activity throughout all of Spain, whereas in 1701 uprisings took place only in the kingdoms of Aragon, Valencia, and, much later, Catalonia. On the other hand, there was a great increase in the land armies sent against Spain, though they lacked the support of a navy which fought the Anglo-Dutch forces to great advantage, effectively supporting the military operations [in the War of Spanish Succession]. One can also find analogies in the behavior of the Spanish in both the earlier and the later campaigns. The entire country was infested by guerrillas. Food was destroyed; communications were cut; barracks and convoys were seized; patrols and the patients in hospitals were massacred; villages, houses, and mountain positions were fortified and defended with dreadful tenacity. In addition there was a lack of cooperation among the united French armies and their generals. Moreover, all the disorders and extraordinary events customarily found in revolutions were increased by the fury of fanaticism.

Although these two wars were analogous, their results were opposite. The reason might be found in the political situation of

4. In the War of Spanish Succession (1702–13) Louis XIV's grandson, Philip, Duc d'Anjou, inherited the Spanish throne as a result of King Charles II's deathbed testament. France and Spain were forced to fight a European alliance to guarantee Philip's inheritance.

Europe, which was quite dissimilar at the two periods. Northern Europe was occupied by its own war, which continued after the War of Spanish Succession. The German Empire was partitioned in favor of France and Austria; the small states had a multitude of private interests; Emperor Joseph had died; changes had taken place in the policies of Queen Anne; and, above all, there was the difference in Europe's anxiety over the aggrandizement of Louis XIV's power and the terror that Napoleon inspired. Moreover, in this war we again find England constantly active and obstinate—the eternal ally and protector of all of France's enemies. The Anglo-Portuguese armies, commanded by Lord Galway, opposed our armies just as those of Count Lippe had in 1762.[5] History offers only a continual succession of similar events, and those who complain of the wars in our time can read how rare are periods of peace and happiness on this earth.

The following paragraph is [part] of a memorandum that I sent to Marshal Masséna and Prince Berthier[6] in October 1808. It contained a number of prudent and moderate views on the Spanish war and ended with this prophetic passage; it will be easy for me to prove it was not written afterward, like so many other accounts, since the copies I sent can be found in the papers of the two marshals.

If these dispositions are not followed, if our armies indulge in their usual disorderly behavior, if they reduce the people to the point where they have lost everything, if they drive well-intentioned men to despair, if they add to great anger and passion the need to avenge religion, country, liberty, and family, if they provoke insurrection everywhere throughout the country—then I am not afraid to say that this war will be the most difficult and longest that France has ever undertaken. In the circumstances in which we now find ourselves, the most fatal result will ensue. We have now only one ally, who

5. Henri de Massue, Marquis de Ruvigny, Earl of Galway (1648–1720), commanded the allied army against the Franco-Spanish forces in 1706–7. Although he seized Madrid in 1706, his army was decisively defeated by the Duke of Berwick at Almanza on April 25, 1707. Count Frederick William Schaumbourg-Lippe-Buckeburg (1724–77) entered military service in 1743 and fought in the armies of several German states. In 1762 he served as commander in chief of the Anglo-Portuguese army against the Franco-Spanish forces and played a major role in the reorganization of the Portuguese army.

6. Louis Alexandre Berthier, Prince de Neufchâtel et Wagram (1753–1815), enlisted in an engineer unit in 1766, but he was soon attracted to the *état major* and served Rochambeau, Lafayette, Luckner, and Biron in this capacity. In 1796 he joined Napoleon's Army of Italy in a similar position and although created marshal in 1804, continued as Napoleon's chief of staff until 1814.

remains attached to us solely because of its interest in sharing the spoils; we are surrounded by vassals who are subservient only because of our brilliant successes and the strength of our arms, by formidable neighbors who possess great armaments, and by sovereigns who are pained by the memory of humiliations and losses. Finally there is this eternal enemy, whose commerce, which we have failed to intercept, provides the financial means for arming an entire country of insurgents against us. Like a relentless torrent of lava, our army is quite able to march across Spain and devastate the countryside that might provide food for us. Yet we shall always find fierce enemies in front of us, and we leave even worse ones behind. Our armies will pursue elusive armies that always flee and disappear toward the sea, only to reappear again a few leagues beyond, while invisible hands destroy everyone who does not remain with our army. What will become of our forces as they pursue these elusive enemies who renew themselves unceasingly; as, fighting in arid countries, they suffer from hunger, fatigue, poor climate, and the deprival of many necessities? What will Europe do when she sees our veteran commanders and soldiers, the backbone of our armies, destroyed and devoured by countless disasters while young conscripts are pushed into the cadres; when she sees our exhausted treasury, far from being maintained by the war, collapse into this abyss?

Let no one accuse me of creating fantasies. Nothing I am saying here is entirely new. We experienced much of it during the War of Spanish Succession, which lasted for thirteen years. Such misfortunes must be avoided, and we can succeed if strength and power are linked with wise policies. Perhaps with such measures disaster can be averted.

At the period when our campaign in Portugal commenced, the French armies occupied a large part of Spain. Marshal Soult had under his command the troops of Marshals Mortier and Victor and General Sebastiani.[7] After the battle of Ocaña (November 19, 1809),

7. Nicolas Jean de Dieu Soult, Duc de Dalmatie (1769–1851), enlisted in a royal infantry regiment in 1785, was promoted to general of division in 1799, and took part in Masséna's Zurich campaign. Created a marshal in 1804, he served at Austerlitz, Jena, and Eylau and in 1809 fought Sir John Moore's army at Corunna. Invading northern Portugal, he occupied Oporto on March 29 and remained there until he was driven out by Wellesley. Soult was named major general of the French armies in Spain on January 14, 1810, and within a month had invaded and conquered most of Andalusia.

Édouard Adolphe Mortier, Duc de Trévise (1768–1835), became a second lieutenant in 1791, general of division in 1799, and marshal in 1804; he commanded Masséna's fourth division at Zurich and a corps in the campaigns of 1806–7. Sent to Spain in 1808, he commanded the 5th Corps at the second siege of Saragossa.

Claude Victor Perrin, Duc de Bellune (1764–1841), enlisted in the artillery in

he entered Andalusia and soon began the siege of Cadiz. Thereafter the corps of Marshal Mortier advanced in the direction of Badajoz to Zafra. A kind of army of the interior and the Royal Guard maintained the capital and a few of the surrounding cities. General Suchet succeeded in pacifying Aragon, which had been humbled by the siege of Saragossa, where the leaders were annihilated and patriotism was exalted.[8] Suchet besieged Lérida, where fortune smiled and gave him the success which had been denied to the Grand Prince de Condé.[9] Marshal Macdonald occupied Catalonia and defended it against continual attacks by the mountain people.[10] With a division in the north, General Bonnet had to hold Asturias against attacks by the rebels and the Armies of Galicia.[11] With only a few troops Generals Séras and Kellermann protected Biscay and Old Castile as well as a line of direct communication with France.[12] The corps that were to form the Army of Portugal were situated as follows: the 8th Corps, commanded

1781 and was named general of brigade in 1795. He served under Macdonald in Italy in 1799 and became a marshal in 1807. Victor was at Marengo, Jena, and Friedland and in October 1808 went to Spain with the 1st Corps. He seized Madrid in December 1808 and the next July encountered Wellesley at Talavera.

Horace François Bastien Sebastiani, Comte de la Porta (1772–1851), a Corsican, became a second lieutenant in the French army in 1789 and general of division in 1805; he served at Arcola, Marengo, and Austerlitz and undertook several diplomatic missions for Napoleon to Turkey. In 1809, after his role in the capture of Madrid, he was given command of the 4th Corps.

8. Louis Gabriel Suchet, Duc d'Albuféra (1770–1826), joined a cavalry regiment in 1791, became general of brigade in 1798 and marshal in 1811; he served in all the major battles of the first Italian campaign, at Austerlitz, Jena, Friedland, and in the second siege of Saragossa. He was given command of the 3rd Corps (Army of Aragon) and achieved notable success in Catalonia.

9. Louis II, Prince de Condé (1621–86), called "Grand Condé," was a brilliant French general who won the battles of Rocroi, Fribourg, Nördlingen, and Lens. Involved in the Fronde, Condé allied himself with the Spanish against Cardinal Mazarin but was ultimately restored to favor after the Peace of the Pyrenees in 1659.

10. Étienne Jacques Macdonald, Duc de Tarente (1765–1840), became a lieutenant in 1785, general of division in 1794, and marshal in 1809. He served at Marengo and was minister to Denmark in 1801. Disgraced in the "Moreau affair" during 1804, he did not serve actively again until 1809; the following year he took command of the 7th Corps in Spain.

11. Count Jean Pierre Bonnet (1768–1857) enlisted in 1786 and served in the Italian and German campaigns through 1799. He became general of division in 1803 and went to Spain in 1808.

12. Count Jean Mathieu Séras (1765–1815) entered the army as a lieutenant in 1791 and became general of division in 1805. He served with the Army of Italy, 1794–1801; he commanded an infantry division in Masséna's corps of the Grand Army and was wounded at Wagram. Séras was given one of Junot's divisions in 1810 and sent to Spain where he was charged with the defense of León.

by the Duc d'Abrantès,[13] was at Valladolid with units extending beyond Astorga, which was captured on May 6 after a siege of fifteen days. Marshal Ney,[14] with the 6th Corps, was between Salamanca, his headquarters, and Ciudad Rodrigo, which had suffered little. The 2nd Corps had remained at Plasencia after the battle of Talavera; it was now placed under the command of General Reynier.[15] He had restored the bridge at Almaraz and moved on toward Mérida.

In this state of affairs the Marshal, Prince d'Essling, arrived at Bayonne on April 30. Rumors had spread along the way and particularly at Bordeaux that he would enter Portugal at the head of one hundred thousand men.[16] The instructions I received from the Prince informed me that he was going to take command of the Army of Portugal, composed of the 2nd, 6th, and 8th Corps. The 2nd Corps, with headquarters at Garrovillas on the Tagus and one division at Mérida, remained for the time being with the Army of Andalusia. The 8th Corps had many conscripts. The Prince was governor-general of

François Étienne Kellermann, Duc de Valmy (1770–1835), acted as his father's aide-de-camp and became general of division in 1800; he served in Napoleon's Italian campaigns and at Austerlitz. As a divisional commander during Junot's invasion of Portugal, he fought at Vimeiro and negotiated the Convention of Sintra in 1808. Returning to Spain in 1809, he commanded French-occupied districts in northern Spain, first at Valladolid and then Salamanca.

13. Jean Andoche Junot, Duc d'Abrantès (1771–1813), enlisted in 1791 and served as Napoleon's aide-de-camp in 1796; he later became governor of Paris, general of division, and ambassador to Portugal. Placed in command of the French army for the invasion of Portugal in 1807, Junot was forced by Wellesley to withdraw after the battle of Vimeiro and the Convention of Sintra. In 1810 he was appointed commander of the 8th Corps before it entered Spain.

14. Michel Ney, Duc d'Elchingen, Prince de la Moskowa (1769–1815), enlisted in 1787; he was promoted to general of division in 1799 and marshal in 1804. He served Masséna in Switzerland in 1799, took part in the battle of Hohenlinden, pacified Switzerland, and commanded the 6th Corps at Elchingen, Jena, Eylau, and Friedland. In 1808 he was sent to Spain with the 6th Corps.

15. Count Jean Louis Reynier (1771–1814) joined the army as an adjutant of the *état major* in 1792 and later served as chief of staff in the Army of the Rhine. He was disgraced in the Egyptian campaign and did not receive a command until 1805. Reynier served as Neapolitan minister of navy and war in 1808; two years later he was made commander of Soult's old 2nd Corps in Spain.

16. When Napoleon planned to go to Spain himself in 1809, he ordered Henri Clarke, minister of war, "to assemble 80,000 infantry and 15,000 or 16,000 cavalry by the beginning of December." On November 23 the Imperial Guard was alerted for duty in the Peninsula and five days later Berthier was named chief of staff for the French army in Spain. See *Correspondance de Napoléon, Ier*, No. 15909, Napoleon to Clarke, October 7, 1809, XIX, 648–49; No. 16021, Napoleon to Clarke, November 23, 1809, XX, 49–50; No. 16028, Napoleon to Berthier, November 28, 1810, XX, 54.

Old Castile, of the Kingdom of León, of Asturias with Santander, and of the province of Soria. It was announced that a large detachment of the Imperial Guard would arrive at Burgos and Soria. The Prince was to drive the Spanish into Galicia, besiege Ciudad Rodrigo, harass the English army, and threaten it with detachments to prevent it from marching either along the left bank of the Tagus or toward Madrid.[17] In either case, he was to maneuver on its rear in such a way that the enemy would be caught between the army of King Joseph and the Army of Portugal.

The English cantoned near Almeida with twenty-five thousand men and an equal number of Portuguese, not including an English division situated near Elvas and Badajoz. Ultimately, the Prince was to prepare to march with the 6th and 8th Corps on the right bank of the Tagus toward Lisbon, while the 2nd Corps marched on the left bank. This army was to be fed and maintained by the people of the countryside. Finally, the Prince was obliged to communicate with both the 3rd Corps, situated near Saragossa, and the king at Madrid, but was to receive orders only from the Emperor. Along with his instructions he was given only two or three rather poor accounts about Portugal and none of the maps or reconnaissance which were essential for such a difficult and unfamiliar country. There were many reports in Paris, but unfortunately we did not have them.[18]

Our trip to Spain was to be made by convoy; the dangers and the difficulties were singularly magnified because guerrillas could be alerted several days in advance. Our train was considerable, but the capture of a prince was a strong temptation to the partisan bands. We had an escort of only two hundred cavalry, who were not worth fifty infantrymen in the wooded passages of the mountains. Nevertheless, our trip was quite peaceful. Instead of the deserts that we expected, we found Biscay to be well cultivated and very green. At

17. Napoleon wrote, "I do not choose to enter Lisbon at present, because I should not be able to feed the town [and] the immense population. . . . The summer must be spent in taking Ciudad Rodrigo, and afterward Almeida; the campaign must be managed methodically and not by disconnected expeditions." See *Correspondance de Napoléon Ier*, No. 16519, Napoleon to Berthier, May 29, 1810, XX, 447–49.

18. One of the reports given to Masséna by Berthier described the Portuguese of Beira, through which he would march, as "thieves—avaricious, treacherous, brutal, haughty, of ill-humor, and as wretched in body as in spirit." See Gachot, "Masséna en Portugal, 1810–1811," LXI, 21.

Vitoria we had proof that our presence was welcome, for as we arrived on a Sunday the inhabitants of the city came toward us in large numbers. At nightfall the dances and the songs, the guitars and the castanets, gave a happy and festive atmosphere to this fair city which contrasted strongly with our notions of Spain.

While passing through Villafranca, the Prince found his first opportunity to express the sentiments that motivated him. The lieutenant in command there thought it was his duty to have an insurgent hanging from the gibbet all the time to serve as an example; he boasted of his punctuality in replacing the corpses that fell with men who had not been put on trial. The Prince became very angry and declared he would have him expelled from the city, although it was outside the limits of his jurisdiction. Never has the Prince acted without humanity and justice. The unfortunate have always found safety and protection with him.

At Vitoria, General Séras was absent. He had gone with a few troops toward Bilbao near Santander on hearing reports that the English had landed there and that Marquesito Porlier[19] was marching on Santander to the left of General Avril,[20] who was retiring toward Torrelavega. Simultaneously, another regiment of the enemy was moving toward Reinosa to cut his retreat. We had no news of General Bonnet, who was commanding in Asturias. It was not probable that the English had landed between the detachments of Generals Bonnet and Séras unless with a very strong division or a very small party. It was probably an insignificant communication between their vessels and the shore. Nevertheless, the Prince wanted to wait at Vitoria for the news. General Séras returned in the evening. There was nothing true in the reports.

19. Juan Díaz, Marquesito Porlier (1788–1815), served as a midshipman at Trafalgar and in 1808 joined a Valencian regiment. As a result of his guerrilla activity, the Junta of Asturias made him a colonel. In the campaign in Galicia, Porlier was given the title "El Marquesito" or "little marquis." The regency promoted him to a captain general of Asturias until the return of King Ferdinand VII. As a result of the king's reactionary policies, he proclaimed the Constitution of 1812. Betrayed, he was seized, tried, and executed for treason on October 3, 1815.

20. Baron Jean Jacques Avril (1752–1839) was promoted to lieutenant in 1775 and general of brigade in 1795; he served with Hoche in the Vendée, Masséna in Italy, and Junot in the first Portuguese campaign. After the Convention of Sintra, he was returned to Spain where he ruled as governor of Bilbao until his recall to Paris in 1810.

The next day we left; it was not necessary to cross the Ebro to recognize that we were in Old Castile. We had hardly crossed the boundary when we saw a very different country, as uninviting as Biscay had been agreeable. One might say that all industry stopped beyond the obelisk that marked the boundary. The Ebro was a torrent only one hundred yards wide, carrying reddish water amid the sand, but crossed by a beautiful bridge at Miranda. Beyond it we saw the defile of Pancorbo, twelve to fourteen thousand yards long and about sixty yards wide. The road crossed the Sierra de Oca [Obarenes] through an immense and hideous break in rocks that rose vertically on both sides to a very great height. At some points it was only the width of the road and a little stream that ran into the Ebro. At the western exit of the defile, the village of Pancorbo was located. This unique passage, controlling the entrance to Castile (for a distance of several leagues), was defended in front by a fieldwork with cannon. The peak of the rocks to the right was occupied by masonry fortifications, and halfway up the slope above a village were two little positions, one of which had guns. On the opposite exterior slope were two advanced works or lunettes. Occupying the height, the fort was situated to facilitate control of the defile. Our troops were garrisoned there.

This gorge had a singularly curious geological construction. It appeared to be the result of a violent separation in the middle of the chain of rocks. This formation was isolated from the principal range of mountains which separates the waters of the ocean from the Mediterranean: we crossed it the next day at Monasterio.

Burgos did not offer anything of interest to us. Nevertheless, we admired the cathedral and went to visit the castle where French valor was later to be demonstrated. The defense of the castle was especially honorable to General Dubreton, since the post was insignificant by itself.[21] Placed on the summit of an elevation, the position was formed by an old castle, where a battery for seven or eight cannon was being built, and a neighboring church which had been joined to it. All this was enclosed with a rather skillfully outlined but irregular earthen

21. Baron Jean Louis Dubreton (1773–1855) entered the army in 1790 but did not become general of brigade until 1811; he served in the Vendée, 1793–96, in the Marengo campaign, in the invasion of Santo Domingo, and in Holland and Germany. Sent to Spain in 1811, he successfully commanded the garrison of Burgos against Wellington's army for 34 days in 1812.

wall with some redans and bastions. Under it was another wall made of palisades, forming a glacis surrounded by small exterior posts without magazines. The fort was dominated by a hill about 260 to 300 yards away, which could be reached under cover and where some works were being built. The Prince visited the constructions. There was a plan for a permanent fortification, but the scheme was of little use because of the position of the city.

On our arrival at Valladolid, the Duc d'Abrantès, with a very brilliant staff, came out a league to greet the Prince. There was a line extending from the gate of the city to the palace, where we descended [from the carriage]. The first division of the 8th Corps occupied Valladolid.[22]

After taking care of the immediate needs of the 8th Corps in Old Castile, the Prince left for Salamanca with General Junot and General Éblé,[23] commander in chief of the artillery, to see and talk with Marshal Ney. I was the only aide-de-camp to accompany him. I made the trip in the Prince's open carriage with General Éblé. There I began my acquaintance with this distinguished man, who honored me with his close friendship. The conversation turned to General Moreau.[24]

22. When Masséna reached the palace of Charles V at Valladolid, he was greeted by Junot and his wife. Some embarrassment occurred when the prince's young traveling companion, dressed as a cavalry officer with the Legion of Honor, alighted from the carriage and entered the palace—it was his mistress, Henriette Leberton. *Chef d'escadron* Marbot, one of Masséna's aides-de-camp, recalled, "Imagine the astonishment of the two ladies. They stood petrified and did not speak a single word! The Marshal had the wit to restrain himself; but he was deeply hurt when the Duchesse d'Abrantès, pleading indisposition, left the room just as Junot was leading in Madame X—— [Leberton]." See Jean Baptiste Marbot, *Mémoires du général baron Marbot* (5th ed., Paris, 1891), II, 334; Laure Permon Junot, Duchesse d'Abrantès, *Mémoires de madame la duchesse d'Abrantès, ou souvenirs historiques sur Napoléon, la Révolution, le Directoire, le Consulat, l'Empire et la Restauration* (Paris, 1831–33), XIII, 66–67. It should be noted that Pelet does not mention this woman anywhere in his manuscript, although he must have been in constant contact with her.

23. Count Jean Baptiste Éblé (1758–1812) became a cannoneer in his father's regiment at the age of 9. As general of brigade in 1793, he served in the Army of the Rhine under Moreau; he was attached to Ney's 6th Corps in 1804, and became King Jérôme's minister of war in 1808. Napoleon appointed him to command Masséna's artillery in 1810 and in 1812 he was instrumental in saving the Grand Army on the Beresina.

24. Jean Victor Moreau (1763–1813) was chosen a battalion commander in Dumouriez' volunteers, became general of division in 1794, and commander in chief of the Army of the Rhine and Moselle in 1796. In 1800 he won a brilliant victory at Hohenlinden, but in 1804 he was indirectly implicated in a plot against Napoleon, arrested, tried, and ultimately exiled. He was killed while serving with the allies against France in 1813.

General Éblé had been very close to him. He praised his self-control a great deal, as well as his forbearance which was sometimes a weakness, his politeness, his good nature, and his talents, though they were not of the highest order. Moreau had frankly acknowledged he did not feel he was born to command when he compared his talents to those of the man who has since become his enemy [Napoleon]. For a long time he refused the offers of his friends and protégés to incite either war or partisans [against Napoleon]. General Éblé did not exaggerate the merits of the campaigns in which, as commander in chief of the artillery, he himself had taken such an extraordinary role. Éblé admitted that the battle of Hohenlinden, the most beautiful jewel in Moreau's crown, had been won in part by chance. Several times later on, I brought the conversation back to this point. General Éblé's opinion did not change.

We were then crossing a depressing sandy country covered in part with small and oddly shaped pine trees. On the right bank of the Duero there were large flat hills, with square and abrupt slopes which formed the basin of this river and of the Pisuerga. The Duero, escarped and about one hundred yards wide, was crossed by a beautiful bridge which seemed never to have been repaired, like most of the structures in Spain. Beyond the Duero the woods extended as far as the Adaja, which seemed to be deep and swift; it was 19 feet deep and at least 50 to 60 yards wide. Its bridge was completely isolated and appeared to be an excellent post for brigands. Villages were rare and poor on this road, which was simply traced in the middle of these wastes and across slightly undulating ground where the rivers had little slopes and were usually swampy. Medina was a small city, formerly very large, rather well built, and attractive for this country. Around it we saw ruined walls extending into the distance. Its old castle had triple walls built by the Moors; we searched for something arabesque.

Marshal Ney came to meet the Prince and the latter entered the Marshal's carriage. We found many troops outside Salamanca. The 50th and 59th Line were under arms. Both regiments looked like magnificent, truly elite units to those of us who had just left the armies of Wagram, whose ranks were full of conscripts. All the soldiers of these regiments had had several years of service. Most of them had taken part in the campaigns of 1805 and 1806, as had the entire 6th Corps.

Yet the reputation of the 50th and 59th Line was not the most illustrious. The entrance to Salamanca was also brilliant. The reputation of the Prince had overcome the pride and the apathy of the Castilians who gathered to see him. The three generals talked together until eleven o'clock that night, and we left very early the next day.

The 6th Corps, formed since the Camp of Boulogne, was still under the command of the Marshal. With him at Elchingen, Jena, Gutstadt, Preuss-Eylau, and Friedland, it had covered itself with glory. Therefore it was very attached to its commander, who had always done whatever was necessary, sometimes at the expense of strict discipline, to retain the love and devotion of his soldiers. At this time the 6th Corps included only eight regiments or two divisions. Later on, a few regiments from the first expedition to Portugal and some unattached troops of the third division were joined to it. These additions were always regarded as foreign to the corps in the eyes of the other soldiers and the Marshal. He kept garrisons at Toro and Zamora.[25]

The 8th Corps was made up almost entirely of new or foreign regiments and one third of the infantry in the fourth battalions had been formed very recently. The remainder of the units had been part of the first Portuguese expedition. Its provisional cavalry regiment had been created with third and fourth squadrons. The first division of the 8th Corps occupied Valladolid, and the two others were at Astorga and León. The dragoons were at Valencia de Don Juan.

At this time General Reynier's 2nd Corps was close to Andalusia at Zafra, where it had replaced the 5th Corps of Marshal Soult's army. The general was engaged in scouring all the land between the Tagus and the Guadiana to reconnoiter Badajoz and Olivenza. The army of La Romana was in front of Reynier, and he could not communicate directly with us because the bridges of Almaraz and Alcántara had been destroyed by the enemy. The 2nd Corps was composed of old regiments with a few conscripts. Most of them were members of the first Army of Portugal. The 2nd Corps had taken part in Marshal Soult's expedition on Oporto; honorable, perhaps, but nevertheless with disastrous results which it had not yet forgotten.

Following is the information which we received about the English army. I am conveying it just as I received it from the deserters and

25. For the composition of the corps see the Appendix.

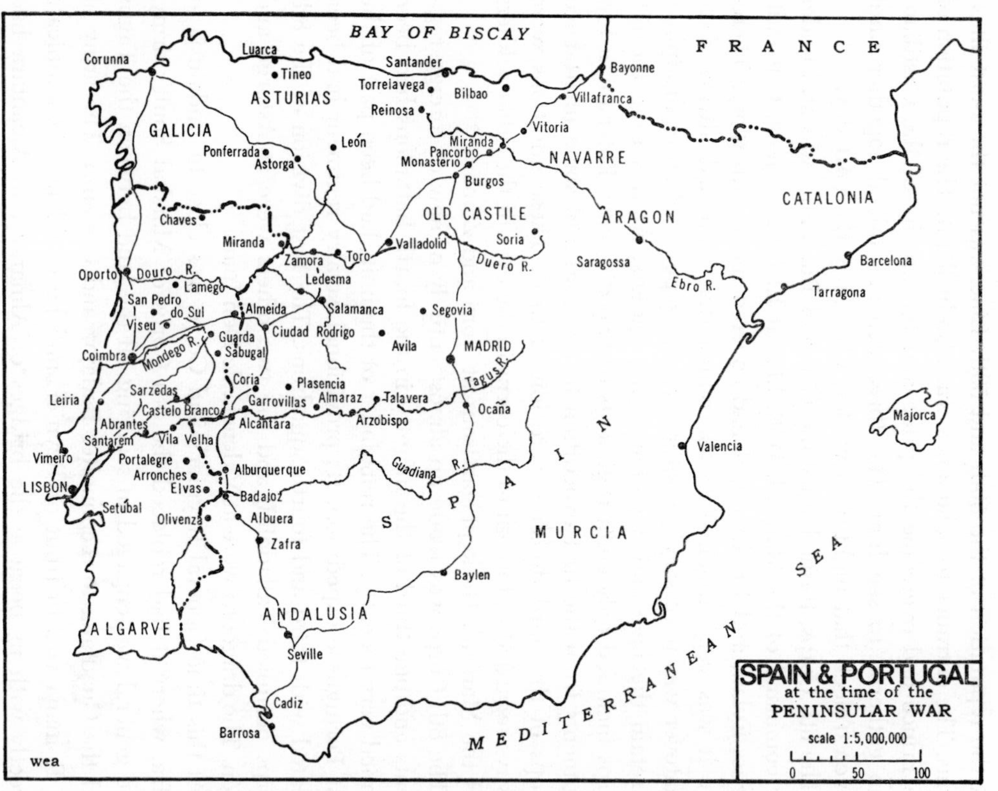

Spain and Portugal at the Time of the Peninsular War

spies. I have not found other material in my Journal which would enable me to give a more exact account of their army. Lord Wellington, who commanded it, had his general headquarters at Celorico for a short time. After receiving substantial reinforcements, his troops had increased in number to thirty-five thousand men, and they were now occupying the areas surrounding Pinhel, Almeida, Guarda, Belmonte, and Trancoso. The right wing, composed of both a British and a Portuguese division, was placed near Abrantes and Castelo Branco under the command of General Hill.[26] It was linked with a corps of ten thousand Portuguese, supported by a few English detachments cantoned near Portalegre and Arronches. There was talk of another Portuguese corps near Elvas. In the direction of Miranda and Bragança there were three thousand English troops with a unit of seven or eight thousand Portuguese. The advance guard under the command of General Craufurd was at Gallegos. A few detachments and depots occupied the rear at Viseu, Coimbra, Oporto, and Lisbon. Ships were anchored in the harbor of Lisbon and Figueira.[27] The British army had already gained fame in several exploits. One segment had fought in Egypt, in Calabria, in Denmark, at Corunna, and at Vimeiro, as well as at Talavera, where it acquired more glory by its valor than by the tactics of its commanders. It seemed destined to purge the English armies of the dishonor of the first campaigns of the Revolution.

26. Masséna's information was remarkably correct, for Major General Lowry Cole's Fourth Division occupied Guarda, Major General Thomas Picton's Third Division was at Pinhel, Lieutenant General Brent Spencer's First Division held Celorico; Brigadier General Robert Craufurd was posted between the Côa and Azaba rivers with his Light Division; and Major General Rowland Hill's Second Division occupied the Portuguese frontier in the vicinity of Portalegre. Before the end of March Wellington had 34,964 rank and file in the British army in Portugal. See Public Record Office [hereafter cited as P.R.O.], W.O. 6/50, Liverpool to Wellington, April 24, 1810.

27. Although Wellington was determined to defend Portugal, he was continually urged by anxious officials in London to complete all preparations for the evacuation of the British army. By May transports totaling 45,000 tons and a fleet of men-of-war were waiting or en route to embark both the English and Portuguese armies, as well as any citizens who felt they would be in jeopardy if the French army occupied Portugal. See Arthur Wellesley, *The Dispatches of the Field Marshal the Duke of Wellington, during His Various Campaigns in India, Denmark, Portugal, Spain, the Low Countries, and France, from 1799 to 1818*, ed. John Gurwood (London, 1835–38), Wellington to Stuart, March 1, 1810, V, 536–39; Wellington to Liverpool, January 24, 31, 1810, V, 446–49, 482–84; Wellington to Stuart, March 18, 1810, V, 561–64.

The Portuguese troops had been armed, clothed, and enregimented by England. British officers led these troops, with each regiment under the command of a colonel or major. The deserters put the strength of this army at forty thousand men. Its capabilities were still unknown; nevertheless, its training had been carefully given and good service could be expected from it in its own country, especially with superior forces, supported by an English army. Most of the militia had been set up like the regular army and had been similarly clothed, armed, and regularly paid. The militia had been trained and disciplined by the British officers commanding them. Finally there was another kind of militia composed of *ordenanza,* that is, a *levée en masse* of all Portuguese peasants. Organized under the command of canton chiefs called *Capltão Mor,* they were assigned to protect the country, defend themselves against small detachments, cut the enemy's communications, and engage his rear guard.[28]

These various militia units totaled well over one hundred and fifty thousand men. In a period when the court of Portugal neglected the army completely, the principal hope of defending the kingdom rested on the militia. It had long been accustomed to this type of service, and maintained a sort of military spirit which was reinforced by a national hatred of Spain — its natural enemy. In 1810 it had been mobilized in units forming several separate corps under the orders of the English officers Wilson, Trant, and Miller, and the Portuguese Silveira and Bacelar; the latter was an old man, loyal and honest, but nothing more.[29] He had supreme command of the various corps, which

28. By the first of May the Portuguese army included 51,280 troops of the line, 54,229 militiamen, and 329,016 *ordenanza.* See P.R.O., Stuart de Rothesay Papers, 1801–14, F.O. 342/19, "Mappa Geral en rezumo da Forca armada em todo o Reino em mez du Abril de 1810." On June 5 Wellington wrote, "The Portuguese army are in a good state. We have arms for the militia, and upon the whole we have an enormous military establishment at our command." *Wellington's Dispatches,* Wellington to Villiers, June 5, 1810, VI, 170.

29. Sir John Wilson (1780–1856) enlisted in the 28th Foot as an ensign in 1794; he served in the West Indies and Egypt and went to the Peninsula with the 97th Foot in 1808. He served with the Lusitanian Legion in 1809 and then was made chief of staff to Portuguese General Silveira. In 1811 he became governor of the province of Minho and commanded its militia.

Sir Nicholas Trant (1769–1839) became a lieutenant in the 84th Foot in 1794; he served at Roliça and Vimeiro, organized a regiment from among the students of the University of Coimbra, commanded a militia unit, and was made brigadier general in the Portuguese service. Although an English officer named Miller who commanded a Portuguese unit is mentioned in Pelet's and other manuscripts on the Peninsular War, no specific details about him could be located.

he later transformed into a kind of army behind us along both banks of the Mondego. The general command of all the Portuguese forces had been given to an Englishman, Marshal Beresford.[30]

These diverse troops were cantoned, for the most part, between the Tagus and Douro rivers. Therefore Wellington concentrated the bulk of his forces and almost all of his army between these two rivers. More particularly, the important and famous position of Guarda was occupied as in the campaign of 1704. This line, which formed a chain of placements between the Douro and the Tagus, was covered on its front and left by the Côa River, on its right by the Serra de Meras and by the gorges of Sabugal, Penamacor, and Castelo Branco, and up to the Tagus by the Zezere. These sites covered most of the principal lines of operation against Lisbon by way of Abrantes and Coimbra. In front of these positions was the fortress of Ciudad Rodrigo, which guaranteed a bridgehead on the Agueda—the first line of defense between the Douro and the Sierra de Gata. The beautiful fortress of La Concepción was on the Turones River. Lastly, Almeida directly covered the excellent line of the Côa River and provided the English with a way of defending its left bank or attacking the flank of any army attempting to pass behind these various lines; the English could occupy their lines with either Portuguese troops or militia. Lord Wellington could unite his armies for offensive as well as defensive operations, and he could bring them forward in very little time to cover or deliver Ciudad Rodrigo, only eight or ten leagues away, by marching on the left flank of forces attacking the fortresses as well as all along the endangered frontier points in Beira.

Francisco da Silveira Pinto da Fonseca Teixeira, Condes de Amarante (1763–1821), fought against France and Spain in 1801 and became a lieutenant colonel in the 6th Cavalry two years later; he supported the regency government in 1808 and was appointed military governor of Trás-os-Montes. He played an important role in the defense of Portugal during both Soult's and Masséna's invasions and in 1812 was promoted to lieutenant general.

Manuel Pinto de Morais Bacelar (1741–1816) enlisted in a cavalry regiment of Chaves in 1756, was promoted to brigadier in 1802, and became military governor of Beira in 1808. In 1809 he was supreme commander of the militia and *ordenanza* of Beira and Trás-os-Montes e Douro with headquarters at Lamego.

30. Lord William Carr Beresford (1768–1854) became an ensign of the 6th Foot in 1785, general in 1808, and marshal in the Portuguese army in 1809. He served throughout the Empire as well as on Moore's retreat to Corunna, at Oporto, Talavera, Albuera, etc. In February 1809 he began the reorganization of the Portuguese army, and his efforts were rewarded at Bussaco in 1810. See Andrew Halli-

The English General could communicate by way of Miranda with the Army of Galicia, under the command of General Mahy, whose corps had advanced to Ponferrada and Puebla de Sanabria. On his right Wellington had the Spanish corps of General La Carrera, four thousand men strong, with a similar number of militia whose headquarters were alternately at Peñaparda, Robleda, and Puebla de Azaba.[31] This corps formed the extreme left of the Marquis de La Romana's army. With four officers on half pay [?], the latter maintained the fortress of Badajoz, where the Junta of New Castile was established. The inhabitants of Badajoz complained that the marquis did not protect the country and that he did not leave it pacified. The Spanish divisions, three to four thousand men each, occupied the following positions: Ballesteros at Olivenza, Mendizábel at Campo Maior, Sol* at Alburquerque, Dinnaz [?] and O'Donnell at Cáceres and Mérida.[32] Butrón, with two to four thousand horses, was six leagues in front of Badajoz. We were told that Wellington, vigorously pressed to hold Ciudad Rodrigo, had responded that his assistance was sought everywhere, in Andalusia, in Galicia, at Badajoz, and that he would do his best.

The English army had very active allies among us, right up to our cantonments. The *Quadrilhas* or Spanish bands, better known by the

day, *Observations on the Present State of the Portuguese Army, as Organized by Lieutenant-General Sir William Carr Beresford* (London, 1811).

31. Nicolás Mahy (n.d.) was a Spanish general who commanded a unit of some 6,000 men in La Romana's army after the retreat of Moore. In 1809 he engaged Ney's forces near Navia de Suarna on the Ser River. General Martín de La Carrara (d. 1811) was a divisional commander in 1809. He successfully attacked a French garrison at Santiago on May 22, 1809, fought at Alba de Tormes and was later killed in Murcia.

32. Pedro Caro y Sureda, Marquis de La Romana (1761–1811), served against the French in 1793–95; he went to Denmark with 15,000 Spanish soldiers to support the French in 1807 but escaped to British transports with many of his troops when he learned of the war in the Peninsula. He served loyally with Moore and Wellington and died behind the Lines of Torres Vedras.

Francisco Lopez Ballesteros (1770–1833) served in an infantry company from Aragon; he was made brigadier and served at Santander and in Asturias. He commanded a division of La Romana's army in 1810 and served in the Peninsular War through 1812. Gabriel de Mendizábal y Iraeta (1764–1833) enlisted in 1793, became a lieutenant general in 1810, and finally commanded the Army of Estremadura. He fought at Alba de Tormes and served throughout the Peninsular War.

Carlos O'Donnell is the least known of the O'Donnell brothers who served in the Peninsular War. He commanded a division of La Romana's army near Cáceres and led his troops behind the Lines of Torres Vedras in October 1810. A year later while he led a division in Joachim Blake's army his forces were involved in the disastrous defeat of Saguntum near Valencia.

name of guerrillas, had spread throughout the provinces; united rather than organized, they changed their leader frequently and their soldiers each day. Often weak and forced to retreat deep into the mountains or deserts, they were strong and daring at other times, but they were always forced to hide from our troops. The guerrillas were composed successively of vagabonds and smugglers, common in the various provinces; of shepherds living in the mountains; and of remnants of former enemy regiments dispersed by our victories. Some of them were motivated by the love of their country, others by zeal of religion and the hatred of the French or by their national pride, and they would go to join these bands. Before long the atrocious barbarity of the Spanish, not provoked at the beginning, brought forth vengeance and reprisals, which in turn fomented the insurrections. The war spread in proportion as the passions excited the easily aroused Spanish minds. The peasants, moved by exaggerated tales of guerrilla successes, or perhaps more concerned with the booty they gained, increased this tumultuous rabble. This life was singularly easy because of the frugality of the Spanish peasant's life, his stubbornness, and the total destitution in which he lived; he left almost nothing behind when he took his coat and bag. The women remained alone in the villages. The less ugly were hidden, and we usually saw only the ugly señoras, old men, and children.

Various leaders gained control of the guerrillas, who would subdivide or gather together but who were formed around a nucleus of troops that seldom left. A number of leaders had become quite famous. They were known by the names of Friar, Curé, Doctor, or Shepherd, depending upon their former profession. The best known were Empecinado ("the implacable"), the Marquesito de Porlier, and Mina.[33] The latter formed a veritable army in the state of Navarre and organized

33. Juan Martín Díaz, El Empecinado (1775–1825), enrolled as a volunteer and became a successful guerrilla leader in northern Spain. Promoted to the rank of general by the regency, he captured Sigüenza and Cuenca in 1811. He was involved in a revolution against Ferdinand VII, and after it was crushed, he was imprisoned, tried, and hanged.

Francisco Espoz y Mina (1781–1836) first served in a battalion commanded by Charles Doyle but in 1809 became a guerrilla leader in Navarre. He claimed to have fought 140 battles and killed or captured 40,000 Frenchmen. In his famous proclamation of December 14, 1811, he announced, "In Navarre we declare war to the death, without quarter, without distinction for soldiers or officers, including the Emperor of the French." Opposed to Ferdinand VII's reactionary policies, he finally sought asylum in France.

a good military government. Among those leaders, a few showed great courage, ardent patriotism, and great strength of character. They possessed remarkable natural or acquired talents for war. They helped to save their country and fought for it with great stubbornness, quite remarkable in a cause that seemed lost. A free Spain should have erected altars to them, but instead they found scaffolds when they asked for the liberty for which they had shed so much blood. In the moment of crisis Spanish leaders with neither soul, heart, nor intelligence sacrificed these men who could have restored to the Spanish name as much glory as had been acquired under Charles V.

As a matter of fact, the major Spanish operations had failed so miserably at the beginning that their armies were easily dispersed by our regiments. The Spanish had almost given up the idea of holding the country and had shut themselves up in a few places. With the exception of isolated corps that were always withdrawing in front of us and that remained in the service of La Romana or Mahy or in Catalonia, their efforts were reduced to the bands of guerrillas who had very little rapport with each other and rarely acted in common. Thus they lacked a center of operation and overall direction of their movements, but from one end of the kingdom to the other most of the Spaniards were animated by two passions—to do as much harm as possible and to support their bands and the English by all means. Each one would do everything possible in relation to his own position, strength, and courage, and he would become in turn a spy, a soldier, a messenger, and, it must be said, quite often a killer. Everything was sacrificed if it inconvenienced the enemy, and even women would use every means at their disposal.

The guerrillas attempted only small operations. They tried to destroy us in detail, falling upon small detachments, massacring sick and isolated men, destroying convoys, and kidnapping messengers. They never attacked unless they were ten to one, and they halted only in the most inaccessible places, defending themselves to cover their flight. Always faithfully warned of everything that occurred, they found all possible help on their expeditions. Their operations were seldom completely successful. They never risked great losses, and when their surprise attacks did not succeed they would draw back in great haste, dispersing for some [future] point of concentration. Hiding their arms, they would come and mix among us like peaceful farmers. The nucleus of the bands and their leaders usually found safe asylum by crossing the limits of the French jurisdiction, or at the least enough tranquility to reorganize themselves. Later on the people, especially the bourgeoisie, got tired of this interminable war whose weight fell almost entirely on them from every side. The guerrillas irritated them very much. They punished the burgers rigorously because of the contributions, in both money and supplies, they furnished our troops and the information they were forced to give us.

The bands of insurgents were more bothersome for individual soldiers in our army than dangerous to the army itself. They brought delays rather than obstacles to the operations by compounding the two greatest difficulties of the war—food and communication. In addition, they were extraordinarily useful to the enemy by forming an excellent corps of light troops and a whole network of spies. Aside from fettering all our movements, they furnished the enemy with precious information on our forces, our plans, and our position, and almost all the dispatches they wanted, as well as great numbers of prisoners. Meanwhile it was almost impossible for us to obtain the least notion about the armies that opposed us. This forced us to play with our cards on the table while the enemy hid their game very carefully.

Nevertheless, it must be said that the British General ennobled the aid he obtained from the guerrillas by turning it to the profit of humanity. If each object—letters, carriages, artillery, etc.—had a fixed price, men also had a price put upon them according to their rank. Thus Spanish greed saved many victims from Spanish barbarism.[34] However, it must also be admitted that the English were accustomed to speculate; they gained considerably from this trade since, aside from the advantages derived from guerrilla operations, they were also able to buy cheaply prisoners that would otherwise have cost them very dearly. Thus the bands of Spanish insurgents and the English

34. On May 1, 1810, Wellington wrote to Liverpool, "The great impediment to desertion is the danger of being murdered, which all the soldiers of the French army incur in Spain, when they wander from their quarters, and are found singly, or in small bodies, by the inhabitants of the country. This impediment was in some degree removed in the last year, by the offer of a reward, by General Cuesta, for every soldier of the French army brought in by the peasantry; and it is probable the same measure would produce the same effect at present. The reward, however, must be offered by some person whose character is known in the country, and in whom the people have confidence." See *Wellington's Dispatches,* VI, 78–80.

army mutually supported each other. Without the English the Spaniards would have been quickly dispersed or crushed.[35] In the absence of the guerrillas, the French armies would have acquired a unity and strength that they were never able to achieve in this country, and the Anglo-Portuguese army, unwarned of our operations and projects, would have been unable to withstand concentrated operations.

Such was the situation of the several armies at the middle of May when the Prince returned from Salamanca to Valladolid. Since the beginning of the campaign, I had been treated by him with the same kindness he had shown me during the previous war in Austria. Now, as far as military affairs were concerned, he gave me his complete confidence. I worked with him every morning. He spoke to me frankly about all his plans and let me read all the dispatches, even those of the government or the army corps. Often he ordered me to answer dispatches strictly related to military affairs, and later on I took complete charge of his correspondence. One morning he had the following conversation with me, which I copied word for word in my Journal. "You are destined to remain with me for a long time. I order you to tell me your opinion always, especially on matters related to the service." "I have done so for a long time," I answered, "with everything that is of any importance. I give you my word of honor never to let a single occasion go by." He added, "I am a man. Passions and pride can get the best of me and hinder me from seeing or agreeing on what would be best, but be assured that within a quarter of an hour I will have recovered and give you the justice you merit." I assured him again that no consideration would stop me from fulfilling the duty that he had imposed on me and that I would redouble my zeal for the service. God knows that I have never failed this commitment, and I often went beyond the limit that our respective positions seemed to prescribe and permit. He told me if he ever found himself away from his headquarters, I would probably have to replace him, and from that moment on I would be in charge of all the important movements of

35. Ney wrote to Soult on April 18, 1810, "Despite all the measures I have taken to destroy the bands of guerrillas, we have not yet been successful. These brigands continue to torment us, interrupting our convoys and cutting off our isolated men and weak detachments. . . . We would only be able to see an end to these small [guerrilla] wars if we were able to employ all the cavalry, but this would only be possible if the English army . . . had evacuated the Peninsula." See Bonnal, *Ney*, III, 310–12.

the army as well as the strategic work concerning the topographic section and military correspondence. He also installed me in his administrative office and often had me write extracts or résumés of correspondence and reports on the state of affairs. I was to start the latter work immediately. Finally, he charged me to collect all the information on Portugal; he ordered me to see General Kellermann and Colonel Gabriel Donnadieu the next day since they could furnish us information that we thought would be helpful. The Prince also expressed the desire that his son accompany me on all reconnaissances where he could learn something about the practice of the profession.[36] I find it necessary to go into these details to show where I stood with the Prince and to justify all that I will say later. Even without witnesses to this conversation, many people have seen me with him and can testify whether or not I have exaggerated.

In his correspondence Marshal Ney had already proposed a plan to march against the English, give battle, and return and carry on the siege of Ciudad Rodrigo, since he assumed the English intended to lift the siege. He insisted on this project during the conference, and in his usual manner he returned to it several times in his correspondence, without supporting it with any solid reasons.[37] The Duc d'Abrantès, with his 8th Corps, was to help the 6th Corps, which was charged with the siege. He proposed to place the first division at Ledesma, the second at Salamanca, the third at Toro and Zamora; one dragoon brigade between Zamora and the Orbigo and the other on the road from Salamanca to Rodrigo; moreover he planned to repair the breach at Astorga, supply it for one month, and put a French garrison there to stop the Galicians. These dispositions of the troops kept them too far from the enemy point of attack. But in this destitute and deserted country, food regulated everything and it was necessary to adopt these dispositions.

36. Jacques Prosper Masséna (1793–1821) served as an aide-de-camp to his father in the Wagram and Portuguese campaigns.

37. When Masséna arrived at Valladolid on May 10, Ney wrote to him immediately, "It seems to me a combined march [by the 6th and 8th Corps] on Viseu, headquarters of Lord Wellington, will decide the fate of the campaign." See Bonnal, *Ney*, Ney to Masséna, May 10, 1810, III, 319–20. After visiting Ney at Salamanca, Masséna wrote to King Joseph, "I will decide perhaps to march with two united corps to fight the enemy." Masséna to Joseph, May 17, 1810, Archives de Masséna, MSS, LI. These archives are now in the possession of André Masséna, the 6th Prince d'Essling, at Paris.

I immediately took care of the first report on the state of affairs on May 20, relative to the project of the Portuguese campaign and the siege of Ciudad Rodrigo. The following are the plans concerning the details of the maneuver. After establishing the respective positions of the two armies and making general dispositions of the government's instruction, I added: Marshal Ney wants to march toward the British at Viseu, fight them, and then return to carry on the siege of Ciudad Rodrigo, leaving a corps of five thousand men in front of this fortress and the heavy artillery at Salamanca. Afterward he proposes the siege of Almeida. I believe I see several problems in this project. First, it means fighting a useless battle, the greatest mistake in war and a great crime because blood is uselessly spilled. This battle could not be decisive because of the country in which it would be fought. Moreover, it is not without danger because many of our troops are new, and although the nucleus of the army is considerable, we would be obliged to leave a great number of detachments along the route. Second, it would remove the army from the provinces it is now supposed to occupy and pacify. Third, to pursue and engage the enemy in Portugal would draw us step by step toward the sea, fomenting insurrections behind us either in Beira or Spain. Fourth, if Madrid were exposed the enemy could threaten the corps at Badajoz, reinforced by only a few troops, and delay the siege of Ciudad Rodrigo since it would be necessary to leave the artillery at Salamanca. Sixth [*sic*] and finally, this battle is completely contradictory to the instructions received. The great advantage Lord Wellington has over us is that he can bring his entire army onto the field of battle while ours is considerably weakened by isolated detachments. Nevertheless, despite what has been said of the intentions manifested by the English and Spanish, I dare to believe that the English will attempt no important action against the siege, however small the observation corps opposing them, with Ciudad Rodrigo and Almeida behind them. This siege, carried on before an enemy whose troops are only a long march away (a distance of eight or ten average leagues), should be undertaken only after successfully moving all the necessary food and material for the artillery and engineers to the fortress in order to push it with great vigor. It should be covered by an adequate corps posted on the banks of the Turones and the Azaba. It would be good to fortify the most accessible point of this line in order to give the remainder of the army time to arrive in case of an attack by the English. Although it is probably not in their plan to attack us, we should not present them with a certain advantage by exposing a very weak corps in front of them. The troops destined to reinforce this observation corps should not be farther away than two marches or twelve to fifteen leagues.[38]

The Prince received this first report favorably and adopted its conclusions. Thus Marshal Ney was limited to fulfilling the orders he had already received to continue siege preparations and to do everything possible to approach Ciudad Rodrigo.

General Bonnet had attacked the enemy on the Narcea, driving them to the frontiers of Galicia. After sweeping the mountains of Godán and Tejera, he placed himself between Luarca and Tineo. Meanwhile a unit of three thousand Galicians, advancing toward Luarca, was driven back with the loss of three cannon and several hundred men, among whom were twenty officers and a major general. The guerrilla leaders occupied the mountains between Asturias and León from where they could infest all the valleys. Insurrection was increasing in intensity [?], and the inhabitants were beginning to desert the villages. General Bonnet resolved to take the troops of General Cacault into the mountains.[39] The Curé and Empecinado recruited by force in Old Castile, and once more they infested the countryside as the army corps approached Ciudad Rodrigo. General Kellermann asked for no less than eight thousand men to insure the safety of his government in Valladolid.

38. Ney waited for some response from Masséna until May 20 and then wrote, "I believe the trip Your Highness made to Salamanca was to determine plans for military operations appropriate either to invade Portugal and force Wellington to battle" or to take measures to continue the siege of Ciudad Rodrigo. Ney requested an immediate response, concluding his rash letter, "I beseech Your Highness to inform me of your decision, because if you do not, I will give orders . . . to return [the troops] to their old cantonments . . . until Your Highness has made a decision." Ney must have regretted his words a few hours later when he received Masséna's decision to continue the siege. The Prince, shocked by Ney's attitude, responded, "Your letter has singularly astonished me. I am unable to conceal from you that I am not accustomed to such a manner." See Bonnal, *Ney*, Ney to Masséna, May 18, 20, 1810; Masséna to Ney, May 21, 1810, III, 321–22.

39. Baron Jean Baptiste Cacault (1769–1813) enlisted in the 58th Line in 1784 and was promoted to general of brigade in 1809. He served in Martinique, with the Armies of the Center, Ardennes, Sambre and Meuse, and Italy, 1792–1801; attached to the Grand Army, he fought at Eylau, Dantzig, and Wagram. In 1810 he was given command of the third division of Junot's 8th Corps but remained in Spain as commander of Ciudad Rodrigo.

Amid all these movements we pursued the insurgents with vigor. Then, for the first time, I had the fortune to save a victim of this cruel war. An unfortunate peasant had just been condemned to death by a council of war. Fortunately, I was approached; I was easily able to obtain permission from the Prince to have the man sent back to King Joseph: the Prince could not give a reprieve, but this was equal assurance of commutation. It was certainly a way of doing good for its own sake, for we must admit that the Spanish showed themselves to be implacable; nothing affected them. They had been cruel and even ferocious. If some Frenchmen took limited reprisals against them later, it was only after they had been driven to it by the spectacle of their atrocities.

During the entire time that the Prince remained in Spain, he tried to win back the inhabitants by the kindness and justice of his administration. He established the most severe order in his government and the most austere discipline among the troops. Exactions were stopped, requisitions restrained and regularized, abuses sought out, pursued, and punished; no one found reprieve under any pretext. The Prince himself provided the best possible example and had the officers follow it. He stopped the scandalous traffic in prisoners of war by freeing the captives. The military authorities were at last restrained and the civil administrations constantly protected. All the supplies of the army were regularized and paid for; provisions of individuals were paid for by themselves and those of the troops with army funds. Based on vouchers and amounts of contributions, these measures did not please some of those who had fought in other countries.[40] Finally, justice reigned as much as possible amid the horror of war. The Prince reprimanded anyone who caused trouble, listened to all recriminations, and avenged any grave injury. Yet so much good could hardly negate the hatred the Spanish had for everything that was French. Nevertheless, I wanted to believe that the name of Masséna was venerated in the

40. Pelet's estimate of Masséna's character is overgenerous; on three separate occasions Masséna was disgraced or denounced for financial misappropriations. When Napoleon appointed him to serve Joseph in Naples, he warned, Masséna "is a good soldier but entirely dominated by his greed for money." On one occasion he was forced to repay 3,700,000 francs extorted from Italian officials. See *Correspondance de Napoléon Ier*, No. 10311, Napoleon to Joseph, June 3, 1806, XII, 525–26; *Lettres inédites de Napoléon Ier (An VIII–1815)*, ed. Léon Lecestre (Paris, 1897), Napoleon to Eugene, April 22, 1806, I, 67–68.

provinces he had governed. My greatest happiness was to support him with all my strength in the good he did there.

At the end of the month of May the weather was horrible—rain, cold, and sleet. This limited preparations for the siege considerably as well as the transportation of the artillery. Nevertheless, the Prince wanted to move to Salamanca. Marshal Ney departed immediately for Caridad, a convent situated near the besieged fortress, taking food and forage for a month since he could not find anything in the vicinity or within a very great distance.

We remained at Salamanca for some time. The city was on the right bank of the Tormes, a torrential river 240 to 260 yards wide, with small islands in it. The river was crossed by a bridge, and, it was said, half remained from Roman antiquity. In fact the arches were semi-circular, small, smooth, and the pillars decorated with pilasters, while the non-Roman part of the bridge had been built in the same style but without embellishments. The city of Salamanca was rather large and poorly constructed; its streets were inferior and it was situated on irregular ground, but there were some beautiful buildings. I will limit myself to saying a few words about its magnificent cathedral. I never passed in front of it without stopping there for as long as I could. It was a vast building of Gothic-moresque style in the shape of a Latin cross with five naves; the extremely high ogival vaults were supported by extraordinarily slender and fluted pillars.[41] This gave the edifice an air of lightness, daring, and immensity which impressed me. Then I would wonder, contrary to my former ideas, whether this architecture would not have been preferable to the Greek style of our churches. For comparison, in the middle of the cathedral behind the altar was a very pure Greek decoration. These Greek styles appeared better adapted and more convenient for smaller dimensions. Standing close to the dome, I often contemplated the multitude of pillars rising toward the sky, similar to the trees in a forest, and spreading their diverse arcades just like the branches of a tree. The indentions that covered the building, the arabesques, the spires, and the openings added

41. The New Cathedral (Catedral Nueva) at Salamanca was begun in 1513 under the direction of Antonio Egas and Alonso Rodríguez but not completed until 1733. The southwest tower is 360 feet high; the building itself is 340 feet long and 158 wide. The exterior is both late Gothic and Baroque and the interior late Gothic.

to the illusion of lightness. However, all this was intermingled but was not monotonous.

The cathedral was also extravagant on the outside with its extremely high steeple. Ceremonies were celebrated here with great pomp and solemnity. The organ contributed singularly to the admirable effect. Unfortunately the choir was cut off at its end, as in most of the great churches we had seen in Spain, which damaged the general effect of the building. I had seen the Cathedral of Burgos, which was highly praised; to me it appeared much less beautiful than the one at Salamanca. Space does not permit me to describe the beautiful square of Salamanca, its university, and the mansion where the prince lodged. This building, constructed of beautiful granite with an exterior Ionic pediment and a courtyard decorated with two rows of Ionic and Doric porticoes, honored Spanish architecture by the purity of its design.[42]

Our engineers had constructed a fort at Salamanca to defend the city and the bridge which it overlooked. This fort, or rather this garrison keep, encompassed a vast area of ground on the western side of the city next to the surrounding wall, which had been used in part; it was adequately protected because of the elevation and the escarpment in front of it. Toward the center of the city the surrounding wall was formed by a kind of bastion front with masonry parapets and gun embrasures, by the walls of a large convent, and finally by a section flanked by a reverse. A palisaded moat extended along the interior of this part of the wall. This temporary fortification was set up merely to cover the fort from a coup de main or to hold until there was a regular approach and the establishment of artillery.

Each day it became clearer that the multiplication and division of the commands in Spain were seriously hampering our operations, both the submission and pacification of the provinces and their administration. The need for a vigorous central authority was constantly felt. Every military commander, from the most insignificant to the most important, already isolated by difficulties in communications and the transmission of orders and instructions, increased his isolation by concentrating all his resources within the limits of his own territory. All the commanders avoided each other instead of combining their forces

42. Salamanca and its buildings made a deep impression on the French soldiers who passed through its gates. See Colomb, "Journal of André Colomb," *Journal of the Society for Army Historical Research*, XLVI, No. 185 (Spring 1968), 14.

and operations. Their strength, which would have been considerable if a common center of action had been utilized, was annulled because of division. This resulted in a passive and inert system that was restricted to the capitals of each command or to a few lines of communication, leaving the insurgents to control the countryside except at rare moments when it was necessary to collect contributions and requisitions. This situation presented us to the inhabitants of the towns as avaricious parasites, unable either to subdue or to protect them. Each commander, circumscribed in the cities or towns under his jurisdiction, was more preoccupied with his own interests than with his military duties; thus nothing advanced.[43] The same lack of centralization also occurred among the Spaniards, but their great numbers made up for what they lacked in order. Always constant in their determination to harm the French, they achieved their goal and succeeded in one way or another. Moreover, they communicated among themselves with great ease and received very rapidly decrees from the Supreme Junta of Cadiz. If the Junta was not obeyed everywhere with great speed, insurrections occurred, at least in those areas that we did not occupy with a major force, and this created millions of enemies for us.

The Prince was impressed by these problems and attempted to remedy them by establishing an excellent plan of operation from which he sent a kind of report to the Emperor. He proposed to concentrate all the troops and divide Spain into three great commands. The 2nd, 5th, 6th, and 8th Corps with the troops of Generals Bonnet and Séras would occupy the northeast and conquer Portugal. The armies of the south, presently limited to blockading Cadiz and isolating it from the rest of the country, just as Gibraltar was by the camp of San Roque, would go into Andalusia and the Kingdom of Murcia. The corps of Suchet and Macdonald would protect Aragon, Catalonia, and Valencia, and complete the conquest of those areas. Finally the Army of the Center, under the command or at the disposition of King Joseph and formed by all the divisions of these French governments, would

43. The problems faced by the military commanders in Spain are exemplified in a letter from Ney to Berthier on April 18, 1810: "It would be very desirable for the Emperor to come to Bayonne to regulate the principal operations and give each army corps positive instructions on the conduct to be followed. This seems to be the only way to avoid all the orders and counterorders that constantly arrive from the King's headquarters and that are almost always as impracticable as they are contrary to the interests of the Emperor." See Bonnal, *Ney*, III, 310–12.

be made mobile and organized into brigades creating a great route [?] between Burgos and Madrid. This system of mobile columns would replace that of garrisons. While the troops, supported by combined movements, pursued the Spaniards, they would destroy the nests of guerrilla bands and dismantle the fortified places or do everything to entice those carrying arms to join our side either by the regularity and justice of the administration or by clemency and pardon. The first operation was to attack the English and chase them out of the Peninsula, since their presence supported and encouraged those with evil intentions, at the same time that it intimidated those who supported us or were tired of the war. The Prince then proposed to attack the British army immediately and enter Portugal without bothering about the fortresses of Ciudad Rodrigo and Almeida; this course did not appear completely proper to me. Perhaps he was listening too much to public opinion. Finally, to complete this project it would probably have been advantageous to form a special government for the country between the Ebro and Pyrenees; that area could easily have been occupied with battalions of the national guard and a few troops of the line at the most difficult points.

It is certain that if this project had been executed in its entirety, it would have had favorable results. Meanwhile, to comply with government instructions, the fortresses had to be seized before any further operations could be contemplated. The conquest of Portugal could not be undertaken without either the assurance of a strong base or the establishment of an intermediate depot, since all the country behind us was considered enemy territory. Indeed, the pacification of Spain could not have been completed without destroying the smallest nests of insurrection and, of course, strong fortresses like Ciudad Rodrigo, the seat of the Junta of Old Castile, situated near the mountains on plains rendered impracticable by the poor roads. For the same reason it was equally necessary to take Almeida and overthrow England's powerful influence, no less dangerous for western Spain than for northern Portugal. In short, if we had followed another line of operation along the banks of the Tagus for the conquest of Lisbon, it would have been more prudent to destroy these pockets of resistance and insurrection, which would have seriously agitated the right flank and rear of this line.

Chapter Two

THE SIEGE OF CIUDAD RODRIGO

It is truly remarkable that in the midst of the immense progress that was made in the science of war during the eighteenth century, the attack and defense of strongly fortified places did not advance beyond the achievements of Vauban.[1] The modifications that have been added since then are so few and are still so controversial that they are scarcely worth considering. It is often said that Turenne, Condé, Villars, and Saxe would be critical of present trends in military science;[2] nevertheless they would be amazed to see the order and rapid progress as well as the precision in maneuvering large forces, which they criticized, claiming that armies should not exceed fifty thousand men since not even that number of men could be put into battle. They would be astonished at the immensity of our projects, which encircle in one sweep those objectives which were the ultimate goals of their long operations. Only Vauban would find himself at home amid these innovations and

1. Sébastien Le Prestre, Marquis de Vauban (1633–1707), was a military engineer who directed 53 sieges for Louis XIV. He strengthened the French frontiers, constructed 33 fortresses, and fortified 300 additional cities.

2. Henri de la Tour d'Auvergne, Vicomte de Turenne (1611–75), was one of France's most brilliant commanders. He took part in the Thirty Years War, was involved in the Fronde, directed the French armies in the War of Devolution and the Dutch War, and conquered Alsace. Claude Louis Hector, Duc de Villars (1653–1734), commanded French armies in the War of Spanish Succession; he was victorious at Friedlingen and played a major role in the decisive battle of Malplaquet. Maurice, Comte de Saxe (1696–1750), served Louis XV in the War of Austrian Succession and won the battles of Fontenoy, Raucoux, and Laufeld.

would continue to dictate axioms to his followers. Perhaps this is the highest praise that can be given to that illustrious man, who first systematized this art and even developed techniques for artillery which have never been outdated in siege warfare. If anyone could surpass his methods, it would be the officers of our day, who have distinguished themselves by their vast knowledge and unrivaled application. Yet all that our engineers have been able to do is perfect field fortifications by adapting them more effectively to the terrain, extending their use to all strategic combinations, and augmenting them by the application of various principles of permanent fortifications. As a result, in the various countries where we have made war, there have been masterpieces of temporary defense which have been admired by foreign officers. We are especially indebted to this distinguished group of engineers for having reduced the science of fortifications to a common knowledge by writing so many excellent works within the reach of almost everyone. It is now a disgrace not to have a knowledge of it.

During the recent war Spain provided many examples of an obstinate defense, a trait found quite often in its history; recently it has brought more honor to the character of the Spanish people than has the ability of their commanders. We saw the city of Saragossa match the resistance of the town of Xativa and obtain a generous reprieve from the French which the grandson of Louis XIV refused to [grant].[3] In its defense, it surpassed the famous siege of Barcelona in 1713 and almost equaled those of Sagonte and Numance.[4] The French engineers gained great honor from the siege because of the ability and skill they demonstrated in their new attacks, and for their obstinate struggle in overcoming the Spanish fanaticism. The conquest cost them one of their most distinguished members [Lacoste], but it assured the submission of Aragon, which lost the nucleus of its forces. Moreover, it was the forerunner of a series of brilliant sieges, one of which was un-

3. Xativa (Jativa), a town in the Spanish province of Valence, was besieged by Philip V's forces in 1707. The inhabitants of the town, supported by a small English garrison, defended the walls, contested the town street by street, and finally retired into the castle where they held out for two months until famine forced them to surrender. Thereafter Philip V had many citizens put to the sword and the houses burned and razed.

4. After an extensive siege Barcelona fell to the forces of Louis XIV and Philip V in the War of Spanish Succession. Sagonte was taken after a heroic defense in 219 B.C. by Hannibal, and Numance succumbed to a protracted siege by Scipio Aemilianus in 133 B.C.

fortunately tarnished by cruelties that are seen today only among barbarous nations. At the other end of Spain there was another famous siege and the details should be given.

Everywhere a siege is a rather routine operation; nevertheless, the imagination is staggered by the enormous inventory of supplies and equipment that is necessary. A siege seemed impossible when one considered the work needed to undertake it, the time necessary to collect all the supplies, and the number of wagons required for transportation; this was especially true in the center of Spain, where everything was lacking and there was no hope of finding assistance in the cities, where communications were so bad and difficult, and where wagons and horses were rare. An outdated fortification that would have been considered unimportant in Flanders or even in Germany and would not have merited a full-scale attack or defense became a first-class fortress capable of stopping the army attempting to besiege it. Such was the situation at Ciudad Rodrigo, where the obstacles of the countryside, the inclement weather, and the lack of every necessity forced us to collect food for the besieging corps from a great distance and thus constituted a more effective defense for the city than its walls, its ample garrison, or the large English army nearby. Although we had devoted considerable time to preparations for the attack, we were not quite finished by the end of May because the sieges of Tarragona [*sic*] and Cadiz had absorbed all the personnel and material brought into or found in Spain.

Ciudad Rodrigo, built in the thirteenth century on the ruins of Mirobriga or Augusto-briga, had been continually fortified to protect its population, which seems to have been considerable and was now almost ten thousand people.[5] This fortress, situated in the middle of a flat plain on the banks of a river that was quite easy to cross during ordinary weather, had no particular relationship with the Spanish frontier. The same thing could be said about the [nearby] fortress of La Concepción; it was even more isolated from all natural obstacles and seemed to have been constructed only to observe Almeida as the latter had been built to watch Ciudad Rodrigo. The city was one of the stag-

5. Pelet correctly estimated Ciudad Rodrigo's population. According to a register kept at the convent of Santa Cruz, there were 10,000 inhabitants in the fortress. See André Delagrave, *Mémoires du colonel Delagrave, Campagne du Portugal (1810–1811)*, ed. Édouard Gachot (Paris, 1902), 42n.

ing areas for Spanish troops whenever there was a war against Portugal, and it served also as a depot on the frontier. The fortress thus played only a limited role in the military system of Spain. However, for us Ciudad Rodrigo had another kind of importance. The Spaniards considered it impregnable. It had become an active center of insurrection, and in some ways the capital of northwest Spain, because the Junta of Castile resided there. It included a garrison and considerable armaments. Finally, its proximity to both Portugal and the English army facilitated their communications with the insurgents of the neighboring provinces. For the insurgents it was the last hope of resistance and once it was in our hands their submission was assured.

The fortress was located on a plateau along the right bank of the Agueda. The escarpment facing the river was rocky and on the northeast side it descended in a gentle and slightly inclined slope. The plateau dominated all its environs except in the direction of Teso,[6] which linked it to the neighboring mountains. Teso dominated the fortress by a few feet. The countryside on the right bank of the Agueda was cut by sandy, rather deep ravines separated from each other by a few slight hills. Four thousand yards away were a number of knolls standing in a semicircle; they were steep, rocky, and covered with trees. On the other side of the river were the elevations of Manzano, rather steep and partly covered with woods, which extended to within twelve hundred yards of the city. All this countryside looked arid to us. The bad season and the cantonment of our troops must have contributed to this state because the area was said to be rather fertile.

Ciudad Rodrigo had two walls. The first one was an old hewn-stone structure thirty-five to forty feet high with a rather restricted terreplein and embrasures cut in the crest. The wall was formed in a curved line without any salients or recesses, and there were only a few towers on the flanks. The establishment of guns even on an angle was very difficult toward the river where the escarpment made an attack almost impossible. The wall was less thick and not terraced there. After the fortress had been taken and retaken during the War of Succession, the old

6. Teso, often referred to as Grand Teso or Grand Teso de San Francisco, was an elevation 105 feet above the valley floor and only 600 yards from the fortress. It dominated the main wall by 42½ feet. For details see Donald D. Horward, "The French Invasion of Portugal, 1810–1811" (Ann Arbor, Mich.: University Microfilms, 1962), pp. 103–7; Jacques Vital Belmas, *Journaux des siéges faits ou soutenus par les français dans la péninsule, de 1807 à 1814* (Paris, 1836–37), III, 215–18.

wall, now without a moat, was screened in 1710 by a low wall [fausse-braie] which ended, supporting both flanks, at the escarpment on the Agueda.[7] Toward the north the wall presented five salients with as many recesses, and toward the east there were four bastioned fronts of unequal width, poorly laid out with extremely small flanks, in the middle of the curtains. These curtains, resting almost against the old wall, left very little space for communication with the ramparts; often with steps, this area was only a few feet in width.

The new enciente, 18 to 20 feet high, had a dry moat 20 to 24 feet wide and 9 to 10 feet deep, with the escarp and counterscarp covered by uncut stones. This new wall was only half shielded by the crest of the glacis, and the old wall could be seen in almost its entire height. During the siege we doubted there would be any covered way, and at least there did not appear to be any palisade. The old castle, with a triple wall capable of lodging only a few hundred men, was far from any point of attack; only a small keep offered refuge for the garrison if an assault was launched on the main square. Any important interior defenses or even ordinary entrenchments were very difficult to construct because of the restrictions of the two walls and the proximity of the old wall to the houses of the town. Nevertheless, it was easy to isolate any breach by either trenches or barricades. The elevation of the ramparts also made house-to-house defense inside the city more difficult. A very flat demilune in front of one of the middle bastions was the only outside work of the fortress. However inadequate this description may be, it should be clear that the fortifications were imperfect, and even at the time of their construction they were less than adequate. If one of Vauban's systems with detached works had been applied to the old wall, which would have been excellent as a keep, and extended along the slope of Teso, Ciudad Rodrigo would have made an excellent stronghold.

The Spaniards had tried to create a kind of third wall toward the east by fortifying the convents of San Francisco and Santo Domingo and the suburb located between them. The works were linked together and covered by a line of field fortifications with some salients in the

7. In 1706 Ciudad Rodrigo was besieged by an Anglo-Dutch-Portuguese army which established two batteries at the convent of San Francisco and thirty mortars within 180 feet of its walls; the city fell after a nine-day siege. As a result, the new wall had been erected to prevent any similar attacks in the future.

form of redans or bastions. These works, still incomplete, rested in part against the enclosed walls of the suburb, and the sides were flanked by the convents, which had crenels and were entrenched more carefully. The convent of Santa Cruz on the north[west] had been put in a good state of defense, but it was separated from that of San Francisco and its extensive fortifications by Teso, whose base meandered along between them; and when the height of Teso was occupied they fell. In neglecting this important height, the engineers of the garrison had shown themselves no wiser than those of the past century. Like their governor they displayed more zeal and devotion than talent. Our engineers immediately busied themselves with Teso while the weak garrison, lacking resources and unable to extend itself, was forced to remain in the fortress. Teso could be fortified only by a permanent work or something similar.[8] There were no entrenchments on the left bank of the Agueda, and as a result the end of the bridge was occupied without much resistance.

General Andrés Herrasti[9] was the governor of the fortress, and his garrison was made up as follows: three battalions of chasseurs from Ciudad Rodrigo; a battalion each of regiments of Avila, Minorca, and the provinces of León and Valladolid; the militia of the city and environs; and finally 800 artillerymen of both army and navy and 600 [*sic*] horsemen of whom 200 were lancers. These troops totaled 7,000 or 8,000 men with 900 sick.[10] The place was very well supplied with food and munitions of war. Each soldier received his entire ration and there was an abundance of powder. The armament consisted of 125

8. Although the governor of the city had posted a Spanish infantry unit on Teso, Loison, realizing its importance, quickly drove them from the hill when the fortress was invested.

9. Andrés Pérez de Herrasti (n.d.) was born in Granada and entered the Spanish military at an early age. He had reached the rank of general by 1810 when he was given command of Ciudad Rodrigo and made a member of the Junta of Old Castile. For a valuable account of the siege, see his *Relacion histórica y circunstanciada de los sucesos del sitio de la plaza de Ciudad Rodrigo en el año de 1810,* published at Madrid in 1814.

10. The three volunteer battalions of Ciudad Rodrigo had 867, 720, and 835 men respectively; the battalion of volunteers of Avila included 857 men; the Minorca regiment consisted of 706 infantry; and the Segovian regiment (León and Valladolid) had 317 men. There were approximately 375 effectives among the artillerymen and trainees, and 310 noncommissioned and commissioned officers. In addition the guerrilla chieftain Don Julian Sánchez commanded 240 lancers and perhaps 50 guerrilla infantry. There were 100 cannon and 18 howitzers or mortars in the fortress.

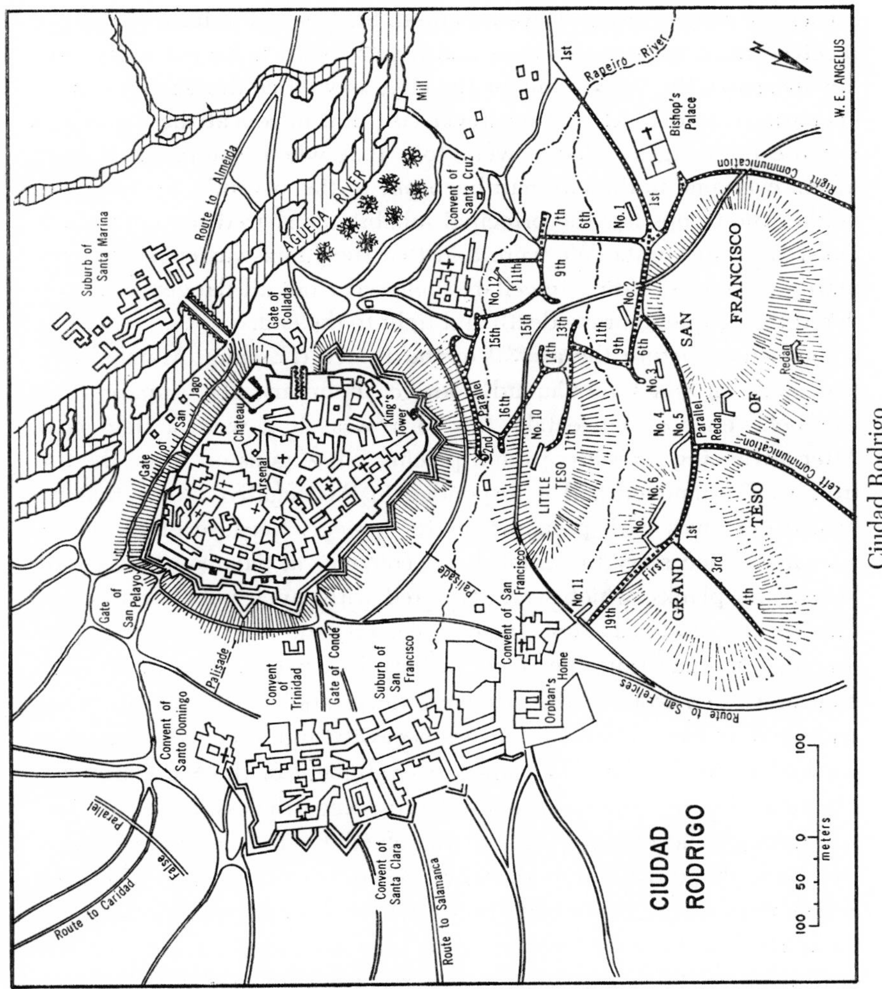

Ciudad Rodrigo

pieces, of which 8 to 10 were mounted. Such was the information we received from spies or deserters and it was found to be exact. By various measures the inhabitants of the city, as well as the garrison, were encouraged to defend it at whatever cost and to repeat the marvelous defense of Saragossa. They were told that when Astorga had been taken, everyone in the city had been put to the sword.[11] Nevertheless, neither the troops nor the principal inhabitants shared the enthusiasm and zeal of the Junta. We were told that the Junta was composed primarily of priests, hiding in cellars sheltered from all dangers; they ordered the people to brave death and fight to the end.

Some time before the arrival of the Prince d'Essling, Marshal Ney had made an attack on Ciudad Rodrigo [February 11]. Apparently it was believed possible to take this fortress as if it were a field post. After advancing some troops and placing a few guns on Teso, the fortress was summoned and it responded in the negative. After that we busied ourselves with preparations for a siege. Because of the shortages it was necessary to demolish the convents at Salamanca to secure beams and planks, which were gathered with much pain. From every direction the necessary tools [were collected] and a great number were forged. For some time the siege artillery had been gathering in Salamanca. The environs of the city were devastated for a great distance, and we were forced to furnish every necessity and to concern ourselves particularly with food. The transport equipment of the 8th Corps was placed at the disposition of the 6th Corps. Nevertheless, the roads, laid out through the countryside and dissolved by the continuous rains, were in such a terrible state that the first convoy of artillery, which left Salamanca on May 29 for San Muñoz, where the *parc* was provisionally established, did not arrive there until June 4—taking six and one half days to travel twelve leagues. A few repairs were made at the worst places, and the following convoys arrived there in two or three days by hitching eighteen mules to each piece. Nevertheless, we lacked teams for our artillery and had only one third of the necessary animals for the

11. When Astorga surrendered to Junot on April 10, 1810, approximately 2,700 soldiers of the garrison were sent to France as prisoners of war and 1,500 peasants who had served on the walls were sent to their homes. See D. José Maria de Santocildes, *Resumen histórico de los ataques, sitio y rendición de Astorga; de su reconquista y del segundo sitio puesto á la ciudad . . .* (Madrid, 1815); D. José Gómez de Arteche y Moro, *Guerra de da independencia. Historia Militar de España de 1808 á 1814* (Madrid, 1868–1903), VII, 144–75.

siege equipment. The same difficulties applied to everything else. The engineers, who had only their tools to carry, began work on the gabions and fascines. Preparations were still far from complete when the Marshal announced that we would be ready to start the siege on the earliest favorable occasion.[12]

On June 1 the 6th Corps, which was responsible for investing the fortress, was disposed as follows: the first brigade of the division under Marchand camped with its right at Pedrotoro and its left in the direction of Caridad; the second was in front of the convent of Caridad on the height of Cantarranas. The first brigade of Mermet's division was on the right of a ravine at Pedrotoro, four thousand yards from the fortress, and the second brigade occupied Sancti Spiritus. Loison's division was on the heights of Palomar with the right opposite Cunejera near a ford of the Agueda; it faced Teso and the fortress. From this camp all the siege operations could be observed perfectly. The light cavalry was used for the outposts; the 10th and 11th Dragoons occupied Tenebrón and Tamames in order to protect the army depot established in the village of Tamames, and the *parc* was advancing toward San Muñoz. The 3rd, 6th, 15th, and 25th Dragoons with an artillery company were to go to Caridad under the command of General Gardanne.[13] Communication with Salamanca was established by way of Alba de Yeltes, Cabrillas, San Muñoz, and Matilla.

This army corps suffered to an exceptional degree during the entire

12. Pelet's information is inaccurate and misleading. See note 17 below.

13. Count Jean Gabriel Marchand (1765–1851) was trained as a lawyer but gained command of a battalion in 1791 and became general of division in 1805. He served at Toulon, in the Italian campaign, in the Tyrol, and commanded a division of the 6th Corps at Jena and Friedland. Accompanying the 6th Corps to Spain in 1808, he was defeated by a Spanish army at Tamames in Ney's absence. Count Julian Augustin Mermet (1772–1837) joined the cavalry in 1787 and was promoted to general of division in 1805; he was in the Vendée until reassigned to the Army of Italy. Serving with the 6th Corps, he entered Spain in 1808.

Count Louis Henri Loison (1771–1816) enlisted in 1787 and was promoted to general of division in 1799; he was with Napoleon on the 13 Vendémiaire, served with Masséna in the Zurich campaign, commanded a unit at Elchingen and Scharnitz, and in 1807 accompanied Junot into Portugal, where he gained his sobriquet "maneta" (one-handed). He accompanied Soult in the second invasion of Portugal and commanded Ney's third division in 1810.

Count Claude Mathieu Gardanne (1766–1818) enlisted as second lieutenant in 1780 and by 1799 was general of brigade; he served in the campaigns from 1792 to 1797 and was at Genoa during Masséna's defense. After service at Austerlitz, Jena, and Eylau, he was appointed to command a brigade in Junot's 8th Corps.

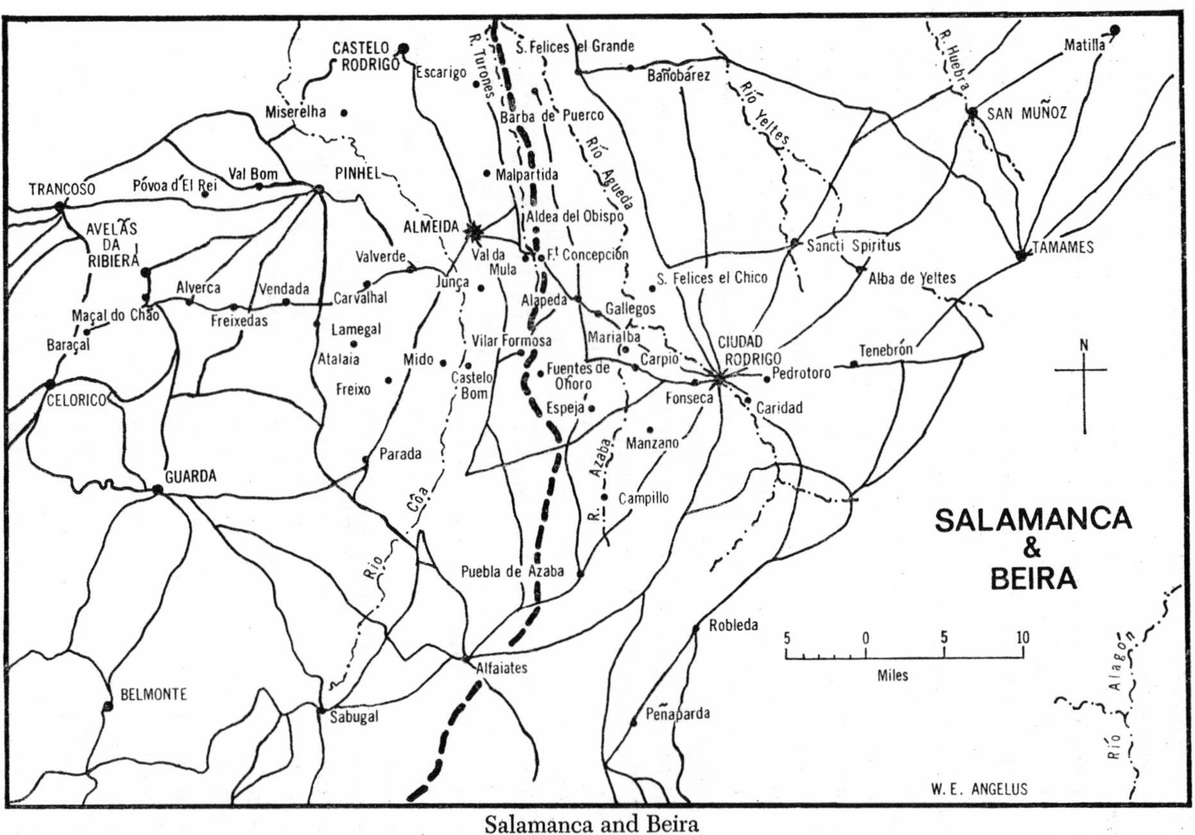

Salamanca and Beira

siege, and from the very beginning water gushed out everywhere, even on the highest ground. Soldiers were in the mud under the Genoa barracks and exposed to almost continual rain and extreme variations in heat and cold. They never had wine or brandy and often no more than half or even a quarter ration of bread, although the Marshal had stated that he had food for a month, even for the 8th Corps. No preparations had been made for ambulances, and the troops lacked cartridges even at the beginning; there were not enough for one battle, and yet there were people who talked only of attacking the English. Without barley, the cavalry suffered considerably from green forage, and the saddles were deteriorating.

On June 3[14] the Prince went to Ciudad Rodrigo with General Éblé to inspect the troops that surround it and to decide definitely on the principal dispositions for the attack. We passed through Matilla and Cabrillas, where the relays and escorts were located, and except for one league of cultivated ground around the two villages we found only wretched country, deserted, almost uncultivated, and covered with weeds and green oaks. The terrain was a little rough as we came out of Salamanca, more level toward the middle, with stony hills and ravines between the Yeltes and Ciudad Rodrigo. Farther on I expected to find better country and more cultivation as we passed through Castro and Robliza. Besides, all the roads, laid out across sandy terrain or along the plains, were easily damaged by the smallest convoys. The Matilla had a narrow bed and a little water. The Huebra River was 16 to 20 yards wide and the Yeltes 70 to 80 yards. These rivers crossed relatively flat countryside, but their banks were dismal and barren of the trees which beautify the streams in most countries. The inhabitants had begun to return to their homes. There were many of them, especially at Matilla, where they found protection with the commander of the Hanoverian Legion stationed there.

Upon our arrival at Ciudad Rodrigo, we went to visit the bridge set up on the Agueda above Caridad; its purpose was to provide communication for the corps assigned to invest the fortress from the left bank. This bridge, not yet finished, was on trestles and all the wood

14. There is some question as to the exact date of Masséna's visit to Ciudad Rodrigo. Letters from Masséna to Berthier on June 5 and from Ney to Junot on June 6, 1810, both stated that Masséna arrived at the fortress on June 1. See Belmas, *Journaux des siéges*, III, 275–80.

needed for its construction had to be carried from Salamanca. The water was then five feet deep, and there was danger it would rise at any moment. The bridge, already protected by the heights of the right bank which butted against the cove, was later covered by a lunette for one hundred and twenty men. It seemed appropriate to occupy the entire plateau in front as well as the flanks of the small area separating it from the Agueda in order to facilitate the retreat of a detachment placed on the left bank. Later we established another bridge on the lower part of the stream closer to Cunejera, where more difficulties were encountered due to the rising water, which increased the width of the Agueda to 120 or even 140 yards instead of 100 as we had expected. This position being less favorable, it was necessary to cover it by two nearby redoubts placed slightly to the right.

Early the next day the Prince went on horseback to inspect the troops. The divisions of Marchand and Mermet were superb, even in the midst of the mud. Each company of Maucune's brigade had set up great eagles [made] of grass in the front line of battle.[15] The Prince also rode around the fortress, reconnoitering its two walls and the entrenched suburb. The point of attack, generally coinciding with a [preliminary] plan, was fixed for the north section of the city on three salients toward the right which formed a kind of priest's cap. The terrain and [defensive] works, far from hampering the first dispositions agreed upon, on the contrary confirmed the advantages the ground offered. The reverse of Teso, which lay six to eight hundred yards from the center of the fortress, covered our approach and allowed us to start the establishment of the first parallel there or elsewhere. The crest of Teso assured our domination, or at the least an elevation equal to the parapet of the old wall. The entire old wall, as well as one-third of the lower enceinte, was exposed, and this permitted us to breach both fortifications from a distance of five hundred yards with our first batteries. The ground between Teso and the Agueda was low and easy to open. The river covered the right of our trenches, and there was shelter at the end of the glacis, one

15. Baron Antoine Louis Maucune (1772–1824) became a second lieutenant in 1786 and a general of brigade in 1807; he served in Italy from 1792 to 1803 and in Prussia and Poland in 1806 and 1807. He commanded a brigade of the 6th Corps when it marched into Spain in 1808, where he served until recalled.

hundred yards from the moat. Moreover, this [north] part of the fortress was the most isolated from the general defenses and the lateral fronts. Its defective profile offered dead angles and was undefendable except from the recesses; as a result, the crossing of the first moat was not very dangerous because of the limited length of the face. In order to approach the fortress we had only to seize the convent of Santa Cruz, and perhaps San Francisco could be safely neglected since these two posts would fall successively if we followed the approaches at the foot of Teso.

An attack on the other sections of the city presented more difficulties and less advantage. The fronts to the east were covered by the suburb, which we would have to approach and take with the sword—a deadly operation whose dangers had been shown in this Spanish War. Moreover, after seizing the suburb we would have been almost as far from the wall as from the summit of Teso and would have been forced to make our approach on regular terrain that sloped gently but was dominated by the wall. These fronts were curved so as to protect each other reciprocally, like a decagon. Their defense would have been very effective if the besieged had been clever enough to throw lunette-salients in the shape of half-moons before each front. In attacking the section of the fortress projecting to the south, we would have had abrupt and broken terrain for the approaches, an earthen salient from which to open the breach and debouch, very few sites to establish regular and enfilade batteries, and finally it would again have been necessary to seize half the suburbs.

The Prince and the Marshal seated themselves in front of the camp of Loison's division; from there they decided on the dispositions for the attack. The engineers and the artillery agreed [with the plan] because the enthusiasm of the 6th Corps overcame their usual opposition. The Marshal had started by keeping Colonel Valazé away from the direction of the siege, although he commanded the engineers of the army [*sic*].[16] The artillerymen announced that within three hours

16. Éléonor Zoa Dufriche de Valazé (1780–1838) entered the École Polytechnique in 1798; he became captain of engineers in 1803, colonel in 1810, and lieutenant general in 1830. After Austerlitz and Friedland, he took part in the siege of Saragossa and in 1810 was attached to Junot's 8th Corps and sent to Spain. Valazé directed the siege of Astorga in April 1810 and became involved in a controversy with Marshal Ney. According to Mme Junot, her husband recommended that

the fire of the enemy would be silenced, that in a few days the fortress would be captured, and that with the establishment of the first battery a breach would be opened in both walls. These pronouncements should be noticed because conditions changed as the siege continued. As soon as he arrived at Caridad [May 30], the Marshal had announced that everything was ready, that he could begin the siege and even complete it without the 8th Corps, and that there was enough food for two army corps.[17] The Marshal now found difficulties everywhere; at times there were problems about the banks of the Agueda and at other times about the corps on the left bank which confronted the English army. He wanted to have command of the entire 8th Corps. The Prince answered him, writing his replies on the Marshal's own letters. There was little agreement and even some bitterness between them. It appeared to us that the trenches could not be opened for several days more. It was true that the weather delayed our efforts because of the continual rain which threatened to inundate our works; water even seemed to ooze out of the stony elevations. On our return to Salamanca, the Prince told me he had written at the end of the month [of May] to request the rank of colonel for me, because I was only a *chef de bataillon*

Valazé direct the siege of Ciudad Rodrigo although he was only the commander of engineers of the 8th Corps. However, since General Joseph Lazowski, appointed by Napoleon to command the army engineers, had not arrived, Ney's chief engineer, Couche, was directing the siege. Masséna sent Valazé to Ney, who returned him with the comment that "the Prince d'Essling . . . is not going to upset my *état major*." The Prince again sent Valazé to Ney, who returned him with an insubordinate letter beginning, "I am a Duke and a Marshal of France like you; as for your title the Prince d'Essling, it is not important outside of the Tuileries. . . . When it pleases you to disarrange the *état major* of the army appointed by the Prince de Neufchâtel, you must understand that I will no more listen to your orders than I fear your threats." According to Mme Junot, Masséna was furious and shouted, "I want this young man to conduct the siege, and by the devil in hell, Monsieur Ney shall bend his knee before my will, or my name is not Masséna." The letter, quoted in d'Abrantès, *Mémoires*, XIII, 86–91, has since been proved a forgery though it has been quoted by numerous biographers of Ney; see, e.g., Andrew Hilliard Atteridge, *The Bravest of the Brave, Michel Ney, Marshal of France, Duke of Elchingen, Prince of the Moskowa 1769–1815* (New York, 1912), pp. 191–92. See also Bonnal, *Ney*, III, 325–28.

17. The investment of Ciudad Rodrigo was premature, but this was not Ney's fault. In letters of February, March, and April, Soult ordered Ney to invest the fortress "as soon as possible [or] compromise the success of the campaign." See Bonnal, *Ney*, Soult to Ney, February 18, March 19 and 22 (referred to in Ney to Soult, April 4), April 14, 1810, III, 297, 309, 313. In fact, Ney, convinced of the premature nature of the investment, procrastinated for almost three months. See Bonnal, *Ney*, Ney to Soult, March 17, 29, 30, April 4, 1810, III, 297ff.

and he then had five other officers with the same grade among his aides-de-camp.

As a result of the food situation, the Prince sent the following orders from Salamanca to the 8th Corps, though some of the orders were changed in their execution. Solignac's division was to be placed at Ledesma, Lagrange's division at Salamanca and along the communication road, and Clauzel's division at San Felices el Grande, a vital point and probably the only one where the enemy could maneuver to threaten the siege.[18] In 1704 Berwick had occupied this position to advantage.[19] The Prince sent his aides-de-camps, François Cavailher and Despenoux, to reconnoiter the country situated between the road from Salamanca to Ciudad Rodrigo and the Duero, and the road from Zamora to Toro.[20] We were in effect without maps, since that of Lopez, in spite of its large scale, was poorly marked, the roads and rivers horribly drawn and the terrain even more poorly represented.[21] The two aides-de-camp were to bring back a written reconnaissance of information on the defense and occupation of the country, and to make the needed corrections on the Lopez map.

18. Baron Jean Baptiste Solignac (1773–1850) enlisted in 1790 and became general of division in 1808; he served at Novi, in Masséna's Italian campaigns, and with Junot during the first invasion of Portugal. He returned to the Peninsula with Junot's 8th Corps in 1810. Count Joseph Lagrange (1763–1836) enlisted in 1791, was promoted to general of division in 1801, and served as Jérôme's minister of war in Westphalia. After fighting in Italy, Egypt, and Holland, he was sent to Spain in 1808. Count Bertrand Clauzel (1772–1842) was a second lieutenant in 1791, general of division in 1802, and marshal in 1831. He took part in the campaigns of Novi and Santo Domingo and marched with Junot's 8th Corps to Spain in 1810.

19. This name appears to be Bervier in the manuscript but in all probability should be Berwick.

20. Captains Cavailher and Despenoux were two of Masséna's fourteen aides-de-camp. They ranked in the following order: Pelet, J. B. A. Marbot, Casabianca, Ligneville, Barrin, B. A. Marbot, Renique, Porcher de Richebourg, Barral, Despenoux, Prosper Masséna, Cavailher, d'Aguesseau, and Victor Oudinot. In addition there were four orderly officers: Beaufort d'Hautpoul, Perron, de Briqueville, and Octave de Ségur. Two other officers, Jourdan and Rippert, were often included in Masséna's staff. For additional details see Marbot, *Mémoires,* II, 337–42; François Nicolas Fririon, *Journal historique de la campagne de Portugal, entreprise par les français, sous les ordres du maréchal Masséna, prince d'Essling, du 15 septembre 1810 au 12 mai 1811* (Paris, 1841), p. 59.

21. Thomas Lopez's map, published in 1779, was based upon local maps supplied by civil and ecclesiastical officials. The routes were copied from Juan Bautista de Castro's "Itinerary," officially known as "Roteiro Terrestre de Portugal," published in Lisbon in 1748. Lopez also used Castro's "Mappa de Portugal," published in 1762, and Thomas Jefferys's maps of Portugal drawn in 1762. The map scale is two leagues to an inch.

Cavailher, ordered to choose a central position for one division of the 8th Corps between Ledesma and Rodrigo, chose Aldeadávila, but the lack of subsistence did not permit its occupation. The other aide-de-camp, Despenoux, announced that General Mahy, with four to five thousand Galicians, was near Ponferrada and that there were also a few thousand Spaniards at Puebla de Senabria and Alcañices. At Bragança or Miranda there were two to three thousand Portuguese but no British. Within a few days Wellington had collected his best troops around Almeida.

During this period the enemy made some movements. They appeared in front of Astorga and invested that square-walled fortress. Situated on a small hillock which dominated the neighborhood, it was defended by numerous towers although half were almost in ruin. General Lauberdière was posted there with a fairly good garrison.[22] The enemy stayed only a few hours, retiring when Colonel Prévôt* arrived with some cavalary. The Spaniards had also attempted to surprise the town of León and kidnap our commanders and the French sympathizers, using several bands of twenty men led by Spanish officers. All these detachments, composed of experienced veterans, were vigorously attacked and taken or killed. Only one band succeeded in kidnapping a single commissioner and his treasury. The next day the commander evacuated León because of a false rumor of the arrival of a corps of four to five thousand men accompanied by the regiment of Castile. Some time later *chef de bataillon* Cristophe Antoine Stoffel, an officer of the *état major,* was sent to General Bonnet; he entered León and occupied it with eighty men until the arrival of Colonel Prévôt, who followed with a few more troops. Some of the Spaniards wore red uniforms and at first this led us to think that they were supported by the British. Before long everything was calm and peaceful. General Sainte-Croix had a rather brilliant affair at Alcañices, where he captured a few prisoners.[23] This young general officer, who

22. Count Louis François Bertrand du Pont d'Aubevoye de Lauberdière (1759–1837) attended the École Militaire and became a second lieutenant in 1776. As a lieutenant colonel he was sent to Ireland, where he was taken prisoner and held until 1800; after the campaign in Germany, he was promoted to general of division and sent to Spain. Within two years he served as governor of Zamora, Toro, León, and Astorga.

23. Count Charles Marie Robert Escorches de Sainte-Croix (1782–1810) was first attached to Talleyrand's ministry but in 1805 volunteered for service with Masséna's army and served as his aide-de-camp in the campaigns of 1806 and

had all the talents and qualities necessary to distinguish himself in war or to succeed brilliantly in any career, was hardly known by anyone. However, he excited such enthusiasm among the recruits of provisional squadrons of dragoons that they rivaled the veteran regiments, even against the English cavalry.

As our troops evacuated some areas of the Kingdom of León and drew closer to Ciudad Rodrigo, the insurgent bands returned to those areas and raised new reinforcements. A few of these groups had united into bands comprising a considerable number of men. That of the Curé included up to seven or eight hundred men; patrolling the area along the road from Salamanca to Valladolid, he kidnapped a detachment of sixty recruits as a result of the stupidity and stubbornness of its commanding officer. Others fought along the road to Zamora, and *chef d'escadron* Marbot, attacked by some, lost a few dragoons from his escort near Peñaparda. It was claimed that among the guerrillas there were many deserters from our own German troops and even a few French. Many of the insurgents wore our uniforms, which they picked up from convoys or from our dead men. It was even said that a few of our officers had joined them and that others supported them. In fact, from time to time we heard the guerrillas being given commands in French—shouts of "tighten the ranks"—and a few of them marched and fought with some order. Should we be surprised that there were a few worthless fellows in our forces, among so many men from so many countries who had grown accustomed to shedding blood in battle and to living by pillaging and marauding?[24] Should we not instead applaud the great number who endured fatigue, wounds, and privation far from their homes and remained only because of a sense of honor and discipline?

Marshal Ney had sent a cavalry reconnaissance on Marialba, Carpio, and Manzano, and they found only a few British who retreated. Ney forced the guards occupying the bridge back inside the fortress. Our engineers had gone forward to Teso and traced a work. The Marshal

1807. After fighting at Lobau and Wagram, he was promoted to general of brigade. Sent to Spain in 1810, he commanded a cavalry brigade of Junot's Corps until killed at Vilafranca.

24. Foreign troops in the Army of Portugal included 345 Hanoverian Chausseurs in the 2nd Corps, 1,158 infantry of the Hanoverian Legion in the 6th Corps, and 1,008 Irish infantry and 986 Prussian soldiers in the 8th Corps. For details see the Appendix.

now announced new delays and strongly insisted on the occupation of the left bank of the Agueda to guarantee our approaches from reverse and enfilading fire. The Prince sent General Fririon, the chief of staff, to the Marshal and gave me orders to accompany him.[25] We found that the roads were becoming more and more wretched; they had turned into streams and even torrents. It was necessary to have oxen pull the general's extremely light carriage from the mud, and up to ten horses were employed to haul the empty caissons. The Marshal had five squadrons across and above the bridge, and he was planning to station an equal number below the bridge when it was completed. We found he was not very positive about the strength of the corps that was to occupy the left bank. At times he was content to observe it only with cavalry, and at other times he planned to send two infantry divisions with all the cavalry to advance and cover the siege.

We discussed these various dispositions with the Marshal. Above all [we agreed that] it would have been wise to delay the operation until everything had been prepared and collected, and to act according to [regular] principles. In the present situation, it was possible to make a distinction between simply besieging a fortress and blockading it so that nothing could enter. However, this fortress had more munitions and troops than were needed, and nothing could prevent messengers from communicating with the English army. Therefore, we only needed to post a few troops on the other side of the Agueda to warn of enemy movements, with posts strong enough to cover our bridges and prevent the enemy from establishing himself on the flank of our trenches. Yet if we wanted to advance an army corps, how far would it go when the enemy was only eight leagues from the Agueda? Would we approach the enemy, or stop midway? Could a battle be fought against an enemy fort with a river and two small poorly defended bridges at our back? Could we rely on the supposition that the river would remain fordable, when we could see that the mountains were still covered with snow? And finally if the English started marching, was it certain that they would march straight toward Ciudad

25. Baron François Nicolas Fririon (1766–1840) enlisted in the army in 1782, was promoted to major in 1794, and general of brigade in 1800; he served at Hohenlinden and was with Masséna in Italy and at Essling. He was appointed chief of staff of the Army of Portugal in 1810.

Rodrigo and not maneuver on our left flank, or rather on the village of San Felices el Grande and the lower part of the Agueda? From there they could throw an advance guard on the Huebra, and not only cut off at Salamanca the army engaged in the siege, but also force us either to abandon our artillery or remain in front of the fortress to protect it. These were the options of the British army, which, without jeopardizing anything, could put us in a rather embarrassing situation and save Ciudad Rodrigo. Would we be concerned if, by chance, the enemy marched toward the fortress under fire from our trenches? If he dared to do so, would it not be a great disadvantage either to wait for him there or to reinforce the army's right for a battle? Why should Wellington tempt the fate of his army in such a daring operation while he held the excellent fortresses of La Concepción and Almeida, and the line of the Côa, behind Ciudad Rodrigo?

The dispositions [proposed by Ney] would, in effect, have two divisions of the 6th Corps along the Azaba, Clauzel's division at San Felices el Chico, Solignac's first brigade at San Felices el Grande, and the cavalry along the Agueda and toward the left; however, several bridges on the Agueda would be necessary above the mouth of the Azaba to facilitate communications among the divisions as the enemy moved, or, in case of a retreat, around Ciudad Rodrigo. But above all the enemy would have food and the resources to transport it while we lacked everything. Furthermore, by this disposition the right bank of the Duero would be opened, as well as the north of Spain. Finally, we rejected any idea of questioning the government's formal orders to besiege Ciudad Rodrigo and limited ourselves to threatening the enemy.

The Marshal listened to all this reasoning with patience but was not convinced. Nevertheless, he seemed satisfied that the disposition of troops around the fortress had been made too hastily before preparations had been completed.

General Fririon and I went to see the city with Bertrand Constantin and Delachasse-Verigny. Opposite the suburb there were a few works set up six to eight hundred yards away to cover the troops against gunfire, and on Teso two types of lunettes were advanced successively to within five or six hundred yards of the moat. The houses on the right toward the Agueda were protected by our troops and the convent by the enemy. In the front of this [rudimentary] kind of line, our sharpshooters were posted in foxholes wherever possible. From one of these holes I could see the first wall all the way down to its base. It appeared to be resting against the houses, and beyond the second wall there was no covered way. The latter was no higher than fifteen feet and the moat, which could be seen running along it, seemed to be eighteen feet wide and eight to nine feet deep. At the end of the glacis, I also recognized a mound or projection almost parallel to its crest, about twelve feet high.

We had heard a good deal of talk about a supposed breach, and I think we had even taken account of it in our dispositions at different times. I could actually see that a new wall had replaced a gap and some of the old wall that extended from the castle to the gate opening toward the Agueda. But the hole was the result of an explosion that had taken place seven years earlier and it had been carefully closed. Moreover, it was located in a recess which would have been very difficult to reach by the approaches. It also appeared to me that it would be possible to batter a breach in those two walls from our projected parallel, for the enemy balls went well beyond Teso while ours struck men on the ramparts quite often. All the ground including Teso itself was covered by very sharp stones and was always quite wet; on some flat areas our horses would sink up to their chests. We had been told that the besieged were relying so heavily on the rain for their defense that they had placed a crucifix in the water at Ciudad Rodrigo to obtain rain.[26] That night [June 23] the convent of Santa Cruz was stormed and seized by a hundred skirmishers from a battalion the Marshal had organized for the siege. The command of this unit had been given to Captain François, who led the attack with the support of three companies of voltigeurs or grenadiers. The doors were broken down with axes, and we fought with bayonets; twenty-one Spaniards, including one officer, were killed. Captain François and three of his soldiers were wounded, but no one was killed on the French side. Later we had to abandon the position because it was

26. In a letter to Berthier, Masséna complained that the rain had not ceased since the beginning of May. "The roads are completely impassable. . . . It is true that as far as anyone can remember, we have not seen the rains as heavy and as continual as in this season." See Masséna to Berthier, June 5, 1810, Correspondance: Armée de Portugal MSS, Carton C[7]8, Service historique de l'armée, Vincennes.

too remote. The next day General Loison made a reconnaissance on the heights of Carpio, and he placed a few troops on the left bank of the Agueda beyond the bridgehead; the left was extended toward Fonseca by vedettes to link with the squadrons of General Milet.[27]

That night we slept with General Marchand's division. The conversation there was only about the lack of food. The shortage was so severe that we could not obtain bread, forage, or lodging for our escort of five dragoons. According to several of the officers, abandoning the siege was the only way to relieve this misery. Fortunately, soldiers usually complain a little more than is necessary; otherwise everything would seem hopeless. The scarcity intensified the lack of unity that existed among the troops of the army. This dissension was carried to such a point that General Taupin[28] of Clauzel's division wrote that he claimed all food supplies on the right bank of the Yeltes; he would shoot anyone who came there searching for grain. If necessary, he would send a force to recover a herd that belonged to him. The quartermaster general, Lambert,[29] who had just arrived, received orders to divide the food exactly between the army corps, to send rations immediately to the 6th Corps, and to have ovens established at Pedrotoro and Alba de Yeltes.

The Prince received letters from the Major General, Prince de Neufchâtel, which confirmed the dispositions the Prince had adopted. The Prince was ordered to act methodically, not to hazard anything, and to prepare for the siege of Almeida. The cavalry was to be united in a reserve corps under the command of General Count Montbrun.[30] Lagrange's division was dissolved; its supplementary battalions were to guard Salamanca temporarily and later to be united with other

27. Baron Jacques Louis François Milet (1763–1821) became a second lieutenant in the 8th Dragoons in 1792 and general of brigade in 1800. He served at Marengo and in the Grand Army between 1805 and 1807, and during the invasion of Portugal he commanded a cavalry brigade in Trelliard's division.

28. Baron Eloi Charlemagne Taupin (1767–1814) enlisted as a second lieutenant in 1791; he became colonel of the 103rd Line in 1805 and general of division in 1813. Taupin served at Diernstein, at Austerlitz, in Prussia, and was attached to Soult's 2nd Division when it entered Spain.

29. Jean François Lambert, quartermaster general (d. 1837), was an army paymaster who served in Germany, Italy, Holland, Switzerland, etc., until he was attached to the Army of Portugal in 1810.

30. Count Louis Pierre Montbrun (1770–1812) enlisted in 1789 and became general of division in 1809. As a cavalry officer he served in the Armies of Italy and the Rhine and in 1808 was sent to Spain.

troops to form another division. Séras was ordered to support the right of our operation and to occupy León, Astorga, and Zamora. The 65th Line was incorporated into Solignac's division and the 15th Line into General Clauzel's division. General Reynier, placed at the Prince's disposal, was to remain at Alcántara and extend his troops toward Ciudad Rodrigo as soon as we began action there. Finally, it was announced that twenty thousand men of the Young Guard were to form our reserve and maintain the country behind us. It would certainly have been helpful if all these dispositions had been put into execution before the artillery was placed in front of Ciudad Rodrigo, but everyone was in a hurry and the suffering of the troops would not allow any delay.[31]

The besieged made several sorties, but none had any success. The largest one was that of June 6. In the morning six hundred men who attacked the posts on Teso were pushed back by a reinforced company. Around nine o'clock a similar number of bourgeoisie in their white coats and stockings came out toward the houses along the lower part of the Agueda to try their strength. Three companies of grenadiers or voltigeurs received them with bayonets and threw them back on the glacis. Finally at noon the attack was renewed by twenty-five hundred to three thousand men protected by artillery placed on the lower wall and even outside along our flank. Our voltigeurs sustained their positions with firmness. As soon as they saw the advance of four reinforced companies sent by General Loison, supported by eight other companies placed behind Teso to fall on the flank of the Spanish, the voltigeurs charged against the enemy, pushed them back with bayonets, and pursued them all the way to the foot of the glacis, causing considerable losses. The advance posts of the fortress were withdrawn successively and ours took up positions four hundred yards from the works. During the night of the 13th the investment was completed between the suburb and the Agueda above it. A detachment of three hundred men took positions within half distance of the guns' range. This worried the enemy very much, and they used two hundred workers to palisade the gap between the right side of the suburb and the fortress proper. For the next two days the enemy opened heavy fire on our positions.

31. For details of this dispatch to Masséna see *Correspondance de Napoléon Ier*, No. 16504, Napoleon to Berthier, May 27, 1810, XX, 438–39.

The night of June 15 to 16 had been designated for opening the trench.[32] The Marshal gave skillfully conceived instructions that were very well executed. Two thousand two hundred laborers, divided into seven detachments led by engineer officers and preceded by nine companies of grenadiers fifty steps ahead, marched to the ground where the parallel was to be built and lay down on their stomachs. Five battalions had already been placed there earlier in the night to support them: one was behind the bishop's palace, three in the two works on Teso, and one to the left and slightly behind Teso. These protected battalions were to keep their positions during the day, and the grenadiers were to relieve the unarmed laborers in the trenches. A segment of the detachment was placed in the communication trenches, which were started at the same time as the parallel. One false attack was directed against the suburb [of Santa Marina] across the bridge and another against the extreme right of the large suburb [of San Francisco]; these diversions attracted the attention of the enemy. Moreover, discipline and silence were so well observed during the actual attack that the fortress directed all of its very heavy fire on these other points and the workers were not disturbed. Thus our losses were very low although we had opened up twelve hundred yards of parallels for an average distance of 510 yards and in stony and very difficult ground. By the time the enemy realized their mistake, the trenches were already three feet deep and four feet wide. They fired all their artillery and muskets simultaneously but without causing much trouble. The total loss for the day was fifteen dead and forty-nine wounded during the various attacks.[33] The battalions of trench guards were relieved at noon, and these shifts continued every day in the same manner. The workers were paid one franc per day and seventy-five centièmes for each night.

The next day a Spanish officer deserted, and he confirmed these same details about their tactics and the garrison. Every day the government announced that the British would help, but the troops

32. Impatient about the deliberate movements of the French before Ciudad Rodrigo, Wellington wrote to his brother, "This *bicoque* has been in part invested for nearly two months; and a fortnight has elapsed since the guns moved from Salamanca; and the French are not yet in possession of the ground they must have for the siege. This is not the way in which they have conquered Europe!" See *Wellington's Dispatches*, Wellington to Wellesley, June 11, 1810, VI, 186–88.

33. There were actually ten dead and seventy wounded. See Koch, *Mémoires de Masséna*, VII, 66.

did not expect it. The rains continued and we encountered a few springs of water that obstructed our works considerably because the lower part of the parallel filled with water and delayed our progress.

A very lucid report from *chef de bataillon* Constantin furnished me with some details on the approaches for the attack. The first five nights were spent perfecting the parallel and the communication trenches. They were ten feet wide at the bottom, three feet deep, and had four-foot parapets with two banquettes. On June 18 the parallel was extended on the left by a 120-yard reverse after the enemy attempted a sortie to seize it. General Éblé located and determined the emplacement for the batteries on the 17th and the work was completed only during the night of the 19th to the 20th. At first there were six in number. The first battery was on the right before the bishop's palace, the others to the left of the parallel on the heights of Teso.[34] It was not until the sixth night [June 23–24] that two approaches were started in front of the parallel, one of 224 yards and the other of 160 yards. On the ninth night two reverse approaches were added on to the first approaches. The work had slowed down a little. The same night of the 23rd to 24th, the Marshal ordered an attack on the convents of Santa Cruz and San Francisco because they had begun to obstruct the approaches. Santa Cruz was taken and held in spite of stubborn resistance. San Francisco, still quite far from us and more easily recaptured, remained with the enemy.

Meanwhile, the Prince, within a few hours of the siege, remained at Salamanca to finish the reorganization of the army and to arrange for the vast needs of his government. He was also able to survey the movements of the enemy beyond the Duero. It was obvious enough that Wellington was not going to attempt anything before we opened fire, which had been fixed for the morning of June 27 and not earlier than the 26th. On the 24th the Prince left for Ciudad Rodrigo and arrived rather early at Caridad. The Marshal had just left. The same day General Gardanne, after making a reconnaissance in front of the British posts, established his troops on the banks of the Azaba. The Prince was warned at midnight by General Éblé that the bombardment was to begin at four o'clock in the morning in spite of what had been previously agreed upon and announced. The Prince immediately

34. For the complement and location of each battery see Belmas, *Journaux des siéges*, III, 226–27.

called General Fririon and me and sent us to the Marshal with all speed. We had hardly arrived when the Prince himself came, complaining vigorously about the haste and the disastrous effects it might have. Despite the explanations I was convinced, and it was later confirmed, that the Marshal did not expect the Prince there that day; he hoped to overwhelm the fortress at the outset and have it fall at the first fire. The Marshal wanted to capture it before our arrival and get the credit alone. Nevertheless, as I have indicated, all the arrangements had been made to commence fire. The Prince did not give contradictory orders, and he went to the camp to see its effects.

At dawn every battery opened fire at the same time with all forty-six of their guns. At first the city appeared disconcerted. Initially it replied with rather sporadic and uncertain fire; later there was a more intense fire from a number of guns which were superior to ours and of a larger caliber. Soon guns were firing vigorously from both sides and the noise was terrible. Those who had never before seen a siege believed that everything would be destroyed. Nevertheless, there was little result on either side. In our camp the first day resulted in a few accidents occasioned by our haste in opening fire. A small powder magazine for the batteries, not sufficiently covered, had exploded, resulting in the loss of a few men. The next day the Prince, finding that he was too far from the trenches, ordered a hut to be built for him near Casasola, a small house on the left and very close to Teso.

The Prince ordered that his aides-de-camp, Captains Jean Barrin and Cavailher, inspect the trenches daily and submit a report to him. Captain Barrin was a well-decorated old engineering officer who had lost an arm at Wagram, but he did not want to leave the Marshal and had continued to serve him with the same diligence and much zeal. Captain Cavailher had had his thigh pierced during the same battle; he was an old geographical engineer officer, full of valor and a true comrade in arms, with whom I did part of my studies. I became a soldier in 1800, and we had been together since then.

Our firing continued with some success, and the Prince ordered it to be increased. We fired vigorously and by salvos. I visited the entire trench network. It was not very safe anywhere, but the enemy appeared to be demoralized (a word coined by our armies to indicate dejection). They fired occasionally from a few guns or howitzers. The old wall had been damaged; the parapet of the lower wall was shattered up to its crest. We walked outside the trenches for a long time. About three o'clock the Prince returned to the camp and summoned the fortress. The rather frequent deserters reported that the garrison strongly desired to capitulate, but the feelings of the people and the Junta were diametrically opposed. The response of the governor was circumspect and polite.[35] He said the place was not yet ready to surrender, and he asked to send dispatches to Lord Wellington; this was refused.

At four o'clock in the morning the Prince went to reconnoiter the line of advance posts. We crossed the bridge to the right. There the Agueda was deeply embanked, narrow, and frequently fordable. It was like this up to San Felices el Grande, where it was said to be almost inaccessible because of rock-covered banks. We followed the Almeida road to Marialba, a poor village one and a half leagues away, near the confluence of the Agueda and the Azaba. The Azaba was thirty-six to forty yards wide and deeply embanked at the bridge of Marialba, where the road descended through a sharp defile. Toward Carpio it was less deep, and higher up it flowed at ground level on the slopes or glacis. This bridge was occupied by posts of British infantry and cavalry.

We followed a large undulating plateau covered with crops as far as Carpio, which stood on a height within cannon shot of the river. There the British posts ended and those of the Portuguese and the Spaniards began. Toward Marialba, Lorcet's brigade of the 3rd Hussars and 15th Chasseurs was posted. The brigade of Cavrois included the 15th and 25th Dragoons around Carpio, while General Milet, with the 3rd and 6th Dragoons, occupied the gap between the left of these troops and the Agueda above the bridges. These cavalry units, with a few infantry battalions and a battery of six pieces, were under the command of General Gardanne. [In case of attack] the

35. Ney sent an aide-de-camp, Captain Esménard, with a summons for the governor: "I am pleased to render justice to you for the fine defense, and the courage that your soldiers have shown . . . but these efforts will destroy you if you continue your defense much longer. You will then force the Prince d'Essling to treat you with all the rigor the law of war authorizes." See Belmas, *Journaux des siéges*, Ney to Herrasti, June 28, 1810, III, 286–87. Herrasti responded: "After forty-nine years of service, I know the military law of war and my military duty. I will know . . . when the circumstances are such as to request capitulation after taking care to protect my honor, which is more dear to me than life itself." See Herrasti, *Relacion histórica*, Herrasti to Ney, June 28, 1810, pp. 84–85.

line would contract on the right bank, extending itself on our left with General Trelliard and four regiments of dragoons.[36] According to information given by deserters and spies, General Craufurd, the commander of the enemy advance guard, was either at Gallegos or Almeida.[37] At his headquarters Craufurd had the 1st Regiment of German Hussars, two battalions of light infantry, and two artillery batteries; at Fuentes de Oñoro the English 95th Rifles, a thousand men strong; and at Vilar Formosa five regiments of British infantry with two Portuguese regiments. His advance post was composed of the hussars and light infantry. The Prince ordered Taupin's brigade to a station on the left between Marialba and Carpio and the brigade of Ferey beyond.[38] We carefully studied the terrain that might be our battlefield if the enemy decided to disturb the siege by marching directly toward us. It consisted of great plateaus, slightly inclined, rather exposed, and well adapted to all kinds of maneuvers. The front of the Azaba could be defended with advantage, but the enemy would not fail to advance toward our left. This part of Lopez's map was rather exact. Returning, we examined the fortress from a completely different point of view; this inspection allowed us to uncover new information and rectified what was already known.

Meanwhile, after four days of fire, the siege was not advancing.

36. Baron Jean Baptiste Lorcet (1768–1822) enlisted as a lieutenant in 1792 and became general of brigade in 1799; he served in Germany, Italy, and the Vendée. In 1808 Lorcet was sent to Spain, where he assumed command of Ney's cavalry after Auguste Colbert had been killed; he remained with the Army of Portugal until Fuentes de Oñoro.

Louis Joseph Cavrois (1756–1833) enlisted in 1776 and became a general of brigade in 1795. He was captured by the Austrians and later by the British. He fought in the revolutionary battles of Valmy and Jemappes and served with the Army of the Rhine until he was sent to Spain in 1808 where he commanded a cavalry brigade.

Count Anne François Trelliard (1764–1832) enlisted in 1780, became a general of division in 1806, and served with French armies in Germany and Holland. He was at Ulm and Austerlitz and was sent to Spain in 1808 where he commanded in La Mancha.

37. Robert Craufurd (1764–1812) joined the army as an ensign with the 25th Foot. He served in India, Ireland, and Argentina before his promotion to brigadier general in 1807. He served with Baird and Moore in the Peninsula and as commander of the British Light Division he was engaged in most of the fighting with Masséna's army.

38. Claude François Ferey, Baron de Rosengath (1771–1812), enlisted in 1788, became a general of brigade in 1803, and general of division in 1810. He served in the French armies in Italy, Germany, and Poland, and was given a brigade of Loison's division before it entered Spain.

There was noticeable deliberation and hesitation in the operation. The trenches were making little progress. The approaches were sometimes poorly laid out. A few of them were enfiladed, especially on June 29. The fire of the enemy regained its superiority; our guns fired little, and already four of our pieces of 24 were *évasée* [flared]. A battery firing against the convent of San Francisco produced little effect; two mortars and two howitzers were placed there. The next day a report appeared that seemed to have been inspired by the Marshal; it presented events in quite a different light than when first announced. It claimed that the haste in the firing and the attempts to open a breach had not produced the anticipated effect; hence we were obliged to examine our remaining resources. Because of the shortage of large projectiles, because of the reduction of smaller and mobile guns [?], and because eight or ten more days were required to complete the approaches, it was proposed to reduce or even suspend fire in order to advance the breach batteries. This was not the time to make such assessments. They should have preceded and regulated the premature bombardment. Apparently it was an attempt to blame the error of rushing the siege operations on the Prince, who had ordered the batteries to fire. Since the Marshal had announced the hasty surrender of Ciudad Rodrigo in Paris, we thought this report was made to justify the delays and relieve him of the responsibility for erroneous decisions.

The Prince was furious. Nevertheless munitions were disappearing, food was being consumed, and soldiers were suffering considerably. Five engineer officers were casualties. Many artillerymen had been killed. Poor use of the remaining munitions could reduce us either to a bloody but fruitless attack on a partially completed breach or to the disgrace of raising the siege. The Prince concurred with these observations; but to stop all subversion at its roots, he renewed his order that Colonel Valazé take command of the works; he gave General Éblé the specific task of supervising the batteries in order to reduce the firing without suspending it. He then gathered the general and superior officers from the engineers and artillery at the Marshal's camp. There he gave his orders. Valazé took command of the engineers, and Couche [whom he replaced] kept his hopes for advancement. We had made a mistake when we began our siege so poorly. A plan of attack and operation should have been made in consultation with the engineers and artillery; moreover, it should have been commanded by the Prince. According to the reports of the artillery and engineer officers, the original plan had called for this procedure.

Henceforth it became necessary to entreat the Prince to maintain as much moderation as firmness in his relations with the Marshal, for under the circumstances he truly had reason to complain about him. Disagreement was apparent on every occasion. The Marshal would say, "Give your orders since you command." "I will give them to you" [the Prince would respond]. [Ney:] "You should never have accepted a command over a comrade." [Masséna:] "You! You could not have done so, but I have been accustomed to command for a long time, and for several years I have even commanded you as though you were one of my brigade or division generals." Two days later the Marshal thoughtlessly remarked in conversation, "If you ordered me to take the suburb, I would disobey you." And at this very moment he was withdrawing his support on the right flank at the convent of San Francisco, though its occupation was strongly urged because it impeded our trenches and its capture would necessarily result in the fall of the suburb.

In this way the rivalry of these two great men manifested itself and it was later to have very fatal results. On the one hand [Masséna] had authority of command and maturity, together with an old tradition of conquest and sometimes of commanding with rigorous strength, especially when he encountered opposition or pretentious enemies. On the other hand [Ney] had all the fervor and strength of virility, the ardor of an impetuous and turbulent character, a self-esteem that wished to recognize only an equal in his old chief; he strongly resented carrying out Masséna's orders and seeing conquests taken that he himself had initially spoiled or promised. Finally, there were eminent titles and high military reputation on both sides. The Prince's reputation had been established by brilliant exploits over a long period of time, and the Marshal's was founded on immortal victories won during the conquest of so many kingdoms; in these achievements he attributed a greater role to himself than he had actually played, but he was supported in effect by the intimate favor of the sovereign and by great influence at the court. The situation had great potential for trouble, but without making excuses for either man, they should have heeded and obeyed their country and honor before everything else. Nevertheless, the more Marshal Ney thought or believed that he had just reasons for complaint, the more it was necessary to show forbearance for his conduct, and there was a real need for this toward the end of the campaign. He needed Roman virtues to master so much passion, and these are not common in titled people. These examples cited are few in number, and more specious than substantial, and would not withstand critical examination. Besides, we have always experienced grave disadvantages in the rivalries of men of equal rank. Perhaps it was an even greater mistake for the government to put two marshals together. However, it was thought wise to have a replacement immediately at hand on such a distant expedition, for accidents occur frequently during war.

As far as my position allowed, I went to the trenches almost every day to see the battery of mortars that was intended to strike the convent of San Francisco, already afire in two places. I found that the emplacement of the batteries was excellent both for enfilade and for ricochet at the point of attack on both walls. Yet we did not have this type of battery; all were direct or at most oblique, although the utility of the latter was contested. I talked about it to the Prince. I detailed the advantages of my proposed batteries to him and Colonel Valazé. It was necessary to write twice to the Marshal to obtain the battery, which did not start firing until July 7, though not without success. The next day I found the trenches well advanced. Colonel Valazé had generated great activity there and given it excellent direction. Despite a heavy bombardment of bombs, grapeshot, and musketry, he had placed six hundred gabions and opened four saps. The approaches were nearing the reverse, located at the foot of the glacis. It was also getting close to the abutment of San Francisco or Calvary.[39] The breach of the lower wall appeared to be sound and soon practicable [for an assault]. The breach in the upper wall was still escarped, but now the revetment had partially collapsed. We could already see the buttresses holding the earthwork. The convent of San Francisco was occupied during the night with little loss. The vast suburb [of San Francisco] appeared to be entirely abandoned. A few Spaniards could be seen in the farthermost houses, and our

39. This hill, often called Calvary or Little Teso, was situated between (Grand) Teso and the fortress. It was 56 feet above the valley floor and less than 200 yards from the breach.

men were able to go individually through most of the suburb to search for a little food.

The Duc d'Abrantès took command of two brigades of infantry and cavalry on the other side of the Agueda. The probabilities of a movement by a part of the English forces diminished with each day of firing. Also our advance posts announced that the English outposts diminished every day. At night we could see a few signals from the fortress; it fired little. Orders had been given to be ready to mount horses in case the garrison should try to escape. Some felt that escape was impossible while others maintained the contrary, declaring it was inconceivable that most of the garrison would thus flee. Yet we had three sentry [posts] ready.

Our posts stopped a priest, a member of the Junta, who was leaving the fortress disguised as a peasant in order to get to Lord Wellington and claim his long-promised help.[40] Under the threat of being hanged, he acknowledged his mission and declared that he was to warn the fortress by signals in either case [if the English planned to send help or not]. Finally, he promised to give the negative signals. He was taken to the heights of Manzano where we saw him make some kind of a signal. At first I did not look at this man because the spectacle of helpless misfortune has always touched my soul. Yet he interested me immediately. I found much devotion and patriotism in his actions. Everyone did not think the same, and his presence excited more anger than I would ever have been able to imagine. Initially, it was necessary to defend him from insults; we placed him with the sentries at the Prince's quarters, giving him protection rather than guards. Taking him some food was almost a crime. "Gentlemen," I shouted, "do you not admire the heroism of the Romans and that of our French? Why do you have contrary feelings about similar actions? Which one of you would not act the same way if ever your homeland [was invaded]?"

These feelings about the fate of our France had always haunted me. I could not foresee its misfortune then and I am proud of it; but after reading of all the triumphs of the century of Louis XIV, I was

40. The curé was Don Sebastian Gallardo, a member of the cathedral chapter of Ciudad Rodrigo. The French induced him to write to his nephew Agapito Gallardo, chaplain of the third battalion of volunteers, describing Masséna's anger with the garrison for its continued resistance. See Herrasti, *Relacion histórica*, pp. 48–50.

afraid to contemplate the deplorable ending. When I witnessed the restoration of Poland, when I saw the entire population of Mohilew, amid the inept attacks by the famous Bagration with his columns marching on the other bank of the Borysthenes, they were clamoring in the face of God for their rights, lost for half a century under foreign domination. They formed an armed confederation to defend those rights and united around the brave Poniatowski, who also honored me with his friendship.[41] Then I thought, "If ever our France were invaded, if ever in my old age I should see the foreigner in our land"; yet who would have believed then that twenty months later those Frenchmen who were delivering the people at the other end of Europe would bend their heads under the enemy yoke and let themselves be conquered twice in one year!

Everybody expected that the curé would be treated as a spy and shot. They even complained that he had not yet been. I first prevented his death and then kept him alive in the face of very great enmity. However I found in the Prince all the help of a compassionate heart. In a very touching conversation he told me how, at the siege of Toulon, he had taken into the fort of St. Catherine more than two thousand inhabitants, men, women, and children who came out of the city, and had thus protected them from the severity of the revolutionary laws. As I became more helpful to the Spaniard, I also became more interested in his conversation. I can still see him with his African complexion, his haggard and silent face, his fixed and firm eyes, wearing the black jacket of a peasant and a large hat for protection against the rays of the burning sun. Beside him were some scraps of food for which he was obliged to me. Seated on the corner of a rock among his enemies, he watched the ruin of his country. This climate, these bare rocks, this arid country, this black face full of religiosity and fierceness, brought back recollections of captive Israelites after the destruction of Jerusalem. The man had shown great character when he responded to the first insults of the soldiers with some kind of disdainful "Well, shoot me." He seemed unconcerned about his unfortunate fate; he accepted my care and consolation as

41. At Mohilew, on the banks of the Borysthenes (Dnieper), Marshal Louis Nicolas Davout took up a position on July 20, 1812, with some 30,000 men to await a Russian army of approximately 45,000 men commanded by Peter Bagration (1765–1812). The Russians attacked on July 23 and were repulsed. Marshal Joseph Poniatowski (1763–1813) was nearby with supporting units.

something that was due him. Yet the hate and vengeance that followed him were not unreasonably motivated. A Frenchman in his situation would have been torn apart in an instant and endured a thousand torments and a thousand deaths at the hands of the Spanish. Many of our men had suffered greatly because of them, or had watched the martyrdom of their comrades and found their bodies horribly mutilated. One of our officers, who gloriously escaped from the enemy's prison, reproached me because of the insults and wretched treatment he had experienced at Ciudad Rodrigo itself, and while crossing Spain from Galicia to Cadiz. "Yet you crossed it," I would tell him. Ultimately the poor priest reached safety. He escaped by running away from the 6th Corps; indirectly I was responsible.

During the night the artillerymen had traced the breach battery on the abutment [of Calvary] between Teso and the fortress about twelve hundred yards away. The works were very difficult because of the bedrock which had to be excavated. The artillery fired little. The large suburb [of San Francisco] was entirely occupied by our troops. There were continual rumors of a retrograde movement by the British. Was this caused by the announcement of General Reynier's march, which they had discovered in an order of one of King Joseph's Spanish officers? General Trelliard had learned very little during two reconnaissances on Campillo and Villarejo.

At dawn we heard artillery, and the noise caused considerable anxiety because of the direction from which it came. Above all, I was afraid of an enemy movement on San Felices el Grande. The source of the noise was a reconnaissance of the Duc d'Abrantès, who advanced to within one league of Fort La Concepción with the brigades of Lorcet and Sainte-Croix, supported by some infantry. He said that he had seen ten battalions and twelve squadrons of the corps of Craufurd and La Carrera on the heights. Adjutant Commander Rippert went there at the order of the Prince, and he saw nothing more than confusion. General Montbrun, who had just joined the army, advanced with his cavalry from Carpio beyond Espeja. The fortress, hearing the fire there, responded as strongly as possible but the firing diminished and ended rather weakly. The approaches continued very slowly. Meanwhile the new breach battery, noticeable from the outside, was twelve feet thick. The communication trenches between the convent of San Francisco and the parallel were open. Considering the state of the siege, the Prince sought to end further defense because the English were withdrawing. He wanted to send the curé into the city to ask the Junta to accept capitulation with some lenient terms. The priest refused absolutely, saying he would be hanged there because he had not been hanged by us. He now saw that he was safer in our camp than among his furious compatriots. He was given food regularly, and everyone became accustomed to see him around. It is difficult for the French to hate for long.

The Prince sent me to the Marshal to give him the results of the reconnaissance. The Marshal did me the honor of talking about our operation. With regard to a movement by the enemy, he thought it would be difficult for them to advance on San Felices because of the nature of the Agueda's banks, and a march on the other side of the Duero River would be almost impossible because it would expose central Portugal more seriously and seemed contrary to the existing state of affairs. In order to initiate broad maneuvers it seemed to us that Lord Wellington would have to attempt something on Coria and Plasencia. Such a move would be the most threatening to us, not only because of Madrid, but also because it would put him in the best position to defend Portugal. Yet if he marched into the midst of our forces, the 2nd Corps, the Army of Interior, and the Army of Portugal could easily gather a considerable number of men; and at the same time Lord Wellington would be vacating the entire north. Finally, the Marshal agreed it was quite probable that the enemy would do nothing for Ciudad Rodrigo. We could not agree on the means to be used against this fortress. The Marshal said he had learned to know the Spaniards and the war could be ended only with the most terrible examples. I replied by indicating that Europe and France would react with abhorrence to such brutality.

The Prince wanted to inspect the position of our advance guard and that of the enemy, for we rarely put complete confidence in the reconnaissance of the light troops. We found Ménard's brigade[42] behind Marialba and that of Sainte-Croix in the village itself; from there we could see a few defense dispositions prepared by the enemy with artillery epaulements on the left bank of the Azaba. The country

42. Jean François Ménard (1756–1831) entered the army in 1775 and was promoted to general of brigade in 1802. He commanded the first brigade of Clauzel's division in 1810.

beyond the river, sloped gently toward Gallegos, was covered with a fine harvest. Some of our men occupied half of the village. The enemy had a post nearby, but it was hidden by the heights. The Prince had me reconnoiter and sketch the country between the Azaba and Gallegos. We returned to eat lunch in Palacios at the Duc's quarters, where the commanders had long dissertations on theology, literature, and politics.

At last the ricochet battery started firing at four o'clock in the morning. It was placed at the foot of the convent of San Francisco and linked to the first parallel. On this day it fired a great deal; it was extremely useful, but also severely harassed. The bombardment was expected to make the ramparts uninhabitable shortly, but they used poor artillerymen who did not know how to fire ricochet. The enemy fired from every side with bombs, grenades, and muskets. I inspected the trench very closely and found most of our batteries under repair. Each one had several pieces or platforms out of service. At the breach battery some fifty feet of epaulement had been overthrown by enemy bombs, and its firing was delayed for twenty-four hours. The mortar battery at San Francisco had been withdrawn to Santa Cruz. The second parallel that troubled the fortress on July 3 was still in good condition, but it could not be protected in its entirety because of the enemy fire. The front of the sap reached to within fourteen or sixteen yards of the crest of the counterscarp; it extended to the right and left on such steep terrain that our approach, although enfiladed, was protected by the elevation opposite the angle of the breach. In order to blow up the counterscarp we had a mine gallery that was already twelve feet deep. All this was protected from grenades which our sappers nimbly picked up with their shovels and there was not as much damage done as we feared in spite of their proximity [to the enemy]. The engineer officers, Joseph Coffinal and Jean Schmidt, were wounded. The trenches had been regularized and made wide and deep. Some approaches had been hit, but they were protected as well as possible. In the evening a deserter, a second lieutenant of light cavalry, announced that Julian and his lancers had escaped by one of the fords on the Agueda.[43] He also told us that La Romana

43. Don Julian Sanchez was the son of a wealthy landowner from San Martino del Rio. With a small army of approximately 300 lancers and perhaps 500 infantry, he waged a private war against the French to avenge the honor of his family; his sister was raped and his father's house pillaged by French soldiers.

had come to solicit aid from Wellington on behalf of the besieged and that the latter had refused on the pretense that we had sixty thousand men in front of the fortress. The English General was well aware of our exact situation, for the couriers he so often captured had already informed him of the state of the army. Moreover, Wellington had our corps before him long enough to know the strength of our force. It was also said later that La Romana was coming with eight thousand reinforcements.

Meanwhile, the fatal hour was approaching for the unfortunate fortress. Everywhere there was talk of assault, of vengeance by the sword, of examples to be made, and we got tired and upset of hearing it. The soldiers, sometimes so charitable, demanded the fortress as a prize to compensate for their hard work, tedious hardships, and great privations. The officers sanctioned their demand by their conversation, and I yelled at them, "We called Suvórov a barbarian because of the atrocious massacres of Praga and Ismail.[44] Do you want to imitate him? What example shall we give when we leave Spain to enter Portugal? My name will never be attached to such horrors." They accused me of becoming soft. They would have charged me with pusillanimity if they had dared. One needed courage to show himself humane and just among all those passionate men. I would take refuge with the Prince, and each time he assured me that the fortress would be saved from such fury. Meanwhile, all the army talked only about burning the whole city and massacring the entire garrison. Individually, very few of these men would not have been capable of a good action; moreover, they were agreed that such an act of war would be an atrocity.

I see no reason to omit this paragraph, though it is a little off the subject of my Journal, since we have been accused on every side of casting off all humane feeling and becoming blind and even furious satellites of glorious despotism. Every night I took a walk by myself under the shining stars. The days were not beautiful there, but the nights were superb. Then I looked toward heaven [and thought of] my mother and absent friends. I found a little consolation and my

44. Marshal Alexandre Suvórov, Prince Italiski (1729–1800) commanded Russian armies in wars against Turkey and Poland. He massacred many Poles after capturing Praga, and thousands of Turks were butchered when he seized the city of Ismail. His army was defeated by Masséna's forces in the Zurich campaign.

soul was somewhat more peaceful. This immensity where everything praised the grandeur and the name of the Creator was so close to the place where men combined madness with every means of destruction. How could one be a soldier with a good heart and a pure soul? One should comfort humanity everywhere. There was virtue everywhere and there were *las casas* [?] in all classes.

At night I found the breach battery ready to fire again, a little oblique and sloping. The mine gallery was sunk to a depth of thirty or thirty-six feet. The enemy fired consistently, concentrating all their guns on the new battery. Within a quarter of an hour I counted twenty-six enemy bombs against seven of ours, and the latter did not seem to be well aimed. The Prince was anxious about the delays, so contrary to his characteristic optimism, and the work continued very late at night. The next day, at four o'clock in the morning, the breach battery commenced firing from the four pieces of 24, and it continued the entire day [July 9] with great success.[45] Enormous pieces of masonry were carried away, the buttresses caved in, and sod started falling down. The major batteries, also firing on the breach, began to exchange fire with the enemy guns. The Spaniards ceased fire for one hour and started again, but with less strength. The ricochet fire was poor and sporadic, but the mortars were frequent and effective. The fortress appeared to suffer greatly. There were two little [sorties] during the night, but they were forced to retire very quickly. The one on the left of the Agueda was sent to gather enough food for the herds, and the second, making a false attack at the other end of the city, was very slow and poorly protected. At night a large number of aides-de-camp went to the trenches to see the effect of the battery. The revetment showed more and more damage, especially at its base. Sod was falling down, but the parapet was not entirely overthrown. One could see a gun of the battery, but the extremities of the fronts were still standing. At the gallery we reached the counterscarp and made a "T" for two mine chambers. I reported to the Prince on the state of the breach.

At three o'clock in the morning the mine blew up and threw the counterscarp down into the moat, filling it completely. This success almost cost us dearly. Our friend Valazé was thrown back a moment

45. On July 9, 1,689 shells and 420 bombs were fired at the fortress.

earlier under a hail of grenades that fell on his head and chest.[46] For several days he lay between life and death, and for a long time he suffered the effects of his cruel wound; nevertheless, it did not prevent him from entering Portugal before he was completely recovered. At daybreak five pieces of 24 started firing again with new violence. All the batteries were firing simultaneously on the poor city, especially against the breach. Bombs were falling down with great rapidity and excellent marksmanship. On every side arose thick clouds of dust and smoke, pierced by the flames of the fires. The wreckage of buildings and walls was tumbling down with great noise, and several of the small magazines exploded periodically with tremendous detonations. The city seemed to be overwhelmed by so much firing. It responded rather weakly with the guns located on the *pavillon* and the *cavalier*; there were a few bombs and some musketry. The Prince sent me to the tower of the convent of San Francisco, already three-fourths ruined, to see if the breach had been entrenched. The tower shook under my step. I did not see any traverse to the fascines against the enfilading artillery and only slight indication of a weak palisade on the crest of the breach. Then Couche, Constantin, and Sprünglin arrived; they were to command the first assault troops.[47] They thought they saw epaulements and barricades in the breach traverse. Returning, we accompanied General Ruty on an inspection of the batteries.[48] They were firing perfectly, and we went uncovered from one end to the other. I told him that this was the most flattering compliment that could be paid to the artillery. The enemy followed us with some miserable gunfire. From the tower of the church the breach appeared

46. Valazé directed the packing of the mine chamber with 800 pounds of powder. Captain Cathala planted the charge in the counterscarp, and Captain Coffinal ignited the charge. The counterscarp exploded with an extraordinary blast leaving a breach 25 feet wide after the debris had settled.

47. An assault column, commanded by Major Delomme of the 6th Léger, included three grenadier companies from the 6th Corps. This column was preceded by an advance guard of 100 elite, 50 sappers, and 100 trench workers under the command of Captain Emmanuel-Frédéric Sprünglin. See Sprünglin, "Souvenirs," *Revue Hispanique* (Paris, 1904), pp. 436–37. A second column of 6 companies of infantry followed the first column. See Ney to Masséna, July 10, 1810, Archives de Masséna, LIV.

48. Count Charles Étienne Ruty (1774–1828) became a second lieutenant in the artillery in 1793 and general of brigade in 1807. Promoted to lieutenant general in 1813, he was made commander in chief of the artillery of the Grand Army. He served in the Army of the Rhine, fought at Aboukir and Friedland, and commanded the siege artillery of the Army of Spain.

very sharp and narrow. However, seen successively from different points, it appeared to be thirty to thirty-six yards wide and to have an inclination of forty degrees. A cannon was brought forward and hollow shells were fired against this ramp to soften the incline.

At the Marshal's quarters I told the Prince about the breach. There everybody seemed to be revolted at the proposition of a new summons. Everything was ready for the assault and everyone wanted the violence and fury [of a storming]. Fortunately, the Prince grasped the horror of sacking the city and decided to do everything in his power to prevent it. Since three or four hours of bombardment were still needed to make the breach easily practicable, the Prince ordered that the city should be summoned at four o'clock for the third time, and if it had not lowered its flag after a quarter of an hour, then the signal for the assault would be given.

While waiting, we made final preparations. The battalion of the *tirailleurs du siège* was to march ahead, supported by five companies of grenadiers, seven of voltigeurs, and five battalions of infantry. The troops gathered in the camp and marched to the trenches to the sound of music. Soldiers were everywhere.

There was no response to the summons. Someone was needed to inspect the state of the breach. The Marshal asked for three volunteers in the battalion of tirailleurs; a hundred stepped forward. The Marshal told them, "You will be killed, but you will die as honorable men." The Prince ordered me to accompany them. The commanders of the engineers and the artillery came along. Those three grenadiers were superb, marching like heroes, and proudly announcing to everybody that they were going to open the path to glory. They were electrifying, and they electrified me. I could feel that I too was a grenadier and a volunteer, marching at their front. Arriving on the counterscarp, they went quietly up the two breaches. In a few seconds they were at the summit firing their guns on the fleeing garrison; they shouted "Vive l'Empereur!" several times and recharged their arms. It was necessary to call them and order them to come down; since they had not received a single shot, they wanted to begin firing again. Their names were Thirion, corporal of the 50th Grenadiers, and Bombois and Billeret, carabineers of the 6th Léger. Thirion was the most excited; coming down, he offered me some brandy to drink. I drank — it was from a brave man. We had only taken a few steps in the trenches when we heard, with rapture, shouts of peace. Peace from the same voices who had demanded an assault only minutes earlier. I climbed on the parapet of the trench and saw the white flag beside the breach. I ran to announce this news to the Prince, since he was on Teso where he could not see the flag very well. Others arrived ahead of me, but I presented my three heroes. The Prince gave them his purse, but they refused, saying, "My Prince, we did not do this for money but for honor and country." This was an ingenious way of asking for the Cross [of the Legion of Honor]. It was promised to them, and they received it.

Meanwhile, the Marshal had already gone to the breach where he conducted negotiations in his own name and according to his own fancy.[49] He secured the entrance to the ramparts with a few companies. As a result of a mistake by the governor, the fortress surrendered at discretion instead of the usual capitulation which would have followed a regular surrender. Later I was told that Governor Herrasti presented himself to the Marshal in the breach. The Marshal put his hat back on after greeting him and the Spaniard replaced his hat also, retaining much of his dignity. The governor was fifty-five years old, with a good face and bearing. I think he was responsible for raising the first piece of cloth he could find while the clergy of the Junta were still protesting from deep within their caves. The Prince went to the breach and returned with the Marshal. I went into the fortress to take a look. It was dreadful. We entered by the breach. Everything adjoining it had been crushed, pounded, and destroyed. The ruins and devastation extended to the middle of the city. At every step one could see collapsed or burned houses. We went all along the ramparts; our posts were already established. The garrison had been shut up in their quarters after surrendering their arms at the general quarters of Casasola. As soon as I arrived there, the Prince, anticipating what was going to take place in the city, had me return.

I found everything in great confusion. It was already midnight. We did not have time to take all the necessary measures to maintain order in the midst of so much confusion. Obviously, those who had planned the arrangements for the assault did not think of police measures. The

49. The artillery commander of one of Junot's batteries recorded that Herrasti appeared in the breach in civilian dress and Ney responded, "Monsieur le gouverneur, after such a brilliant defense, you should not be afraid to wear your uniform; you honor it as much as it honors you." See Jacques Louis Hulot, *Souvenirs militaires du baron Hulot, général d'artillerie, 1773–1843* (Paris, 1886), p. 310.

Prince designated Adjutant Commander Rippert as commander of the city, but in the darkness he could not be everywhere. The Spanish garrison increased the confusion to its maximum, becoming involved in and directing the pillaging. Some of them took our soldiers inside to the good sites. Others led soldiers who were outside over the lower wall and through the posterns. At first even the guards allowed the excess and joined in it. I must say this so that everyone understands my horror at such conduct and does not accuse me of tolerating it. Some of the junior officers of both nations joined in the pillaging. They did not blush in carrying off shameful plunder with their own hands. Others, more skillful and experienced, had prepared in advance to take the most valuable objects in the city, and later some of the inhabitants were secretly put in prison and forced to purchase their liberty.

When I entered the city, I realized there was no way of imposing any restraint except with saber thrusts. A few other officers and I struck right and left at the pillagers, no matter who they were. My eyes were impervious to distinctions of rank, and if I recognized anybody I only hit harder. I complained vigorously to the post commanders. Little by little they were able to call in their men and send them on patrol. If the disorder did not stop completely, at least word spread that it was not allowed or tolerated; thus, it took place secretly in a few isolated corners. Besides, the pillaging generally did not go beyond the stealing of a few worthless objects, since the inhabitants had taken precautions. The thieves found their match almost everywhere. Seizure of the smallest object was disputed, often with blows and threats. Some toothless old women clutched their ragged garments as thieves tried to tear them away. An emaciated servant with scarcely a breath of life, seeing that I was protecting him, fell on the conquerors arrogantly, hitting them so ferociously with an enormous ring of keys that I was ready to turn on him. Finally, after spending part of the night establishing order, I took some rest, elated and consoled in seeing that we had become masters of the fortress with the least possible damage; moreover, we had helped to save the city despite the outburst of so much armed passion.

I do not claim to minimize the horror that such pillage should inspire in all men of honor nor minimize the fault of commanders who should have taken greater precautions to prevent it, but the principal blame must fall on the fortress authorities. They refused to submit to an ultimatum even when they had no right to hope. They surrendered at discretion, raising the white flag at a moment when we were almost masters of the breach. The fortress thereby abandoned itself to the terrible laws of war. With troops other than French ones, the garrison would have paid dearly for their unreasonable passion. We also believed that the presence and the authority of the Prince contributed substantially to saving it. Everybody had the time and the opportunity to express the most secret feelings in his heart. The Prince had declared his intentions very clearly and opposed those who asked for the destruction of the unfortunate fortress. As a result the word spread throughout Spain that it was he who had saved Ciudad Rodrigo. The Marquise "N" told me on my arrival at Salamanca, "We know your Prince alone prevented everyone from being put to the sword."[50]

Early next day the Prince entered the fortress and walked along the rampart. We found superb artillery and counted 125 cannon, most of them made of bronze. There was a great abundance of ammunition, 250,000 pounds of powder, 12,000 cartridges, etc. The garrison, consisting of about 7,000 men, had deposited their arms at the arsenal and left behind them six flags.[51] Governor Herrasti was presented to the Prince, along with the brigadier commander of the artillery [D. Francisco Ruiz Gómez] and two engineer officers. The brigadier claimed he would still be fighting if there had been more garrison troops. This Spanish boasting reflected the poor leadership the officers had shown during the siege. Nothing had been done to defend the breach or even to obstruct it. They had only erected a few pieces of wood as a palisade which grapeshot could have swept away. Since the narrow old wall and its terracing were supported from the inside by a revetment wall, two strong traverses at the end of both breaches — or at least at the end of the superior breach — would have been sufficient to stop us and make us clear it out completely. Thus we would have been

50. It is ironic indeed to compare the treatment of Ciudad Rodrigo by its French conquerors in 1810 with that of its English liberators on January 19, 1812. After General Picton's Third Division captured the city, an uncontrollable orgy of pillage and destruction broke out among the English troops, who burned large sections of the town and killed many Spanish citizens. Yet the Spanish government awarded Wellington the title of "Duke of Ciudad Rodrigo."

51. According to Major Husson, who inventoried the captured arms, the French took 118 guns, 82,477 projectiles, 269 wagons, almost a million cartridges, 147,100 pounds of powder, and 7,225 small arms, etc. See Belmas, *Journaux des siéges,* III, 310–11.

forced to establish an outwork under the plunging fire of the great tower or to push a new mine chamber through the old wall to open it. All these operations would have delayed us several days. If these traverses had been placed at the lower wall, we would have been forced to attack the breach twice through some kind of a moat passage across the lower wall. It was evident that a few workers and a few hours would have been sufficient. The Spanish engineers and artillery had not been very effective in the most ordinary artillery dispositions, not to mention what a little imagination might have done to strengthen the fortress outwardly. Only the cannoneer had fired perfectly. The defense ended at the very point where that of Saragossa had started, but the ardor of those old days was long gone. All that remained was some subdued bravado.

In general, the people and especially the landowners were tired of the war. They only wanted it to end one way or the other. Many Spaniards declared themselves on our side, and a few entered the service and took up arms for us. A much larger number secretly hoped that our victories would put an end to the burden and turmoil of this civil war. In this part of the country, the great majority damned the British for supporting the disorder and doing nothing to protect them. The inhabitants of Ciudad Rodrigo cursed them more violently, especially when they broke their word of honor and betrayed the confraternity of arms which had been sworn. Everywhere it was undebatable that if a yoke had to be borne, that of the French was infinitely better. I found this opinion boldly expressed in a Spanish work by some member of the Cortes; it was very well reasoned and written, but violent against the British army and its commander.[52]

The capture of Ciudad Rodrigo was the final blow to the insurgent

52. Herrasti complained to the Spanish minister of war in a letter of July 30, "The valor, the fortitude, and the sacrifices of the garrison and the inhabitants deserved a better fate. They have had the misfortune of not being supported by the arms of our allies after defending themselves for such a long siege with firmness and vigor." Belmas, *Journaux des siéges,* III, 315–19. Even the English questioned Wellington's judgment in not supporting the fortress. A young English engineer officer, John Burgoyne, wrote of Ciudad Rodrigo, "Why it is thus deserted to its fate, after solemn promises being given to relieve it, appears extraordinary. . . . If we are not able to attempt some effort in favour of this devoted place now, I fear we cannot expect much success in our operations, when all the arrangements and combinations of the enemy are made." See John Burgoyne, *Life and Correspondence of Field Marshal Sir John Burgoyne,* ed. George Wrottesley (London, 1873), I, 83.

band's power in the north of Spain. In order to achieve the submission of Spain, we had only to force the English to embark. Why was the Army of Portugal not given enough troops to force the British to depart? Why were all the army corps involved in the conquest of Portugal not forced to cooperate sincerely and simultaneously with us?

Two thousand people, made up equally of garrison and inhabitants, perished in Ciudad Rodrigo; on the last day alone they numbered three hundred.[53] The firing had been terrible against the entire city. There were children crushed by bombs, and few houses escaped damage. It was necessary to find masons, carpenters, and glaziers for the house of the general in chief before he could occupy it. After the departure of the Prince, useless exactions increased the misery of the unfortunate inhabitants. Members of the old Junta, priests, and citizens of the urban militia were arrested. These vexations were accompanied by some extortion which made them even more odious.

Before leaving for Salamanca, the Prince ordered the following dispositions. The left of the 6th Corps was to occupy Aldea Nueva de Azaba, with the right at Marialba, two strong detachments at Gallegos and Espeja, and the reserve cavalry at the disposition of Marshal Ney at a central point to his rear. With regard to the 8th Corps, the right of General Solignac was to be at Ledesma and the left at Vitigudino with the communication posts at Pont de Yecla. The right of General Clauzel's division was to occupy San Felices el Grande; the left to hold San Felices el Chico with a line of communication through Bañobárez. The two army corps received orders to communicate frequently and push their reconnaissance as far ahead as possible toward the front, as well as to the left of the 6th Corps and the right of the 8th Corps. Thus placed, the army corps mutually supported each other. Ciudad Rodrigo itself was covered; its trenches were being filled and the breach repaired. The army could move to the right bank of the Douro in case Lord Wellington wanted to maneuver in that direction. The right bank of the Tagus was guarded by General Reynier's new position. General Loison was at Gallegos and General Marchand remained

53. French casualties in the siege totaled 14 officers and 168 men killed, and 39 officers and 1,009 soldiers wounded, of which one-third were seriously incapacitated. See Belmas, *Journaux des siéges,* III, 306–9. The Spanish garrison had 461 dead, 994 wounded, and approximately 5,500 taken prisoner. See Herrasti, *Relacion histórica,* p. 130.

at Ciudad Rodrigo, where the headquarters of the 6th Corps were established.

The Prince ordered me to make a summary report of the siege. I will not include it here since it appeared in the newspapers of the day just as it was sent. I first recognized the Prince as commander in chief and for his role in the conduct of the siege, but he wanted to create as large a role as possible for the Marshal. Meanwhile the Marshal complained bitterly during the following days that we dared to praise him, although I only wrote "that he had done everything that could be expected of a great captain." On the contrary, the report of the engineers of the 6th Corps gave all of the credit to the Marshal and only indifferent mention to the Prince and did not [*sic*] cite the active and profitable command of Colonel Valazé, who had been honorably wounded. The Prince did not learn anything about that report.

Lieutenant Jourdan soon brought us news of General Reynier. The 2nd Corps had been at Mérida during the month of June, making frequent expeditions toward Alburquerque, Compo Maior, and Portalegre. This officer left as the General was marching toward Coria; Reynier arrived there soon. The news was brought by an officer of the 6th Corps detached from Gata.

Subsistence was one of our principal concerns, for the meager supplies found in Rodrigo had been eaten by the 6th Corps. Again the scarcity tormented us because we were surrounded by an abundant harvest; the environs of Rodrigo and the Azaba had completely changed in appearance after a few weeks of sun. They were covered with beautiful fields of ripening wheat. The Prince, aware of the abilities of French soldiers, had the insight to allow them to gather the harvest and provide their own food. He had them search for and make some sickles, which were sent to the army corps; he ordered the mills on the various rivers repaired, and he sent a few of the local engineers to the region of the Agueda. He prescribed the arrangements necessary to collect the grain and bake it into bread. The quartermaster general was charged to employ all his resources to replenish the magazines in order either to create a reserve of food or to aid those corps unable to find a sufficient quantity of grain.

The Marshal complained that his troops were on half rations. He asked permission to send two divisions to the rear toward Tamames and Salvatierra, with detachments at Béjar, Baños, and Castanar; to gather provisions there. Simultaneously, he announced that the enemy, thought to be forty thousand men at present, were making a retrograde movement which would give us the fertile plains of Argañan. Moreover, the previous day rumors spread through Salamanca that the British were abandoning Almeida and blowing up a part of the beautiful fortress La Concepción, which they had disarmed. News of the retreat came from everywhere. General Reynier wrote from Coria that the detachments at Portalegre and Castelo Branco were retiring on Abrantes. This certainly was not the moment for troops of the 6th Corps to make a retrograde movement. At first the Prince wanted to establish them on the communication line between Ciudad Rodrigo and Salamanca in order to place them closer to the food magazine, which was difficult to transport. To accomplish this, the Prince had to send Séras's division toward Bragança and Miranda on the frontier and move the 8th Corps between the Agueda and the Azaba. He also wanted a division of the 6th Corps near Almeida and La Concepción, another division at Ciudad Rodrigo, and a third in the rear to allow it to rest from the fatigue of the siege.

The British movement was not caused by the capture of Ciudad Rodrigo but rather because of the concentration of our army and the advance of the 8th and 2nd Corps along their flanks. It was evident the British general wanted to be able to react to our movements and anticipate us if we tried to move along our left side toward Lisbon, and he wanted to be on the alert until we had made a decision to besiege Almeida. It was equally clear that his movement of concentration was made to collect his entire force on the position at Guarda or at least on the other side of the Côa, while Almeida was to be left to itself. On the basis of this premise the Prince ordered the Marshal to make an extensive reconnaissance on Almeida with five to six thousand infantry and adequate cavalry, and seek to communicate with the fortress. He sent an aide-de-camp from the Marquis d'Alorna with a letter for the governor and a proclamation for the Portuguese.[54]

54. Dom Pedro de Almeida, Marquis d'Alorna (1754–1813), was a member of an illustrious Portuguese family that was persecuted by the ruling house of Bragança. He served in the Spanish army against the French in 1793 and was named commander in chief of the Legion d'Alorna in 1798. Prince John expelled him from court in 1806. Therefore when Junot invaded Portugal in 1807 d'Alorna welcomed him as a liberator. Junot named him governor of Alentejo and inspector general of

Chef d'escadron Casabianca, who carried the letter, was ordered to accompany the Marshal on his reconnaissance, but the Marshal would not allow him to do so and sent him back rather briskly. He returned to us the next day with news of the evacuation of Fort La Concepción.

The Prince learned that the Marshal had left Rodrigo; he immediately sent orders with an ordnance officer, Pierron,* not to undertake anything important before his arrival, which would be very soon. Thus on July 24, at eight o'clock in the evening, he sent me to see what was happening to the 6th Corps. This was always the extent of his orders and instructions to me. I started with a few dragoons in miserable weather. The rain was extremely heavy. It was so dark that I was unable to see a silver-white horse walking immediately ahead of me. We got lost in the woods of Matilla. After riding a long time, we finally reached a convent, a frequent refuge for brigands. My dragoons knew it well. Without noise we started again in the right direction. Some distance away we saw the light of a fire; we expected to find some shepherds there and ask them for directions. We advanced very carefully and I had the fire scouted; there were a large number of peasants around a great fire. The rain was still very heavy. We did not ask for any directions, and we did not encounter anyone else. I arrived at Rodrigo at nine o'clock in the morning, exhausted, a little sick from the previous day, and all for nothing. I learned that a battle had taken place. The troops of the 6th Corps had taken positions on this side of the Côa and the enemy on the other side.[55] Having no reason to go to the Marshal nor any pretext to proceed to the 6th Corps, I decided to go no farther.

the Portuguese troops in several provinces of northern Portugal. After the Convention of Sintra, he was warmly welcomed in Paris by Napoleon, who hoped to enlist his support for the French cause. D'Alorna and several high-ranking Portuguese officers accompanied Masséna into Portugal to provide the prince with confidential information and to add an air of legitimacy to the French operations.

55. For details of this action see below, pages 89–90.

Chapter Three

THE SIEGE OF ALMEIDA

At this time our military glory shone at its brightest and was undiminished by any significant reverses; our armies experienced only rapid conquests and great victories. In fact, they did not calculate either the number of their enemies or the force of the obstacles they faced. Thus, as soon as the Army of Portugal had been formed, everyone dreamed of the immediate invasion of this kingdom and the entry into Lisbon. Nobody took the British army into consideration; they thought only of its destruction. But after the siege of Ciudad Rodrigo and the preparations for the siege of Almeida, many people began to whisper. Accustomed to see the conquest and the fall of strong fortresses, they wondered about the delays and the work involved in siege warfare. Moreover, they accused the Prince of slowness, of not understanding the true nature of the war, and even of becoming old.[1] These reproaches were even stronger because everybody expected that he would act vigorously and that as soon as he arrived there would be immediate victories. These reactions were also due to our custom of winning and the excessive confidence it inspired in us. There was also a morale sickness, much more dangerous for the army, because our troops were more susceptible to it than they had

1. When General Maximilien Foy of Reynier's Corps saw Masséna in September 1810, he wrote, "He is no longer the Masséna with the sparkling eye, the changeable face, the intensive figure whom I saw in 1799 and whose head resembled the bust of Marius. He is only fifty-two but looks more than sixty." See Maurice Girod de l'Ain, *Vie militaire du général Foy* (Paris, 1900), pp. 100–1.

been in other countries. This sickness occurred when the troops were not animated by great enthusiasm or involved in great projects or lacked talented commanders. More than anyone else, the Prince certainly had all the qualities necessary to excite the confidence and admiration of the troops, but the soldiers were already wearied by the attacks against Ciudad Rodrigo; they had become apathetic as a result of the delays in the works of the last siege, the inclement weather, the lack of food, and finally of having been denied the prize which they believed legitimately belonged to them.

The complaints and the spirit of opposition, created and sustained throughout the entire campaign as a result of the foregoing circumstances, were further multiplied by the troubles that accompanied the invasion. Commanders and officers, who had allowed themselves indiscreet discussions about military affairs during the past few years, first created and then sanctioned discord by their example. Commanders went along too easily with the general opinion, and they suggested and openly supported projects acceptable to the troops but contrary to the plans of the Prince, although such projects were not well conceived. This opposition lacked even the excuse of blind submission to passions and rivalries which first excited them, and only worsened the situation; but it is useless to anticipate events. Most of these malcontents were ignorant of the orders of the government and totally unable to form sound opinions on such matters. After I was initiated into confidential affairs, I could see how faulty their judgments were. Their ideas were usually induced by military operations without any knowledge of the data on which to base them. These men usually knew nothing about the most elementary things necessary for making such decisions.

Meanwhile Marshal Ney wished to make the reconnaissance ordered on the 21st. The enemy had already moved his posts near Almeida as our troops approached the fortress. The Marshal left Ciudad Rodrigo at midday on July 23, and Marchand's division started the next day. Leading Loison's division, the Marshal attacked the enemy and after a bloody fight threw them back across the Côa River; this action constituted the first investment of Almeida. But not satisfied with this success, the Marshal tried to cross the Côa, with its immense and very deep ravine and high banks full of rocks, where the enemy could find a suitable hiding place. Up to this time our troops had been completely successful, for the enemy losses were three times ours. We had captured a flag.[2] The Marshal, unable to cross the Côa, established some posts around Almeida and established his own troops there. Loison's division moved to Val da Mula on Portuguese territory; Marchand's division, with the headquarters and General Montbrun's cavalry, were at Aldea del Obispo; Mermet's division was at Almeida; and as a result of these movements the enemy concentrated his forces at the position of Guarda.

I can find no information in my Journal about this engagement. Newspaper accounts reported that the entire rear guard of General Craufurd was attacked with great boldness under the cannon of Almeida. The enemy were charged by the 3rd Hussars and turned toward the right by General Ferey; this probably determined their retreat to the other side of the Côa. It appeared that the enemy had suffered considerable losses, especially in the number of officers killed. General Éblé at Ciudad Rodrigo refused to follow the Marshal, and he told me the latter left suddenly on the 23rd although he had not considered such a move until noon. At that time neither the chief of staff nor the artillery of the 6th Corps knew anything about it. Did the Marshal hope to take Almeida or once again obtain some great advantage over the English army? He had announced to General Éblé that he was going to besiege and take the fortress and at the same time defeat the enemy. However, the previous day he had claimed to be in difficulty and asked for the 2nd and 8th Corps to support his flanks. The movement nearly succeeded; yet it might have become serious and even dangerous.

The Prince arrived [at headquarters] as soon as possible and wanted to go to the 6th Corps. He was very angry, but fortunately we were able to stop the Prince at Ciudad Rodrigo and prevent an altercation between the two great men. He finally sent General Fririon and me to the Marshal. We arrived very early at Aldea del Obispo and found the Marshal still in bed. The general addressed him courteously.

2. The French attacked the British positions before Almeida at 6:00 A.M. on July 24 with Loison's infantry and Montbrun's cavalry. Craufurd was surprised and his Light Division was driven back on the only bridge crossing the Côa. Regimental officers initiated several counterattacks that delayed the French advance and saved the Light Division from a humiliating defeat. The English were able to retreat across the river, but their casualties totaled approximately 350 men. The French casualties reached 117 killed and 410 wounded. For details see Horward, "Invasion of Portugal," pp. 182–90.

He answered very cautiously that he had been ordered to reconnoiter and probe the fortress, that he had followed his orders but that nobody appreciated what he was doing for the others, that the enemy had resisted him, that he had fought an excellent combat (he boasted a good deal), and also that the Prince should not have gone to Salamanca. I listened but did not want to join the conversation and even less to make any reply. Nevertheless, I began by saying that after finding forty thousand enemy before him and requesting [permission] to execute a withdrawal, he had, without warning the Prince, advanced with his whole corps instead of making a simple reconnaissance. It was not surprising that the Prince had been worried about an unexpected movement. The Marshal seemed rather embarrassed by what I said, but got out of it by again boasting of his operation.[3]

Returning to the Prince, we did not repeat any of the Marshal's disrespectful remarks but described his moderation, his willingness to take orders. We further said that he proposed to take charge of the siege, as well as send brigades on Pinhel, which we occupied, and Guarda, now said to be abandoned; or dispatch his brigades to the rear to gather food. The Prince accepted all this favorably, but in the evening he received a letter from the Duc d'Abrantès, requesting the siege for his corps. At the same time, the Duc confided that the Marshal had asked him to make a forward movement to support his own, but that he awaited the Prince's orders. The Prince was displeased with the situation. This correspondence was obviously contrary to discipline and the good of the service. Nevertheless, before employing his authority as commander in chief to effectively control affairs, sometimes dangerous when used against powerful men who meddle, the Prince wanted to use his personal authority to humble this haughty spirit.

As a pretext for seeing the Marshal, the Prince used the necessity of making a reconnaissance on the fortress of Almeida. Therefore he left with Generals Fririon, Éblé, d'Alorna, Lazowski,[4] and Ruty, and

3. This was more than a reconnaissance, as Pelet suggests. Masséna wrote Ney on July 21, "No doubt, if you press near the English, they will abandon Almeida or they will blow it up as they did at Fort La Concepcion. In consequence, I desire that you support General Loison with your troops in order to push the enemy on Almeida." See Archives de Masséna, LI.

4. Baron Joseph Félix Lazowski (1759–1812) graduated as an engineer in 1784; he enlisted in 1794 and was promoted to general of division in 1809. Lazowski was sent on a mission to Turkey in 1794 but returned in time to take part in the Egyp-

he paid me the honor of letting me ride along in his carriage. He overwhelmed me with affection and kindness and repeated what he had already told me at Valladolid and had frequently said since then. We conversed along the following lines during the trip and on the return: The Prince admitted that he had made a mistake in returning to Salamanca and acting like a little Bonaparte there. I proved him incorrect, noting his various duties, but I did concede that he should have returned [to Ciudad Rodrigo] a little sooner. He talked to me about his troubles with the Marshal, whose inappropriate comments had influenced the younger people. The Prince had remained aloof, but still the rumors continued and the guilty allowed the entire army to repeat them. We talked about the forthcoming siege and the one that had just taken place. I pointed out all the mistakes I noticed in the direction of the first siege. I asked the Prince to take charge of the new siege himself and to begin it only when all the preparations were completed, and then to conduct it with the greatest rapidity, regularity, and exactness. The Prince wanted to send the 2nd Corps to Alfaiates to threaten Guarda. I proposed, in accordance with the orders received from Paris, to place a force opposite Salvatierra on the Erjas to maintain communication with Madrid and to position a strong detachment at Penamacor to threaten Guarda. I also suggested that we maintain considerable strength at Alcántara, with a good position on the left bank of the Tagus, and guarantee passage and observe the country between the Tagus and the Guadiana. This entire project was adopted and I prepared the orders after alighting from the carriage.

The Marshal came out to meet the Prince and they ate at his quarters at Aldea del Obispo. There was no talk about what had taken place. The Prince went immediately toward the fortress; everyone else fell behind. The two marshals approached it with General Fririon; the generals of engineers and artillery and I followed them. We arrived within eight hundred yards of the city and then advanced as far as the water mill; there was a good view from which to judge the works.

The bastion system had very small demilunes with limited flank curtains and a sentinel path. At this point the revetments were well

tian campaign. He commanded the engineers of the 1st Corps under Bernadotte in 1808 and of the 4th Corps under Masséna at Essling. In 1810 he was attached to the Army of Portugal.

covered and its fire was low, but it seemed possible to uncover a vulnerable point somewhere else. Everything on the outside seemed to be well prepared and leveled. The fortress had the courtesy to fire some shots. The Prince then went to inspect the troops of Generals Simon[5] and Marchand, sending the generals of engineers and artillery to finish their reconnaissance around the place, though they did not complete it until the next day. While we were there, the enemy attempted a sortie. On that day [July 26] there were three sorties of several hundred men to gather up the piles of grain which the enemy had not been able to collect because the investment had been so rapid. Each sortie was easily repulsed. The last utilized four cannon and the enemy lost one of them. Only one company opposed them. An Englishman, William Cox,[6] commanded the Portuguese garrison, and he said they would not surrender until the last moment. He had only two English officers as aides-de-camp with him.

The Prince slept at Aldea del Obispo. The Marshal arrived at his quarters early the next morning. General Loison was already there. They had to decide which corps would conduct the siege. The Marshal wanted to do it himself and he began to minimize the ability of the English; he talked about the ease of protecting the country beyond Almeida and at the same time of conducting the siege with very few soldiers. Then the Prince decided to recommend the 8th Corps for the operation and said to the complaining Marshal, "You will be able to lend it a few of your troops." After much discussion the Prince quoted the letter written to the Duc; he showed it with some ill humor and sternly reproached the Marshal. The Marshal was about to answer in the same tone; however, as I have previously mentioned, the 8th Corps was too weak for this operation anyway. Thus, seeing a way to retain the siege, he contained himself: he spoke highly of the British army and exaggerated the difficulties of the siege, the danger of employing weak forces beyond the Côa, and the difficulties of crossing it. He talked to everybody, even to me. At last he got his way and convinced the Prince, who had intended all

5. Édouard François Simon (1769–1827) enlisted in the infantry in 1792 and was promoted to general of brigade in 1797. He was sent to Spain in 1809 and given a brigade in Loison's division.

6. Little information exists on William Cox, who was appointed to serve as lieutenant colonel of the Portuguese 24th Line. By the fall of 1809 he was a brigadier general in the Portuguese service and the governor of the fortress of Almeida.

along to give him the siege but wanted to make him believe he might not obtain it. Then it was decided that it would be better to watch rather than occupy the left bank of the Côa, that the 6th Corps would conduct the siege, and that the 8th Corps would be in reserve to support it, while General Montbrun's cavalry would go to the left beyond Robleda to subsist there and form a junction with General Reynier. Trelliard's division would remain at the Marshal's disposition. As far as I was concerned, I would have preferred to see the left of the 6th Corps at Freixedas, the right beyond Pinhel, and the headquarters in that city [Pinhel]. I wanted the 8th Corps to conduct the siege and the 2nd Corps echeloned slightly to the right. However, during the conference these ideas were discussed again and again [without result]. Returning to Ciudad Rodrigo, the Prince ordered the Duc d'Abrantès to have Clauzel's division ready to march so that it could be at Almeida within three hours, supported by two regiments of dragoons. To accomplish this it was necessary to reconnoiter and prepare crossings on the Agueda and to keep Solignac's division ready to support and follow the movement.

We lacked information about Portugal, although everybody tried to give us some. From the very first I had been worried about Almeida; moreover we had no diagram. The Marquis d'Alorna, lieutenant general in the service of Portugal and a former commander in chief on this frontier, had set up the works that carried his name. He had been stationed at Almeida a long time and had drawn up plans for work done on the fortress. He should have been able to give me exact information. He was a very amiable man with excellent manners, witty, well read, literate in French; he had many agreeable talents—in other words, he was an accomplished gentleman with exquisite manners. He was sociable with everyone and paid me much attention, which did not stop me from speaking the truth, but at least this proves I did not like to be too critical of him. In addition, he was zealous, devoted, and conversed fluently on military matters or any other subject. The marquis was always ready to tell us everything except what we needed to know, and to answer any questions he was not asked. Thus, after counting several times on his fingers, he assured me Almeida had seven bastions and therefore seven fronts. However, Colonel Valazé gave me a little memorandum prepared by a French artillery officer in 1808, which described only six fronts at Almeida. The marquis

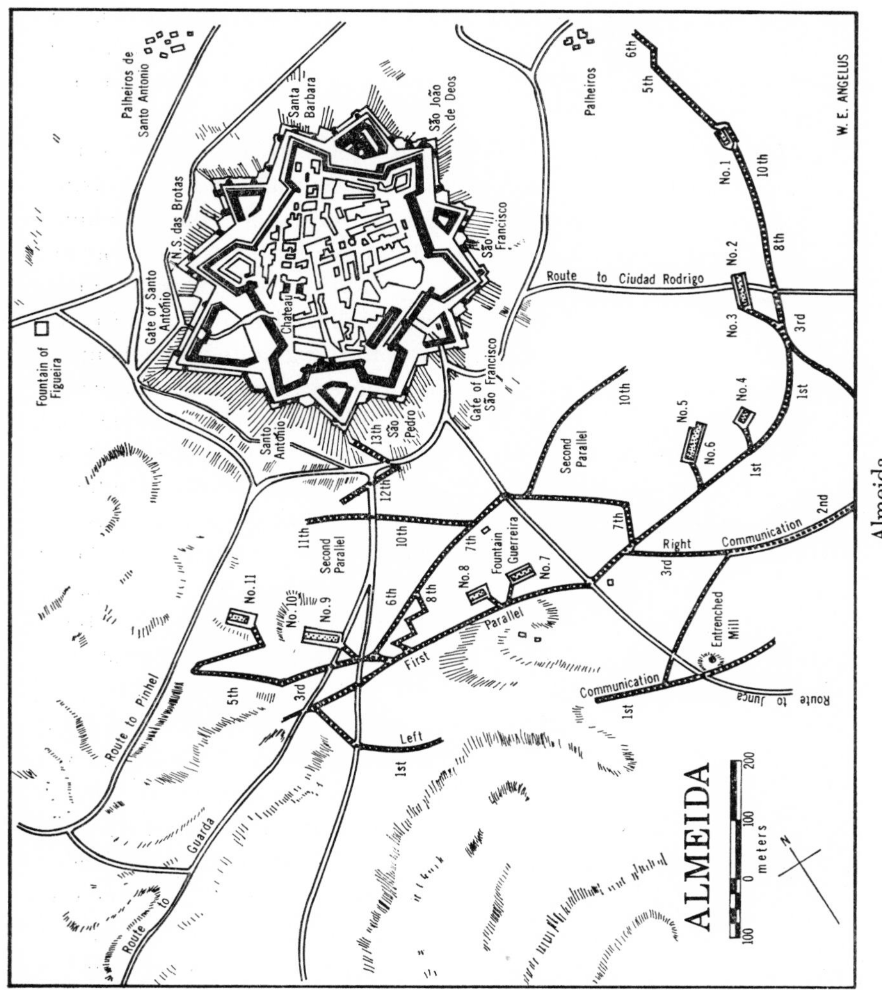
ALMEIDA
meters
100
0
100
200
W. E. ANGELUS
Palheiros de Santo Antonio
Palheiros
Santa Barbara
São João de Deos
N.S. das Brotas
Gate of Santo Antonio
Chateau
São Francisco
Gate of São Francisco
Santo Antonio
São Pedro
Fountain of Figueira
Route to Ciudad Rodrigo
Route to Pinhel
Route to Guarda
Route to Junca
Second Parallel
Second Parallel
First Parallel
Right Communication
Communication
Left
Entrenched Mill
Fountain Guerreira
No.1
No.2
No.3
No.4
No.5
No.6
No.7
No.8
No.9
No.10
No.11

Almeida

protested and assured me there were seven. This question was resolved by the map and a reconnaissance, and we found there were six. I have reported this incident to show how we were helped and served.

The fortress was a rather long and irregular hexagon. The outline was quite defective as a result of the flank curtain and some flanks perpendicular to the fortress. The fronts were short; the demilunes were small and did not cover the flanks of the bastions except on the northwest front, where there was one strong salient of outstanding width; the salient toward the east was smaller. The moats, thirty-six yards wide, were dry and partially cut into the granite.[7] The counterscarp was covered with granite as was the escarpment of the works. The covered way was in fairly good condition, well palisaded and furnished with beams, but without a fortified esplanade. The bastions on the north, south, and east had massive towers. In the middle of the fortress, but closer to the northwest front, arose an immense but very old castle with four enormous towers surrounded by a large moat. It was used partially as a magazine and lodging for the garrison. The wall, approximately thirty to thirty-five feet high, had been carefully repaired. The British had apparently taken the utmost care of everything in the city for some time.

Almeida was on a small plateau inclined slightly toward a crest where the old castle was located. The terrain in the vicinity was slightly broken and offered almost continuous cover to those attacking, but it had little depth, and enormous ledges of extremely hard granite were often visible. These blocks were larger as one approached the Côa, where they seemed to emerge from the ground as if sown on the surface, presenting a veritable image of obstacles. The fortress was about three thousand yards from the river, and the interval between was filled with vineyards and cottages interspersed with many trees. The terrain became more and more difficult as one approached the valley; it was impassable toward the north, but more accessible in the direction of Junça. The roads that ran from the bridge toward that village were protected by the fortress, but the main road itself was not entirely under its domination. Thus Almeida was unable to contri-

7. Baron Hulot observed that the demilunes lacked adequate profiles to protect their adjacent bastions, the pitch of the glacis was too steep, and the moat lacked the necessary depth and breadth. See Hulot, *Souveniers,* p. 314.

bute to the defense of the Côa or the single and very difficult exit there or across the valley; hence it did not fulfill that very purpose for which one might reasonably assume it had been built. Though I did not have time to see if there was any way to link the two fortresses, it seemed to me at a glance that the goal had been to make Almeida the counterpart of Ciudad Rodrigo.

The attack had been initially fixed on the western front between the bastions of Santo António and São Pedro, which were at the end of the oval and consequently more detached from the adjacent fronts. The other end was covered by a rather good demilune with a keep. Later the attack was limited to the bastion of São Pedro on the southwest, no doubt because the large demilune, on the lateral front to the right, took a wide reverse, and it was impossible for us to rake a section of the fortress which could observe our approaches. Reasonably favorable terrain permitted us to establish the first parallel 360 yards away and start the approaches about 600 yards from it. This was the part of the city reconnoitered by the Prince.

The preparations for the siege of Ciudad Rodrigo had been lengthy and required infinite care and effort. Most of the provisions had been used up in front of the fortress, and what was found there did not compensate for what had been expended. Two hundred and fifty thousand pounds of powder, part of it damaged, would be inadequate for this siege. General Éblé threatened to bring supplies from Bayonne, which would have meant an endless journey. This man, though brave and trustworthy, was too pessimistic. Listening to him, we could not believe that a siege of Almeida was possible for a long time. Nevertheless, it was done, and rather quickly. If one can neglect nothing in business, especially in warfare, it is also unnecessary to believe everything that people say. Moreover, General Éblé was already hard at work. He took me to see his artillery *parc* in the convent of San Francisco, where he had put seven forges in operation. The sights of several cannon were being replaced with iron angle sights. Twenty-seven cannon were already on their carriages. An immense quantity of various kinds of provisions had been prepared and loaded; much of it had come from Metz. Even the powder had come that far. A large number of projectiles had been found under the ruins of the powder magazine, abandoned there for seven years as a result of Spanish apathy. It was necessary to unearth and sort them according to caliber.

Nevertheless, we were most troubled by the lack of artillery horses; those we had were exhausted and poorly nourished, and dying like flies.[8]

What was lacking, above all, was money, which everyone called "the sinews of war." The treasury chests had been emptied before our arrival, since the men as well as the officers of each army corps had received their arrears, gratuities, extraordinary pay, etc. Collections were very difficult and they produced less and less as the troops moved out farther into the provinces. The countryside they occupied had been overrun and crushed and could not pay anything. Neither France nor Madrid furnished funds. As a result of all these difficulties, the paymaster extended credit and he came to ask the Prince to guarantee it. This took him on his weak side. Since the Prince was not generous enough to imitate the conduct of Marshal de Brissac,[9] he satisfied himself with an obvious and continued disinterest, but his example was not followed by everybody. Later the paymaster reserved funds for the expenses of the quartermaster general and refused the funds that had been assigned to the engineers and the artillery. The Prince authorized them to carry out the orders militarily in case of a new refusal, to avert repetition of this business. I will say that we entered Portugal almost without a penny in the chest, just like the people who went to conquer the treasures of Brazil and Judea. Afterward we had to consolidate for the most urgent expenses and look for resources in hands that were not always clean.

We also experienced a great shortage of food in the midst of a very fine harvest. Truly, so many articles were lacking that I cannot mention them all. The administration seemed to be there only to hinder the service and not to help us. It was also difficult to give the laborers the grain collected by our troops. In the villages, and especially in the bivouacs, the troops could not find any method to have bread made from the grain. Nevertheless, the administration believed that

8. General Éblé complained to Berthier, "Although the distance [from Almeida to Ciudad Rodrigo] is only seven leagues, the poor state of the horses and the difficulties of the roads force us to employ two days for this journey and to double the teams. The dearth of subsistence augments the difficulties still more, and the loss of horses sometimes rises to 15 a day." See Belmas, *Journaux des siéges,* Éblé to Berthier, August 11, 1810, III, 373–75.

9. Charles de Cossé, Comte de Brissac (1504–64), was a famous and exacting French marshal during the reign of François I.

everything had been accomplished when it had set up a few stations where nothing went wrong and had sent in a few reports describing some new projects. Although we were encumbered with wheat, we lacked the means to use it. We proposed to buy grain, and while the rations could not be distributed, the sutlers were selling bread to the soldiers. These abuses came from several sources, and we had the time neither to pinpoint nor to eliminate them. The army transportation was quite insufficient for the artillery and especially for the food, and the latter could not be obtained from the provinces. The isolated system of the governors was a primary obstacle; an even greater problem was the opposition of the inhabitants. It was not motivated by patriotism, for the proud and avaricious Castilian, who hid his wagons to escape our requisitions, would put himself at the service of our sutlers. A few of the latter often paid the complete cost of large convoys. General Loison finally acquired a *parc* in this manner; he paid the ox drivers, the commanders of a platoon, and moved them beside the Duero. A few corps still had their wagons, but little by little their oxen and those used to draw the *parc* were eaten; soon only the wild ones were left.

The Marquis d'Alorna had gone to Pinhel with *chef d'escadron* Casabianca; they found only an old woman there. Later some of the inhabitants came back asking for a garrison to protect them, offering to gather food for the army. We learned that our advance troops were causing considerable disorder. The Prince had vigorous letters written to the corps commanders which were to be passed down through all the companies.[10] The Marquis d'Alorna always interceded in favor of the Portuguese. His patriotic sentiments were revived with fresh intensity at the sight of the troubles his countrymen suffered, but it was a little late after the Rubicon had been crossed, and the English were behaving even worse than we were. The marquis returned to Pinhel to reassure the inhabitants and to take back the militia commander to whom I had given a letter. The Marshal did not permit the marquis to pass since no order to this effect had been

10. Masséna wrote to his commanders, "We have seldom seen French armies where we can cite as many disorders as we have had in Portugal. Rape, pillage, and murder seem to be the order of the day there. Recently, in a village on the Portuguese frontier, some unknown soldiers raped three girls after murdering their father. . . . Unfortunately, I am able to cite fifty more examples as revolting." See Masséna to Ney, August 7, 1810, Archives de Masséna, LI.

given. The most severe orders were issued under which the different commanders were held responsible for halting the pillaging and the horrors being committed.

General Reynier, in a very long and verbose letter, wrote that he was going to echelon Merle's division toward Penamacor and that Heudelet's division was at Zarza la Mayor with a regiment at Alcántara.[11] He said the bridge at that city could not be rebuilt; thus he kept his ferry boats at Alcanetar. Simultaneously he sent a few troops toward Salvaterra to make a reconnaissance on Castelo Branco, while the light cavalry and 31st Léger occupied Penamacor. Thus the General contained Wellington's entire right flank and watched the left of the Tagus River; however, he had established his ferries too far away from him. At the very same time [July 30 and 31] General O'Donnell with four to five thousand men, following far behind La Carrera, arrived on the left bank of the Tagus in front of Alcanetar, after uselessly attacking a tower with about forty men hidden inside. The Spaniards used artillery against the tower. After a stubborn defense, it was taken and the ferries burned. General Reynier announced these events from Penamacor and complained considerably of the dispersal of his corps, listing many arguments. The 2nd Corps found fifteen cannon at Penamacor and four cannon, two of them without carriages, at Monsanto. The General kept watch at these two important posts, which had been occupied without opposition although everybody depicted each of them as a kind of fortress.

The Prince ordered me to answer General Reynier forcefully. I did so, reminding him of the Emperor's instructions and of his recent orders to concentrate and keep his troops within four or five marches of us during the siege of Almeida, to have a good defensive position within his reach on the left bank of the Tagus, and to go there himself; he was also to contain O'Donnell and stop him from making an attack toward Toledo. Finally, he was to observe Hill who, after crossing

11. Baron Pierre Hughes Merle (1766–1830) enlisted as a private in 1781 and was promoted to general of division in 1805. Merle served in Spain during the Revolution and was attached to the Grand Army before Austerlitz. In 1808 he returned to Spain in Soult's 2nd Corps and served as a divisional commander in Reynier's Corps during 1810. Count Étienne Heudelet de Bierre (1770–1857) became a lieutenant of volunteers in 1792, and after Austerlitz he was made general of division. He served with the French armies in Germany between 1793 and 1806 and fought at Jena and Eylau. He was given a division of Reynier's 2nd Corps before it was attached to the Army of Portugal.

the Tagus at Ródão and marching on Atalaia, had returned to Castelo Branco with Beresford's Portuguese. This force had as much infantry as the 2nd Corps and more cavalry. These movements on the other side of the Tagus were not dangerous for us; however, they were probably linked with those of Wellington and designed to stop us or give us trouble all the way to Madrid, and this was what happened.

Marshal Ney announced that his reconnaissance had found the enemy in front of Guarda and Trancoso, but that the English were concentrating at Celorico. Soon after, he asked for food, although when he had requested the siege of Almeida he had pretended to have enough food and to be in need of nothing. The Prince gave him ten thousand rations per day; the disposition was to be made by the quartermaster general.

During our stay at Ciudad Rodrigo, I encountered by chance my curé of the trenches. It seemed that he did not feel any need to thank me for my services. Nevertheless, he came to see me with tears in his eyes and with great protestations of gratitude, which was quite unusual for him. I wanted to do something more for him, and I used my influence to place him in the cathedral chapter. Later I learned he was one of our worst enemies; he had stimulated enthusiasm during the siege to the point of beating the women to force them to carry food and munitions to those defending the ramparts.

Since nothing is unimportant when one is painting the customs of a country, I noted several typical Spanish characteristics in my Journal as I became acquainted with them. A rather pretty woman where I stayed was always asking favors of me. One night when she began to flirt, I said to myself: "Here is a request for a favor, and tomorrow she will not even look at me." I was not mistaken one moment. She wanted leave for a wounded Spanish officer, and I agreed to it immediately. I had also seen how patriotic German women act, and I had been touched in a different way. They used to cry as they listened to tales of how their troops had fought; they cried as they gave every kind of help to their wounded; they asked generously for everything possible for their compatriots, but they did not feel they could do so without politeness or gratitude toward a munificent enemy. I will not mention the patriotism of the Poles. It would put women of a certain country to shame. Moreover, all those proud Spanish women, unlike the Poles, did not know how to stop their flirting once they had started. Often they used it to serve their vengeance.

The Prince asked Generals Éblé and Lazowski to report on their reconnaissance, their plans for the attack, and their operations at different stages of the siege, which were to be analyzed and carried out at the precise time. He urged them to do so because the troops were suffering and the food was being exhausted. The generals sent their report. They could not be exact about anything yet, neither the time to open the trenches nor details of the approaches, but generally they did agree on the system of attack. Preparations continued at Ciudad Rodrigo, but not with the kind of activity everyone expected and circumstances required; moreover there were delays because of the lack of funds. The engineers lacked transport for all the tools and sandbags that were essential in this rocky country.

General Séras had occupied Puebla de Sanabria on July 28 with 1,100 men; he said it was stronger than Astorga. Actually, this city had an old wall in fairly good condition and a castle built of hewn stones. Of the three hundred Spaniards who guarded it, two hundred had been sabered and fifty taken prisoner. The general found twelve bronze cannon and two thousand cannonballs there. The occupation of this city was rather important since it closed one of Galicia's principal lines of communication with the right bank of the Duero and the two enemy corps occupying Ponferrada and Bragança. Séras requested immediate concentration of his division, which was scattered in the province of Valladolid and kept there by the governor. The latter complained that guerrillas were seen more frequently than ever. Moreover, the governor had just published an order of the day, declaring absolute independence. The Prince wrote him a severe letter with the injunction to retract his order immediately and allow Séras' division to leave at any time. Later the same governor retained the very important 44th Flotilla Battalion, which was part of the Army of Portugal. The Prince ordered him to let it go or suffer grave consequences. Everywhere we met with obstacles and impediments, even from those who were supposed to be helping us.

Meanwhile General Séras, no longer able to maintain his position at Puebla de Sanabria, withdrew with 1,100 men; he left Colonel Graffenried with 350 Swiss soldiers, 8,000 rations of bread and biscuit, 70 oxen, 6 mounted cannon, and 6,000 cannonballs to defend the little city. As soon as he learned that the enemy was surrounding Puebla de Sanabria, General Séras advanced to Mombuey. Unable to go any farther because of his limited force, he notified the commander of the city. General Kellermann started off immediately to support him. The Duc d'Abrantès received orders to send some of his forces, which were still near Zamora. At the very moment when everyone was marching to help him, Graffenried surrendered, although he still had food for four days. He claimed that the enemy had bombarded much of the town and that his Swiss soldiers refused to enter the castle.[12] The Spanish abandoned Puebla de Sanabria in such great haste that they burned the gun carriages and left the garrison's arms, as well as bags full of cartridges and three barrels of powder. General Séras entered the next day and took thirty-two Spanish prisoners of whom two were officers. General Bonnet sent better news from Asturias, where he held the insurgents shut up in the mountains.

At this time Lieutenant Aliberti of the 8th Line at the head of sixty men fell on six hundred Spaniards.[13] At first he pushed back their skirmishers and gained some ground on them, but he was finally surrounded. After defending himself for a considerable length of time, Aliberti and his men marched en masse and reached Old Castile, where they took refuge in a house to gain a little cover from the numerous enemy and take some advantage of the location. The enemy set fire to it. Lieutenant Aliberti went through the wall into an adjacent house; it too was burned. Our men had to defend themselves against both the fire and the attack of these furious Spaniards, who were the more enraged because they had to burn their own homes. The soldiers ran successively from one house to another until they reached the last one. There they were at length dazed by the fire and forced to come out; throwing themselves against the enemy, they reached an isolated house and succeeded in occupying it, while keeping the Spaniards at a distance. At six o'clock in the evening, after nine hours of fighting, the Spaniards retreated. Some time later a

12. On August 10 Swiss Major Graffenried surrendered the 2nd Swiss infantry after a ten-day defense against a Portuguese force commanded by General Silveira and a Spanish detachment directed by General Francisco Gil de Taboada. See Koch, *Mémoires de Masséna,* VII, 133.

13. Lieutenant Aliberti was wounded on August 7 during a reconnaissance in Old Castile. See Aristide Martinien, *Tableaux par corps et par batailles des officiers tués et blessés pendant les guerres de l'empire (1805–1815)* (Paris, 1899), p. 135.

major came to the assistance of those brave men, and he found twenty-seven men killed, twenty-five wounded, and only eight without wounds. Lieutenant Aliberti had been wounded twice. The Prince requested the Cross [of the Legion of Honor] for him and two Crosses for his detachment. We were happy to be able to tell of such heroic deeds. Unfortunately we could not know of all those who honored such bravery back in France.

The preparations for the siege were still running into many difficulties and advancing very slowly. The Prince sent me to hurry the Marshal and General Lazowski. I found General Lazowski outlining his project after posting Loison's division six hundred yards from the city. He agreed with the Marshal and Loison that the trenches would at last be opened on the night of August 19; everything would be started at the same time, the parallel and the communications trenches. The artillery would be ready to start its work the next day and to open fire seven or eight days after the trenches had been opened. The general was obliged to borrow everything from the artillery. The artillery always announced it was ready; yet it had to request a delay because it was not ready.

General Reynier announced that O'Donnell had departed toward Alburquerque, leaving one thousand men in front of Alcanetar to prevent any repairs on the ferries. The General sent reconnaissances and messengers whose reports left us in great doubt. A few said that General Hill[14] was retiring toward Sarzedas and Sobreira [Formosa], while others said he was going beyond the Tagus to Vila Velha, and that the cavalry was taking the road to Abrantes. At last an officer was sent to General Hill, bearing a flag of truce, to obtain precise news; he advanced as far as Alpedrinha. A Portuguese general, Lecor,[15] commanding a corps of four to five thousand men, let him pass. He was stopped by a British general to await orders from General Hill. He was told that Hill occupied an entrenched position at Monte Gordo or the

14. Lord Rowland Hill (1772–1842) was appointed to the 38th Foot in 1790, and in 1803 he was promoted to the rank of brigadier general. He served in Ireland, at Toulon and Minorca, in Egypt, and in Hanover between 1793 and 1805; in 1808 he was given a brigade in Portugal, where he fought at Roliça and Vimeiro. He marched with Moore and Wellesley in 1809, and before the battle of Talavera he was given command of the Second Division, which he led during Masséna's invasion.

15. Carlos Frederico Lecor, Baron de Barão (1764–1836), commanded a Portuguese unit and was attached to Hill's division during the French invasion in 1810.

Serra das Talhadas, with his left at Estreito and his right extended toward Vila Velha, to guard the bridge on the Tagus. At the time, I thought his position was along this river and on the Zezere, or at least extended to one or the other of these two support [positions], and that the advance corps would form some kind of an advance guard, able to retire into a defensive position.

General Reynier indicated that Hill's division was composed of six to seven thousand British infantry, eight or nine hundred horses, and four to five thousand Portuguese situated on the right bank of the Tagus. Furthermore he reported that several regiments of British infantry had just arrived by the road to Abrantes and Pedrógão, but he was unable to find out whether these were additional reinforcements or troops being sent to the rear. We were also told that Beresford was at Guarda and to the right of Wellington near Celorico. The English sent officers through the villages to force the peasants to arm themselves and abandon their homes; they announced the arrival of La Romana and their determination to wait for us in their entrenched position rather than march toward us. Finally, the people of the country told us that troops of the 5th Corps had appeared at Zafra beyond the Guadiana while General Reynier labored to establish a rope bridge on the broken arch of the bridge of Alcántara.

The Prince received a dispatch from the Major General that designated new plans for our entry into Portugal, different from the ones given in our earlier instructions. The dispatch read: "The Emperor asked me to express his extreme satisfaction with the important capture of Rodrigo. He lets you decide on a battle against the English. You will enter Portugal at the beginning of September. You will have twelve thousand men under the command of General Drouet."[16] This letter, dated July 29, was in answer to that of the 11th. A few days later, all the recommendations [for promotions] in the 6th Corps were returned under the pretext of requesting records of service.[17] This was

16. Jean Baptiste Drouet, Comte D'Erlon (1765–1844), enlisted in a volunteer battalion in 1782; he was named general of division in 1803 and marshal in 1843. He served in the Armies of the Moselle and Sambre and Meuse from 1793 to 1796. He was at Zurich, Hohenlinden, Jena, and Friedland and he commanded the 9th Corps sent to reinforce Masséna in 1810. For details of Drouet's instructions see *Correspondance de Napoleon Ier*, No. 16732, Berthier to Masséna, July 29, 1810, XX, 642–43.

17. Pelet was indeed correct in blaming Berthier for obstructing promotions. On July 21 Napoleon wrote to Berthier, "I send you back the Prince d'Essling's pro-

a point of friction between the Prince de Neufchâtel and the Prince d'Essling, for many of the records had been attached to the report.

For a long time we had been accustomed to such tricks and we were often the victims, particularly me, the oldest officer of the Prince's [staff]. After having been a lieutenant from 1802 until 1805, I had to wait eighteen months to become captain. During that period I [served in] the Italian campaign, at Austerlitz, at Gaeta, in Calabria, and finally in Poland; moreover I had been wounded at Caldiero and exhibited conduct at Gaeta I dared call glorious.[18] Marshal Berthier had always detested Marshal Masséna without being able to aspire to the honors of such a rivalry; he had not even acquired the right to show jealousy. Moreover, he never neglected an occasion to indicate his feeling to those serving under him. If any external influence or petty jealousy was detrimental to the success of my work, he was the source of it. Any other conjecture was a dream without any basis. Although Prince Berthier had never done anything by himself, the simple composition of reports or instructions, either written or [verbal], carried by the officers in their missions, gave him enough latitude to bring about results favorable to his views. We found too many contradictions in the orders given or communicated to us and in the movements executed by the other armies.

The enemy made movements all along their line of forward posts. The telegraph at Almeida was kept busy during the whole night with the one the English maintained between Lamegal and Carvalhal. Every indication seemed to threaten an enemy advance, and there was even

posals for granting rewards on account of the capture of Ciudad Rodrigo. Let me know the names of the individuals mentioned in the dispatches relating to the capture or to the details of the siege, and tell me what rewards you propose. Let me also know what regiments were employed in the siege; they alone have a right to be rewarded." See *The Confidential Correspondence of Napoleon Bonaparte with his Brother Joseph, sometimes King of Spain* (London, 1855), II, 132. Ney was also concerned about these promotions. He wrote to Masséna on August 30, 1810, "I do not understand all the difficulties experienced by my army corps unless they may be to force me to request my recall to France. In order to put an end to all this jealousy and in the hope that my regiments will obtain the justice and rewards that are due them for their distinguished conduct at the siege of Ciudad Rodrigo . . . I beg Your Excellency to ask the Emperor if I can be relieved as commander of the 6th Corps and that I be permitted to return to France." Bonnal, *Ney*, III, 367–68.

18. The battle of Caldiero was fought by Masséna against the Austrians in October 1805; the fortress of Gaeta in Calabria fell on July 19, 1806, after a siege of five months.

talk of a general operation in the center to deliver Almeida. General Reynier also announced movements. Hill had a strong detachment at Ladoeiro forming a position ahead of his line. He had ordered provisions for a large corps in the same village. Although in this state of affairs an attack from the enemy was still not probable, General Reynier withdrew his detachment from Penamacor to Monsanto and Penha Garcia, and he momentarily suspended his operations beyond the Tagus.

The Prince, skeptical of these movements, noticed their coincidence and the relationship with attacks on Puebla de Sanabria and Alcanetar. He warned the various army corps, approved General Reynier's measures, and remained at a central point until the movements of the enemy became clear. He sent me to Marshal Ney with considerable authority to send officers from Malpartida or his headquarters to the 2nd and 8th Corps, and to halt a large convoy of advancing artillery. He also sent the Marquis d'Alorna to Pinhel to get more precise news from the inhabitants. I left with the marquis, who wanted to see the Marshal only after I had.

The Marshal received me with his usual demonstrations of kindness, while underneath he blustered, thundered, and forgot himself. I remained with him two or three hours, talking about the siege, about his positions, and about the movements of the enemy, but he had not received any fresh news. He took the trouble to give me the most exact information on the disposition of his troops. His advance guard was in the center, with a reserve of three battalions of the 66th Line (1,800 men) and the 3rd Hussars forward on the road to Celorico. On the right a battalion of the 15th Léger was posted one thousand yards behind Pinhel; a company was in the city, and the cavalry was one or two leagues ahead. Toward Freixedas on the left, one battalion of the 22nd Line was flanked on the extreme left by the 15th Chasseurs; the line of his advance guard was protected, and all its retrograde movements were concentric. The countryside in front of him was very poor and arid, but an advancing enemy could be seen from very far away; beyond was an excellent plain extending to the inaccessible Côa. As a result, there was nothing to fear on this front, and the Marshal would be able to support his advance guard and any attack on the Côa. Above the river toward his left he had a good position at Castelo Bom, and two brigades were deployed to march, with the army corps ready to follow. On the right the 15th Dragoons occupied Almendra. From this side the enemy would run into a dead end between the Douro and the Côa, both of which were impassable; he would be attacked from the front by the 8th Corps and on the flank by the 6th Corps, making any operation impossible. The Marshal was very clear on this ground and went into great detail. That same day he sent fifteen companies and some cavalry to the town of São João da Pesqueira with orders to put three or four companies on the other side of the Douro facing the city, and to send a reconnaissance in the direction of Viseu.

The Marshal hoped to collect some food and at the same time seize a strong post of enemy infantry with a cannon which held Vila Nova de Fozcoa. He talked to me at length about his procedures for harvesting grain, the duties of his soldiers, and in great detail about the food. Little by little his soldiers had organized a good system of marauding to gather food. Each one brought back anything he found. Then a value was determined for every item—a measure of grain, a cow, a pig, a goat, etc. Each soldier or company could get what they lacked by exchanging these items. Unfortunately, this manner of subsistence could not exist without great disorder. It was carried out at the expense of those who had their possessions taken without compensation or reclamation. But since it was impossible to find any inhabitants in the country, it was impossible to pay or give a voucher for anything taken. Nevertheless, on this subject it occurred to me that according to our invasion plans or extensive campaign maneuvers (and this is what occurred), we should organize a food commissariat within each regiment, just as there was one for funds, clothes, equipment, etc. There would be a common center in each divisional headquarters to make all distributions and to regulate consumption. Quartermasters or commissioners would be in charge, and during the wintertime they would remain at the supply depot in the rear.

The Marshal talked to me about the Spanish war; about Marshal Soult, who he claimed had missed Lord Wellington three times; and about Wellington's politics and those of his brother. The Marquis d'Alorna arrived, and the Marshal told him that the discussion was finished since he had received the new orders of the day. The poor marquis, eager to enter the conversation, suggested that the enemy could attempt an operation toward the Pass of Perales and place themselves between Reynier and us. The Marshal seized upon this idea, which was not completely irrelevant, and discussed it with cruel bitterness. We talked again about the siege, and he said it was necessary to spare no expense, although he knew quite well that we probably lacked funds. I hinted at a few details of the Major General's dispatch, and this did not please him. I also told him about the arrival of twelve thousand men under General Drouet, and he made a face as if it had been reinforcement for Wellington himself.[19] At last, after having stopped me from leaving several times, he allowed me to go, astonished by his unusual good nature.

Going over to General Lazowski on the other side of Almeida, I approached the front of attack and examined it closely. I noticed it was possible to see most of the wall revetment. Everywhere the enemy was working unprotected. The terrain did not appear to be as bad for our works as I had been told it would be. I found the general still sketching his plan, and from it he described his project for the attack, now reduced to a single bastion. We talked about it for a long time and he made several requests; one was that the artillery would commence its batteries in two days. I returned to Ciudad Rodrigo at eleven o'clock at night after having stayed on the road twenty-one hours, most of the time in the saddle. If I mention these circumstances, it is only to prove that I was not being spared, that I did not spare myself, and also that I had not seen everything in the Prince's council that I am writing about.

I made my report to the Prince, who was suffering impatiently from all the delays in the siege. I praised the dispositions taken by the Marshal and his extreme moderation. I vigorously insisted on handling him with caution, especially for the sake of his army corps, on the usefulness of both the Marshal and his corps for the campaign, on the dangers of a rupture, and on the trouble that friction would bring. The Prince complained of the frequent correspondence of the Marshal and the Duc d'Abrantès with the government. This could only prejudice his

19. Many observers believed that Drouet had little ability as a military commander. Thiébault declared, "The Count of Erlon was certainly one of the most estimable men I ever knew, but so thoroughly established was the opinion of his weakness as a general that, without noticing it, everybody spoke of him as the Count of Erlon, nobody as *General* d'Erlon." See Paul Charles Thiébault, *The Memoirs of Baron Thiébault*, trans. A. J. Butler (London, 1896), II, 290–91.

authority and perhaps even his person. He was not ignorant of the adverse gossip that was being spread, some of it a disgrace to its authors. I did not know who had the baseness to repeat this gossip to the Prince, but there were vile souls, masked by high position, who came to pay him their respects. I opposed all this [dissension] and did everything possible, as I still do, to mitigate the great anger and discord between these two great men in the interest of the Prince himself and of the campaign, as well as to gain for myself the satisfaction that all honest souls feel when they are doing what is right. According to a report of the Marquis d'Alorna, the Prince issued a dreadful order making officers responsible for the pillaging and horrors committed by their soldiers. He renewed it later and made examples which unfortunately were not effective in stopping the evil, produced in part by ———.

At last, during the night of August 15 and 16, the trenches were opened, the same date as the ridiculous siege of 1762. The first parallel was cut along its entirety, three hundred and sixty yards from the fortress. The communication trenches were also started toward it. Together they included a development of twenty-four hundred yards of works. During the day the trenches were covered almost everywhere or else masked by gabions; these gabions were filled with bags of earth and set up where the rocks could be cut only with mines.

Despite our closeness to the fortress and the difficult terrain, there were very few losses. The Prince remained at Ciudad Rodrigo because of the solemnity of the day,[20] and the next day he came to the trenches with Generals Loison, Éblé, and Ruty. The latter now disagreed with the engineer officers. After some discussion they refused to put the previously accepted projects into execution, especially the establishment of all the batteries on the first parallel. They claimed that the distance between the first parallel and the fortress was not what it had been said to be, and they did not want to open their works that night until the trenches were improved and far enough advanced to protect them, nor even to erect a few elevated batteries which would harass the fortress and protect our workers. The principal subject of discussion was the breach batteries. The engineers wanted to try them from the first parallel itself; they pleaded the length of time, the danger, and the

20. August 15 was a "solemn" day because it was Napoleon's birthday.

difficulty of establishing them on the covered way, and even their uselessness since we had unmasked the entire revetment up to the rocks where it was built. The artillerymen were afraid the battery would be too far away from the wall to destroy it, and they would be obliged to advance their batteries, which was often the case. The Prince sent for General Lazowski, who could not be found, and then for the Marshal, who had gone to another part of the trench. When he returned, we talked for a long time about the difficulties of crowning the covered way, which seemed avoidable to me. I asked General Lazowski to lay out two projects for the approaches; one would be for the breach battery initially placed between the first and second parallel, while the other would be established on the side of the moat. It should be noted that we were dealing only with a rather poor fortress and a Portuguese garrison, commanded by a foreign general. As a result, we could treat the city in a somewhat unceremonious manner.

We spent part of the day riding. It was hot and tiring. I fell asleep for a few moments in the trench thinking about home. It was the feast day of my village. There was dancing in front of my door while [in fact] I was under the cannonballs of the enemy. Happy pictures of my *patrie,* fond memories of my childhood, kept coming back to me, and from far away I took great pleasure in those dances that I had always avoided in real life. These memories have accompanied me everywhere and inspired me with a universal friendship that made me see a brother or sister in everyone of my own age, a father or mother in all the old people, and a paternal house in the habitation of mankind. Wherever I went, these feelings suggested to me the desire, the need, to prevent evil and to do all the good that I could. The feelings softened my heart but not my soul, for everywhere they reminded me that I had the honor of being born a Frenchman and that there was nothing great or even heroic that I was not capable of doing.

The Prince established his headquarters at Fort La Concepción, in the vacant lodging of the governor. We went to the casemate where we lived together with our horses. I had taken the gateman's room, which served as a kind of a study next to our casemate. The mess hall was in the casemate which we found to be the least gloomy and the kitchen in the one next to it. Two or three casemates had been reserved for two companies of grenadiers of Taupin's brigade, who were on duty. We remained in this fort for a month, and it deserved the cursory examination I made because it was unusual to find works of such perfection in Spain.

The fortress of La Concepción, destined solely to contain a garrison for the protection of the fertile plains of Argañan, was completely isolated from the frontier system. Situated on the crest of a hill between the Turones and Oñoro rivers and overlooking the village of Aldea del Obispo, it was perfectly laid out, defiladed, and constructed. The skillful engineer in charge had calculated everything perfectly, quite unlike the usual practice. The major elements of this regular square bastion, along with the salient demilunes and all the improved details, had been planned and laid out so that all its extensions ended in low ground and were protected from enfilade and reverse fire. After careful study [of the terrain], a system of works had been erected four hundred yards to the northeast on an elevation overlooking the neighboring heights and the deep valleys; a blockhouse protected on all sides from crossfire opened toward the gorge. Nevertheless, the fortress was subject to a general plan of enfiladement. Good esplanades with reverse fire covered each front, and a large covered way enveloped the whole. This way communicated with the fort by a double *caponniere*; midway it had a small construction, nearly oval in shape (similar to a very large redoubt), surrounded by a moat. Cavalry horses destined to protect the countryside were kept in this structure, which had the necessary gates for easy ingress and egress. The fortress was constructed entirely of cut granite. The curtains, formed by casemates, were situated along the entire width of the ramparts. One could see only a little earth inside the bastions. The ramps, the traverses, the talus, the openings of the embrasures—everything down to the channel at the bottom of the moat—showed great care in construction. The good covered way also had a revetment wall; it surrounded the fort and glacis all the way down to the bottom of the two valleys in a well-defined slope. Since the English did not want to leave their troops in the fort, they abandoned it, and the Spaniards refused to maintain it. The English blew up most of the demilunes and a few flanks of the bastions when we entered Portugal. It was necessary to complete the demolition so it would not be left to the insurgents. The Prince ordered the salients of the bastions mined. To complete this task effectively, I vainly asked that one curtain be blown up because a strong square remained for defense after the bastions had been destroyed.

We lived there almost as though we were in barracks. Before long a café was opened there. The officers had very little to do and found the days very long. There were games going on in a few of the casemates; there were punch, warm wines, gambling on race horses, and toward the end all kinds of military amusements. I was so busy I did not have any time to waste. After my daily work, there were long talks with the Prince and preparations of the plan for the campaign.

All my pleasure revolved around my association with two friends of war, Benôit Édouard Beaufort d'Hautpoul and Cavailher, whom I had the good fortune to keep in contact with the Prince. We three lived in very close friendship. This kept us constantly isolated from the rest of the *état major*. For a long time I found in them every quality, every talent, and every virture that can be found in the most diverse of characters. I was the happy link that united them. There was as much impetuosity, ardor, and passion for arms in the first man as there was moderation, composure, and perseverance in the second. Brilliancy was opposed to stability, mental vivacity to excellent judgment, enthusiasm to an almost unimpassioned sagacity; but in both there was the same affection, the same devotion, the same sensitivity, and the same exaltation of honor and patriotism. Some of their qualities were of constant intensity, while others often appeared in crises but were no less strong and tender. If I had been forced to choose between these two very different characters, I would certainly have been embarrassed, but I was blessed with the friendship of both.

If in ordinary life, friendship possesses so much sweetness and strength, if it is the most positive source of happiness and consolation, what is it amidst the difficulty and uncertainty of a military career? It is especially there that one feels strongly the need to share the ecstasy of success and the pains of defeat! It is there too that friendships become more sure, more sacred, and almost eternal. In the calm of society it is difficult to understand man; challenges are rare and easy to overcome. Perhaps our friendships had more charm and strength because they were intertwined with the vigorous struggle for glory and experienced great vicissitudes. Such were the attachments that never weakened among us. During this cruel campaign these friends were my confidants in everything that strict duty did not force me to keep to myself. They helped me in every way with talent and admirable sacrifice. They consoled my bitterness, softened my pain, and gave me some peaceful moments in a situation where I found only enemies. As a result we were always together and involved with each other. We fled the noisy show of happiness all around us.

At Fort La Concepción we used to walk in the neighborhood every evening. One day we made a charming discovery and our walks became so interesting that we made as many as possible. In an isolated spot in the middle of a small wooded area of green oaks, we met—a republic of ants. We took great pleasure in watching them. We contemplated their work, their pyramidal home, and their long roads. In these industrious "people" we recognized an image of human passions, tenderness toward children, avaricious foresight, and even a picture of our wars. We used to bring them enough to fill up their storehouses each day or as often as possible.

King Joseph had been anxious about the appearance of O'Donnell. He wrote to the Prince in his own hand to express a few fears on this subject and on the concentration of Spanish corps threatening Madrid. He asked for the deployment of some troops toward Plasencia and signed himself as "your affectionate friend." I answered him with a fine letter, demonstrating that there was no need to worry and that we were protecting him from a distance by vigorously menacing the English army.

The Prince had a hut built near the trench. Two aides-de-camp were always ready there to give him an immediate account of everything taking place. Despite the very chilly weather and a strong wind at sunrise, he went to the hut to settle a disagreement between the engineer and artillery generals. They discussed their project at length in his presence. The engineers wanted to reduce the distance between the parallel and the fortress, and finally it appeared that the batteries as well as the breach guns would commence simultaneously the next day. I went into the trenches and visited the works every time I could approach them. The parallel was splendid, quite improved and relatively safe from right to left, as were the communication trenches. The fortress fired a great deal and most accurately. Its shells and bombs were landing with great effectiveness. During the return trip the Prince announced that the enemy had invested Astorga and that the Portuguese peasants were arming against us. The adverse conduct of our advance guard contributed considerably [to the feelings against us], and Wellington was doing everything he could to arouse the enemy to fight us while he remained inactive. Orders were given to the 8th Corps and to Séras to help Astorga, defended by General Jeanin.[21] The enemy withdrew with the approach of these troops.

The Marshal had some [fire] signals placed on the line of advance posts; he announced that they had burned and that five hundred men had gone in front of Pinhel; on the basis of these facts he constructed a long six-page letter of projects and movements, etc. He wished to concentrate Generals Bonnet, Kellermann, and Reynier; nevertheless he added that the reports from deserters announced the concentration of the English behind Celorico. The Prince had a rendezvous with him at the hut. There was a long conversation between the two, and then the engineer and artillery generals arrived and took part in the discussion. I thought the Marshal, seeing the progress of the siege, was clearly pleased to have support for his plan to attempt another attack on the English like that of July 24. Loison, the good advocate, approached me and censured the Marshal's behavior, telling me, "We know whom we should obey." He intended to go and say the same thing to the Marshal. He was the oldest general of division in this army corps and the only one who would have anything to gain by dissension.

The Prince had already given me orders to make a reconnaissance of the Côa with Cavailher in case of an enemy attack. We made a reconnaissance which would be very useful to any army following us. Our report found its way into the papers of the Prince at Salamanca because this area was the theater where we had our only battle line with Lord Wellington. The plateau between the Turones and the Côa was smooth, rather gentle, and not very rocky. On each side of its elevation or summit were old guard or signal towers. Erected in the time of the Moors, it was said, they were capable of containing some ten men, and most of them were linked together. They were called

21. Baron Jean Baptiste Jeanin (1769–1830) became a lieutenant in 1792; he was promoted to general of brigade in 1808 and to lieutenant general in 1815. Jeanin served in the Army of the Rhine, went to Egypt with Napoleon, and fought in the Austrian and Prussian campaigns of 1806–7. Sent to Spain in 1808, he served there for three years.

atalaya. There was a tower in every town, and they were placed about four to six thousand yards apart. The slopes of the valley where the Côa flows were full of rocks, cut by ravines and precipices, and sparsely wooded. From a distance the slopes presented the appearance of an amphitheater of piled rocks. In this part of the country there was only one very difficult road, almost impossible for the artillery to descend; it went through Castelo Bom to Mido. It took us half an hour to descend and twenty minutes to climb back up. Castelo Bom, a village along a slope on the right bank, was once surrounded by walls, but they had now collapsed in ruins. The bottom of the valley was rather broad. The bridge was eighty yards long and the river not very deep. The left bank was less steep but no less difficult. The plateau beyond was rather uniform and covered with ripe grain, which was cut by a detachment of a hundred soldiers from the third division. There was not a single man in the village and only a few women. Toward Almeida the main road, descending to the Côa by endless turnabouts, was no less difficult, and its bridge was built up on rocks. Above the valley, toward Junça, where a few paths ran, the road became wider and more accessible. The road across the right bank was not as poor. Toward the north the valley ended, presenting a heap of rocks strewn about, a picture of true chaos, and we had all kinds of difficulties slipping through with our escort horses. Night was about to overtake us in this awful labyrinth, and we hurried toward the cultivated land, which we reached at last. It was ten o'clock at night when we entered the fort, although we had left at four o'clock in the morning.

The following day Captain Cavailher continued the reconnaissance to the Douro, and he found the Côa less difficult nearer the Douro. This entire countryside was granite and we saw only diverse variations of granite. There were sometimes immense blocks and at other times the large surfaces were very smooth and slippery. Although in general the stone showed rhomboidal forms in its cracks, it became round on the exterior like rolled pebbles. At other times the formations presented great masses of prismatic shapes. The quartz appeared pure and often crystallized in flat white or various other colors. The water, running clear and pleasant, decorated the landscape, but this was its only ornamentation since the trees were thin and the buildings would merge, surrounded by these rocks.

The Prince wanted to commence the firing, which was still delayed. He went to examine the trenches and the batteries in the greatest detail with Generals Éblé and Lazowski. General Bardet[22] was on duty for the day and Beaufort, the engineer officer in the trench, had just been slightly wounded. The approaches were becoming uninhabitable under the noonday sun. Movements were extremely difficult, and a terrible reflection off the sand created a suffocating heat. Although the workers had to break up the rocks with petards if they could not be removed, the works advanced rapidly enough. The batteries were completed; a great number of the platforms and embrasures had been established, but they were still masked from the enemy. Thirty-nine cannon had been moved through the fields with a great quantity of provisions. The engineers opened large straight lines from the first parallel which crisscrossed each other to form a double approach. These approaches were quite advanced and improved, reaching the lowest point between the fortress and the ground of the attack. However, it had been necessary to make a reverse on the left because the approach was under water. General Lazowski asked that as many cannon as possible be set up there to counteract the fire from the fortress, and that the guns not be risked separately. He also wanted the two breach batteries placed in the extensions along the fronts of the bastion of São Pedro, 300 and 360 yards away. They were to be armed with the largest caliber, even at the expense of the main battery, to begin bombarding the salients. I had been suggesting this for a long time. At last, after much debate and many pleas for the intervention of the Prince, General Éblé, the best and most devoted man in the world and a devil of an artilleryman, consented to change the caliber of the two cannon. However, he asked for a written order from the Prince, who promised it to him. Meanwhile the two generals, in agreement as much as possible, expressed mutual satisfaction.

Battery No. 1 had been designated as a ricochet battery; it was improperly situated and the more useful howitzers were put in its place. This battery, as well as No. 11, was heavily bombarded, but fortunately the ground protected both of them. General Éblé had confided

22. Baron Martial Bardet de Maison-Rouge (1764–1837) enlisted in the 70th Line in 1781 and was promoted to general of division in 1814. He served with the Army of the Sambre and Meuse and with Augereau's forces in Batavia in 1798, and was attached to the 6th Corps before it went to Spain.

in great secrecy to the Prince that he expected three 10-inch mortars from Madrid at any moment and that he had kept five pieces of 24 in reserve at Rodrigo. This decision delayed the fire of the batteries, but assured him not only of numerical superiority in cannon but also that his positions would encompass one third of the city. As he left, the Prince entrusted to the engineers and artillery the decision of when to open fire. They said it might be the next day but more probably on the morning of August 26. Although they claimed to be ready, they were happy to have more time. The engineers were to start two half parallels that night.[23]

A young British officer who had been made prisoner was taken to Fort La Concepción. He was only a charming child sent from the 2nd Corps where he had been for a while. I had him brought to headquarters for an exchange. I urged him to introduce himself to the Prince when the latter went for his walk, and ask to be returned to his own people. I was convinced that his youth and gracefulness would influence the Prince more strongly than any possible recommendation. Unfortunately, the Prince was not very well disposed at that moment since he was displeased with the conduct of the British regarding our own men taken prisoner. He therefore did not agree to the request as I had expected.

General Reynier wrote that the troops reaching General Hill from Lisbon had been placed on the left above Atalaia and that one of our officers with sixty Hanoverian chasseurs had been taken near Ladoeiro. General Reynier was ordered to prepare to march at first warning and to follow General Hill if he made a movement or sent an overwhelming detachment in our direction. Simultaneously, the Duc d'Abrantès was to march on San Felices el Grande. Our intelligence reports announced the arrival at Guarda of the old Bishop of Oporto, a member of the Regency who had just been named in London as Archbishop of Lisbon and Patriarch of Portugal.[24] This bishop-patriarch-elect was reputed to be a rather mediocre but obstinate and passionate man. He was al-

23. For the complement and location of batteries, see Koch, *Mémoires de Masséna*, VII, 150–52.

24. António de S. José e Castro (d. 1815), became Bishop of Oporto in 1798. He was appointed Archbishop of Lisbon and Patriarch of Portugal; moreover, he played an influential role in the policies of the Portuguese government as one of the Governors of the Kingdom. He brought Oporto under attack by attempting to defend it in March 1809 when Soult's army reached the city.

ready well known for the misfortune he had attracted to Oporto. It was said that he complained in England about the desertion of Ciudad Rodrigo and that he carried orders to Lord Wellington to defend Almeida and the Portuguese frontier. Moreover he ordered the inhabitants, under penalty of death, to abandon the country which we entered and to destroy everything ahead of us, promising compensation and rewards. Those who did not obey him were to be rigorously punished. He fulminated terrible punishment against those *ordenanza* who did not arm themselves; he threatened with a council of war the militia captains who did not organize insurrection.[25] Finally, he announced reinforcements for the Allied army. His arrival created much commotion and excited great enthusiasm among the Portuguese. There was much talk about raising the siege by a double movement on the Côa, above and below the fortress. The British and Portuguese senior officers had held a great banquet at Misarela to reaffirm the union and eliminate any divisions that might exist. It was said that the British artillery was beyond Guarda on a rather extended line.

The foregoing is mentioned as an opportunity to examine the reciprocal positions of the armies, rather than as a subject of grave anxiety. I was apprehensive only about the left. However, it was expedient to prepare as rapidly as possible, for if the enemy was going to attack it would probably be on the 27th or 28th. I went to speak to the Prince; he saw me the next day. I was immersed in the problem. After supper I took a walk alone. I dreamed. I made up plans. The enemy could not put themselves in a dead end between the Côa, the Douro, and the Agueda. Although the Côa was quite passable parallel to Castelo Rodrigo, they could not make any frontal movement because of the rocky ravine of the Côa; therefore they would have to move on the left by Sabugal and Alfaiates. Should the 8th Corps be moved there? If so, would the right be uncovered? What danger would there be if the right bank of the Tagus was evacuated for four or five days while the 2nd Corps moved temporarily to Alfaiates? If the enemy wished to start on the road to Madrid, would he have time to do so before the

25. Wellington actually issued orders for the mobilization of Portugal. He wrote to Lieut. General Stapleton Cotton on August 4, 1810, "Send round to the people that they must retire from the villages, and let the magistrates know that if any of them stay, or if any of the inhabitants have any communication with the enemy, they shall be hanged." *Wellington's Dispatches,* VI, 324.

end of the siege? I stopped with this idea. I thought I had found the right solution.

I then went to the Prince's quarters. I spoke excitedly to him about my project, and he agreed with it. At ten o'clock he woke me up and had me write a dispatch to General Reynier. "Go immediately to Alfaiates, observe Sabugal and its flanks closely, leave communication posts en route to Madrid, especially at Talavera and El Puente del Arzobispo, which are in a good state of defense, and establish a few necessary posts to reoccupy your position and send news of the enemy." This dispatch left a few minutes later in the hands of Captain Ledoux, and the next day duplicates were sent. From this moment, our siege was well guaranteed, but it was possible to derive even greater advantage from these dispositions, as we were soon to see.

At last the day arrived for beginning the attack against Almeida. We reached the fortress in a thick fog, and the firing started after six o'clock. Although eleven batteries were firing simultaneously, the sight was not very imposing to those accustomed to genuine battles—not too much noise and little effect. On the other hand, the fortress fired considerably and very well. Everybody was standing in front of the Prince's hut. He sent me to inform the Marshal of his arrival. As usual, I found him absolutely alone in a hut he had built to the right of the attack. He told me coldly that he had nothing to say to the Prince. On my return I went by the first parallel to judge the shots. They were low, short, and had little effect. A few fell in the second parallel and killed some of our tirailleurs. Nothing had been damaged, and only a few cannonballs and ricochet shots were falling in the *gazonnements* and embrasures. However, the city was firing more strongly than ever; yet it did very little damage. Orders were given to throw a few bombs. They damaged and set fire to a few houses, but the flames were soon extinguished. The firing continued the whole day on both sides.

We returned to Fort La Concepción. After supper I took a walk by myself, for it was good to be alone from time to time. Night was approaching. Sitting beside our ants, I read a few lines from Tacitus and went from the awful pictures of the tyrants of Rome to the contemplation of our little people. Suddenly I felt the earth tremble strongly under my feet. I heard a vast and deep noise. It was an awful explosion. My first thought was for our powder, but the concussion was too great. "It is the fortress," I shouted with a feeling of horror and joy. "It is certainly ours!" My thoughts passed quickly to our army. Now it would be able to concentrate against Wellington's army, which was scattered weakly in cantonments. I said to myself, "Fortune has given us Almeida, but it has also given us Wellington and his army. His scattered cantonments must be attacked if he tries to withdraw his artillery and its baggage, or else he will have to abandon everything to save the British army. Thus he will have to flee with his dispersed regiments and unite them again beyond the Mondego or perhaps even farther away."

Meanwhile, I ran in all haste toward the fortress, where everyone was in great suspense. Soon an officer arrived from the trenches and announced that he had seen an awful explosion in the middle of the fortress followed by a violent fire, and that a rain of huge stones and debris together with a small piece of artillery had fallen on our approaches.[26] All my anxieties were put aside. The fortress continued to fire weakly and unreliably while our own bombs increased the ravage and the most frightful miseries. The old castle had completely exploded along with eight hundred barrels of powder, an enormous quantity which destroyed the whole fort. While all this was happening, I mentioned my project of an advance. Everybody was too agitated and excited to pay any attention to it. Only one dispatch was prepared for the Major General. I stopped its consignment until the next day.

We were on horseback very early [the next day] to go to Almeida. The Prince asked me to come with him as he usually did, regardless of whom else he had with him. Adjutant Commander Rippert and the Marquis d'Alorna were right behind us, and they could hear what we were saying because at the end we were talking angrily and very loudly. (Here I will turn to my Journal for a description of what took place, as an example of the manner in which it was kept, although not every event will be as detailed.) On the way I again proposed to the Prince an immediate march against the enemy if the fortress surrendered as he expected. I pointed out to him that Wellington was not ready yet, that he expected the fortress to resist us for six to eight

26. Sprünglin related that he and Ney were reconnoitering the fortress; they had just dismounted to observe the French fire when the explosion occurred. He recorded, "It resembled the eruption of a volcano, and the memory has not diminished after twenty-six years." See Sprünglin, "Souvenirs," p. 445.

days,[27] that he would have the greatest difficulty withdrawing his artillery from Guarda to Celorico and Pinhanços, that he had at most a very weak line of posts in front of us, and that his army was dispersed, unprepared, and in its cantonments, while ours was united. The 2nd Corps was at Alfaiates or very near, almost the entire 8th Corps was at San Felices el Grande or beyond, while Hill was still quite far away. I added that we had the Côa behind us. With the disposition of a few large cannon it would afford us excellent protection during a retreat and guarantee the bridge road. Moreover we had the fortress of Almeida; its defense must still be in a good state, and we could immediately arm it by drawing in all of the siege *parc* there, still intact. Besides there was still Ciudad Rodrigo, and also the [expected] arrival of General Drouet with twelve thousand men. The Prince received my advice as though it had been given by a young man. I persisted because I was strongly convinced. He resisted and finally became almost angry. I still went on speaking. He countered with the difficulties of collecting food and the impossibility of living over there. I answered that the movement would be limited to two or three marches and that we could make five or six days' biscuits for the troops. Finally, I let the Prince think about this idea. The fortress was not firing any more. We could not see the tower, the church, or the castle. Everything appeared turned upside down. At the hut, we thought there had been negotiations. The Prince had brought an ultimatum along. He sent it with Captain Gania and one of Marshal Ney's officers.[28] He ordered me to go and see what had taken place. I had already been to the trenches with General Fririon, and we found General Simon ready to send an ultimatum on his own initiative.

I walked forward with the parliamentarian. Only two were allowed to go in. I yielded to the Marshal's representative and waited at the barrier. While talking with the Portuguese officers, I examined the fortress in detail, surveying all the profiles and counting the officers

27. Governor Cox expected the fortress of Almeida to hold out 90 days. See *Wellington's Dispatches*, Wellington to Wellesley, August 20, 1810, VI, 373–75.

28. Apparently Pelet was unaware that Masséna had sent General Fririon to Cox with an ultimatum. See Fririon, *Journal historique*, pp. 31–32. The ultimatum declared, "The town of Almeida is burning. All my siege artillery are in their batteries, and it is impossible for the English army to come to your aid. Render yourself to the generosity of the Armies of His Imperial Majesty. I offer you honorable conditions." See Belmas, *Journaux des siéges*, Masséna to Cox, August 27, 1810, III, 382–83.

[?]. The Marquis d'Alorna arrived on horseback. As soon as he was recognized by the garrison, they shouted, "Long live Marquis d'Alorna." There was a general concert of "vivas" with all the shakos up in the air. The more recalcitrant officers were forced to be polite. Everybody was greeting each other, and there was an uproar. Meanwhile the negotiators were gone longer than the Prince desired. I tried several times to break up their parley. I sent messages, and the Prince also sent two. Finally our officers returned.[29] William Cox requested the conditions on which we would treat. The Prince said capitulation; this was later accepted. I was to be one of the negotiators. The generals left and I remained to arrange the capitulation. Captain Gania and I carried it.

After waiting at the barrier, we were blindfolded and made to cross two or even three fronts to reach the governor, who was in a postern closely resembling a jail. Governor Cox was thirty-four or thirty-five years old, tall, noble, a handsome figure with the shrewdness of self-discipline, the appearance of a strong character—in all, *un bel anglais.* He read the ultimatum but was unwilling to accept it. We talked. The conversation began on a serious note, then became pleasant, then light, and was always carried on in an agreeable way. The door of the casemate was closed and we could see only two or three officers; several incidents prolonged my stay there. I sent a message to the Prince that Captain Gania was sending two officers charged to negotiate with him. I told the governor the way things were, and I told him the truth about the state of affairs. At last I left with the two officers, one a major of artillery and the other an officer attached to the governor.[30] Without being blindfolded, they mounted their horses and we went to find the Prince at the mill tower. The Prince demanded the acceptance of his conditions. We discussed them for a long time. At last the major agreed to sign. The captain insisted that the garrison should not be made prisoner. The Prince sent me back with the major and the signed capitulation. I had to wait for more than an hour. Then I learned that

29. Pelet refers to the second summons, when Gania was accompanied by Captain Sprünglin of the 6th Corps. See Sprünglin, "Souvenirs," p. 445. This second ultimatum announced, "I am displeased that you do not wish to accept the honorable capitulation that I offered you. I now inform you that I will recommence firing. . . . I suggest you sign and return the capitulation you have in your hands." See Koch, *Mémoires de Masséna,* Masséna to Cox, August 27, 1810, VII, 155.

30. The Portuguese negotiators were Fortunato José Barreiros of the artillery and Pedro de Mello of Cox's staff.

the garrison wanted to surrender, that all the powder had exploded, that there were only thirty-seven damaged barrels left, and that there were no more bombs or shells. Governor Cox insisted that Lord Wellington would arrive on August 28 and end the siege. A few troops of General Simon were ready to enter and take over the barrier. I gave them orders to remain in their ranks.

At this time Adjutant Commander Rippert brought me a copy of the capitulation.[31] He entered with me although his eyes were still blindfolded. Governor Cox, who had earlier been agreeable and frank, now seemed worried and preoccupied. I gave him the exact words of the Prince—to allow the garrison to return home if they desired, but to insist on the rest of the capitulation terms. I complained that he had kept me waiting for a long time, and he apologized. I fixed the time I would wait for an answer. He gave me his ultimatum: "that the garrison would be free to go home on their word of honor, that the British would be allowed to return to England on the same terms, and that the door would not be opened until the next day at noon." These conditions were written down next to our articles. I did not persist lest the talks break off. I parleyed with Governor Cox in a different way. Finally, I realized that he wanted to gain one day and give Wellington time to maneuver and prepare himself. This seemed to prove he was not expecting him the next day, for in that case he would have proposed a conditional capitulation. On the contrary, I insisted that we occupy one gate immediately. I proposed all the articles to him separately, but he wanted to combine them. He offered his word of honor and some hostages at the moment the capitulation had been signed but continued to insist on the commitment to leave at noon. At last I offered liberty to him, the other English, and the garrison prisoners on their word of honor. He did not want this and at times became a little angry. He served us Oporto wine, and I was a little suspicious of his kindness. I was allowed to return with my eyes uncovered and I saw, in part, the results of the disaster. The Prince did not want to consider

31. According to the capitulation terms, the garrison would evacuate the fortress with the honors of war and become prisoners, while the militia would be permitted to return to their homes. The officers were to keep their swords and personal effects, and the property of the citizens would be guaranteed. The French would take the supplies remaining in the fortress and care for the sick of both nations. See "Capitulation d'Almeida," August 27, 1810, Correspondance: Armée de Portugal, Carton C[7]9.

the proposed conditions. I agreed with him, against everyone else, convinced that the governor would be forced to come to an agreement and that Lord Wellington would withdraw. The Prince wrote that he would commence firing again if they did not accept his conditions immediately.

At this time the Marshal took me aside and proposed the same project I had suggested in the morning, that is, to march against the British. He was with General Loison and talked to me with great confidence because I was the man of the hour. I was forced to oppose this project, which was so dear to me, and to exaggerate its difficulties. I assured him that it was now too late and that by the next day the English would be ready. He claimed Lord Wellington would attack us. I showed him it was impossible. Then he again spoke to the Prince to accept the conditions; everyone wanted the same thing. The Prince still wanted to propose the conditions that I had suggested. I assured him that the governor had given me his ultimatum but that he only wished to gain time. The Prince did not go any further.

We opened fire again in a vigorous manner. There were always five or six bombs in the air. With the entire military staff, we waited in the wretched mill tower during an awful rainstorm until one or two o'clock in the morning. As we returned, the sky was completely black and we could not see a thing. We had the greatest difficulty following, and we frequently got lost going to find our horses at the field hospital. Then we went to the right on a wide road and, finally, to the left. We rode without knowing which way to go. After traveling to the left for more than two hours, we found the main road to Val da Mula and, without doubt, the road of Nova de Avel; we arrived at the fort very wet and weary.

Poor Colonel Jacques Pavetti and *chef d'escadron* d'Oraison of the *gendarmerie* were not as fortunate, although they had left at the same time. They rode all night and until eight o'clock in the morning; then they arrived in a village where they were massacred [*sic*] along with two gendarmes.

At eleven o'clock in the evening the governor of Almeida sent a signed copy of the capitulation that I had left with him. The only restriction was that the militia would be free to return to their homes after giving their word not to serve until exchanged. This was accepted and the firing ended immediately.

General Fririon went to Almeida very early to execute the Prince's orders. He did not want anyone to touch the provisions, in order to maintain them intact for the army reserve. No one else was to enter the city with the exception of General Brenier,[32] who was named governor, and a battalion to occupy the posts. Governor Cox created difficulties because he had not received a copy of the capitulation signed by the Prince. I wrote to General Fririon that if the governor raised new arguments we would open fire again and complete arrangements to blow up the door and take the city by storm, since our second parallel already touched the end of the glacis. Finally our troops entered. Five thousand men of the 24th Portuguese Line, the militia, and one company of cavalry left with the honors of war. They deposited their arms outside the barrier. The Marquis d'Alorna was ahead of them. They were wildly enthusiastic about the return of their old general in chief. As one of the most renowned men of Portugal, he was surrounded with many well-known officers. They received the marquis as their savior and proclaimed him the defender and the avenger of the country. They asked his help and swore to assist in breaking the chains of the British who had just abandoned them so infamously.

Those who had seen the manner in which the French army was received during the first Portuguese expedition; those who knew how heavy and odious the English yoke had been for the inhabitants; who knew the intrigues and the severity with which the British cabinet had founded and maintained its usurpation, the anger of those proud descendants of de Gama, Alburquerque, de Castro, and Ataíde who had been subjected everywhere to the British in insignificant posts; and finally, those who knew how much difference existed between the Portuguese and the Spaniards with regard to the progress of civilization and enlightenment—all these had hoped there would be a party to counterbalance the influence of the faction that had sided with the British, if not a complete revolution in our favor. In fact, if the English

32. Comte Antoine François Brenier de Montmorand (1767–1832) entered the French service in 1786 and reached the rank of general of division in 1811. He served with the various French armies in Holland, Germany, and Italy until 1807, when he was assigned to Junot's corps for the invasion of Portugal. Bernier marched with Séras's division and served as governor of Almeida from August 28, 1810, until May of the following year when he was reassigned to the Army of Portugal.

had put a little less of what we call *politique* into their conduct and campaign, had employed less rigor in their orders for the evacuation of the country and fewer punishments when their orders were not obeyed, and had shown less finesse in their military movements, they would have been abandoned by the inhabitants and the Portuguese troops. Then we would have confirmed conjectures that the events of the last year justified only too well.

The large number of Portuguese in our midst, most of whom belonged to the first families of the kingdom, had hoped for such an event for a long time and had tried to make us share their hopes. Many of them seemed to be able to influence those of their compatriots whom they contacted. The most conspicuous one, the Marquis d'Alorna, whom I later saw die in Russia, had been in our ranks since 1807. At that time he obeyed only the orders and politics of his sovereign. He was certainly very far from having hostile sentiments toward his country. He believed he served it, and he finished a memoir on the conquest of Portugal with these remarkable words: "Since my country is destined to be occupied by troops whom no one can resist, I must hope, for the good of my compatriots, that it is invaded quickly rather than disputed step by step." Thus, like a minister of peace, he followed a foreign army to mitigate the misfortunes of invasion and ward off the tempest ready to fall on his country. Nevertheless, he was declared a traitor along with his followers. A price was put on his head by those who organized a war of extermination, by a Regency which had accepted the English oligarchy against the true interest of Portugal and which was subject to a foreign army from the Thames or the Seine; by a Regency which—indifferent to the inhabitants—claimed the right to dispose of this distant kingdom, usurp its government, and declare that those who followed the flags of the opposition were traitors. Accordingly, could Junot have used the same right when he dominated Lisbon? On which side was justice then? Who can recognize it positively when surrounded by these political storms?

The Marquis d'Alorna issued a patriotic proclamation to the Portuguese that was directed only against the English. The Prince also issued a proclamation which I found in the work of Captain Guingret.[33]

33. Captain Guingret published his *Relation historique et militaire de la campagne de Portugal, sous le maréchal Masséna, prince d'Essling* at Limoges in 1817. He served in the 6th Léger of Marchand's division during the invasion of Portugal.

I cannot remember whether it was sent from Paris or was made in the council. Nevertheless, both of them were written with commendable moderation and according to principles very different from those professed by the English. We urged the inhabitants to remain quietly at home and not to join a war that was foreign to them. From intercepted dispatches, private reports, and the response of the peasant bands summoned to put down their arms, everything permitted us to hope that Portugal would be able to detach itself from British arms. The conduct of the garrison at Almeida seemed to fulfill the wish of the true Portuguese.

The Prince was wrong to believe in the oaths of honorable warriors and to eagerly seize on this means of ending the war with the least possible bloodshed. He consented to the formation into regiments of those who wanted to take service with us. The Marshal named the officers and General Pamplona took command.[34] Those who applauded this excellent idea, perhaps more than anyone else, have bitterly blamed him since then. These Portuguese troops were encamped at Aldea del Obispo; a few dragoons brought us their six flags. We found 119 pieces of artillery in Almeida. Moreover, there were a few mountain pieces and a great deal of food.[35] Despite very stringent orders, everybody entered the fortress before nightfall. We remained in the neighborhood for a long time, but I was unable to gain the dismal satisfaction of visiting it, although I hoped to examine the fortifications and see the destruction.

It has been said that this disaster was terrible. The entire city seemed to have been uprooted from its foundation. Five hundred people either perished in the castle or were crushed by the collapsing houses.[36] A

34. Manuel Inácio Martins Pamplona, Condes de Subserra (1760–1832), began his career by joining a cavalry regiment at Santarém. He served in several foreign armies and in 1797 was given command of a Portuguese infantry regiment. Placed in command of the 9th Cavalry in 1801, he was promoted to brigadier in 1806. When Junot invaded Portugal the next year, Pamplona collaborated with the French. He served on Masséna's staff in 1810 and was proscribed by the Portuguese government.

35. According to Major Bouvier, who compiled an inventory of the fortress, the French captured 172 guns of all calibers, 605,695 cartridges, 2,885 small arms, but only 39 barrels of powder. The quartermaster general gathered 300,000 rations of biscuit, 10,000 rations of salted meat, 24 tons of wheat, 25 tons of rice, 80 tons of maize, 2 tons of beans, 150 tons of straw, 80 tons of barley, and 34 barrels of wine. For details see Horward, "Invasion of Portugal," pp. 234–35.

36. The French casualties numbered 62 dead and 377 wounded, and the Portuguese lost over 500 in the explosion; 5,000 more surrendered on August 28. For details see Horward, "Invasion of Portugal," pp. 235–38.

piece of 24 was thrown over the parapet into the moat. Other smaller pieces were hurled several hundred yards away. The wall was cracked and all the houses shaken and damaged. The Portuguese artillery officers from whom I obtained these details presumed that the accident happened in the following way: since the entire castle vaulting was bombproof, a few people had been permitted to take refuge in the artillery magazine, where there were more than four thousand shells. According to a few men who survived, it seemed that one of our bombs had fallen in the middle of the courtyard and rolled down to the magazine, where it exploded. At this unfortunate moment thirty militiamen were loading barrels in the principal magazine to take to the batteries. The fire of the artillery magazine spread to this enormous amount of powder and the whole castle blew up and along with it the larger part of the city.[37] One of the most horrible spectacles I have ever seen was that of an unfortunate soldier carrying his one-month-old child in his arms; the mother had died during the night and he had no idea of how to get any milk. I had him get a mare.

General Reynier arrived at Alfaiates with the first division; the second was at Navas Frias under General Soult with the cavalry beyond Sabugal.[38] General Reynier received orders to move toward the Tagus and stock enough biscuit provisions so that he could march about September 10. He left part of his artillery with a secure guard beyond the pass of Navas Frias.

Lord Wellington had gone to Alverca and Beresford to Avelãs da Ribeira. There was also talk of a general advance of their army. The Prince told me at this time he knew the enemy was going to attack him, but I neglected to ask him where he obtained this information. Nevertheless, I remained convinced that they would not attack, and if

37. Pelet's account of the explosion is supported by the artillery officers Hulot and Noel. See Hulot, *Souvenirs,* p. 316; J. N. A. Noel, *Souvenirs militaires d'un officier du premier empire, 1795–1832* (Paris, 1895), p. 107. The Portuguese historian Luz Soriano also recorded this incident with minor modifications, basing his account on the statements of an eyewitness. See Simão José da Luz Soriano, *Historia da guerra civil e do estabelecimento do governo parlamentar em Portugal, 1777–1834* (Lisbon, 1866–90), Segunda Epocha, III, 73n.

38. Baron Pierre Benôit Soult (1770–1843) enlisted in the 33rd Line in 1788 and was promoted to general of division in 1813. He served in the French armies in Germany and Italy and was present with Masséna at Zurich and Genoa. After fighting in Italy in 1805 and Prussia in 1806, Soult was sent to Spain, where he was appointed to command his brother's cavalry in the second Portuguese campaign in 1809. He commanded Reynier's cavalry during Masséna's invasion.

they were marching, it was only to push our advance guard back on the other side of the Côa. This could be done very easily, and they could pretend to be attempting something in support of Almeida for the honor of their arms as well as for political utility. If Lord Wellington had wanted to help Almeida there was still time for him to advise the governor by telegraph and march on the 27th or the 28th. Governor Cox, who had served him so well, could have withstood our fire despite its intensity.[39] He would only have had to use grapeshot in his cannon against any main assault and wait. Lord Wellington would have found many unfortunate people in the city, but any harm done could have been repaired with thirty wagons of powder. Besides, at the beginning the British General had more than enough troops to advance and impede us or even force us to raise the siege by maneuvering in front of our left, since we would be forced to leave four to five thousand men at Almeida to guard our trenches with cannon and prevent the enemy from marching toward Rodrigo, whose breaches were not yet repaired. Nevertheless, immediately after our entrance into Almeida, all the intelligence reports mentioned only the retrograde movement of the enemy army.[40]

I prepared the report on the siege of Almeida. The Prince first asked for it to be written rather colorfully and then he wanted it toned down. I started the work and after completing a good third of it, I became aware of the customary difficulty of trying to satisfy the Prince. I even got a little angry and left my report as it was. It ended as follows: "This is the second fortress the British army allowed us to take right

39. Cox described his predicament to Beresford in a letter dated August 30: "The painful task has fallen to my lot of acquainting your Excellency that I was reduced to the necessity of surrendering the fortress of Almeida . . . on the 27th inst., at 10 o'clock at night, in consequence of the unfortunate explosion of the great magazine of powder in the castle. . . . I was deprived of the whole of my artillery and musket ammunition, with the exception of a few made-up cartridges . . . and 39 barrels of powder which were deposited in the laboratory. Upwards of half of the detachment of artillery, and a great number of infantry soldiers, besides several of the inhabitants, were destroyed by the effect of this terrible explosion. Many of the guns were dismounted upon the ramparts, the works were materially injured, and a general dismay spread amongst the troops and inhabitants of the place." See *Wellington's Dispatches* (1852 ed.), IV, 257–58.

40. After the fall of Almeida, a Portuguese officer was reputed to have said to Wellington, "If you are unable to defend us, why do you stimulate our resistance and cover our unfortunate country with blood and ruins? If you are in force, deliver battle; if you are too weak and cannot obtain reinforcement, retire and leave us to compromise with the conquerors." See Fririon, *Journal historique*, p. 34.

under their guns, although they had haughtily promised to protect Spain and Portugal. Their manner of retreat had been so well prepared that they disappeared while destroying the country they had undertaken to protect. Simultaneously, we were marching toward it after having reduced Almeida."

It took four days to form the garrison of Almeida into regiments. These units became the brigade of General Pamplona, and he had very good rapport with them; weapons were returned to the men after they had taken an oath of obedience and fidelity to France. But enemy emissaries entered their camp and worked so effectively on their minds that half of them deserted with their weapons. We hoped to keep those who remained behind, and as a matter of fact there was little desertion after that. A few of the officers who had taken the oath came to see the Prince, along with some of the cavalry officers, to renew their vows. Almost all of them left in the end. The cavalry, which had not moved for twelve days, departed one morning, leaving its horses behind. The Prince then ordered the arms taken from those who remained and had them sent to France immediately as prisoners of war.[41] He regretted very much that he had not kept this nucleus of troops. They might have detached and brought over to us many of those who were in the British pay, especially when the English neared the sea and the news spread that they were preparing to embark. As a result of this unfortunate attempt, the Prince was averse to the idea of forming corps with foreign deserters when it was proposed to him later on. Nothing equaled the confusion and chagrin of our poor Portuguese generals who had counseled the Prince on this measure and guaranteed its success.[42] The individuals who predicted disasters were usually wrong, but when Fate proved them right they did not neglect to point out that they had predicted everything and foretold the unfortunate outcome.

At last we received news of Colonel Pavetti and *chef d'escadron*

41. The 24th Portuguese Line and three militia regiments were taken into the French army. Only the governor, two English officers, and the Portuguese colonel of the 24th Line were sent to France as prisoners. See Masséna to Berthier, August 30, 1810, Archives de Masséna, LI; *Wellington's Dispatches* (1852 ed.), Cox to Beresford, August 30, 1810; Wellington to Stuart, August 31, 1810, IV, 252, 257–58.

42. The desertion of the Portuguese troops marred the French victory and caused considerable dissension, skepticism, and disgust among the French officers and men. Many believed Masséna's lack of judgment negated their victory at Almeida. See Guingret, *Relation historique*, pp. 33–34.

d'Oraison. They had been attacked by the peasants at Nova de Avel. The former was badly wounded and the latter slaughtered along with two gendarmes. The guilty were identified. The Prince wanted to have them tried, and he sent a senior officer with a detachment to seize them. This officer did not execute his orders; he took two peasants from the village and had them shot. He returned and announced this to the Prince, who was furious and had him arrested. He wanted to have him broken in rank for taking the lives of two men who had not been declared guilty.[43]

43. As a result of poor intelligence reports, Pelet's information was partially inaccurate. In fact d'Oraison was shot by the peasants and his body stripped by the village women. Pavetti and the two gendarmes were captured, garroted, and after degrading treatment conducted to Wellington's headquarters at Gouvea. Wellington wrote to Masséna complaining that several men in the village of Nova de Avel were shot and a number of houses were burned. Colonel Pavetti was sent to Tomar, but since arrangements could not be made for his exchange he was taken to Lisbon, where he was mobbed by an angry crowd of Portuguese. See Burgoyne, *Life and Correspondence*, I, 104; *Wellington's Dispatches*, Wellington to Masséna, September 24, 1810, VI, 464–65; Wellington to Stuart, September 14, 1810, VI, 440–41.

Chapter Four

PLANS AND PREPARATIONS FOR THE INVASION OF PORTUGAL

The fortress had been taken. The conquest of Portugal was now ahead of us, and a campaign plan was therefore needed. In the eyes of certain people this was all that was necessary. In general greater efficacy is attributed to plans than in reality they have. Until now our honors and successes had been attributed more to the management of the Committee of Public Safety than to the burning patriotism of our troops, as though events could be foreseen or directed from afar and did not change from one moment to another. The enlightened military men, and those people who take the trouble to think, know that plans of war, necessarily reduced to a few points or principal ideas, cannot be prepared far in advance. They must be created for, or at least be responsive to, the needs of the moment.

This is the way in which great generals have always acted. Likewise, Napoleon improvised his positions in this fashion, without taking any obstacle into account and often after announcing the results far in advance. Yet he would modify his position at any moment to reflect circumstances and the movements of the enemy, and the latter, though well advised in his methods, were always taken by surprise. The ultimate of the art was to anticipate the plans of his various adversaries and oppose them on the field with maneuvers designed to impede them. This was what he had done in all his campaigns and battles. But the ultimate masterpiece consisted in opposing a fairly well conceived plan executed by a vastly superior army. By the very fact that one cannot oppose force with equal force, everything must be calculated with extreme precision. The greater the danger the more serious become the errors. Further, circumstances change more easily for the army on the defensive; each enemy movement and each moment creates new variations and with them the need for new plans.

Thus, while the defensive is infinitely superior to the offensive, a defense of actions and movements is not entirely inert and passive. For this reason, our campaign of 1814 was the most admirable of any that we made. Above all else it is noble to fight for a great country against vastly superior armies, to charge the middle of their columns, to stop their front ranks, to move on their rear, to attack them in detail, to paralyze their movements, and to force them to withdraw in succession. But it is not "defensive" to yield terrain except under extreme pressure or abandon it methodically when the forces are nearly equal. The greatest names and the most magnificent plans cannot make this anything else but the art of losing the contest. This is what is called the science of retreat, and later we will give it just evaluation. As for retreating with superior forces, this must be called "systematized consequences."

Nevertheless, let no one believe that a campaign plan is a matter of indifference or one that can be neglected with impunity. I am only objecting to the excessive confidence given to these projects in order to prove that the merit of creating a plan is nothing compared to its execution, since it must be changed or modified at each moment; moreover, the best of plans cannot remedy a mediocre general's conduct of the war. Unfortunately, this was where we were weak, for self-styled strategists were everywhere among us.

Besides, the orders of the Major General extricated us from the most intricate and important part of the campaign plan. In order to invade the kingdom in the month of September, the fortresses we had just captured were designated as bases of operation. The capture of Lisbon was fixed as the major objective of the operations. The Prince was the master of subsequent movements. All he had to do then was confirm the establishment of the designated base and choose the direction for the lines of operation. In going beyond the details determined by the government, we had to take account of the strength of the army, which was then [64,947] men, while that of the enemy army was larger [*sic*] at [59,454].[1] The difference in these ratios increased to our disadvantage as we moved farther from our own base and the enemy neared his. Also the political situation and the nature of the country ahead of us were similar to those behind us in relation to the movements and subsistence of the army.

Following are the various data on which our entire plan for the campaign was founded, as well as the resources put at my disposal for working on it. We possessed only the maps of Jeffreys and Lopez, the inaccuracies of which have already been mentioned. There was also a poor little map by a Portuguese major, not to mention several even more defective ones drawn on the previous maps. A few private drawings had been given to us, but they could not be of any help; they showed even more errors, for their scale was larger. Meanwhile there was excellent material in Paris that I have seen since. Although it would not have been enough to draw a complete topographic map of Portugal, copies would have enlightened us considerably during our operations if they had been sent and used to fill the gaps found in our information. These aids were withheld and the only thing that the Prince was able to obtain from the Depot of War at the time of his departure was a kind of geography of Portugal. Composed of very incomplete manuscripts translated from works printed in this country and a military reconnaissance of the kingdom, the document carried a note in the corner with the signature of Dumouriez [?], which appropriately reflected his abilities.[2] Finally, there were some very insignificant materials on the campaign of the Gallo-Spanish army in 1762. General Thiébault sent us two good memorandums on Portugal. The presence of this distinguished general would have been very useful to

1. For details on the complements of the French and British armies in September 1810, see the Appendix and Donald D. Horward, *The Battle of Bussaco: Masséna vs. Wellington* (Tallahassee, Fla., 1965), pp. 159–71.

2. Charles François Dumouriez (1739–1823) obtained a commission in the army and served during the Seven Years War; he turned to the secret service and finally became foreign minister in a Gironde cabinet in 1792. Three months later he became commander in chief of the Army of the North. Dumouriez commanded at Valmy and Jemappes and conquered Belgium and Holland. Driven back at Neerwinden, he continued to command a French army until he defected to Austria in April 1793. After roaming the European continent, Dumouriez finally settled in England in 1803, where he resided until the collapse of the Empire. Dumouriez's *État présent du royaume de Portugal en l'année 1766* was published in Lausanne in 1775; it was used by both the French and the Allies during the Peninsular Wars.

our army.[3] A single conversation with him at that moment might have enlightened us on everything. However, we had been given a fatal quantity of itineraries, notes, inventories, and statements of every description which contradicted each other; they were either based on misinformation or apparently drawn up to confirm the specific systems or campaign plans of their authors. Yet this is not what an individual writing a military report should do. The misfortune was that none of these self-styled strategists had gone over the ground they were describing, and they could not answer the only thing we asked them. "Can a carriage go on this road? Is this river deep? Is this range of mountains impracticable?" In the end I felt obliged to compile an extract of the best accounts and attach it to a few ideas on a plan for the campaign in Portugal.

Yet we should have had an inexhaustible source of excellent information. Since this was the third expedition to Portugal within three years, we had generals, staff officers, engineer officers, and entire army corps who had taken part in the first campaign; French émigrés who had gone into the Portuguese service, including the Count de Chambors, *maréchal de camp* de Vioménil, and *chef de bataillon* Auguste Pierre de Fontenilles, who had abandoned the Spanish service in Madrid; in addition there were a great number of Portuguese officers.

The presence of the Portuguese officers was particularly disastrous for us. Without making a dismal listing of all the errors transmitted to us in the information that the Prince or I requested, I will cite only one, but vital, example. On August 15 an engineer captain who had taken part in the campaign of 1807 gave me the following information at Ciudad Rodrigo. I copied it word for word in my Journal the same day. "Beyond the confluence of the Zezere the country becomes flat. The bed of the Tagus becomes wider. There are only scattered hills and everything is very approachable. The heights of Santarém are not

3. Baron Paul Charles François A. D. H. Thiébault (1769–1846) enlisted in the army in 1792. He served in the *état major* throughout most of his military career and was promoted to general of division in 1808. He served with the armies of Germany, Italy, Naples, and Portugal and in 1809 commanded the province of Burgos. Thiébault became governor of Salamanca in 1810 and in October of the same year he became chief of staff for Drouet's 9th Corps. Thiébault's "Plan d'une nouvelle campagne en Portugal" was drawn up at Burgos on January 12, 1810. It can be found in an appendix of his *Relation de l'expédition du Portugal, faite en 1807 et 1808, par le 1er corps d'observation de la Gironde, devenu armée de Portugal* (Paris, 1817), pp. 332–46.

high; they are accessible and practicable on the summit but not defensible. It is the same all the way to the sea, for the heights of Montachique are rounded plateaus, accessible to all armies, and adequate for marching or maneuvering in any direction from the Tagus. Beyond the Tagus to the sea there are a great number of mountain ranges." From this vague description how could we anticipate the inaccessible positions and the rock walls, the terrible English [positions] of which we had heard nothing? The government should have informed the Prince of their existence before he left Paris. This paramount mistake was to have a disastrous influence on our entire campaign. We must not lose sight of it for a single moment, for if we had had exact knowledge of the terrain our plan would have been completely different.

How was it possible that officers who had lived in Lisbon so long did not have a better knowledge of its environs, although they were always talking about it? How was it possible, with the entire army of the Duc d'Abrantès maneuvering in the mountains before and after his battle of Vimeiro, that no military officer had been impressed by their configuration or the advantage that could be derived from them? How could those who planned the conquest of Portugal have failed to establish a genuine plan for its various defenses? We were even less fortunate in what we had been told about the military topography of Portugal, about the inaccessibility of the Serra da Estrêla and the banks of the Zezere, the nature of the Tagus and the country in general, the roads, and the positions of Bussaco and Murcella.

According to everything we had been able to learn about the kingdom, Lisbon appeared to be a common center where the Tagus, the Serra da Estrêla, and the lines of communication united. The lines of communication were located either on the southern flank or between the capital and the mountain; finally, the two lines to the north joined below Santarém. The routes beyond the Tagus were completely unfamiliar to us because of the location of our bases and the necessity of crossing the river twice. The Tagus and especially the Serra da Estrêla had been described as impassable obstacles which definitely divided the various lines of communication. The lines, traced among the rocks, were without ramps and bridges on the numerous deep rivers; they crossed very difficult country, steep mountains and valleys, and the terrain was uncultivated or at least semi-barren. Only the obstacles encountered by detachments in 1807 were mentioned. Finally, the enemy had worked everywhere to augment the obstacles which we would encounter.

While we were ignorant of the enemy's most important works, we knew some details about his first line of defense. On the most direct road to Coimbra, between the Mondego and Serra da Estrêla, they had carefully fortified the position of Ponte de Murcella, which was already very formidable, rendering it almost inaccessible. Between the mountains and the Tagus, there were a great number of defensible positions, inaccessible posts, mountains, defiles, and ravines. Beyond Castelo Branco, in the Talhadas where all the roads met, the enemy had prepared another very strong entrenched position, further enhanced by the nature of the terrain.[4] Other entrenchments barred the mountain road on the left toward the Moradal. Thus the two great communication lines to Coimbra and Castelo Branco were cut. We had been told that some good roads extended on the right bank of the Mondego through open, easy, flat country up to Coimbra, and that by this means we could turn the position of Ponte de Murcella. The double crossing of the Mondego would not delay us, for this river was not very wide near Celorico and had very little water in it. Such was the terrain.

With this configuration it would have been very difficult to establish a regular base of operations. In the first place, our two fortresses were not connected, their zone of activity did not extend beyond the range of their cannon, and they were on two completely separate rivers. If a line were drawn between the two fortresses, far from being perpendicular to the various lines of operation, Ciudad Rodrigo and Almeida would have been parallel or at least very oblique. Moreover, in our circumstances, four hundred and fifty miles from our frontiers and in the middle of an insurgent country, it would have been impossible to establish such a base; or at least it would have had the dual role of

4. Wellington took special care to have John Wilson disrupt the vital Estrada Nova, which passed through the Serra da Guardunha to the village of Sobreira Formosa and joined the main road from Lisbon to Castelo Branco. All the important roads behind the Allied positions were repaired and improved. An extensive network of fortifications composed of redoubts and trenches was thrown up at Ponte de Murcella on the Mondego and near the mouth of the Zezere. See *Wellington's Dispatches,* Wellington to Beresford, January 23; Wellington to Bacelar, January 26; Wellington to Wilson, February 18, 1810, V, 436ff.

facing the interior [east] as well as the exterior [west]. But how could one conceive of a base which was only a simple line; it would not have had a productive and friendly country behind it where we could gather replacements for the extensive and multiplying daily requirements of the armies. Our fortresses were simply a point of departure for the army, of concentration for its detachments, or a depot for supplies in transit to or from the corps. They were a link in our communication lines, a warehouse, and, in truth, was anything else needed? I dare not make any more fundamental criticism of the system of bases and imaginary [operational] lines.[5] Heretofore this concept had appeared to me as a speculative theory of councils rather than an outcome of wartime experience.

Nevertheless, it seemed to me as it had to Bülow[6] that the principal purpose of the formal bases was limited to a system of magazines and transportation for the various supplies necessary for an army, especially for food. However, as soon as one abandoned (as we had always done) the system of magazines and the continuous string of convoys, the ostensible bases lost their principal merit because in most European countries replacements could be moved along at the same time as troop reinforcements formed into large detachments. In fact, we conducted the campaign with hardly any bases, and it would not have been any more successful even if we had had ten thousand additional men. Even with the best possible base, the results would not have been altered if the maneuvers had been made in the same manner. The same considerations did [not] apply to the defensive measures that were employed to cover the frontier, because one must think about protecting his own country against all probable attacks before advancing. These defensive resources could be combined with operations of

5. Pelet adds in a footnote: "In our day, Napoleon in his campaigns . . . did not worry very much about his bases when he threw himself over the Apennines in the middle of the Austro-Sardinian army, at Ulm on the rear of the famous Mack, at Jena on the left flank of the Prussians, at Vienna and then at Wagram in 1809 on Archduke Charles's line of operations, at Marengo, especially where he dashed down from the top of the Alps amid Melas's army. . . . For a defensive line of operation, Napoleon never had a more beautiful interior or eccentric strategic line than at Dresden or between the Seine and the Marne or the tactical line of Leipzig, Brienne, and Fleurus. Nevertheless, we have seen the results."

6. Dietrich Heinrich, Baron von Bülow (1757–1807), was a Prussian military historian and tactician. He published *Der Geist des neuern Kriegssystems* (1798), an attempt to apply geometric rules and fixed principles to all military operations, as well as several other works.

the army and with its line of supplies, or they could be used as a reserve or point of support when necessary. But I believe that we should not mix up aspects that are entirely defensive in nature with those which are completely offensive. On many occasions we could eliminate the defensive consideration. Although our provinces in Spain had to be considered as enemy [territory], in actual circumstances they would become even more belligerent if the English were able to enter them. Therefore it was necessary for detached corps to prevent the advance of the English, to protect the collection of requisitions, and to maintain such little tranquility as had been preserved.

The nature of the terrain between the frontier and Lisbon would permit only very simple and direct lines of operation through its narrow passages. Considering the obstacles separating the border and the capital, opposite an alert and superior enemy, we could attempt none of the great strategic maneuvers which were so brilliant and advantageous. Everything was reduced to choosing the most direct line, the terrain where the English would be least able to resist, where we would have the greatest latitude to maneuver in case of a main attack, where the roads would present the fewest obstacles, and, finally, where we could hope to find some trace of food. Double lines were rejected because of the size of the army as well as the nature of the country. The enemy would be able to throw himself on either line or between them as we approached Lisbon, where the ground became less difficult. Besides, double lines were never useful in the case of very marked superiority because it was extremely difficult to set up a double operation except on very extended terrain. In this case Lisbon was everything. Oporto was unimportant in comparison and anything done in that direction would have been entirely to the detriment of the principal goal. Moreover, the country beyond the Douro was extremely difficult, its population numerous and bellicose, and it would have been necessary to send a considerable detachment on that point to contain the country and to maintain itself there. A secondary line of operation on the other side of the Tagus would not have been without difficulty because of the numerous forts located there. In addition, such a line would have been completely separated from the main army since a detachment would pass through Idanha a Nova and Castelo Branco. These two secondary lines, on Oporto or on the left bank of the Tagus, would subsequently have become accidental lines at best, either after completing the conquest of Portugal or when it would become necessary to give up the occupation of Lisbon.

From all these considerations we drew up our plan for the campaign. Our base was formed by the two fortresses, Ciudad Rodrigo and Almeida, or rather the segment of the frontier maintained by them. A corps was to be left around these fortresses to retain communications, to facilitate their provisioning and the arrival of our replacements, and to await the army corps charged to occupy that area. Séras's division, placed on the right of the Douro, covered a part of the Kingdom of León. In addition, it was announced that the Army of the Interior would maintain Estremadura between the Tagus and the Sierra de Gata. After this had been determined, our line of operation was directed by Viseu on Coimbra in order to avoid the long passage by the left bank of the Mondego and to outflank the position of Murcella. We were ignorant of the relation between Murcella and the Serra de Bussaco, but we should have guessed it from the maps. Yet we did not consider this relationship because of the previous assurances given us on the impossibility of crossing the Serra da Estrêla with an army corps. In effect, if General Hill, who was posted at the Talhadas, could not join Lord Wellington, the latter would never have dared to cross to the other side of the Mondego, and he would have tried to effect his junction toward Tomar or Leiria as rapidly as possible. In our plans we expected, with some reason, to find the English gathered there to deliver battle. From Viseu we would march toward Coimbra, by way of Mealhada and San Antonio de Cantaro, and from there finally toward Lisbon. A detailed order was to be drawn up for operations as far as Viseu; new orders and successive deployments were to be given there and at Coimbra. It was recommended that the army hurry to reach that city before the enemy had time to make any dispositions for its defense. If the city was too formidable, the army would maneuver to cross the Mondego at some other point.

The detachment left near the fortresses was to collect men and matériel destined for the army; this unit was to form a convoy and march when it was replaced [by the 9th Corps]. Our communications with Spain were to be maintained by the 9th Corps and later, as announced, by the Young Guard.

This, in outline, was the project on which I was employed and the nature of the work that was usually delegated to me by special order of the Prince from the beginning of the campaign. This plan was decided upon, as I have already said, and I spared no trouble nor pains to collect information from all sides. If our intelligence had been more exact perhaps our operation would have been less defective. When the Major General announced that the operation against Portugal was to be established along both banks of the Tagus, and while General Reynier was still on the other side of that river, I had proposed to the Prince in my first report, drawn up on May 20 at Valladolid, that we march quickly on our left toward Abrantes and forestall the enemy with demonstrations against Almeida. That project would have been advantageous, especially in regard to the actual defense of Lisbon; nevertheless, it would have been difficult to be completely successful. Subsequent orders and the siege of Almeida changed these dispositions.

This is a good place, I think, to examine the system of defense adopted by the enemy and to give the reader an advantage we did not have—that of seeing the various developments of the two armies and more particularly the opposite principles under which they were directed. In this way the reader can see the mistakes that were committed and will be able to judge the excuses made for them. Later on we learned that the actual system of Portuguese defense was viewed quite differently by the government of this country and by the British ministers. The latter, concerned only with protecting the harbor and the settlements at Lisbon, set up strategic plans which made the capital the center of all the projects and lines of operation. They had taken every care to render it unassailable and to concentrate all the defenses of the kingdom there.[7] They seemed ready to abandon and destroy the country, leaving it deserted and uninhabitable. At the same time the English prepared fortified defenses on each line of operation and on every road. These defenses were linked in an uninterrupted chain from the Tagus to the Vouga, and they were occupied by corps of armies [*sic*] to guard against threats from any side. Finally they put

7. On October 20, 1809, Wellington wrote his famous memorandum to Lieutenant Colonel Fletcher on the establishment of the Lines of Torres Vedras. "The great object in Portugal is the possession of Lisbon and the Tagus, and all our measures must be directed to this object. There is another also connected with that first object, to which we must likewise attend, viz.—the embarkation of the British troops in case of reverse." *Wellington's Dispatches,* V, 234–39.

a few British governors in the frontier fortresses to force the Portuguese to defend themselves. These dispositions were accompanied by orders to the inhabitants to arm themselves under pain of death, to organize insurrections on our flanks and rear, to destroy everything and completely abandon the countryside as the French army advanced, and to kill isolated men or small detachments that fell behind. It was said that these orders were immediately reinforced by a number of military executions.[8]

If the essential idea of preserving a country could hypothetically be eliminated from the defense scheme, or if the British deployments were considered as forming a system of defense to be executed with tenacity step by step, prolonged patriotically until the last extreme in order to dispute every inch of sacred territory, certainly this plan would be praiseworthy because of the sequence and management of its various strategic dispositions and even of its rigors. Yet, when it is considered as the organized devastation of a country that one could not or did not want to defend, especially of a foreign country for the sake of interests that were alien to it, only a Machiavellian cabinet could applaud such projects and through its pernicious influence find means for putting them into execution. Who else would now dare to approve a system that instantly spread the evils and violence of war to a whole kingdom, bringing more evils than twenty years of continual war? One may look at every circumstance of our campaigns, subject as they were to so much bitter criticism and complaint, and not find anything to compare to such a terrible system.[9] If we examine this project itself, and the way it was executed, and consider the movements of the British army as the result of fixed plans, it seems to me that there were two distinct elements in the project—two thoughts, one which was conceived and one which was executed. In effect, what was the good of so much care for the intermediate positions, especially for the junction of

8. Wellington wrote to Lieutenant General Leite on February 28, 1810, that the irregular Portuguese troops were expected to be prepared to "do the enemy all the mischief in their power . . . not by assembling in large bodies, but by impeding his communications, by firing upon him from the mountains and strong passes with which the whole country abounds, and by annoying his foraging and other parties that he may send out." *Wellington's Dispatches*, V, 529–30.

9. Pelet comments in a footnote: "In withdrawing to Bayonne, if the French army had destroyed all Spain or if, even to save the unique position of Brest, it had devastated all of France from the Rhine to the sea, what would the panthers in the pay of England have said . . . ?"

forces, if the goal was not to concentrate this superior force on the threatened line of operation? Why unite their troops if they were not going to take advantage of their strength to oppose and halt the invasion, if a minor flank movement could so easily be opposed, and if a large army could withdraw toward the capital and abandon the whole kingdom? Moreover, with this strategic and clever plan, well conceived and executed with various locations carefully chosen on good maps and verified on the terrain, it would have been possible to establish an excellent system of defense for Portugal and afterward an actual system of attack. But this is not my goal, and there is little point in discussing these matters any further.

I have felt it necessary to go into these details to prevent anyone in similar circumstances from falling into the traps into which we fell. I am not afraid to express them after having proudly admitted them to the man least able to forgive military errors [Napoleon]. And now it is time to leave these vast fields of hypothesis and principles and return to our operations in Portugal.

The catastrophe of Almeida had surprised the two armies, both of whom had expected at least eight [*sic*] days' resistance before the fortress surrendered. Each side had counted on this time to prepare the operations to be executed after the siege. We were even less ready than the British army; they had only to withdraw and destroy their surplus food, prepared far in advance along their line of operations. We, on the contrary, had to gather, with the greatest of difficulty, the immense quantity of supplies necessary for an army entering an enemy country, especially an insurgent territory transformed into a desert. During the sieges our food was consumed as fast as we gathered it, because we lacked the means to bake much bread beyond the daily consumption. Therefore it was necessary to start preparations for all kinds of foods. Yet the impatient men who quietly consumed it without taking the trouble to think, did not delay in complaining loudly about what they called our inaction. Without doubt they believed that after the capture of Almeida there was nothing more pressing or more simple than to hurry to take Lisbon, as if it were a part in a promenade after a performance. Yet we would need every kind of food for at least twenty-five days for the entire army, with some reserve in case of any unexpected trouble, in addition to many and indispensable kinds of supplies and a method of transportation to carry them along the numerous bad roads. Finally, a gigantic munition and artillery train would be needed, for it was also necessary to think about preparing implements of war for the soldier after we had given him something to eat. The imagination is staggered by a calculation of the amount of munitions expended during a single day of battle.

Soon our preparations took on new activity, though it did not produce great results at first. The difficulties seemed to increase progressively. General Éblé, who left nothing to chance and was accustomed to the most regular accuracy and abundance in resources, became very annoyed and grieved. According to him, everything was lacking in his campaign equipment: horses, caissons, guns, cartridges, not to mention the less important provisions which would become useful at one time or another. He was losing up to twenty or twenty-five horses a day. Ammunition wagons could not be improvised. There were only 700,000 to 800,000 cartridges in reserve—that is to say, a second distribution for 15,000 men, or what would be used in a minor combat by the whole army. Finally, we did not have a single gun in the *réserve parc,* nor a piece of 12, nor an eight-pound howitzer for bombarding even a small shack or a simple blockhouse. The engineers immediately put some workers on the roads along the left bank of the Côa in the directions of Pinhel and Celorico, and through Freixedas and Guarda. The regiments brought such items as had been left temporarily at Salamanca and Rodrigo; in fact, there was very little.

As for the military administration, we were in even greater trouble because our difficulties were just as great and our resources just as inadequate. During the sieges we had been limited to procuring food for the army corps and had prepared almost no biscuit reserve for supplying the troops or reinforcements who were to follow the army on the campaign. The two fortresses, Almeida and Ciudad Rodrigo, absorbed much for their magazine, and we had to regulate and limit those supplies before we left. On entering Ciudad Rodrigo, we had been told there was a reserve of 300,000 rations of biscuit, and that had now been reduced to 120,000. Pack mules, food wagons, and all kinds of equipment were lacking, and the country offered no transportation, nor were the funds in our treasury sufficient to accelerate the various preparations. We were concerned primarily with food and munitions of war. How many other things of prime necessity were missing! In the first place, shoes were deteriorating rapidly, sometimes after four days of rain, and without them it was impossible for the troops to march; moreover, it was impossible to give them extra shoes because each man already had one pair in his knapsack. Clothing and accouterments were used up or lost quickly during the war, as was the equipment necessary for temporary hospitals and ambulance service. Many were surprised that we were not marching. They should rather have been astonished when we started to march.

The acute lack of every resource was due primarily to the condition of the countryside in which we were located; nevertheless, it must be admitted that the government could have helped considerably. While it gave formal orders to enter Portugal, well aware of the various kinds of obstacles we would have to overcome, the government could at least have furnished us with most of the resources. The two most important were at its disposal: first, money, and second, men. With these, everything would have been easier for us; it would have been sufficient to send us what was presently going to other areas. After deciding once and for all the great question of whether it was advantageous to occupy Portugal and chase out the English, the government should then have supplied the proper orders and resources and directed the system of war in Spain toward one goal or the other. My opinion was that the expulsion of the British would have been followed by the pacification of the Peninsula.[10] Nevertheless, toward the end, Napoleon seemed to realize that it was advantageous to keep the English there so they could not go to other more dangerous points.[11] It was not surprising that this operation was alternately right and wrong according to the successive changes taking place in Europe; and our campaign suffered from these variations. It was equally possible that orders had been given which prescribed the division of forces and that all these arrangements were changed and thwarted during their transmission;

10. Pelet's conclusion was in agreement with that of Wellington, who wrote to Dom Miguel Pereira Forjas, the Portuguese minister of war, "I truly believe that if we are able to continue the war in the Portuguese and Spanish Peninsula, Europe will not be lost; and I believe also that if we are able to maintain ourselves in Portugal the war will not end in the Peninsula." *Wellington's Dispatches,* Wellington to Forjas, March 8, 1810, V, 556–59.

11. Pelet adds in a footnote: "No doubt Napoleon feared the presence of the English in northern Europe. Once embarked they could do no great damage in Spain or the most important coastal points—Lisbon and Cadiz."

the least delay or alteration was enough to cause trouble at certain times. I have already mentioned my opinion of the Prince de Neufchâtel, and his subsequent conduct proved that his devotion was not entirely reliable.

Be that as it may, the great difficulties of the war and the inadequacy of our resources were so well known that it was thought Masséna's expedition had been sacrificed to Napoleon's jealousy of him. A few people who exercised great influence in our various governments have carefully insinuated such suspicions to the Prince. As far as I am concerned, I see only bad faith and no basis in these suppositions. The Emperor's military glory, which had always shown with the most brilliant luster, had risen above that of everyone else during the great campaigns. Only the most profound blindness could conceive any doubts on this subject.

Meanwhile the Prince worked with the greatest diligence on all details of the corps and administration to accelerate our preparations. But the many obstacles and hindrances he could not overcome filled him with disgust and ill humor at times, especially when he considered the way in which the government seemed to have abandoned him; he could already foresee all the dangers of the expedition. The Prince did not hide them nor the probable results if he were not more effectively supported and later helped. He often talked to me about all the difficulties of our position. Perhaps they would have stopped anyone else, but they were shattered by the unshakable strength of his character. This small army was formed in part by provisional corps and new regiments; it was full of conscripts and included only fifteen [actually twenty-two] infantry regiments; it possessed insufficient matériel, lacked many indispensable items, and was without money to procure them. Diminished by the losses during the sieges and by the garrisons occupying the fortresses, decreased by several divisions which had been part of its complement but were now to occupy the country behind us, the army was already reduced to half of the troops that Dumouriez [?] had requested for such an operation, and to almost one-third the number required by General Thiébault and others who formulated the plans. It was deprived of the guard reserve, which was to disengage our available divisions; and the twelve thousand men of the 9th Corps, promised as reinforcements from the beginning, were kept in northern Spain at the very moment we were preparing to start our march. The Prince had only depleted provinces from which to draw resources, and they were badly disposed toward him and would not give any more food or money since most of the population was hostile and animated by violent hate. We were faced with a strong army, abundantly supplied and supported by powerful auxiliaries everywhere. It was very difficult to conquer an insurgent and devastated nation far from the frontier of France and bordered by the sea where we were still forbidden to go; yet it was more arduous to hold Portugal than to invade it; and even if we had first occupied Lisbon, it would have been very difficult to maintain ourselves there and dominate the entire kingdom.

Nevertheless, during these times of glory the confidence of the French army was so great that they never doubted anything, and now they hoped for easy victories. Masséna, who more than any other person helped to create this heroic assurance, was far from lacking confidence. Yet, without sharing the popular opinion about the English army, he expected a laborious campaign, difficult and vigorously contested. However, relying on himself, on the proven valor of our soldiers, on the devotion of his comrades on the field of honor and the battlefield, and finally on the reinforcements solemnly promised, he marched boldly toward this struggle which appeared worthy of him. Anxious about the suffering and the privations that his army could not avoid and the sacrifices to which they were exposed because of their weakness, he was gratified to think that he had been purposely chosen for such a difficult and intricate operation and that he intended to triumph over the many obstacles. Portugal would be conquered as gloriously as northern Italy had been and as brilliantly defended as Switzerland; and if necessary the marvels of the siege of Genoa would be repeated at Lisbon. I said to myself, "Let everyone do his duty; ours is to advance and that of the government is to support us." Masséna would conceal nothing about his position from the government.

More than once the Prince complained to the Major General of the many obstacles that seemed to have been amassed against him. He complained especially about those whom his obstinancy could not overcome, pointing them out so that something could be done about them. He kept a record of the delays caused by all the problems that daily postponed the start of the campaign. But because of the time required to correspond with Paris, all his letters were simply reduced to reports from which we did not expect even an answer, let alone any help. This was one of the principal dangers of the war in Spain.

The Prince had requested the promotion of a few of his officers who were old companions in his service. It was now the only thing he really had in his heart, since his ambition had been more than satisfied. The Major General sent 102 Crosses for the siege of Rodrigo but did not bother to say a single word about the special requests of the Prince. The latter was very angry. Already exhausted by so many mortifications and impediments, he was more offended by the silence than by a refusal and called it the ingratitude of the government. With his notion of sacrifice, devotion, and great deeds, he became irritated to the point that he wanted to quit this army which seemed to have been completely abandoned. He even fixed the time of his departure with me. I beseeched him, in the name of the army, of his glory, of his retirement, but for a long time he would not change his mind. Finally he dictated a very strong letter to the Major General. The Prince complained bitterly, describing all the difficulties of his situation, and then in another letter, just as strong, he renewed our requests. The next day he wanted to write particularly about me to the Emperor, with whom he had not yet directly corresponded. I persuaded him with all my power that this was clearly against my interest, fearing that it would embitter the Prince de Neufchâtel against him, create more trouble, and damage his peace of mind and the success of his operation. He insisted for a long time. I opposed him, saying "that I preferred his confidence and the great kindness and honor he gave me rather than all the ranks in the world." The Prince, deeply touched, assured me he would never forget such conduct or disinterested advice. Nevertheless, eight days later he wrote to the Emperor without my knowledge to make the request.

Before starting the campaign, the Prince wanted to be completely assured that the Emperor knew the exact situation of the army and the state of affairs in every detail. Thus he decided to send one of his aides-de-camp, *chef d'escadron* Casabianca, to Paris. He was a young officer, full of merit, whom Napoleon liked very much. By his noble character he had shown himself worthy to carry a name that had been illuminated by the finest examples of heroism and filial devotion. Like his uncle and cousin, he was also to die gloriously on the field of honor, on the banks of the Svolna at the head of the 11th Léger.[12] Casabianca carried the flags taken at Rodrigo and Almeida,[13] but he was charged more specifically to speak to the Emperor about the exact situation of the two armies, the campaign plan, the absolute need for reinforcement and supplies which could be sent later with the new corps, the state of the provinces the army was leaving behind, the friction already very apparent between the Prince and the Marshal, and the extreme necessity of solving all these problems before the most fatal results should ensue.[14] Finally he was expressly ordered to declare that the Prince, relying faithfully on the promised help, was devoting himself to the execution of the orders received.

Meanwhile the enemy army withdrew after our capture of Almeida. Our reconnaissance on Guarda and the other points on the line of the advanced posts had encountered neither troops nor inhabitants. On September 4 Lord Wellington's headquarters were at Gouveia and those of Beresford were close by at Moimenta da Serra. It was said that they were withdrawing to the position of Murcella. They had placed Silveira on our right at Freixo de Espedrada to harass the rear of our march as he already menaced our cantonments. Toward the left General Hill had definitely concentrated at the position of the Talhadas, with detachments at Castelo Branco, Alpedrinha, and Fondão. There, he was on the crossroads which led into Beira and Spanish Estremadura and disposed to defend the approaches to Abrantes and the Zezere. It was said he was making preparations to withdraw on Tomar.

Thus all the reports seemed to confirm our idea that Lord Wellington

12. A battle took place at Svolna (Soolna) between the Russian general D'Auvray and Marshal Nicolas Oudinot on August 11, 1812. Casabianca died of wounds on August 14. See Martinien, *Tableaux*, p. 416.

13. The two battle flags of the 24th Portuguese Line captured at Almeida in 1810 are now in the possession of André Masséna, the 6th Prince d'Essling.

14. Casabianca was instructed by Masséna to tell Napoleon that the "army is full of ardor and enthusiasm, but it has very few resources; that the English retire burning and destroying everything, arming the peasants and carrying them away; that all the towns are abandoned and pillaged; that everything indicates great misery for the army; that the gentle means I had hoped to employ at first to gain the support of the Portuguese have failed; that the harsh privations the soldiers experience alter the mildness of their character and carry them to excesses that exasperate a furious people already prejudiced against us." Koch, *Mémoires de Masséna,* Masséna to Casabianca, ca. September 14, 1810, VII, 178–79.

had divided his army by this damnable Serra da Estrêla, said to be as impracticable as the great Alps, in order to cover his flanks and at the same time to guard the two great lines of operation which could be opened to Lisbon along the reverse sides of the mountains. As soon as our army unmasked its movements, all their efforts would be devoted to delaying us, and the enemy would end by concentrating their force at Leiria or Tomar. One cannot deny that these calculations seemed very plausible to us. Yet later a report announced that General Hill was preparing to march on Ponte de Murcella and Viseu. We committed the error of ignoring this information because it was so contrary to everything we had been told; but it could have informed us of the excellent shuttle system used for the defense between the Tagus and the Vouga which we could have tried to stop. This report was mixed with the great amount of information, often contradictory and entirely improbable, that one received daily in the army. General Hill was to leave his artillery on the southern side of the Serra da Estrêla and it was probable that his *parc,* as announced, was moving to Tomar. All this was clear enough afterward, but during the war it was necessary to guess how many alternatives were presented by the genius of men, the caprice of fortune, and the way affairs go. This march of General Hill, executed across the bridge of Pedrógão, would have been worthy of praise had it not been completely useless. The English did not take advantage of what they achieved by it.

The 6th Corps remained in the positions it had occupied during the siege, extending only to the right and left on our side of the Côa to find food more easily. The 8th Corps occupied the banks of the Agueda, with the headquarters of its two divisions at Barba de Puerco and San Felices el Grande. The 2nd Corps was withdrawing from Alfaiates to reoccupy its old positions on the Erjas and the Tagus. General Reynier had his headquarters at Zarza la Mayor, where O'Donnell appeared at the first news of our division's departure. When he learned of their return, he left in great haste to move to the other side of the Tagus. Thus if we were harassed on our flanks, at least we were assured that as we left the country the enemy would again occupy it with relatively poor troops; yet they caused enough trouble by encouraging the inhabitants to rise up and close in on our rear when we advanced. The 5th Corps which could have held O'Donnell had withdrawn on ———.

This was the state of affairs at the beginning of September, when we decided on the plans for entering Portugal. Like everyone else I found myself delayed because of the shortages we experienced in obtaining every kind of information. I worked until the last moment to collect all available materials. I had to begin by correcting the map, or rather by drawing a new one based on the confused and often contradictory notes. Then, with little information, I had to learn the military topography of the kingdom in order to draw up some kind of description; to gather the most certain and probable data on the movements and disposition of the enemy; to establish a general plan of operation from all of this; and finally to detail the particulars of the marches, day by day or in series.

Meanwhile, since the first of the month I had been setting up the various reports and analyzing the principal elements of the campaign plan. I presented them to the Prince and read them in the presence of General Reynier. Both of them made various objections that I later contested after I explained and developed my thesis again. The Prince adopted the plan, dictating a few notes and some new deployments to me. He ordered me to continue my work with the plan; after that we were busy every morning and for several hours each day.

At last, when the plan was nearly agreed upon, the Prince sent me to give it to General Loison, a rather witty man, who conversed well about everything, especially war; actually he talked about it better than he made or understood it. Nevertheless, he knew Portugal rather well, but perhaps he was too confident and too intimate with the Prince. I found him at Junça, and he approved my report and project with much praise. He came with me immediately to talk with the Prince about it. The Marquis d'Alorna was there. He also approved of the plan, offering some embellishments which included several detachments of small units for the rear guard, on the flanks, for bridges, and such other positions as rivers, etc.; he would not have left two divisions together. His observations were rejected and his proposals not accepted. At last the basic plans were definitely recognized as advantageous and were adopted. I busied myself working out tables of the marches for the army corps in accordance with the itinerary that had been developed; they were repeatedly corrected and changed. The Prince even added a few supplementary dispositions. From all this, I formulated the General Order of March, checking it carefully because of its importance. And I was sure that it would be carefully picked over by the commanders. I also prepared copies of the itinerary map I had drawn. They were sent to each corps commander with orders to modify or correct the mistakes on the map which they already had. We sent a schedule of the marches for each column and unit, clearly showing the day-by-day situation of each army corps, the advance guard, the *grand parc*, and the general headquarters, with the distances to be traveled, the distance between the columns, the roads to be followed, and observations on the principal modifications in the orders.[15] I had never known such procedures to be employed before in the *états majors*. Nevertheless, carelessness can result in very dangerous accidents. These methods should be followed especially in countries where good maps are lacking. In other countries it is necessary first to agree on the map to be used in the correspondence, and then always to use copies of it for fixing the disposition of troops in a more precise manner or particular way. I strongly regret that nothing remains of my little map.

At first the General Order of March did not indicate the day the movement would start; the various days were merely numbered. It included only four marches, that is to say, only as far as Viseu, through an area we could hope to cross without encountering the enemy, and the only one about which we had detailed information. The orders of march were to be revised from time to time according to the locations and movements of the British army. The first instructions included ordinary details of the arrangements for the marches, those for the police and for the discipline of the troops, and a few particulars in case the enemy was encountered or extraordinary difficulties occurred in this unknown country. The corps commanders and the advance guard were requested to send several officers of the *état major* for orders every evening. The soldiers were to have biscuit for six days and one pound of rice, together with fifty cartridges in their knapsacks. The corps carried fifteen days' food[16] but because of the difficult roads they had

15. The "Dispositions générales pour l'entrée en Portugal" can be found in Correspondance: Armée de Portugal, Carton C[7]9.

16. See "Journal de l'expédition de Portugal, 15 au 27 septembre, 1810," Correspondance: Armée de Portugal, Carton C[7]9. According to this journal, the French army had ten days' rations. For additional details, see Horward, *Battle of Bussaco*, p. 26n.

only as many artillery wagons as were absolutely necessary. Everyone else marched along with the *grand parc.* Finally, the corps commanders were expressly ordered to inform the general in chief immediately of all enemy movements and to maintain the greatest regularity and most exact troop discipline during the march and in camp.[17]

The Prince set up a list of orders and instructions for all the governors of the provinces and commanders of the fortresses that he was leaving behind; he took special pains with Ciudad Rodrigo and Almeida, which were indeed becoming his depots. The breach of Ciudad Rodrigo had not been entirely repaired, but it had been cleared and covered with countersinks and palisades, and revetments were erected rapidly. Only twelve hundred men were left in each of the fortresses, along with sixty horses and a good supply of food for several months.[18] In his instructions the Prince requested the governors, especially the governor of Rodrigo, to guard against surprise from outside as well as from the inhabitants. The governor was to collect all the army sick and provide for convalescence depots in the suburbs. He was to detain small detachments and even isolated men en route to Portugal. The governor was to form marching battalions of five hundred men and send them on with food and all the provisions he had received. The governors of the fortresses were to carefully conserve their siege food and gather everything they could find for the army and for shipment. The governor of Salamanca, Rouyer,[19] the prefect of the province, and the *ordonnateur en chef,* Pierre Clapier, received orders to organize convoys for the army and to accelerate the arrival of grain at these two fortresses. General Gardanne remained near them with the 10th Dragoons and an infantry battalion to protect the supplies. He was also to gather the detachments and form a marching corps. When the

17. Masséna issued an order to be read to all regiments: "All the soldiers, having their food with them, will have no pretext for leaving their ranks, and the line officers are expressly ordered to march en masse by columns. The strictest surveillance, in this regard, is more important, because bravery will not insure success if it is not accompanied by discipline and good order. The conduct of the inhabitants will be determined by their first reaction" to the French. Fririon, *Journal Historique,* "Order of the Day, September 14, 1810," pp. 37–38.

18. Actually 3,368 men were left in garrison at Ciudad Rodrigo and Almeida. See Horward, *Battle of Bussaco,* pp. 39–40.

19. Baron Jean Victor Rouyer (1756–1818) entered a National Guard unit as a captain in 1789 and served within France until 1799, when he joined the Army of Italy. Promoted slowly through the ranks, Rouyer served at Marengo and in Prussia, Poland, and Spain before he was made general of brigade.

9th Corps arrived and his operations were ended, Gardanne was to join the army. The governor of Valladolid carried the spirit of independence so far that he gave orders that the provisions he had sent to Salamanca must be returned if his wagons could not be replaced. Contrary orders were issued, but of what use were they when we were about to leave?[20]

Lord Wellington wrote to complain that the forward posts had shot a few *ordenanza* or armed peasant insurgents, in compliance with the terrible law of war. He supported his complaint rather poorly by the example of Colonel Pavetti, who arrived at the British lines after he had received six grave wounds and seen his friend and two gendarmes massacred.[21] He seemed to have written the letter himself in very correct French and he signed his name without any title. In answer we deplored the cruel extremities which exemplified the brutality of war despite the humanizing influence of civilization; such cruel ravages were almost never seen among the civilized nations.

The departure of the army was fixed for September 16. The Major General was informed of this and of all the related dispositions. The Prince protested that his sense of duty and devotion alone could induce him to enter Portugal notwithstanding the [supply] delays and the army's deficiencies. He also warned Berthier about the state in which he was leaving the provinces of his government; he stressed this point strongly and cautioned of the need to increase this area proportionally as he advanced into Portugal.

20. General Kellermann was governor of Valladolid in June 1810; he withdrew his wagons and deposited the grain at Medina del Campo rather than transport it to Masséna. As provisions accumulated, they began to decompose because Quartermaster General Lambert did not have adequate wagons to transport the grain to Ciudad Rodrigo. Lambert complained to Masséna, "The orders of General Kellermann paralyze the transportation and will make us short of everything. I am not afraid to accuse him; he is destroying all administration by his unprecedented and culpable resistance. Some provisions exist in abundance at Medina while we starve." See Lambert to Masséna, July 15, 1810, Archives de Masséna, LI.

21. Wellington wrote to Masséna on September 9, 1810, "It disturbs me greatly to learn that you have issued orders to the French army not to take prisoners among the Portuguese *ordenanza,* and that the French army, obeying this order, shoot all of this corps that fall into their hands. . . . I beg you to give the order that the officers and soldiers of the *ordenanza* taken prisoner enjoy equally with the other troops of the Portuguese army the rights and customs of war. . . . If the French army continue to shoot the prisoners of the *ordenanza* . . . these orders . . . will be the cause of misfortune for the soldiers of the French army who fall into the hands of the Portuguese troops." See *Wellington's Dispatches,* VI, 419–20. For details of Colonel Pavetti's capture, see above, pages 125, 131–32.

The army corps received the necessary orders to start marching and begin the entry into Portugal. Going through Monsanto, General Reynier arrived at Alfaiates on the 12th and Guarda on the 15th. Marshal Ney moved Loison's division, which formed the advance guard, to Freixedas the same day, supported by another division; he even advanced the rear guard. As a result, the entire 6th Corps was on the other side of the Côa. The 8th Corps was concentrated at Escarigo with the *grand parc* and baggage on the left bank of the Côa.

The final orders for preparations having been given, the army started to execute the first day's march on the 16th; it was placed as follows: the advance guard was at Celorico on the banks of the Mondego in case the enemy wanted to contest the crossing, the 2nd Corps was at Guarda, and the 6th Corps at Alverca. The 8th Corps at Póvoa d'El Rei was obliged to halt at Pinhel as a reserve for the 6th Corps if the latter encountered the enemy. The headquarters were at Freixedas. The reserve cavalry, marching to the rear of the *grand parc* and baggage on the road to Pinhel, would cover this column movement. If the English occupied Celorico in great force, the 2nd Corps was to move on the English right, across the bridge at Ladras to gain the position of Aldeia da Serra in the rear. The 6th Corps was to attack the bridge at Celorico in the center with one division and try to outflank the enemy by the ford of Santo António. The Marshal would hold one division in reserve for this maneuver and would move a third division on the left of the enemy toward the ford of Ferreira. The 8th Corps, five leagues away, at the disposition of the Prince, was to move rapidly to support the 6th Corps or on the left of the enemy.

The Prince formed his own guard from an elite company of [100] men of the 3rd Dragoons.[22] It was commanded by Captain Duret, a good soldier and a pleasant man whose companionship was very agreeable. I had the sorrow of seeing him killed by a cannonball in the battle of Moskowa. Everyday the 6th Corps was to furnish one regiment to guard headquarters; a battalion of marines was later in charge of this duty. In these last moments, I was pleased to see one of the officers of my old corps, Captain Jean Richoux, a well-educated and meritorious geographic engineer; he proved to be of little use.

22. Koch, *Mémoires de Masséna,* VII, 570.

Chapter Five

THE BATTLE OF BUSSACO

At last we were starting on our long-announced expedition, closely watched by all of Europe. The war continued only in Spain. The sham siege of Cadiz and the interminable preparations for the siege of Tortosa received little notice, for all attention was riveted on Masséna and Wellington.[1] It was at Lisbon that the fate of the Peninsula was to be decided and perhaps the destiny of the world; if the British were forced to abandon the capital they would lose all their influence in Spain. No other part of the country offered them the same resources or advantages, and they would lose the means of maintaining their army and fomenting insurrection. Portugal would submit and Spain, exhausted and discouraged, would follow its example as soon as it was abandoned. Then England would find itself isolated and blockaded on its island. It would lose hope of renewing its intrigues with the governments conjoined in the Continental System. Then France could preserve its preponderance in Europe which could only increase with its excellent army of three hundred thousand in Spain, composed of the best corps available. Any other outcome of the expedition could only

1. Marshal Macdonald, commanding the Army of Catalonia, and Suchet, with the Army of Aragon, isolated and besieged Tortosa in December 1810. On January 1, 1811, the fortress surrendered after only a three-week defense, giving rise to speculation of treason. The French troops of Soult reached the walls of Cadiz on February 4, 1810, following the conquest of Andalusia. The siege dragged on until the summer of 1812, when Soult was forced to withdraw his army.

bring the opposite results. The English would recommence the war against us at the expense of the entire Spanish population. The efforts of France were carefully watched by the powers of Europe, and France needed prompt success to prevent any changes in its policies, while its enemies gained by waiting.

According to the General Order of March on the 16th, the army was to occupy a line from Guarda to Póvoa d'El Rei, with the advance guard at Celorico. Marshal Ney, instructed to move only his advance guard to Freixedas on the 15th, had advanced there with his whole army corps. On the 16th he had marched on Celorico instead of halting at Alverca as he had been ordered. Thus the isolated 6th Corps was in a position to reveal the goal of the army's operations twenty-four hours too early, whereas from its position at Alverca it would have been able to march forward on the Mondego or on the flank by the Zezere. The Prince was notified of this development at five o'clock in the morning. He sent me immediately to give the Marshal written orders to stop wherever I should meet him.[2] Thus I was unable to see Almeida, where the Prince was to stop.

Crossing the Côa, I found the defile very long and difficult, still filled with the wagons of the 8th Corps' *grand parc*. Beyond, there was a rather extensive plateau and then Valverde, Vendada, a gorge with a stream, another defile, and the village of Freixedas, about five leagues from Almeida. The countryside here was better cultivated but still sprinkled with enormous blocks of granite. I was traveling as fast as possible to reach the Marshal. Before we reached Freixedas an unfortunate soldier, riding between an officer and myself, was shot on the road from eight hundred yards away. Without doubt, it was done by one of the peasants we had met earlier, and as a result of my kindness they had not been inspected by my dragoons. Freixedas, a large village on an elevated and rather rugged hill, offered a good position for several thousand enemy troops and a counterposition for our retreat. Alverca, a pretty village six leagues away, framed a defile, and a league

2. Masséna informed Ney on September 13 that Reynier's 2nd Corps would occupy Guarda by the 15th. Since Masséna neglected to tell him that Reynier would remain at Guarda on the 16th, Ney incorrectly assumed that the 2nd Corps would be marching to Celorico on the 16th. He therefore believed that his corps would have to complete two marches on the 16th to avoid becoming entangled with Reynier's advancing columns. As a result Ney's corps marched 21 miles to Juncais on the 16th. See Horward, *Battle of Bussaco*, pp. 42, 45.

and a half beyond rose the hills which separated the waters of the Mondego and those of the Côa. They were elevated and difficult. From there I could see Celorico, in its basin; Maçal, a rather nice village (eight or nine leagues away); and Baraçal (ten leagues away) on a beautiful plain at the bottom of the Mondego valley, well cultivated and planted with vines. I estimated all these distances by sight, perhaps influenced a little by my fatigue and annoyance. The Mondego was only a trickle of water in the middle of a bed of large rocks, some sixty yards in width. The city of Celorico appeared in outline on the top of a hill; it was embanked and had a strong defense toward the bridge and the mountains. On the north the city descended on a gentle and flat slope toward the plain and the Mondego, and during ordinary times it did not form any obstacles. By this flank the town could be turned and left behind or advantageously attacked. Thus it could not be considered as a defense position.

I finally found the Marshal in Celorico. He was with General Mermet, who left before long. Then he became angry about the meaning and wording of the order.[3] He said the Prince opposed him personally and that people advising His Excellency were set against him. In the middle of his outburst and declamation, General Reynier arrived in the course of reconnoitering the country, as was his excellent habit. He embraced the Marshal and expressed his surprise at finding him there because he expected to see only his advance guard. According to the General Order he had received, he expected to find him at Alverca. The General soon left us and I returned to the conversation. Speaking forcefully, I convinced the Marshal that he would expose his army corps by trying to move his position to Mangualde the next day, that he had disrupted the harmony of the movements, that he had prematurely revealed the goal of our operation, and that the Prince had many reasons to reproach him. I ended by telling him that because of their high position they should see more of each other. The Marshal agreed that he was wrong in not going to see the Prince. He added, "You have his complete confidence and you deserve it. Well, I am going

3. Masséna wrote to Ney on the evening of September 16, "I am unhappy to see that you have not conformed to the instructions I gave you. It has completely disarranged the march of the army. Therefore I desire you to remain where you are. If my letter finds you at Juncais make no movement tomorrow so the other two corps may be able to take their battle positions." See Correspondance: Armée de Portugal, Carton C[7]9.

to tell you why I have not gone." I expected some serious confidence. He gave me such a frivolous pretext that I could not keep from laughing nor take it upon myself to respond seriously. The Marshal quickly admitted the necessity of frequent communications to halt indirect reports and intrigues; moreover, he readily recognized the impropriety of his forward movement and promised to remain at Celorico the next day. I returned to Freixedas at around nine or ten o'clock in the evening. I told the Prince to sleep peacefully, and I went into a corner to do the same.

I reported our whole conversation frankly to the Prince and he laughed. He too recognized all the advantages of seeing the Marshal frequently; on the way we discussed only this subject. The Marshal was waiting for him at Celorico and the Prince was well satisfied. The 6th Corps had stopped at Juncais with its advance guard at Fornos. The 2nd Corps came to Celorico in compliance with the General Order, and the 8th Corps was to be at Venda do Cepo. All the corps experienced the greatest difficulties with their artillery, which was still far behind. The enemy was withdrawing, but already the country was in revolt up to the very gates of Almeida and Rodrigo. The Prince received the news that a battalion escorting food from Zamora to Almeida had been stopped at San Felices by insurgent peasants and had not been able to go any farther.

Celorico was completely abandoned. We found no inhabitants there except for a few infirm old men. The English had ravaged and destroyed everything. There was not a single piece of straw left for our horses. Our troops finished the devastation. How could we stop them when there were no inhabitants to complain and ask for help? Yet the countryside was well cultivated and laid out, and the villages were beautiful with white houses. We were struck by the difference as soon as we had crossed the frontier between the last village of Spain and the first of Portugal.

The army continued its movement. The advance guard was at Pisini[4] occupying the banks of the Dão, the 2nd Corps at Fornos, the 6th Corps at Mangualde with a division at Quintela observing the course of the Mondego and another division at Macieira. Part of the artillery

4. Pisini appeared in the "Dispositions générales pour l'entrée de Portugal," but no village of this or a similar name is shown on any map of Portugal.

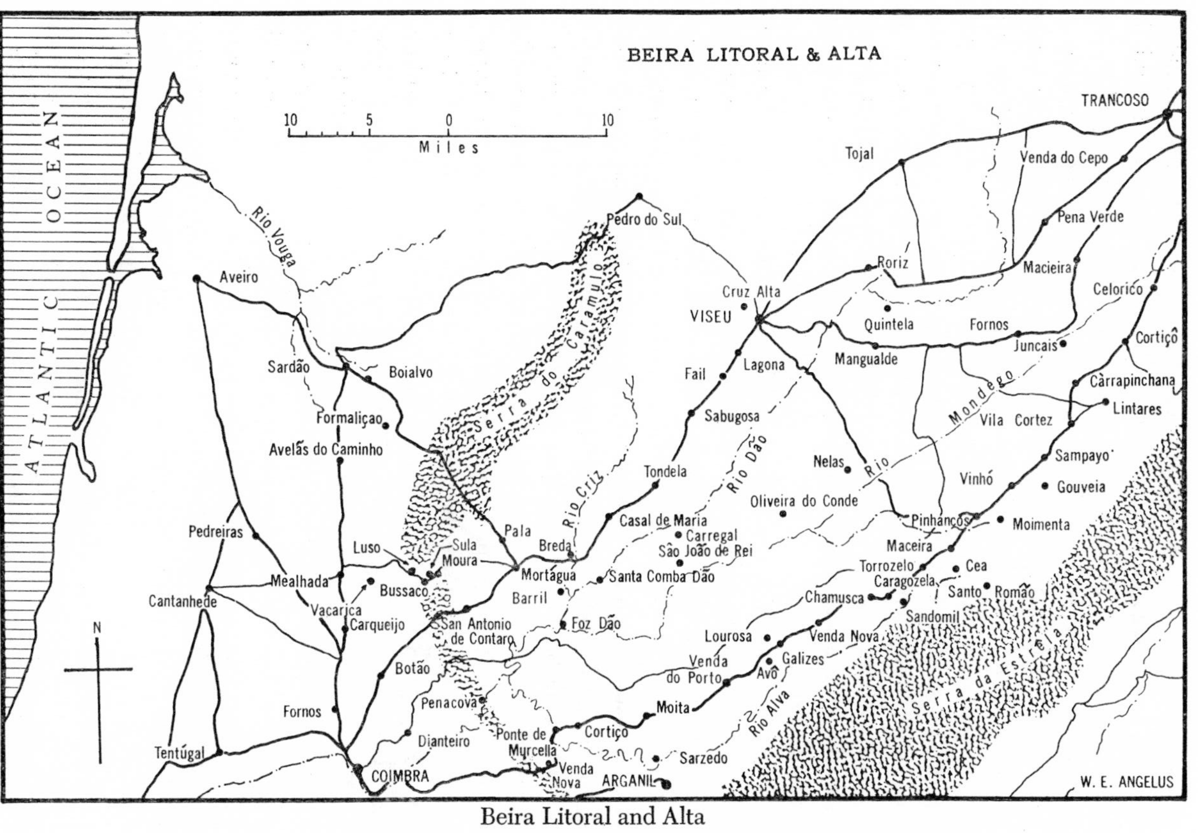

Beira Litoral and Alta

and the baggage of the 2nd and 6th Corps went through Trancoso. The 8th Corps was at Tojal with one division at Pena Verde and the reserve cavalry at Trancoso. Headquarters were at Mangualde. We found that the roads were always difficult since they had not been repaired by the British, although the country was better. At the bridge of Juncais both banks of the Mondego valley were very abrupt and steep;[5] the river had only a little water and its bed was eighty yards wide. The bridge, high and flat, was formed by five unequal arches. Here we found mementoes of those ancient masters of the world, the Romans, whose empire we believed we were renewing. After twenty centuries, the ancient remnants of this bridge again saw the unconquered eagles.

Fornos was a large and beautiful village on the slope of the mountains, which were even higher beyond the Mondego. There we admired the first of many olive trees, but we had only rather poor griddle cakes to eat. "There is only oil here," said one passing soldier. "Oil," said Bavastro, getting off the mule. "I am going to make you a capon dish," and he made an excellent and extremely appetizing salad of biscuit. Bavastro was the famous corsair, well known for a number of splendid achievements and honorably mentioned by General Thiébault during the siege of Genoa; he received decorations of honor in Spain and France before the renewal of the order of chivalry.[6] He had always shared the good fortune of the Prince, and he now followed him with the hope of arming a few vessels when we reached Lisbon, because he wanted to repeat on the ocean the exploits for which he had become famous in the Mediterranean. Frank, loyal, and a good sailor, he followed his trade of privateering as others practice the most disciplined professions; one could rely on his kindness until the moment of boarding. Quite unpretentious, he amused us and was even more interesting because he accomplished the most courageous and brilliant acts as if they were quite ordinary. He recounted his exploits

5. The narrow defiles beyond Juncais made the movement of wheeled traffic extremely difficult. Several wagons were wedged into the passes and the men of the 6th Corps were backed up for several miles. See "Journal de l'expédition de Portugal 15 au 27 septembre," Correspondance: Armée de Portugal, Carton C[7]9.

6. Thiébault incorrectly described Bavastro as Masséna's cousin; they had gone to sea together as boys and were close friends. Thiébault depicted him as a "man who would have been extremely well suited . . . [to be a privateer] had his honesty been on a par with his courage." See Thiébault, *Memoirs*, II, 36.

with vivacity and charming simplicity as if he were on stage excitedly acting them out. To his accompaniment of shouts, gestures, glances, Bavastro added the sound effects of gun, cannon, or sea and wind. Speaking half in French and half in Provençal, he created very picturesque descriptions. Born a man of the sea, he had had little education. Perhaps he lacked only a greater stage and a little more good fortune to become a Jean Bart or Duguay-Trouin.[7]

The country beyond Fornos was extremely rough and covered with pine and chestnut trees; half way across it there was a deep valley full of rocks. Beyond, the country became flat and more open to our left. The range of the Serra da Estrêla, quite high and covered with rocks, appeared completely impassable. A Portuguese officer was serving as a guide that day; he passed by his home without stopping to see it or asking for any news of his family. I was troubled for him. Perhaps he did not care, but at the least he appeared very quiet. We finally arrived in Mangualde at night; it was a large and beautiful village with a magnificent country house. The wine of this part of the country was excellent when aged in the bottle. Without liking Portuguese wine one could still rejoice in substituting it for the abominable wine of northern Spain and the awful goat skins. Yet the amateurs celebrated the latter; they did not sing about the bottle any more but about the goat skin which had taken its place in song as well as in conversation.

We left rather late. Therefore I had enough time in that country to visit the castle and its gardens. Everything was beautiful and seemed magnificent. There were engravings of Italy by Volpato, the Morpheus of the drawings of Canova and Piranesi, and a few paintings.[8] Everything reminded us of what we admired in the country of *beaux arts* and showed us a people worthy of appreciating them. This type of scene, repeated so often in Portugal, impressed us more strongly after leaving the ignorance of Castilian barbarism. Everywhere we discovered art objects, engravings of libraries, and great numbers of

7. Jean Bart (1650–1702) enlisted in the Dutch navy but became famous as a corsair sailing for Louis XIV during the War of the League of Augsburg. René Duguay-Trouin (1673–1736) was a privateer who sailed for Louis XIV and Louis XV. By 1709 he reportedly had captured 300 merchantmen and 20 warships.

8. Giovanni Volpato (1733–1803) was an engraver who worked for the Duke of Parma. At Rome he was employed by Gavin Hamilton to engrave several plates for Hamilton's *Schola Italica Picturae.* Antonio Canova (1757–1822) was an Italian sculptor of the neoclassic period. Giovanni Battista Piranesi (1720–1778) was an Italian engraver and architect of the same period.

French books; moreover, we did not find the same stubbornness and patriotism we had seen in Spain.

The 6th Corps marched to the middle of the village. I saw it go by as I stood with the Marshal at his window; it passed in the most noble and majestic manner in three very tight ranks. In every respect these regiments appeared to be elite corps. Here is one example of their singular type of discipline. One of our aides-de-camp encountered a soldier who offered him a good mule for twenty francs. The officer offered him double if he wanted to take it to headquarters. "No," answered the soldier, "my captain has promised to make me a corporal. I have been out of the ranks for the last ten minutes and if he does not see me there immediately I will not have my grade any more." The soldier offered the same mule to a *cantinière*[9] for fifteen francs although it was worth six hundred. I certainly could not praise such robbery; nevertheless, this kind of discipline changed considerably later on.

We left at noon. The road to Viseu was fairly good but the crossing of the Dão offered some difficulties. The city appeared attractive from afar. We found it completely abandoned. It had been spared by the advance guard, but the arrival of the columns of the 6th and 8th Corps caused some disturbances that each attributed to the other. At first we remedied the confusion, but it was entirely impossible to stop the disorders in vacant houses. As soon as we arrived, the Marshal came to pay a visit to the Prince, and I noted this event because I thought it was the first time since our arrival in Spain, and it did not happen often. The advance guard marched directly to Fail on the Coimbra road, the 6th Corps was a little to the rear of Lagona, the 8th Corps was at Roriz or Cruz Alta beyond Viseu, and the 2nd Corps was at Mangualde with one division marching on the left of the Mondego at the request of General Reynier. The reserve cavalry should have been at Tojal with the *grand parc* and the baggage, but the latter was so delayed that its wagons had hardly gone beyond Trancoso. Headquarters were established at Viseu. The army corps saw almost none of the enemy, except for the 8th Corps, which encountered a detachment of seven to eight thousand [*sic*] soldiers and Portuguese peasants formed in a corps said to be gathered near Lamego.

9. A *cantinière* was usually a female sutler or canteen keeper attached to a regiment of the French army.

The interior of Viseu was actually unsightly. The architecture of the churches and the buildings was not beautiful, but the surroundings were delightful and the scenery beyond was charming. Fine promenades and beautiful gardens surrounded the city. The luxuriant vegetation delighted and surprised at the same time. The trees were magnificent; cedars, aloes, a few palm trees, and many laurels gave a foreign atmosphere to this cheerful countryside that made it even more lively to us. Beautiful and swiftly running waters, often shaded by stately weeping willows, enhanced the splendor of this vigorous and vitalized greenery and added a charm found especially in the warm countries. We enjoyed finding oriental characteristics on the great number of fountains around the city and along the roads of Portugal.[10] Without doubt it got its ancient name, *Vicus Aquarius,* from the abundance of water around it. All kinds of orange and lemon trees were laden with unripe fruit, and grapevines as large as trees displayed their last grapes. Ancient traditions added to the interest inspired by the beautiful view of the country. Near the city there was a wall six hundred yards in diameter, formed by an earth entrenchment twenty-five to thirty inches high. Some said that it was a Roman camp from the time of Sertorius, while others attributed it to Lusitani Viriatus.[11]

Viseu furnished little in the way of food and useful provisions but a great quantity of oranges, fruit, jelly, and abundant wine. Those who found so much charm in the scene of beautiful nature and in the industry of man, developed here to a rather high degree, were distressed at the prospect of the inevitable destruction which the passage of the army would bring. For them this was a very sad picture of a deserted city, momentarily occupied by conquering soldiers accustomed to sparing nothing.[12] Even the hospitals, with all the sick, had been

10. Although Pelet does not mention it, when the French reached Viseu, they found that the springs and wells had been poisoned by the inhabitants before they fled the town. This practice was repeated in each major town through which they passed. See Jean Baptiste Lemonnier-Delafosse, *Campagnes de 1810 à 1815 ou souvenirs militaires* (Le Havre, 1850), pp. 78–79.

11. Quintus Sertorius (d. 72 B.C.) was a Roman general who attempted to unite the Lusitani against Rome and foster national feelings among local leaders, but he was assassinated by a disaffected officer. Viriatus Lusitani (d. 139 B.C.) was a Lusitanian leader who successfully defended the country against several Roman armies; he signed a peace treaty with Rome only to be assassinated by bribed officials.

12. At Viseu the discipline of the army began to deteriorate noticeably. Great numbers of soldiers deserted their regiments and during their search for plunder

left without assistance. We immediately sent some guards and doctors there. At least the inhabitants, when forced to abandon their homes, had not burned or destroyed them as we had seen during some of our campaigns, and it was not long before they returned. The day after our entry we saw the governor of the neighboring district arrive with his secretary. He protested strongly against the iron yoke of the British and against the horrid harassments employed to force the inhabitants to flee. He gave us little information about the enemy but a great deal about the country, which he knew quite well. He summoned his wife and the inhabitants to come back. We saw the effect of his assurances by the return of many people as well as a few priests.

The troops were strung out between the Criz River and Viseu, and we could already see that we would be obliged to stop there. The 6th Corps moved its advance guard, which was that of the army, to Tondela and the next day to Casal de Maria, while the other divisions were situated at Tondela and Sabugosa. General Reynier posted a division at Nelas to observe the Mondego, and protected the Ponte do Oliveira while his small advance guard was at Carregal; replaced by a division later on, the advance guard pushed as far as Santa Comba Dão. These two army corps sought to occupy the right bank of the Criz without a fight.[13] The 8th Corps was cantoned around Viseu. The artillery of the army corps, most of it in need of some repairs, was concentrated near the city. During the night of September 21, the 2nd and 6th Corps received orders to carefully reconnoiter the terrain and passes and collect all necessary information on the roads they had traveled. The 6th Corps was to march through Mortágua to Mealhada, and the 2nd Corps by the Ponte de Criz and San Antonio de Cantaro to Coimbra. The 2nd Corps was instructed particularly to observe the movements and positions of the enemy on the Alva toward Ponte de Murcella. Both corps were once again forbidden to march and engage in combat without receiving new orders. They were to support each other mutually. The 8th Corps with the *parc* and the cavalry was to follow the 6th Corps by one day's march. If the artillery of

committed shocking excesses against the Portuguese who had taken refuge in the hills. An officer of the 6th Corps recalled, "Some soldiers conducted themselves in an abominable manner toward women and the inhabitants they captured." See Guingret, *Relation historique*, p. 46.

13. For details of the French advance, see Horward, *Battle of Bussaco*, pp. 49–63.

the 2nd Corps was unable to pass through San Antonio de Cantaro, it was to follow the 6th Corps.

As soon as we arrived at Viseu, the Prince ordered me to present to him the rest of my work on the campaign plan, or give a new report on the present state of affairs. I gave it to him, and the original is still in my hands. One must never forget our ignorance of the topography of this country, especially what we had been told about the impassability of the Zezere and the Serra da Estrêla; we believed that direct communications between Lord Wellington and Hill were impossible except through Tomar. Here is an extract from my report: "The army has unmasked the provisional goal of its operations by reaching Celorico. Lord Wellington can see that we wish to go first to Coimbra. He is obliged to concentrate his troops there, and he can only defend his approaches by uniting with Hill's forces. The Mondego is fordable at this moment; it is necessary to take advantage of it as quickly as possible. If the conditions of the artillery, wagons, and food permit, we should march on Coimbra and attack by threatening to outflank it, and then ford the river before the English troops are united. We must move the 2nd Corps there as rapidly as possible, with the 6th Corps following by one march. The 8th Corps and the remainder should follow on the main road to Mealhada. If the Mondego cannot be forded, it will be impossible for us to force a passage without barges or boats. Moreover, if Coimbra is too strongly occupied and entrenched, as it is said to be, it will be necessary to threaten the city and force the Ponte do Oliveira in order to seize the position at Murcella and thus outflank Coimbra. It is to be feared that Lord Wellington will unite and combine the defenses of this city with that of the Alva because they are so close to each other."

The Prince approved these dispositions, but we still had no news of the *grand parc* or of the cavalry. The next day two soldiers, sent as messengers, announced that the baggage convoy had been attacked near Valverde by a force of soldiers and peasants. The 65th Line was sent in advance of the *parc*. General Clauzel was ordered to make a reconnaissance in the direction of São João [da Pesqueira] and Lamego, and also to send a few troops there to harass the rear of the militia and attack them if they could be overtaken. An officer of the *état major*, marching with the headquarters baggage, arrived on the

22nd with detailed news of his battle and, even better, of his victory against five thousand men.[14] The officer repeated his news so often to the Prince that the latter finally turned his back on him, saying "It is beautiful, it is romantic," which it was not at all. Since all the baggage wagons were marching in units according to the size of their load and the strength of their teams, it seemed certain that the united corps of Silveria and Trant went after them but were unsuccessful. The *grand parc* was still quite far in the rear.[15]

As we entered Portugal our poor opinion of the maps was confirmed. In effect, many of the villages were not shown and a very large number were incorrectly placed. The rivers, the roads, and, even more, the contours of the terrain were inaccurately shown. However, despite the imperfections in the map, drawn according to our information, it was infinitely superior to that of the printed maps. Still it was necessary to use them for the country we crossed between Viseu and Coimbra. This work was not enjoyable for anybody, and it was impossible for me to apply myself as much as I would have wished. In fact, it must be acknowledged that we did it in a very tiresome manner. Our French-speaking Portuguese had nothing to teach us about these districts or the other areas. We had to use their translations to obtain any information and then unscramble the many variations and obscurities of the translators and obtain details that were difficult to grasp and express. The Marquis d'Alorna brought us many people—the governor, priests, hunters, and smugglers—and they all worked with us. However, our lack of reliable information was so acute that we believed our troops had already passed the defensive positions on the Criz. We had been told that the Serra de Alcoba was

14. A Portuguese detachment of 2,000 militia, 200 horsemen, and 5 pieces of artillery under Colonel Trant marched from Moimenta da Beira to Tojal to intercept the *grand parc*. De Fontenilles, in command of the artillery column, deployed his forces in a semicircle to await the support of his Prussian escort, almost a mile behind. Although he attempted to parley, the Portuguese attacked. The few escort troops still with the column put up a determined resistance until the Prussian infantry arrived. The French had 8 killed while the Portuguese left 39 dead and 2 wounded on the battlefield. See "Rapport fait à S. A. le prince d'Essling par De Fontenilles," September 20, 1810, Correspondance: Armée de Portugal, Carton $C^7$9.

15. If Trant's attack had been successful, the entire invasion might have been postponed or cancelled. Captain Noel of Junot's artillery observed that if the column had been disabled or captured "the invasion of Portugal would have been impossible for us." See Noel, *Souvenirs,* p. 116.

between the Criz and Moita whereas the mountain chain was beyond Moita. Duplicates of our work proved this. It was also difficult, even impossible, to understand the connection and strategic relationship between the abutments of Murcella and Serra de Alcoba. To complete our ignorance, General Reynier, who had always furnished us the best information on the enemy, lacked or at least neglected to send intelligence reports to us after he had gone beyond Foz Dão, despite the formal order he had received on the 21st.

It was only on September 23 that the leading column of the *grand parc* arrived; it had been announced that all of it would be at Viseu on the next day. General Montbrun also arrived with part of his cavalry. The enemy had exposed himself at several points along his column and had made a few attempts [to halt us] that were easily repulsed. We were stopped at Viseu not only by the delays of the *grand parc* which could not be left behind, but also because we still had to wait for the food wagons in order to give the troops a fresh supply of biscuit before sending them forward; this country furnished almost nothing toward our subsistence. Finally, we were obliged to make repairs on all the artillery wagons of the army corps since they were badly damaged by the poor roads.[16] Those of the 8th Corps had arrived by the 24th. General Éblé asked vainly for the wagons of the *parc*.

Few people were aware of all these details. As soon as their horses were saddled or their bags filled up, most of them were surprised when we did not start marching immediately, and they complained. But what would they have said if they had had to march without provisions or fight without ammunition, for nothing less than that was involved. How fortunate were the ancients, with only a few arms, fighting with pike or sword, and nourishing themselves on a little flour. How often had I complained about the baggage, which they so correctly called impedimenta although they had only a small quantity. In this regard, everything I feared occurred, and even more. First, there was the junction of General Hill, who would not have reached Lord Wellington if we had been able to leave Viseu the day after we arrived, since he could not have received his orders before the 18th

16. According to *chef d'escadron* Marbot, Masséna's second aide-de-camp, the French delay at Viseu was ordered by the Prince so that Mme Leberton would have time to recuperate from the strenuous journey to Viseu. See Marbot, *Memoirs,* II, 108–9.

or 19th and had a great distance to cover before rejoining his army.[17] I was also afraid that the Mondego would rise and fluctuate during that autumn season as a result of recent thunderstorms. Yet what could we do to surmount such obstacles when we could not even predict marches of only four or five leagues on the road to Trancoso, which had been designated as rather good. Every day we were supposed to leave, and each day brought us new delays.

General Reynier occupied the banks of the Dão and started to reconnoiter Foz Dão. When his cavalry approached, bands of armed peasants fled. General Loison and the advance guard had gone across the Criz, although its bridge had been cut and the enemy had boldly announced they were ready to defend the crossing. There he had some light skirmishing and a few were wounded. The 6th Corps made some dispositions to assure the possession of the other side of the Criz and all its crossings. Orders for movements and schedules for the marches, together with the maps of the terrain to be crossed, were sent to the army corps. The 2nd Corps was to march on Coimbra through Carvalho, Bemfeita, San Antonio de Cantaro, and Dianteiro, while the advance guard and the 6th Corps would proceed through Mortágua, Luso, Carqueijo, and Fornos. These two army corps were marching almost parallel. In reserve, the 8th Corps and cavalry were following one day behind the 6th Corps, ready to support the 2nd Corps in case of attack, since it was the pivot of a flanking movement. The *grand parc* marched behind, escorted by one regiment of dragoons and three battalions of infantry under the command of General Gratien, who protested vainly against this position.[18] The headquarters followed a little behind the 6th Corps. The 44th Flotilla Battalion had just been designated to form its usual garrison.

On September 23 two rivers, the Dão and the Criz, were crossed and their passage assured. General Reynier was at Santa Comba Dão, and he advanced a few troops near Mortágua. General Loison was at

17. Wellington alerted Hill to the French movements toward Guarda on September 15 and two days later the Second Division was marching north. Hill was at Espinhal on the 20th but did not reach Bussaco until the morning of September 26. See *Wellington's Dispatches,* Wellington to Hill, September 15; Wellington to Liverpool, September 20, 1810, VI, 441, 457–59.

18. Baron Pierre Guillaume Gratien (1764–1814) enlisted in 1787 and became general of brigade in Loison's division in 1809. He was assigned to units stationed along the French frontier between 1792 and 1802 and he served with Bernadotte in Holland and Jérôme in Westphalia until sent to Spain with Loison's division.

Couto do Mosteiro with troops near Barril. He asked for support since several enemy regiments had appeared in front of him; he thought it was only Craufurd's division crossing the Mondego at the same time as he was; but Craufurd was helping to cover the movement of their whole army. The peasant insurrection deprived us of any definite news about the enemy. It was said the English army was massing around Coimbra. This did not seem probable because of the state of the Mondego and the direction of its flow. Furthermore, the enemy continued their destruction, destroying and burning everything.

The army commenced its movement and was set up in a line: the advance guard at Breda, the 2nd Corps at Cancela, the 6th Corps at Casal de Maria, the 8th at Sabugosa, and a division at Viseu where the cavalry reserve remained and the *grand parc* was forming. The last of the artillery and food wagons finally arrived and essential repairs were finished on the various artillery. At last the long-awaited departure took place; we hurried it as much as possible. The advance guard received the order to move on the summit of the Serra de Alcoba, the 2nd Corps to Bemfeita, the 6th Corps to Mortágua, the first division of the 8th Corps to Casal de Maria, the second to São Joaninho, headquarters with the reserve cavalry to Tondela, and the *grand parc* to Sabugosa. The country beyond Viseu was uneven, rather good, and covered with chestnut trees, and the roads were passable though there were frequent acclivities and declivities. We were told that the enemy had shown themselves opposite the advance guard above the defile of Moura.

The 2nd Corps was to go within one league of San Antonio de Cantaro, the 6th Corps to Luso, the 8th Corps with the headquarters to Mortágua, the reserve cavalry to Breda, and the *grand parc* to Casal de Maria. The 2nd and 6th Corps encountered the enemy's advance posts near the Serra de Alcoba, where its army was posted on the crest of the mountain. They took positions in front of it at eleven o'clock or noon. Marshal Ney's aide-de-camp, Captain d'Albignac, announced this news to the Prince, who was marching at the head of the 8th Corps to observe the army's maneuvers. Before long another aide-de-camp brought him a copy of a letter the Marshal had just written to General Reynier.[19] The General had reported what was

19. In fact, Ney's first aide-de-camp was sent to Masséna's headquarters, 22 miles in the rear at Tondela, before 8:00 A.M. and his second aide-de-camp was

occurring ahead of his column and asked what he was to do. The Marshal answered him (more or less), "If I were the commander in chief, I would not hesitate for one moment to attack the enemy and throw him back, but since we have a generalissimo, it is necessary to wait for orders."[20] The Marshal sent only one copy of his reply with General Reynier's letter.

As a result of this information, the Prince went beyond Moura on the Coimbra road as fast as possible and found the two armies as follows: The enemy crowned the summit of the mountain, where the walls of the convent of Bussaco could be seen, with artillery along a line for more than eight or even ten thousand yards. To the right, beyond the road of San Antonio de Cantaro and extending quite far through the posts and militia units, was General Hill's division, which had just joined the army within the past few days.[21] The center was near the convent and straddled the road to Coimbra. The left was also extended very far up to a detached abutment that was almost perpendicular and slightly in front of the summit; the enemy had placed a

sent at 10:30 A.M. with Reynier's letter. Apparently Masséna set out from Tondela around 10:00 A.M. for he reached Mortágua, 14 miles away, at noon and wrote to Ney, "On arriving at Mortágua I heard the firing cease and I think you should continue your march, pushing the enemy toward Luso. If they still hold, please inform me immediately by one of my officers who is near you and I will join the 6th Corps." See Masséna to Ney, "midi" September 26, 1810, Archives de Masséna, LI.

20. In response to Reynier's letter, Ney wrote at 10:30 A.M., "I think a great part of the Anglo-Portuguese army spent the night on the crest of the mountains that dominated the entire Moura valley. . . . Since this morning, the enemy has marched by his left and seems to direct his main columns toward the road of Oporto. . . . I have sent one of my aides-de-camp to the Prince d'Essling this morning to tell him they are in our presence, and that it will be necessary for him to come and take part. If I commanded, I would attack without hesitating a moment, but I believe, my dear general, that you would compromise nothing if you echeloned on the right of the enemy." See William F. P. Napier, *History of the War in the Peninsula and in the South of France from A.D. 1807 to A.D. 1814* (New York, 1864), II, 516.

21. Loison informed Masséna of the presence of the Allied army on the Serra de Bussaco on the evening of September 25. Therefore, if Masséna had been at the front line early on the 26th, he would have found on the mountain only 34,000 men, of whom at least 14,000 were changing positions. Spencer's First Division was occupying the positions vacated by Cole's Fourth Division and the latter was moving to the north. In addition Hill's Second Division did not reach the mountain until the morning of the 26th. Thus if Masséna had been able to attack the Allied army early on the morning of September 26, he would have had a good chance of success. See Bonnal, *Ney*, III, 390; Burgoyne, *Life and Correspondence*, I, 110; William Tomkinson, *The Diary of a Cavalry Officer in the Peninsular and Waterloo Campaigns, 1809–1815*, ed. James Tomkinson (London, 1894), pp. 40–42.

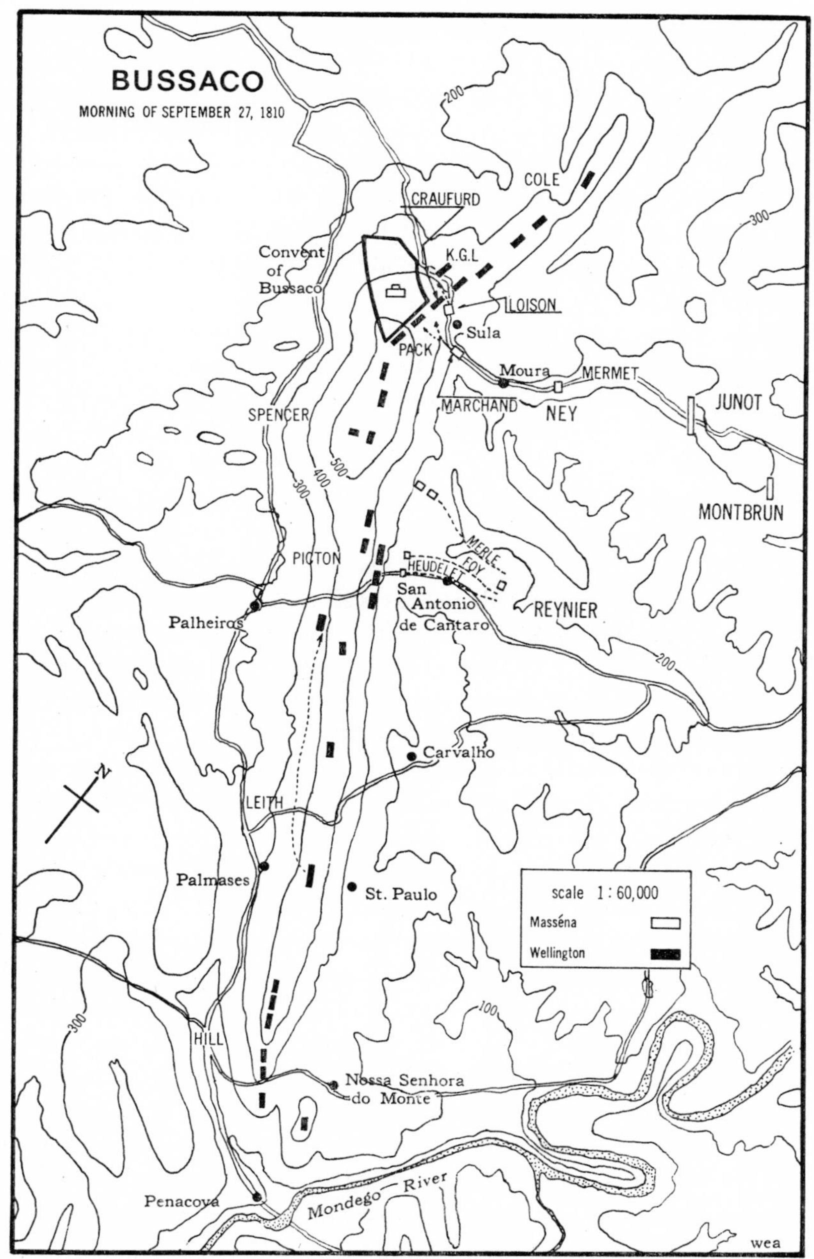
BUSSACO
MORNING OF SEPTEMBER 27, 1810
COLE
CRAUFURD
Convent of Bussaco
K.G.L
LOISON
Sula
PACK
Moura
MERMET
MARCHAND
NEY
JUNOT
SPENCER
MONTBRUN
PICTON
MERLE
FOY
HEUDELET
San Antonio de Cantaro
REYNIER
Palheiros
Carvalho
LEITH
Palmases
St. Paulo
scale 1 : 60,000
Masséna
Wellington
HILL
Nossa Senhora do Monte
Penacova
Mondego River
wea

Bussaco

redoubt at its extremity. When our army advanced, we saw a full line whose deployment indicated at least sixty thousand men and consequently the greatest part of Wellington's army. The 6th Corps was massed in front of Moura, ten thousand yards from the village on the main road. The 2nd Corps, on the road of San Antonio de Cantaro to the left, was four thousand yards from the 6th Corps. The 8th Corps and the reserve cavalry, scheduled to halt at Mortágua and Breda, had received orders to move immediately into position, but they were still far away.

Closer to the Serra de Alcoba, the terrain became more irregular and mountainous. The road was also worse; the main route followed the right bank of the Dão, one league away, although Lopez's map placed it on the left bank. The Criz flowed in a deep valley full of gullies, eight hundred to a thousand yards wide at the top. These mountains were third-degree schist, with gentle, rounded slopes, and covered with heather. The principal mountain range bore several names: Alcoba, Bussaco, Luso (because of the convent and a village with the same name found there), as well as Caramulo and Bèsteiros. The range was much higher than the mountains adjoining it and dominated them by a considerable degree.[22] The slopes were very steep, and it took about three-quarters of an hour to climb to the crest, which appeared extremely sharp from the other side. There was no connection between the range and the terrain the 6th Corps occupied and the irregular conglomeration of hills that extended to Mortágua or the extremely low and narrow passage where the Coimbra road passed; beyond this obstacle was lower Moura, where both sides of the gorge descended in deep ravines. Farther on, the mountain rose up immediately to its full height and proved to be perpendicular. Thus we could only debouch against the [mountainous] position through this extremely narrow defile, which was at the same time the closest point where we could establish the artillery, since the ravines became wider and turned obliquely behind us. On the slope of the mountain we could distinguish an abutment, a little inclined toward our right, where Loison's division was to climb. The center road turned right from lower Moura and seemed to cut the mountain obliquely. Horizontally and to the left, a very poor road ran across the mountain on a

22. The Serra de Bussaco has an elevation of almost 1,800 feet above the Moura valley.

berm or a small plain below the enclosure of the convent of Bussaco. The road to San Antonio de Cantaro and the terrain where the 2nd Corps was posted were likewise connected to the principal range by an abutment descending from it. This point appeared less steep and difficult.

Having perceived the nature of this terrain as soon as we arrived, I urged anyone in the engineers, artillery, and *état major* who would listen to me, to remedy the very grave drawback of this exit, which was the only one along the entire center of the position; moreover, it had ineffective artillery emplacements for exchanging fire. Above all I pointed out that we should not venture beyond this treacherous bottleneck. We should make the gorge wider and more practicable and prepare the small abutments in front of or behind us for the emplacement of a few guns; they could be removed without much trouble. Nobody wished to believe or listen to me.

Meanwhile the interview between the Prince and the Marshal had been rather sharp. In front of everyone the Marshal loudly expressed his desire to attack and conquer all. He spoke in the same way to the Prince, who at first did not want to listen to him and was in rather a bad mood. Leaving his troops some distance behind, the Duc d'Abrantès arrived and the conversation became more animated. The reserved Reynier arrived and added more coals to the fire. They surrounded and excited the Prince and seemed to want to push him into a battle. It was not necessary to do this. "Gentlemen, you want it," he shouted. "Well, we shall attack tomorrow when the army is united." "Are you giving us orders now," they asked? "There they are."[23] The Prince had us sit down on the ground, General Fririon and myself, and he dictated the following dispositions to us: "The 2nd Corps will commence the attack and the 6th Corps will do likewise when the 2nd has nearly reached the heights. The 8th Corps will come and place

23. This council of war took place on the night of September 26. According to Koch's sources, Ney, Junot, Éblé, and Fririon now opposed an attack while Reynier and Lazowski thought it might succeed. Ney suggested a withdrawal to Oporto but Masséna replied, "The Emperor has ordered us to march on Lisbon, not Oporto, and he has his reasons. The capture of Lisbon ends the struggle while that of Oporto only prolongs it." Koch, *Mémoires de Masséna,* VII, 191–92. Fririon suggested an attempt be made to turn the position, but Masséna retorted, "You are of the Army of the Rhine, you like to maneuver; this is the first time that Wellington appears disposed to offer battle. I will profit by the occasion." Fririon, *Journal historique,* p. 47.

itself in reserve behind the 6th Corps with the cavalry as a third line." The Prince added several deployments verbally.

General Reynier made a few observations on his attack and said that he would be drubbed. The Prince replied that the 6th Corps was going to break through and make the effort; the rest was less important. As for me, I would have preferred another arrangement which seemed better adapted to the terrain, but the first plan was good if everyone was willing to execute it well. I would have preferred the 2nd Corps to be the hammer, supported by the 8th Corps and by one large division of the 6th Corps; the latter would maneuver and attack only at the end. In the system adopted, the brigades of the 6th Corps would mount three attacks, *tuyaux d'orgue* [formed like organ tubes]. The first, that of General Loison, would move forward on the point already indicated; the second would start marching by the horizontal main road when the first column was one-third of the way up the slope; and the third column, on the road to the left, would move after the other two. The artillery would advance by the horizontal road and exchange fire with the enemy while the second brigades of the 6th Corps, in reserve, would advance progressively. At the same time, the 8th Corps would hold itself in reserve for the 6th Corps as prescribed. The 2nd Corps, attacking in two columns by brigades, would draw nearer to the left of the 6th Corps to close the enormous gap between the two attacks. I have copied from my Journal because these reflections were made afterward in calm consideration. They were well based although they might seem a little disorganized.

The Prince and the commanding generals spent the rest of the day examining and reconnoitering the position of the enemy. In order to force the enemy to show all their forces, we made some preparations for the attack. The enemy formed immediately and crowned the ridge. The preceding evaluation was generally confirmed. The *chef de bataillon* of the Légion du Midi was wounded as he returned to headquarters at Mortágua in the evening, and the Prince sent me to him.

The Prince d'Essling certainly made a mistake in allowing himself to be pushed into attacking the Allied army on difficult terrain. However, if his intention was to maneuver, and if he had made his decision in the presence of the British, he would have been blamed for his haste. Those very men who maintained silence in the councils, on the seat of the tribunals, or in the benches of the church will, with heated passions, probably censor our illustrious warrior for not having mastered his emotions on the field of battle. But who would dare reproach Masséna for having doubted victory? If I allow myself to criticize him in any way, it was because he did not expose himself to encourage all of his troops in the midst of this terrible game of passions. He did not take active direction of his columns, he did not allow the noble cry "*à mon commandement*" to be heard from one end of the army to the other, and he did not show the famous sword of the *fils chéri de la victoire* to his men and to the enemy. In addition he did not force the rivals under his command to cooperate in his triumph by controlling the maneuvers of their army corps and divisions as if they were battalions and companies of the same regiment.[24] If he had done so, the Prince would have proved that the battle was necessary and that the British army had foolishly exposed itself to great disaster. The Prince thought that it was enough to give written orders and that his presence would overcome the hidden malice as well as the resistance of his men. He left the secondary dispositions to his lieutenants, and the battle miscarried. He was blamed for attacking. What would have been said if he had avoided the battle by maneuvering? He was blamed for not attacking immediately. That very evening several of our corps were still in the rear while the enemy had been gathering for two days.

We were on the line long before daybreak. General Reynier's troops, marching for a long time, reached the foot of the mountain and began to climb it. Loison's division was by the passage and turned toward the right; it advanced from the bottom of the valley and soon began to ascend slowly en masse. The English army appeared on the crest, forming a full and continuous line interrupted only by numerous batteries. They had withdrawn all the advance posts from the foot of the mountain, but halfway up the slope a line of skirmishers was established, sustained by small posts and strong reserves. The various vulnerable points such as rocks, groups of trees, hedges, etc., had

24. Masséna made several other errors in his battle plan. He did not provide for the use of his artillery, which was reduced to impotence along with the cavalry. His reconnaissance on the 26th was ineffective and the attacks were not coordinated. The 2nd Corps, although smaller than the powerful 6th Corps, did not have a reserve, while the latter was supported by the 8th Corps. For details, see Horward, *Battle of Bussaco,* pp. 72ff.

been carefully reinforced. It was claimed they had even cut the main road. The abutment, defended by a redoubt on their left, extended a little and they could see our right from the reverse. Moreover, I noticed nothing concentric in this position and its curve (if there was one, as mentioned by General Wilson and pointed out by Rocca) was not very perceivable and could not be of any influence whatsoever.[25] The acute elevation of which Wilson spoke helped the English because our troops were exhausted by the climb and because of our difficulty in attacking several points simultaneously on a wide front. It was for this reason that several enemy corps were able to act concentrically on the fronts of our two columns, but the same thing would have happened on a straight line against two isolated columns.

The first division of the 2nd Corps continued climbing the mountain, which was not as steep at this point; it successively forced back the enemy pickets and overthrew their posts. From afar we saw these masses with their whitish capes; they seemed to be suspended from the steep slopes of the mountain. On the other side and indeed at the opposite end of the battlefield, Loison's division ascended fighting on one abutment after another. Stopping for an instant before each enemy post, Loison captured it immediately. Some areas were weakly defended by the English skirmishers, others had to be stormed with vigor. A few detached companies on the left had carried upper and lower Moura. This division broke through and pushed the last line of reserves; soon it was about to reach the crest.

I followed it with my eyes and my prayers. I saw it on the crest. The enemy pieces which had vainly fired on it were forced to flee at a gallop, at the instant we thought we had captured them. Already a well-sustained fusillade commenced as our line formed. The front of the column was received head on by the British striking force. The troops of the right and left, not contained by anything, threw themselves on our flanks. Their batteries, previously unable to fire on the

25. General Robert Wilson wrote: the "combined army thus posted, extended along the ridge of Busaco for nearly two leagues . . . and formed the segment of a circle, whose extreme points embraced every part of the enemy's position." See his *Narrative of the Campaigns of the Loyal Lusitanian Legion* . . . (London, 1812), pp. 291–92. Albert Jean de Rocca recalled, "The position occupied by the British and Portuguese on the crest of the hill, formed the arc of a circle, whose two extremes embraced the ground over which the French advanced." See his *Mémoires sur la guerre des français en Espagne* (2nd ed., Geneva, 1887), p. 52.

columns because of the elevation, now caught the column from the side as it advanced and cut it to pieces. The first platoon was thinned by the fire, overcome by numbers, and thrown back on those following it. The latter fell on the body of the column. Some British and Portuguese units, sent to help the line of skirmishers, moved on the left flank of Loison at this instant and increased the disorder by their fire. The brave men who earlier had marched toward death or victory with so much assurance and intrepidity, who had so much perseverance against overwhelming fatigue and obstacles, who were exhausted by so many efforts, were pushed back and overthrown. They descended much faster than they had been able to climb. General Simon arrived on the crest first; he fell into the hands of the enemy, dangerously wounded.[26] But either we had made a great mistake or the corps did not want to succeed. The division was not supported, there was no reserve ready, and our artillery was too far away and poorly placed. It was only much later that guns were placed on both sides of the passage, as I had been preaching since the previous day. For, under the circumstances, an unimportant officer only seemed like a busybody. The enemy quickly followed the scattered troops of Loison's division. When they got close enough, a few shots from our cannon halted and turned them back, but it was too late. The attack had been repulsed and our soldiers, unable to keep their ranks on the steep slopes, re-formed themselves only at a safe distance.

On the left the 2nd Corps had some success at first. As a result of the terrain the artillery fire, although far away, supported the march of its columns; a heavy cannonade continued on that side. The first division skirmished vigorously while climbing. At last it reached the summit. The column began to deploy as if at an exercise, while the fire of the platoon was well sustained. The division of General Hill [*sic*] hastened from every direction to throw itself against the front of the column as it maneuvered. They attacked its flanks, stopped its deployment, smashed it with grapeshot from their field pieces, and finally

26. General Simon, his jaw "broken and almost hanging down on his chest," was taken prisoner by a private of the 52nd Foot. Furious over his capture, Simon demanded the right to meet Craufurd in single combat to determine the outcome of the battle, but his request was denied because he was already a prisoner. See George T. Napier, *Passages in the Early Military Life of General Sir George T. Napier*, ed. W. C. E. Napier (2nd ed., London, 1886), pp. 125–26; John Kincaid, *Random Shots from a Rifleman* (London, 1847), p. 84.

pushed it over the slopes and forced it to descend. Of the commanders marching at its head, General Merle was seriously wounded while General Graindorge[27] and the colonel of the 2nd Léger were mortally wounded. The first brigade of the second division, organized as a reserve, wanted to attack and support the retreat of the first. It met with superior forces and was obliged to withdraw with some losses; General Foy, commanding it, was seriously wounded.[28]

Such was the result of those two isolated attacks; on the basis of the manner in which they were directed, one could not have expected any other result from two points so formed and removed from each other. Meanwhile we did not lack troops. Two good divisions of the 6th Corps had their weapons on their shoulders, the 8th Corps was in reserve at the rear, and the noble cavalry of General Montbrun was still farther away waiting for a signal to advance. The enemy could see these dispositions, they could count the number of our battalions, and they had only to remain quiet. It was around seven or eight o'clock.[29] We had enough time and men left to throw back the British. The losses we had just sustained were almost nothing. A little disorder could be very quickly repaired. However, an attack is not started a second time in the same way when the situation and circumstances are difficult or when the soldier can persuade himself that it is impossible to succeed and that it is not his fault if he has not swept the enemy away. It was necessary to change the strategy by attacking at other points or resorting to maneuvers immediately. This was not done, and it was easy to anticipate the results of the day.

27. Baron Jean François Graindorge (1770–1810) enlisted in 1791 and 14 years later became general of brigade. He served in the Armies of the North and the Sambre and Meuse until he was transferred to Masséna's Army of Switzerland. Given a brigade in Lannes's corps of the Grand Army, Graindorge fought in Austria, Prussia, and Poland. In 1807 he accompanied Junot into Portugal and died after the battle of Bussaco.

28. Count Maximilien Sébastien Foy (1775–1825) attended artillery school and became a lieutenant in 1792; he was promoted to general of division in 1810. He served with the Armies of the North and the Rhine and Moselle until 1799, when he was attached to Masséna's army in Switzerland. Foy commanded a brigade in Junot's army in 1807 and during Soult's invasion of Portugal in 1809. He fought at Vimeiro, Corunna, and Oporto, and served as Masséna's messenger to Napoleon in 1810–11.

29. After the battle was ended, a truce was agreed upon at approximately 4:00 P.M. while the surgeons and health officers administered to the wounded still on the field. See Wm. Napier, *War in the Peninsula,* II, 406; José de Santo Silvestre, "Diary of Brother José S. Silvestre," in George L. Chambers, *Bussaco: Wellington's Battlefields Illustrated* (London, 1910), pp. 149–51.

As Loison's division was thrown back, a brigade of Marchand's division was pushed forward, but too late. It occupied the abutment beyond the passage of upper Moura after a dispute with the enemy; each occupied it successively. The English maneuvered and fell back as soon as they received some cannon fire. Our brigade, attacked on its flank by artillery, was thrown to the left of the road. After fighting for some time, it found itself almost entirely dispersed into groups of skirmishers, and in the end it was necessary to support this unit with the second brigade. Thus we covered the entire slope below the convent of Bussaco while the enemy successively reinforced their line of skirmishers, hidden behind the rocks and the trees, but these Allied troops were not allowed to stay there very long. They were recalled by horns and replaced by fresh troops—an excellent method neglected by us for too long. Our system permitted the French regiments to be dispersed during a battle and in the end only the officers and the bravest soldiers were left, and they were completely disgusted, even with having to fight for an entire day. The Portuguese were interspersed among the British; they acted perfectly, serving in the covered positions. Nevertheless, our skirmishers gained ground on the enemy and from time to time pushed them beyond the reserves, which they were obliged to reinforce.

To our right, Ferey's brigade of Loison's division, less engaged than the first, fell back to the position it had left on the abutment. Covered by posts halfway up the slope, it held there all day long despite the continuous attacks of the enemy. Simon's brigade came to re-form behind it. To the left General Reynier had taken a position at the foot of the mountain and also with posts halfway up its slope, but free from useless bickering, which tired the army and was without advantage or glory. In the center the Prince placed Mermet's division at the bottleneck to reinforce that of General Marchand. The light cavalry formed its line on a long abutment along the left. At its extremity Clauzel's division was established to join the 2nd and 6th Corps. Solignac's division remained massed on the main road near the reserve cavalry. From that time on the army was generally formed in a battle line. The spectacle must have been impressive for the British atop the mountain and might have exaggerated the size of our forces, for everything was exposed.[30] In such circumstances one is always ready to exaggerate objects a little and assume that everything is not exposed.

The enemy surveyed all our movements and worried about them. They maneuvered on their side, presenting the fronts of their columns and moving their artillery along the crest. We could distinguish their headquarters north of the convent of Bussaco on a little elevation. At least, we could see all their artillery arriving and departing. We could distinguish the long blue coats, the little white feathers, and the batteries of field glasses. The enemy line was impressive and even formidable above the amphitheater of rocks. I thought I saw several long mountain pieces and their implements carried by mules; the limber boxes and chests appeared to be carried by other mules. In general there was a great deal of artillery in that position, but it produced insignificant results because of its excessive elevation. The batteries could not fire straight ahead for their plunging cannonballs hardly reached our battle line. With great difficulty they began some cross fire on the climbing troops, but we were protected from their fire most of the time. Our artillery did not have many batteries and it lacked emplacements for deployment, but the enemy, afraid of our cannonballs, withdrew as soon as a few fell in their ranks.

Thus the day passed, skirmishing and losing men uselessly. I cannot express how much aversion I have always had for skirmishing. It is difficult to imagine how much it costs in casualties or, as one might say—drop by drop. Two new attacks against the position, just like the first, would not have been more deadly. I could not resist saying a few words. The skirmishing ended on our side and the enemy started it again. As a matter of fact, it was extremely difficult to stop bickering except by withdrawing our troops, and this was not without inconvenience for either advantageous terrain or the morale of the army. However, I do not think skirmishing can be allowed for its own sake

30. On September 26, 1810, a British officer of the Second Division recorded in his journal, "My regiment had no sooner piled arms, than I walked to the verge of the mountain on which we lay, in the hope that I might discover something of the enemy. Little, however, was I prepared for the magnificent scene which burst on my astonished sight. Far as the eye could stretch, the glittering of steel, and clouds of dust raised by cavalry and artillery, proclaimed the march of a countless army; while, immediately below me . . . thousands of them were already halted in their bivouacks. . . . The numbers of the enemy were, at the lowest calculation, seventy-five thousand." See G. Moyle Scherer, *Recollections of the Peninsula* (London, 1823), pp. 107–8.

in any case, unless it is to prepare attacks, cover movements, or momentarily detain the enemy at one point while they are being attacked or outmaneuvered at another. General Reynier had wisely withdrawn his troops and taken up positions. There was hardly any more fighting in this direction.

During the afternoon the Prince, after considering the results of the battle for a long time, sent someone to reconnoiter the terrain on the flanks to determine a way of making a maneuver in either direction to turn their inaccessible position and, as a result, the enemy, who believed themselves victorious. Some light cavalry of the 2nd Corps marched toward the Mondego to examine the roads, the banks of the river, and what was occurring near Murcella. Specifically, Captain Beaufort was charged with this reconnaissance. They went a considerable distance and found many armed peasants supported on the heights by a few detachments of troops. They observed that the enemy seemed to be effectively holding the flank where it could have been threatened. General Sainte-Croix had been sent toward the right by the road to Boialvo and Sardão, which opened on the plain of Coimbra in the rear of the enemy. He went boldly up to Boialvo with twenty picked dragoons. He was not able to see the terrain very well because of the darkness, but he had favorable information and at length he passed beyond the crest without finding either lines or enemy detachments. From the report of these two reconnaissances, it was about decided that the movement would be to the right. Thus the anecdote of Lieutenant G. [?] about the peasants who suggested this movement and that of Captain Guingret about the Marquis d'Alorna are refuted.[31] The Marquis's information should have been given to us at Viseu before the movement and not on the battlefields; there he was hardly given a chance to talk.

Toward evening the enemy, holding half the slope with a strong line of skirmishers who were seated and even lying down, was reinforced by large reserves, but several times we pushed them back as far as the summit. The enemy extended their line on both flanks as if to take a night position and form a chain of advance posts. Later they pushed their line forward and again started the fight. I did not know their goal, unless it was to recover the ground we had seized and not to

31. Guingret said that "the Marquis d'Alorna had suggested this wise move to the Prince." See his *Relation historique,* p. 81.

abandon any part of the battlefield to us. This useless attack was repulsed by our infantry with the artillery hardly becoming engaged. The enemy line was forced to retire even higher. Ours was formed and we remained there without any indication that the fighting might start again. Mermet's division replaced the exhausted division of Marchand which had lost many men during the firing. It occupied both upper and lower Moura with its posts extended to the height of upper Moura.

It was not only on the line of battle that hard fighting was taking place. The emotions of the commanders were also directed against each other. As early as nine o'clock in the morning the Marshal and the Duc d'Abrantès proposed to withdraw our troops, to abandon Portugal, and to retire into Spain. They claimed that we should not have started and that we were not strong enough. In a word, they seemed to counsel dishonor for the Prince and the army. For his part, Reynier was saying coldly that his troops wanted to do nothing more. I did not hear these opinions there because I was staying discreetly away, but the Prince told me about it in the evening, adding: "This is what is going on, my dear friend, and if some misfortune happens to your general, I want you to know what might have caused it." Could we attack again with such men? As for me, I ardently wanted to, but did they want to win? No![32] Moreover, they exaggerated our losses, the strength of the enemy, and the impregnability of their position. They dared to say it before their colonels and in front of their troops. "Well," said the Prince, "if I had lost twenty thousand men, if I did not have a single extra shot, I would still fight." We saw that the 6th Corps in front of us was in a very good position. We went to observe the 2nd Corps. Although it was said to have suffered very much and to be discouraged, the fact was that the 2nd Corps still expected to renew the attack and even desired it.

In the evening we saw six mounted Englishmen going through the enemy line amid cheers. It was Lord Wellington. It is said that his army believed him dead. How was this possible since they did not attack and our balls could not carry that high? Perhaps they were congratulating themselves on their success? A strange acclaim; they had not been pushed out of an impregnable position and they had

32. On a percentage basis, the French lost more officers in the battle of Bussaco than in any other Peninsular encounter.

dared to sustain the surprising shock of two French divisions.[33] They effectively proved the renown that our arms had acquired. They believed they were the victors because they had not been vanquished; and we were blushing because we had not taken more than half the battlefield and had not completely defeated them. Nevertheless, those shouts of victory made us sick. We could not pardon Wellington any more than we could the ostentatious and false inscription we had just read at the bottom of a picture where he [Wellington] was represented on foot: "INVICTO WELLINGTON LUSITANIA GRATA." Was such indiscreet praise merited at that time? Is it even now?

The Prince spent the night in the little hamlet of [Sardeirinhal ?] one thousand yards from the line, between the 6th and the 2nd Corps. His baggage was in the rear and we could find nothing. The Prince set up his headquarters in a wretched peasant house. He had only a little hay to sleep on and he covered himself with his general's overcoat; his food for the whole day was one glass of water. I happened to have a single bottle of Madeira wine in my saddlebag. I implored him to accept it, but he refused. I felt some kind of religious scruple about touching it. It was broken later during the night. The sight of this great Prince's miserable lodging after such a day touched me strangely. I wanted to remain near him. He wished to be alone. Later I went to lie down on my bed of hay. Completely exhausted, I got a little sleep but not before having many gloomy thoughts and great sorrows. What would we do the next day? Could we maneuver on the flanks? What should we do with such leaders, with an army whose maneuvers were limited by its generals or partially by itself, with such valuable baggage, all of it vital in the midst of this waste? At least I was not worried about the enemy's offensive movements. Nevertheless, I was unable to get over the sight of our French attacks being repulsed. This was the first time that I had seen defeat when the forces were relatively equal. This was how we felt and thought then and have ever since, despite our misfortune. The only idea to which I have not become accustomed is the defeat of a French army. How often I re-

33. The number of French involved in the attack was approximately 26,000 men, while the Allies employed roughly 17,800 soldiers. Nevertheless, Fririon declared that 26,771 Frenchmen had attacked 50,000 Allies in "an impregnable position." See Fririon, *Journal historique*, p. 52. Lieutenant Colonel William Napier, on the other hand, stated that 65,000 Frenchmen attacked 50,000 "mixed and inexperienced troops." Napier, *War in the Peninsula*, II, 410.

proached myself for not guessing the relationship of the positions of Murcella and Bussaco and Hill's movement. In addition we had Portuguese officers who had commanded or operated throughout the country; yet they could not tell us anything. How long I reproached myself for not having reconnoitered the point of attack better, but I did not have enough horses. Yet I was spending all my moderate inheritance, which was hardly sufficient now for my service expenses.

That cruel night passed, just as so many others no less bitter have passed since then. In the morning I had some soup and coffee, and I found myself a little more reconciled to life. We saw there had been no change along the line of the two armies. During the entire day we stayed in each other's presence. There was some feeble skirmishing and a few momentary cannonades, but this was no longer the time to attack. When there are great obstacles to surmount, it is necessary to profit by the first élan, especially with our soldiers, whose imagination is inflamed or extinguished so easily. They had become indifferent through the failure of their effort. The continual view of those steep mountains exaggerated their difficulties, and the talk of their commanders confirmed their beliefs. They were already accustomed to blame any failure on either the impossibility of achieving victory or the mistakes of the generals.

Now I will again let my Journal speak for me. I have suppressed a few lines in it because some reflections are too bitter to confide to anyone. I went below the British skirmishers to examine and detail the position. I looked at it and the enemy headquarters, still on the rocks, with dozens of field glasses aimed at us. My reconnaissance was not as valuable as bullets, but I could see everything clearly and recognize each uniform. Returning, I learned that hideous rumors had been circulating. It was said the Prince had attacked an unassailable position just as a second lieutenant might do. I had just examined the position again and recognized the truth of what I had thought the day before—that it was possible to force it. The Prince had ordered the attack, but it was the Marshal commanding the 6th Corps who had taken the principal disposition. Adjutant Commander Béchet de Léocourt, his chief of staff, came to talk to me in confidence, and he magnified the difficulties. "But," I asked him, "did you want to attack all by yourself?" "No, never," he answered me. "Then do you recognize this writing?" I showed him a copy of the impertinent letter from the Marshal to General Reynier, which I had in my pocket. "Read." "I would never have believed such a thing," answered this brave man, and I immediately hastened to the Prince and told him, "I may be shot or made prisoner. Keep this letter. It is too important for me to keep on my person."[34]

Nevertheless, the Prince, the Marshal, and the Duc were meeting together. They renewed the conversation of the previous day. Now a council of war was proposed with the corps commanders and the commander of both the engineers and the artillery. This proposition was rejected vigorously. I suggested making a reconnaissance of the outlets on the right and left. The Prince had General Reynier's cavalry march, and on the left the reserve cavalry advanced toward Boialvo. I sent Richoux in that direction to accompany General Montbrun. The enemy were fortifying their positions. I proposed to the Prince that we fortify the position on our side to give the impression that we wished to hold it. The order was given to General Lazowski. I wanted this done so we would be able to occupy it with a few men while having the freedom to maneuver elsewhere with our troops. These fortifications took a long time but the engineers as well as the artillery worked to smooth the pass and cover the batteries. General Reynier was there. The Prince continued to talk with his generals. He had me come to give details on the terrain and then he said to them, "I would certainly like to know your opinions." They wanted to discuss again the dangers of the expedition. "That is not the point. The question is this: Should we attack or maneuver? In the latter case, should it be on the left or the right of the enemy?" I withdrew a little and tried to put together some information on the roads to Boialvo and Murcella from the reports of our guides, who included a priest who had been following us. During the discussions a ball ricocheted above the heads of these great men. How much Destiny would have been changed if that ball had been slightly lower!

The question posed was not easy to resolve. Everybody had been negative about an attack, but it was more difficult to have agreement on an alternative. With a more agile army and better commanders, I would have preferred a movement on Murcella as being more deci-

34. See footnote 20 above for the text of this letter.

sive and offensive. There was the disadvantage of descending into a mountainous country where we could not obtain any food, but the movement was advantageous if we continued to Tomar or Pombal. A maneuver in the other direction, through Boialvo, was wiser, more prudent, less offensive, and took us into a fertile country. The *parc* had not arrived at Mortágua until late in the evening and was still disorganized. This movement, to be made by our army in front of the enemy, disturbed me. At last a decision was made. The 8th Corps would form the advance guard and march on Boialvo, the 6th Corps would follow, and the 2nd Corps would form the rear guard. The baggage would march, covered by Gratien's brigade; meanwhile, the Prince dissolved the *parc* and ordered the divisions to take what belonged to them. It would have been wise to leave an entrenched corps in attendance to cover the maneuver.

In accordance with the dispositions made by the Prince, I drew up the orders outside in the rain. The orders were not ready until seven o'clock, and the movement, scheduled for nightfall, did not start until almost dawn. If it was possible, I hoped that the retreat could be delayed one day, but so often precautions are useless. Clauzel's division made a movement and retired by its left to the first position in the rear. The enemy appeared to follow our operation very attentively with their glasses and were also quite anxious about what was occurring on their flanks. They maneuvered and moved their troops from the left to the right and vice versa; they put them in columns and then in battle array. They also moved their artillery. By this time the commanders were exaggerating their losses to such a point that the 6th Corps, which had claimed to have twenty thousand men ready for anything, was now claiming only twelve thousand men and citing a great number of losses. Meanwhile the quartermaster general and the chief surgeon reduced the number to seven or eight hundred wounded for the center [of the army]. (I do not pretend to guarantee this number of wounded, which is far from the evaluation that is generally made. Just because the loss of the 6th Corps was seven to eight hundred, one cannot assign the same number to the 2nd Corps, which actually attacked with three brigades but only skirmished during part of the day. Yet, on my word of honor, I affirm that this number was given to me and in my opinion it is almost exact. Thus the entire estimate of the wounded cannot exceed fourteen hundred.[35]) With regard to the wounded, the English behaved perfectly. They returned them and notified us where to find them. We also had praise for the monks of Bussaco.[36]

In the evening the baggage and the artillery started to file off, but it was done a little too early. We were harassed, wet, hurt; and we warmed ourselves with difficulty. Night arrived; it was ten o'clock and then eleven. Solignac's division, placed near us, had not yet moved. Our fires were brilliant. Nothing had been overlooked in the orders, but, seeing the congestion at headquarters, I could hardly conceive of the possibility of clearing the army away; much care and activity would be necessary to do so. I pointed this out carefully to the Prince who, in a bad mood, sent me to the Duc d'Abrantès. The Duc was near Mortágua. I looked for him but got lost and roamed around the village part of the night. At last I entered the village and found it full of wounded. I talked to General Gratien about a means for evacuating them. There were none. I pressed him. I pleaded with him. He promised to do everything he could. At last I reached the Duc, who was about to leave.

Meanwhile, that hazardous night was dark and rainy, and this, added to my worries, drove me to despair.[37] I expected a "hurrah" at any moment, and I shuddered to hear a cannon shot. I also dreaded finding the position already occupied by the enemy. It was four o'clock and the 8th Corps, which should have been on the crest of Boialvo, was still filing through Mortágua. There I waited for the

35. In all, the French had 515 killed, at least 364 captured, and 3,608 wounded, a total of 4,487 casualties. The Anglo-Lusitanian army suffered 1,252 casualties, of whom 200 were killed and 1,052 were wounded or taken prisoner. For details see Horward, *Battle of Bussaco,* pp. 128, 172–75.

36. According to Brother José de Santo Silvestre, the British attempted to aid the wounded French by carrying them to large bonfires built to keep them warm until they could be treated. In addition an English cavalry regiment brought 70 wounded Frenchmen to the Convent of Almas and the monks remaining at the monastery cared for them. See Silvestre, "Diary," in Chambers, *Bussaco,* pp. 151–66.

37. Regarding the French withdrawal, Guingret recalled, "We left at night [September 28–29], carrying our wounded with us; those who were not severely wounded rode cavalry horses; the others, suffering grave wounds or fractures, were carried by their comrades. . . . The unfortunate soldiers strained to hide their suffering. . . . The bodies of those who died during this distressing march were placed on the edge of the road to point the way . . . for the troops that followed." See Guingret, *Relation historique,* pp. 77–79.

Prince. He arrived at dawn. It was still raining but I lay down for a few moments on wet hay. Never will I suffer as much as I did during that cruel night, when exhaustion and rain were nothing compared with my mental anguish and many fears. Our troops were naturally in disorder on that night march along a single road, so narrow and unfamiliar, in mud and continuous rain. The columns were interrupted, the regiments extended to infinity, the army corps had intervals or wide gaps between them, and the divisions had not started when they should have. Moreover, the artillery and cavalry increased the disorder among the infantry. If the enemy had arrived in that region, so familiar to him, or if he had fallen on the rear or flank of our columns, on the artillery, or on the wounded, how would it have been possible to set up a defense and resist?

I accompanied the Prince for a while, then he told me to go to the Duc so that he would halt after one league to reunite his men. I marched with the 8th Corps. When it stopped beyond Tarrastal, I went forward to reconnoiter the country. There was a very thick fog. I prayed for it, and I rejoiced because of our movement. Yet, I was always apprehensive of cannon fire from every direction. Trotting along with Richoux, I finally arrived at 7:30 A.M. on the crest of Boialvo and Caramulo; from there an immense horizon could be seen. The sun came through and I noticed the abandoned enemy position two leagues away on my left. It was a beautiful but quite accessible crest that would have offered the enemy an excellent way to reach us. Beneath our feet was a magnificent plain unfolding to the sea, and our dragoons' posts were only one and a half leagues away. I was in ecstasy. I can say that my soul was overflowing with happiness. After contemplating this magnificent spectacle, I hurried to the Prince to report what I had seen. In passing, I announced the news to the Duc. He did not want to believe it. Finally, I reached the Prince and told him of my joy. Everybody was so happy that I was overcome with compliments. I said to His Excellency, "Today you alone have vanquished all of your enemies."

The wounded received care. Orders were given not to leave a single one, not even the worst wounded, and to place them on cavalry horses or carry them on stretchers. We started marching again. Everybody was entranced on [reaching] the heights. The Prince was in rapture.

We went to Boialvo. The 8th Corps was at Avelãs de Caminho, the 6th Corps on the crest, and the 2nd Corps two leagues to the rear. The English movement had commenced at two o'clock in the morning; it was already known in their army at midnight that they were withdrawing.[38] The English moved by Murcella and by Mealhada on to Fornos while the Portuguese retired toward Mealhada. Our cavalry had gone forward to Pedreiras. Thus the two armies were going to be on the banks of the Mondego, which was not defensible in spite of the rains. Arriving at Boialvo, we busied ourselves with a new itinerary. I took it to the Marshal the next day.

38. By 7:00 P.M., September 28, Wellington was well aware of French withdrawal because of the clouds of dust rising above the valley. He began formulating plans to retire, and at 2:00 A.M. on September 29 the English divisional commanders had received their instructions. An hour later Picton's Third Division marched down the western slope of the mountain to Casa do Canonigo Paes while the divisions of Spencer, Cole, and Leith began to retire toward Mealhada. The Second Division recrossed the Mondego river and marched south. See Burgoyne, *Life and Correspondence*, I, 114.

Chapter Six

THE MARCH TO LISBON

It is with reason that books are praised when they make us think and when they are not based on worn-out material. It seems important that the historian should limit himself to recounting or clarifying facts, leaving each reader at liberty to appraise them; he himself should abstain from making any judgment. Indeed, why is it necessary for him to praise virtue or good conduct, and condemn crimes, vices, or the weaknesses of men? The facts speak for themselves, and on the basis of them posterity establishes its irrevocable decrees. Nevertheless, in affairs that are subject to particular principles and a regulated course of events, or on occasions when fortune has played so important a part in events and opinion always fluctuates doubtfully, it seems that the historian cannot prevent himself from searching for the influence that fate or man has exerted. At the same time, he also looks for the mistakes that have been committed and for the probable results that would have followed if events had been regulated according to generally accepted rules. However, since these memoirs are very personal my principal goal is not to write a history, prepare an impartial judgment on the campaign, or offer young military men an occasion for studying their profession.

Now that the maneuvers at Bussaco are almost settled, I am going to examine the mistake of others, as I have frankly admitted mine, and without making any comparison or reproach, for I am in the presence of such colossal reputations. Amidst confused prejudice and contemporary passions, I am forced to detail my assertions and submit them more specifically to the criticism of my friends and to the public.

It has always appeared to me that the British General, Wellington, committed several major errors in this one operation. I have praised his general plan of defense and the flexible position he established between the Tagus and the Vouga; yet I am forced to remark that it is difficult to recognize the author of this defense as the same man who showed himself so unfamiliar with the science of topography and positions as to perch himself on inaccessible rocks with such a vast army. The army could maneuver neither forward nor backward. Nevertheless, this kind of mistake is common to most generals, who believe the best positions are inaccessible; they are incapable of recognizing a good position on favorable ground, which is usually level. If the British General were asked for an account of the ten days that passed between our crossing of the Mondego at Fornos and the attack of the 27th, he would have to deny that concerted action had been calculated in his plans and movements. If this liaison had existed, it could be maintained that he would have prepared other means of defense at Bussaco than simply cutting the bridges on the Criz. A skillful strategist would have probably preferred to defend the banks of that river with the position of Bussaco in reserve.

Having drawn these general observations together as much as possible, I will now discuss the specific mistakes I observed. First, the Allied army, in this position, lacked the means to withdraw in the face of a strong attack which might have encircled it. Once its lines were driven in, it could not have stopped its descent from the mountain, either at Coimbra or even at the sea. Second, this movement, already considerable for any army, became even more dangerous due to the intermixing of troops. While the English General had confidence in his compatriots, as they deserved, he would have been in a hazardous position if a single Portuguese corps had fought ineffectively and weakened or had laid down its arms; then the entire defense would have been swept away or overthrown.[1] Third, the English

1. The English were also apprehensive about the performance of the Portuguese troops, although the 1st and 3rd Portuguese Caçadores ("Hunters"), serving with the Light Division, performed valuable service during the summer of 1810. Captain William Tomkinson of the 16th Light Dragoons recalled, "The army is in most

army had no means of taking the offensive again whatever happened. The most it could have done was to send a few detachments to pursue us; without this [excuse], it would have been unpardonable not to follow the retreat of the two divisions that had attacked, or at least the movement of our army. Fourth, not only had the English General paralyzed the movement of his lines, but he had also rendered his cavalry useless since they were unable to move along the sharp slopes or charge on the narrow crest once our troops had climbed it.[2] The plunging shot of their artillery was without effect. Obviously, in a mountainous country cannon must be accommodated only in well-pronounced abutments or well-marked recesses, and their fire cannot be aimed perpendicularly but by the flank or obliquely; however, this type of terrain did not exist at Bussaco. Fifth, even if the English general was unable to move his entire line, nothing prevented him from marching one or two of his best infantry divisions with the mountain artillery and some of his light cavalry. If this entire force had attacked us on the night of the 28th–29th, as we have already determined, misfortune would have beset us. Such an attack would have been quite easy during the English withdrawal, for they could still have maneuvered on the Mondego and joined the main body on either of the two banks.

Sixth, once the English General had decided to hold the position at Bussaco, he should at least have made some defensive dispositions for reinforcing the various posts, such as barricading the two villages of Moura and the approaches to the excellent pass [beyond Moura], which were naturally his first line of defense, as well as a few other points on the road to San Antonio de Cantaro. Its slopes should have been reconnoitered and its flanks assured. He should have occupied the approaches to the Boialvo road as well as those on the right and posted the outlying corps of Trant, Silveira, Wilson, etc., there in advance of our baggage train. Thus he would have stopped the front of our column, given himself time to extend his flank along this posi-

beautiful order [at Bussaco], and the Portuguese as fine-looking men and as steady under arms as any in the world. The only doubt rests with them; if they do their duty, and the business becomes general there can be no doubt of success." See Tomkinson, *Diary*, p. 42.

2. Wellington actually posted 210 men of the 4th Heavy Dragoons behind Stopford's brigade on the plateau of the mountain. See *Wellington's Dispatches,* Wellington to Liverpool, September 30, 1810, VI, 471–76; Tomkinson, *Diary*, p. 42.

tion, and come to bar the passage ahead of us in two hours. If he had stopped for an instant to worry about his communications with Lisbon, he would have gone the same way, as far as the direct road from Viseu to Aveiro.[3] Seventh, if Lord Wellington really intended to fight the battle at Bussaco, and if his army were truly victorious, why did he not stop on the plain before Coimbra? There was a distinct probability that the French army, numerically inferior and weakened by the previous day's attack, would have stopped and attempted to maneuver. Since the English would have been between us and the goal of our operation, there was little for them to fear. The Mondego was not an obstacle, and nothing prevented them from withdrawing simultaneously on the city and the fords. A few defensive preparations on the left bank of the Mondego would also have detained us, and the English army would always have had its retreat guaranteed on the Lines of Lisbon. The English cavalry was mounted perfectly and its artillery very well teamed; and the superiority of its forces gave them considerable chance of success in level country. Whatever the projects of Lord Wellington were, he should have ascertained whether this demonstration would not have stopped our march; in his situation, I still believe it was an error not to have attempted it.

Thus the English General, at the head of an army much more numerous than ours, was extended on a line of eight to ten thousand yards at Bussaco. Exposed there to the terrible hazards of an attack without any chance of withdrawal or success, deprived of the use of arms, and neglecting to assure the flanks of his position, he did not attempt anything against an army maneuvering in front of him with an immense collection of baggage. Finally, he withdrew in great haste as if he had been beaten. There fate saved him from himself. What should have been a cause for blame has become an occasion of exaggerated praise and the basis of a colossal reputation. Nevertheless, if

3. Wellington was well aware of the weakness of his position along the Boialvo road and the Caramulo Pass. As early as September 19, he issued instructions for Colonel Trant "to proceed as expeditiously as possible to Agueda and Sardão. . . . When at Sardão he will be on the left flank of the army, and will cover the road over the Serra leading towards Oporto." *Wellington's Dispatches,* Bathhurst to Beresford, September 19, 1810, VI, 455. Trant was delayed by his commanding officer, Bacelar, and did not reach Sardão on the road to Boialvo until the afternoon of September 28 with 1,500 militia. See Charles William Vane, Marquess of Londonderry, *Narrative of the Peninsular War from 1808 to 1813* (3rd ed., London, 1829), II, 302–11. For details, see Horward, *Battle of Bussaco,* pp. 136–38.

the English army had been effectively attacked according to one of the proposed systems in oblique order and by *tuyaux d'orgue* [formed like organ tubes] on five points of their position, and if the fronts of our columns had been united by small attacks on their whole line, the enemy would not have been able to throw their entire force on two isolated points and envelop them. Even if the English General had immediately guessed our movements and distinguished the true worth of those various attacks, his troops would still have believed they were attacked along their entire front in a position which was represented to them as unassailable. Perhaps in the future they would have watched the rear with some anxiety. Therefore it seemed that only fate presided over Wellington's movements, or that he sought a sham battle at Bussaco, or finally, as it was said, that he only wanted time to embark his baggage and place a large flotilla at Figueira.[4] Yet, if this was the case, he had been warned of our movements since the arrival of Marshal Ney at Celorico on the 16th.

Justice imperiously demands that, from my own impressions, I give some counterbalance to what I have just written. Masséna also made mistakes, but according to Turenne, a good judge in this matter, in war the one who makes the fewest is the best general. Our Prince knew his commanders well and had already learned at his own expense what could be expected from them, and that it was necessary to force them to win when it was to his benefit. Hence he should have left to them nothing concerning the fate of the battle. He should have maneuvered the army himself, directing their divisions instead

4. Wellington's decision to fight at Bussaco has been questioned for 150 years. Several eyewitnesses suggested that his reason might have been to gain time to destroy his magazines and prevent their falling into French hands. See Noel, *Souvenirs,* p. 119; and Silvestre, "Diary," in Chambers, *Bussaco,* p. 154. Another participant declared that the battle was fought for political considerations, especially for its influence on the English and Portuguese governments. See Wm. Napier, *War in the Peninsula,* II, 397–99. A nineteenth-century historian suggested that his purpose was to nerve the troops for the defense of the Lines at Torres Vedras. See Louis Adolphe Thiers, *History of the Consulate and the Empire of France under Napoleon,* trans. D. F. Campbell and J. Stebbing (London, 1894), VII, 217. Charles Oman implied the battle was fought to delay the French advance. See his *History of the Peninsular War* (Oxford, 1902–30), III, 394–96. All these interpretations and assertions certainly have some validity; however, they can only cast doubt on the abilities of Wellington. There can be no question whatsoever that Wellington fought at Bussaco to turn back Masséna. His dispatch clearly indicated this, but writers have refused to take him at his word. As early as September 24, he confidently wrote, "I shall do everything in my power to stop the enemy here." *Wellington's Dispatches,* Wellington to Stuart, September 24, 1810, VI, 466–67.

of relying on written general orders. In this intermediate role, he first placed confidence in his commanders that was close to presumption and then condescension that almost resembled weakness. Once he saw their dangerous intentions completely unmasked, he should have rectified the dispositions taken, and done this himself instead of sending officers who were ignored.

At eight o'clock in the morning, there was still time to assume, under his command, one fresh attack based on an entirely different system or on some broad and clever maneuvers. Then what would the two armies have said if they had seen the Masséna of Zurich and Genoa leaving a rear guard on that famous defile [beyond Moura], broken sharply by an entrenchment, and the length of his line covered with skirmishers. After first extending himself slowly toward the left, with his troops descending to the bottom of the valleys and behind the abutments, he would finally have exposed this maneuver proudly, a masterpiece of strategy and boldness. Reaching the dismantled position of Ponte de Murcella with flags unfurled, he would have advanced toward Tomar or Pombal. If the baggage prevented him from trying this excellent movement, why did he not make it during the first night? It is true that he would have had to employ all his spirit to arouse that rather dilapidated machine and all his old activity to conduct such a very difficult maneuver. It must be admitted that the Prince had reached a point [of laxity], a frequent peril of human greatness, as a result of the excessive good fortune which seemed to intoxicate wisdom, experience, genius, and all the moral strength of men. Victory and fortune had spoiled its *enfant chéri*. Successful, victorious, and accustomed to regard as easy and ordinary those things that others judged impossible, Masséna, it seemed, had only to present himself to obtain them by a single glance. Great difficulties and impossible obstacles were required to arouse him. But then what a man! Who would not have been discouraged at the sight of the problems up to this point [September 27, 1810] which could have been predicted but were now surrounding him. The commanders loudly demanded that the expedition be abandoned, pretending they were too weak; they showed their ill will, which had just become evident in their maneuvers. With an inferior army whose ardor and confidence were influenced by the commanders, in extremely difficult country, without roads, surrounded on all sides by mountains and the most complete devastation, and suffering every deficiency, Masséna faced a superior army shouting victory, an armed population, and vast deserts around him without a single inhabitant nor a kernel of wheat. As for any prospect of retreat, Spain was on fire and rebelling in the areas we had just left. As for any hope of assistance, a few vain promises had been given from far away by suspicious men in whom the Prince had never placed complete confidence. None of this could touch his great soul. Only Masséna could order the march forward. If there were a few faint shadows around this giant of glory, he can be recognized by these great traits.

I am pleased to render justice to the conduct of the two armies in the action; ours showed itself worthy of what it was, but also worthy of doing better. The English army acquired merit by resisting our attacks. I would like to believe the enemy had no need to be protected by those insurmountable barriers. The Portuguese established their reputation there and learned they were a force to be reckoned with in the military system of Europe. I do not have any further comparison to make between the two armies. They have been judged by the acclamations of "Bussaco."

The army approached the Mondego. We followed the 8th Corps on to Mealhada through Avelãs de Caminho; it went as far as Carqueijo. The front of the 6th Corps, already as far as Formaliçao, stopped to wait for its artillery instead of going to Mealhada as it had been ordered. The 2nd Corps, instructed to occupy Pedreiras, was forced to stop for the same reason at the foot of the mountains. We first crossed a beautiful country of well-cultivated slopes interspersed with woods, and soon after this a beautiful plain covered with oranges and citrus fruit, laurels, and olive trees; it was a beautiful garden as far as Coimbra. We looked with suspicion at the position of Bussaco, which appeared to be as sharp as the blade of a knife. Two days earlier the Portuguese were telling us that it had a magnificent plateau for cavalry, and this was the information we were given. The crest, so sharp from north to south and so inclined toward the east, was more accessible from the west.[5] Before Mealhada we saw the camp of Vacariça, where the enemy had gathered the previous day. We had little information concerning their movements. They were said to be at Fornos, displaying only four or five regiments of English cavalry.

5. The plateau atop Bussaco varied from 300 to 500 yards in width.

The advance guard was ordered to get news of the enemy and push them on Coimbra. The Duc sent Sainte-Croix with an infantry brigade. We heard the cannon before Carqueijo. The Prince went forward, and we entered Fornos as the English were being driven out. We arrived near the village of Pedrulla [?]. The enemy had fourteen squadrons on the plain. The Duc had set up only a weak position on the right against them; it was necessary to reinforce them on our left. The Prince sent me ahead into the village. I found seven or eight hussars waiting in ambush there. We fired point-blank with our pistols and they fled. I reconnoitered the point of attack. I gave directions to the pickets and then to Taupin's brigade; the dragoons were vigorously pushing on the plain. Montbrun was there with two of his regiments and those of Sainte-Croix.[6] They paused for a short time on the banks of the Mondego and then went forward. We reached the river and Coimbra without realizing it. We kept on going.

Near the city I found an English officer who announced that our wounded, who had been captured and carried from Bussaco, had declared themselves prisoners in Coimbra; if [their status was] not [acceptable to us], the enemy would defend the passage of the bridge. But the enemy were also leaving their wounded in our power, which counterbalanced the advantage. This proposition was accepted so as not to endanger the fate of the city by fighting in the streets for so few men. In a conciliatory gesture, I went and relieved the post with the English officer. Everybody wanted to enter the city in spite of the Prince's orders. General Pamplona, named governor of Coimbra, stopped them, but some entered through the breaches in the surrounding walls. Three or four of us advanced. There were still a few English in the city and they were taken. I tried to prevent this since I considered myself a parliamentarian with the officer. We found Coimbra in frightful abandonment—not a soul was there and all the houses were closed. It had the solitude of a tomb. The posts were relieved. With the English officer I set up lodgings for the Prince at the bishop's palace. No

6. Sainte-Croix encountered Allied troops composed of the 1st Hussars of the King's German Legion and the 16th Light Dragoons under Captains Georg Krauchenberg and C. Somers Cocks. Unable to halt the French advance, General Stapleton Cotton brought up three more cavalry brigades and Captain Robert Bull's horse artillery. Masséna took charge of the operation and drove in the English center, forcing Cotton's men toward the walls of Coimbra. See Koch, *Mémoires de Masséna,* VII, 205–6; Tomkinson, *Diary,* pp. 45–46.

one was in the palace to open the doors. Therefore it was necessary to break them down. Soon my dragoons found Madeira wine. We established ourselves in his grace's library and we drank his wine—Captain Henry Mellish, Octave de Ségur, and myself. The captain, as Lord Wellington's first attaché, was an adjutant general.[7] He was as pleasant as an Englishman could be to us. We spoke for a long time about many things; both of us courteously, in a good patriotic way. He was telling me that they would fight, they would wait for us, they knew our situation as well as we did, they knew of our movements on the right bank of the Mondego two days before their execution, and they had seen and followed our movements on their left at Bussaco. He said we had attacked poorly. I agreed with that, and I gave as a reason our ignorance of the locality. There was much discretion and modesty in our talks. Lord Wellington could only improve his reputation in this war, whatever the outcome might be. The defense would be long and skillfully planned. Debating this point, he asked about another officer who was a prisoner. I sent for him; it was Lord Percy.[8] We drank to another meeting, to an early battle—it would be better than the last; they could have attempted it in front of Coimbra. Many compliments were made about the Prince, and many respects were paid to the great nation, noble loyalty, and admiration was expressed on both sides. Meanwhile I attacked their system of war, which could not be well defended.

I returned rather late to Fornos to see the Prince, together with Count Oudinot, but not without glancing at the beautiful museum of natural history and the department of physics of the famous university, as well as the observatory and the library, those sanctuaries of science and the arts; my love of this had never abandoned me, even in the midst of war.

7. Lieutenant Colonel Henry Francis Mellish (1780–1817) was attached to the Light Division during the retreat to the lines. He was described as an "all-around sportsman and many-sided gentleman, who was scholar, soldier, and lover of every manly pastime in one." Mellish was a born gambler who "loved anything on which he could back his fancy." Even in the Peninsula "his passion for gambling could not be restrained," and Wellington was obliged to send him home "lest he demoralize everybody else." See Joseph Smith Fletcher, *The History of the St. Leger Stakes, 1776–1901* (London, 1902), pp. 117, 180–188.

8. Captain H. Percy was captured at Celorico and Wellington corresponded with Masséna about providing him with money and personal belongings. Percy served as Wellington's aide-de-camp during the Belgian campaign and carried the Water-

Captain Mellish did not give me a single clue to their system of operation nor let me know how much they were relying on their entrenched positions.[9] It seemed that I had been talking only about a truly skillful war of maneuvers and positions. Yet all my ideas remained fixed on the system of operations which could have been established on both sides of the Tagus and the terrain situated beyond Tomar and Leiria, between that river and the sea, which I have referred to as the pocket of the Tagus because of its elongated form. I did not have the pleasure of seeing Mellish again, but he came to the advance post and always left a message of goodwill for me.

The Prince did not enter Coimbra until the next day. The measures he had prescribed for the protection of the city were not completely executed. Guards had been set up at the gates but the walls were ruined. The soldiers of all the army corps were able to enter through the walls and the posts became useless. Moreover, these very measures had been thwarted by those who were supposed to be executing them. The day before our entry, the enemy had begun regularized pillage. The Prince's indignation was fully aroused when he saw this celebrated city completely ruined. The day before, the solitude had appeared terrifying to me, but the next day I was astonished to see the city filled with drunken men and plunderers. Houses were broken into, shops upset, nothing was left untouched.[10] A great quantity of food was lost in the streets among the furniture, clothing, candles, jams, and quantities of various commodities. In the streets we noticed magnificently bound books, sumptuous editions from all countries, beautiful and rare pictures, desks of Japanese lacquer, and rare objects from China. There were bivouacs in the streets and squares, surrounded by

loo Dispatch to England. See *Wellington's Dispatches,* Wellington to Masséna, September 17, 1810, VI, 449–50.

9. Pelet expands this observation with a footnote on the Lines of Torres Vedras: "I found no mention of this in my Journal before October 7 or 9 at Rio Maior, and I would certainly not have neglected to mention such an important discovery sooner since I never omitted less important ones. Moreover, I recall well that we did not have any knowledge of it until the last moment." See p. 222 below. This refutes Oman's statement that Pelet claimed knowledge of the Lines on October 5. See Oman, *Peninsular War,* III, 406n.

10. Captain Noel of the 8th Corps recorded, "With my own eyes, I have seen officers of the *état major,* hatchet in hand, break in the doors of shops, then place a sentry there to enable them to pillage at their leisure. What a sad example for the soldier! How can we be respected? . . . I regret to say that General Junot, whose corps first entered Coimbra, did nothing to hinder them." See Noel, *Souvenirs,* pp. 121–22.

many precious objects, lost and wasted, and there were frequent fires endangering the city with acute disaster. A few bodies of people who had been killed according to military justice when the enemy troops left could also be seen. The sight of the first inhabitants eager to return, hoping to reenter and save their fortunes, added to the grief because of their quiet sorrow and dejection. How horrible war is, when it is shown without the varnish of glory and generosity which hides its awful truth. But how could we have prevented these misfortunes in a city open on all sides and entirely deserted? Divided by the Mondego, it had to be occupied by our troops since the whole army could not cross the river immediately. Here many of the horrors must be blamed on those who had forced the entire population to desert their homes rather than on men who were driven by hunger and searching for something to appease it in those abandoned homes. For the most part these men had allowed themselves to become drunk, and as a result they had caused some troubles.[11]

The Prince received the Duc d'Abrantès coldly. Shortly after receiving reports of what had happened, he wrote a thundering letter ordering him to move immediately to Cernache.[12] Meanwhile orders were given quickly. The city was cleared and numerous posts were established. Frequent patrols passed through the streets. The plunderers disappeared before them, only to hide themselves in the cellars of houses that were not military lodgings and there carry on their ravages. The soldiers were detained in their camps, but how could one contain the vile horde of domestics who followed the army—the *cantinières*, sutlers, and laborers? How could we punish them by death when, after all, they were only finishing the devastation of the enemy.

But in the middle of all these excesses, we nevertheless saw a few sparks of virtue that were resplendent. Many officers watched night

11. Taupin's brigade of Junot's corps reached the city first and began indiscriminate pillaging. There were large magazines of rice, wheat, biscuit, green vegetables, coffee, tea, chocolate, etc., in the city but much of it was wasted. The quartermaster general and his officers complained to Junot, who frivolously responded that it was improper to employ such a small detachment to maintain order; yet he did nothing to halt the disorder. See Delagrave, *Mémoires,* p. 90 and note; Guingret, *Relation historique,* p. 83.

12. Masséna reprimanded Junot in a letter dated October 2, 1810: "I am discontented with the conduct of the 8th Corps and I may be forced to replace it in the battle order. . . . I am commander of the Army of Portugal and I have the power to send back to France those who fail in their duty." See Correspondance: Armée de Portugal, Carton C^{7}10.

and day to prevent disorders; second lieutenants and even soldiers themselves strongly opposed any disorder. A fire began in the midst of pillaging, but help was brought. The very men who had dishonored themselves by their rapine came and threw themselves into the thick of the flames as if to purify themselves.[13] All of them shared their bounty with the sick and wounded, even those of the enemy. The places where we found some miserable abandoned old men were taken care of, and the hospitals were entirely respected. A little later some domestics exposed themselves to expected dangers so their wounded masters would not be abandoned. We found a band of health officers and employees who had decided to remain in the military hospital that had been established. The surgeon of the 2nd Léger had showed them a noble example in refusing to leave his colonel, Merle, who had been seriously wounded. This benevolence could be found in the French army better than in any other, and those subjected to the misfortunes of war received heroic and touching treatment and kind compensation from them, while one would search vainly for it in the cold character of soldiers of northern nations or in the exalted passion of the men of the south. If the Frenchman was sometimes undisciplined, he never lacked generosity.

Coimbra was a very pleasant city. In population, size, and renown, it was the third city of Portugal. It was situated on the slopes of beautiful hills covered with vineyards and olive trees. The houses were white, surrounded by beautiful convents that seemed to sparkle amidst the trees that kept their shining greenness forever. On the tops of the various hills we could see the cathedral, the buildings of the university and its observatory, and the convent of Santa Cruz with one of the most beautiful gardens in the world; these surroundings formed delightful sights and the most beautiful scenery. The interior of the city was rather agreeable. Mme du Châtelet [Voltaire's confidant] spoke with much severity of its university and the observatory, but to me the university appeared worthy of praise because of the articles and the order found there.

13. Captain Lemonnier-Delafosse described this fire, which threatened to engulf the entire city. The 31st Léger was sent to fight the blaze and prevent it from spreading. The troops entered the houses and carried the furniture out into the street where they stacked it; hence "each street of this neighborhood resembled an auction sale." See his *Souvenirs*, pp. 79–80.

Coimbra and Santarém claimed to have been the cradle of Camoens, who lived in poverty and unhappiness like Homer.[14] The areas that had refused to help the illustrious poet were now fighting for the honor of having given him birth—sad consolation for merits usually unrecognized and often persecuted until they are avenged by posterity. We were shown the house where Inés de Castro lived, the stream by which she sent notes to her unfortunate spouse, and the fountain where she came to weep; it was still called the "fountain of tears."[15] We could not keep from shedding tears at the scene of that tragic love, praised in the languages of Europe; but the memories that Don Pedro I left in the hearts of the people were even more touching than his fame as the new Titus: he said that "A king who allows one day to pass without doing good does not deserve the title of king." And what was even better, he always justified those beautiful words by his conduct.

The hills that surround Coimbra were joined to the mountains of Bussaco and Murcella. In their midst ran the Mondego, which divided the city into two unequal parts, the larger on the right bank. The opposite bank was higher and appeared easily defended without the neighboring homes. Above the city was a vast and very fertile plain, cultivated in wheat and corn, through which the Mondego ran before going straight south. This torrential river had then only a few streamlets of water scattered in the middle of its sandy bed, which was 240 to 260 yards wide. However, everything indicated that it often filled the whole bed and became a formidable barrier. Flat boats served as the ordinary communication by means of a small channel between Coimbra and Figueira, a port situated at the mouth of the Mondego and the usual station for a flotilla. There the English had embarked their supplies, along with many of the principal inhabitants and their wealth. We were told that the embarkation had been performed so quickly that some thirty Portuguese, the richest of Coimbra, had drowned there.

14. Luís de Camoens (1524–80) was a Portuguese poet and the greatest figure in Portuguese literature. He wrote the *Lusiads,* an epic poem concerning the history of Portugal and its people.

15. Inés de Castro (d. 1355) was a Galician lady-in-waiting who fell passionately in love with Pedro I of Portugal. Although she was banished by Pedro's father, Alfonso IV, their love continued. The king had Inés murdered, but when Pedro ascended the throne he avenged her death. Pedro I was reputed to have reorganized the legal structure of Portugal.

The Prince busied himself with a number of measures to maintain order and police Coimbra. A governor had been named. The Prince established some provisional authorities from among the first individuals who had reentered the city. They were soon followed by a large number of inhabitants who had been outraged by the rigorous orders of the English and Portuguese generals, whose proclamations were still hanging on the walls, and frightened into hiding by the death penalty with which they had been threatened. They were hiding not so much because of our approach as because of these persecutions. In the streets we found a few bodies of people who were said to have been killed by military order before the departure of the troops. Most of the Portuguese complained bitterly about this loathsome tyranny and about having been chased from their homes. Actually, with the exception of the homes already plundered or evacuated in advance, everything was still in order and seemed to have been abandoned only a moment earlier. The authorities had not taken any measures to protect the hospitals; the aged invalids and some old nuns were dying of hunger. The authorities had destroyed very little except what was found in the public magazines or the principal depots. We could have collected a considerable quantity of food had it not been for the pillaging and devastation that took place. Nevertheless, a few magazines were formed. We organized a hospital for our sick and those who had been wounded in the previous battle. They were put under the protection of the entire city, which was held responsible for them in a proclamation written in Portuguese and widely published—it was quite unlike those that had been left by the English. The decree urged the inhabitants to remain peaceful and quiet, to return to their homes, and not to become involved in a foreign war. In addition the Prince took hostages among the more important people, who were to answer more particularly for those whom we left among their compatriots.

Everything seemed to indicate that the English were going to embark at Lisbon, since a group had already done so at Figueira. We were even told they had held the position at Bussaco only to cover their final embarkation. All the reports, from the Portuguese as well as from our own people, repeated the same assertion, and the most important inhabitants of Coimbra confirmed it by their remarks and their eagerness to reenter the city. Accustomed to being themselves deceived or sacrificed, the inhabitants did not believe what had been said about their defense before Lisbon, since the English had just lied to them by announcing a complete victory at Bussaco. Thus, without sharing this general opinion, and only according the same respect to the enemy that they had shown us, it was certainly possible—in our ignorance of their preparations and Lines—to believe that the fate of Portugal was to be decided by a new battle between Coimbra and Lisbon. According to what we had been told, we could not doubt our success on open terrain. If the enemy were beaten, we could be in Lisbon within eight days. If the battle was indecisive or a complete defeat for us, our army could retire to Coimbra in the same length of time and establish itself on the Mondego. Thus, either by the success of an important conquest or by the fear of our arms, inspired by our return, we knew we could rely on the faithfulness of the city of Coimbra for a few days.

It was on such calculations that the Prince, forced to leave the wounded and sick whom he was unable to transport with him, decided on the following arrangements. The city was entirely open and hardly adequate for entrenchments. Therefore a brigade was needed to guard it even though the soldiers would have trouble maintaining all the posts. There were many disadvantages in reducing our army, already limited in size, at the very time that we expected to encounter the enemy. We decided it would be best to place the hospital in one or two of the large convents that were close enough together to be entrenched and capable of making a good post, and to collect there the provisions necessary in case they were surrounded by enemy militia. We would also leave a detachment in garrison there, strong enough to defend the gates against the peasants and form its own police guard. This unit was fixed at one hundred men. Every engineer officer and all the companies of sappers were employed in putting this position in a state of defense. The convent of Santa Clara and a neighboring convent, advantageously situated on the left bank of the Mondego, were chosen since they were closer to the army and the units we proposed to place between them and the army. Only the sick and wounded who could not follow us were left, along with the officers whose condition did not permit movement. These arrangements taken for the defense of the hospitals were not concealed from the army. As a result the seriously wounded officers were carried behind the regiments; among them was Colonel Merle, who died, carried by his soldiers behind the 2nd Léger. I pointed out the weaknesses in the hospital defenses to all those who talked to me, and the commanders of the army corps were warned. Thus the number of wounded was reduced remarkably. I dare to state, after the calculation established above [Chapter 5], that the losses did not go beyond fourteen to fifteen hundred men, not counting the lightly wounded who followed the army along with the crippled and their attendants. The very large number of five thousand mentioned in the English newspapers, according to the reports of Colonel Trant, should be greatly reduced, for such a number of casualties would be appropriate only in an army of eighty to one hundred thousand Frenchmen.[16]

All kinds of falsifications were included in the official Portuguese reports. It was said that we had already lost forty thousand men during the month of January. In that case our losses would have exceeded our strength. I am now looking at part of this report.[17] Colonel Trant had considerable difficulty attacking these unfortunate wounded in the hospital, who, according to what he said, killed several of his men and wounded twenty-five, including the colonel of the regiment of Penafiel. He was only able to capture the hospitals with the help of a capitulation. Therefore the preparations had been satisfactory, since these hospitals were defended vigorously against a whole corps of militia. The French surrendered only after negotiating modifications in the terms of capitulation and the various rights of war and people, without consideration for the respect that all brave men feel toward honor-

16. In the hospitals of Coimbra Masséna left 3,506 wounded and sick with a guard of 146 men of the 44th Marine Flotilla and 1 doctor, 28 surgeons, 9 pharmacists, 20 hospital aides, and 3 commissariat administrators. See "État sommaire des blessés et malades laissés à l'hospital de Coïmbre," certified by Fririon, in Koch, *Mémoires de Masséna,* VII, 585.

17. In the following sentences Pelet is referring to the capture of the French hospitals of Santa Clara and Santo António by Colonel Trant with 4,000 militia on October 7. Although the militia units of Miller and Wilson were also nearing Coimbra, Trant resolved to attack the hospitals at once. The French garrison and some 200 infirm soldiers barricaded Santa Clara and put up a determined resistance. The French finally surrendered after inflicting some 30 casualties on Trant's men; despite Trant's promise of protection, more than 10 Frenchmen were massacred. See Wm. Napier, *War in the Peninsula,* II, 414; Luz Soriano, *Guerra civil,* Trant to Beresford, October, 1810, V, 219–22. Trant collected his prisoners, supplemented by the 300 stragglers gathered by Miller and Wilson, and marched toward Oporto. Despite their wounds, Trant marched the prisoners 64 miles in 4 days. For details see Horward, "Invasion of Portugal," pp. 379–81.

able unfortunates, and for our conduct toward their wounded compatriots remaining at Coimbra. The Englishman, Trant, abused the prisoners. The most horribly wounded were grossly insulted by being made to serve in some kind of victory celebration, as atrocious as it was ridiculous, that he wanted to give himself on entering Oporto. He all but gathered up the sad fragments of our dead on the field of battle and put them under the eyes of the ferocious scoundrels of that city.

These were the only trophies the English obtained in this campaign and they were praised highly. The hospitals were the subject of violent reproaches with which everyone later overwhelmed the Prince d'Essling. I will not go into anything to justify his arrangements and I do not have the slightest merit to remark on this presumed mistake, but how abandoned were these wounded if they were able to defend themselves for some time? Was the Prince responsible if the enemy violated what is most sacred among men, that is, the law of hostages, of capitulation, and finally of humanity?[18] What army has ever interrupted the course of its success to guard its wounded and, by dividing, exposed itself to be beaten in detail? Could we guess what was going on at Lisbon? If we had left a brigade at Coimbra, it would have been swiftly surrounded by the corps of Miller, Wilson, and Silveira, who entered Coimbra the next day. It would have been besieged and starved or, if able to escape, would have definitely abandoned the unfortunate wounded. Then the Prince exposed himself to another mistake, but in this error he honored himself. Near Molianos he received news from Coimbra which included a report on the excellent conduct of the inhabitants who were returning in throngs; in fact, a

18. Napoleon was indeed concerned about Masséna's loss of the hospital at Coimbra. He said to Foy, "For an army to lose a hospital is like losing a flag. I have never lost a hospital in war." See Girod de l'Ain, *Foy*, Foy to Masséna, December 4, 1810, pp. 347–50. Oman condemned Masséna for leaving his hospital at Coimbra; however, in a footnote, he mentioned Wellington's abandonment of 371 Allied soldiers when the French entered Coimbra. Indeed, there was less reason for Wellington to abandon his wounded than Masséna. Masséna was in a belligerent country, 135 miles from his base of operation, lacking sufficient supplies, without means of transportation, and commanding only the territory occupied by his troops; nevertheless, he did leave a small garrison to protect his hospitals. On the contrary, Wellington, in an ally's country, was less than 125 miles from his fortified position by good roads, had ample supplies and transportation, and was supported by the entire population; yet he decided to desert his wounded although he knew quite well they would certainly fall into French hands. Hence Oman's criticism seems biased and unfounded. See Oman, *Peninsular War,* III, 407–8, 412n.

deputation of provisional authorities came to renew their pledges and ask for the return of hostages. The Prince generously took them at their word and, faithful to his system of mitigating the severity of the war, returned the hostages. At the same time the ferocious peasants of Trás os Montes, led by a foreign soldier, were unwilling to respect the pledge of those hostages and the promise made by the inhabitants of Coimbra. We did not think of taking vengeance on this type of treachery, but it is difficult to attribute the deplorable consequences to us.

Another unfortunate victim of this atrocious system of war departed from Coimbra. The Prince wanted to send an officer to Paris. A Portuguese captain, Mascarenhas, presented himself for the mission; he had great devotion and a desire to distinguish himself. He had ability and wished to take charge of this honorable but perilous mission. The captain wanted to disguise himself in order to slip easily through the mountains to reach Almeida. Unfortunately, he was notably tall and had a face that was easy to recognize. He imprudently showed himself in the streets of Coimbra in his disguise. This was enough, and he was certainly sold out. Not long after being arrested, he was ruthlessly hanged as a traitor. Who was guilty of treason in this struggle in which the English and the French wanted to subjugate Portugal? Who could decide which side had committed treason in the absence of the old government, and, amidst the confusion of the parties committed to both of the two foreign nations, each in turn enemies of the prince regent and masters of the country? There was no one among the British noble enough to take up the defense of Mascarenhas![19] They sacrificed him not long after our generosity prevented the death of the curé of Rodrigo and many of the other victims; it saved that entire city, taken by

19. In fact, Wellington sharply disagreed with the Portuguese government's treatment of Mascarenhas. After a visit from Mme Mascarenhas and her daughter, he complained bitterly to Charles Stuart, a member of the Governors of the Kingdom: "Although I told them that I could not interfere in any concern of the kind, I cannot resist stating to you my sense of the injustice which the Portuguese Government are about to commit. In the first place, I cannot get over my sense of the right which every subject of Portugal had to take which line he pleased, under the proclamation of the Prince Regent when he withdrew from Portugal. In the next place, I must observe that, under the 18th article of the Convention [of Sintra], the safety of the persons who served the French is guaranteed to them. . . . I cannot but think that the Government will be guilty of a gross injustice and murder if they put this young man to death, upon the ground of his having served the French." See *Wellington's Dispatches*, Wellington to Stuart, February 14, 1811, VII, 260–62.

assault, from the sword. The garrison of Almeida was given its liberty, and we sought everywhere to reduce the horrors of war.

I had given the unfortunate young man a note for my poor mother, together with a wrapped pastille of Seraglio, innocent booty found by someone else in the streets of Coimbra. Why should I hesitate to mention your name, Mother, in these personal memoirs when I find your name constantly in my Journal! Deceived by my pious strategy, you still thought that I was safe in Paris for a while, but soon you will be trembling at the exaggerated dangers of those who are in Spain. Now I am happy to relieve you of any such sorrow. The only one I have to reproach is myself. I am happy to be able to thank you, in your humble home and honorable poverty, for those days that belonged to us twofold—by the continuous care for your only child and by the great love you shared all your life with my father, the best of men, and myself! At last I am pleased to be able to devote myself entirely to these pleasant tasks—to the memories of our glorious works, and also to my mother.

Meanwhile Lord Wellington wrote a seven- or eight-page letter to the Prince dated September 24. It was well written and honored both of them. "It is necessary," he said, "that I take with me those I am unable to defend. How could you, who have increased the glory of the French armies with soldiers who were for a time without uniforms, treat the militia with severity? I am very sorry for you personally because of the trouble that has resulted from the ruin of this country, but I cannot save it in any other way."[20] It was said that Lord Wellington was a very brave man and very loyal personally, but British politics!

I was extremely busy during our stay at Coimbra, even more so than during the marches. It was necessary to make reports to Paris, orders, and those eternal maps based on the intelligence reports. The enemy army was withdrawing in three principal directions. The right flank crossed the Mondego in the direction of the mouth of the Alva and then moved toward Ponte de Murcella and on to Tomar. The center

20. Wellington wrote, "It appears that you demand that those who enjoy the rights of war must wear uniforms but if you remember, you have added to the glory of the French army in commanding troops that did not have uniforms. . . . The question is only if a nation which is invaded by a formidable enemy has the right to defend itself by all the means within its power. If this right exists, Portugal is justified in activating the *ordenanza.*" *Wellington's Dispatches,* Wellington to Masséna, September 24, 1810, VI, 464–65.

retired through Coimbra on the road to Pombal. Finally, one large detachment with the cavalry passed through Figueira. Did this corps embark or go toward Leiria? We were still ignorant about this. The Prince decided to follow immediately in the direction of Lisbon while reconnoitering his flanks. As a matter of fact, the 8th Corps had been moved to Condeixa from the outset, the 6th Corps was a little to the rear on the road from Cernache [?], the 2nd Corps was at Venda do Cago, the *grand parc* was completely dissolved and distributed, along with the equipment, among the army corps.

The arrangements for the defense and administration of Coimbra took three full days, and it was on the fourth that we were able to leave the city. With a lump in our throats, we passed under the walls of Santa Clara [after] cross[ing] the beautiful bridge on the Mondego. Beyond there was a slope with olive trees, rocks of slate, undulating country, and beautiful views of Coimbra, followed by Venda do Cago, a tavern, Cernache, a hamlet, and Condeixa, a large and beautiful village with many country houses. Beyond, as far as Redinha, we traveled three short leagues rather quickly. The region became ugly. There were forests of oak or pine interspersed with a few areas of cultivated ground and several large ravines that presented good positions for the two armies. The site at Redinha was very good for defense. Redinha was a large village on the left bank of a stream surrounded by ravines. In the evening there was a superb illumination from the fires of the 6th Corps. We had found the debris of enemy wagons, a few stragglers, and a large number of dead horses. An advance guard had been formed under the orders of General Montbrun with the brigades of Sainte-Croix's dragoons, Lamotte's[21] and Soult's light cavalry, and Taupin's infantry. It had followed the enemy on to Figueira and from there it swung around on Pombal. The 8th Corps was beyond Redinha, the 6th Corps behind it, and the 2nd Corps at Rabaçal, marching on our left along the old Lisbon road. The reserve cavalry, under the command of General Trelliard, was behind the 6th Corps.

21. Auguste Étienne Marie Gourlez Lamotte (1772–1836) enlisted in 1793 but was wounded and left the service in 1795. He returned to the army before the blockade of Gaeta and was promoted to general of brigade in 1809. He served at Novi in 1799, and between 1805 and 1808 he commanded a cavalry brigade in the Grand Army. Lamotte was sent to Spain in 1808 and he returned to the Peninsula attached to Junot's corps. He took command of Ney's cavalry before Almeida in 1810.

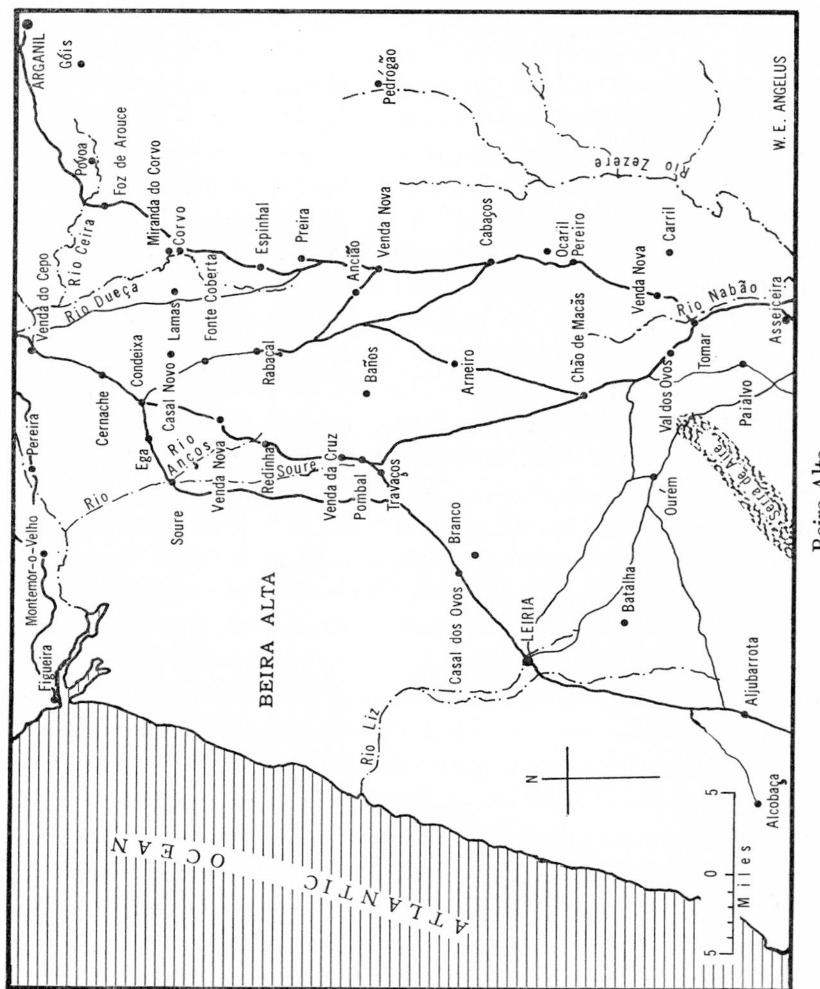
ARGANIL
Gôis
Pedrógão
Póvoa
Foz de Arouce
Miranda do Corvo
Rio Ceira
Corvo
Venda do Cepo
Rio Dueça
Espinhal
Preira
Ancião
Venda Nova
Cabaços
Ocaril
Pereiro
Rio Zezere
Carril
Venda Nova
Rio Nabão
Assejceira
Lamas
Fonte Coberta
Condeixa
Casal Novo
Rabaçal
Baños
Arneiro
Chão de Macãs
Tomar
Val dos Ovos
Paialvo
Pereira
Cernache
Ega
Rio Anços
Venda Nova
Redinha
Soure
Venda da Cruz
Pombal
Travaços
Montemor-o-Velho
Rio
Soure
Branco
Ourém
Serra de Aire
Figueira
BEIRA ALTA
Casal dos Ovos
LEIRIA
Batalha
Aljubarrota
Rio Liz
N
Alcobaça
5 0 5
Miles
ATLANTIC OCEAN
W. E. ANGELUS

Beira Alta

The advance guard at Leiria had taken or killed several of the enemy. An order was issued to reconnoiter in the direction of Tomar with the light cavalry. The 8th Corps marched beyond Pombal; the 6th Corps and the reserve were behind. The 2nd was at Arneiro, always on the left. The artillery was slightly delayed and would join us after a short march.

The headquarters were at Pombal, where there was a beautiful road with embankments at the low spots; it was rather broad and well kept at a few places but very sandy. The country was ugly as we left Pombal but it became more beautiful along the road as we approached the Soure. The positions were still against us. If the enemy wanted to hold behind this stream, they could extend on our right from Condeixa or on the left they could have a kind of mountain with protruding abutments. Pombal, two leagues from Redinha, was a rather pretty and well-built little city with decent houses. The English had plundered the city and grain had remained behind in the streets; they had abandoned the town to its inhabitants before forcing them to flee. Always the same reports; it was said the enemy were detested by the country and the army. The Portuguese soldiers threw away their powder and did not want to fight against us, but against the British. There was no news from the advance guard or the 2nd Corps. I visited the city with the veneration that a great name [Marquis de Pombal] always inspired.[22] We felt his presence everywhere although he was damned by everyone. Without the Marquis de Pombal, this town would be no more than a *bicoque*. Portugal was still unimportant, and he did not have a grave yet! Perhaps his ashes will not be respected! His lead bier, covered with black velvet, was still lying at the Capuchine convent. The town hall was not very large, but the buildings adorning Pombal were substantial.

We left early in the morning for Leiria. There was a beautiful road leaving Pombal with plateaus of olive trees and pines. Three leagues from Pombal were the Madalena River and a valley one hundred and

22. Sebastião José de Carvalho e Melo, Marquis de Pombal (1699–1782), was a Portuguese statesman during the reign of King José I. After serving in the diplomatic corps, he became secretary of state for foreign affairs and war in 1750. He dominated Portugal until Queen Maria assumed the throne in 1776 and exiled him to Pombal. He expelled the Jesuits; curtailed the power of the church and nobility; reorganized the educational, legal, and military systems of Portugal; and encouraged the development of industry, especially wine production.

twenty yards wide. The river ran at the foot of the southern slope; there a good rearguard position for us was within cannon-shot of the other slope. It was almost perpendicular to the road and defensible on three hills, with the right above a configuration and the left at a village. I had it drawn. Above Leiria was another rearguard position for us where the artillery could enfilade the road for a great distance, even on the flanks, and the reverse could be taken for an infantry position; nevertheless, it was not as good as the preceding one.

Leiria was a pretty town of three thousand souls in a kind of basin that was surrounded by green hills with churches and white convents at the tops. In Leiria all the houses, the same color, were grouped around hills of sharp rocks, covered with laurels and crowned by an old half-ruined Moresque castle. All this had a fine and delightful effect. But when we entered we found the houses deserted. One mansion was on fire; remains of dead horses and remnants of plunder were in the streets. We lodged in the highest part of the city at the bishop's palace. I worked to set up a miserable itinerary map. I talked with General Loison and then with the Prince about the positions of Montachique. The advance guard was at Molianos pushing some reconnaissances on Santarém and Obidos. The 8th Corps was in front of Leiria, the 6th Corps around it, and the 2nd Corps in the rear, with the reserve still farther behind. In the evening my friends and I climbed among the ruins to the Moorish castle, where we seemed to find remnants of all ages. We entered an abandoned chapel, formerly surrounded by a wide wall, which perhaps had been an ancient mosque. Among the debris of so many centuries and on those walls, already darkened by the shadows of night, a religious and dismal silence reigned. We had moral and melancholic reflections on time passing by and on the men and nations that appear and disappear so quickly. It was said that Sertorius founded Leiria. Before him the Greeks had come, the Carthaginians, and who else? After him came the Vandals from the north, then the Moors from the Orient; now here we were in this country that had influenced the two Indies with its exploits! What will be left of all of us soon, beyond the evil that we have prevented and the little good that we have been able to do?

We left early in the afternoon during a terrible rainstorm with the prospect of seeing it continue the entire day and even during bivouac and through the night. Because there was said to be only one house at Molianos [?], we passed by the superb monastery of Batalha on our left, built in memory of the victory of Aljubarrota over the Castilians on August 14, 1385.[23] We regretted very much not being able to gaze on this magnificent monument, whose superb drawings I had admired at Coimbra, now that such occasions had become rarer in the Peninsula, but the bad weather and my duties prevented me. We crossed a rather well-cultivated country. The banks of the Liz were very fertile and Leiria was found at the confluence of the Liz [and the Lena]. As we went farther away from the city, the country became more barren. Finally, we saw only mediocre plantations of olive trees and a range of mountains on the left. It was covered by clouds, rain, sleet, and wind that struck us cruelly in terrible gusts. As we traveled along the road, the Prince talked to me about the operations to be made. The small village of Venda do Carvalhos had a superb inn. I was very sorry we did not set up general headquarters there. Finally, one hour later, we arrived at Molianos, which was surrounded by olive trees. It was a miserable collection of miserable huts. I was delighted when I saw that there were several of them, and I took one of them for myself. My comrades, the Marbots, arrived and shared my hut. The two brothers, then *chefs d'escadron* and aides-de-camp to the Prince, were very good officers who had been attached in the same capacity to our most illustrious marshals, Masséna, Lannes, Bernadotte, Soult, and Davout. They were the sons of General Marbot, to whom the Prince was very attached.[24] The hut gave me more pleasure than the most magnificent

23. At the battle of Aljubarrota King João I of Portugal, supported by English archers, defeated an army of King Juan I of Castile, assuring Portuguese independence. The monastery of Batalha, one of the most imposing structures in western Europe and now the Portuguese tomb of the unknown soldier, was built by João in honor of Santa Maria da Victoria.

24. Jean Lannes, Duc de Montebello (1769–1809), entered the army in 1792 and within eight years was promoted to general of division. In 1804 he received his marshal's baton. Lannes served in both of Napoleon's Italian campaigns and the Egyptian campaign and commanded the 5th Corps of the Grand Army from 1805 to 1808. He defeated a Spanish army at Tudela in 1808 and captured Saragossa in the following year. In 1809 Lannes was recalled to take part in the Austrian campaign and he was killed in the battle of Essling.

Jean Baptiste Bernadotte, Prince de Ponte Corvo (1763–1844), enlisted in the army in 1780 and was promoted to general of division in 1794. He became minister of war in 1799 but resigned before the 18 Brumaire. Made a marshal in 1804, Bernadotte become the crown prince of Sweden six years later. He joined Russia and the sixth Coalition against France in 1812; thus he took part in the defeat of

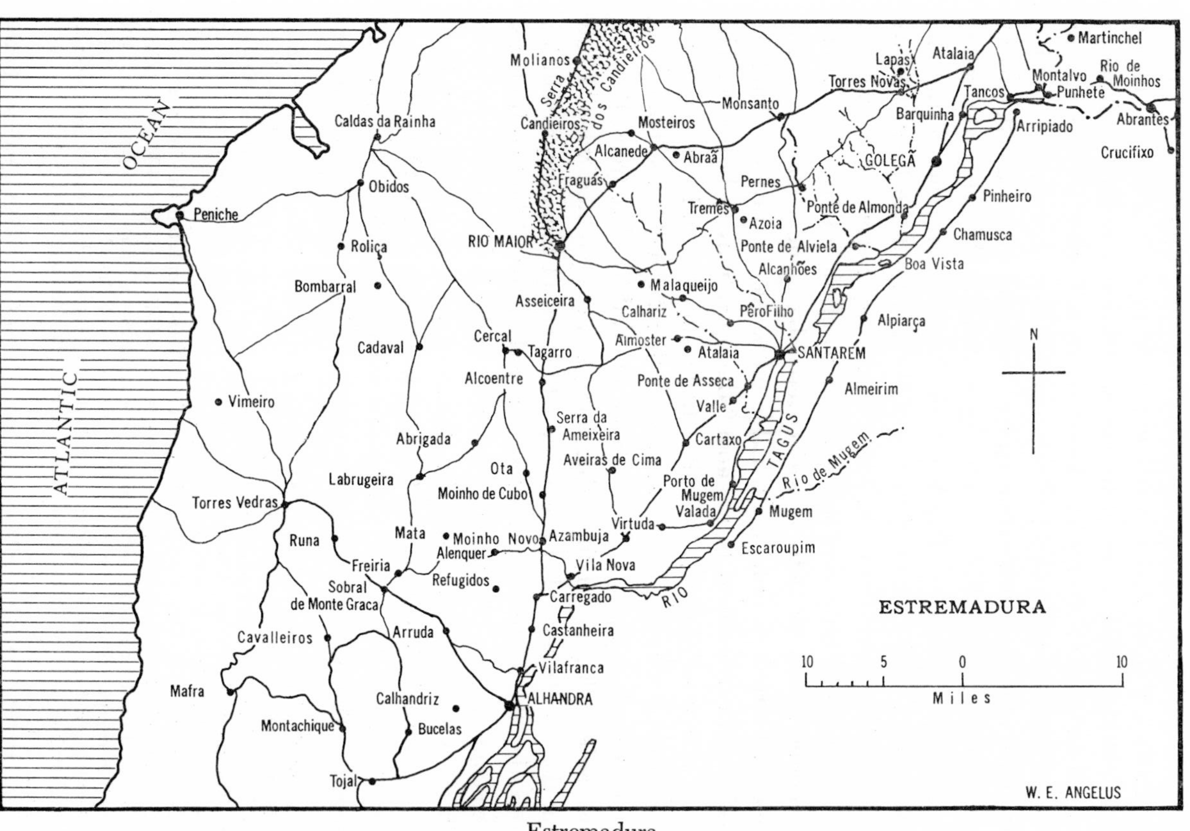

Estremadura

palace elsewhere. Some soldiers had already lit the fire. We found some hay and a few figs, but the frightful weather continued. The day was spent warming and smoke-drying ourselves in very thick smoke. Later on we told stories and debated. Discussions were of great help; without them we would have slept all the time. Finally we ate supper. Soon after, I lay down in the hay beside my horses, somewhat annoyed since I was far from my inseparable friends. The day had not been too disagreeable. The advance guard was at Rio Maior. Sainte-Croix had encountered the enemy and pursued them near Candieiros. Close to Alcoentre General Cotton had shown five regiments and six guns.[25] Sainte-Croix had maneuvered and the enemy withdrew, believing they faced the entire advance guard.[26] We could see the enemy infantry from a distance. The 8th Corps stopped near Candieiros, the 6th Corps was at Molianos, the 2nd Corps at Porto de Mós, and the reserve was in the rear on the main highway, which was still good despite the rain.

We left so early that it took me a while to join the Prince, who joked with me about my delay and then told me some stories about what his grandfather and grandmother had told him when he joined the army. "Go, you are good-for-nothing and lazy. You are only good enough to be a soldier. Get out of here." Then he talked of his disputes with

France. He served in the armies of the Republic and commanded the 1st Corps of the Grand Army from 1805 to 1808.

Louis Nicolas Davout, Duc d'Auerstadt, Prince d'Eckmühl (1770–1823), entered the army in 1785 and attended the École militaire. Promoted to general of brigade in 1794, he became a marshal of France in 1804. After serving with Dumouriez in Belgium, Davout was attached to the Army of the Moselle. He took part in the Egyptian campaign and commanded a corps of the Grand Army at Ulm, Austerlitz, Auerstadt, Eylau, and Friedland. In 1810 Davout was appointed commander of the Army of Germany.

Jean Antoine Marbot (1754–1800) enlisted in the king's guard in 1773 and became general of division in 1795. He served in Germany and Spain during the early campaigns of the Republic, represented Corrèze in the Council of Ancients, commanded a division of the Army of Italy, and died at the siege of Genoa.

25. Sir Stapleton Cotton, Viscount of Combermere (1773–1865), became a second lieutenant in the 23rd Royal Welsh Fusiliers. Fifteen years later he was promoted to major general; in 1812 he reached the rank of lieutenant general. He served at the Cape and in India between 1796 and 1799, and in 1808 he was dispatched to the Peninsula. He commanded the cavalry of the Allied army during the Oporto campaign, served at Talavera, and was active during Masséna's invasion.

26. Sainte-Croix surprised Bull's artillery battery at Alcoentre. However, Captain Cocks rallied the 16th Light Dragoons and seized the bridge into the village until the artillery could escape. Tomkinson of the 16th Light Division blamed General Stapleton Cotton for negligence in this affair. See Tomkinson, *Diary*, pp. 50–51.

Napoleon, "My sword is as good as yours; I can set myself on your right or your left"; about his stubbornness during Moreau's trial; and about the Life Consulate and the Empire.[27] During those latter events it had never been possible to obtain any action from him.

Each day the country was the same as the day before—pines, olive trees, windmills with eight sails, a rather flat plateau, and a good road without slopes or valleys. Candieiros was a miserable hamlet. We climbed slightly toward Alta Rio Maior and then descended rapidly through several turnabouts which, I believed, could have formed another position for us, but the descent would have needed examination. There was the sad sight of numerous inhabitants returning home, carrying children in their arms. They said there was an immense number, chased away by the English, on the banks of the Tagus between Azambuja and Vilafranca. It was said the enemy was entrenched at Alhandra and Bucelas. Generals Reynier and Foy had a map showing the area from Rio Maior to Lisbon; it was some kind of a drawing done quickly and based on good information, but the sketch was very poor. Richoux was with General Reynier copying it. Foy reminded me to remember that during the battle of Bussaco he had had two horses killed under him before being wounded himself.

Headquarters were established at Rio Maior, a small town where the enemy had some repair shops and magazines that had been destroyed or moved, although traces still remained; there were four thousand cartridges and some wood and iron. It was still raining, and I spent part of the day working. The advance guard was beyond Alcoentre occupying Santarém; it pushed a reconnaissance on Roliça, near Alenquer, and beyond Santarém. The 8th Corps was beyond Rio Maior, the 6th Corps around it, and the 2nd Corps behind it. Having been forced to take the Royal road, the reserve was three leagues in the rear. The 25th Dragoons were sent toward Peniche. General Lazowski went to reconnoiter the road to Ota and Bucelas, and the entrenched position near Alenquer. Colonel Jean Lecamus Camus, Baron de Moulignon, and *chef de bataillon* Nempde, with four companies of marines and one of pontoniers, went to Santarém; the former to gather the boats found on the Tagus and the latter to search for a

27. Masséna was a member of the Corps Législatif. In August 1802 he voted against the modification of the Constitution of the Year VIII which gave Napoleon the office of First Consul for life.

defensive position around the city. Both of them were to reconnoiter the Tagus for the establishment of a bridge.

The army marched for Alcoentre, only two leagues away. The country was mountainous and it seemed to me I could see two excellent rearguard positions for the enemy which must furnish us some defense as well. The 8th Corps marched on Moinho de Cubo, the 6th Corps was on the right of Alcoentre, and the 2nd Corps was to the left. It was still raining dreadfully and it increased twofold on the way. I was obliged to lodge in a great castle outside of town where several of my friends were. I established my quarters in a beautiful and well-selected library, but our soldiers and the enemy must have damaged it for there were some remains of vandalism. The sad remnants distressed me: Herculean paintings, pictures of Rome and Paris, botany, etc., and the *Encyclopédie* had been trampled on. I was some distance away from the house of the Prince, who summoned me continually. He had ordered a delay in order to unite the troops and their artillery.

Beaufort and Richoux had already copied General Reynier's maps. I took them to draw the mountains, which seemed to have been traced incorrectly. The Prince requested these maps repeatedly. At last I took them to him and he made his dispositions for the next day, although he had earlier attempted to extend our stay until the arrival of the intelligence he expected from Santarém and Alenquer. The day before, he had ordered an attack on Vilafranca, and he sent Cavailher there again to reconnoiter the entrenched positions. We occupied the town. General Montbrun moved on to Sobral, accompanied by Cavailher. General Lazowski sent only one kind of plan for Alenquer, having mistaken the city for the indicated position; he declared it of little value for defense. On that basis, the Prince sent the 8th Corps in front of Alenquer, the 6th Corps to Ota, the 2nd Corps toward Moinho de Cubo, the cavalry to Alcoentre, and the advance guard to regroup itself at Carregado. I went to the Marshal to talk about these dispositions and I told him to reconnoiter the roads to Ota. He engaged in conversation on this subject and on the army in general. This time he seemed to be seeing things in the proper light and agreed with our views about the Tagus. That evening he sent word that the roads were good, then the next day that they were bad. If this was true, the 6th Corps would be thus situated: one strong division at Ota reconnoitering the exits of Vila Verde and Labrugeira by Torres Vedras, and two other divisions in the direction of Moinho de Cubo. The administration's wagon train was abolished to provide horses for the artillery, which lacked them.

The army started marching toward the designated positions. Instead of leaving at 6:30 A.M., the Prince left at 6:15 A.M. and almost alone. I hurried to follow him. He talked to me agreeably and considerately on the inconvenience of galloping after him, insisting that he had left at the time he had set; then we talked about military affairs. One short league from Alcoentre was Serra da Ameixeira with a large and beautiful church on a small hill near a small stream. Two leagues away was Moinho de Cubo, with an isolated house, a castle, and a large stream; on the rather high southern slopes there were other positions for the enemy. The counterposition could have been useful to us. The sandy road had deteriorated somewhat, and the arid country was covered with pines and a few olive trees; to the left was a great plain and a stream which appeared to be rather wide. Little was known about the road to Alenquer. We stopped at Moinho Novo, a hamlet situated on both banks of a broad but shallow valley. The map indicated a road on the right slope but there was none; behind was the junction of the road to Caldas da Rainha, marked by an inscription. We had all those Portuguese with us, and we had to discover it ourselves. Finally, we followed the main paved road to the junction of Santarém. There we turned toward Carregado, where we left the road in order to go on to Alenquer along a paved road.

The headquarters were at Alenquer, a small city situated at the bottom of a valley and on the steep right slope. The 8th Corps was still there. The Prince sent this unit forward to Sobral, but the enemy had occupied the village. They were quickly chased out by the troops of Clauzel's division after little resistance. I saw General Sainte-Croix at the window of the Duc's [residence]. He paid me a number of compliments and two hours later he was killed by a cannonball that cut him in half at the kidneys as he was coming out of Vilafranca. Accompanied by General Montbrun, he was going along a low road to examine the position of the enemy. A random shot from a boat on the Tagus fell at a spot where he should have been safe. While this sad event was occurring, I had fallen asleep for a short time. I dreamed that Sainte-Croix had just been killed and that I was saying, "We must not speak evil about the dead." What a dream about this life. Until then Sainte-Croix had been singularly protected by fate. What a blow! What an example! At least we are left only with regrets. I was affected very much by this loss. General Sainte-Croix had played a very great role, but he had not liked me and often proved it. It is not important. I was very upset by his death. The Prince saw his body the next day and cried bitterly about this young man, whom he had liked very much.

General Montbrun took command of the banks of the Tagus from Abrantes [southward]. He was ordered to gather all the necessary materials for a bridge and the installations of the army. Taupin's brigade was reunited with the 8th Corps. General Reynier moved to Carregado and beyond it. Soult's brigade, in that village, marched on to Santarém. A battalion of marines was also directed to the city. The 6th Corps remained encamped at Ota and Moinho. Cavailher, returning from Sobral, waited for us at Alenquer. He had seen nothing in detail because the clouds covered the crest of the mountains; however, he gave us exact information, unfortunately too late, on the nature of this ground that we were learning to recognize and on the entire fortifications of the enemy.

Chapter Seven

BEFORE THE LINES OF TORRES VEDRAS

At last we clearly discerned the English system of operation and the goal of their movements, which we had scorned until then. We had been ignorant of their plans, and it was impossible to guess them when we were given not only inexact but totally false information. We had been led along in the footsteps of the English army to this inaccessible area where they could brave our efforts and ingenuity for a long time. The cruel ravages carried out by the enemy reinforced our ignorance, for it seemed they would not have abused a country they wanted to save. One must never lose sight of this central idea, for otherwise we could be accused, with reason, of a lack of foresight and even of stupidity.

It is clear from our discussions at Coimbra that we had no indications of their plan. The first notions, initially very confused, came to us on October 7 and more specifically on the 9th, for I copied it in my Journal after our departure from that city. General Loison, who came frequently to visit the Prince, spoke of it first either because he had heard some fresh news, or because the locale and his anxiety brought back memories of this country, which he and his division had occupied for a long time in 1807. Whatever the case may be, he should have spoken very succinctly, for it seems to me that the least spark would have produced an explosion of ideas on such an important subject. In effect, only a few words on the nature of the mountains would have indicated to us the enemy's system of occupation with its fortifications, its signals, its militia, and its system of maneuvers with the entire army behind that impenetrable barrier.

However, it would have been necessary for these few comments to make a precise and accurate impression. Although the word "lines" had not been pronounced before Sobral, I admit that I would have paid it little attention without exact particulars of the terrain, since the maps marked this expanse as nine to sixteen leagues [wide] and almost as flat as it had been represented to us. (Lopez's map indicated some ten leagues from Vilafranca to the sea by Torres Vedras and sixteen leagues from Santarém to Peniche—the defense positions indicated by the reports we had collected.)

For a long time it had been a military axiom that all attacks on lines were to force them. In effect, without overburdening this chapter with a long exposition on the principal and numerous situations that confirm these theories or give examples of all the different types of lines broached and seized, it is sufficient to remember that, as obstacles, temporary fortifications are nothing in themselves if they are not defended by adequate troops and artillery. The more these obstacles are extended to form a line, the more impossible it becomes to man them sufficiently in ordinary times. For if the defenders are spread along the line, their formation is like a cobweb and easy to pierce. If they want to maneuver behind the line in order to concentrate on a point of attack, it is certainly very easy for an [opposing] army, even with inferior numbers, to master its movements, confident that the enemy will not attack or follow during maneuvers. The army can menace all the points on the line by detachments of cavalry and light infantry, by cannonade or demonstrations, and by concentrating troops on exposed points either by a night march or by rapid movements. The point attacked is overwhelmed by artillery and easily breached by columns of attacks; and the line of fortifications is pulled down immediately. The troops that are met, retreat a distance on each side and the defensive army, either scattered or at least disconcerted, does not have any recourse except a distant withdrawal. If a fortification line is continuous, the more concentrated the obstacles, the better the defenders find themselves confined; if the line is intermittently manned, it presents a great expanse with many openings through which attackers can enter. For a line of fortifications to include every advantage, it must almost be reduced to the area a defensive army can occupy when deployed as usual. A line formed by detached works provides points of resistance and support or a pivot for maneuvers. Behind an excellent defensive position it is possible for an army to brave the attacks of a very superior enemy and to hazard bold countermaneuvers; attack columns can hurl themselves forward through a formidable rideau on any points in a solid formation or on a single point formed in oblique order. Finally, in a second line with excellent reserve, retreating or broken troops can swiftly re-form themselves.

Thus the first announcement of the enormous English Lines did not make a very great impression on us; however, everything was different from what we had experienced in other places. The Lines were of such an extraordinary nature that I daresay there was no other position in the world that could be compared to them. In effect, it was not enough to encounter this formidable wall of rocks, supported on one side by the sea and on the other by an immense river. Behind it was a great capital with its arsenals, workshops, magazines to furnish all needs, workers of every description, artillery depots, and numerous batteries where large caliber guns were concentrated. Moreover, the population of the kingdom was deluded and influenced enough to construct and defend all those fortifications; there was sufficient time to prepare them in advance, an open sea to feed everyone, and a large unencumbered fleet. Alentejo presented a further means either of subsistence or of retreat. If a single circumstance had been defective, on the other hand, the system would have collapsed. We would have searched vainly in our memories and experience for examples or applications of such circumstances. We found only this maxim: "In war one must foresee, expect, and protect against everything."

The English Lines, enveloping twenty to twenty-four thousand yards, barred the terrain between the Tagus and the sea. The right extended from Alhandra; the center was at Monte Agraço, or Mountain of Grace, facing Sobral;[1] and the left reached through Torres Vedras to the sea. There was a very narrow defile in front of Sobral, and beyond the mountain rose up again suddenly like a gigantic wall of

1. Monte Agraço or Sobral de Monte Agraço may be a derivative either of *graça* or *agrado,* meaning "grace," or of *agraço,* signifying "unripe" or "premature."

rocks extending on both flanks; it was this formidable barrier that the English had crowned with works. On both sides of the passage two deep valleys full of ravines opened out and extended all the way to the sea and the Tagus. They served as the first obstacle of the primary defense line and as a kind of ditch at this line. These were the valleys where the rivers of Arruda and Torres Vedras [Sizandro] flowed. Thus the terrain we occupied was joined at only one point to the range of mountains and this was at the very depressed defile of Sobral. Every part of the mountain not covered by rocks or absolutely inaccessible, all the avenues, and all the small detached abutments useful for observation or flanking the base and slopes had been carefully entrenched to form their first line. One could find every type of field fortification among the thirty-two works. The works were armed with 141 pieces in position, manned by 10,040 Portuguese troops;[2] and they were surrounded with unattached militia and a multitude of *ordenanza*. Finally the first line was defended more particularly by the English army. Its divisions and their artillery, distributed from place to place, were free to move and to act behind the curtain of fire against attack columns. A system of signals placed on the highest points, with frequent communication along the whole line, reported on our long and difficult movements in the middle of the valleys and rocks. Orders flew back and forth.[3] The roads and the other methods of communication had been improved. All this assured Lord Wellington the means to gather quickly all manner of defenses on any points that might be attacked. It was said that the center of this general system was before Sobral. Behind the first line the enemy had a second one, even stronger; according to the inventory, it was furnished with 65 works and 206 cannons, and manned by 15,400 men. Finally a third line was estab-

2. The first line at Torres Vedras was constructed as an afterthought of Captain John T. Jones, who suggested that the fortified positions before the major line (the second) be formed into a contiguous line. When this work was completed, the fortified posts had been transformed into what was known as the first line. It included 69 works with 319 pieces of artillery manned by 18,683 men. For details see John T. Jones, *Journals of Sieges Carried on by the Army under the Duke of Wellington, in Spain, during the years 1811 to 1814; with notes and additions: also Memoranda Relative to the Lines Thrown up to Cover Lisbon in 1810* (3d ed., London, 1846), III, 94–96.

3. The telegraph stations on the first line were located at Alhandra, Monte Agraço, N. S. de Socorra, Torres Vedras, and behind Ponte de Rol at redoubt No. 30. Each station resembled the deck of a vessel with mast and yardarms. See Jones, *Journals of Sieges,* III, 90.

lished at São Julião to cover the embarkation points. It was defended by 11 fortifications, 89 pieces of artillery, and 3,850 men.[4]

The career officers for whom I principally worked will not be displeased to find that I have included a detailed survey of this formidable line. I have copied from my Journal, which I consider an official report of the campaign, however imperfect it may be. Although reconnaissances were made at various periods, I have put them all together here despite some repetition and lack of order; it will be easier to judge the true state of affairs, the local color, and the circumstances from these quotations. I must mention here the deplorable fate which prevented me from carrying out my reconnaissance from one end of the line to the other. Our troops never occupied the terrain facing the left. In order to satisfy an indiscreet curiosity on my part, I did not want to provoke troop movements and, even less, the slightest fighting. Moreover, the decision not to attack had been made at this time, and it had become quite useless to know the left in detail. It was enough for us to know—by limited inspection, by our reports, and by definite information—that it was no less carefully fortified than the right and the center.

The Prince went to Vilafranca [on October 13] to observe the enemy positions, the 2nd Corps, and the Tagus. He ordered me to go and examine the center of the Lines at Sobral. From our reconnaissance, he added, "I shall decide." I had already wanted to ask him about following this course and I would have done it the day before if I had had better horses. I could hardly do my regular duty, for the rain was still very heavy, although it slowly diminished and the weather became clear. Richoux came with me. The road was steep, narrow, and wretched for riding horses; nevertheless, it was well repaired in some places. Ten dragoons followed, but only one arrived with us and his horse had lost a shoe. I climbed a hill with some peasants, but they did not know or did not want to tell me the name of any village. I descended to Sobral, which was full of our troops. Its exits toward the defile and on the flank were barricaded with large barrels. I went to the left and found the Duc there: I talked about his position. Then

4. By the time the fortifications before Lisbon were completed, the second line included 15,442 men with 215 guns in 69 positions. The third line around Oeiras at São Julião was ultimately composed of 5,350 men and 94 guns. See Jones, *Journals of Sieges,* III, 92, 97–99.

Colonel Valazé arrived and we climbed up on a mill. The Duc pushed the enemy and they moved very far on our right. We attacked. Solignac's division in the rear fired and Clauzel's division advanced a little. We followed these movements, Valazé, Richoux, and I. We then went and caught a few balls that the enemy directed toward us when he was not firing at the soldiers. After two hours of fighting, we retained this necessary position, although it was useless in itself. We had forty casualties, of whom eleven were officers. In the evening we occupied some of the abutments on our side of the passage. The enemy had many men in the village of [Enxara dos] Cavalleiros, which was said to be on the communication route between Torres Vedras and Montachique. In the evening the enemy marched some of their troops from Torres Vedras toward the center and halted them above the village of Cavalleiros; a corps was formed there the next morning. Meanwhile the appropriate countermovement was performed. One rather strong camp still remained at the same point.

I examined and studied the defile of Sobral, the streams to the right and left, and the various slopes on the Tagus and the sea. I recognized the inaccuracy of our map and drawings. I went toward our left to reconnoiter it; we arrived on the observation point at dusk with seven or eight voltigeurs. A few moments afterward two hundred enemy came to this same point. Opposite Sobral I could see the crest of Monte Agraço, Mountain of Grace, where a large work of 360 to 400 yards' deployment with 14 to 15 feet of relief was covered with seventeen embrasures. We noticed some countersinks and palisades, and inside the fortification were barracks or traverses and perhaps even a redoubt or blockhouse covered with sod. This work occupied a kind of hill which was higher than the mountain range. To the left, on the slope, we saw a redoubt or some kind of lunette; another work was on the right and farther back at the bottom of a rock-step; and finally there was a third one forward. They were like three satellites around a great entrenchment of two thousand men which seemed to be the center of the first enemy line.[5] It reminded me of the English redoubt [Fort

5. The fortlet atop Monte Agraço had 25 pieces of artillery and was maintained by 1,590 men who controlled the road through Sobral. To strengthen the flanks of this position, one supplementary redoubt was established on the right and three on the left to protect its vulnerable extremities. In all, fifty guns protected this position, while four miles to the rear two additional fortifications were constructed with seven pieces. See Jones, *Journals of Sieges*, III, 94.

Mulgrave] at Toulon as drawn by St. Paul. In this way the crest of the mountain was crowned from place to place with large works for a distance of eight to twelve thousand yards from Sobral to the Tagus, even where certain points were covered with rocks and seemed inaccessible. There must have been twelve to fifteen of them. I was not able to complete my inspection and examine everything. The shoulders of the road and the extremities of the abutments were also defended by works. On every crest were signals, a league apart. It appeared that the enemy's first line of works extended from Alhandra to beyond Torres Vedras with the center at Sobral.

Behind this first line was the second line of Montachique, extending on one side from the Tagus through the swamps of Tojal and advancing to the other side on the sea through the ravines of Cheleiros and the mountains of Sintra. The line had only five to six thousand yards of accessible ground; the rest was covered by great natural obstacles. Behind the second line the enemy could maneuver in response to all our movements, which could be relayed by Allied signals from a very great distance. Thus we could achieve nothing after piercing the first line. Moreover, these works were not of a nature to fall after having been outflanked, but had to be attacked with cannon. They were a firm support upon which the enemy could pivot or at the least depend. If the first formidable line was pierced, the second line still remained to assure the English retreat.

It would have been very difficult to advance the artillery and climb [the mountains] when all the roads and passes were cut, to have the infantry clamber up without the use of roads when the ground was rocky and wet, and to march under the fire of heavy artillery brought from Lisbon and the seacoast. Afterward we would have found fresh troops on the crest, concentrated there by means of signals along the whole line. Moreover, considering the situation in general, the enemy had every means of resistance—powder, shells, etc., in great abundance—while we lacked everything and the rain had cost us more cartridges than a battle. The enemy were at the gates of Lisbon, where they could shelter their wounded and sick after the first battle; they were near their vessels and assured of withdrawal in case of a rout; they could even consider themselves very close to London, while we were a thousand leagues [*sic*] from France and lacking in everything.

What could we do after a battle of uncertain outcome if we had two thousand wounded? Where could we place them? How could we care for them? To whom could we confide them in case of withdrawal? As for the composition of the armies, the enemy were assured of their retreat, confident of the fortifications on which they had been laboring for more than a year and of the thirty to forty thousand Portuguese inside—troops whom a [French] division could put to flight on the plains, but who would fight like other soldiers when they saw behind them the last corner of their country, the sea, and the dishonor of desertion.

Although our soldiers were young and had not made war or been disheartened by making it, our officers had to push them, even though they were disgusted. Moreover, certain people did not wish to succeed. They had contrary desires or interests—but everything cannot be written down. These people worked solely on the morale of our troops. Not able to preach infamy directly, they exaggerated the difficulties and the losses we had suffered. They hinted at the impossibility of an attack and talked about the possibility of disastrous events, etc. What could be done in such a state of affairs, with so many serious troubles, such troops and commanders, and an army that diminished and deteriorated everyday, against positions that were said to be not only impregnable, but even unassailable, and defended by a very large army? There were said to be more than thirty thousand British, since they had received reinforcements during recent weeks, and thirty-five to forty thousand Portuguese regular troops not counting the militia and *ordenanza*.[6] We could attack, maneuver from the right to the left, clear some of the enemy at a few points, and seize the works in the fog or at dawn. But if we were not sure, very sure, of breaking through to Lisbon, could we risk it? Therefore we had to temporize, study the position of the enemy, try to remain there, establish on both banks of the Tagus a temporary land blockade of Lisbon, where an immense population was crammed, and wait for reinforcements. Then what would the English General do? Unfortunately, at that moment we

6. At a conservative estimate, Wellington's disposable force behind the lines included 20,000 Portuguese militia and *ordenanza* and 8,000 Spanish troops occupying the fortifications, while his field army included 35,000 English and 24,500 Portuguese troops by the end of October 1810. See Oman, *Peninsular War,* III, 431–32, and for more details Luz Soriano, *Guerra civil,* Segunda Epocha, III, 218–31.

could not find sufficient material for a bridge over the Tagus, but we could gather it. If there were no boats, we could use rafts. It was necessary to entrench the positions we occupied before Sobral and Vilafranca to retain them more effectively and to make the remainder of the troops more available. I started a long line of reasoning on our position, but I was never able to put it into any order. This subject made me think, and I followed it; nevertheless, I gave the foregoing report to the Prince; one day it will have some interest and become the material for memoirs.

Going from the right to the left with Valazé and Richoux, I indicated to the latter the important points to seize the next morning. Afterward we witnessed a kind of minor combat where we should have maneuvered instead of attacking, for I am opposed to useless action. I had not seen the place where, it was said, the enemy had employed fifteen hundred men, but they could have been on the reverse of the abutments mentioned earlier. I returned to General Solignac's quarters, where I made a report to His Excellency, based on the principles I have indicated, on our position in Sobral, on the enemy at Outeiro,* and on a large fortification above the general position. I included a sketch that Richoux drew and ended my report with the following words: "Here you will find the precipitous rock of Bussaco crowned by every kind of field fortification that can be constructed, along with formidable artillery."[7]

According to what the Prince had told me when he left, I thought he would come in the morning [October 14] since he had finished very late the night before. I thought it was useless to leave [Sobral] in the middle of the night only to return at the break of dawn. In the morning I went to examine the positions again, since the weather was sufficiently good and clear. Again I saw all the works and one entrenched village near Torres Vedras. There were numerous redoubts on the garden heights at Mafra. There we noticed an encompassing wall together with a large number of new redoubts on the slopes to the left of the great central work.

As I returned to Sobral, the Prince arrived. I accompanied him be-

7. In Pelet's report to Masséna dated 7:00 P.M., October 13, 1810, he declared, "The mountain on which we find the principal work of the enemy rises before Sobral as that of Bussaco above Moura." See Correspondance: Armée de Portugal, Carton C[7]10.

yond the village and then conducted him on the left to the barricade of barrels barring the defile at the front of the village. General Clauzel had placed a few guns on several points behind the barricade. After His Excellency had carefully examined the position, an attack was proposed to him; I did not know against what point. The Duc condescended to call me in, but this was the first time I had heard talk of an attack. At the bottom of the main road the enemy had the village of Outeiro full of troops but somewhat cleared out since the previous day. On the enemy's left was a pine forest in front of a hamlet, and the heights of an abutment extending toward Cavalleiros were full of Englishmen. Moreover, the passage was occupied on each side by a trench which protected the English skirmishers. The attack on Outeiro was naturally made on its left (west), which was much more accessible than the abutment that was truly the key point of the position; the right (east) was pronounced and extended almost perpendicularly from the bottom of the Arruda River. We climbed the hill by a mill. We cannonaded the enemy trench and chased them out. Then they drove us out rather vigorously. There were very few shots on our right, but many on our left, and we sent most of the troops on this spot since it was the most difficult. The enemy presented a considerable number of soldiers, and they had a rather strong camp on our right beyond Cavalleiros. I have already mentioned it. I was always afraid that the troops there would march on our rear. This would have been unfortunate for the 8th Corps, which I found placed all by itself, unattached to the rest of the army and too isolated in view of its actual strength. I spoke about this to His Excellency. The firing went on for a long time, and there was cannonading from both sides. Our skirmishers gained some ground on the left.[8]

The Prince, who only wanted to see the strength and the behavior of the enemy, gave orders to cease fire and withdraw. I had a long and important conversation with His Excellency, and he ordered a reconnaissance of the positions, the terrain, and the roads in the valley. Beaufort and Cavailher were charged directly with these reconnaissances. The Prince agreed with me on the enemy positions, finding

8. The French attack was carried out by General Ménard and the fourth battalion of the 19th Line. They were opposed by the 71st Foot of Spencer's First Division. The French casualties numbered 120 while the English lost 67. See Noel, *Souvenirs,* p. 125; Delagrave, *Mémoires,* p. 100; Oman, *Peninsular War,* III, 443–44.

them inaccessible for the moment. Since the position of the 8th Corps was poor, he stopped on the way to give the Duc orders to place Clauzel's brigade one league ahead of the second brigade, to withdraw his artillery somewhat, and not to delay one moment in doing so.[9] General Fririon wrote the dispatch and I copied it. In returning [from Sobral], I took some bearings on the enemy position. The Prince gave orders to General Reynier to occupy Arruda and to the quartermaster general regarding the administration of food, since we had found a considerable quantity at Vilafranca. There was a large quantity of oats at Sobral, but the enemy had burned it.

The Prince wanted to see the right of the English Line again [on October 15]. I accompanied him beyond Vilafranca. In order to see the general effect of their right, we climbed a very steep height to reach the crest of an abutment opposite one occupied by the enemy.[10] The country was rich in the great quantity of its wine; the wine presses were magnificent. We stopped on a crest near two mills, a good half league from Vilafranca. We were three thousand to thirty-six hundred yards from the enemy line, which effectively covered the entire crest with closely knit works. The positions appeared carefully done, but none of them was as strong as the one at Sobral. It was true that on one abutment there was a square construction with four great towers at the corners. It was so dominant that we thought we were looking at a stone wall and a parapet of fascines. I thought it was an old fort that had been restored, for certainly its profile could not have belonged to a field fortification adapted to the locality. I also thought I saw an angular work with a keep on the summit of the same abutment. I was wrong; what I saw was a great redoubt with a signal post and a small advanced breastwork. The remainder of the line was outlined by tents. Everybody also said that the enemy had cut away the mountain to make the slope more perpendicular. Several horizontal roads, crossing the various summits, had been widened with the earth thrown up

9. Orders for Junot's redeployment can be found in a letter from Masséna to Junot, 7:30 A.M., October 15, 1810, Correspondance: Armée de Portugal, Carton $C^7$10.

10. After his reconnaissance, Masséna wrote to Ney on October 16, "The enemy is dug in up to the teeth. He has three lines of works that cover Lisbon. If we seized the front line of redoubts, he would throw himself into the second line. . . . I have already visited the line three times to the right and left and I see great works bristling with cannon." Correspondance: Armée de Portugal, $C^7$10.

on the outside. This was contested. I maintained my opinion and it was at last verified by some men passing by, and this was how things were determined![11] Yet General Reynier saw the opposite. However, I am only reflecting some generalizations about the Line without describing it in detail. Someday I will follow along and describe the line from the right to the left. Beyond the works with towers—toward the west—the slope of the mountain became steeper. We saw rocks and works farther apart and less frequent, but we could see others on summits beyond those of Sobral which were perhaps another great abutment of the mountain range; it seemed to be attached to the range toward Montachique. Those works must have belonged to the enemy's second line and formed some support and reserve areas for the right wing. Not everyone agreed with me on this, but when I was convinced about something and believed it to be material or important, I persisted and the others agreed—the rest was unimportant. The previous day I had also reconnoitered the entrenched mill which almost blocked the horizon and the large earthwork of Sobral in the distance. The latter had made signals that the mast placed beyond us had repeated. The enemy had a telegraph station at Vilafranca communicating by two lines with Castelo Branco and Almeida. At present they derived a major advantage from the signals; somewhere in my memoirs I had once proposed the same idea for the defense of rivers (that of the Adige, I believe), suggesting their placement on church towers.

Deserters told us that the enemy had seven divisions of English troops in front of us and that the Portuguese defended the works. The divisions were divided along the front of the position in the following order: Hill was to the right; then Craufurd, Picton, and Spencer[12] were

11. Pelet's judgment was indeed correct. The slopes were increased in pitch and the rough terrain was blasted into perpendicular precipices by the engineers. Military roads were constructed or improved along the reverse slopes of the fortified chain of mountains to connect the redoubts and facilitate the rapid movement of Wellington's army. See Jones, *Journals of Sieges,* III, 87–89.

12. Sir Thomas Picton (1758–1815) became an ensign in the 12th Foot in 1771, but in 1783 he was placed on half pay for twelve years. In 1794 Picton went to the West Indies, where he served for more than a decade. Promoted to brigadier general in 1801, he secured a unit in the Walcheren expedition eight years later. Picton arrived in the Peninsula in 1810 and was given command of Wellington's Third Division, which he commanded at Bussaco and Fuentes de Oñoro.

Sir Brent Spencer (1760–1828) was commissioned in the 15th Foot and in 1805 he was promoted to the rank of major general. He served in the West Indies intermittently from 1790 to 1798 and the following year in Holland. Spencer participated in the Egyptain campaign and the Copenhagen expedition; in 1808 he was

charged with direct defense or with attacking the flanks of our attacks. General Hill, the second in command, had the strongest division and twenty-four pieces of artillery; the others had twelve guns, aside from those of the works. The enemy had worked on the Lines for more than a year and had gathered the peasants of the surrounding countryside there. They had conceived a perfect defense for this country and had executed it completely to their advantage. The capital was all important for them, and in preserving it they had preserved everything. Nevertheless, they had ruined the country for a very long time to come and we would complete its destruction! It was very difficult, if not impossible, to force the Lines without losing a dreadful number of soldiers.

Earlier, we could have seized the Lines easily without great loss, but that time was past. After reflection I can now clearly prove that the attack of the three enemy Lines would have cost us half of our actual army. Then what would we have done at Lisbon? The sea, so favorable for the enemy, would become an insurmountable barrier for us. If they landed troops at Peniche immediately, we would have been blocked between the sea and the Tagus. On the day after our triumphant entry into the capital, we would have had to think soberly about evacuating it in order to avoid the supreme misfortune of leaving half our wounded there. In this regard, the Prince said that even if the enemy evacuated Lisbon he would enter only with the greatest precautions. How was it possible that, of all the people who had written about the attack and defense of Portugal, not one had understood the crux of the matter and the system that was so favorable to the British? With so many Portuguese among us, why had none of them been able to enlighten us about the aspect of the topography nor tell us that there were mountains, which were so easily defended, rather than representing them only as hills? And what about the others who had traveled in this country and already made war here? As for me, I believe I would have been able to recognize this as a theater of operation for the enemy where their flanks would be strongly assured and could not be turned or outmaneuvered from any distance. I had clearly seen the advantage of the terrain on the map. I was always mentioning the "pocket of the Tagus," for this was the name I gave to it. I had told

sent to Portugal where he took part in the fighting at Roliça, Vimeiro, Bussaco, and Fuentes de Oñoro.

everybody that if we fought, it would be there. I expected that there would be some fieldworks, as there are anywhere, but a chain of forts on such lofty mountains, which they had been working on for fifteen [*sic*] months (is it possible we had not been warned of it?)—this burned me up.

For some time I had wanted to examine in detail the position of the enemy from Alhandra to beyond Sobral. I decided to do that today. Beaufort and I mounted our horses early in the morning and left for Vilafranca, where the colonel of the 17th Léger ordered his adjutant major to accompany us. The advance posts of the enemy were on a small detached hill ahead of their Line. The Line was on a very extensive abutment which appeared to descend almost directly to Sobral. However, near the middle the Line was crossed by a rather deep valley called Calhandriz; it dropped into the Arruda River, which rambled downward from the Line, swerving toward the east. The right of the enemy position rested at Alhandra. The position was barricaded in several places, and the church was defended by a breastwork that raked the road and the main highway behind Alhandra. On the other side of the stream a long entrenchment was dominant where one could see embrasures established on one side of the Tagus; it seemed to me the entrenchment had to go up beyond the church. Behind the abutment, this field fortification rose toward the east to a summit about sixteen hundred yards away; the entrenchment was crowned by a great principal work covered with sod, and the embrasures also appeared to be masked. We could count ten to eleven embrasures on the side facing us. Ahead of it there were some remnants of breastworks to cover the approaches. Previously I had believed this position to be angular. There was a signal post on this main work. From the summit there was a detached perpendicular abutment, and at its extremity was a large work which presented some type of towers to defend the faces; there were at least two of them made of masonry which may have been old mills. From the summit to Alhandra I counted five redoubts traced according to the formation of the terrain. Each one was broached by embrasures and before them was a long escarpment.[13]

13. This position Pelet describes at Alhandra was designated by the English engineers as No. 1; it had 13 guns and was occupied by 1,000 men. The fortifications above Alhandra were Nos. 2, 3, 4, and 114. They had a total of 9 guns and 1,100 men. See Jones, *Journals of Sieges,* III, 94.

Was this a berm enfiladed by the works of a widened road? Could there be some kind of faussebraie? At least I had watched men and mules marching there and crossing without the men ever disappearing into any recess, which indicated there was no moat nor parapet.

To the west of this summit, where several little abutments were connected, was the valley of Calhandriz which rose toward the south. This position showed several works on both its slopes, and three redoubts were united toward its extremity; it seemed as if they were intended as a reserve between Alhandra and Sobral or for the defense of some communication line in the bottom of the valley and on the road from Sobral to Santo Antão do Tojal.[14] There were rocks on the west exit of the valley and the crest was partly unoccupied because of its steep slope, but everywhere there were small posts formed by three tents. To the east of the same exit, the enemy worked on the slope of a hill and appeared to be cutting its grade as if to make a road there. The country we crossed was tortuous and very cut up. Since part of the journey had been made on foot, it had been a little long and there was no way to continue on to Sobral. Now we had to think about withdrawing. Moreover, we were at the extreme right of our lines, at the advance post of the 2nd Corps. The posts of the enemy formed a point that descended into the Arruda valley, and it would have been necessary to come the long way around to reach the 8th Corps. Thus from the village of [Cachoeiras?] we went through the fields in the direction of Alenquer. We descended with much difficulty to the Arruda River, which was very narrow and rocky in this area; higher up, near the village of Arruda, it ran through a rather pretty little plain, whereas lower, before Carregado, the valley became somewhat wider. Communications were difficult enough in this country because of the nature of this stream and its numerous tributaries. In our desire to hurry, we got farther away and found ourselves again in the middle of nowhere. As we returned we discovered a pack of dogs which had fled with the inhabitants, but they did not approach us—it was as if they recognized us as enemies of the country. Actually they ran away at our approach and prowled, hunting for food; all they could find was an immense quantity of dead horses. At one turn of the road we saw a

14. Pelet is referring to the works designated by the English as Nos. 115, 116, 118, 119, 6, 120, 5, 121, 122, 123, 124, 125, 7, 8, 9, 10, and 11. These fortifications had 74 guns and were manned by 4,180 men.

comical scene. There was a sad marauder with tears in his eyes. He was looking at a broken jug and the wine that had spilled. He had probably gone six or eight leagues to search for it. He had been drinking intemperately, and his emotions and regrets had increased inordinately. Thus he made the whole squadron laugh. The unfortunate donkey, companion of his tired days but not of his pleasures, had fallen, and all the happiness of the plunder was shattered. He seemed to be saying, even more bitterly than the shepherds of Gaster, "It is broken, the most beautiful jug." And he left, abandoning in the middle of the road the animal which was no longer useful to him.

I intended to continue my reconnaissance and recommence from where I had quit on the right of General Reynier. I returned to an abutment on the left of the Arruda valley that dominated it perfectly and was joined to our hills of Sobral. This abutment was truly inclined and covered with rocks in the direction of the unassailable enemy. The middle of the crest was guarded ineffectively by the Légion du Midi and the 32nd Léger (five hundred men) commanded by General Ferey. Behind him on the road to Sobral, he had the Hanoverian Legion with three cannon, but the guns were quite useless, poorly placed, and would have been better left in the *parc*. The posts of the 8th Corps began on the right of General Ferey and extended toward Sobral. Between General Ferey and the 2nd Corps there was a single post of *chasseurs à cheval* and a few men of the 31st Léger. The posts of the various army corps did not communicate with each other. At the same time there was a major gap behind them through which the enemy could drive directly on Alenquer by way of Refugidos or some other village above it, with a more direct road going between Carregado and Alenquer. General Ferey was placed there to observe the rocks; his post was near Refugidos. The weather was foggy. I could see the enemy lines only with difficulty and little of the new structures in the distance. During a break in the weather I distinguished two signal posts and the works from the valley of Calhandriz to Sobral. With difficulty I could see several great works on the crest and many other smaller works or entrenched mills occupying the various secondary slopes of the abutments, defending the approaches of the roads. The enemy cannonfire plunged deeply into the bottom of the Arruda valley. Passing through the village of Arruda, I was shot at several times as I went back to Sobral past the farmhouse on the main highway. I had taken along an inaccurate drawing made by an officer of the 2nd Corps.

The enemy had worked extensively above the entrenched mills and on our right at Sobral. He had covered the foot of the mountain with works which descended to Runa and Torres Vedras. I could see this only with difficulty because of the dense fog, and I saw even less of what was beyond. On our side we were moving earth. We were erecting a few works on the abutment of a mill ahead of the 86th Line. There were a few other works near Sobral and Outeiro, and the avenues were covered with fortified posts. Clauzel's division defended Outeiro and extended up to the foot of the enemy entrenchments. The first brigade was cantoned at Sobral whereas they [Junot and staff] had written us a few days before that there were only one hundred men in this village; the second brigade was behind, the third near Feria,* and the cavalry was on the right, but the enemy occupied the foot of our reverse which dropped into the [Sizandro] River from Torres Vedras to Runa. The enemy was on the right and behind the 8th Corps. Thus this corps still formed the advance point. The exit from Arruda was masked only on its left, and the road from Runa to Alenquer was perfectly open on its right. I could not see anything, but I expected to substantiate the notions I had acquired from a distance about the mountains of Montachique and Mafra and the enemy position behind Torres Vedras. Nevertheless, I could see the rear of the 8th Corps and the valley with the Alenquer River. On my return I received an order to go to Santarém. I was in a hurry, but I wanted to return later to the position assigned to the 8th Corps; that is, from Mata, Pipa, and Refugidos, with a strong advance guard at the head of the valley of Freiria (the one to the left, which started below Freiria and extended toward the position of General Solignac), and a single detachment ahead of Sobral. Everything was quiet in this position, where I would not have wanted to command for a quarter of an hour. It was sufficient that we held there for a month for the sake of persistence. Such are men, and they are all the same.

As I examined the surroundings of Arruda, it had appeared to me that they presented less difficulty than any other point for an attack on the enemy lines: the various valleys culminated there, the roads

Jean Jacques Pelet
(painted after a portrait
in the Pavillon des Armes,
Vincennes)

André Masséna

The New Cathedral at Salamanca, Spain

The Roman Bridge over the Agueda River at Ciudad Rodrigo, Spain

Ciudad Rodrigo as Viewed from the French Positions

An Aerial View of Ciudad Rodrigo

An Aerial View of Almeida, Portugal

Segment of a Curtain and Bastion at Fort La Concepción

The Bridge over the Côa River below Almeida where Ney Attacked Craufurd's Light Division in July 1810

The Mondego River at the Southern Tip of the Serra de Bussaco

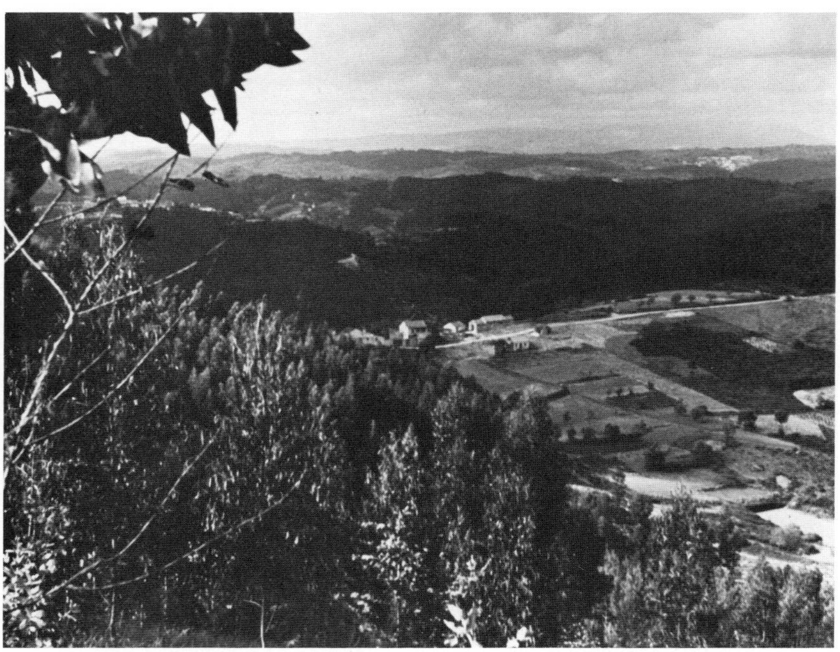

The Village of San Antonio de Cantaro as Viewed from the Allied Positions

The Ridge of Bussaco as Viewed from the French Positions

The Boialvo Road, North of Pala, Route by which the French Outflanked Wellington after Bussaco

A Fortification Overlooking the Village of Torres Vedras

The Tagus River from Santarém toward Cartaxo

spread from there on to the opposite mountains, and the latter connected and encompassed the position of the enemy from Sobral to Arruda and beyond, extending parallel to the position from Torres Vedras to Alhandra. One of the advantages of such an attack was the rocks that formed our reverse in the valley opposite Arruda; they had a few pieces of artillery in case of misfortune and would insure a firm retreat to the attacking corps; we would be able to come and re-form under the guns with great safety. If I have time I will return to this point and sketch this part of the enemy line the best way I can. Perhaps one day we will attempt to attack it with some reinforcements.

These were the formidable lines that Lord Wellington had for defending his English army, which consisted of five strong infantry divisions, one division of light infantry, and one of cavalry now numbering thirty-four to thirty-six thousand men, as well as a great part of the Portuguese army, said to be thirty-five to forty thousand men. Two-thirds of the regular militia corps formed into regiments, clothed and armed like those of the army, were estimated at the same size. Wellington had at his disposition an immense number of armed militia or *ordenanza* raised en masse, totaling more than one hundred thousand men. These peasants were not capable of maintaining themselves on a battlefield, but placed in two or three lines on the less exposed points, thrown out as skirmishers, hidden in the rocks, forming a cordon on the Tagus, they could be quite useful and leave the major part of the English and Portuguese forces unencumbered. Wellington had also asked La Romana for Spanish aid. The division of O'Donnell had already arrived and that of La Carrera was announced. If these men could not be of great utility on the Line, they were of value to the English troops against the people of Lisbon and for guarding the most important points of retreat, which Wellington would not in all probability have dared to give to the Portuguese.

Meanwhile, despite these formidable ramparts and so many troops, Lisbon was not quiet. With every possible consideration, the Regency suggested to the public that they put their precious objects safely aboard the man-of-war *Vasco da Gama* and the frigate *Phoenix* while the government embarked all its papers and funds.[15] Likewise they in-

15. Wellington expressed some concern about the attitude of the Portuguese behind the Lines; on October 6, 1810, he wrote to Charles Stuart, a member of the Portuguese Regency, "All I ask from the Government [Portuguese] is tran-

vited the public to bring their papers and money to the English vessels. The government punished the militia who absented themselves from their corps by deportation to the African possessions and confiscation of their wealth. It declared that all officers not present were deserters. Under threat of the most severe punishment, it prohibited the smallest gatherings and the spread of news or rumors. Finally the government amassed all kinds of ordinances and measures, which proved how little protected from danger they felt themselves to be, and how enslaved they were by English domination.[16] Moreover, even before our arrival in Portugal the Regency, under the pretext of a conspiracy, had expelled those of the principal inhabitants of Lisbon who had not subordinated themselves to the interest and passions of this faction. Some had been thrown into jail and others had embarked for Brazil; included among them were two men of the first families of the kingdom, distinguished by their talent, merit, and wealth.[17]

quillity in the town of Lisbon, and provisions for their own troops; and as God Almighty does not give 'the race to the swift or the battle to the strong,' and I have fought battles enough to know, that even under the best arrangements, the result of any one is not certain, I only beg that they will adopt preparatory arrangements to take out of the enemy's way those persons who would suffer if they were to fall into his hands." See *Wellington's Dispatches,* VI, 493–94.

16. On October 13 the Governors of the Kingdom issued the following statement to the people of Lisbon: "Portuguese, the march of the enemy army, already weakened by the lack of men, announces battle is very near. . . . The God of armies will bless our army and give us complete victory. The Governors of the Kingdom, the Marshal General, the army, and all the nation hope they have reason to expect it. However, it is necessary to protect yourselves against false rumors that may be spread by the malicious on this occasion. Do not be afraid of the passage of troops, the arrival of the wounded, and the constant movement of transports and other necessary movements that are the consequences of war operations. You must not believe any news that is not announced by the Government whose frankness has already been proven to you. It will take all the measures to punish the evil who dare to spread false rumors with the severity that circumstances demand. Portuguese! let us have quiet, confidence, obedience, and we will be content." See Colleção da Academia das Sciências de Lisboa.

17. When Charles Stuart learned of the seizure of Portuguese nationals, he wrote to Wellington, "I was surprised a few days since to learn that domiciliary visits had taken place throughout Lisbon and a number of persons named in the enclosed list confined in the forts previous to embarkation for the islands. The partisans of the enemy are very willing to throw the odium of every violent act on the councils of His Majesty's Government. . . . When the Principal Souza hinted to me the doubts and suspicions of many persons in [his] employ, I had written that gentleman. . . . After I heard he had nevertheless carried his threat into execution I did not fail to communicate with the Government, both for the purpose of expressing my repugnance [and] . . . enquiring the causes which had led to this unusual exercise of arbitrary power. . . . I regret however to say that suspicions, personal animosities, and groundless fears appear to have been the sole causes of

After praising the great strategical plan of the English in Portugal—although separating it from their system of devastation, which I regarded as the worst in a period of calamities and war horrors—I cannot refrain from praising the manner in which the two Lines of Lisbon were built and occupied. For the development of the art, it is to be hoped that a description may be given by the Portuguese and English officers.[18] This can now be done without danger, for the concealment of such matters is ridiculous and as useless as it is difficult to do, since details can be uncovered by the simplest inspection of a good map or by a stroll that many people have made; furthermore the works must have been pulled down or ruined by now. An officer charged to re-establish these Lines would certainly change many of the details. However, what cannot be praised is the complete inertia, the continued English defense in front of a much weaker army, and especially against the advance guard, the 8th Corps, which was poorly placed and separated from the rest of the army; they had only to reach out with their long arms to seize it. For a month the position of the advance guard and its cantonment seemed to be a challenge and an insult to the English army.

Here is a very important question to decide. Was that position assailable and, more particularly, was it so for our army? The extracts from my Journal have already shown what my opinion was at that time on the great difficulty of attacking the Lines,[19] the advantages guaranteed

an explosion calculated to gain the unthinking part of the public, and unnecessarily to increase the hatred of the higher classes to the Government by carrying affliction into their families, and humiliating the pride of persons, who with some justice will long retain a strong sense of the injury they have experienced." See P.R.O., F.O. 342/21, Stuart to Wellington, September 15, 1810. For more details and a list of those transported, see Luz Soriano, *Guerra civil,* Segunda Epocha, III, 89–92.

18. John T. Jones published *Memoranda Relative to the Lines Thrown up to Cover Lisbon* in 1829 and three years later a French edition appeared. Jones's volume included not only a detailed analysis of the Lines but most of the correspondence relative to its construction.

19. Long after the war ended, Marbot said that General Hill told him, "If the French had attacked within the first ten days after their arrival, they would have easily penetrated together with the confused multitude of peasants in the midst of whom the English armies could never have disentangled themselves nor made any regular disposition for defense." Marbot also indicated that Masséna wanted to attack the English positions but that Ney and Reynier refused to carry out the orders. See Marbot, *Mémoires,* II, 128–29. Marbot is obviously incorrect on this point, for Masséna wrote Ney on October 16, "I do not believe this is the moment to attack the enemy. A check would destroy all our hopes and would overthrow

for its defense, the point that appeared most suitable for attack among all those we had reconnoitered, and finally the morale of our army and its commanders. Added to this were our numerical returns, which were not above [40,792] men at that time;[20] in every way these figures showed an enormous disproportion to the strength of the enemy and their position.

Likewise we will find fresh developments of this opinion in various memoirs. The reinforcements that I requested were only twelve to fifteen thousand men (that is to say, the strength of the 9th Corps) to form our reserve, while our entire army would attack. It was this lack of a reserve to harbor any columns repulsed by the enemy that worried me the most. If the army had as few as fifty thousand men under arms, we could have broken through and overthrown the English despite their great strength because we could have induced them to extend themselves by movements along the whole Line and along the Tagus, forcing them to send detachments onto the other bank. Also, as the danger increased, the English would be less able to rely on the Portuguese; for their own safety they would find themselves forced to keep reserves and even garrison troops on the beach and in Lisbon. As for my opinion, I always thought that Lord Wellington relied more on the state of our situation than on his systems and Lines. Not until the month of March did I give up hope of seeing those Lines forced or evacuated.

When it was realized that we could not consider attacking the English Lines, at least for the time being, we still did not give up hope of forcing them someday. The Prince was unable to take any other course than the one he adopted, as much for the honor of arms as for the good of the operation. Waiting for relief, and believing that the entire 9th Corps would soon arrive as had been announced, he was obliged to remain in position before the enemy and maintain the ground we had seized under their cannon as long as subsistence permitted. During this time the Prince busied himself with future operations and prepared the measures for undertaking those which appeared most expedient. Consequently his care and attention was divided between the English Lines, the bridges to be built on the Tagus, and subsistence

the state of things, so we will indulge in temporizing." See Correspondance: Armée de Portugal, Carton C710.

20. Koch, *Mémoires de Masséna,* VII, 575.

for our troops. Later on, if he renounced Lisbon, he would have to choose among various movements. First, he could retire on Coimbra and occupy Oporto. This would give him a country rich in every way but would seriously compromise his line of communication with Spain, necessarily established on his left. Second, he could march beyond the Zezere and on Castelo Branco, through a difficult country—arid and devastated. Third, he could maneuver on the Tagus, occupy Alentejo, and open up Old Castile; this was preferable to any other scheme. Fourth, and finally, he could move tentatively between the Rio Maior and the Zezere and reserve the choice from among the three other operations if no aid arrived. This movement was executed during the month of November.

Marshal Ney had received orders to choose a central site for his first two divisions, to send the third to Pipa on the hills of Sobral as a reserve for the 8th Corps, and to link this unit with the 2nd Corps. The Prince put General Trelliard at the disposition of the Marshal. He was posted at Alcoentre with two regiments of dragoons and a detachment of infantry at Rio Maior. The posts of the 6th Corps extended up to Cadaval; its food magazines were at Vila Nova. The Duc d'Abrantès had orders to hurry the entrenchment that had been indicated on the defile of Sobral and to guard it with the greatest care. General Reynier had received similar instructions and in addition was to occupy the village of Arruda and send the 8th Dragoons to Ponte Santa Ana on the Tagus. General Montbrun was to gather all the boats he could find on this river and attempt a coup de main on Abrantes. General Éblé went to Santarém to collect the materials and necessary articles to establish a bridge on the Tagus. The Prince also asked him to make some powder.

The quartermaster general received orders and instructions to gather grain, which was available in large quantities at Santarém and Vilafranca, and to distribute it among the various army corps, bake bread for headquarters, and organize a hospital at Santarém, as well as the other necessary establishments for the army. Moreover, he was to form magazines for the articles that could be gathered and to replace the various scarce items which could be found in the countryside only with great effort and care.

The Prince had ordered me to find a central position to accommodate the entire army in case of an attack (or to deliver an attack), although this was not expected on the part of the enemy. I thought I had fulfilled those conditions with the hills of Vila Nova and Moinho Novo. I showed them to His Excellency from a distance while accompanying him to the 2nd Corps. He sent me to reconnoiter them with his son. I found that the post of Vila Nova, where the left of the position was to rest, was excellent; it was covered by two streams crossed by a single respectable enfilade. The houses were on a small ridge dominating an open and regular plain. In the rear, hills surrounded and covered the village; with a few barricades it would be an impregnable point from the front. On the south toward the Tagus the terrain was nearly under water, though in summer it would have to be covered with cavalry. The position, extended in the north by these hills, was distorted on the summit with lacerated slopes cut and divided into many wooded abutments. It crossed the small stream of Cubo and followed its left bank to Alenquer through Moinho Novo. There we found a limited rideau, gently dominating the small plain preceding it, and much more favorable with its possibility for sweeping fire. The site, turned slightly to the right, rested on some small hills which slipped away to insignificance at an easily defensible village. The position extended some forty-eight hundred yards; it was slightly concentric and cut the two main communication roads with Coimbra and Santarém. At the same time it had both an advantage and a weakness since a withdrawal made in either direction would become entirely concentric. However, since the line was a strong defense, this weakness had its remedy. If the army wanted to withdraw on Santarém, the right, after disputing its ground, could go through a slight pivot backward on the continuous hills below Guerreiros. On the contrary, the left, after fighting dearly for the town of Vila Nova or removing troops to reinforce the center, could easily march parallel to Guerreiros along a very good road that followed the uniform crest of hills whose slopes were very abrupt. Then the first line could bend back on a new position at Ota, Cubo, and Guerreiros.

Later on, sketching the country between the Tagus, Liz, Zezere, etc., because I had missed this piece of ground in a moment of haste, I found the hills of Vila Nova so cut up and their slopes so full of ravines and covered by woods that it appeared difficult to occupy the position with troops without some minor fieldworks. This position pleased me very much and I never passed it without some interest.

Thus, when I disapproved of a position as abrupt and escarped as the one at Bussaco, it was only because I was completely convinced of my principles and not for the pleasure of finding fault. On my first trip I met Marshal Ney and another time General Reynier. I spoke to them about this plan for a position and they approved it strongly.

The Prince wanted to examine the ground accompanied by the commanders of the 6th and the 2nd Corps; none of these gentlemen found it acceptable. They could not understand how I could propose that slight rideau of Moinho Novo, and they paid hardly any attention to the escarpment of the hill of Vila Nova. We became very unpleasant about the subject of positions, and little [of our conversation] was based on the usage and advantage that could be obtained from them. Few men were capable of understanding and appreciating the refinements of terrain. It was necessary to make a continuous and thorough study; without that, we could find positions only on the highest mountain. Twice I was asked for my opinion. I stated it in a few words, observing that I did not look on this position as a means for hiding the whole army from the enemy and rendering it inaccessible.

According to military principles, one could never see without being seen nor maneuver without being the object of maneuvers. But what I had hoped to find there were very strong points to support the flanks and a few positions to cover the other parts of the line, and, for the remainder, all the advantages of terrain for fighting with superior firepower or for making a favorable counterattack, maneuvering with various arms. In addition, I mentioned the previous opinion of Marshal Ney and General Reynier. We went to Moinho de Cubo. I was limited to making an extensive study of the terrain. His Excellency began to talk about the operations, the principles, the legions, the discipline, etc., because this was how all our conferences ended. As we returned, I indicated from the top of the mountain of Alenquer to my two good friends, Cavailher and Beaufort, and also to Richoux, the terrain each one was going to study. We had a magnificent view from the summit of the mountain.

It is appropriate here to talk a little about the beautiful country that we occupied. Alenquer, our headquarters for a month, must have been a very beautiful city in time of peace. Built at the bottom and on the southern slope of an excellent valley, it had been left by the enemy in complete devastation and it was soon entirely ruined and horribly dirty as a result of the continual bivouac and passage of so many troops. No cleaning was done; manure and all kinds of debris filled the streets, and plague would have come in any other season.

This agreeable city had become merely a military colony. One expected [to hear] only the roll of the drums, the shouts of soldiers, and the noise of metal artillery wheels. When some of the curious visited the church, they rang the silent bells; this unexpected noise reminded us of old memories and sad thoughts, and we found ourselves even more struck by the destruction surrounding us. I cannot paint all the effects of these contrasts, so common in military life, such as the little fountain of Aspern running peacefully amidst the horrors of a burning village retaken fourteen times in two days, and the sundial in the middle of a battlefield, impassive as eternity, marking the last hour for the conquerors as well as for the conquered, and vainly telling these men that the fires of war are blind.

The proximity of Lisbon had attracted most of the inhabitants of Alenquer. The others did not dare to return home, for we had become masters of the city and they were frightened by the threats of the English and the Regency. We did not find either children or old men in the city. Two or three days later we saw a few old nuns; I sheltered and confined them in a small house. One of them came to our quarters daily to search for their bread of sorrow and anything we could add to it. At first the inhabitants of the country fled and hid. They did not dare return to the villages inhabited by foreign soldiers. They had no less hate for their pretended protectors and liberators. Most of them were roving in the woods, eating grass and wild fruit. Good God! What shelter did these unfortunates find? How many must have died during the six months we remained in this country, maintained by food that extreme necessity forced us to wrest from them.

Among other establishments, Alenquer possessed a handsome paper mill. It was not completed because the entire mechanism had to be brought from England. I could not keep from admiring the details! I often walked around this newborn factory, and when I compared this noble product of human industry with our profession, which was always accompanied by ravage and destruction, I sank a little deeper and enjoyed war a little less. Several hundred feet above the paper mill a charming little house had been constructed on ancient ruins and nestled in the rocks. We lodged there, away from the dirt of the city.

Thus we overlooked the beautiful valley and the delightful surroundings of Alenquer. Although the inside of the town was depressing and even hideous, the surroundings were still charming; every side offered a picturesque view and everyone wished to make a few drawings, always including a lively military scene. Around the house were orange and lemon trees, aloes throwing their flowery stems some twenty feet in the air, and enormous cacti extending their wide blades. Olive trees covered the hills; and here and there palm trees, as if with plumes and embellishments, crowned the scenery decorated by the great white flowers and soft green of the magnolia trees. The brown rocks brought out this greenery, in turn glittering delicately or dimly; swift and abundant waters, shadowed by the bending branches of gigantic weeping willows, refreshed everything. Everywhere both the beginning of winter and the soft influence of spring could be felt; the first buds were mating with the last flowers of autumn. Amidst the universal grief of the inhabitants, Nature maintained her brilliant ornaments, and this good mother seemed to be inviting all her children to enjoy her wealth in peace. We not only admired its beauty but walked far without fear of ambush or murder as we had in Spain.

We found the vineyards untouched, still covered with half-dried grapes, and the corn fields still covered with their harvest. Sometimes we saw wretched-looking peasants made even more hideous because of their misery. Everywhere individual soldiers were running about and gathering provisions, first for themselves and then for their companies, making wine, flour, bread, and taking advantage of all the things that would soon become vital to them. The usual goal of our walks, at the bottom of the valley, was the estate of the Grand Huntsman (a member of the Regency of Portugal), where a rather impressive house was inhabited by a few peasants. All the country was siliceous and the numerous mountains were formed by small fragments that were just like broken tiles. The fountains often showed inlaid limestone.

Our life was very simple. I am speaking of that of my two friends and myself. We lived very retiring lives when errands or work for the Prince did not call us outside, or when we did not have to prepare projects inside. Maps took most of our time. There had not been any operation for which I had not drawn several plans. I drew them for every contingency I could think of and finally, when the combinations were exhausted, my imagination transported me into the English camp. I examined what they could do against us, and often I wrote down those daydreams. I destroyed those dangerous plans quickly, but there is a stimulating one left from which I might give an extract. Besides, this is one of the best ways to work for those who want to study the profession of war.

We formed a small and very incomplete library, but it, along with our walks, provided our only amusement. On our trips and in the neighborhood of Alenquer, we had found most of the good French books. In Spain the mere possession of a great number of them would have carried us into the arms of the Inquisition: Voltaire, Rousseau, Helvétius, Condorcet, Dupuis, Raynal, our classic novels, even the works of Restif de la Bretonne. Specifically, there were many works on the Revolution, books in which its principles were praised and developed, and finally some military works, among which I had Puységur. What was interesting was that our literature was much more abundant than that of any other people; although these people had lived for such a long time under the influence of the English, the works of the latter were infinitely less numerous in the libraries where I had been. There were a great many of them, and only a few large villages where we could not find the *Encyclopédie*.

Nevertheless, we were always perfectly tranquil, while many people worried and even despaired. I was concerned only about a change in position because I knew about the confusion that usually existed during the movements of several corps. I was especially apprehensive that the rainy season would catch us in a precarious position and inconvenience us very much during our retrograde maneuver. I predicted this outcome amid contradictory opinions of every kind. This matter alone worried me and made my soul sad. The Prince, strongly thwarted in so many ways, was not always very gracious. Even if his brusqueness was not aimed at me, as everybody knows, it sometimes disgusted me and prevented me from communicating with him as frequently on minor things. In the meantime, it was necessary that all our work be connected and certain things, though they seemed unimportant at first, later became essential. Beginning with some fixed principles or bases, the plans were to be prepared in advance and brought successively into execution. The best plans, if proposed too abruptly, can fail and this was very rarely understood; thus many very good plans were often ignored.

Finally, one more thing must be said in order to complete the picture. We began to experience the harm of destitution. Now everything would follow. The provisions of an aide-de-camp were not very ample. I had more maps and paper than anything else. We could not find anything to replace what was used up. My hat no longer stayed on my head, my boots were getting bad, we did not have any soap and almost no candles or coffee. We had only what was strictly necessary. Our lodgings were without furniture and open on all sides. I was sleeping on a poor mattress, the worst in the army, because I was one of those who were least bothered by it. Yet this adventurous situation, not only full of boldness and hazard but also brilliant with glory, pleased and thrilled me so much that there are few memories in my life with as much charm for me. Perhaps it was the pure air, the beautiful climate, which made us appreciate life more—this could have contributed much to my attitude. Nevertheless, more than anything else, I liked all the old scenes, the strong emotions of war, and the great movement of the soul in the midst of success or reverse. Some memories ennobled us, others touched us; between the two we found an almost equal charm but very different lessons.

Opinion on the English Lines was fixed, and everybody looked toward Santarém. That position was vital for us, as much for its defensive position as for its proximity to the Tagus, its dockyard, and the various kinds of provisions we found in the city and its environs. The Prince had to make up his mind. The first reserves, the depots, and every type of magazine were to be established at Santarém. He sent me to the city while he went to visit the enemy works in front of Sobral again.

The city of Santarém, running north and south, was three times as long as it was wide. It was constructed on a kind of plateau fourteen to sixteen hundred yards in diameter, and it radiated in spokes in all directions; the abutments extended two thousand yards toward the Rio Maior but were much shorter and abrupt toward the Tagus. The abutment in the center, near the river, had a fort or castle rising from the city and surrounded by old, deteriorating walls. To the right and left on the riverbank were two suburbs, an abutment, and a Capuchine convent that formed the western extremity of the city. Toward the Rio

Maior three abutments descended in successive slopes; dominating each other and the entire plain where the river flowed, they enfiladed the road, crossing it for fourteen to sixteen hundred yards. In the valleys there were two roads separating the three abutments; the one toward the north was the main road to Lisbon, and the road to Abrantes went in the opposite direction. Accordingly, we could distinguish two systems of military occupation for Santarém. The first could be established on the ends of the abutments by strengthening the summits and the heads of the valley approaches, especially toward the Rio Maior. This defense, which extended rather far at first, could be successively concentrated on the various crests of the abutments. The second system was limited to defending the city or the plateau on which it was situated; there the fortification would play a much greater role than in the preceding project, and the various convents surrounding the outside of the city, toward the north and the west, could be advantageously employed for its defense.

The first system would require twelve thousand troops—with fewer than eight thousand it could not be used. Thus Santarém would become a position for an army corps. In this connection it would be difficult, for the troops held there would be backed up to a river and could be blockaded by an equal or even inferior number. In such a case it was too much like the celebrated position of Pirna.[21] As a very large bridgehead, it would be quite effective, but we could not consider establishing a permanent bridge at Santarém because of the terrible inundation extending along the left bank of the Tagus. These various difficulties disappeared once we limited ourselves to the occupation of the city. It then became a depot, a relatively well-fortified post, but one that could be surrounded and yet resist the pretense of a siege. Then the city was excellent for covering the depots and even the bridges, either by a temporary operation or by implementing a system to withdraw the bridges during the temporary floods, since they were not absolutely necessary. A garrison of only 2,500 to 3,000 men would be needed for that.

The Rio Maior, running 3,000 yards west of Santarém, crossed a wide and flat plain of 1,400 to 1,600 yards that was often covered with

21. Pelet's handwriting here is almost illegible, but the word appears to be Pirna, a famous Saxon city on the Elbe, surrendered by Saxon troops to the forces of Frederick the Great during the first year of the Seven Years War.

water. This river was 16 to 20 yards wide and 8 to 20 feet deep. The bridge was slightly closer to the right bank and bore the name of Asseca; the stream covered the first position at Santarém perfectly. The Rio Maior swerved to the right, parallel to the Tagus, probably through a discharge canal, leaving a rather wide, very wet, and difficult plain obstructed by the hills of Santarém between it and the river. Toward the right, the first bridge (Celeiro) was half a league away on the Rio Maior and had to be cut to insure the plan. Lopez's map showed shocking inaccuracies for this whole region.

I found Nempde, of the engineers' *état major*; he had been at Santarém for a few days to take care of the defense project. He had been considering it in its greatest scope. I believed it was expedient to limit it to a fortified post. By examining the various plans from both points of view and reducing, in consonance with the strength of the army, the garrison which could be placed there, we further limited the latter system. We sought to divide the town and concerned ourselves only with the areas indispensable for covering the bridges and the major establishments. Finally, in accordance with this rather good plan and the terrain, we resolved to occupy only the castle and the abutment to the west (that of the convent of Capuchine) and the small section of plateau which connected them, where there was a large convent suitable for defense. After many discussions we generally agreed on details.

I lodged at General Éblé's quarters, and I talked to him with so much strength and conviction about the importance and extreme necessity of the bridge that he said to me, "And you too, my friend! Here, do not break my heart." And he carefully employed two words that were sufficiently revealing: "'*tout manque*'—materials, workers, tools, money, and resources of every kind." Everything was lacking because the enemy had either taken everything from the Tagus or destroyed it. There was not even a sack of coal in the whole city. I brought orders to take the timber from a public building;[22] it was only the poorest type of wood and could not be of any use. The forests were far away,

22. Masséna wrote Éblé on October 18, "It will be necessary to surmount all obstacles; we must demolish the houses to obtain planks and beams, and iron and nails. Collect all the rope in the country [for the bridge]. . . . You will employ all the extraordinary means at your disposal to succeed there." Masséna also instructed him to construct two flying bridges and added, "Time presses and it is necessary to do all and to employ all . . . our resources." See Correspondance: Armée de Portugal, Carton C⁷10.

and we did not have any means of transportation. This worthy man was in despair, for all the needs of the army fell on him. He had been able to capture only two barges, one of which was going to be repaired. Together we went through the city, the suburbs, the private houses, and the convents, but there was nothing anywhere. We collected some rotten planks, but only in small quantities. The general had gathered some debris overlooked by the English in a kind of arsenal; anchors were made from axles, a few axes were forged because we had to begin by procuring the basic tools. Yet after wood, iron was necessary, then tar, rope, oakum, and also laborers to work with all of this. He had only three craftsmen in his artillery. Still this was the least of our worries for we were accustomed to finding such craftsmen in our armies and we knew well that all kinds of artisans could be located. Later the 44th Marine Flotilla was a great help. I spoke to the general about a battery to be established on our bank of the Tagus in order to stop the enemy from setting up one on the opposite bank. The enemy lost no time in doing this. My advice was neglected, and we were sorry later on.

General Montbrun was also at Santarém, preparing with great commotion for his expedition to Abrantes. He expected to take the town with his cavalry after crossing the Zezere with fifty swimmers.[23] The general regarded his expedition as glorious and easy. I was thinking the opposite. He pushed me vigorously on this, and on the necessity of explaining myself frankly—certainly a matter in which I had never been at fault. On my arrival at Alenquer, I found his report reinforced with all my explanations. At our approach the enemy had burned the bridge over the Zezere; its waters were very high. They had four regiments in Abrantes and many cannon,[24] and they announced the arrival of La Romana and the entry of Silveira into Leiria. Montbrun left the next day and was not able even to pass the Zezere. At Chamusca, on the other side of the Tagus, he saw twenty-seven boats he wanted to

23. Montbrun's forces included the 76th Line, the 11th Dragoons, a company of marines (44th Marine Flotilla), and four pieces of artillery. When Montbrun advanced on October 21, his men were instructed to search each house for sulphur, but unfortunately the cavalry, lacking discipline, pillaged the houses and destroyed large quantities of supplies. See Masséna to Montbrun, October 22, 1810, Correspondance: Armée de Portugal, Carton C^{7}10.

24. Abrantes, commanded by Governor Lobo, was defended by the 22nd Portuguese Line, or Serpa regiment, and the 13th Portuguese Line from Peniche.

seize, but he made too much noise and lost them.[25] Loison did not succeed any better against Abrantes when he was sent there. One could surprise a town when the garrison had been removed or was poorly guarded, but after the first moments the attack had to be renounced.

I also had orders to take care of the food and hospitals. I walked through the city of Santarém with the administrators. This country yielded a great deal of wheat; the houses were full of it. Part of it had been wasted, but much still remained. We found rations for fifteen days for the whole army in Santarém. We labored with donkeys and forage parties to collect the wheat into a magazine. Food was the worst problem for the administration. Meanwhile one of the villages in the neighborhood, where all the inhabitants had remained, promised to furnish thirty bags of flour every day in return for a similar amount of wheat, and some orderlies were sent for their protection. A storehouse was organized, but meat was lacking since the inhabitants had moved all their cattle to the other bank of the Tagus; yet we were sure to gather some inland. The hospitals were in a very deplorable condition or, rather, nothing had been done. Everything was lacking. We had sick people and a building but no doctors. The administrators requested a permanent commander and a small garrison of some laborers for the city. I should have left immediately but, detained by so many matters, I wrote to the Prince to give him an account and to ask him for the necessities.

A few inhabitants had returned. I consulted the important ones on the nature of the country and its communications. I drew up statistical bulletins of its production and its customary resources at that time, and I noted the roads. According to the inhabitants, the tide on the Tagus was noticeable as far as Valada, and the river rose very strongly and suddenly. Opposite Santarém it spread one league over the low and flat left bank. The Tagus was pleasant during the summer and autumn; it had been like that ten days earlier! A part of Hill's division, the in-

25. Unable to cross the Zezere, Montbrun requested reinforcements, and Loison was dispatched to Golegã with the 66th Line and 500 men of the 39th Line. In the meantime Montbrun learned that 27 boats were on the southern bank of the Tagus below Chamusca. Instead of waiting for Loison, he sent 50 swimmers across the river on October 25 supported by his artillery. Although most of the boats were seaworthy, the swimmers returned without them, apparently to await reinforcements. Before Montbrun could make arrangements to seize the boats, they were burned by the Portuguese. See Fririon, *Journal historique*, pp. 91–92; *Wellington's Dispatches*, Wellington to Liverpool, October 27, 1810, VI, 553–54.

habitants and their belongings, the animals on the right bank, everything, had crossed the Tagus a few days before our arrival![26] We could see that here the Tagus was 380 yards wide, while above and below it extended as much as 400 to 600 yards. In some areas it appeared to be full of sandbanks, islands with alluvium, and abandoned beds. Between Vila Nova and Santarém it was contained by dikes. A dry period would permit us to recover the fords on the Tagus. In that case there would be no more fear of famine. A few detachments of foragers would insure us of an abundance, the numerous boats lined up on the opposite bank would be at our disposal, our bridges could be organized immediately, and the results of the campaign would be changed. We were not fortunate enough for that! I complained bitterly to the inhabitants of Santarém about the conduct of their compatriots: "You treat us like barbarians. You authorize it, by forcing us to conduct ourselves like barbarians." This was the first time we had seen armed peasants in front of us. The right [*sic*] bank was covered with them. Reassured by the width of the river, they walked proudly along with their guns on their shoulders and were sometimes bold enough to shoot. Meanwhile, on our side many peasants remained in their villages far from the main roads.

When I returned and gave an account of my mission to the Prince, I found him a little angry with my report. I had put too much concern, too much devotion, and perhaps too little restraint in it. He talked to me in an immature way of the commander's calculations, but he quickly returned to his senses.[27] Turning to another subject about which I knew nothing, he declared that except for me he considered all those who proposed that we march to Oporto as his enemies. I then realized

26. On November 1 Major General Henry Fane's cavalry and a Portuguese brigade were transferred to the south bank of the Tagus and two weeks later Hill was alerted that his Second Division would soon follow. On October 18 his division began to cross to the southern bank of the Tagus. See *Wellington's Dispatches,* Wellington to Fane, November 1, 15, 1810, VI, 568–70, 624; Wellington to Hill, October 19, 1810, Hill Papers, Add. MSS 35093, in the British Museum.

27. Pelet's sympathetic two-page report to Masséna on the problems confronting Éblé concluded, "Meanwhile, I believe I am able to assure you of the complete validity of the report made by General Éblé and all that he has said to you." See Pelet to Masséna, October 18, 1810, Correspondance: Armée de Portugal, Carton C[7]10. A day later Éblé wrote to Masséna, "M. Pelet is obliged to have informed Your Highness of the few resources the country offers for the construction of a bridge and the difficulty of establishing it satisfactorily at Santarém on the supposition that nothing would be lacking." See Maurice Girod de l'Ain, *Grands Artilleurs: Drouot, Senarmont, Éblé* (Paris, 1895), pp. 428–29.

there had been talk about it in my absence. This project was dear to the hearts of those who missed the wealth of Lisbon and coveted that of Oporto. As for me, without lowering myself to vile calculations of self-interest, I would have preferred to abandon Beira Baixa for the riches and pleasures of the Vouga and the Douro.

I would have gone anywhere—to the Algarve or Trás-os-Montes—rather than leave Portugal. Yet above all I preferred the left bank of the Tagus and a system of operation based on both banks of the river, convinced that the position at Santarém was not adequate for the establishment of permanent bridges and as a consequence not adequate to become the center of our operation. It could only serve as a temporary passage and give us fortified support on the Tagus and the Rio Maior. Beyond that, all my considerations centered on the upper reaches of the river and pointed to Punhete at the mouth of the Zezere on the Tagus. If the locality permitted, we could establish a permanent double bridge and a triple bridgehead like that of Modlin[28] and become masters of the two great obstacles that divide the heart of Portugal, as well as of operations in Alentejo, Beira, and Estremadura. This point would become the center and the hub of all our operations. It was on the basis of such considerations that I answered the Prince without, meanwhile, concealing the advantages we could reap from Oporto, one of the wealthy towns of Europe and a city where there was a Portuguese government opposing Lisbon. This was an advantage we would want to maintain in its entirety for the profit of the army by placing there strong men of incorruptible honesty. The Prince sent me back to the quartermaster general to organize the military administration of Santarém. I talked with confidence to him. I permitted myself to give him a few insights into the future. "Sir, I am doing my duty," he told me. And I answered him plainly (as would a Royal prince) that at war "he who does only his duty does not do much." The quartermaster general was angry. I protested my innocent intentions. Finally he was pacified.

Whatever care we took, if the corps had waited to receive the necessary food from the administration, they would have run a great risk of doing without. It must be admitted that the quartermaster general

28. Modlin was a great fortified depot constructed on the Vistula River for the Grand Army before the invasion of Russia began in June 1812. After the retreat of the army, this position held out against attacks by the hostile German population.

was not equipped for such circumstances. The grain found in the country had not been distributed equally among the different corps. Those who had grain kept it, and the others lacked it. This happened particularly to the 8th Corps, placed as it was between the enemy and the remainder of the army. The 2nd Corps had found a quantity of wheat nearly sufficient for its nourishment at Vilafranca. The soldier scorned corn at this time, but he was soon forced to search carefully for it. The enemy had ruined all the mills; yet the dexterity of our soldiers soon had most of them repaired. Whatever was lacking was improvised in some other way. The grain was pounded or crushed between rocks rolled against each other. The regiments hulled and cooked for themselves in their cantonments or in the villages closest to the camp. They sent men great distances to search for everything that was needed—grain, cattle, and wine, which they found in great quantities in the caves of Cartaxo and Azambujeira. The soldiers applied themselves with much more fervor to these forages. We saw them in continuous lines [that ran] from their quarters to those beautiful hills, returning with the precious jugs on their backs or on donkeys. They scattered far and never returned without their tribute. They showed a special knack on these expeditions. When they went into a new region, they reconnoitered it from the highest points and by intuition went directly to their prize.[29] Then they left a few men to warn them by signals when anything happened. In these circumstances they showed inexhaustible activity, skill, and ingenuity that would have been worthy of admiration if discipline had not suffered from their continued vagrancy and if, because of their isolation, some excesses had not been committed.[30]

In the midst of these hard-working bees there were some hornets. The latter established themselves in houses where they could find plenty of food. Living quietly in their new domains, they would send someone to the camp from time to time to assure themselves there had

29. The Portuguese devised a system of burying their grain in large chests in the gardens surrounding their homes. However, the French soon learned their secret by observing the vapors rising from the ground early in the morning. See Lemonnier-Delafosse, *Souvenirs*, pp. 93–94.

30. These marauding parties, composed of men from each company and commanded by an officer, were expected to procure food for the regiments. In columns of 200 or 300 men, they were sent far behind the lines to gather supplies by any possible means. The marauding columns would divide and subdivide as they attempted to encompass more territory; thus small columns led by noncommissioned officers often became bands of starving, violent, undisciplined men ready to commit any crime for food or booty. See Noel, *Souvenirs*, pp. 128–29.

not been any movement; however, if they had heard any gunfire we should have seen them running as fast as possible into their ranks, for the worth of our soldiers has never been denied. This type of provisioning occasioned considerable waste, but whatever its disadvantages and even its dangers, it was becoming impossible to do otherwise. One-third of our soldiers, if not half, were always out of their camps on regular forage parties and on those carried out secretly for their own profit. The enemy could not be ignorant of this, and they knew our men were going very far away, especially toward the end.[31] This extreme reduction in our strength never induced them to attack us. It might also seem that this dispersion of our entire army would have caused enormous losses or even destroyed it in a few days. Nevertheless, we lost very few men because of the marvelous instinct that directed them and the valor they often displayed in these partial engagements. The enemy did not know how to profit by these advantages, although they might have pulled back some light corps in a system of mobile columns to capture or destroy our isolated men. They certainly did not know how to employ such tactics because they had not displayed enough refinement in their plans to have willfully neglected this tactic.

General Loison had been sent to the Zezere with the 66th Line and part of Marcognet's brigade, which had furnished a garrison at Santarém. He was ordered to attempt a coup de main on the entrenchments of Abrantes, as well as to occupy both banks of the Zezere and watch Tomar, where there was a regiment of dragoons. General Montbrun, still posted before Punhete, had been put temporarily under his orders. Fortunately General Loison did not judge it necessary to venture an attack against Abrantes; it would not have succeeded after the way the enemy had strengthened the place.[32] At Barquinha he found

31. Most of the bands of marauders traveled distances of 30 to 50 miles from their regiments. They remained away as long as 10 days, and as soon as they returned new columns of marauders would leave. See Lemonnier-Delafosse, *Souvenirs*, pp. 94–97. Masséna was rightly concerned about this situation and instructed his corps commanders to halt the practice. "Different reports have been made to me that one-third of the regiments scatter a great distance from their cantonments to maraud. This cannot be tolerated at any time. . . . You will please give strict orders that the roll be called each day in each regiment of your army corps." See Masséna to Ney, Junot, Reynier, and Montbrun, October 25, 1810, Correspondance: Armée de Portugal, Carton C[7]10. There are slight variations in the letters to the corps commanders.

32. Loison's column, which also included the 6th and 11th Dragoons, reconnoitered Abrantes on November 4. They encountered a Portuguese unit at Rio de

some materials—rope and wood—for the bridge. A few boats seized on the Tagus were also brought back to Santarém. At the same time the army corps received general orders to redouble their surveillance and push frequent reconnaissances on the enemy line, as much for their own safety as to harass the English and to keep them in fear of an attack.[33] These orders were renewed more vigorously two days later after a report from General Reynier announced a movement in the English Line from the right to the left. This occasioned a kind of alert. Everybody was on guard except in the Prince's quarters, where we knew what to believe. There were also some rumors of a movement by the 5th Corps of the Army of Andalusia which was, without doubt, following the troops of La Romana. Lord Wellington, writing a letter on behalf of his prisoners, paid tribute to Marshal Ney by announcing the return of the Marshal's nephew, who had been a prisoner in England.

The beautiful weather continued for several days after the interminable rains which were so fatal to us during our march; the rainy season was drawing nearer. I dreaded this terrible rain very much, first because of the Tagus, then because of the unpaved roads and the streams we encountered at every step! It was an excellent aid for the English, rendering the approaches to their Line more impracticable and our movements more difficult everywhere. This country was very windy, and the winds from the sea covered us with immense clouds that burst into over-abundant rains. It was no less damaging to the fragile arms of our windmills, since the soldiers had not become accustomed to maneuver quickly enough to protect them. Meanwhile, we were not hurt as much by this bad weather as we had feared.

The Prince prepared general dispositions for the army in case of an enemy attack. Thus all the movements were known, and everyone could go immediately to his position in the manner indicated. When

Moinhos and drove it back some two miles into the city. *Chef de bataillon* Nempde of the engineers then made an extensive reconnaissance of the town, diagraming its fortifications and noting its weaknesses. See Masséna to Junot, November 4–5, 1810; "Reconnaissance des ouvrages et des approches de Abrantès faite le 5, 9bre, 1810, par Nempde," Correspondance: Armée de Portugal, Carton C^{7}10.

33. As early as October 16, Masséna instructed his corps commanders, "It is always necessary to have the enemy fearful of being attacked at one time or another. How shall we make them fear us? By strong reconnaissances on all points of the line; these will keep him under arms day and night." See Masséna to Ney, October 16, 1810, Correspondance: Armée de Portugal, Carton C^{7}10.

the map was completed, I occupied myself with the dispositions. In the guidelines he gave me, the Prince had fixed a line of retreat through Leiria. I prepared a report which is still in my papers. I projected the different marches on the map. I thought I had foreseen and calculated everything. The movements were combined and balanced step by step. The 8th Corps would go successively to Ota, the 6th Corps to Guerreiros, the 2nd Corps to Vila Nova, and the cavalry behind the 8th Corps, with Loison and Montbrun marching in reserve directly to Rio Maior. When I took my work to the Prince, I found him excited. Without listening to me, he dictated other dispositions. The 6th Corps was to go to Alcoentre, the 8th Corps to Guerreiros, and the 2nd Corps to Vila Nova.[34] I permitted myself to point out that the line was very long, parallel to that of retreat, instead of perpendicular as it should be, and that it would be necessary to protect Ota in order to support the movements of the 2nd Corps, especially when it retreated through the long and difficult hills of Vila Nova. His Excellency paid no attention. If I had been in command, I would have returned entirely to my first positions at Vila Nova, Moinho Novo, and Camarnal, which were supported up to the hills of Alenquer with three roads (to the rear) abutting on the recessed position of Ota and Cubo, since it was decided to abandon Santarém and that line of retreat.

It had been a month and a half since we left the Spanish frontier. The 9th Corps was supposed to arrive soon, and the Prince had every right to think that it would proceed toward the army immediately. It was with this hope that His Excellency plunged into Portugal. However, he was becoming even more worried because he had not received any information; the presence of the 9th Corps was indispensable for subsequent operations.[35] The Prince was relying on requests that had already been made. Meanwhile the Prince had been thinking for some time of sending an officer to Paris to give news of the army and to

34. For details of the plans for an immediate withdrawal in the event of attack, see "Disposition générales pour prendre position sur les coteaux Aveiras [*sic*], October 28, 1810," Correspondance: Armée de Portugal, Carton C710.

35. Napoleon was also anxious about the fate of Masséna and his army. He had had no direct news of the army since it crossed the Côa into Portugal in September; his only source of information was the English newspapers. On September 18 Napoleon instructed Drouet to communicate with and support the Army of Portugal, and ten days later he wrote to Berthier, "I am most anxious that he [Drouet] should go to Valladolid as soon as possible to watch the rear of the Army of Portugal." On October 12 he instructed Berthier to order Drouet to continue his move-

demand reinforcements or new orders. It would have been better if he had worried about this before our arrival at Alenquer. The Prince only informed me on October 27 about his project to send General Foy with a detachment of four to five hundred men through Tomar and Ponte de Murcella. This assignment was certainly the greatest mark of confidence His Excellency could give, and the most advantageous occasion for receiving some reward; consequently, Foy was named general of division. The Prince gave him very extensive instructions, details of our movements as well as of the various obstacles we had encountered and those that now delayed us, and a rather poor drawing of the enemy lines and the terrain we occupied.[36] The general left from Santarém carrying orders for General Gardanne to rejoin the army with his detachment by marching through Tomar or any other road that he judged suitable.

The Prince surveyed the waters of the Tagus with the greatest care. Graduated gauges were prepared at Santarém and Vilafranca to observe the varying elevations of the river. If the river fell slightly, we

ments toward Valladolid "according to the turn of events in Portugal." As the days passed without news from Masséna, Napoleon became even more concerned. On November 2, when he learned that Drouet was still at Valladolid, he thundered to Berthier, "It is necessary that you inform him [Drouet] that I am anxious for him to make a diversion to reopen communications with the Prince d'Essling." On the following day, after reading more English newspapers, the Emperor wrote angrily to Berthier, "Make General Drouet understand that I am most anxious for news of the Army of Portugal; that it is important from every point of view, and that the communications must be reestablished so we may have information. . . . Six days later, genuinely alarmed, Napoleon issued orders for Drouet to advance into Portugal, supported by 7,000 to 8,000 men of the Imperial Guard between Burgos and Valladolid. "It is absolutely necessary to obtain news of the Army of Portugal and afford it aid." However, Napoleon did not obtain direct information about Masséna's army until Foy arrived on November 22, 1810. See *Correspondance de Napoléon Ier*, Nos. 16921, 16963, 17036, Napoleon to Berthier, September 18, 28, October 12, 1810, XXI, 148, 182–84, 250; *Mémoires et Correspondance politique et militarie du Roi Joseph*, ed. A. Du Casse (Paris, 1855), Napoleon to Berthier, November 2, 3, 9, 1810, VII, 358–64.

36. In the report Foy carried to the Emperor, Masséna declared, "For twelve days I have been in front of the works of the Anglo-Portuguese army. It is behind three lines of entrenchments which have been in preparation for eighteen months. . . . I am not able to attack fortifications supported by formidable artillery and an enemy twice as numerous as us. The lines have given them great advantage and I would have to compromise the army of His Majesty, the Emperor. I would not have the strength to give battle in open country and in the actual state of things, I limit myself to observing all his approaches. . . . Since our departure from Almeida, the army has declined by 7,000 to 8,000—wounded, dead, and missing. . . . We did not find any inhabitants in this entire country through which we passed." See Masséna to Berthier, October 29, 1810, Archives de Masséna, LI.

had everything to hope for, as the enemy had everything to fear. If we could take advantage of a ford, the crossing would be effected immediately. If we had to wait for the construction of the necessary boats, it would be impossible to think about crossing for a long time, and our operation might become impossible. On their side the enemy carefully guarded all the usually fordable points, and opposite Santarém they placed cannon which fired on everything that showed its face. They kept a battery with a strong detachment of Portuguese infantry at Escaroupim facing Azambuja, and numerous posts of peasants were lined up along its entire bank. Lord Wellington had already made General Fane and the English troops cross.[37] Thereafter the Santarém area seemed to be the quarter in which we would have to operate; moreover, all the Prince's attention was directed to that end. He had sent General Fririon to Santarém.[38] The general wrote several reports on the difficulties and impossibilities arising on every side; he was assured that the English would not move on our front. The Prince extended the army to facilitate its subsistence and to move it slowly toward the Tagus. Moreover, he decided to go to Santarém in order to accelerate the work there and to take advantage of every available means of throwing a corps on the other side of the Tagus if the waters receded a little more; it would either establish itself there or seize the boats still on the enemy bank.[39] Finally, he had to prepare cantonments for the army to occupy after abandoning the position at Sobral because the rainy season and its miseries were approaching. We could already see the moment when lack of food would force our withdrawal. The Prince searched everywhere for money to put at the disposal of General Éblé for his bridges, since the paymaster's chest had been exhausted for a long time.

37. Sir Henry Fane (1778–1840) entered the 6th Dragoons as a cornet in 1792. Accompanying Wellington to Portugal in 1808 as a brigadier general, he served at Roliça, Vimeiro, and Corunna, as well as during Masséna's invasion of 1810–11.

38. Concerned about Éblé's progress at Santarém and skeptical of Pelet's report of October 18, Masséna sent Fririon to Santarém to observe and "put everything in your notes to make a report to me." See Masséna to Fririon, October 25, 1810, Correspondance: Armée de Portugal, Carton C[7]10.

39. On October 29 Masséna left for Santarém to determine the validity of the report given to him by Pelet and Fririon regarding Éblé's progress in gathering material for a bridge across the Tagus. During the previous twelve days Masséna and Éblé had exchanged a series of letters characterized by recriminations and acrimony. Masséna's trip was actually made to allay his concern about Éblé's efforts and abilities. For details of this disagreement, see Horward, "Invasion of Portugal," pp. 432–43.

The Prince left early for Santarém. According to a special disposition that surprised everybody, he left me at Alenquer with secret authorization to open his dispatches and to communicate them to General Fririon, who was also staying at Alenquer with part of the main *état major*.[40] I saw this worthy general very often. I was constantly honored with his kindness during the entire campaign. At that time, he confided to me the ridiculous gossip about the Marshal whose affairs I was now guiding. The general knew quite well the part I played in affairs and how it was sometimes insignificant and disputed. The Prince established relays on the road and left several of his aides-de-camp to carry the reports of the advance posts to him each day.

Adjutant Commander Jacques François Delelée went to reconnoiter the position for the 8th Corps, which had been established according to the orders of the Prince. I pointed out to him that the left was at the confluence of the brooks of Ota and Guerreiros. Then I went to General Reynier to receive his information on the country beyond the Zezere. The General claimed that the area was rather productive, that the roads were not as bad as we had been told, that the rains which threatened us were not so heavy, and that the swelling rivers were less considerable. We hoped to find fords as we reascended the Tagus. He strongly advised, and so did I, maneuvers on the other bank and even a siege of Elvas and Badajos so that our war in Portugal would not be interrupted. However, he wanted to make these expeditions by occupying Abrantes and remaining along the Zezere, while I thought we could hardly keep both banks of the Tagus with a bridgehead at Punhete; thus we could not consider the sieges unless we received reinforcements. The General thought that the army could withdraw through Castelo Branco into Spain if necessary, but Estremadura was so depleted we could not hope to find any food there. In addition he promised to send me a few written notes, which amounted to very little. More than ever, I found that he had great difficulty expressing himself. After hesitating and searching for words for a long time, he

40. Before leaving for Santarém, Masséna wrote to Fririon, "My first aide-de-camp, M. Pelet, remains at Alenquer with orders to open all the letters addressed to me. He will communicate to you all those that are relative to the service. You will respond to the requests and give answers within your jurisdiction, as if they were mine. . . . Will you please have some confidence in my first aide-de-camp; he has mine and he should merit yours. You will communicate with him in order to make emergency arrangements while awaiting my presence or response." See Fririon, *Journal historique,* Masséna to Fririon, October 29, 1810, pp. 95–96.

could not express himself any better. He was very busy with the topography of the country. At his quarters I saw a section of the English Lines from Sobral to Alhandra, drawn very well by the artillery officer Enoch*; there was the course of the Tagus from Alcántara to Almaraz, one of the immediate surroundings of Lisbon, and finally a plan of Peniche showing five or six fronts on an isthmus, but with flat bastions or great square towers.

The Duc d'Abrantès gave very vivid descriptions of the misery of his army corps. We must agree that it had finally become excessive. Later it was to suffer the most. However, he had already asked to evacuate the position or to be relieved; yet at that time he was still far from such extremes. We exchanged a few prisoners. There were some difficulties on the subject of Lord Percy, whom the English were requesting. It was impossible to send him back because he had lived with us for such a long time and knew not only the strength and composition of the army, but also the most secret details of our headquarters, where he lived unconstrained. They also refused unconditionally to receive Portuguese officers in exchange. In addition our [repatriated French] prisoners praised their good treatment by the English very much because they had not seen the convict ships of England, and they complained bitterly about the Portuguese. In returning, our men were intentionally made to pass through several parts of the first and second Lines covered with impenetrable works. They had seen the Spanish troops of La Romana there in very poor condition. The friction prevailing among the various troops was obvious. On our side, we placed some detachments on the road that the English prisoners were to follow in order to increase their estimate of the strength of our small army. Deserters announced that four English regiments of reinforcements had arrived, the 11th Foot was presently disembarking, the light cavalry was returning from Spain to Portugal, the rear guard had crossed the Tagus at Lisbon, and there were rumors of an English attack if they were not attacked themselves; others confirmed the arrival of La Romana. English newspapers announced the capture of Almeida and claimed incorrectly that Portuguese officers had been involved in it, whereas the governor was incapable of any resistance after that tremendous disaster.[41]

41. Governor Cox claimed that several Portuguese officers led a revolt against him after the explosion and forced him to surrender. The English maintained that

Alenquer was a very important position. In the first place, the largest elements of the headquarters were still located there, and this created a considerable number of people and great congestion because of the wagons; it was also the point of retreat for the 8th Corps. Meanwhile, as a result of its slopes, the bridge, and the long road, the city formed a very narrow and difficult defile at the bottom of an extremely deep valley. As soon as we arrived, I reconnoitered the neighborhood. Subsequently I established a system of occupation and defense which I indicated to Major Pierre Charles Morel, the commander of the 82nd Line, garrisoned there. Alenquer could be turned and taken on the flank along the right by roads that descended from Sobral into its valley, and on the left by another road that descended onto the main highway between Alenquer and Carregado from the crest of a height dominating the city to the west. Two bridges beyond the limits of the city would have to be carefully defended. The garrison was to occupy the summit near the road from Sobral and provide as much resistance as possible; they were to descend it successively to the entrance of the city and then ascend to an elevated position to give time for the evacuation of headquarters by the insignificant road to Moinho Novo. In withdrawing, the troops would send some men toward the right to reinforce the garrison, marching by two roads which descended toward the center bridge; there they would start their defense again on the other side of the stream. When one of the bridges had been forced, the garrison would withdraw along three roads, two of which took them to the mountain on the east where they could hold for a while. What increased the importance, or rather the dangers, of this position was that the guards of the 2nd and 8th Corps were so poorly placed and linked that the enemy could move directly on Alenquer by Arruda and Refugidos.

In the other direction the road from Runa through the valley to Alenquer was neither guarded nor observed. Moreover, from a distance the enemy could turn and reach the 8th Corps on its point of

Colonel Fortunato José Barreiros, who commanded the artillery, and Francisco Bernardo da Costa de Almeida were instrumental in the collapse of Portuguese morale. Wellington complained to Stuart, "The Major commanding the artillery was the person employed by Cox to settle the capitulation for him. He went out and informed the French of the exact state of the place after the explosion, and never returned!! Masséna has made him a colonel!!" See *Wellington's Dispatches* (1852 ed.), Wellington to Stuart, August 31; Wellington to Liverpool, September 5; Beresford to Wellington, September 4, Cox to Beresford, August 30, 1810, IV, 252–58.

retreat by either or both of its flanks. We could see how easily Lord Wellington could have seized the weak 8th Corps in order to extend himself by the heights of Alenquer to Moinho Novo or Vila Nova right into the middle of our army. He could destroy it, at least partially, by sending the English and elite Portuguese forward, leaving the others in the Lines. We could also see how necessary it was for us to defend this unique exit with all our resources. This gave me an idea for the retrograde movements of the 8th Corps, but I was not able to communicate it to anyone at that time. I kept it in mind, convinced that my weak voice, contradicted in moments of tranquility, would be heeded in a moment of danger. In general, I was waiting for this moment because we did not understand these maneuvers very well and executed them even less effectively.

The withdrawal of the 8th Corps was to take place according to the same principles. General Ferey, detached from Loison's division, was to march along his left, extending by the crest of the hills and retiring through Refugidos to take a position above Carnota. (If those who have good maps of Portugal find some mistakes in these localities, let them remember we had very bad information on the names of these various places.) The 8th Corps would be obliged to march its artillery toward Alenquer at the first gunshot and withdraw slowly without starting its defense until Clauzel's division had arrived parallel with Solignac's division, because of the roads that came from Outeiro and Arruda on its left; then they were to halt the enemy on the two crests for as long as possible. The troops were to descend along the road running through Mata in the valley of Alenquer and through the positions above the Quinta de Dom Carlos, thus defending the approaches of the valley and Alenquer. The 8th Corps was to draw near the city in echelon and, after mounting the summits, one brigade was to place itself on the right of General Ferey, who was to withdraw by the road to Carregado if the 2nd Corps was still holding and the enemy did not push him too vigorously. Naturally, General Reynier had his position behind the stream of Carregado, strongly reinforcing his right toward the summits. As soon as the artillery of the 8th Corps had gone beyond the defiles of the city, the corps was to defend all of Alenquer just as its garrison would have to do on a smaller scale if the enemy continued to push it determinedly.

The 8th Corps was also to cover the march of its artillery on Cubo and keep a few pieces, the lightest ones, to hold back the enemy as long as possible. It was to place them along the crest and, if necessary, set fire to the tall buildings of Alenquer to stop the enemy artillery in those narrow passages. The 82nd Line was to take a position on the hills to the east of the city to insure the flank of the 8th Corps during its movements on the minor road to Moinho Novo; then it was to withdraw parallel with the crests.

The Prince announced that he had done a good deal of work in Santarém and its neighborhood. In effect, he already had troops on the left bank of the Zezere. Two bridges were prepared, one of boats and the other of barges. He planned to have the troops cross at Tancos, where the Tagus was very narrow and there were some facilities for a crossing. General Trelliard gave an account of the reconnaissance ordered on Leiria. He did not find anything in the city. Pombal was also without troops. A brigadier of Trant's forces made an appearance there in mid-October with two thousand infantrymen and five hundred horses, and had them withdrawn toward Coimbra. The corps were informed about the officers whom the Prince had named provisionally to fill vacancies. An English officer said one of their detachments had seized Crosses and certificates in the mail. The latter information made me and my friends rather anxious. A few days later I wrote to Fitzroy Somerset,[42] first aide-de-camp of Lord Wellington, at the same time that I sent a letter from the Prince to His Excellency requesting the return of the Marquise d'Alorna, who was said to be confined in a convent. The lady was not returned to us, but Somerset consented to send me a large parcel of private letters.

General Fririon, visiting the line, ordered Loison's division to give food and flour mills to the 8th Corps in order to prolong its stay in position. He returned very worried about the enormous gap he found between the 8th and 2nd Corps, which had not been filled at all nor even masked by Ferey's brigade [as ordered].[43] As a result of this gap,

42. Lord Fitzroy James Henry Somerset, Baron Raglan (1788–1855), was Wellington's military secretary after December 1810; he replaced Lieutenant Colonel James Bathurst, who was recalled to England. Somerset assumed these functions at the age of 22 and served in this capacity until the end of the war; he ended his career as Lord Raglan in the Crimean War.

43. Fririon, describing the untenable position of the 8th Corps, declared, "The village [of Sobral] can be considered as the center of a circle and more than half of its circumference was occupied by the British." See his *Journal historique*, pp. 106–8.

it was necessary for the divisions of the advance guard to tighten up on the left, at least when the gunfire began. The 2nd Corps was also to bear toward the right near the village occupied by General Soult; then the positions would nearly be connected and closed. General Reynier announced that the English advance posts of the 6th Foot had been replaced at Alhandra by the Guards. This led him to assume that General Hill had made some movements on the left bank and that he had Craufurd's or Picton's division before him. The ford of Escaroupim on the Tagus that he carefully observed was still more practicable, and the enemy withdrew the cannon, leaving only the Portuguese troops there. Reports from the rest of the line did not mention these troop movements. It was true that the Duc d'Abrantès was as negligent about his duties as General Reynier was careful. Rumors that the 5th Corps had marched were renewed. Another disembarkation of English troops at Figueira was announced, along with the concentration of militia near Ourém. Marshal Ney moved his headquarters to Azambuja. The Prince placed Loison's division near the Zezere. He sent the 6th Léger to Santarém and General Marchand with two of his regiments to Tomar. Simultaneously, he gave orders to General Reynier to occupy Vila Nova, General Fririon to visit the positions at Sobral, and me to examine those at Alhandra and Arruda.[44]

General Reynier wrote that the enemy had arrived and were bombarding Vilafranca. He could only counter with a few soldiers; his line was extended greatly and could be attacked with advantage. The Duc d'Abrantès announced that the English were gathering twenty battalions in front of him, that he was suffering excessively from lack of food, that several regiments were reduced to the last extremity, and that his cavalry always experienced some losses when contending with the enemy horsemen. All these letters requested that the positions at Sobral and Vilafranca be abandoned, and it seemed they were all written for the same purpose. When I made the various reconnaissances mentioned at the beginning of this chapter, I found that the 8th Corps was still at the extremity of the abutment of Sobral, despite the orders the Duc d'Abrantès had received twenty-four days earlier. Contrary to

44. Fririon, however, said that he reconnoitered the positions of Clauzel and Solignac at Sobral while Pelet examined Ferey's posts guarding the valley of the Arruda. Fririon strongly recommended that the 8th Corps be withdrawn before it was driven out. Pelet apparently made only a few notes on his reconnaissance; thus Fririon's son criticized him for it in 1841. See Fririon, *Journal historique,* p. 105.

the reports he had sent, the 8th Corps was not linked any better with the 2nd Corps, whatever had been written on this point.

The Prince sent orders for me to go to Santarém.[45] Passing through the position of Moinho Novo and Vila Nova, I saw again what appeared to be a good site for a battle, whatever the great men might say. In my dreams, I hoped to receive them there—our small army against all the combined forces of Lord Wellington. I passed through the impregnable city of Vila Nova. The paved road from Santarém turned round the foot of the hills of Azambuja and Cartaxo and crossed several valleys that came down from Aveiras. These valleys presented a few rearguard positions for us, easily turned by their right if the summits of Aveiras were not occupied. The principal one of these positions lay to the east of Azambuja, with its left resting at the convent of Virtudes. The Tagus ran about a league from the road through a beautiful plain, but the plain was restricted to the foot of the hills by the artificial bed of the Rio Maior, which collected the waters of all the hills and could serve to support the left of these defense positions. The environs of Azambuja and Cartaxo were beautiful and covered with vineyards, olive trees, etc. The villages in other areas were superb with sandy moors and pine forests. The English telegraph line began at Vilafranca and passed through Azambuja, Santarém, and Atalaia.

The Prince greeted me with great kindness on my arrival at Santarém. He told me he was thinking about positions and wanted me to work there with him. The Prince talked to me about his work at Santarém. He had rather quickly collected forty-two boats there or on the Zezere and with twenty more he would have what was needed to cross the Zezere. A bridge was established at Punhete on the Zezere and another was then placed at Martinchel. The Prince also talked to me about the position of the troops which he had in this area and that of the army in general, and of his intention to canton there. The 6th Corps would be in the neighborhood of Tomar, Loison's division guarding the Zezere, the 8th Corps at Torres Novas and Golegã, the 2nd Corps at Santarém in charge of the bridge, the cavalry near Leiria and forward to scout, and the headquarters in Torres Novas. We occupied ourselves for a long time with the details of these troop dis-

45. In a footnote at this point Pelet explains that the remainder of the chapter was copied directly from his Journal. In all, perhaps 10 or 15 percent of the entire manuscript was taken verbatim from his Journal.

positions, the commanders of the corps, and the moment to execute the general and particular measures. I was not always of his opinion, but we ended agreeing to his original idea, and he dictated the principal articles of the instructions to me. This work did me much good. I could only benefit even when I did not feel bound to yield to the Prince's reasoning. This was excellent training from the *état major*. The plan itself was excellent.

The army would occupy a productive country. It could be moved on the enemy position from the roads of Leiria and Tomar to the Mondego, from the route of Castelo Branco and Guarda, and on the Tagus to prepare the bridges. They would wait for reinforcements, provisions, instructions, and orders. Once the bridges were established, the army would be master of Portugal (except for the capital) since it would be able to move in any direction. Finally, cantoned in a beautiful country, the army would recuperate and rest from its numerous marches and bivouacs.

Meanwhile Abrantes, protected from a coup de main, would require a vigorous operation or even a regular attack, as I had always thought. I had hoped we would not trouble about the Zezere at this moment, or that only a trestle bridge would be built there in order to have a position on the left bank. Then we could gather all the materials for one bridge on the Tagus. If, as the Prince assured me, he could have it completed in fifteen or twenty days, the army would not leave Vilafranca and Alenquer, and these positions would be strengthened and occupied as noted below. As soon as we reached Santarém, the enemy would send a strong detachment on the left bank of the Tagus and disturb our crossing, especially if they occupied the suitable points with entrenched batteries. Because of their system of signals and the bend of the Tagus, they could detach many troops and they would always be warned in time of all our forward movements on Vila Nova and Alenquer; they could thus take measures to avoid being caught in the Lines. Then we would occupy Alenquer with one division of the 6th Corps, with an advance guard on a height half a league away and posts in the valleys. Castanheira, the gorges of the valley of the Arruda, and the Tagus would be occupied by another division; there would be posts on the heights to the right. Finally, the third division of the 6th Corps would be in position at Vila Nova with a brigade at Moinho Novo and cavalry as far as Alcoentre. This disposition was safe and the enemy could hardly attack. It menaced the enemy vigorously and in such a way as to hold them in check and stop them from separating their forces. The 2nd and the 8th Corps would have been cantoned temporarily between Vila Nova, Alcoentre, and Santarém. While waiting, we would be working along the Zezere and the Tagus on the barges that would form the bridge. At the moment the troops at Santarém were to erect the bridge, the 6th Corps would make a retrograde movement. Then we could attempt a coup de main in force on both banks against Abrantes, but it was better not to think of this yet.

This retrograde movement was perfectly safe because a single division of the 6th Corps as a rear guard could hold the English army at Vila Nova for a whole day. This division would then be able to retire quietly in front of the enemy between the Tagus and the hills, and finally we could accommodate the army in the position of Rio Maior and consequently make defensive preparations there. Whereas a British detachment on the left bank would obstruct us very little during the construction of the bridge, it would give great stability to Abrantes while, on the other hand, the attention of the enemy army would be turned to this river and to Alentejo, which they would devastate and evacuate. One great advantage of this disposition was that it retained for us a foothold opposite the enemy lines and the means of attacking them immediately if our reinforcements arrived. We would abandon this operation only when we were assured of that on the Tagus. The 6th Corps had enough food to subsist in the area for some time. We were also awaiting the first result of General Foy's mission, but the Prince had his plan in mind and since there was not one point of agreement between our two views, it was impossible for me to develop a system based on proper principles, as distinguished from a plan based strictly on inspiration. When one does not listen for a long time or read and is sometimes angry and moody, and when fate has already spoiled his project, he has good reason to believe that what has been successful for him in the past is the best thing to do. Nevertheless, I opposed some dangerous and unimportant dispositions in his plan. The Prince postponed a decision until the next day. Everything was set up later except for a few modifications which provided some latitude to assure that the movement would be well executed and mutually supported by the various corps.

In the second [*sic*] long conversation with Vacherat [Masséna's secretary], he mentioned a singular assertion that had been made about me in the *Journal de Lisbonne* [*Gazeta de Lisboa*]. Although the statement flattered my vanity, it would be dangerous if such rumors should ever reach the ears of the Prince or the Emperor. Unfortunately, the story was very generally accepted; the role I played was rather honorable but certainly hazardous and greatly envied. Nevertheless, I will show myself worthy of that role. If it did not make a fortune for me, it flattered my pride so much that I could not complain, whatever the cost. Yet it was hard to see myself credited with the responsibility for events over which I had no direction and blamed for those I found myself forced to support openly or silently—if fortune smiles it will not be for me; so, frequently I will have to remain silent. (I had constantly predicted success or failure in this campaign without being able to assist the one or prevent the other. But I have not been as unfortunate as I might have been, and I owe it only to myself. If what was said about the *Journal de Lisbonne* is correct, those who saw the statement will remember it. I myself will certainly not repeat it. But in some way those rumors have forced me to write this Journal.) On one side [Masséna's], there was immense glory, consummate experience, excellent service in warfare and administration, great military genius and innumerable victories, brave actions and brilliant conquests; and on the other side [Pelet's], a little theory, study, application, and the desire to do well. The balance was not equal! Moreover, without the overwhelming evidence which drove one to try and brave everything, could one run the risk of recommending a project that he could not execute himself and that might involve far-ranging consequences? Could one then defend his opinions? Could one persist? Could one fight?

The passions of the Prince did not always permit one to reason with him. I always did it on an important occasion! More than once I vigorously opposed him, but there were few remedies for our difficulties. On the other hand, all the generals envied the way the Prince treated me. The commanders who were offended by it believed they had reason to be! What could I do about it? Complain? No! My only ambition had always been to have duties above rank. I believed this is what characterizes men! My friends worried about all this. As far as I was concerned, deep inside I was proud of my role, yet I wanted to answer only for those things I did.

We talked with the Prince about all his troubles, the annoying obstacles, and his disgust. Everyone irritated him and he complained about everything. The Prince had great finesse and understanding of men; he did not always take into account their good qualities nor judge them favorably. His attitude was the result of knowing too well the world and affairs. Much politeness and moderation were required to hide it, but he did not always do this. We talked about a concentration at Ourém. General Montbrun was sent there and found nothing. Another reconnaissance, directed to Cabaços on the road from Tomar to Murcella, encountered some men and a Portuguese prisoner was taken there. According to him, three army corps were in the area under the command of Lieutenant General Bacelar, who was now at Botão beyond Coimbra; the first force, behind Cabaços with six thousand men, was commanded by Trant; the third unit of eight thousand men, almost all militia or peasants, was at Coimbra with Silveira. The latter was always withdrawing in front of our reconnaissances. Earlier we had announced the presence of numerous troops, including fifteen thousand English at Peniche or Figueira.

The Prince spoke of sending someone to Paris and asked for my advice. I told him that it was difficult for me to point out someone and I added, "As far as I am concerned, I am always ready to do anything for you, wherever you will judge me most useful." "You are needed here too much," he had the kindness to tell me. I was willing to make the trip because of my devotion to him. I felt it was important that the progress of the campaign be well presented and discussed in Paris by a man who knew the country and the situation, and could go into it deeply with the Emperor; but above all the man would have to be fully devoted to the Prince and to this task. In offering myself I had fulfilled my duty to His Excellency and toward myself. But I did not say anything more about it.[46] I asked him only for one company of infantry to assure going by the most direct road. As I expected, the Prince ordered me to return to Alenquer and watch the withdrawal to see that everything was carried out according to orders. After lunch he sent me the instructions and orders, which would not be given until later in order to avoid indiscretions. By having me come to do this

46. It would certainly have been unwise for Masséna to send Pelet to Paris with Sainte-Croix dead. During the previous five years he had relied upon one or the other of them for help in preparing and coordinating the complex details of his maneuvering corps or army.

work, the Prince gave me splendid proof of his friendship and confidence.

As I passed 2nd Corps headquarters, I had to talk to General Reynier about our movement. I briefly discussed the successive dispositions on Carregado and Vila Nova, giving some opinions on them and on his position in general. I dined with him and the grandson of General Eliott, the governor of Gibraltar.[47] He was a marine lieutenant who had arrived from the Indies to get married in London and to see his brother. He had intended to follow the advance-post line to join his brother at Arruda but he stopped to eat figs in a valley where he was captured by our post. He looked extremely clean by comparison with us. He had come from Plymouth in ninety-two hours on a ship of the line which brought a regiment of reinforcements that was to be followed by another. A second convoy was being prepared at Plymouth. This young husband, twenty-three years old, was taking his fate rather well; he announced that since he was rich and the husband of a pretty wife—who appeared to be stylishly dressed in the picture he showed us—he no longer wanted to serve on an English packet. He told us that he had arrived in fifty-two [*sic*] hours, passing through a storm, and taking water throughout the vessel. What a contrast to our correspondence from Paris! In one week Lord Wellington could have everything he desired from London, freely and with great certainty, while we needed more than a month and a half to obtain a very simple answer from Paris, if one arrived at all. The English were taking great advantage of their convenient communications by sea—even to the point of employing them to bring forage for their horses from England. In view of their mastery in extracting food from the coast of Spain or from barbarous Sicily, how could one believe that they did not have enough subsistence for all their troops and even for the refugees in Lisbon; yet it was said that the latter often lacked food.[48]

47. George Augustus Eliott, Baron Heathfield (1717–90), served with the Duke of Cumberland in the Seven Years War and in 1775 was appointed governor of Gibraltar, which he successfully defended during a three-and-a-half-year siege.

48. An *Edital* of October 19, 1810, issued by Francisco da Mendoça Arraes e Mello, Prosecutor of Lisbon, complained that a Royal *Aviso* of October 8, limiting the price of food and hoarding, was being ignored. Therefore, "those who are trying to make a fortune on the public misery and those who are hoarding and monopolizing . . . in order to raise the prices, will be punished by being forbidden to sell and their shops will be closed." On the same day the Prosecutor issued an *Edital* forbidding merchants to purchase the cattle brought into the city by refugees; the municipality wanted to buy them for the destitute of Lisbon. An

As the time for our movement approached, I increasingly regretted that I had not reconnoitered the left of the English Lines toward Torres Vedras and the sea. One day or another we might retrace our steps to attack that position. At the least we needed a description of it for others or even for ourselves. We also lacked information about a piece of terrain between Alcoentre and Aveiras. I urged everyone to complete these gaps. Two battalions of the 25th Line at Labrugeira and Abrigada were echeloned up to São João to permit *chef de bataillon* Antoine Calmet Beauvoisin to reconnoiter and sketch the enemy's left. He went there, but I never received his report. Richoux went toward Aveiras and I was no more fortunate with him. Yet in case we had to march forward this would be one of our lines of maneuver or attack. Everybody was talking about the movement and many had already started it.[49] Those guilty of indiscretions came primarily from the administration. The commanders, in whom we were forced to confide, divulged all the movements in order to get the best lodging and to make their arrangements. From the first days, they started a procession of travelers and baggage and it continued, augmented by the *état major.* Such blunders always occurred among those who had nothing to risk from the enemy. At the least we should have burned the equipment that was departing without orders and thereby revealing such a difficult and important move to the enemy.

The Prince fixed the moment of our maneuver for eight o'clock in the evening of November 14,[50] repeating his order that I was to follow it. The 8th Corps, which was to march through Moinho de Cubo and Guerreiros on to Aveiras so as not to disturb the movement of the 2nd

Edital issued by the *Câmara* of Lisbon on November 9 prohibited the exportation of oil from the city, and ten days later another *Edital* established bread control, eliminating high-grade bread. See Colleção de Academia das Sciências de Lisboa. These *Editals* give some indication of the stringent regulations enacted by Portuguese officials to secure food for the refugees in Lisbon.

49. Wellington had been anticipating the French withdrawal for several weeks. In fact, he was surprised that the French were able to remain as long as they did before his Lines. Although the French were to retain their positions for eighteen days more, on October 27 he wrote to Liverpool, "All the accounts which I have received of the distresses of the enemy for want of provisions would lead me to a belief that their army could not remain long in the position in which it is placed, and it is astonishing that they have been able to remain here so long." See *Wellington's Dispatches,* VI, 545–46.

50. For details of the French withdrawal, see "Dispositions générales pour un changement de position de l'armée," November 10, 1810, Correspondance: Armée de Portugal, Carton C[7]10.

Corps, received orders to take the road from Moinho Novo and Vila Nova because someone, I did not know who, had given the Prince a new itinerary from Alenquer to Aveiras. There are a few comments to make about the preparatory dispositions for the movement. I would have preferred to have a stronger rear guard and troops at Mata until the moment when Clauzel's division fell back toward General Solignac as General Ferey marched toward Carregado. These details were rarely well applied to the terrain, but it was useless to quibble about such points when we could not change anything. An order was also given to destroy the mills and other buildings as if we were leaving these positions forever. However, what advantage could result from such destruction? General Reynier had the good sense not to touch any of his.

I could never give up the idea that one day or another we would return to attack the enemy in his Line. I left our positions with the deepest regret. I particularly feared that the English would fortify their positions in such a way that we would have to pay very dearly for them one day. As long as we stayed there, I explored the Line to determine what the enemy could do and how we should attack them. First, it seemed clear to me that the enemy would want to occupy the exits of the valleys of the Tagus, Arruda, and Alenquer. Their Line, extended along both banks, was limited on one side by the bridge of Carregado and on the other by that of Alenquer. The positions of the entrenched hills were such that it would be necessary to outflank them either through Alenquer or by going higher up the valley to its origin. I was also apprehensive that they would fortify the mills and hills of Sobral. An excellent position for them, it was the key to various roads we had occupied so poorly when we chose the points beyond the hills while our flanks and rear were unsupported. If the enemy knew their profession, they would hurry to secure the position of Sobral and the gorges of the valleys. Thus I had never suggested abandoning them completely. I examined the means of turning the first line through Alenquer. The stream was inaccessible except at a ford below the paper mill and beyond the last bridge of Amour.* There it was possible to cross it and climb the mountains under the protection of artillery placed above the road to Ota. This would require an attack by skirmishers from tree to tree to bypass and turn Alenquer, while threatening all the bridges. The mountains on the east were accessible for artillery to their summit by the Ota road and the guns could fire on the city; they could even attack the town from an oblique angle or in a sweeping movement. The enemy could cover the whole slope with skirmishers, especially the balustrade of the road-ramps leading to Sobral. I took the directional points for such an attack. I was still in the mountains on the night of the 14th, and I abandoned them as I would a most precious conquest; it always seemed that it was man's nature to become attached through pain, privation, and difficulties as well as through enjoyment.

During the night we had an alert. At one o'clock in the morning General Fririon sent me a letter from the Duc d'Abrantès announcing that a strong mass of enemy infantry had been seen at the bottom of Arruda and at some other points. A few deserters had reported that we were to be attacked, and this report was finally confirmed by a peasant who had been forced to abandon Arruda because of poor treatment. The letter was communicated immediately to the commanders of the corps. I did not believe this news, and I tried to go back to sleep. Meanwhile the hour when I wanted to get up arrived, and I could not stay in bed any longer. The moon was covered by clouds and there was a rather thick fog. I paced to and fro on a balcony, listening and awaiting the event. While thinking about the conduct that Lord Wellington was obliged to follow in such a case, I amused myself by drawing up a plan of attack against our army, leaving myself enough time also to make a counterplan, always for my own instruction, though I did not completely finish the first one. These project studies appeared to be excellent for training officers, and I worked on such exercises as much as possible. They were like a novel about the campaign, conducted from both sides according to the strategic principles of the war. Nevertheless, morning came slowly and nothing happened. I was rather calm during the night because I had my dispositions well in mind. The alert had awakened the entire administrative corps; everybody remaining left at the break of dawn. During the whole day there was a continual procession of people departing. They had known for a long time about the movement that was to take place during the night. The baggage, donkeys, and mules followed continuously along the crest of Pipa. The enemy must have seen all this with field glasses, in addition to the reports from the spies.

How could we stop all this mischief? It would have been necessary to start at the roots—to unpack the baggage and give orders to march or move at the last minute or as late as possible.

Because of the rumors of the alert, Marshal Ney arrived at General Fririon's quarters that morning, announcing that he had come from Azambuja to put himself at the head of his troops, and he asked for the Prince. He complained when His Excellency was not there and then vented his rage against him and against the manner in which he was treated. He now said that we should have established ourselves at Coimbra and not gone beyond it, and that if he could leave for Paris he would give an account of everything. This time he said nothing against me.

Many claimed that Mermet's division had started its movement a little too early. I was not aware of this nor did I believe it, but it was certainly a fact that he had extracted a great deal of food from the country on the other side of the Monte Junto, that he had never lacked any, and that he had even left a considerable amount behind. Another fact was that several regiments of the 8th Corps, who from the very beginning clamored and complained so loudly that they were dying of hunger, had actually suffered much less than was reported. They could have procured resources in the area where General Mermet went, but the 8th Corps hardly ever came out of its position; besides they had lost or left behind a great deal, particularly the officers, who had considerable provisions. In a trick of the trade, Solignac made a reconnaissance on Arruda and gathered fifty thousand rations left by the others. I found many ears of corn on a threshing-room floor at the bottom of the 65th Line's camp. The regiment would have collected this corn if it had found itself in such need. The 2nd Corps lost and abandoned a great deal of grain. Finally, all this proved to me that we could have lived in those positions for twenty or twenty-five more days. How important would it have been to do so? Yet the corps commanders did not stop complaining until they withdrew. All this disheartened me.

I was continually anxious, since I had heard some cannon fire the day before. The enemy knew our movements, confirmed by many indications. In two days he had four deserters from our foreign corps. Thus after determining our retreat, he could make a show of attacking us and then announce this advantage to all of Europe. The English did not make such an attempt even though they had absolutely nothing to lose. Our movement took place very quietly although few precautions were taken, and it was never obstructed by the enemy, who marched even more quietly.

Chapter Eight

THE WITHDRAWAL TO SANTARÉM

The army was ready to start marching and effect its withdrawal. In general, maneuvers or tactics have too often been confused with what might be called march maneuvers or strategic movements. The former, executed according to fixed principles and on level terrain, are elementary geometric problems for which it is easy to determine number and duration and rapidly calculate strength, whatever the number of troops in movement. The latter, which elude strict reckoning, are subject to an infinite number of outside influences, to all the variations presented by numerous obstacles, to delays and negligence, to the condition of roads and the marching columns, and to the passions of men. Regular maneuvers or tactics can be undertaken in the presence of the enemy. At all times such maneuvers must derive their strength from within, and the tactician who directs them, despite his limitations, holds it in his power to ascertain their exact effect even if he has not calculated them to the foot or minute.

The second, the march or strategic maneuvers, are irregular by their nature, always executed beyond the reach of the enemy, that is to say, beyond their immediate attacks; and they are covered by a powerful corps that can sustain the first impetus with either rapid movements or dispositions. These operations are necessarily executed on any type of terrain and on any road in the region where operations take us, even where we cannot expect to find main routes. Most of the time, the troops will be forced to march by the flank, and the inconveniences of such order are well known. This is why such movements are extended for immense distances and elude the attention of the commanders directing them; thus, their difficulties increase in every way. In any case the problems are great, but they become even more considerable when one withdraws near the enemy. Then precautions must be multiplied in proportion to the many possibilities that impede the strict execution of orders. First of all, it is necessary to conceal information from the enemy with the greatest secrecy or, even better, to deceive him of the actual goal by making demonstrations. The marches must be calculated with the greatest possible exactitude, taking into consideration all the delays that may be occasioned by numerous accidents, hazards, etc.; they must be in harmony with the topography of the land, with the disposition and support of troops and artillery, especially when the army moves rapidly toward the designated position as soon as it is safe. The marches must be executed with rigorous precision, and each commander and officer must employ general vigilance everywhere. Finally, it is necessary that the orders encompass and explain every aspect; it would even be advantageous to draw up general orders together with particular instructions for the troops, because all the minute details vitally influence the flank marches. It is no doubt useless to tell the columns to march by section all the time; yet it is hoped they will be maintained in such order. However, in spite of the many precautions and efforts, these marches are always ineffective if they are not combined with offensive demonstrations. Moreover, this is certainly the most favorable time for the enemy to attack a maneuvering army with reliable and well-deployed troops. We have seen the maneuvers of Bussaco, we are going to see those of Alenquer, and a little later we will see those for the withdrawal of the army.

Our movement was ordered for eight o'clock [in the evening of November 14], but it could start earlier because of early nightfall and the moonlight. That of the 8th Corps was to commence later. Although its movement should have been more rapid than the others, the 8th Corps was extremely slow. Nevertheless, this corps had been ready for a long time; it had sent off a major part of its artillery and baggage during the preceding days. It further made the mistake of withdrawing its advance guard post around nine o'clock or earlier, so that the first enemy patrol on guard advanced as far as an abandoned bivouac and from there opened fire on us with shouts of joy. It was past midnight when the front of this corps, formed by Ferey's brigade, arrived in Alenquer. The directions for the march were not very definite, and in addition they had been altered somewhat by an order to go through Moinho Novo and not by Cubo; thus it was necessary to have the 8th Corps turn back since it had already moved in the latter direction. After midnight the Duc arrived at General Fririon's quarters, where I was. We talked together.[1]

The Prince had ordered the 8th Corps to stop at Moinho Novo on the 15th. This was certainly an error. I suggested we go beyond it. The Duc did not wish to do so. I pointed out the danger of a battle at this point if we decided to stay at Moinho Novo, and this settled the matter. I continued to insist on the road to Cubo, thinking that the Prince's order indicated he was apprehensive about this direction and that Ota might have been abandoned earlier. It was my opinion that we should follow the road indicated in the original orders without stopping at Moinho Novo. From this village we would advance on Guerreiros because the enemy, aware of our movement, could move in force on Guerreiros and attack us during the march of the 8th Corps, but we did not expect this. I urged the Duc not to stop until he arrived on the height between the hill and Guerreiros; there he would find himself covered by the stream, close to the 2nd Corps, and in Aveiras just as surely as if he had come directly by Cubo. The Duc followed this advice. Because of the state of the road, it was also decided that the remainder of his artillery would go to the right of the mill of Vila Nova along the main highway to Azambuja; from there it could join his army corps by the road from Azambuja to Aveiras in case of attack. The Duc then left.

General Fririon wanted to go to General Reynier's quarters at Carregado. The latter had made good dispositions; his advance posts had orders not to leave the line until seven o'clock in the morning and to be ready to withdraw briskly. General Soult had command of the rear guard. Thus the march of the 2nd Corps had been perfectly covered. After reconnoitering the posts of the 2nd Corps, the enemy advanced

1. For Fririon's description of the French withdrawal from the Lines, see his *Journal historique*, pp. 114–19.

to them only to withdraw when they saw them occupied. The movement of the 2nd Corps did not start until very late, when it had been announced that the last troops of the Duc d'Abrantès were leaving Alenquer; this was after three o'clock [A.M.]. At four o'clock Heudelet's division was on the march and we all departed. Leaving General Reynier at Vila Nova, we stopped part of the day at Azambuja. That night we slept at Cartaxo.[2] The enemy followed our movement with some cavalry. It was said that a column had been seen passing through Moinho Novo, but this was not certain. Our advance posts were at Vila Nova, the 2nd Corps was between that village and Azambuja, the headquarters were in the latter, and the 8th Corps was at Aveiras de Cima.

We heard the rejoicing cannon at Lisbon. It was agreed that our movement would have great consequences: it would inspire confidence in the Portuguese soldiers, revive and animate the kingdom, give new energy to the insurrections in Portugal and Spain, cast new luster on Lord Wellington and the English army, and finally might have great influence on the events of Europe. For us that influence might be fatal and far-reaching. It was not even certain that the morale of our army had not suffered a little, or whether they believed in the literal meaning of the word "retreat," which had been mentioned so casually. (Events are built on such little things and are so interrelated that it was possible nothing would have happened, perhaps not even the subsequent misfortunes, if my project to retain Alenquer had been executed, for then there would no longer have been any pretext to delay crossing the Tagus.) With regard to the disposition for our movement, it was good enough, but it should have been made during the day with the army united en masse in a manner to form itself on the hills of Vila Nova and fall on the English if they showed themselves outside of their Lines.

According to the reports, the enemy followed our movements feebly, although they had been given three days' warning by the movement of our baggage and by the deserters. It was said that their divisions were just descending beyond the pass of Sobral and that their advance guard had only moved to Alenquer.[3] That is to say, they had traveled

2. Details of Reynier's withdrawal can be found in Pelet's letter to Masséna, November 15, 1810, Correspondance: Armée de Portugal, Carton C[7]10.

3. On the morning of November 15 a thick fog obscured the terrain occupied

two leagues that day [November 15] while we had only weak pickets along the streams of Vila Nova. Nevertheless, the English General could not have been afraid to compromise himself, for his flanks and rear were rather well protected.

The enemy sent a few men before our advance posts during the night [of November 15].[4] It was said that two of their columns were marching on the roads from Vila Nova and Moinho Novo. The 8th Corps, receiving orders to advance on Cartaxo, descended through Azambuja and delayed the movement of the 2nd Corps, which was not able to march from Cartaxo to Santarém until much later. The 8th Corps established itself in the latter city and its vicinity. I accompanied General Fririon there. The Prince left the city rather early in the morning for his headquarters at Torres Novas. At the moment his carriage left, the enemy saluted him with Congreve rockets[5] and a few fell near His Excellency. It was alleged they were fired because of his presence; the shots were intermittent. It appeared that cannonballs and shells had also been fired from a battery with eight embrasures built on the bank of the Tagus; two smaller batteries had been placed below it, but I did not see any cannon in either one. I saw the Congreve rocket. It was a cast tube three to four inches in diameter and twenty to twenty-two inches long, with a sharp cone at one end and a spherical bottom. The lower part had a chamber filled with flammable material, while on the outside there were two rings for a long

by the French army, and after it had lifted Wellington's pickets were duped by "some stuffed-straw gentlemen occupying their usual posts. Some of them were cavalry, some infantry, and they seemed such respectable representatives of their spectral predecessors, that, in the haze of the following morning, we thought that they had been joined by some well-fed ones from the rear; and it was late in the day before we discovered the mistake and advanced in pursuit." See John Kincaid, *Adventures in the Rifle Brigade and Random Shots of a Rifleman* (London, n.d.), p. 15.

4. An English soldier following the French retreat recorded, "We could not advance one hundred yards, without seeing dead soldiers of the enemy stretched upon the road, or at a little distance from it, who had lain down to die, unable to proceed through hunger and fatigue. . . . Their retreat resembled more that of famished wolves than men." See "Journal of a Soldier of the Seventy-first regiment from 1806 to 1815" in *Memorials of the Late War* (Edinburgh, 1828), I, 83.

5. William Congreve (1772–1828) attended the Royal Academy and was appointed to the Royal Laboratory at Woolwich. He completed his rocket in 1808 and it was used the following year against the French fleet at Basque Roads. Wellington's forces attempted to employ the rocket in the Peninsula, but it was erratic and ineffective. Congreve wrote *A Concise Account of the Origin and Progress of the Rocket System* in 1807.

stick as with any ordinary rocket. They were fired, it was said, like the latter, by placing them on two supports.

Santarém was filled with artillery and caissons. We trembled, the general and myself, to see those fires we had heard so much about falling from the sky. We did not see or hear anything else. How could the enemy neglect to take any action? They knew very well there was only one passage through the city and that it was congested. On the other hand, if we had placed a few batteries as I suggested, the enemy would have been contained. The Allied army marched in two columns by the roads of Alcoentre and Vila Nova. Its cavalry and advance guard stopped at Azambuja and Alcoentre,[6] and they were followed by the divisions of Spencer and Leith.[7]

We left at eight o'clock [on the morning of November 16]. As we came out of Santarém we saw a hideous mud field three-quarters of a league long, often covered by the Tagus. Beyond, steeply inclined hills rose above the river; they had a few passages and defensive positions. Two leagues away there was a partially cut bridge on the wide Alviela; it was a good post and was the left of the position that was to be reconnoitered. The right of this position, covered by the Alviela, had to be at Pernes and to extend along the hills on the left bank. The advantage of this position was that it was central for the 8th and 2nd Corps as well as for the troops at Golegã. It intercepted the two principal communication routes of the area. The plain of Golegã began three leagues from Santarém; it was flat and smooth, without the least undulation. The plain was still covered with growing corn; it bordered the Almonda, which made a large detour there. Four leagues away, Golegã, on a rideau and behind a pond, also offered a good position with its left on the Tagus, its right covered by the Almonda River, and some good locations for posts. Another position to be reconnoitered—

6. Wellington ordered his army forward in pursuit at approximately 3:00 P.M., declaring, "We must make our first movements with caution, as I heard last night that the enemy had a reinforcement on the frontier of Upper Beira on the 9th." See *Wellington's Dispatches,* Wellington to Craufurd, 10:20 A.M., November 15, 1810, VI, 623.

7. Sir James Leith (1763–1816) attended military school at Aberdeen and was appointed second lieutenant in the 21st Fusiliers in 1780. Following his service at Toulon in 1793, he was sent to Ireland where he was promoted through the ranks until he became a brigadier general in 1804. With Moore at Corunna and Chatham at Walcheren, Leith joined Hill's division in the Peninsula in 1810, but Wellington soon gave him command of the Fifth Division of the army.

like the one before Golegã, centrally located for either a withdrawal or a point of concentration for the three army corps—was at Torres Novas, which had a plain of olive trees. We had crossed through the 8th Corps, and during a halt we met General Solignac. After an extended conversation the general pulled me aside and said: "Always be careful, because everything that goes wrong is blamed on you." This comment hurt me to the bottom of my heart. "Well, what can I do? Can I remonstrate with a warrior who is so illustrious and covered with so much glory? Must I continue to be responsible for the actions of others, for faults I do not commit and from which I suffer so acutely at times? Ah, why am I not far from here for a while? It would be my greatest desire to have this [Foy's] mission to France in order to escape from the eyes of envy and evil."

The Prince changed his dispositions for the headquarters of the 8th Corps from the middle of Golegã; he placed it at Pernes with the first division. This position was on a better line, closer to the 2nd Corps, and could reinforce it more easily. The Duc was at Golegã when we went through. He told me that he had had three soldiers condemned to death for pillaging. In shooting them, they actually aimed at only one, but all three fell down. He said, "Bury all those rogues." Two of of them were untouched. "Well, since heaven has saved you, let this be a lesson to you and the others." We arrived [at Torres Novas] and gave an account to the Prince, who was furious because the Duc had not been the last to leave Sobral and was not where he was supposed to be. Thus are we all blind to our own mistakes. His anger had been better spent on the abandonment of food by the army corps in their respective positions.

The previous day [November 16] General Reynier had arrived at Santarém as we were leaving. Thus we were not able to wait for his corps to be established. It appeared he was followed, or more accurately, that he had neglected to observe a position west of Cartaxo, and that General Soult, in placing his posts near Valle, fell in with strong detachments of the enemy. No doubt they had marched through the hills and found themselves at the Valle bridge at the same time as the 2nd Corps. This resulted in the loss of grain gathered at Porto de Mugem, which should have been evacuated earlier. General Reynier, finding Santarém full of the sick, artillery, boats, and baggage, feared that if he were forced to evacuate this position he would be blamed for losing all of them. He began shouting like a demon, and he wrote to the Prince that he had the enemy army on his rear, that he was going to be attacked, and that he was waiting for orders.[8] The Prince became angry as usual and ordered him to hold at all costs. Then he called me and sent me back to Santarém again. I carried new, more precise orders to General Reynier.[9] For my own part, I was to act according to circumstances. I was in a hurry to arrive. Various men told me they had heard gunfire, that I would encounter the evacuation of the sick and the doctors, and finally that there was a thunderous rumble in the background which sounded like a very heavy cannonade.

I halted General Clauzel's artillery and hurried to General Reynier's position. Two or three thousand enemy infantrymen and several hundred horses had crossed the Ponte de Asseca. One of their cavalry regiments had crossed the bridge below Asseca and deployed in battle formation on the plain. We could not see any artillery; a few posts with mounted sentries covered the left of their line. There was considerable smoke in the rear near Cartaxo. Our troops occupied the two abutments on the side of the main highway, reinforced by artillery. We had put some abatis on the summits and the most accessible parts of the gorges. Lastly, the 31st Léger guarded the height opposite the bridge with four pieces. The 4th Léger and the light cavalry were near the right. The 47th Line, in reserve near the city, was in a good defensible position with its left pulled in and supported on the Tagus,

8. In a report which reached Masséna before 3:00 A.M. on November 18, Reynier described the deployment of his corps as dangerous indeed. With an exposed right flank, a narrow defile obstructing his escape route, encumbered by the artillery of the 6th and 8th Corps, and hampered by a large hospital, Reynier recommended immediate evacuation of Santarém rather than running the risk of a defeat in which he would lose both artillery and hospital. See Koch, *Mémoires de Masséna,* VII, 266–67.

9. Although noticeably annoyed by Reynier's frantic dispatch, Masséna climbed out of bed and wrote to him: "I have sent my first aide-de-camp with positive orders to remain at Santarém. I will come to you with the entire 8th Corps immediately as I have already said this morning. . . . In calculating all that is possible in war, we cannot conceive of the possibility that Lord Wellington is before you with his entire army. Cut the bridges you entrenched, reconnoiter your terrain well, and you will see that extensive preparations are necessary by the enemy to attack you. You are to be en masse with your army corps. The 8th Corps is not far from you. I reiterate the order to remain at Santarém and only as a last resort are you obliged to retreat on Golegã or Pernes." See Masséna to Reynier, 3:00 A.M., November 18, 1810, Correspondance: Armée de Portugal, Carton $C^7$10.

but its right unsupported. General Reynier still claimed that considerable forces were before him, menacing his right, where some troops had marched, though we could no longer see them. I maintained that only Craufurd's [Light] Division had followed us and that we were seeing its first brigade, while the second was in reserve at Cartaxo.[10] The General said that the enemy, observing that all our projects were directed toward the Tagus, wanted to oppose them. I responded that according to their well-known system, the enemy would oppose us only on the left bank.

General Reynier returned to Santarém at five o'clock [the evening of November 18]. He had the sick and those in danger hastily evacuated as well as the caissons, the baggage, and finally everything else he could. He persisted in his ideas, and I in mine. He told me he was going to send an account to the Prince. I also wrote to the Prince, describing our positions and that of the enemy, indicating my opinion and my fears for the right.

The position of Santarém, by itself and with the Rio Maior, was very strong and capable of a good defense on its front by an army corps. However, its right was unsupported and could be easily outflanked one or two leagues away by four or five bridges on the Rio Maior. Our whole army would be needed to occupy the position near the right, but an entire united army was also needed to attack it; such an attack was not without great dangers consequent on marching through the narrow passes with the difficult hills of Aveiras in the rear.

During the day [November 19] we heard no more firing on the line. I had arisen early to write in my Journal. Later I thought I heard gunfire. I ran to the position but found nothing. After General Reynier examined the ground and saw that the enemy regiment had evacuated the plain on the left, that the troops occupying the plateau had descended the slope which had seemingly increased their number, and finally that there had been only two guns, he still claimed that the

10. This probe by the Light Division was initiated to determine if the French were in strength. With the cavalry of Slade and Elder, supported by Ross's light artillery and the 88th Foot, Craufurd advanced toward the causeway over the Rio Maior into Santarém. Reynier's 4th Léger repulsed them. When Wellington arrived to observe the action, he wrote to Hill, "The enemy are still too strong for us this day at Santarém, and I have delayed the attack upon them till tomorrow morning, in order to have the assistance of the 1st division. If they stay, we shall then attack them." See *Wellington's Dispatches*, Wellington to Hill, November 18, 1810, VI, 626.

whole enemy army was there and that he had seen other enemy troops filing off toward the bridge. Moreover, he claimed they were opposite it but concealed by the hills. I still maintained my earlier opinion. On the right and along the Rio Maior road, he showed me two masses which he called two regiments, but which I believed were much less considerable. He then added that it was absolutely necessary that I go and report all this to the Prince. I told the General that I did not have any horses, that he should send an officer or soldier if he wished, and that it was my wish to remain there since the Prince desired it. He still responded in the negative. He pressed me, saying that I knew the road, that I could give information to the Duc, and finally that his officer would be captured. After that I did not answer any more. I said to him, "You do not want me to stay. You want to get rid of me. I am leaving out of deference." I could have resisted, but there would have been indignant cries and I had already had enough complaints without valid reason. Yet he certainly wanted to get rid of me, unless he was in a great hurry [to send word to the Prince] because he feared an attack. I told General Reynier that I had already given an account of his position to the Prince, that I would never tell him that an entire army was there when I did not see more than five thousand men, and that we could not unite our army for so few men.[11] He claimed that all of Craufurd's [Light] Division was behind those two regiments (which were the 16th Dragoons and 1st Hussars), that they were unable to cross because of the waters but would attack our right. This little discussion took place in front of his astounded *état major*.

I left quietly, taking the road to Pernes because the Prince had written that he would go to that village without saying positively whether he would advance as far as Santarém. Half a league away I was collared by one of General Reynier's officers with a note for the Prince which he was supposed to show to the Duc as he passed. It declared that a great number of enemy columns were descending from the plateau into the valley of Valle, that others were marching opposite the right, and that in a quarter of an hour we would be attacked. This note made me even more apprehensive about the 2nd Corps than I

11. Pelet wrote to Masséna on November 18, 1810, "I think the troops that he [Wellington] exposes before us and has dispatched, are to assure him of our movements and the dispositions that we have taken, and to pursue us in the event of retreat." See Correspondance: Armée de Portugal, Carton $C^7 10$.

had been because it was so positive. I urged my horse forward vigorously. An aide-de-camp of the Duc, to whom the General had already cried out in distress, told me that I would find Ménard's brigade on the road. It had stopped and was camping at Torre do Bispo. I spoke to General Ménard. I showed him the letter and persuaded him to start marching on General Reynier's right; he went there immediately.

I also proceeded toward that point with a battalion. Although I complained about General Reynier's conduct, my zealous conduct showed him how much I was above such trifling matters. At last, near Pernes, I met the Prince, who was very upset with General Reynier because of his fear and the dispositions he had taken. I made my report pure and simple without adding anything, although the Prince wanted me to agree that the General was frightened. We were riding rather fast but bearing a little too much to the right; I knew that it was unguarded and that some enemy parties were roaming there. Actually, it was claimed that we had passed a large detachment of enemy cavalry. I do not believe this.

We reached Alcanhoes and from there Santarém, where the Prince went around the position with the Duc d'Abrantès, who had followed him and General Reynier. It seems that His Excellency showed some discontent with the latter. This was not unreasonable, for I saw nothing that I had not seen when I was there previously. There was nothing new, with the exception of troops that were said to be marching on their left, and that I did not see. They were seen better, it was said, from the abutments on the right. With the exception of the first day when I went there briefly, I never had an occasion to return. Thus I did not know the area very well. The abatis General Reynier had started was well advanced and in a rather good state, but that is all he had done. After staying at this point for some time, wandering around and doing nothing, we returned to Santarém. An order was sent to General Fririon to have Clauzel's division march to Torre do Bispo, Gratien's brigade to Pernes, and General Thomières'[12] regiment

12. Baron Jean Guillaume Thomières (1771–1812) volunteered in 1793 and within 15 years was promoted to the rank of general of brigade. He served in the Army of Italy and fought in many of the major battles of Napoleon's first and second Italian campaigns. Attached to the Grand Army, he acted as one of Lannes's aides-de-camp in Austria, Prussia, and Poland. With Junot in Portugal in 1807, Thomiéres fought at Roliça and Vimeiro. He commanded a brigade of Masséna's army in 1810–11 and was killed at Salamanca commanding the seventh division of the Army of Portugal.

between Pernes and Torres Novas, while General Solignac's regiment and another regiment of the 6th Corps occupied Santarém. General Loison was ordered to have the 6th Dragoons march. This order, as well as the one for the departure of the 6th Léger, had already been sent to him. In case of an enemy movement I sent orders to Calmet to reconnoiter immediately the line from Torres Novas to Golegã, as I have indicated above.[13]

We mounted our horses very early [on November 20] with the Prince and the Duc, and picked up General Reynier on the way. We descended on the main highway to go to the front of the position on the Asseca causeway. The 31st Léger was there, with four cannon which I thought poorly placed; two cross-fired on the causeway, but at an elevation of more than 170 to 200 feet and two were on the right but slightly lower. I would have wanted these guns as low as possible, with all four raking the causeway; the two outside guns, completely covered by good breastwork and embrasures if necessary, would be able to strike in the center or on the flanks. We cut trenches for the infantry in the main highway and made a few defensive preparations that had been completely lacking. I saw nothing new that morning. The enemy had given us some alerts; they were told to attack or leave the advance post alone, and this is what they had done. We bore to the left. There we found a reentrant angle with the Tagus; its sides were the hills and the apex touched Santarém. The middle was covered by vineyards, fields cut by ditches, and the old bed of the Rio Maior. It was crossed by the road from Porto de Mugem which ran straight toward Santarém. I found this point weak; however, it was improbable that the enemy would go and dig themselves into this dead end, although it was favorable for defense because of its narrowness and its hedges, houses, etc. Little was needed to secure it completely.

We saw a few launches, or at least barges, on the Tagus. Since nothing indicated offensive preparations at the moment, the Prince seemed resolved to return. He ate at General Reynier's quarters and gave the order that we would be on horseback in an hour and a half. Luncheon was interrupted by some firing. It was announced that the enemy had taken dispositions for an attack. Columns were marching

13. For additional details of these deployments, see Fririon, *Journal historique*, pp. 116–17.

and troops were being deployed. When we arrived, there were at most 150 skirmishers advancing to reconnoiter our left with a squadron of cavalry in the rear. At length a battalion was seen making its way on the left, with two cavalry regiments filing toward the Tagus. The fusilade lasted for some time.[14] The Prince gave me orders to leave with the Duc and accompany him on a reconnaissance; he was supposed to make it on our right at Tremês and Alcanede, examining the enemy's positions and those we could occupy against them. I was to return directly from Tremês to Santarém the next evening to give an account to General Reynier. The shooting continued sporadically. I left with the Duc and his *état major*. We went to Pernes and I slept at Junot's quarters, where everybody took care of me.

The Duc d'Abrantès became slightly ill and I had to make the prescribed reconnaissance quickly with General Boyer,[15] his chief of staff. Pernes was on the right bank of the Alviela and at its confluence with the Abraã valley, whose stream surrounded and partially embraced it. Just above Pernes the Alviela turned toward the hills on the east. These circumstances, and the ease of defending or cutting the bridge on either bank, made Pernes an excellent post; it would cover perfectly the right of the position at Alviela between that village and the Tagus. The stream, rather wide at this point, ran full to the brim and was difficult to cross; it frequently covered the entire bottom of the valley. This position was a league and a half long and ensured a retreat from that of the Rio Maior. From Pernes to Alcanede through Ornes,* Abraã, and Alqueidão, we found some small mountains, not very formidable, rather stony, and covered with beautiful pines and a few olive trees. The road that crossed the mountains dropped on the west to Tremês; on the east it stopped at the Alviela. General Godart was

14. Assuming that only a rear guard held Santarém, Wellington sent the Light Division between the Tagus and the Rio Maior on the left, Pack's brigade toward Ponte de Celeiro on the right, and Spencer's First Division across the causeway for a direct assault on Santarém. However, once he realized the strength of the French forces in the town, he recalled his columns. See Andrew Leith-Hay, *A Narrative of the Peninsular War* (4th ed., London, 1850), pp. 189–92.

15. Pierre François Boyer (1772–1851) volunteered in 1792 and the following year became General Scherer's aide-de-camp. He was promoted to general of brigade in 1801 and reached the rank of general of division in 1814. He served in the Army of Italy in 1796–97 and the next year was attached to Kléber's division for the Egyptian campaign. He was captured by the English while serving in the West Indies and after his exchange was appointed as Junot's chief of staff for the 8th Corps.

at Abraã guarding that region.[16] Alcanede was a rather large village at the crossroads of the routes from Rio Maior, Leiria, Ourém, Torres Novas, and Santarém. It was the best of the points where the enemy could launch a heavy attack on us. Alcanede offered little means of defense, but a position could be established on the hills in the rear, and afterward at Ponte el Quinta de Alviela. In front of Alcanede the country was rather open, with several small roads coming from Rio Maior, São João de Ribeira, and Malaqueijo. To its right was the main road to Leiria along the very accessible reverse of the hills of Mosteiros. Adjutant Commander Grandseigne was at Alcanede with his two dragoon regiments and a battalion of infantry. He had sent a reconnaissance on Rio Maior, where nothing had been found; this completely assured us that there would not be an attack. His troops had been forced to swim across a stream.

[On November 20] the Prince wrote that he had recognized two English cavalry regiments of Anson's[17] brigade near Azambuja and Malaqueijo, and that a prisoner declared they had been cut off from their army because of the flooding streams. The Prince ordered Clauzel's division and Grandseigne's brigade to march on Tremês through Romeira to attack them, while General Soult marched against them by Pêro Filho. Grandseigne should have been directed on Rio Maior, but it appeared evident to me that this attack would not produce anything;[18] the English regiments would cross the streams in some way or the enemy would make such a show of artillery on the opposite bank that the action would be limited to an exchange of cannon fire. These two regiments were the ones that we had already seen from Santarém and that General Reynier had claimed were Craufurd's advance guard, while I had maintained they were only a corps of flankers thrown between the Rio Maior and the Rio Fráguas to threaten our right and relieve the enemy's left. The orders from the Prince were very slow.

16. Baron Roch Godart (1761–1834) entered the military in 1779 and after a temporary resignation reached the rank of general of brigade in 1809. He served in the various armies in Germany and Italy and in 1803 joined the Grand Army at Boulogne. Godart served at Caldeiro with Masséna, at Ragusa with Marmont, and in 1810 was given a brigade in Junot's 8th Corps.

17. George Anson (n.d.) fought at Talavera and during Masséna's invasion commanded a cavalry brigade (16th Light Dragoons and 1st Hussars of the King's German Legion) as a major general.

18. For additional details of Grandseigne's movement on November 20, see Fririon, *Journal historique,* pp. 117–18; Koch, *Mémoires de Masséna,* VII, 270.

Adjutant Commander Grandseigne was ready to leave. I went ahead of him to Tremês, where I found General Clauzel marching. He had orders to escort our reconnaissance, but his direction was toward the right. With eight dragoons I started on the left through Romeira, on a branch road that the enemy occupied. I approached as close as possible to reconnoiter them. Finally, I went to Azoia, a beautiful, well-kept village crowded with inhabitants and peasants who had taken refuge there. It was an island of peace and happiness in the middle of a tempestuous sea. I allowed my dragoons to refresh themselves, and I went on to Santarém. From Alcanede to Tremês the road was rather bad but practicable. Tremês appeared to be located on some kind of a passage formed by the tributaries of the Rio Maior, opening from the right and left, covering a great plateau to which Tremês was the key; it made a rather good post. The countryside was indistinct and difficult to reconnoiter at a gallop because of its levelness. It was beautiful from Tremês to Santarém, slightly undulating, easily practicable, with good roads and small, well-cultivated valleys. There were few villages and many houses, usually surrounded by olive trees.

On arriving [at Santarém], I saw General Reynier, who still claimed that the whole combined army was there before him and that Lord Wellington had his headquarters at Cartaxo. He maintained that the enemy army would have attacked if it had not been for the flooding, but at least he was much calmer. I asked him why he was so sure, and he replied that it was because he knew the enemy's method of making war. He smiled cunningly, and contrary to his usual appearance he looked like a person who was lying to himself and wanted to bluff someone else. Moreover, I found a look on his face which pleased me very much. He told me that General Soult had pushed back the advance posts of the English regiments and had taken a position during the night. The next day he would go there himself.

I was proceeding quite slowly through Alcanhoes toward Pernes when I heard some shooting at Malaqueijo. The enemy withdrew before we could take any action against them. I found the Duc much reassured, ridiculing General Reynier, who, according to him, was compromising the dignity of a corps commander with all his commotion. Going to Torres Novas with dragoons who knew the road well, I lost my way completely, as anyone might do, crossing through that flat country covered with olive trees and streaked by a multitude of poorly traced paths across the ground or the heather. Later they were marked, but this did not help matters much. The Prince inquired persistently about the morale of his generals, and in fact their attitude alone was the only thing that was impaired and dangerous.

Again there were new vexations from General Reynier. He now wrote that he had been informed by peasants and deserters that the enemy was going to attack on three points: the English on our left, the English and Portuguese on the center, and the Portuguese alone toward Leiria. He added that in effect Marshal Beresford had crossed the Rio Maior and was near Malaqueijo with six Portuguese battalions and the English cavalry. The Prince gave him instructions and orders to defend and guard his line, recommending various dispositions. The Prince and I talked about this situation, and I said that as long as the enemy had English divisions on the other side of the Tagus and had not made any movements near Rio Maior, we should feel safe.[19] If they were going to attack us, their three approaches (for an army of 60,000 men) were: the road to Santarém; the route from Aveiras to the bridge of Azambujeira and Calhariz; and finally through Alcoentre and Rio Maior on Alcanede to seize our front and move on our flanks. This last attack was the most important for them and the most dangerous for us. The Prince told me this was incorrect and he showed me his ideas in his own way. He repeated his explanations in the presence of General Solignac, who approved what I had said.

General Fririon came up, he said, to give a lesson to a young soldier. He claimed that I was infatuated with the idea of Santarém; my proposition was not that at all, and I confidently defended my opinion without support.[20] He ended by saying that if the enemy were maneuvering

19. Pelet was correct in his observation about Wellington. Once Wellington realized the French had decided to remain at Santarém, he wrote to Hill, "I have received Fane's letter of last night from Abrantes, which almost induces me to believe that I have made a mistake in sending you over the Tagus at all; and I am certain that you should proceed no further up the river than Chamusca." See *Wellington's Dispatches*, Wellington to Hill, November 19, 1810, VI, 626–27.

20. It seems extraordinary that Pelet regarded Fririon as a close friend and praised him highly. See pages 262 and 375 of this volume. Fririon, on the contrary, made numerous attempts to discredit Pelet. No doubt Fririon, as Masséna's chief of staff, resented his reliance on Pelet when decisions were to be made. It was not until 1841 when Fririon's son began the publication of his father's work, *Journal historique de la campagne de Portugal, entreprise par les français, sous les orders du maréchal Masséna, prince d'Essling, du 15 septembre 1810 du 2 mai 1811,* that Pelet took up his pen to defend himself. When extracts of the *Journal*

on him he would not do anything, but he would be quite worried if they were maneuvering on Leiria. This did not disturb me very much in the present situation because that point was too far away from us and the Tagus. Nevertheless, when we were alone, I told General Fririon that I continued to believe what I had at first proposed. The enemy, after leaving us safely in our positions in front of Sobral for thirty-five days, when they had only to come out of their entrenchments to punish us, would not attack us now nor campaign against us since they quite reasonably expected to see us leave again when we had consumed our food, which was already rather low. Furthermore, in spite of all this reasoning, if Wellington decided to attack us, he would march, as I have already said, in three columns and would try to maneuver first against the right at Santarém, which must necessarily be reinforced. After all this discussion, the Prince went to Pernes. On the way he talked about sending General Fririon [to Paris]. I supported this idea because at least it would stop the general in chief from doing anything without well-defined motives and Fririon was a witness he could not get rid of. The Duc was not at his headquarters.

According to the three Portuguese prisoners captured the day before, there were very few troops. An Englishman said that Lord Wellington was at Mafra and that on the day of our movement four or five thousand English had left for Lisbon. Ten thousand troops had remained in the Lines and the remainder with the Portuguese had followed us. There was nothing new from General Clauzel or Grandseigne. What is more, when I was sent to Paris,[21] the Emperor assured me that the entire English army was before us and that we were going to be attacked, until a general who had arrived from London opposed an advance, finding our position too strong. I could not believe that this was true because I had not seen anything that announced the presence of the English army. In fact, the troops had remained near the Lines while General Hill was already on the other side of the

first appeared in the *Spectateur militaire,* Pelet wrote to the director defending his actions and those of Masséna, declaring that the *Journal* had "not been very truthful." For Pelet's letters of May 5, June 11, 28, 1841, see "Correspondance relative à la publication dans le Spectateur Militaire du Journal historique de la campagne de Portugal par M. le Commandant Fririon, 1841," compiled by Pelet. These documents are in Carton 916 of the collection "Mémoires historiques," located at the Service historique de l'armée at Vincennes.

21. Pelet was finally sent to Paris with details of Ney's insubordination on March 23, 1811. See the Epilogue.

Tagus, perhaps sent to harass us at Abrantes during our presumed retreat. If Lord Wellington had truly intended to attack us, he would not have detached such a considerable force as Hill's, which included some fifteen thousand men. Certainly he would have known that the surest way of disengaging the Zezere, the Tagus, and Abrantes was to attract our attention at Santarém. Moreover, if Wellington had wanted to overrun our position and force the Rio Maior, he could have taken his principal forces to the bridges at Celeiro, Secorio [?], Calhariz, etc. I think he was still searching to give the appearance of a battle for the sake of his army and ministers, and all these demonstrations were reduced to testing our position and finding out if we intended to establish ourselves at Santarém. These considerations also proved to me that he had not judged our movements well and that he believed we were on our way toward Castelo Branco or at least the left bank of the Zezere.[22]

Indeed, I found in an English letter printed by our newspapers that preparations had been made for an attack against our rear guard by Brigadier General Craufurd, a Portuguese brigade under the orders of General Pack, and the brigade of W. Erskine[23] reinforced by the rest of Spencer's division. General Craufurd was to attack our left, Erskine our center with a brigade of the Guards, and lastly General Pack was to turn our right flank with the Portuguese, probably by the Celeiro bridge. When General Spencer arrived, he was petrified at the mere idea of this plan and declared it impracticable. They found that the

22. Pelet's assessment of Wellington's plans was again correct. When Wellington first learned of Masséna's withdrawal to Santarém, he wrote to Fane, "The enemy intended either to retire across the Zezere, into Spain, or across the Tagus into Spain, or across the Zezere, to attack Abrantes." See *Wellington's Dispatches,* Wellington to Fane, November 15, 1810, VI, 624–25.

23. Sir Denis Pack (1772–1823) enlisted in the 14th Light Dragoons in 1791 as a cornet and reached the rank of colonel in 1810. He became a brigadier general two years after his services with the Portuguese Brigade. He served in Flanders, Ireland, the Cape, and South America between 1794 and 1807. In 1808 Pack was sent to the Peninsula, where he served at Roliça and Vimeiro. Fighting at Corunna and Walcheren, he played a significant role during Masséna's invasion in 1810.

Sir William Erskine (1769–1813) entered the army in 1786 and became a lieutenant two years later. He was in Flanders in 1793–95 but then served in Parliament from 1796 to 1808, when he was promoted to the rank of major general. He was sent to the Peninsula in 1809 and commanded the Light Division during Masséna's retreat while Craufurd was on leave in England. As a result of his recklessness and indiscretions during the spring of 1811, Erskine was transferred to Hill's forces. After Erskine exhibited signs of insanity, he was relieved of command.

French were more numerous than they had thought. What would this general have said if he had seen us perched on the rocks of Bussaco? A short time later, all attack became impossible on the Rio Maior because of extensive flooding from the rain.

I could not induce myself to believe that Lord Wellington was at Cartaxo, and in that I was completely wrong. This kind of error often occurs in war when one wants to make absolute judgments based on his own premises, because each one looks at them in his own way. Nevertheless, what was the good of placing the headquarters so close and what reason other than politics explained why they appeared to press our flanks and contain us by their proximity? Without a bridge on the Tagus, the location of their headquarters looked quite strange to me in view of this extraordinary tactic. With so many resources at his disposal, why had Wellington not constructed any bridges, since the tide was not felt beyond Valada? Certainly his numerous boats would have been insufficient to supply him there and if we advanced against him in any way, he could not do otherwise than withdraw into his Lines and move General Hill along the left bank beyond Alhandra.

It seemed likely that the movements of the two armies would be temporarily suspended. They would retain their respective positions until they wanted to start new operations again. This was becoming evident from the slowness and even the timidity with which the English army had followed our retrograde movement. This movement could have been fatal if the Allies had either attacked vigorously along the main highway or had maneuvered in that direction and pursued the 8th Corps; they could well have outdistanced the 8th Corps at Guerreiros or at least pressed it very closely. This simple march through Aveiras, Marmeleira, and Tremês would have overwhelmed all our dispositions. A rather strong attack on the 2nd Corps would have had the same results from the very first moment, if we were to believe General Reynier's misgivings. It was true that we could hardly believe that the English General, with such a great superiority of forces, preferred to remain strictly on the defensive and leave us the choice of operations, the time to prepare them, and all the offensive postures. One could not argue that it was quite important for Wellington to force us to withdraw still further and renounce our plans for bridging the Tagus.

All things considered, we preferred a line of operations on Leiria and Coimbra rather than on Castelo Branco; we were so far away from the latter that it would have been necessary to initiate a ninety-degree pivot to the rear to approach it. If Lord Wellington were to maneuver at the same time against the right of our position and our communications with Pombal, he could have forced us to make a broad movement and abandon the Tagus. But to do so he would immediately have had to concentrate before Rio Maior and Alcanede General Hill's fifteen thousand men that he so inopportunely sent on the other side of the river. Such an extensive movement on Alcanede would have cornered us between the Tagus and the Zezere and, with the two rivers at our back, threatened us with a more distressing attack than if we had placed the whole army in line on the Rio Maior or the Alviela. A small detachment of the Abrantes garrison would be sufficient to burn our preparations for the bridge on the Zezere. If we attacked the enemy, he could oppose us with more troops, and he could always control his withdrawal. Thus a strong detached unit, accompanied by attacks on Alcanede and Pernes, would be sufficient to force us to evacuate the country and throw ourselves quickly on Tomar or on the other side of the Zezere. On the one hand Lord Wellington would have separated us from the 8th Corps and the Tagus, and on the other he would have pushed us toward adverse territory. In the latter case, he knew very well that we could not have tried any open attack against Abrantes since it could not be besieged or forced with pieces of eight and six against larger calibers. Simply by establishing batteries across from Punhete, he would have made it impossible to construct any type of boat on the Zezere because of the easterly inclination of its flow and the difficulties of its passage. Wellington would have been free to place bridges at Barquinha and even at Tancos, and to maneuver as much as he wanted on both banks of the Tagus by those bridges and the one at Abrantes. We would therefore have found ourselves confined between the Tagus and Abrantes. We would then have lost all the fruits of our labors at Santarém and Punhete and been thrown back on Castelo Branco and faced the passage of the river beyond Vila Velha without any resources for constructing new boats. The English General believed he had opposed our plan to cross the river by moving General Hill on the bank opposite us. This only thwarted us momentarily and reassured us about an attack! Such a large detachment might have caused his defeat, as we shall see later.

The following, I believed, was what Lord Wellington should have done without changing his careful system or risking anything. Had he wished to indulge in a little reasoned audacity, without venturing half of what he risked at Fuentes de Oñoro and at Paris in 1815, he would only have had to prepare bridge equipment at Lisbon and cross the Tagus at Chamusca in order to throw himself in the middle of our army when it was extended on a circumference of [more than sixty miles] at Santarém, Alcanede, Leiria, Tomar, and Punhete. What would we have done if Lord Wellington had marched directly on Torres Novas and from there up to Tomar or Pernes? He had enough second-line troops to occupy the entrenched banks of the Rio Maior, its posts, its lines, etc.[24] This was not a recent plan, but I thought about it often then; it would have made me very apprehensive if I had not had an intimate knowledge of the English strategy.

Considering its position, the French army's only goal for the time being was to maintain itself in the heart of Portugal as long as possible and wait for orders and all the reinforcements that it had requested. Until they arrived, it could only prepare for new operations by producing resources to build bridges on the rivers and to reinforce its position and defensive system in a way to extend itself to gather food. While waiting, we could study the countryside, gather materials and information, and prepare the course for insuring its conquest. Rumors on the approach of the 5th Corps continued to circulate, although it was still quite distant. There was also talk about the 9th Corps. An English truce officer asked if Drouet's corps had arrived at Sabugal, in order to learn no doubt if we had any news. All our hopes and hearts were turned toward those two army corps.

The Prince had not seen the 6th Corps for a while. He went to Marshal Ney's quarters at Tomar. The Marshal had written him a long let-

24. Wellington described his intentions as follows: "Their army [French] being collected between Santarem and the Zezere, they are in a situation to be able . . . to maintain themselves in that strong position till the reinforcements, which I know are on the frontier, can join them; and for this reason, and because I was unwilling to expose to the inclemencies of the weather a larger body of troops than it was absolutely necessary to employ to press upon the enemy's rear, and to support the advance guard, I have kept in reserve a considerable proportion of the allied army, some of them still in the cantonments in the line of our fortified positions." See *Wellington's Dispatches,* Wellington to Liverpool, November 21, 1810, VI, 629–32.

ter [dated November 23] on the position of the army and its dispersion. The Prince explained his whole system to him. Never had they separated more content with each other.[25] Returning, I saw a large cannonball of foreign caliber on the main highway, which made me think General Hill's artillery had passed through, going to or returning from Bussaco. On the way, the Prince ordered me to prepare a report describing the basic principles governing our stay in the country. [Regarding the location of] the bridges on the Tagus, I proposed Punhete and Alcántara. As usual, the Prince was far from adopting them. [Concerning] the sieges of Elvas and Badajoz, I suggested we retain one of those fortresses and blow up Ciudad Rodrigo.

The Prince sent me to Punhete to observe the work of the engineers and the artillery. This village was situated at the confluence of the Zezere and the Tagus. At the very beginning of our retrograde movement, General Éblé's workshops for boat construction had been transported to the left bank of the Zezere below Punhete where they were covered from the view of the enemy bank of the Tagus. Since we had plans to throw up a bridge beyond the tip of Punhete, this position was entrenched by engineer officers for the dual purpose of use as a bridgehead and as cover for our dockyard against sorties by the nearby Abrantes garrison.

Near its confluence with the Zezere, the Tagus ran in a very narrow and deep valley, occupying its entire width. The slopes were sharp, full of ravines, often lacerated, and completely barren. On their summits were wide cultivated plateaus, and those on the left bank dominated the ones across the river. At the bottom of this immense ravine, the Tagus cut a bed averaging three hundred yards in width and ran in almost a direct line from Punhete up to Tancos, a village situated on the escarpment of the northern bank. A little upstream from Tancos, in the middle of the river, was the tower of Almourol, an ancient fort built on a rock, flanked by long slender towers, crowned by a great square keep, and it gave a very picturesque effect in the middle of this stony valley. These ruins had not been occupied.

The main highway from Abrantes followed the steep slopes of the

25. Despite the comments of numerous writers on the friction between Masséna and Ney, the present writer is convinced that the relations between the two were characterized by sympathetic support and understanding from December until the beginning of the retreat in March. See Horward, "Invasion of Portugal," pp. 500–42. Pelet's comment here supports this contention.

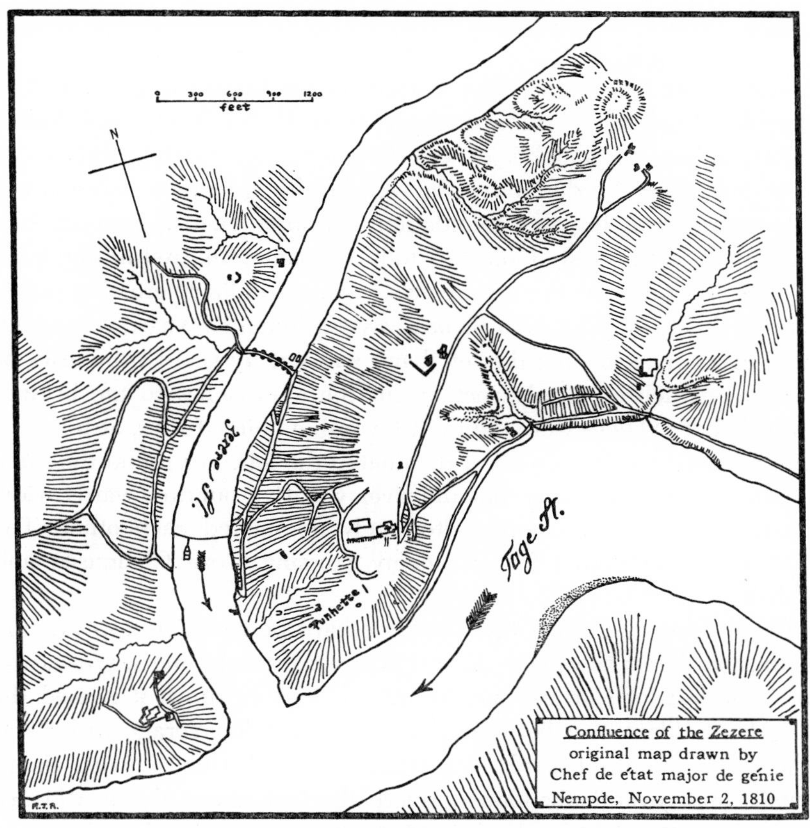

Confluence of the Zezere and Tagus Rivers

river from Barquinha to Tancos and climbed a plateau beyond. Another more difficult road ran along the height of Barquinha to Punhete. A horse path skirted the opposite bank. Opposite Tancos was Arripiado, where peasants were shooting at everything that passed. Near this point the range on the left bank was farther away from the river and left a large plain on the bank. The mountain drew closer to the river toward Pinheiro and Chamusca and then extended, at the distance of a league, as far as the stream of Mugem, where it ended. On its slopes were several torrents that carried a great amount of sand and debris, raising their beds above the slopes of the terrain. Alpiarça and Almeirim were on the crest of a rideau, and at the bottom was the stream of Alpiarça, which ran through low and frequently flooded terrain. Below Tancos the Tagus became wider, with an average width of four hundred yards along the plain. At Barquinha the mountains on the right bank turned away toward the north and formed a beautiful position, perpendicular to the Tagus and linked by Atalaia to the heights of the Almonda. Up to the Alviela the right bank was bordered by the very fertile plain of Golegã, but it was covered by the inundations of the Tagus. Beyond, the right bank again rested on the hills of Santarém. Returning from Boa Vista, I saw that there were two excellent military crossing points close to this town. The right bank was very dominant, sharply inclined, and almost inaccessible; the left bank was cut by small tributaries of the river which could obstruct or cut the approaches to the bridges during floods. These were the most favorable points for us, at least the ones where the right bank best dominated the left. We found the same domination at Barquinha, but the river was five hundred yards wide. Farther upstream the slopes alternately dominated each other. The most favorable points for an enemy crossing were Chamusca and Pinheiro.

Below Santarém, the Tagus could perhaps be considered as running in the middle of the plain since it was consistently one league away from the hills of Cartaxo and Azambuja. Farther down it neared the heights of Vilafranca; between these two cities its average width was again four hundred yards. Its banks were obstructed with dams, canals, and several abandoned riverbeds. Just above the confluence at Punhete, the right bank of the Tagus was low and rather flat up to Abrantes, where it rose considerably, while the left bank was always steep. Nevertheless, the heights were distant from the river opposite Crucifixo. Between this hamlet and Punhete, there were two great bends inclined toward the right bank, and they offered a few advantages for crossing; they also had the drawback of displaying a line of steep defensible hills above the plain that contained them. We witnessed the floods of the Tagus, extending far onto the plains and into the middle of the valley, raising its bed considerably. The river rose above a seventeen-foot perch placed to measure its heights at Punhete. Then it was higher than the Zezere, and its waters flowed into the latter. These ordinary floods came rather quickly and disappeared in the same way. While they lasted, the river was more favorable to us for navigation and for maneuvering the pontoons, but it was also more difficult to stabilize or fasten the pontoons.

We looked at the approximate configuration of the confluence of the

Zezere on the map. We had thought of establishing the pontoon bridge above Punhete, closer to the vertex of the first bend. A few people, especially the sailors, discouraged by the difficulty of going above the tip of Punhete and by seeing boats swept away by the current of the Zezere and thrown close to the other bank, proposed to set up the bridge below. However, we would then have been at the foot of the height and involved from the front as well as the flank.

The Zezere flowed in the middle of a mountainous country through a valley that was equally full of ravines and steep slopes, covered with woods and rocks. The river filled nearly the whole bottom. I had seen it only from the bridge of Martinchel and at Punhete. At Martinchel it was only seventy to eighty yards wide and not very deep. The valleys were very difficult there and much work was needed to make the road practicable. At the Punhete bridge the Zezere was 140 to 160 yards wide when the water was high and a little less in ordinary times. However, as it poured into the Tagus, the Zezere was narrower because of the alluvium on the left bank and the rocks on the right. The slopes were very steep at the confluence and made practicable by means of a great number of ramps. Along the confluence the plateaus on both banks of the Zezere were streaked by deep ravines which reached the surface and cut it in such a way as to impede the entrenched dispositions somewhat. Yet the positions also became much better when it was decided to reinforce their flanks. According to a reconnaissance of the upper Zezere, the valley there was difficult and full of ravines. At the passage of Pedrógão, we descended and climbed again through a multitude of very well-prepared turnabouts, but absolutely no wagon could pass there. It required one hour to descend and another to ascend. Below Martinchel the Nabão flowed into the Zezere. This was another torrent; it crossed a valley that was about one hundred yards wide and similar to that of the Zezere, but its bed was usually not wider than fifty to sixty yards and had little water.

I went to Punhete by the Tancos road. There I found the bridge on the Zezere attached so solidly that it had already withstood the river's heavy floods.[26] It was made up of twenty newly constructed boats. There were another thirty-five boats completed, seven in the shipyard,

26. Wellington claimed that the first bridge constructed on the Zezere was carried away by the floods. See *Wellington's Dispatches,* Wellington to Liverpool, November 21, 1810, VI, 629–32.

and a few unserviceable ones that had been brought from Vilafranca to no purpose. Each of these boats was twenty-nine feet long, six feet wide, and three feet deep. Seven laborers were employed on each boat in the shipyard. It took about six days or more to finish one. Six workers and five days would have been sufficient if the wood had not been so scarce, the materials so poor, and the workers so mediocre. In the construction of these boats, the bottom was first built with the use of lengths and widths attached to six or seven ribs, placed and raised on each side. Once the planks were nailed to the side, they were caulked with oakum and tar. The marines and artillery furnished part of the workers, but it was necessary to search through the regiments for everyone who had worked with metal, wood, rope, and caulkings. The corps lent themselves grudgingly to this, and everybody worked with indolence and negligence. If the enthusiasm of the Prince and General Éblé had been supported, we could have done twice as much. The workers were well paid, but they lacked food since they worked all day and could not go out to gather it. The Prince frequently gave General Loison orders to provide them with food from his harvest on the plain of Golegã. This order was never completely executed.

I went with General Éblé to the dockyards as well as to several of the rope, rigging, and metal depots. He had three forges operating, and the engineers had a similar number. All this was behind the left tip of the Zezere and nearly hidden from the opposite bank of the Tagus. The creation of bridge equipment in the midst of a devastated country, without any resources from the army *parc*, required the total energy, devotion, and talent of this worthy man. He promised more than sixty boats and eleven dingies by mid-December and eighty boats before the end of the month in order to have bridges on the Zezere and the Tagus simultaneously, as the Prince desired. The Prince supported the general in all his troubles, gathering money for him everywhere. Furthermore, he sent for planks, wood, and sawyers from the country, for this was what we lacked most. Finally, he asked for food from all the corps.

General Éblé had not yet fixed any point for the emplacement of the bridges on the Tagus. Nevertheless, he seemed to want to place them above the confluence and the village of Punhete, where the banks would be easier and less congested. The Tagus flowed strongly onto our bank, which dominated the opposite bank from the front and flank, but the far bank quickly rose in a very sharp slope. There was no other crossing near Punhete, and I strongly supported this idea because an operation there would be more secure—since it would be covered by the Zezere against any flank attack. Besides this site was closest to my particular system for occupying the confluence. The only difficulty and reasonable objection concerned the boats' entering into the Tagus from the Zezere, but we tried to reduce those difficulties. Unfortunately, I was not in agreement with the engineers. Their first works had been established on a principle which appeared to be faulty, but it was not possible for them to begin again.

A kind of isthmus formed by the bend in the Tagus and the Zezere and completed by the ravines descending into these two rivers, appeared to be cut crosswise by some kind of fortification line. Conversely, we had projected an oblique line to the isthmus with its defense directed against the waters of the Tagus. Two fortifications were established along the gorge, which could also be enfiladed along its length or taken from the rear and thus leave the streets of Punhete free on both flanks. We had started by the church and could not quit before the building was fraised, palisaded, leveled, and dressed, or in other words completely finished. In order to complete the system, we later started two redans or lunettes and a round redoubt. I visited the works with General Ferey and the chief engineers of the *état major*, who were charged temporarily with their construction. General Lazowski was ill, so I gave my opinion and made my observations. I presented my system of a triple bridgehead and a double bridge. I was challenged on it, and I in turn attacked, demonstrating the weakness of the system that had been adopted, its actual uselessness, and the necessity of rectifying it. They wanted to discuss the general system again. I returned to the local application, as a simple officer of the *état major*; then I requested a note indicating to the Prince only that which was agreeable to the engineers.

During a meticulous supper given by General Ferey at his quarters, despite the miseries in the middle of Portugal, three deserters from Abrantes declared that a noncommissioned officer, sent to that city for information, had announced the march of the French 5th Corps along both banks of the Tagus and the flight of the inhabitants of Alentejo before them toward Lisbon.[27] As a result of this news, the few Portu-

27. On the basis of a report from Hill, Wellington was convinced Masséna

guese troops who had arrived at Abrantes, especially one cavalry regiment, had recrossed the Tagus, leaving the city with only its garrison. Finally, they said that French troops going along the right bank were already at Sarzedas and even Cardigos. I said that perhaps it would be expedient to send ahead to obtain accurate news; this was judged useless and the declarations of the deserters were considered to be ridiculous rumors of the kind so often spread. Nevertheless, they were only too true as far as our side was concerned. The unfortunate column of Gardanne was arriving at that moment almost within sight of our advance posts, or at least a very short distance away. He was less than three miles from Punhete, in the direction of Cardigos, while rather close on the other side of Abrantes [by November 26]. There were no militia between us. On the basis of false information from peasants that we were ruined and dispersed, his column withdrew with the same haste and disorder via the Estrada Nova, which ran along the crest of the Serra da Estrêla, losing many men who were left behind when they became tired and hungry.[28] Perhaps this information had come to us too late, but we should have sent out a few spies, for one must neglect nothing in war. The reconnaissance on Abrantes showed that it would require a full attack.

General Éblé returned with me to Torres Novas in a heavy rain and a thunderstorm. I gave the Prince an account of the state of affairs without blaming anyone. On the contrary, I praised the efforts made by everyone. He flew into a rage about the many delays and difficulties regarding the bridges. I had time to calm him before General Éblé came to his quarters. The latter asked that the number of extra artillery wagons be reduced in each army corps in order to make a general distribution of the wagons and their teams. His Excellency gave this order.

would cross the Tagus and invade the Alentejo. Therefore he began making preparations to evacuate the province. "The passage of the Tagus by the enemy must be resisted as far as may be practicable; and every effort made to prevent them from establishing themselves on the left of the Tagus." See *Wellington's Dispatches,* Wellington to Stuart, December 24, 1810, VII, 68–70.

28. On November 28 a Spanish deserter named Ibanez informed the French of Gardanne's unsuccessful advance with some 5,000 men. When Napoleon heard of this incident, he wrote to Berthier, "The English mock General Gardanne greatly. That idiot was no more than three leagues from the French corps on the Zezere. You will find the entire dispatch. Send it to General Drouet, giving him orders to send this general, who appears to be an arch-imbecile, back to France." See *Lettres Inédites de Napoléon,* Napoleon to Berthier, January 4, 1811, II, 101.

A few days later the Prince wished to see the works of Punhete. We went along the Barquinha road. The defects of the entrenched positions surprised everyone. The Prince, to whom I had made only favorable comments on the entrenchments, found the terrain very poorly occupied and complained to me. In front of General Ferey I replied that since all the works were very advanced I had believed it useless to give my opinion, but that I had discussed and explained my viewpoint adequately in the presence of the general. Then I declared to the engineer officers how unacquainted I was with all these operations, but no doubt I would be involved in it. We then went down to the shipyards and found forty-two boats finished and twelve under construction. In the middle of a discussion on the subsistence, the Prince compelled Loison to furnish some food. Solignac promised to give something more. His Excellency treated the brave and dignified Éblé with great distinction, and he was very satisfied. He told the general in front of everyone that he was worth more than twenty thousand men to the army and then gave one hundred louis [d'or] as a gratuity to the workers.

I felt obliged to keep the Prince at a distance because of the stupid comments I continued to hear, which came from very high levels and were far from flattering. They offended and annoyed the Prince as much as they did me. I saw His Excellency for only a few moments in the morning and during the day when he sent for me about an urgent matter. My personal work was increasing; it was not that I had a challenging subject or anything that could excite me, since the work hardly involved anyone beyond my two friends and myself. Thus I rewrote plans for the conquest and occupation of Portugal twice because the Prince had asked me to, and he wanted to work on them himself. I gave them to him a few days later. He received the plans very graciously and assured me he would have them read to him, and he would add notes. He did not talk to me about them again.

Too often the Prince asked me for a map made by an officer unconnected with his *état major.* I was rather annoyed at having to bother myself with something that did not concern me, and I said so. Then the Prince returned in a peremptory way to his former project of ordering me to take charge of topography for the army; he sent me written orders. From that moment on I was obliged to take care of it, but almost nothing remains of this work in my papers. The task had been poorly started, the positions were wrong and badly placed, the details not exact and still incomplete. Since the Prince asked for this work all the time, I took it upon myself to make for our immediate needs a drawing of all the topographical studies that had been finished and then to proceed with the details, waiting until we had measured a base on the field of Golegã from which we could establish a few triangles and put in the details of the positions when they had been fairly well determined. General Reynier continued to work; he had the kindness to send us very good information on the country that he occupied. We did not get any help from the other army corps. Our map of the region was drawn at a scale of one hundred thousandth. It covered all the country that we had occupied and was to be extended with the movements of the army. Meanwhile, I made a kind of guidebook of the country on the right bank of the Tagus from Santarém and Abrantes up to Soure according to the information that I was able to obtain from the Marquis d'Alorna and the inhabitants. At the last moment Cavailher and Richoux made an excellent and very beautiful survey of the confluence of Punhete on a scale of one to twenty thousand. Beaufort and Captain Jean Louis Million surveyed the course of the Tagus from Montalvão to Vila Nova. A few reconnaissances were drawn in the areas of Castelo Branco, the Zezere, and Leiria. During our withdrawal the terrain we marched through had been drawn more particularly by Calmet and Richoux. At length a rather large number of good reconnaissance surveys were written either by the officers of the Prince or by those of the engineers. This is a glimpse of our topographical work in Portugal.

Meanwhile, the army corps began to complain about the lack of food, although they had hardly entered the territory where they were to live for three more months. Nevertheless, we were accustomed to such complaints and knew what to think; their purpose was always to obtain aid or permission to disperse. Each army corps had gathered all the grain in the region it occupied. Each general and colonel had procured an advance of grain and storage for his troops, and they continued grinding and baking. The officers sent out detachments to bring back the necessary animals. Almost all of them had executed the order to make twenty-day rations of biscuit in case of a movement. A few districts and especially the plain of Golegã had furnished a considerable quantity of corn; it was exploited by both the corps and the administration, who had a great number of peasants working for them. In the beginning we had found a large quantity of wheat at Santarém, on the banks of the Tagus, and near Torres Novas. Situated far from the passage of English troops and the main communication lines, Torres Novas still had most of its inhabitants and provisions. The military administration seized the provisions and made bread, according to custom, first for itself and then for the hospitals and headquarters. The Prince had charged General Fririon to inspect carefully the details of provisioning, which were becoming of major importance. All these resources were eventually exhausted, and it was necessary to resort to large forage parties who fed the corps by extending themselves for great distances, but this practice was accompanied by many horrible excesses.

The first and most constant complainer was General Reynier, who had lost so much grain at Porto de Mugem. He asked to be relieved in order to occupy the Zezere.[29] On the other hand, Marshal Ney wrote long letters full of details of his reconnaissance on Cabaços, where he had not found anything. The reconnaissances beyond the Zezere had encountered a few peasants. The enemy had shown themselves in force at Alcobaça and had posts at Aljubarrota, but this did not worry us as long as we could see the English corps on the other side of the Tagus at Pinheiro and Chamusca. The Marshal proposed a few dispositions to throw the enemy back beyond Rio Maior and onto Cartaxo, thus providing terrain where the 2nd Corps could be cantoned. The 6th Corps would give up villages for two thousand men near Ourém and Chão de Macãs. In this way, we could go on living up until the fifteenth of March. Why fight for this piece of exhausted land, and why throw ourselves beyond the flooded streams when it was quite preferable that our line be covered and inclined toward our support and the Tagus in the rear rather than carried forward? Moreover, the

29. Although Masséna established districts for the various corps to obtain their food, Reynier was appealing for supplies by the first week of December. Masséna then wrote to Ney and Montbrun, requesting 88,000 to 132,000 pounds of food for Reynier. Ney replied, "I am aware of the difficult situation in which the 2nd Corps finds itself with regard to subsistence, concentrated as it is by the enemy. However, with the best intentions, I am not able to send him . . . the grain that you have requested. . . . Your Excellency has placed corn, vegetables, and grain taken at Azinhaga [?] at the disposal of the 6th Corps. We will make this sacrifice in favor of the 2nd Corps." See Masséna to Reynier, December 7, 1810, Correspondance: Armée de Portugal, Carton C^{7}10; Bonnal, *Ney*, Ney to Masséna, December 5, 1810, III, 425–27.

Marshal wrote down all these excellent plans in response to a request for a few hundredweight of grain to be sent to the 2nd Corps. The Prince announced to the corps commanders his intention to prolong the sojourn of the army beyond January 15, to prepare bridges on the Tagus, and to conserve the food that was at their disposal.

Captain Letermiler* of the dragoons, who had been made prisoner at Coimbra, was sent to us in exchange for Eliott. He brought me compliments from Captain Mellish. The captain claimed that as I left I had told him we would be in Lisbon in eight days. I believe he was wrong. Captain Letermiler gave us a good deal of information about the English army. The French prisoners captured at Coimbra on October 7 by Trant's column were taken to Oporto in triumph with a band, and all were so badly wounded they could not walk. They were atrociously insulted by the Portuguese, and a few of those left behind were massacred. The English were very bored in their camps. They said that we had sixty thousand men and that we had not made any movements because we lacked food; they spoke with great respect of the Prince and praised General Reynier highly. They reported a reinforcement of twenty thousand for our army, and they usually mistreated the Portuguese, whether they were soldiers or the bourgeoisie. The port of Lisbon was full of transport and war vessels. Everything was embarked and disembarked according to need. There was much misery and unrest there, and bread was both scarce and expensive in Lisbon. Letermiler had seen three lines of works at Caveira, Alhandra, and one in an intermediate position. He said that King George was quite ill, that England wanted to make peace with Turkey, and that war between Russia and us seemed certain. The English newspapers had been announcing this break with the north for a long time. It was possible that such considerations would influence the measures the government took toward us. This news was highly relevant to our predicament, since we were at one end of Europe. We had sent several peasants toward Castelo Branco to get some news, but no word had reached us about the reinforcements that were to arrive.

[On December 7] Colonel Pierre François Dejean made a reconnaissance with his regiment and a battalion of the 69th Line. He reached the bridge at Coimbra. According to his report, Trant was in the city with four thousand men, Wilson was at Espinhal, and others occupied Ponte de Murcella. The colonel stopped at Venda do Cago and sent a strong reconnaissance on Coimbra. When they showed themselves on the heights, the general alarm was rung, the tocsin sounded, and shouts of confusion were heard. There were some troops in a column on the bridge, but as soon as ours advanced the enemy withdrew on the right bank. The bridge on the Mondego had a broken arch and could be crossed only on planks.[30] During the same day the colonel marched on Redinha, fearing some movement by Wilson on his right or rear. All the inhabitants beyond Pombal had taken refuge in Coimbra; they believed that our army was going to withdraw in that direction. Finally, the colonel brought no news of the 9th Corps.

The Prince wanted to place Loison's division closer to the Zezere, so he relieved his troops at Atalaia with Thomières' brigade of the 8th Corps. The 86th Line left Torres Novas to go there. With the Prince, we were very busy working on the bridges in order to place them on the Tagus because the time for laying them across was continually delayed. All our activities produced only a few letters to General Éblé, but I found a great source of instruction in the discussions, which always took place with great freedom.

The Prince had taken a notion to have me draw up a military topography of Portugal to serve as an introduction for the history of his campaign. He wanted to do the history himself, but he soon laid it aside and ordered me to work on it. I complained to him about the total lack of organized espionage. We were without accurate and frequent news and were always limited to sending out a few miserable peasants. Besides their immediate utility, these intelligence reports would have served us favorably by providing various new hypotheses for us to work out. However, we lacked all the elements—first money and then leadership from our crowd of Portuguese. Otherwise, I said to His Excellency, we would fall asleep and become "bourgeois," as indeed we had. The inactivity was getting extremely tiresome.

In reality we lived at the Torres Novas headquarters in a strange tranquility. Part of my time was taken up with administrative work

30. Dejean's column, which included two battalions from the 69th Line and the 6th Léger supported by the 15th and 25th Dragoons, undertook this reconnaissance during the first week of December. *Chef d'escadron* Robineau, with one hundred men, pushed on from Venda do Cago to the Mondego River. According to Dejean's report, when the column reached Coimbra the citizens "made a frightful disturbance in the town; the drums beat general quarters, the bells sounded the tocsin, and above all we heard the inhabitants screaming, especially women." See Bonnal, *Ney*, Dejean to Montbrun, December 7, 1810, III, 428–30.

and reading in our ill-assorted library, where the number of books grew daily; frequent trips filled up the rest of the day. We were, furthermore, living in a superb country. Torres Novas was a small city in the province of Santarém, seven leagues northeast of that major town. Rather pleasing and well built, it was situated on the right bank of the Almonda at the foot of the Serra de Aire, in a hilly country covered with olive trees and vineyards. The majority of the inhabitants had remained there, except for a small number of the upper class. This formed a great contrast with what we had seen throughout Portugal and proved how violence and cruel treatment had forced the transmigration of the whole population. We were told that charming women beautified the happy climate, but the elite had fled and among those who remained I did not see a single noteworthy girl, for they went out very little. What is more, all our men amused themselves, or thought they were amusing themselves, at Torres Novas. There were gatherings and even theaters for the very formal society where light comedy was played with success. The young men gave many dances. Since there were few women, they admired the *cantinières*, grotesquely adorned with pillaged booty. When they were offered a strong punch, they pretended they did not like lemonade. We had many pleasant stories about those gatherings, which would not be in the best taste.

Torres Novas was surrounded by beautiful gardens planted with orange trees. Now they were full of flowers and fruit. It could be said that we enjoyed a continuous spring, for hardly once were the surfaces of the water covered with ice. We constantly found daisies in the middle of the fields, along with violets and fruit trees adorned with flowers. The environs offered delightful walks on the hills near the aqueduct and on the banks of the Almonda, especially going upstream. The Almonda flowed full to the bank in a bed of rocks, and at the bottom the translucent water could be seen very clearly as it played marvelously amid the black slate rock and pleasant greenery. There were many mills, usually situated on rocks. Each one of their falls made a beautiful cascade, and often several were united as assembled groups. They were a beautiful sight, charming among the dark buildings, with the great waterwheels and the lofty hills that crowned them. Near Lapas we found in the limestone and schistose rocks immense caverns which were sometimes used as homes by the peasants. Every branch of the Almonda provided a charming valley, and each house was isolated with something picturesque about it. However, we always returned to the mills and the streams to find the most beautiful sensations. This country seemed magnificent to us with its pure sky; the sun sparkled on the crystals of the waters and lightened the gay greenery. I have never seen anything more elating in the vicinity of Naples, Calabria, or the most beautiful sights of Italy. How many agreeable walks I made with my two friends, who shared the same tastes and feelings with me, and that very pleasant engineer colonel, whom everyone will recognize without my naming him.[31] This was our group and these our only pleasures! Outside and inside we were always together, and the charms of friendship adorned every moment. It is necessary to make this point, for there are those who cannot imagine war without perpetual battles, gross pleasures, and brutal passions.

However, not everyone was leading such an innocent life. Horrors were committed. The situation was the more deplorable because it was impossible to stop. There was an infamous traffic, and unfortunately since a few inhabitants had yielded it seemed that the others had been deprived of the right to object. Young girls were sold by their parents, and a few brigands, out searching for food, kidnapped young women they met; they had the women follow them and made an odious traffic of them. It was claimed that public markets of this kind had been held, but I was unable to believe it since I had no proof.[32] These ruffians, who believed themselves generous, gave liberty to the unfortunate victims of their violence, but it should be said that most of the women did not want to leave their new masters and go back to the old ones. They preferred licentiousness and the affluence of marauding to purity and abstinence in the deserted countryside. I had only seen these Portuguese women from afar, but there were a great number following the regiments and even a few at headquarters. They were quite free and were attracted by this new type of life. It has been necessary to talk about this baseness since I cannot destroy the memory of it, so that I cannot be suspected of covering it up, and so that it is known how much honest people abhorred it. As a contrast to this infamous conduct, we can cite the conduct of two grenadiers of Clauzel's division

31. Apparently Pelet is referring to Colonel Valazé, who was a long-time friend and companion-in-arms.

32. Captain Guingret of the 6th Léger claimed foragers often returned to their regiments with young peasant girls whom they sold to the highest bidder. See his *Relation historique*, pp. 125–27.

who met some women in a cave and swore to themselves as well as to the women to respect their asylum; they did not break their oath, and they continued bringing them food during the night.

There was also much talk about other crimes committed by isolated men or small groups of marauders in order to obtain the location of secret caches from the unfortunate peasants. The details that were given would make one shiver. However, they could not be obtained from the mouths of the originators or witnesses of such atrocities, and so we must believe that if crimes really were committed, nobody would dare to brag about them. It is well known that there are some men everywhere who brag about crimes and feel a kind of honor in making themselves appear worse than they really are. There are also many others who make a habit and a necessity of lying and exaggerating the falsehoods of others as much as they can. Moreover, we have seen excesses carried out by a few monsters with human faces far too often not to believe that, among such a great number of soldiers—accustomed to spilling blood during the fighting and then left to their own resources—some would not have committed cruelties. But in the French army such crimes were hidden. When we were able to discover wrongdoers, they were pursued and severely punished.[33] Elsewhere such crimes were tolerated, rewarded, and even publicly ordered. If we find ourselves reduced to such extremities that we turn away with horror, who is finally the most guilty—the man who kills his fellowman to prevent his own starvation or the one who murders him as punishment for staying quietly in his home? This is what the enemy has done for us. Severe instructions and the most rigorous orders were given to the commanders of detachments sent on forage detail and to the officers accompanying them; yet, to find food, the officers were forced to scatter their troops and leave the soldiers to themselves. Those marching in units brought back very little.

In addition to the forage parties sent out regularly by the corps,

33. Daily reports of atrocities committed by French foragers forced Masséna to issue a stern circular to his corps commanders: "I understand that the soldiers of different detachments sent to search for food are involved in terrible excesses. Those of the inhabitants who have already furnished all the subsistence within their power . . . are victims of vicious barbarity. You cannot listen without shuddering—they have hung a great number of the unfortunate inhabitants. Make exemplary punishment of the disorders that you see. . . . Give the punishment you have to inflict in public as proof to those who need a lesson to remind them that they are men and French." See Masséna to Junot, January 13, 1811, Correspondance: Armée de Portugal, Carton C[7]11.

from the beginning there were also isolated soldiers and others who ran away from their regiments and marauded for themselves. The latter committed fewer cruelties because it was too dangerous for them. With their insufficient numbers, it was not to their interest to maltreat the inhabitants. Some of them even established themselves as the protectors of the region where they settled. Moreover, they sometimes gathered to confront the enemy and often stopped our forage details from marauding in their area. Finally, one such band styled itself the 11th Corps, a number not found in the Army of Spain. It was said to have been formed under the orders of a corporal who made himself commander and was called General Chaudron. He had taken the decorations of a general officer from some baggage pillaged by his band. There was a great deal of talk about this 11th Corps for rather a long time, but the famous Chaudron was finally caught and shot.[34]

As soon as the most urgent needs had been met, the industry of our soldiers was employed with singular diligence. Each one took over the various workshops in every city according to the job that he had formerly performed. As a result we found as many resources as could be expected in the middle of such general destitution. Hand-written signs announced each type of industry. We saw two watchmakers at Torres Novas. At Tomar soldiers started the manufacture of soap again. At first they made only rather crude products, but the extreme need made it very precious. Some claimed they made considerable money from the soap. The *cantinières* followed the marauders and the detachments at a distance and later on supplied the markets, where objects varied in price constantly according to the supply and the demand. Avid speculators who expected to exploit the wealth of Lisbon followed the army like sharks behind vessels, but their number soon dwindled because they were wasting all their time with worthless secondhand goods. Their principal commerce became the silver that the soldier sold for a low price as soon as it was plundered.[35] Some individuals, whose rank and duties should have kept them from involvement in this

34. According to Marbot, who also spoke of "Marshal Chaudron," "the scoundrel had also carried off numbers of women; and being joined before long by the scum of the three armies, attracted by the prospect of unrestrained debauchery, he formed a band of some three hundred English, French, and Portuguese deserters, who lived as a happy family in one unbroken orgy." See Marbot, *Memoirs*, II, 133–34 (in the French ed., II, 418–19).

35. Any Frenchman who found a pair of breeches could sell them for an ounce of gold, according to Lemonnier-Delafosse, *Souvenirs*, p. 117.

money business and even more from the scandalous traffic, demeaned themselves to the point of concealing pillaged booty and converting the stolen goods into ingots when they should have punished this practice vigorously.

Since November, when we had evacuated the position of Sobral and occupied the left bank of the Rio Maior, affairs had been in the same state. General Reynier spoke of some new troops at Ponte de Celeiro and on the Azambuja road. Nevertheless, everything remained quiet on the line. We were waiting impatiently for news from the 9th Corps or from General Gardanne and for orders from Paris along with answers to the requests taken there by General Foy. Having left Ciudad Rodrigo more than a month and a half before, Foy was to talk about the state of affairs with King Joseph as well as with Marshal Soult. I wished we had sent officers to them and that all these arrangements had been taken when we first arrived in front of the enemy Line and had decided not to attack. These delays naturally halted all our movements and decisions. We could not go to the other side of the Tagus without maintaining a bridgehead on the right bank or on both banks of the Zezere until General Gardanne and the 9th Corps arrived; they would join us either by the Tomar road or by Sarzedas. We had to maintain our line of march with this corps and prevent it from being smashed by concentrated enemy forces or turned back to the fortress without hope of our seeing them. There was no agreement, and there had never been, on the question of determining whether the army, in its present state, could hold both banks of the Tagus or at least occupy a bridgehead on either bank. Moreover, we could wait a while longer since all the reports declared that the corps had enough food to last until January 15, with a twenty-day reserve of biscuit. Even Marshal Ney claimed that he had provisions until March 15, but we were to see him change his story more than once.

The enemy labored for a few days opposite the mouth of the Zezere, on the left bank of the Tagus, and we were informed they had just moved some cannon there.[36] This disposition was easy to predict. We might have been able to prevent it by increasing the demonstrations on both sides of the Zezere toward Abrantes. The enemy wanted to

36. On January 12 Ferey informed Ney of the construction of fortifications and artillery opposite Punhete, on the south bank of the Tagus. See Bonnal, *Ney*, III, 439.

keep our boats from coming out on the Tagus River; he could do even more mischief by entrenching the point where the disembarkation was to be effected. The Prince wanted to see all of this himself, but he had a violent cold and sent me. The cannon which sounded so loud from a distance was only a piece of three that the enemy fired for amusement everyday at noon, when our posts were relieved on the plateau of Punhete. However, the English reinforced this point.

With General Éblé I visited the place where he proposed to throw up the bridge. I talked about the project a great deal, in confidence and friendship, with the brave and worthy general. As long as we had such men on our side, we could scoff at anyone. I spoke to him about my triple bridgehead and of the need to occupy the three opposite banks [both banks of the Zezere and the left bank of the Tagus] and to combine these operations with communications to France, and more particularly to combine the crossing with exterior maneuvers. His works still went forward with the same activity, while those of the engineers followed their previous system. The engineers had not been officially informed that the bridge at Martinchel had been erected and that they could work on its ramps and works. Thus they were not doing anything. Moreover, I was not in complete agreement about [the value of] this bridge. It served only to attract more attention from the enemy and was useful only momentarily although it utilized about twelve boats. On my return, I visited the plateau on the right bank of the Zezere with General Ferey. Like the other side, it was streaked by ravines which could be used for its defense. We could see there some traces of considerable works, with embrasures directed against the confluence. They were linked with a few redoubts, placed along the bank toward the north, to defend a passage of the river. These were probably the works of 1807 that General Thiébault wrote about.[37]

There were rumors in the countryside that Bacelar was in strength near Abrantes and that Silveira had beaten General Drouet. It was later said that it was General Gardanne and that he had been made prisoner. During a conversation with English officers opposite Golegã, a stupid Portuguese said that the net had been stretched around us.

37. Thiébault described these Portuguese redoubts and batteries on the right bank of the Zezere in his *Relation de l'expédition du Portugal, faite en 1807 et 1808, par le Ier corps d'observation de la Gironde, devenu armée de Portugal* (Paris, 1817), p. 63.

Our people responded that it would be broken at any time. There were conversations about plots in and around Torres Novas, of correspondence with the enemy army, and plans for a massacre at headquarters, in combination with some attacks by the Portuguese. The mayor was arrested along with a few of the principal citizens, and a military tribunal was formed to judge them. The Prince did not want to give this affair more importance than it deserved. More specifically, this incident was not to be considered a conspiracy, as many people called it; but safety measures were to be taken and the guilty found. Fortunately, he chose a wise and enlightened man as captain-chairman. The latter proved that this so-called conspiracy was only a chimera invented by a miserable servant and initiated by our commander of the town. Everyone was released immediately.

Perhaps this is the time to talk about the alleged conspiracy which the English claimed as a pretext when they arrested many of the influential inhabitants at Lisbon who were known to abhor their usurpation. They were accused of corresponding with the French army. I must affirm that I was personally convinced there was no correspondence, no secret relations between our army and any part of Portugal, least of all with Lisbon. I think that if such a conspiracy had existed, the Prince would have told me about it in confidence before talking to anyone else, or I would probably have guessed it during the course of events. I was also convinced that the Portuguese who were with us would have been the first to communicate it to me. The English now wanted, as they had just done, to sacrifice all those Portuguese who considered themselves true patriots and enemies of English domination. I have always heard it said that General Gomes Freire, whom our Portuguese considered one of their best military men and commanders, did not want to serve with our army against his country.[38]

Finally, we made a reconnaissance on Castelo Branco that I had sought for several days. General Ferey left with two thousand men

38. Gomes Freire de Andrade (1757–1817) joined the 13th Portuguese Line at an early age; he served in the Russian army during its war with Turkey and with the 4th Portuguese Line against France in Catalonia and Roussillon in 1793–95. He was promoted to the rank of lieutenant general, and when Junot occupied Portugal Freire worked with the Marquis d'Alorna to establish a Portuguese Legion for the French army. When Masséna invaded Portugal in 1810, Freire refused to accompany him. He served in the Russian campaign and returned to Portugal in 1815; however, two years later he was accused of conspiring against the government and executed.

[on December 22]. He had orders not to compromise himself, to protect his communications, and to watch his rear and flanks. He was to send a note to Almeida or Rodrigo with news of the army. I hoped that he would send an officer with a few men to Paris from there. He took an engineer, Captain Treussart, with him; he was a man full of merit and great determination as he had already proven at Corunna and Rodrigo and was later to demonstrate at Wittenberg. General Ferey remained out for a week; he did not find anyone, not even the local inhabitants.[39] The peasants had fled after the English had threatened the death penalty. He reconnoitered the formidable positions of Alvito, Monte Gordo, and Talhadas which General Hill had occupied for a long time. Captain Treussart sent an excellent reconnaissance of that district.

A Portuguese surgeon abandoned the enemy and came to join us because of the persecutions his family had experienced and his fears for his own safety. He told us that there were two Portuguese infantry regiments, the 13th and the 22nd Line, together with three regiments of militia and one of unmounted cavalry at Abrantes—in all four thousand men. There was no one between that point and the frontiers of Spain. There were many cannon in Abrantes but little food. The bridge was pulled back onto the left bank opposite the town, which was on a height a quarter of a league from the Tagus. The enemy had only two regiments of cavalry on the opposite bank at Alpiarça [?] and two at Almeirim, all of them Portuguese. A regiment of eight hundred Spaniards was opposite Abrantes with detachments near Punhete. Five English regiments were near Chamusca and General Beresford was at Cartaxo.[40] There was no news about English bridges on the Tagus. La Romana was at Vila Nova with eight hundred Spaniards and the 5th Corps was around Badajoz, according to the surgeon. A peasant had

39. On December 22 Ferey crossed the Zezere at Martinchel with approximately 2,000 infantry and 400 cavalry. Reaching Castelo Branco on Christmas Day, Ferey learned from the inhabitants about Gardanne's fiasco and the movement of 20,000 French reinforcements toward Coimbra. See Bonnal, *Ney*, Loison to Ney, December 31, 1810, III, 436–37.

40. The brigades of Hill's force were established along the left bank of the Tagus from Abrantes to Almeirim. William Stewart's brigade occupied Pinheiro and Tramagal; Houston's brigade held Chamusca; Lumley's brigade was posted at Almeirim; Fonseca's brigade was established at Mugem; Campbell's brigade occupied Salvaterra; and Fane's cavalry was interspersed along the entire line. See Benjamin D'Urban, *The Peninsular Journal of Major General Sir Benjamin D'Urban, 1808–1817*, ed. I. J. Rousseau (London, 1930), pp. 173ff.

given us a completely contradictory report. Rumors spread about the countryside that troops were reinforcing us, that we already had sixty thousand men including peasants and soldiers, and that we were in a bad position.[41] It was the opinion of the officers and discriminating people that in the end we would remain masters of Portugal. There were severe shortages at Lisbon; bread and meat were three times the ordinary price. The capital was full of refugees. Two Portuguese regiments were at Elvas and one at Cadiz. Including the 24th Line at Almeida, eighteen of the thirty-four Portuguese infantry regiments were available; four were with General Hill[42] and the remainder under the command of Beresford, not counting the militia and ten to twelve cavalry regiments. The surgeon said that there were many French partisans in Lisbon and that the inhabitants of the capital would not flee.

I explained the principles of my plan for crossing the Tagus to the Prince, and he finished by having me read it. His ideas were a little different from mine. He wanted to take the 2nd Corps to Golegã, the 8th Corps to Torres Novas, and the 6th to Martinchel and cross by night; he hoped to throw six thousand infantry and two thousand cavalry on the other bank immediately to support the right on the Tagus and the front downstream, and blockade Abrantes with Solignac's division. Another of his plans was to cross with the 2nd and 8th Corps, with the passage covered by the 6th Corps, which would remain on the right bank. He wanted to execute this crossing even after our reinforcements had arrived and, I believe, without maintaining the bridgehead. We discussed these different plans and their various aspects, such as a strong enemy detachment on the left bank or an attack against our retiring troops. His Excellency's opinion was contrary to

41. Wellington expected the French to withdraw from their position at Santarém momentarily. On December 21 he wrote to Liverpool, "It is certainly astonishing that the enemy have been able to remain in this country so long; and it is an extraordinary instance of what a French army can do. It is positively a fact that they brought no provisions with them, and they have not received even a letter since they entered Portugal. With all our money, and having in our favor the good inclinations of the country, I assure you that I could not maintain one division in the district in which they have maintained not less than 60,000 men and 20,000 animals for more than two months." See *Wellington's Dispatches,* VII, 56–60.

42. The Portuguese troops with Hill included the 4th and 10th Line in Archibald Campbell's brigade and the 2nd and 14th Line in Fonseca's brigade. In addition, Fane's command included the 1st, 4th, 7th, and 10th Portuguese cavalry regiments.

mine. He wanted to attack in the last case rather than in the first because food was a major concern. This would not stop me, for we could only reach Lisbon by attacking and I was so convinced that if we had orders to attack with a few reinforcements, I would want to use such a demonstration pushed all the way [to the capital].

Every morning we worked on these plans. The Prince persisted in his ideas, and I was convinced of mine. Sometimes he condescended to join in our discussion and I spoke with liberty and frankness. His enthusiasm did not always agree with my calculations and reasoning. When I thought I saw the evidence and at the same time the importance of an objective, I supported it strongly, yielding only to the authority of the commander and the individual. Although his ideas were different from mine, I still executed his ideas as if they were mine, and I easily overcame my partiality. Sometimes I would tell him about my work only on his expressed order, or I would wait for his orders to go and see him, to prove both to him and others how little I tried to exert or extend the influence with which he honored me. The Prince made a few notes on the crossing according to his particular plan; he even gave some preparatory orders to reconnoiter the roads and the various localities. The artillerymen had started building their eightieth boat, not counting a few that had been patched up; eleven skiffs and one barge were being completed. Thirty-six wagons were prepared to carry all the equipment.

At last [on December 26] we received news of the 9th Corps. A report declared that a reconnaissance on Cabaços had met a party from General Drouet's corps in the direction of Espinhal; they announced his arrival in that village with a corps of twenty-five thousand men.[43] This news spread quickly from mouth to mouth. Everybody was frantic—great happiness and great plans. We must attack, break through, conquer!

Everyone was preoccupied with their ardor, their interest, and their dreams. Nobody thought of the value of the crossing itself. They pushed or pressed me, but I had already given them my opinion on that. In the morning I again worked on an attack plan in support of

43. Captain Sprünglin declared that he encountered Gardanne's cavalry near Cabaços, acting as Drouet's advance guard, on December 26. See Sprünglin, *Souvenirs*, p. 460. However, Koch maintained that Colonel Mouriez of the 39th Line made first contact with the 9th Corps. See Koch, *Mémoires de Masséna*, VII, 284.

my crossing. The work was not advanced enough; yet it was the way that I hoped we would attack.

Excited by the news, and relying on the number of men announced in the report, the Prince wanted to cross the Tagus at Tancos as soon as possible. He wrote to General Éblé to reconnoiter this point. Then he wanted to establish himself at Santarém, put down the bridge, send his cavalry opposite Lisbon, extend his right to the sea through Alcobaça, direct the 9th Corps toward that point and Rio Maior immediately, and place a few of General Montbrun's cavalry in the village of Rio Maior. That morning I had drawn up not my own opinion but the various possible operations for this situation. I found it too embarrassing to make a decision on such an intricate and important matter, especially when giving advice that others had to execute. My work, entitled "Coup d'oeil sur la situation de l'armée" (28 December), was not completely finished.[44]

Nevertheless, I told the Prince I thought I would commence with the demonstration I had proposed, ready to attack the Lines if the enemy had a detachment on the left bank. In a contrary situation, I would blockade Lisbon for a while on both banks and, if there were enough food, occupy Merceana, Alenquer, Carregado, and Aldeia Galega; if that did not succeed, I would, with good dispositions, attack the Lines. But in such a hypothetical situation we should refrain from reaching Rio Maior until the last moment, because that was a sensitive point which would force the enemy to reenter their entrenchments.

The reported twenty-five thousand men were actually six thousand and they did not even belong to our army.[45] Casabianca came to bring

44. The manuscript that Pelet refers to could not be located in the Correspondance: Armée de Portugal at Vincennes. However, Pelet did note several salient points in a footnote to his manuscript. He suggested an attack against the Allies across the Ponte de Celeiro and through Alcanede to seize Vilafranca, Cadafais, Sobral, Panasqueira, and Bombarral. He also proposed that the 6th Corps cross the Tagus at Barquinha while the 9th Corps held Torres Novas and Pernes, the 8th Corps retained Alcanede, and the 2nd Corps remained at Santarém. When the English withdrew troops from the right bank of the Tagus to reinforce Hill on the left bank, the French would drive down the roads of Cartaxo, Aveiras, and Alcoentre and breach the Lines.

45. The second division of the 9th Corps, commanded by General Michel Marie Claparède, remained in the vicinity of Celorico to destroy the Portuguese militia operating on the rear of Masséna's army. When Drouet arrived at Ney's headquarters, he refused to place himself under Masséna's orders. He wrote to Ney on December 30, 1810: "I am not to unite [with Masséna]; my orders are clear and precise in this regard." Bonnal, *Ney*, III, 435–36.

this glorious news. He had been made a major, but no promotions had been granted for us. I felt this injustice quite deeply. If I were not so French—Everybody appeared to be upset, especially my friends, my good friends who forgot the rejection of their own promotions and worried only about me! But then how often had I taken care of them in my plans. There were no letters either. The mail had remained at Valladolid. General Drouet came to Torres Novas alone [on December 28].

The Prince called me early, for he was quite upset, especially for those of us who had been refused our deserved advancement, although it had been requested so often and so insistently. Foy and Ferey had been named generals of division, but how could I complain? The Prince was always talking about his friends and he treated me with the greatest confidence, especially at that moment; therefore I did not say anything. There was a long letter from General Foy with details of his meeting with the Emperor. He asked why we had crossed the Mondego? Why did we leave the sick at Coimbra? Why stay so close to the enemy? All the answers had been peremptory, at least this was what General Foy said. Nevertheless, the Emperor expressed much confidence and satisfaction as well as an accusation of too much boldness. He was displeased about Coimbra. Moreover, he recognized the difficulty of chasing the British as well as the need to temporize and secure the country.[46] The English newspapers were saying that we had well-fortified bridges on the Zezere and Tagus. When there had been no news of us, bulletins and articles in the newspapers had been complimentary and were based on the same sources. In celebration of the battle of Bussaco, cannon had been fired from one end of French-dominated Europe to the other. A short note in this letter [from Foy] said that the 9th Corps must become part of the Army of Portugal if the English held; that the 5th Corps was marching toward us on the

46. Foy's letter to Masséna announced, "The Emperor declared to me, 'It is necessary that the Prince organize his food, that he entrench himself, that he construct bridgeheads, that his communication with Spain be established with strong posts at a distance of two or three marches apart, and that he continue to hold the country. I will send the 9th Corps to Coimbra and the 5th Corps to Alentejo.' My mission to Paris has produced excellent results. The Emperor appears to be content; yet his anxieties about the fate of the army are great." See Foy to Masséna, December 4, 1810, Correspondance: Armée de Portugal, Carton $C^7$10. For additional details on Foy's trip, See Horward, "Invasion of Portugal," pp. 487–92.

left banks of the Tagus; that the Army of the Interior had orders to send detachments toward the frontier of Estremadura to communicate with us; and finally that once Tortosa was captured, General Suchet would move closer to us.

A letter dated December 4 had arrived from the Major General and it seemed very wise to me because it was based on my system: bridges on the Tagus and entrenchments like those of Spitz in front of Vienna;[47] confine the English army; entrench our positions; occupy the country with fortified posts; communicate with Spain by Cardigos, the Estrada Nova, and Belmonte; guard Alcántara, prepare to attack the enemy on the arrival of reinforcements; and maneuver on his left flank or cross the Tagus. There was an announcement that the 5th Corps again had orders to move between Montalvão and Vila Flor, and that the Army of the Interior had detachments at Coria and Plasencia. (I have extracted an exact summary of this dispatch, which was quite important and must be kept in mind.) The Prince told me that he was content, or at least that he must pretend to be, and that he could only talk candidly with his best friends. What could I say or do in the midst of so much endearment and confidence? I would remain near the Prince as long as he wanted me under any title whatever, but never as an aide-de-camp with someone above me. He was still looking for an officer to go to Paris. I offered myself again; he did not want this. Everyone wanted the assignment, and they spoke of it on all sides. I would have liked to go to present my ideas and system for Portugal. The Prince told me that after we had crossed the Tagus he would send me there to confer with the Emperor on the state of the kingdom and on the resources needed to reduce it.

General Gardanne also returned [with Drouet's forces]. We learned that he had approached us from Abrantes at the time indicated by the deserters. He was near Cardigos with three to four thousand men. On the basis of a peasant's report that our bridges had been destroyed and the army defeated by the enemy, he had withdrawn in haste, losing

47. The accuracy of Pelet's account is attested by the following extract from Berthier's letter to Masséna on December 4, 1810: "The Emperor requests you to establish two bridges on the Zezere, to defend these bridges by formidable works like those of Spitz before Vienna. Your lines of operations and communications are to be established by the route of Guarda, leaving the Zezere, passing through Cardigos, following the crest of the mountains by Campinha and Belmonte." See *Wellington's Dispatches* (1852 ed.), IV, 820–21.

half of his men as a result of forced marches, although at the time we had a great part of Loison's division between Punhete and Abrantes.

General Drouet caused some difficulties when he received orders from His Excellency, [acting] as though they did not pertain to his army. The Prince finally ordered him, on his own responsibility, to go to Leiria with the cavalry and push frequent reconnaissances on Rio Maior. By chance I have found in my papers a letter from General Drouet in which he said that, according to the orders he had shown the Prince, he had entered Portugal only to obtain news of the army; he was never to pass eight days without communicating with Spain and more particularly was never to be isolated from Almeida; and he had under his command the troops stationed in the Sixth Government as well as the Province of Salamanca, the division of Séras, and the fortresses of Almeida and Rodrigo.[48] The order placing the 9th Corps at the disposition of the Prince never reached us. He had marched by the difficult and wretched roads of Espinhal to Pombal through Ancião and Preira. The Prince wrote confidentially to the Marshal to let him know about the imminent crossing of the Tagus and of his intention to leave him on the right bank with the 6th Corps to communicate with General Drouet and to receive the food he would be sending from the left bank.[49] Although this could not have pleased the Marshal, he responded nevertheless that he would willingly do all he could for this

48. Drouet complained to Ney on December 30 of his predicament: "I hope to return promptly to reestablish communications though Castelo Branco, but the Prince has convinced me that this movement would be harmful to his enterprise on the left bank of the Tagus. I have consented to remain at Leiria to divert the enemy who believe my corps has 15,000 men. As soon as this operation is terminated, I will take the position assigned to me in my instructions." See Bonnal, *Ney*, III, 435–36.

49. Masséna lamented to Ney on December 30, "Without doubt, you have learned that the number of troops that General Drouet has led is well below the number we have announced, and there is no chance of the arrival of a second column. . . . We will reach the end of our resources in January . . . [and after this period] it will be necessary for us to go into Alentejo. Thus, I have made all the preparations for crossing the Tagus. . . . The 2nd and 8th Corps will cross the Tagus and you will remain on the right bank. General Drouet, with Claparède's division, which he left at Celorico, will establish communications with you. . . . I have ordered General Drouet to move to Leiria where he will still be able to find food. The cavalry under General Trelliard will remain with him and push strong reconnaissances daily on the Rio Maior. These reconnaissances will make the enemy apprehensive that we soon intend to march on Lisbon. I think he will not fail to recall his troops on the left bank of the Tagus in order to reoccupy his entrenchments." See Correspondance: Armée de Portugal, Carton $C^{7}10$.

end. The English had pushed a reconnaissance on Ponte de Calhariz between the 2nd and 8th Corps and had taken two prisoners.

Thus our ardently desired reinforcements were limited for the time being to a single division of conscripts formed entirely from fourth battalions of which only the cadre had been in battle. These provisional units—good enough to march, to occupy a peaceful country, and to engage in a few disjointed operations—were recognized as inappropriate for the broad movements of an army. Moreover, the division still kept the title of "Army of Spain." If we calculated the losses experienced during the two sieges, in the battle of Bussaco, at the hospital of Coimbra, on our long and difficult marches, and from the continual foraging of our soldiers, it could be seen that these temporary reinforcements did not equal the losses the army had suffered since its formation, even in assuming the replacements to be rather mediocre.

Chapter Nine

PREPARATIONS TO CROSS THE TAGUS

When the army first neared the Tagus, everyone ardently thought about plans for crossing that wide river. Among the most difficult and complicated of all the operations an army can execute are those for the occupation of the enemy bank, for the construction of a bridge, or for the passage of either infantry columns or artillery. Yet such operations are usually successful, and the occasional failure is the result of extraordinary accidents. Among the ancients we see the establishment of bridges not only on the widest rivers, but also on various sea passages. They have left us a tradition of several ingenious procedures that were probably used on only the weakest rivers. Besides the rafts that have been common in all ages, modern men have used only pontoons made of wood or copper. Recently we have limited ourselves to the use of ordinary boats in order to relieve the army of the apparatus of permanent bridge equipment and to make the passages safer. In wars of other centuries, we find memorable examples of bridges on the Rhine, the Danube, and the Po, executed with great success. During our campaigns, the Armies of Germany executed famous crossings and all the rivers were successively overcome by our maneuvers. However, I believe that among all the operations of this type, the works on the Island of Lobau will be remembered in modern military history for a long time.[1] There all the difficulties seem to have piled up in order to

1. Pelet served as Masséna's aide-de-camp in the Austrian campaign of 1809 and in 1824–26 published a four-volume work entitled *Mémoires sur la guerre de 1809, en Allemagne.* It remains one of the most authoritative works on this campaign.

be overcome all at once and to prove by the extent of the enterprise, the diversity of the works, the celerity of the execution, and finally by the successful culmination that there is nothing of this kind that armies can not execute.

With the arrival of Casabianca [on December 26] we approached the time when the crossing was to take place. But in this campaign we seemed to be condemned to hope and wait without ever seeing the realization of our calculations and hopes. The army had received a definite announcement from the Major General of actual reinforcements and of the cooperation of part of the corps in Spain, along with orders to prepare to attack or cross the Tagus while waiting for them. In such a state of affairs, was it possible to hazard an operation as difficult as crossing a river like the Tagus opposite an enemy army that was superior in strength with every advantage, established in the front and on both flanks of our operation, when only the arrival of the 5th Corps would make the passage easy and assured? This was the only operation that could still be executed. We could not consider attacking the English Line with this new directive. The crossing, then, was the only question to decide at the moment. The rules of prudence were for a negative decision, but the prudence of a warrior must be strong and enlightened. Too often weakness, incapacity, or pusillanimity adorn this noble appellation. It is the first determination that military men make when they begin to reason, because it is the safest for the time being, the easiest, and the one with the least responsibility. In warfare prudence almost always lies in boldness. It is in war that such decisions often appear bold at first glance, but when examined carefully and very closely are the easiest and the safest.

It is enough to say that I was not of the opinion of the prudent men. After involving myself in plans for the Tagus crossing, I believed I saw the operation as easy, limited in casualties, and quite advantageous for the army and for our concerns in Spain. Little was needed to convince me; I only asked to share the first dangers and, if necessary, all the risks that would follow. I had just seen the miracle on the Island of Lobau. I had taken an adequate part in the operation, and after it everything else had to appear easy. Indeed, we could well wait a few more days for the arrival of the 5th Corps. Yet, when nearly all the bridge equipment was ready, I was afraid that as a result of more delays and privation the morale of the whole army would be weakened; the force of inertia, spreading secretly, would undermine and carry everything away; and the fatigue of the body and spirit would finally force us to look to our rear. Then all the opposition, diverse interests, and impatience, so natural among the French, would solidify to carry away our final resolution. I was also apprehensive about what usually happened after each of us had been consulted; the worst and easiest decision would be made. Some feelings of pride for our army also entered into my reasoning. I did not want to give the impression that the 5th Corps was coming to raise the blockade and give us a hand in crossing this wide river.

The Prince then had to make the decision that was the best in his position, but his personal character forced him to oppose most vigorously the choice that prudence dictated, believing that he could add some daring. A rather singular thing was that by extraordinary judgment, not the application of definite rules, the Prince guessed the conduct of Marshal Soult from the very beginning and told me, "The 5th Corps will not come, or Soult will accompany it and use it for some personal operation." This was only too true.[2] Meanwhile, he objected to the very precise orders from the Prince de Neufchâtel and at least counted on the other announced reinforcements. Simultaneously, he doubled his regular work. I was at his quarters from daybreak until lunch, and almost every day he had me come for two to four or fiive hours [in the afternoon]. I saw him very rarely in the evening and only for extraordinary affairs. There was not much going on. The daily correspondence with the army corps had no other subject than that of food. The Prince conducted this paperwork with his secretary Vacherat,

2. As early as September 29, Napoleon instructed Soult "to march directly with the 5th Corps on La Romana, so as to hold him in check if he should attempt to cross the Tagus or to attack the rear of the army of Portugal." In mid-November Napoleon learned that Soult had fallen back on Seville "instead of following La Romana and thus threatening the left bank of the Tagus opposite Lisbon." Soult responded on December 31, "If I march 10,000 men to the Tagus as His Majesty has ordered . . . that unit would never reach its destination and it would be surrounded immediately so that I could not go to aid it." On February 6 Napoleon told Berthier to order Soult "to assist the Prince d'Essling in crossing the Tagus; tell him that I hope that Badajoz [under siege since January 28] was taken in the course of the month of January and that he joined the Prince d'Essling on the Tagus around the 20th of January; that if necessary he may withdraw troops from the 4th Corps; that, in short, everything turns upon the Tagus." See *Correspondance de Napoléon Ier*, Nos. 16967, 17131, 17335, Napoleon to Berthier, September 29, November 14, 1810, February 6, 1811, XXI, 186–87, 320–21, 455; Belmas, *Journaux des sièges*, Soult to Berthier, January 22, 1811, I, 470–73.

a commissioner of war. We busied ourselves almost exclusively with the crossing or with the position of our troops and the movements of the enemy. These various topics and the works at Punhete were the subject of dispositions and daily discussions up to the last moment. Besides, we worked much more than I would have desired. It was claimed there were rumors of highly placed and widespread intrigues to remove me from my administrative work. I was very quiet; I worked because of duty and devotion and not ambition. The Prince had known me for six years. I had gained his confidence through my antipathy for all intrigues, doing nothing to curry his confidence and everything to merit it. I had always been known by the motto, "Do well come what may."

The Prince often went to Punhete and I usually accompanied him. This time he wanted to go through Atalaia, and from there we climbed the crest of the height to join the road to Barquinha. This gave me an occasion to visit the position there, which was actually very beautiful. Behind Atalaia on the right was the hill which had a well-isolated, detached, and dominant telegraph on top. From the hill the Tagus was four thousand yards away; there were five or six abutments stacked up, one on top of the other, and on the valleys that separated them. It was a beautiful position to occupy with thirty artillery guns and thirty infantry battalions; that is, two strong divisions with a few fortified defense posts, some abatis, and a good disposition of artillery. The top of this position was quite accessible from the right to the left. Moreover, it overlooked the roads to Atalaia, Moita, and Tancos. In the evening, I examined the left beyond the telegraph designated "S." It appeared that these two telegraphs were established in the directions of Abrantes and Tomar. From the crest we followed a wretched road on the right which took us down to a mill and joined the main road. We found the eightieth boat in the dockyard, built to replace the sixty-third which had been lost when it was carried by the current to the left bank of the Tagus. In addition, there were a few more boats that had been repaired, one barge, two flying bridges, eleven skiffs, and an immense quantity of rigging, planks, chains, etc.[3]

After visiting the yards with the Prince, we went toward the cross-

3. On December 25 General Éblé reported that the eightieth boat was being completed, nine others were in the stocks, and work had begun on a ferry and flying bridge. See Girod de l'Ain, *Grand Artilleurs,* Eblé to Masséna, December 25, 1810, p. 451.

ing point. General Éblé called to me, and the three of us went to examine and reconnoiter the apex of the bend above Punhete again. I sketched the position and the contour of the height. The engineers received orders to take some fortifications for three or four thousand men on the right bank of the Zezere. This was a return to my plans for the confluence, but there were no further explanations. The Tagus and the Zezere were considerably lower, and we saw much of their banks exposed. After the departure of the Prince, I spoke to General Éblé about the possibility of a siege of Badajoz and Elvas. This project seemed very difficult to him. We were no longer collecting the matériel that I had expected. We would need equipment from Almeida and not a single horse was there; therefore we would need several thousand horses and enough time to gather all of them. In addition, there was not a single pickax or shovel. It appeared difficult to start before summer, whatever our speed. We could not rely on the siege equipment attached to the Army of the South and in use before Cadiz. I had also spoken to Colonel Camus. He thought that we should erect the bridge during the day and protect it with three thousand men; that it could be started on both banks; and that two disembarkments would be necessary. Marine Major Reynaud* said that we should embark on the Zezere immediately and go across to the left bank.

The Prince wanted a new plan for the crossing. The basic idea he gave me was that it would be effected by two divisions. Generals Loison and Solignac, still at headquarters, had been assigned this operation by the Prince. I set up two specific dispositions. In the first the 6th Corps would support the passage of these two divisions and take a position on the left bank of the Zezere to mask Abrantes. On the previous day, the three brigades of the 9th Corps would make a reconnaissance on Alcobaça and Rio Maior and move to occupy the bridges at Tomar, Matrena,* and Martinchel. That morning the first brigades of the 2nd and 8th Corps would leave before dawn to go to Atalaia and then Punhete. In the evening the second brigades would move to take a position on the heights of Atalaia, covered by artillery to halt the enemy if he wished to follow their movement. The *parc* equipment, etc., would cross the Zezere by the bridge at Martinchel; the bridge would then be withdrawn on the day of the crossing. Thus the troops would leave their positions and arrive at the bridge in succession so that the crossing of the columns could continue without interruption. The works would be prepared on the Zezere and by the bridge of the Tagus to cover the troops who had crossed or were withdrawing. My second disposition was quite inferior to the first. The various army corps were to leave their positions on the evening of the previous day. The 6th Corps would take a position on the heights of Atalaia and the 9th Corps on the right at Matrena. If the troops did not arrive at Punhete soon enough, and their crossing of the bridge was interrupted, the army would be separated; and the enemy, already warned by the departure of the equipment and able to operate on both areas, could make the passage impossible or give battle to the 6th Corps, which would have two rivers at its back. If the 6th Corps took a position on the Zezere immediately to cover the crossing, the enemy would then be too close to it.

I read this report with all the details of the marches and preparations to the Prince. He approved the plan but wanted the 9th Corps to invest Abrantes, although it seemed to me sufficient to mask it. General Reynier, who had gone to Punhete, proposed to advance against the English by the Rio Maior and obstruct their left in order to cover the passage. This would increase the already considerable distance between our outlying troops, since they were more than two marches apart. Moreover, the difficulty of separating the army into two parts became much more dangerous with a river and only a fragile bridge between them. Our goal was to cross. It was necessary to concentrate on forcing the enemy to extend themselves. General Éblé believed that the preparations could be made in a few hours and the bridge thrown up during the day. The Prince asked him for one extra barge and written dispositions regarding the artillery during the passage and the establishment of the bridge. All this was discussed at length with the Prince; he settled on the first part of my project, only delaying the time of execution because he was still waiting until some fresh communication came from France and the other army, and until we could find new sources of food. Nevertheless it appeared the operation could be executed relatively soon. Furthermore, if the enemy should march on us too vigorously during the crossing, or if their detachment on the other side of the Tagus was too large, the Prince appeared determined to throw all his bridges over the Zezere in order to have four bridges behind him in case of retreat, and then to march vigorously against the

English army. Finally, if the passage could not be made, the army was to move between the Douro and the Mondego.

Nevertheless, everything seemed to indicate that the operation would succeed, and according to the planned dispositions there would not be any serious fighting on the left bank because the enemy was tied to the right bank through Lisbon. The Marshal had extended the 6th Corps in order to gather food. Marchand's division arrived at Pombal, where it found a rather large quantity of grain. General Drouet reinforced his cantonments at Alcobaça and moved Gerard's[4] brigade there because a corps of seven to eight thousand English or Portuguese, coming to reinforce their left, had arrived at Obidos. One of his other brigades was at Leiria with the 8th Corps. General Clauzel occupied Alcanede, and Taupin was at Azoia de Cima and Tremês, supported on the right by the 2nd Corps.

There had been some complaints against the administrative personnel of the army. Their correspondence seemed designed to establish a series of complaints against the commanders while protecting themselves. The administration revealed its existence only through its letters and complaints. The quartermaster general had not given a report since the beginning of the campaign,[5] although he was obliged to make one every fifteen days. He drew up a summary every fifteen days from which I extracted the most important items. It was divided into seven paragraphs: general subsistence, military and auxiliary equipment, hospitals and ambulances, clothing and camp equipment, treasury, postal system, and administrative personnel. Each one of these paragraphs presented what had been done or what should have been done. From September 15 to 30, nineteen food wagons had been destroyed or abandoned in the mountains of Beira and no magazines or depots had been found at Viseu or en route. On October 15, 356 horses were given to the artillery and the wagons were burned. After that, the wagon train had lost 634 horses, and 121 wagons were destroyed

4. Count Maurice Étienne Gerard (1773–1852) enlisted as a volunteer in 1791; he became a general of division in 1812. Following the Revolution of 1830, Gerard was appointed minister of war and a marshal of France. He fought at Jemappes, Neerwinden, and Fleurus and from 1794 to 1808 served with Bernadotte in various capacities. Attached to Drouet's 9th Corps in 1810, he fought at Fuentes de Oñoro.

5. For Lambert's reports to Berthier, see Jones, *Journals of Sieges,* Lambert to Berthier, September 23, October 20, 1810, III, 185–90.

by us. No public funds were found in the occupied country, and the army chest was in such destitution it was necessary to borrow from private individuals for the inevitable expenses. There was absolutely no clothing in reserve. After October 30 the administration worked only for the hospitals and the general headquarters. On November 15 we proposed regimental hospitals for our sick. Only a dozen of those who entered the hospitals died, but we were no longer able to care for the sick there. On November 30 the remaining food caissons were divided among the army corps, who fed themselves. The resources of the ambulances were reduced because there was absolutely no way of finding replacements. On December 15 corn was harvested on the plain of Golegã and the wet corn was dried out by the sun [?]. The death rate was low in the army because of the drop in temperature and the healthy air. On December 31 the reserve supply of biscuits ordered by the Prince was maintained intact. The army corps found grain every day. Although at first we thought eating corn was dangerous, it had only a slight effect; it caused some diarrhea and fever, but we would have no complications as long as wine and quinine remained. The regiments were starting to care for their sick. There was enough linen left to make five thousand dressings at one time. Shoes and clothing of the troops suffered. It was very urgent that replacements be expedited by the minister of war and the Depot of War.

It has been noted that the administrative wagons had been sacrificed to save those of the more important artillery. This measure, which should always be taken, was especially expedient in a country where the administration could do so little for the sustenance of the corps; and where the heavy wagons followed the army on the principal roads with great difficulty and could only benefit the marauders in the difficult country through which they passed. Thus the artillery kept a great part of its resources. General Éblé had made a new distribution of guns, wagons, and teams among the army corps and the *grand parc.* He still had some twelve thousand cannon shot and twelve million cartridges,[6] that is to say, enough for two major battles. There was

6. On January 4 Éblé proposed that 92 wagons be destroyed, leaving 441 to be drawn by 2,566 animals. These vehicles were designated to carry 2,609,420 cartridges and 12,919 artillery shells. See "Tableau présentant l'organization du matériel de l'artillerie," Éblé to Masséna, January 4; Masséna to Junot, Reynier, Ney, January 5; Masséna to Éblé, January 10, 1811, Correspondance: Armée de Portugal, Carton C711.

probably some additional ammunition in the army corps, which could not always give a very exact record since no one complied very well with the instructions of the commander in chief of artillery.

We experienced all kinds of difficulties with General Lazowski, commander of the engineers. He was then ill and worried, but fortunately he had just chosen a new chief of staff, Colonel Valazé, who minimized many of the difficulties by his ability and good nature. The fortification projects on the right bank had just been completed but were too wide, having a deployment of three thousand yards and forming three or four defensive positions and a dozen intermediate posts linked by abatis, often double. This was more like a position for a retreating army than a stable bridgehead which was to be moved closer to the mouth of the Zezere as soon as we had occupied the opposite bank of the Tagus. Colonel Valazé went to rectify all this in the field, motivated by a spirit of compromise and the need to reconcile himself with the artillerymen, who in this situation were the major group in determining the crossing point. I proposed two new plans to him. The first, while retaining the actual bridge on the Zezere, called for moving the entire bridgehead from the right bank to the opposite heights; its left would be supported by a vast gravel surface which was occupied by a work, enclosed and isolated, on the plateau where the chapel of the Concepcão was situated. My second plan, much better and adopted in the actual hypothesis (by the principal army corps before occupying Alentejo), was to establish communications on the Tagus with two bridges above and below the confluence of the Zezere. The regular passage of the Zezere was to be made by means of a barge placed in a site hidden from enemy fire and from the hills bordering its banks. Then the two bridgeheads on our side of the Tagus would be restricted to the two plateaus of the church of Punhete and the chapel of the Concepcão. Both positions were excellent and well circumscribed by large ravines. This plan would be applicable to my system for a triple bridgehead. The one on the left bank of the Tagus would need less development than a first inspection seemed to indicate if we occupied a very strong central point on the crest and descended the Tagus along the two appendages of this common summit. Since the plateau of the church of Punhete was the principal fortification on the right bank of the Tagus and was much more advanced than that of the Concepcão, its cannon could always ensure the establishment of the bridge on the Zezere. This scheme included every advantage; nevertheless, it was necessary to examine the essential part of the terrain on the right bank and consult the artillerymen before proposing it to the commanders. Thus nothing could be decided.

Meanwhile the enemy continued their works opposite Punhete. They opened batteries that were directed against the mouth of the Zezere, and they bordered the opposite bank with entrenchments. We concerned ourselves too much about these works; we already had talked about the impossibility of crossing under their fire. The Prince thought about carrying boats to the other side of the tip of Punhete, pulling them either by hand or on wagons. He sent me there to plan the various ways with General Éblé and to examine the enemy's works. I was to make the trip with Valazé in order to reconnoiter the ground together, but he was unable to go. On my arrival, I visited it alone. The plateau of the Concepcão was excellent, quite isolated, dominant, and made expressly to be fortified in a favorable way. Our works were to be placed either at the end of the plateau, flanked by the rivers, or on the crest of the ravine slopes. As a result they would not be very long. We repaired the old trenches, but they were directed only against the waters of the Tagus and the Zezere and could not be of much help either for defense or for the occupation of the plateau. Then I went over the whole development of the projected work toward the right. North of the road was an immense pile of rocks in the ravines, where one could neither recognize the work of men nor guess that of nature. Beyond was a wide ravine which ended at the bridge opposite Punhete and its left bank. Rocky hills where the bridgehead was to be established dominated the surroundings and overlooked the entire expanse of the Zezere. I recognized the need to dominate all this terrain if we wanted to cover the actual bridges on the Zezere. From there I examined the left bank of the Tagus and the only troops I saw were a camp of five to six hundred men partly hidden, it was true, by olive trees. I did not alter my system for the two bridges on the Tagus and the occupation of the plateaus of the two churches.

I found General Éblé in the dockyards. The boats were finished and they were now working on a large barge for Martinchel and two smaller ones, in addition to a large flying bridge and a smaller one.

The small beams were prepared. I went to look at the confluence again; a battery with two embrasures was aimed aslant at it. The enemy also worked opposite us behind a house and to its right, but we still could not perceive the object of their work. They were establishing a trench along the Tagus across from the mouth [of the Zezere]. I examined the rear of the Zezere, which was not difficult. General Éblé approved the plan of transporting the boats, not by hand but by wagons. He would try it and make his report. It was necessary to hide our movements and at least the site of the transported boats from the enemy; the general expected to succeed with teams of twelve horses. He would make drays from limbers, wheels from peasants' [wagons] as well as from the equipment wagons if he could not get anything better. The general very much wanted me to go to Paris and believed it was quite necessary. Now he came back to my system for the confluence [of the Zezere] and the idea of a triple bridgehead. I proposed to him my project for two bridges on the Tagus and barges on the Zezere. The general vigorously approved them if a ramp was feasible. We laughed and joked together, although he was not much for laughing. Returning, I climbed up on the plateau to determine the number of night fires and noticed only one. In general, the number of enemy troops at this point had been greatly exaggerated; I thought it was much smaller than was said. I also examined the enemy's works above General Ferey's terrace. Again I noticed the trench, a work masked behind a house, some ground that had been piled up, and, beyond, a circular breastwork on a hill. None of them was attached or seemed very formidable. General Ferey wrote in the evening that this excavation was actually one battery with four embrasures. The troops of the third division were young and lacked confidence. General Ferey believed they were rather weak.

In general, everyone talked about the difficulties and exaggerated them. The marines and the artillery were confident—this was important. We continued to fortify the large church. I met the major of the marines; according to him there was little agreement among the artillery. If we came out on the Zezere, he believed that we would be carried far away unless the Tagus was lower and that one hour would be required to reascend and reembark. He hoped very much that the passage would be executed above the confluence [of the Zezere] so that we could drift diagonally and gain considerable time. He found our boats heavy. He wanted less wood; he showed me a trial boat twenty to twenty-two feet in length and six or seven feet in width, with raised sides. The ribs were much closer together; more time would be needed to build such a boat, but it was much easier to maneuver, safer, and lighter. The boats of the Tagus were good for cutting water, even straight ahead. The rafts would also be very good, with plank beams on their frames. My account here may not be very exact, especially since the major had a few complaints about the general in regard to some details of the planning and duties. However, Reynaud was full of confidence. All the boats, except those for the bridge at Punhete, were divided into eight sections, of which one was the advance guard and another the rear guard. The first one was composed of light boats commanded by Captain Parmentier and the officers who once took part in my expeditions to the Island of Lobau. I would embark with them if this were possible. I would jump to the ground first and determine what was happening on the other bank. I would retire after we had established ourselves in order to watch the great battles that would take place on the right bank. It was said that General Hill had come from Almeirim to Chamusca. He was on the left bank with his division, but it would not be he who would stop us from crossing.

By chance I met General Pamplona. Our conversation naturally turned to the state of affairs, and he spoke to me about moving the army near the Mondego and about establishing a government at Oporto to rival the one at Lisbon. Since many people, even General Éblé, were thinking about the ideas that he shared with me, I felt it my duty to tell the Prince what he had said. His Excellency thought there was a connection between the ideas of those who had always supported [a withdrawal to] the Mondego and who now exaggerated the difficulties of the crossing and of living in Alentejo. We examined the latter very carefully from all points of view. It was quite clear that the fate of Portugal was at Lisbon. That city was the center of the English defense. Therefore it was only there that we could conquer the kingdom. Anything that deviated, delayed the operation by that much. We would always have to return and either attack the Line or invest the capital and then establish ourselves on the Tagus. Yet His Excellency said it would be very unfortunate if we could not live in Alentejo, but we must make the attempt. How would we communicate with Spain? It would always be safer through the Estremadura than anywhere else. In short, the enemy must have been frightened to see Lisbon blockaded by land. Above all, they wished to see the French army far away, wherever it went. Consequently, we had to maneuver contrary to the enemy's interest and not according to their fears and desires.

Our army was forced to extend itself far and wide for food, but the English spread themselves without necessity and seemed to want to close all the gaps through which we might reach them. This weakened them considerably and would have given us great advantages if we had been able to maneuver offensively. Without doubt Lord Wellington, seeing extensive preparations against the fortresses in Alentejo, thought that our system of war had changed, that we intended to cover the sieges only temporarily, and that we had received orders and instructions accordingly, whereas the orders we received were entirely to the contrary. Perhaps this was one more reason for trying to save the fortresses and the capital simultaneously by a central maneuver. Thus the English army could be considered as having the sea on their left with a major unit at Obidos, their center in front of Santarém, and their right isolated and separated by a large river from Almeirim to Abrantes. The latter appeared to be reinforced daily.

We saw English infantry battalions and Portuguese cavalry going up the river in broad daylight toward Almeirim and Chamusca. We believed that there were fourteen English battalions, five Portuguese infantry regiments, the Portuguese cavalry, and the Spanish brigade of Don Carlos de España.[7] The Spanish posted opposite Punhete talked about the Portuguese with Castilian bravado. It was further affirmed that the English did not have a bridge on the Tagus and communicated from one bank to the other by boat near Azambuja, where Picton's division was posted. The enemy had shown some apprehension about the trestles erected on the banks of the Rio Maior near the Ponte de Asseca. They asked when we would attack and when we would cross the Tagus; they said we would find only rabble at Lisbon. Lord Wellington had some troops approach and

7. Don Carlos José Enrique de España (1775–1839) was of French origin but fled to England during the Revolution. He joined the Spanish army in 1792 and served against the French until the Treaty of Basel. He rejected French overtures to rejoin his countrymen and commanded Spanish troops against Napoleon's armies.

reconnoiter our lines. At the same time the enemy was working steadily in front of Santarém. They augmented their entrenchment at Sobral and lined the banks of the Tagus with a thick cordon of armed peasants. We could see a great number of huts along the Tagus. Craufurd was still at Valle, with one cavalry brigade on his right near Porto de Mugem and one on his left at Ponte de Calhariz. Spencer's division was at Cartaxo and Picton's was at Alcoentre. A deserter brought us a strange soldier's rumor that Lord Wellington had gone incognito to London and had been there for twenty days. His departure had been carefully hidden. Our spies reported that the enemy was finally fortifying a line from Setúbal to Aldeia Galega through Palmela and also the approaches to Almada and Torre Vilha, as I had predicted a long time ago, and that ten thousand people were employed there.[8] As a result of the arrival of a great quantity of grain from Morocco, the famine had ended at Lisbon but not the discontent; in addition the spies indicated that Beresford's headquarters were at Portalegre, that General Séras occupied Chaves, that new French troops were leaving Almeida, and finally they were repeating the ridiculous rumor that Austria was to furnish an army commanded by Archduke Charles to take Portugal for himself.

Letters from a captured messenger were sent to headquarters. We found only private letters from January 1 to 8. I extracted the following summary for my Journal: Lord Wellington was at Cartaxo, with the English headquarters on the other side of the Tagus. Beresford had gone in front of Marshal Mortier; the marshal's letters announced his arrival. The enemy were still expecting a great battle in front of Lisbon and despaired of success. There were few troops in the Lines, and some Portuguese forces at Alhandra were complaining considerably about the Spaniards; the latter had all crossed to the left bank. Alentejo was being evacuated. Grain had arrived at Lisbon, where there were no soldiers and order was being maintained by only the police legion. Work had been going on for some time on the lines at

8. Wellington anticipated Masséna's intention to cross into Alentejo soon after the French army withdrew to Santarém. On December 5 he traveled to Almada with Lieutenant Colonel Fletcher; they agreed to fortify the area opposite Lisbon to ensure Allied control of the harbor. These fortifications, which extended 8,000 yards, rested on the basin of the Tagus above Mutela. Seventeen redoubts flanked by flèches were erected and linked by a sunken road; they were manned with 7,500 men and 86 guns. Wellington was convinced that Masséna would need siege pieces to breach this position. See Jones, *Journal of Sieges,* III, 37–39.

Setúbal, which were guarded by sailors and marines. Everywhere they were calling us the evil ones, and the Prince was the great devil of victory.[9] It was said that he was on bad terms with his Corsican Emperor. The arrival of General Drouet was known; reinforcements for us were being announced everywhere. There was talk about the army which the Emperor of Austria was sending to Spain, of the difficulties that the English ministry had raised for the regency of the Prince of Wales, of the conditions imposed on him, and of the protests of the royal family.

The movements of the enemy, and especially those on the other side of the Tagus, concerned the Prince very much. For us they were the subject of various conjectures and serious reflections. Would the English post their troops at a central position along the middle bend of the Tagus between Abrantes and Almada, across from the Zezere, and by means of signals move them rapidly in groups on the point where our boats would be directed? Would this not in effect be an excellent way to oppose the crossing? Would these troops confront the 5th Corps as, according to all our information, it advanced, in order to halt or destroy our reinforcements and prevent them from crossing to guarantee our unequivocal superiority (after the march of Beresford and La Carrera, it appeared these English movements were directed toward Badajoz); or would they ultimately take an intermediate position near Ponte de Sor to oppose, simultaneously, both the arrival of Marshal Mortier and the passage of the Tagus? In that case, I was afraid that Marshal Soult would halt when he encountered the front of this corps and later allege that he had a considerable part of the allied army confronting him which we should have contained so that he would have the freedom to advance. As for the supposition of some people that the enemy wanted to attempt a coup de main against the boats at Punhete, I could not bring myself to believe it. The vagueness of our conjectures was increased by the lack of accurate reports, the contradictions between them and our fixed ideas, and the total lack of well-organized espionage.

In discussing all the aspects of these enemy projects, the Prince

9. An eight-page play published in Lisbon in 1811 portrayed Masséna as being tried for multiple crimes against the Portuguese people. Entitled "Processo verbal do desgraçado Masséna, ex-anjo da vitoria: convencido de muitos crimes de lesa magestade," the document can be found in the Biblioteca Nacional at Lisbon.

ordered me to state my views definitely. Then I returned to [my scheme for] a rapid crossing of the Tagus. I had strongly insisted on this plan and opposed any contrary opinion, regardless of who gave it, for the sake of the army, for its system of war, and for the glory of the Prince, who, after concerning himself with this long drawn-out operation, would have to resist anyone who blamed him under any pretext. Nevertheless, since the Prince now reserved for himself the command of the crossing troops, it was of highest importance that the operation succeed completely. I further pointed out to him that the troops he expected to employ were weak, even the worst in the army, and that he should have chosen the elite. I emphasized this point vigorously, and the Prince felt all the weight of my reasoning. Finally, I added that if the enemy had really set up such a large detachment in front of us, we could not remain quiet spectators but must take advantage in some way, either in attacking their position on the Rio Maior or in crossing the Tagus and, at the same time, putting their troops on the left bank between the 5th Corps and ourselves. But it was of the greatest importance to be perfectly certain of their position and what was happening in the vicinity of the army.

In accordance with this analysis, the Prince first ordered the primary dispositions necessary to reinforce the vulnerable points of the line. Taupin's brigade was sent toward the right of the 2nd Corps. This corps, as well as the 8th and the 9th Corps, received orders to make some wide reconnaissances along with combined demonstrations opposite the enemy to ascertain exactly what was ahead of them. Loison's division was tightened around Punhete and on the left bank of the Zezere, and Delabassée's brigade was concentrated at Martinchel.[10] On January 20 the Prince prepared to make a general reconnaissance of the line himself. He wrote everywhere to get positive information; later he sent me with his son to the banks of the Tagus to visit the posts and see what the enemy had in front of us.

With the young duke, I followed the partially flooded banks of the Almonda, which approached the heights of the right bank but was

10. Baron Mathieu Delabassée (1764–1830) served in the French marines from 1775 to 1784, when he became a second lieutenant in a chasseur battalion. He marched with the French armies in Germany from 1792 to 1800. Transferred to the Army of Italy, Delabassée fought in the battle of Marengo and was promoted to general of brigade. In 1805 he was given a brigade in the 6th Corps and served under Ney until March 1811.

contained by dams on the left. The plain of Golegã, entirely harvested, was rather dry and accessible to various branches of the army, even the artillery. From Golegã to the Tagus we crossed one-half to three-fourths of a league of cultivated terrain with a few dried-up branches of the river; its alluvium extended eight hundred or a thousand yards. It was very wide opposite Chamusca. The left bank was a little flat, but rose gradually up to the height of Chamusca. Between that village and Pinheiro the slope seemed to be broken. We could see neither camps nor gatherings around Chamusca. The enemy did not even have posts made up of line troops on the bank, but there was a concentration of peasants with huts every two hundred to four hundred yards. We noticed only one crowd near Chamusca, and it gave every appearance of a headquarters.

An officer sent up on the heights to observe the bivouac fires did not see anything else during the night. Returning through Golegã, we found General Loison, who started to exaggerate the problems in Alentejo, including everything—even the bad air. We followed the heights of the left bank of the Almonda and made out a defensive position there, or at least a position where an army could concentrate when the plain of Golegã was half under water. The inhabitants of these unfortunate districts had gone to gather rotten corn and the remnants of pumpkins in the field so they would not die of hunger. Already great numbers had perished from starvation. They were accompanied by our orderlies for safety. We saw long lines of them. It was a very painful spectacle [to see] a foolish nation condemning itself, through the most blind allegiance, to die of hunger by obeying a foreign army which destroyed and wasted everything, although this country had offered its arms, its homes, and its effort in its defense. What an example for people who subordinated themselves to English policies.

The Prince had been preparing dispatches for the Major General and orders for the Spanish frontier for some time. He still hoped to receive some results from these dispatches on the banks of the Tagus, where we would find food once again. Then he decided to send Casabianca to Paris. His instructions contained many details about the state and position of our army and about that of the enemy, about the various projects and operational plans, the bridges, the need for reinforcements, the advantages of cooperating with the 5th Corps, the particular position of the 9th Corps, and the pretensions of its commander. I gave Casabianca all the information I could about the country, as well as particular and secret details on men and affairs. I had prepared my map on a smaller scale and various copies of the plans for him; finally, I gave him everything I could not use myself. The choice had made many people envious, for everyone desired this mission—the safest road to favor and advancement. Some of them came to provoke me, telling me that I was a dupe. I surprised many of the officers by showing them the special work I was doing for Casabianca.[11]

I began to fear that we would be drawn toward the Mondego. Since I viewed our return to Spain as a last consequence, my report to the Major General was based entirely on the crossing of the Tagus and the occupation of both its banks. I believed it suitable to add in a postscript that if the crossing did not succeed, we would have to fall back toward the Mondego. Nevertheless, I detailed all the reasons for repudiating such a move and for opposing those who had proposed or supported it in Paris. Both of my ideas were approved by the Prince, but I made the mistake of openly showing the disadvantages of the decision that we ultimately adopted. This mistake was later repeated, but I am not sure it should be imputed to me on either occasion.

General Gardanne left at the same time. He had orders to collect everything he found at Almeida and Rodrigo which belonged to the

11. Casabianca carried a dispatch to Berthier declaring, "Until now, we have been unsuccessful in determining a method of conquering Portugal. . . . The lack of subsistence and the poor roads are the greatest obstacles that we face in our military operations. I am convinced that we will only reduce this kingdom when we secure both banks of the Tagus by occupying Alentejo. . . . Then we will be able to move to cut off Lisbon from both sides of the Tagus to profit by all the available resources in Alentejo and the vicinity of Golgau [*sic*]. . . . I will cross the Tagus at the end of January." See Masséna to Berthier, January 20, 1811, Correspondance: Armée de Portugal, Carton C^{7}11. In another dispatch to Berthier also carried by Casabianca, Masséna declared, "After the siege of Ciudad Rodrigo I had the honor to indicate to Your Highness those officers of the general *état major* and my *état major* who have taken a very active part in the daily work of the siege. Following that of Almeida I again requested Your Highness to recommend these requests to the kindness of His Majesty. The services that they have rendered since then have only added to the qualifications that recommend them to your interests. I have the honor to beg you for the following favors . . . Lieut. Colonel [*sic*] Pelet, my first aide-de-camp, for the rank of adjutant commander. . . . These compensations are merited by good service, exemplary devotion, and an activity without limit." See Masséna to Berthier, January 20, 1811, Archives de Masséna, LI.

Army of Portugal and to bring it back immediately. However, rather than compromise their escort of three hundred men en route to the fortresses, they were to return toward us.[12] The itinerary directed them through Cardigos to Pinhal. General Delabassée followed them from Martinchel with a battalion of six hundred men, two or three marches later. The 6th Corps furnished biscuits for this detachment and the Prince gave twelve hundred rations from his private reserve since there was nothing in the magazine, and everything had to be done in this way. Two officers from the Prince de Neufchâtel, who had come into Portugal following the 9th Corps, also left. They did not take all the information that they had requested in the way of reports, maps, lists, etc. They asked us the strangest questions. In general these officers of the Major General assumed, whenever possible, more importance than their Prince himself had. The commanders of the army corps wanted to send some officers to Paris, but His Excellency felt he should prevent anyone from leaving the army without his authorization.

The Duc d'Abrantès wanted to execute in person an extensive reconnaissance that had been ordered for the army corps, and he pushed it to the village of Rio Maior.[13] Only four hundred horsemen were found there. The voltigeurs took the barricades of the bridge in one rush. The enemy withdrew on the heights some distance away. Thus the reports that the enemy had partially evacuated its left seemed to be confirmed, since they no longer occupied the stream of Valle and the bridge of Calhariz forward of the Rio Maior. Moreover, there were only a few poorly supported troops in the village of Rio Maior,

12. Although Casabianca, with an escort of 400 men commanded by General Gardanne, was instructed to march on January 22, he had to wait several days at Martinchel until adequate rations could be collected. His column reached Almeida on January 27 and he proceeded on to Paris immediately. Gardanne, however, found a letter waiting for him from Berthier; he was relieved of his duties and ordered to return to Paris to answer charges of incompetency. See Bonnal, *Ney*, III, 440; Koch, *Mémoires de Masséna*, VII, 298–99.

13. Hoping to force the Allies to withdraw some of their troops from the left bank of the Tagus, Masséna ordered Reynier and Junot to carry out a joint maneuver on Wellington's positions beyond the Rio Maior. Without attempting to coordinate the probes, Reynier sent a column toward Porto de Mugem on January 18. Junot's column, including 3,000 infantry and 450 cavalry, advanced the following day from Alcanede toward the village of Rio Maior, where elements of Pack's Portuguese brigade and Craufurd's Light Division were posted. See Roch Godart, *Mémoires du général baron Roch Godart (1792–1815)* (Paris, 1895), pp. 159–60; Jonathan Leach, *Rough Sketches of the Life of an Old Soldier . . .* (London, 1831), p. 187.

which was doubly important because of its position along the river and on the main highway to Leiria. It was true that the village was not capable of defense because the stream flowed on its west; the position to occupy was on the heights beyond. It did not appear that the enemy had been pursued up there. A deserter arrived on January 19, announcing that Picton's division was at Alcoentre. This reserve position, supporting the defense of the Rio Maior, was more suitably established after the arrival of the 9th Corps at Leiria; the latter had taken the reverse of the line of the Rio Maior. Picton's position seemed to be better linked with the corps on the left situated at Obidos. It was also said that this line was extended to the sea by a chain of posts along the Anoja.*

The Duc, moving on the line of *tirailleurs* to reconnoiter the enemy movement, received a gunshot wound in the face, across his nose. The violent wound did not knock him from his horse. He continued giving his orders and immediately sent his aide-de-camp, Dubuisson, to inform the Prince and reassure him about the accident. The news soon reached the enemy. Lord Wellington did not neglect this occasion to show his courtesy toward the commanders of the French army. He wrote a very polite letter to the Duc, offering his personal services for the wound. It was not as serious as we first thought. We went to Pernes two days later. The Duc stayed in bed, and he did not have any suppurative fever. The ball had been extracted; it had flattened itself against the maxillary bone.[14] The Duc must have had a strong constitution to withstand such a blow. He was soon well, but this accident may have had the most distressing effects on the cruel sickness which ended his days.[15]

Provisions were still our most difficult adversary. Everyone was complaining. All the corps were clamoring, but they clamored more than they suffered; the worst off, the 2nd Corps and the workers at Punhete, were helped by the others. We could not agree on the

14. Junot's surgeon, Malraison, extracted the ball through his cheek and the wound, although serious, healed without complications. See Noel, *Souvenirs,* p. 133.

15. During the Russian campaign Junot exhibited symptoms of mental derangement, perhaps as a result of his numerous and serious head wounds. He returned to France in January 1813 and was appointed governor of the Illyrian Provinces. However, his mental illness forced him to return home. On July 22 he threw himself out a window and broke his leg; it was amputated but he tore off the bandage and died on July 28.

reports. While General Reynier complained, his paymaster wrote that the 2nd Corps had enough food. Each day new complaints came in and each protest received new help from those who were enjoying some comfort, as ordered by the Prince. Nevertheless, our regular marauders found large amounts of grain everywhere. Provisions for the entire army appeared assured, at least until the end of February. Adjutant Commander Marie Xavier Joseph Lefebvre, Comte de Dantzick, sent with a column of eight hundred men along the coast near Alcobaça, brought back a rather large quantity of grain; we also discovered some grain near Leiria and Espinhal. Detachments were sent to those areas. They would leave small garrisons there, and the grain would arrive, carried by mules, donkeys, and finally by the men themselves. We were forced to employ regiments of dragoons for these tasks; the horses carried the large bags and the men carried the smaller ones. But the rather heavy rains, and the flooding occasioned by it, hindered the marauding a great deal; it prevented the grinding of the grain, and we lost a considerable amount of corn at Golegã and on some of the other low plains. There was enough livestock, and the various forage parties brought back numerous herds. It was accurate to say the corps suffered less than the general headquarters because they had more resources and men to employ. We would have been unscrupulous to take any of the supplies which cost them so much in trouble and fatigue.

Unfortunately, the raids were the occasion for many horrors. The men, full of wine, committed violent acts against the peasants they met in order to discover their hidden supplies. The peasants avenged themselves whenever they found isolated or drunk soldiers.[16] The abandoned houses were first pillaged. As they left, the soldiers would set them on fire and the flames soon spread, resulting in frequent conflagrations. No one was there to put out the fires when they started, and no one came for assistance or help. These careless soldiers would allow the fire to feed itself; villages and towns would become

16. A French officer of the 31st Léger recalled, "During our retreat we found four bodies hanging from a tree! Entering the first floor of a nearby house we found a hideous sight. High on the wall, the skin of a man, freshly peeled, was nailed and under it was written in Portuguese, 'French dragoon skinned for hanging our brothers.' Without doubt, he had not committed the crime because the hanging bodies were decomposed. Alas, the poor soldier, taken alone, had to pay with his life for [the crimes of] others." See Lemonnier-Delafosse, *Souvenirs*, p. 97.

its prey. Thus the magnificent convent of Alcobaça and an immense factory still full of woven cotton were burned, and the horrors of war increased in this unfortunate country.[17] We often found hidden caches at Santarém or Torres Novas. We finally ordered full-scale investigations of the larger homes to search for grain which we believed was hidden there.

Toward the end of January the food distribution ceased at the main headquarters; it was reserved for the hospitals. It was necessary to send servants with the forage detachments. The administration found itself punished and suffering more than anyone else, especially among its noncommissioned employees. However, the Prince put all the mules and beasts of burden belonging to various individuals at their disposal. They were taken far away to magazines or grain depots and loaded, three-fourths for the administration and one-fourth for the owners. This furnished some resources. We kept a record of these animals in order to relocate them when needed. We were already short of wine in the *état major* of the army corps. The less prudent soon lacked bread and wheat and had to use corn. Thanks to his care and farsightedness at the start, the Prince performed for his household, composed of some thirty officers, what he had ordered the army corps to do. In his quarters he had a provisioned attic and a well-filled cave. From the very beginning, he put at the head of his little magazine a Portuguese who was to render an accounting only to him. The Prince regulated consumption and based it on strict necessity. Later on it was reduced a little, but until the end we had wine and rather good wheat bread in nearly sufficient quantity. He also had enough to give very valuable help to the sick and to the people at headquarters who were suffering the most.

The reconnaissance of the 8th Corps had all the brilliance the Prince wanted to obtain. He limited the expeditions he wanted to make along the line to Santarém. The Prince only went through Pernes to see the Duc d'Abrantès. Arriving at Santarém, we visited the position. The farthest heights in the direction of Rio Maior were occupied by a large square construction that went down to the Asseca road, which was not blocked at the gorge. The slopes of the wide plateau of Santarém,

17. The convent of Alcobaça has been restored, but some of the destruction committed by the French and Allied soldiers is still evident in the interior of the church.

toward the west and the north, were crowned with abatis and flanked by a few flèches placed in salient areas. There were also several rows of abatis on the plain in the direction of the Tagus. This position was very strong, but its right should have been extended opposite the Ponte de Celeiro up to a hill which could have been entrenched. Then it should have been set up along the stream of Romeira so that it could not be immediately outflanked on this side by a march on Azoia de Baixo. The great weakness of this position was that it offered all kinds of opportunities for a corps wanting to outflank it, from either nearby or at a distance, because of the direction of the stream and the abutments on the line of retreat. Thus this position would become better when we had more troops to place there.

The enemy still had the advantage of the terrain because the hills of the Rio Maior presented a nearly continuous ridge up to the valley of Almoster, and everywhere the heights were near the stream that covered them. For this reason the position was doubly strong and nearly perpendicular to their line of retreat. Only the right between the Rio Maior and the Tagus seemed more accessible, but this area was very wet and the bridges on the river could be blown up. The English had set up epaulements at the points nearest to the Ponte de Asseca. It was said that the latter was barricaded and mined like the one at Valle. They showed few troops but the sun, shining in our eyes, did not allow us to examine their dispositions effectively. In a conversation during the day, General Reynier still advocated his old project of advancing and pushing the enemy into his lines in advance of making and facilitating the crossing.

In the evening we went to a play. Everything was improvised because the Prince was not expected and a performance had taken place the day before.[18] Nevertheless, everything went very well. There was some kind of prologue, naturally made up for the occasion, and it was very well done and well delivered. The actors had gathered, but soon the arrival of the Prince was announced and it was necessary to entertain him well—everybody did his best. One day there were songs and comedy, another probably a battle and triumphs; then they sang about victory and its cherished son. In a few words, the play had well-turned

18. According to Lemonnier-Delafosse, a dramatic society was organized at Santarém and each week a new comedy or tragedy was performed in a playhouse constructed for that purpose. See his *Souvenirs*, pp. 111–12.

verses and was full of zest. They were still playing *Le soldat tout seul le réveil du charbonnier, vade à la grenouillère.* The authors, the actors, the orchestra, the stagehands, the decorators, the workers—all were soldiers and none higher than noncommissioned officers, most of them from the light infantry. The most graceful and the youngest were dressed as women. Costumes were not lacking. Marauding had furnished everything, but the women had not been persuaded to sacrifice their blonde moustaches. It was rather well played and not badly sung. Memory furnished the repertoire for the major parts, while natural enthusiasm filled the gaps. The auditorium was in a church; a rather large part of it had been shot up by us. The choir furnished a pretty decoration of foreground scenery; the wings and backdrop had been found in some great castle. They had skillfully supplied everything lacking and each type of scene was generally found in its analogous decoration. Finally, everything was quite good, except the odor. Since the play was especially for the soldiers, they were admitted by tickets distributed to the corps, but they were crowded together. I found myself better off at Santarém than at our headquarters, for here I slept on sheets, and this was never the case at my quarters as long as we remained in Portugal.

The next day the Prince wanted to reconnoiter the banks of the Tagus. We went along the bank up to Boa Vista, where the heights bordering Alviela ended. These heights were quite high and steep above the Tagus. The river flowed at their foot and formed a rather steep and pronounced bend on the right bank. On the other side, the river was blocked by a small and very narrow but easily fordable branch that peasants crossed in less than two minutes while we were there. Here the Tagus was embanked and narrow, and overall this formed a very good crossing point. All this struck me because I had a confused idea for a plan that only developed somewhat later. From Santarém to Boa Vista, and from there to Golegã, the road was good and rather dry. We ate in Golegã, at General Loison's quarters. The general prodded me, demanding my opinion on Alentejo. I responded that I did not allow myself to have an opinion on such important matters. He answered that he knew I had some ideas, that they would not be without influence, and that he desired to know them. Then I gave my private and purely personal opinion on my plan for the occupation of Portugal, on the necessity of occupying both banks of the Tagus with a triple bridgehead and then taking Alentejo, and on the utility of besieging the fortresses. My plan was contrary to his opinion and even his wishes. Nevertheless, he agreed with me on the advantages that would ensue. While speaking about Golegã, the Prince sent me with his son to Punhete to examine a battery of seven guns the enemy had unmasked against the mouth of the Zezere.

Passing through Arripiado, we saw a strong English detachment performing some exercise, and across from the Zezere we saw an open enemy battery with seven embrasures, but their merlons were so thin and high that I have always wondered if it were nothing more than a disguise designed to protect the firing of the Congreve rockets. They also worked behind a large white, partially demolished house, half on the slope, but we could not guess what was going on there. General Éblé was sick. We visited with Valazé and Beaufort. A new point had been chosen for the establishment of the bridge, but I did not know by whom. It was four thousand yards beyond Punhete, below Montalvo. The only advantage was that there was a nearly level section of field on the opposite bank. However, the field ended in a very steep height that contained it completely; thus we would have to overcome this height after crossing. Moreover, our side of the bank was lower, and the opposite bank was raised in such a way as to dominate ours at a certain distance. Besides, the small artillery positions were close to us and those of large caliber much too far away, while at Punhete they were immediately along the bank. All this was discussed and observed about the terrain. We recognized the advantages the first site had for the bridge as well as for the bridgehead which was to cover it and the general system of works. Then we visited the confluence [of the Zezere], which was the great whipping horse for the opposition because the Zezere narrowed between the rocks on the right and the sand on the left. The enemy battery actually raked the canal and even our workshops. Finally, we climbed on the right bank to the plateau of Concepcão. There I pointed out the system of works that I proposed for both projects, a bridge on the Zezere or two bridges on the Tagus.

I had much to contend with at Punhete, fortunately not with my worthy friends, but with everybody else. They took delight in exaggerating the fortifications of the enemy and the terrible effects they would produce against us. The enemy forces had also increased, and they were compared to our situation to make ours look worse. I could see that the bravest, lacking only the light of knowledge and experience, were terrified by things they would have disdained if seen closer. I fought as one convinced of the superiority of our resources over those of the enemy for such an operation, and as a Frenchman who kept the sacred faith. Nevertheless, it must be said that the spirit of the army was becoming impaired; that of Loison's division had never been very vigorous. I also had to admit that this sickness was gaining in the more knowledgeable branches and in the highest ranks. A man with high rank was able to say, when not in my presence, that we were completely lost, that only a few men would be saved by separating into groups, and that it would be necessary to capitulate.

We crossed a rope bridge which the worthy General Éblé had set up across a ravine eighty or eighty-five feet wide by means of five or six cables to which were attached small beams covered with thick planks. A bridge of this kind, made with good cables, could carry artillery pieces and the largest wagons. The general wanted to carry the experiment to its conclusion. Previously he had had a bridge built behind a battery and the largest cannon crossed it to arm the battery.

We followed the banks of the Tagus on our return. Ahead of us, the sun was setting slowly in a cloudless sky. We saw the ancient towers of Almourol fixed in the distance and then the middle of the wide river basin. The mountains surrounding it were taking on their spring colors. Yet I talked rather sadly with young Masséna about the discussions we had had at Punhete, about the sentiments so unworthy of French valor, and about my regret at seeing a conquest escape that had cost us so much pain. Suddenly we heard the touching and silvery tones of the English horns. They filled our souls with a soft melancholy. How bitter we would have been then if we had supposed that one day those horns would be heard on the banks of the rivers of France.

We found the Prince very anxious. We had gone well beyond the hour that he had fixed for our return. I believed he was uneasy from more than just paternal sentiments. We had to give him an exact accounting of everything we had seen and heard because the moment was approaching when we could no longer hide any part of the truth about our state of affairs and the morale without neglecting our duty entirely. I did not make an incorrect prediction in declaring that the English battery would never fire or be armed. I found it poorly constructed and rather poorly situated on a rise which was too high; in fact, we never saw any pieces there. It was also necessary to repeat all the talk at Punhete, at least that which could be repeated without too much shame. We had to describe the morale of the troops there. I was fortunately able to counter it with the example of Mermet's division situated near Martinchel. It was made up of excellent veteran soldiers who had not suffered very much in other respects. The Prince completely rejected the idea of employing Solignac's and Loison's divisions, which were composed of unreliable conscripts and foreign corps, for the crossing project that he wanted to execute himself. But all the inconsistencies were starting to shake his resolution on the subject of this operation.

General Éblé left Punhete, impatient at the obstacles he endured there. He came to get some rest at Torres Novas for a few days. We discussed the difficulties of his operation with him and the Prince. Now the general saw great and ever-increasing difficulties. He was becoming converted to the idea of the Mondego, but not to the particular projects that were being set for it. Fearful of the sinister spirit that was spreading throughout the entire army and feeling that responsibility for the crossing would fall back on him alone, the general concluded by saying "that although more interested than anyone else in the success of the bridge, which was his work, he would voluntarily make the sacrifice if the Prince felt that he should yield to public opinion." I insisted on the necessity of the passage and I showed how easy it appeared if we could transport forty boats above the designated crossing point and make two or three landings of elite troops and then march with them to the enemy battery. Simultaneously, we could launch the boats and barges on the Zezere even though it was necesary to come out of the river with all the boats under the fire of those alleged batteries. The Prince proposed to move between Abrantes and Punhete, but this was useless since we could go beyond the batteries and fortifications of the enemy without going that far. I proposed Santarém, where the crossing was certain and could be made under the protection of our artillery and the heights. A crossing there had the advantage of cutting the enemy army in half and severely compromising their right. General Éblé objected, declaring that three hundred wagons would be needed to carry the boats and equipment, that they would take three days to move there, and finally that he was opposed to an attack in the middle of the enemy line. I persisted. It seemed to me I would make it there rather than anywhere else. I reckoned, according to the tables of Gassendi,[19] that only two hundred wagons would be needed for the equipment of forty pontoons. It was true that everything was quite heavy, because of the nature of the naturally heavy green wood. Nothing was decided. We did not know whether we would have forty wagons or not. There were a great number of wheels and limbers, and already some twenty wagons were almost ready. I said that forty wagons were necessary because this number of boats was indispensable for the bridge and the disembarkation. The boats were very difficult to unload and load. Thus it would be necesary to launch them directly from the wagons. The next day General Éblé wrote that he would need four days to set up his preparations when we were ready to begin operations. This was almost the same as saying that we should give up completely.

Meanwhile everything seemed to combine to oppose the intentions of the Prince and to prevent the establishment of the bridge. The eagerness that had been shown for crossing the Tagus from the very beginning diminished because of the delays and difficulties in the construction of the boats. The ardent enthusiasm everybody had demonstrated when it was announced that twenty-five thousand men under General Drouet were coming, soon subsided; we knew what to expect—this always happened in similar circumstances. The more one is excited, the more one is depressed afterward. Most of the men, unaware of the content of the last ministerial dispatches, reasoned in accordance with what they could see; they soon asked why we remained in this country, what we wanted to do here, and whether we could not quickly make a decision either to cross to the other bank of the Tagus or withdraw if we did not judge an attack feasible. All the private passions, and the disinterest which was not mentioned when everyone was excited or in action, were heard among the arguments.

The old spirit of opposition, suppressed by the events of the campaign, was now slowly awakening. It began by finding dangers, difficulties, and disadvantages in the Tagus crossing and much more advantage in withdrawing to the Mondego. Before long this opposition ended by raising itself boldly against the first of these operations and

19. Count Jean Jacques Gassendi (1747–1828), a renowned artilleryman, wrote *Aide-mémoire à l'usage des officiers d'artillerie* . . . (1801), a valuable work used by most officers of the Empire.

praising the second. All the opponents united on these two points. A great number joined them because of uncertainty and the trouble that occasioned our apparent inaction. The situation was almost unfavorable for a French army. Some wanted to proceed to Oporto, where they hoped to find favorable occasions for fortune and pleasure, and others toward Spain where their yearning or memories called them, but the greatest number wanted only to change position. Beyond these anxieties about morale, many more alarming reasons existed in the numerical state of the army. The corps were reduced slightly and sickness was inconsequential. Daily losses in the continuous raids were almost nothing, but in regiments to the rear more than one-eighth of the men had lost or broken their guns and were unable to fight. Repairs were difficult. Nothing could be replaced, and the losses were felt still more gravely in the cavalry and artillery.

As long as the Prince could hope to restore those agitated spirits, he stood up against the storm. But he felt that at such a delicate juncture it was necessary to overlook nothing in achieving success. Everything must contribute to the success of an operation which was becoming more difficult in every way. He recognized the absolute necessity of confiding the operation to the best troops, which were in the 6th Corps, and the appropriateness of leaving Marshal Ney in command. Discretion also required that the Marshal, who was to make the crossing, should share the responsibility for the operation so that he would take every precaution. Similarly, discretion also advised us to detach Marshal Ney from the opposition and to gain his support, since he was always eager for battle and the hope of some personal success. This was why the Prince gave me orders to prepare a new project on this new basis.

The new plan for the crossing was calculated for February 5. The 9th Corps would come and relieve the 8th Corps, and the 2nd Corps would remain in position. General Montbrun's cavalry would gather at Ourém. On February 4 the 6th Corps would go to Punhete, Solignac's division between Martinchel and Montalvo, and Clauzel's division to Atalaia. At dusk the 2nd and 9th Corps, under the command of General Reynier, would leave for Torres Novas and Golegã and take a position with the cavalry of the 8th Corps, while General Montbrun's cavalry would be at Bairro, near Martinchel.

It also appeared that we had worked for a long time to form the opposition party. All kinds of interests, often contrary, all the hidden feelings, rivalries, resistance, weakness—everything had been united and intertwined in that league, and by a singular inconsistency they exploded at the very moment when the preparations for the crossing were almost completed. It must also be admitted that the Prince did not do everything he might have to prevent it at the beginning or to repress it later. He would have succeeded, at least in part, by visiting the troops more often in their quarters or during parades, and particularly by seeing the general officers and even special ones more often so that by talking to them he could have enlightened or encouraged them. But the way the army, while always in the presence of the enemy, had to be extended to gather food, hindered frequent visits or any movements of troops that would be detrimental to the specific magazines.

Generals Loison and Lazowski began talking openly to the Prince about the plans of the opposition. He silenced the generals, showing them the government's orders. General Drouet, at Torres Novas, declared against the bridge and never stopped talking in that vein. He even fixed his own time limit for operations. After February 5 he wanted to return to his government in Spain.[20] At the Duc d'Abrantès's headquarters it was loudly said that the passage would not take place and that all the preparations were only a demonstration. Marshal Ney for his part denounced the operation and did not bother to direct any of his frequent trips toward Punhete, where he had one of his divisions. Finally, Generals Marchand and Maucune came to the Prince's quarters to proclaim these opinions as if they were those of the entire army. In fact, toward the end there was an outcry against the passage. Everyone showed themselves against it, the generals and officers and the soldiers who should have been enlightened by them—everyone up to the administration. Moreover, nobody took the trouble to reason properly. No one discussed and everybody babbled. It was a fashion, a rage, that captivated those with half-wills and that was imposed on those with strong wills. Thus popular opinion had a great hold on the French mind, even in the most serious affairs. Strong conviction and

20. Ironically, Napoleon issued instructions to Berthier to place Drouet's 9th Corps under Masséna's command, since Bessières had been appointed commander of north-central Spain. See *Correspondance de Napoléon Ier*, No. 17335, Napoleon to Berthier, February 6, 1810, XXI, 455.

much stubbornness was needed to oppose this universal disorder. Yet what external opposition could threaten it when General Éblé was about to give in? Among the higher ranks, General Reynier alone was constantly for the passage, and supporting him were some good heads, or at least those who believed themselves to be such.

Chapter Ten

INDECISION AT THE TAGUS

Like all great assemblages of men, armies experience internal storms which sometimes agitate and upset them. It seems that the larger the number of men, the more violence these storms acquire. They are produced by passions which spread ferment; the passions catch fire and often bring terrible consequences. The isolated man, dominated by their influence, can abandon himself to his passions, which are always circumscribed by his position. But when he finds himself in a group, the passions of others dominate, inflame, and agitate him with greater vehemence. Thus we see that man's mind moves quickly from one extreme to the other, like the most illustrious armies, and yields to the most contrary passions in an instant. The passions vary in intensity according to the character of the individual. Hence the more volatile, temperamental, and impetuous that men are, the more violent is their imagination, and the easier it is to inflame and change their direction and the less difficult to stir their passions; however, it is also easier to turn them around and change their view.

In order to lead these masses of men it is necessary to have a profound knowledge of this "terrible game of passions," as the first warrior of this world referred to it. Long before he establishes his plans, combines his operations, calculates his maneuvers, and disposes of his attacks, an army general of true talent must not only know how to excite the passions, which is very difficult, but also to take advantage of them once they are in movement—to moderate or finally to know how to subordinate them when he can do nothing better. However, to inflame others, it is necesary to possess the greatness of soul which makes heroes, or to become impassioned while remaining master of oneself. It is again nature that gives this last faculty. It cannot be acquired by studies nor developed by calculated effort. It is part of a general's instinct and exists for war as much as the instincts of a soldier, and without it all the knowledge, theories, and skills are of no use. This is how one is born a general. Without all these qualities, one is only a courtier with a diploma, a dispassionate tactician, or a student of strategy, just as a rhetorician is often no more than a mediocre poet or an impotent orator.

If we regard as admirable the talent of moving passions, of touching hearts, of raising and especially of moderating souls in peaceful assembly, of calming them in tumultuous crowds, what is its value when it is necessary to move a great number of men armed with thunder and to subject them to the severest privations and the most cruel sufferings, to sustain them in the most difficult and perilous occasions, to consign them to the most painful sacrifices, and to lead them to certain death or raise them to the most sublime heroism? Discipline begins the difficult task of forming the soldier, of organizing the regiments and creating artificial power among them, but honor, glory, liberty, and above all love of *patrie* render them capable of the greatest things. Thus, discipline forms an army, passions exalt it; but the latter, by their very nature, must not and cannot endure forever. Likewise, during wartime it is necessary to have a special system for the army, which could be called "high discipline," to maintain it in a wisely balanced movement, in skillful moderation, and in perpetual employment of bodies and minds. However, a single man must direct all the efforts and movements of this vast machine, made up of so many thousand living cells subordinated at all times to its needs and to such sudden passions. The army has only one soul that enlivens and sustains it from the top of the lofty regions it inhabits. This soul is the General.

Of all armies, the one most subject to the influence of passions is certainly the French army, because no army is composed of men as susceptible to enthusiasm and even to exaltation.[1] None, especially

1. Pelet gives an example of this French enthusiasm in a footnote of his manuscript, describing how the Army of Egypt, "filled with admiration, stopped

among modern armies, have shown themselves more aroused by the love of *patrie* and glory. I am speaking of our recent armies. The ease with which all French people prove themselves and become capable of every kind of heroism is a wonderful thing! Where else would one find so much soul and élan! How many miracles have we seen during the last twenty years in all the corners of Europe under the sacred words of *liberté, honneur, et patrie*! The day before Austerlitz I saw French soldiers asking loudly for battle and victory as if each one were going to be the victor the next day. I saw them in the disasters of Russia, surrounded by the dead and dying, succumbing to famine and the cruel cold, displaying their accustomed valor, dying while praying and hoping for vengeance without uttering a single complaint and still keeping traces of French good humor amidst those horrors.[2] I saw brand new soldiers at the end of the Campaign of 1813, which was so rich in glorious action wherever the genius [Napoleon] was directing the battles; with only the rumor of a march on Berlin that would restore all our glory, they became heroes (October 10). Finally, I saw them in 1814 and 1815, showing themselves simultaneously as indomitable warriors and subdued citizens, sacrificing their glory for the peace and safety of the *patrie*.

Moreover, these intrepid soldiers, so susceptible to the brilliant passions of war, seem to have been born with an instinct for it. Often they make war and understand it better than their officers. No one judges military operations and the conduct of generals with more wisdom than they; their judgment is based on all the activity of their imagination, the mobility of their minds, and often the ardor of their passions. Thus French soldiers, more than all others, need to be sustained and even contained, more with the help of confidence and the

and spontaneously clapped their hands when they saw the ruins of Thebes, showing themselves worthy heirs of the glory of Sesostris, Alexander, and Caesar."

2. In a footnote, Pelet recalls the comment that Madame Louise Fusil-Fleury, an actress in Moscow when the French occupied it in 1812, made about him in her memoirs, *L'incendie de Moscou, la petite orpheline de Wilna, passage de la Bérésina, et retraite de Napoléon jusqu'à Wilna* (1817). He writes: "Despite Mme Fusil-Fleury's slight mistake of taking me for a colonel of the Guard, I claim my share of her memoir of Russia. I would not have been flattered, under any other circumstances, to be called 'a very funny man.' However, then I believed there was more merit in showing oneself as such. Certainly it was not callousness on my part. Two days later I distributed all the flour and brandy I had left to my regiment. Hence I saved the lives of many brave men at the expense of what assured my life."

influence of talent than with that of rank. Let no man become a commander if he does not feel he has all the qualities and talents to command such soldiers, if he does not have the same passions, sentiments, interests, actions of glory, and, more specifically, if he does not have a soul tempered like theirs with which they can communicate at all times. It is necessary that this soul show itself shining before their eyes. They will always feel it, and often under this common appearance through which the men of the world cannot see, they will discover and join it in its heroism.

The French armies, above all others, must be kept in a state of motion. In wartime they have no greater enemy than rest, inaction, and the quiet life of the cantons. Then by singular contrast, a rust is formed simultaneously which expands progressively to inhibit all the resiliency and create a disturbance that destroys them. Therefore the soldiers must be kept in a state of mobility by continuous and diversified exercises, frequent maneuvers, changes of quarters, military works, expeditions, and alternate service between the advance posts and the bivouac, instead of being captivated by a shabby attention to attire, by insipid details of discipline, and by routine exercises which are a cause for fatigue of both mind and body. It is also good to reinforce the mental activity of the troops and exercise their imagination in order to divert them from those things we do not wish them to do, and to encourage their noisy games and distract them by amusements and gymnastics.

The habitual use of what we call "*petite guerre*" would be of great utility in distracting and instructing officers and soldiers alike, as long as it is not limited to vain skirmishing, maneuvers without goals or results, and ridiculous display. Attacks on villages, marches, and realistic deployments in every direction; occupation of the country around a position, camp, or terrain which has just been seized and may be threatened; maneuvers against cavalry or flank attacks, etc.; entrenchments quickly formed, then defended, and taken and retaken in a way to give the troops some positive notions of their dispositions and their usefulness—all these offer a multitude of combinations which can easily create lively interest in all the ranks. Through the novelty and amusement involved, the troops who participate in such activities will be able to evaluate them. By means of a few very simple and explanatory orders of the day, one can derive a great source of instruction for an army called to the most prominent duties. Such activities would thwart the numerous military prejudices, private interests, and bad habits, as well as the waste of powder, clothing, armament, etc. But there are remedies and answers for everything. Here it is enough to point them out so everybody can implement them, once it is evident that in this way we would have an army much better instructed, highly skilled, volatile, stable, and lastly more effective.[3]

It was only too true that after long inaction and prolonged rest in their daily canton life, surrounded by the disorders of pillaging, our army had lost some of its military spirit and had seen the ties of discipline relaxed. The dispersal of the corps over such a vast terrain had contributed to maintaining notions of isolation and even rivalry for cantons between the more comfortable divisions. The dispersion of the regiments and battalions had dampened the spirit of the army corps, which was not without its advantages. The continual sight of the inaccessible enemy fortifications; of the wide and important Tagus, the neighborhood of Lisbon—the goal of all our wishes whose entrance was forbidden to us; the misery and the perpetual expeditions of our soldiers contrasted with the abundance in the enemy camp—all this could have influenced the moral strength and confidence of the army. But, I repeat, our greatest enemy was prolonged inaction; from this all kinds of discontent were born: indiscreet wishes based on various interests, a spirit of criticism and controversy, vague complaints, anxiety among some, and finally the league of opposition which agitated the many passions, inflaming and fomenting all the elements of discord. But a thing to notice, forever honorable for the army, was that in such a position there was not the least feeling of fear among the soldiers and hardly any desertion in the French corps. Whereas we can suppose, with some truth, that not half the English troops would have remained under arms after two months in such a situation.

General Reynier was the first and almost the only one to try to amuse his soldiers by various means and to divert their disturbing ideas by games and agreeable occupations. He promoted the establishment of a theater under the cannon of the enemy and each division alter-

3. Omitted here is a long one-paragraph discussion of the classical warrior and his problems. This is the only omission that has been made in Pelet's original manuscript.

nately sent up balloons twice a week. It was a favorable feature of a wise policy in his army corps, which was badly situated and suffered the most from the lack of provisions. Once occupied by diversions, the soldier worried very little about the things surrounding him, and he would show all his French hilarity and work with affection. Sometimes we saw the marauders returning several leagues loaded with some heavy piece of decoration. We established another theater at Punhete, so close to the guns of the enemy that General Lazowski's coachman was killed by a ball while he stood at the door.

I take pleasure in citing these characteristics of French cheerfulness and tranquility in the army. Moreover, confidence was apparent everywhere. From the enthusiasm which manifested itself when news of the reinforcements of the 9th Corps was announced, we saw, in effect, that this feeling was dormant rather than altered. Only one word was needed to inflame the army. This magic word, "Charge," was one of our war cries. Then there would be nothing of which the army was not capable, as there was no one who could excite it more than Masséna. No one possessed the instinct of a great general as he did. He possessed it more than he realized himself—his warrior bearing, his head which resembled those of antiquity, and his quick and flashing eye. (It was thought that after he received a gunshot in the eye his sight would be impaired. It appeared that only one eye had suffered much from the exterior alteration. Moreover, his sight was just as good as I had ever known.[4]) With his bold look, his pleasing wit, his military language, this bellicose genius in the midst of fire had everything to inflame our soldiers, and his character, like his talent, was eminently French. But then, this inaction and all the delays and contradictions had tired even him, and he was worn out. Our war of positions and calculations did not fit his ardent and impetuous genius and his heroic inspirations. He needed a war of actions and movements. Unfortunately he did not have the occasion in the last campaign to show everything that he was.

As long as the Prince could hope to retain by activity and to restore by persuasion these diversely agitated spirits, as long as he could hope

4. Masséna lost the sight in his left eye while hunting with Napoleon, Berthier, and several other marshals. According to Marbot, pellets from Napoleon's gun struck Masséna in the eye; Masséna, however, had the wit to blame Berthier for the careless shot. See Marbot, *Memoirs,* II, 193.

to obtain some success by sheer strength although contested by the opposition, His Excellency held out vigorously against the turmoil. But at such a delicate juncture, he felt that nothing should be left to chance. This was why he was determined, above all, to wait for the cooperation of the 5th Corps and he confirmed this in his resolution. On the other hand, he saw that in regard to the crossing, nothing should be neglected in order to eliminate any doubt of its outcome; everything must be coordinated to make the operation a success, although it was becoming more and more difficult. He further recognized the absolute necessity of confiding it to the best troops in the army, which were in the 6th Corps, and the expediency as well as the advantage of leaving Marshal Ney in command. This is why the Prince gave me orders to prepare a fourth project on this new basis.

The new plan for the passage was calculated for February 5. The 9th Corps would come and relieve the 8th Corps, and the 2nd Corps would remain in position. General Montbrun's cavalry would gather at Ourém. On February 4 the 6th Corps would go to Punhete, Solignac's division between Martinchel and Montalvo, and Clauzel's division to Atalaia. At dusk the 2nd and 9th Corps, under the command of General Reynier, would leave for Torres Novas and Golegã and take a position with the cavalry of the 8th Corps, while General Montbrun's cavalry would be at Bairro, near Martinchel, and Trelliard's would be toward Alqueidão. On February 5 the crossing was to be made by the 6th Corps. Clauzel's division would move and form behind Punhete with General Montbrun's cavalry, and both of them would cross the Tagus immediately after the 6th Corps. The cavalry of General Trelliard would go to Tomar and follow the movement of the rear guard. General Trelliard would start marching at noon and take up a position on the right bank of the Zezere. His cavalry and two brigades of infantry would defend the position of Atalaia until nightfall. These army corps would cross the Zezere during the night, while Solignac's division invested Abrantes.

Now the great difficulty was to induce Marshal Ney, who had announced himself so often and so openly against this passage, to accept the command with frank and complete cooperation. Was it necessary to write to him or to send me, or should the Prince see him? It was decided that the Prince would meet him at Martinchel, that I would go there to take his letter and as usual explain the projects and prepare the way.[5] General Solignac was there [during this discussion]. Amid many flattering remarks, the Prince made a prediction about me that came true rather quickly, and he added, "I want it to be said that he comes out of my school; if I am not unreservedly supported, I will send him [Ney] to Paris." I then made my first trip to Tomar to see the Marshal. He received me very coldly: "What is new?" I presented him with the letter: "You know quite well what it is." After having read it, [he said,] "I will go to Martinchel." This was our entire conversation, and my mission—gone to rack and ruin. The Prince was piqued by this coldness, but this was not the time to show his feeling. I vigorously encouraged him to show himself agreeable at Martinchel and he promised to do so, while giving vent to his great anger at this opposition. His intention was to interrogate the Marshal very carefully to see if he could rely on him for the crossing and to make up his mind accordingly. He sent me to General Reynier a second time in order to learn in detail his plans for the movement on the enemy line and the exact state of his provisions.

A monk arrested at Santarém said that Hill and Beresford were at Chamusca with eleven English regiments, six thousand Portuguese, and two thousand cavalry. Lord Wellington was still at Cartaxo with Spencer's division. Craufurd was at the advance post and Picton near Azambuja with troops at Almeirim, opposite Santarém. He said that La Romana was dead,[6] that the Spanish had left for Badajoz, and that the Prince of Wales was declared regent.

The Prince saw the Marshal at Martinchel [on January 29]. After a few slight recriminations on each other's conduct, they agreed (perhaps too easily) on the need to occupy both banks of the Tagus and on the difficulties of marching toward the Mondego. When everything

5. In this letter carried by Pelet, Masséna suggested that Ney should complete his preparations for crossing the Tagus. "I hope that we will be able to execute this passage on February 1. Since your army corps, composed of experienced troops, is destined to play the principal role, I think it will be useful if we meet." See Masséna to Ney, January 25, 1811, Correspondance: Armée de Portugal, Carton C711.

6. La Romana's death was a shock to everyone in the Allied camp. Wellington wrote to Stuart on January 23, "I am much concerned to inform you that the Marques de la Romana died this day. He was attacked some days ago with spasms in his chest, and he had since been very unwell; but I had seen him every day. . . . Under the existing circumstances, his loss is the greatest which the cause could sustain; and I do not know how we are to replace him." See *Wellington's Dispatches,* VII, 175–76.

was settled, the Prince confirmed the preparations, showing him the last letter of the Major General. Everything went along quite well. The Marshal finally promised to go to Punhete with the Prince to examine the state of affairs and to give food to the 2nd Corps. He said to the Prince, "I can now see that you are obliged to make this crossing. Nevertheless, if I were in your position I would not take it upon myself to do so, but I will execute it willingly." Finally he asked the Prince to do him a favor and send him back to Paris. His Excellency promised to send a dispatch requesting it, whatever the reason. At length they left each other in agreement and as united as possible.

Meanwhile I arrived at Santarém. I talked with General Reynier about his position and that of the Allies; about his needs; about my idea for crossing at Santarém by transporting the boats on wagons, of which he strongly approved; and about operations in general for us as well as for the enemy. He advocated very good principles, far removed from the operations on the Mondego, and strongly attached to those on the Tagus. He grasped the circumstances of the situation quite clearly, but he desired above all that we act immediately. He claimed he did not have enough food for his men beyond March 4 or 5, and for the horses only until March 1. We talked about his diversionary plan to march on the left of the enemy. He made use of the details of his operation and did not insist on pushing any farther than Alcoentre, but on freeing the left bank of the Tagus and attracting Hill with our entire army. I left the General in order to go with the Marquis d'Alorna to see the position on the Tagus and what we could do about establishing an imposing and admirable bridge under the fire of our artillery and in the presence of the entire enemy army. There were streams or discharge canals between the Tagus and the heights, two of them carrying the waters of the Ulme. The marquis said that they were rather wide but not deep, and easily fordable everywhere in dry weather. There was a beautiful position at the belvedere where a marine officer was established as an observer for General Reynier, and where the balloons were sent up. Lately there had been one with parachutes. Then another one sent a whole village on the left bank into flight.[7]

7. Reynier often sent up balloons to celebrate various public occasions. The balloons were constructed with the aid of documents from the archives of Santarém and frequently had a small carriage attached. On at least one occasion, a

At supper I found myself with *chef de bataillon* Brulley of the engineers. He had very good military opinions, sound views on the position of the army, and generous feelings. I shared with General Reynier a project that I had conceived during the night to bring all our boats to Santarém by water, unite the army there, and attack the enemy line at the same time as we made the crossing. The boats would set out during the night. If they were guided there without the knowledge of the enemy (for which we could hope), we could make some visible preparations at Punhete or, better still, we would continue those made during the previous days to detain Hill at this point, and then fall on him with superior strength and destroy him by separating him from Wellington. The General approved, but he was afraid that we could not move the boats. In my proposal, I was still apprehensive that the Prince had found the Marshal recalcitrant. I asked the General if he would undertake the operation once the boats were brought down. He made it difficult. I replied that the Prince would do it himself with a division from each corps. Then the General decided to take charge of it immediately. He would have preferred that the boats be carried and that we make the crossings, one in full strength at Santarém and the other at Punhete, as soon as the position at Punhete had been dismantled. This would create the difficulty of dividing the army and renouncing the operation against Hill since it would actually be an operation and demonstration. He suggested the point of Boa Vista at the mouth of the Alviela, which I had examined another day. This site reduced the trip of the boats and made it easier to launch them into the water; but on the other hand it would be farther away from our attack on the Ponte de Asseca. If Lord Wellington knew his profession, he would attack, if he had not already attacked, at the moment we erected the bridges. Thus it was necessary that Reynier have his best troops there and in a good position.

The General returned to the topic of a diversion on the enemy's left. For a long time we discussed the operation and the idea of occupying Lisbon. Acording to him, this would put an end to everything, and according to me it would not. After having exhausted these dif-

lamb was carried aloft and the Allied soldiers turned out of their entrenchments and mounted the parapets to watch the balloon. While it hovered high above the Tagus, Reynier, with a powerful field glass, was able to determine the number of enemy troops across the Tagus. See Lemonnier-Delafosse, *Souvenirs*, pp. 113–14.

ferent matters, I summarized his requests: act quickly; relieve his light cavalry (I proposed two squadrons of the 6th, and he was satisfied); food for the men; the dying horses; the proposal of the various plans of operation to the Prince; the utility in remaining on the Tagus and taking the fortresses; the positioning of the 9th Corps from Almeida to Alcántara in order to bring the siege artillery; a false operation besides the one on the Mondego, etc. The General had determined the position of Santarém astronomically; he was nearly in agreement with Lisbon ['s astronomers] on his maps; his desk was piled high, etc. We promised to act in concert regarding topography. He strongly approved of the measure for a base near Golegã. His map was at 1 to 100,000th. I went to visit the banks of the Tagus to examine the facility for launching boats into the water. The banks were accessible enough, and beams and planks could be carried on the [men's] backs from the upper city. On my arrival, I reported to the Prince on General Reynier's project and the one that I had conceived. He put off hearing the details until the next day, when he went to Punhete to consult with the Marshal.

My head was full of my new plan. I wrote it down during the night at Torres Novas. I saw the probable ruin of the English army by the destruction of Hill's forces, or at least the possible evacuation of Lisbon and the embarkation of the English, and, finally, the guarantee of our establishment in Portugal in some manner. I may have been wrong. Nevertheless, I am still of the same opinion. So that anyone may be able to appreciate what I was thinking, I am placing the plan at the end of this work.[8] My friends were beside themselves. I will never forget that one of them wanted to spend the night copying my work although he was himself capable of making excellent plans. All those who knew about it were delighted. Everybody, even those opposing it, approved it in the end, when there was no longer any question of crossing the Tagus. Finally a useless experience showed how easy it was to execute. From this first day, I consulted with Major Reynaud and Captain Parmentier at Punhete on the aspect of the project related to the boats. First of all they undertook to bring them down in very little time.

The Marshal had arrived at Punhete before the Prince. Together with

8. Unfortunately this document could not be found at the end of Pelet's manuscript.

General Éblé they went to the point of the crossing. The Marshal approved the operation strongly and found no difficulties where he had seen only impossibilities before. He would undertake its execution with his good divisions. He would seize the batteries by storm, spike and overturn the guns, and establish himself on the summit. I would have preferred that he occupy the bank itself since the enemy could, with strong artillery, push back the troops unsupported by [artillery]. The two marshals seemed to be very pleased with each other, but the Prince was apprehensive about this excessive pliancy of Marshal Ney.

Finally, I was able to propose my [new] and last project to the Prince, who approved it in all its details, claiming that Hill and Wellington would not know what to do for twenty-four hours; at last he deigned to compare this operation to the battle of Zurich. He wanted it executed. He ordered the marine officer and General Éblé to come to him because he did not want to see the former without the latter. Meanwhile, His Excellency was complaining a little; each day he found Éblé colder and more awkward. The Prince claimed that Éblé was succumbing a little to the contagious spirit which was, as a matter of fact, infiltrating his headquarters. I also found the sailors rather uninspired: there was the rain, the moon, and the endless difficulties. I cheered them up, there in the presence of the Prince with General Éblé. The latter praised the project and agreed to help. It was decided that the major would reconnoiter the riverbed of the Tagus with Beaufort and Parmentier, that he would make a report, and that I would complete a map of the river at 1 to 50,000th. A real difficulty was that the moon was waxing. The Prince agreed to wait until February 10 to execute the operation because he had enough food until then. The transportation of the beams was another difficulty, but there were a certain number of planks at Santarém where we could procure others. I gave a copy of my project to General Éblé. When he sent it back to me, he wrote a most gracious and flattering letter on my operation, which he considered not only brilliant but very advantageous and easy for the army to execute.

We experienced a loss very painful to us and very acute for the Prince. Lieutenant Louis Armand Xavier d'Aguesseau, who had served in our headquarters for five years, expired after we saw him dying [a little] every day from a chest disease. Although he was already suffering considerably, we were not able to induce him to leave when we entered Portugal. From that period he continued to decline. For a long time I urged him to leave the army, for which his health was not suited, and to take up the [legal] profession where his name had acquired such great renown. He was the only heir of his great name and he possessed everything needed to distinguish himself in whatever field he embraced. Perhaps if it had not been for this faithful perseverance, I could still count him among my friends, because we had a very close friendship. Everybody recognized his talents, his many noble qualities and virtues, with few defects; but those with whom he lived intimately appreciated him even more because they knew him better. We rendered him full funeral honors. The entire *état major* and a few generals were present there. Octave de Ségur, his cousin, conducted the ceremony and I shed some very bitter tears.

General Reynier announced that an aide-de-camp of Lord Wellington, carrying money for Lord Percy, had said that Marshal Soult was entering Portugal, that Marshal Mortier had already arrived and obtained some success against the fortresses, and that the Spanish troops were before them, asking whether those marshals were under the command of the Prince. Without doubt, this English officer wanted to know if they would advance or besiege Badajoz; they were rather indignant over the capture of Olivenza. He also announced the departure of Napoleon for Spain. This prospect was often discussed at the advance post. We did not believe it, but such a trip could have been combined with the movements of Soult. It was even believed that Napoleon had arrived at Bayonne. Colonel Valazé, returning from Tomar, told me that the Marshal had learned about my latest project, although I could not find out who told him. He said he still did not agree on the crossing, but he would execute it. Cavailher told me that the enemy was worried about the road laid out above Punhete for transporting the boats and that a strong reconnaissance of enemy generals had been seen on the opposite bank.

Each day the Prince became more attracted to my new project. He claimed it was hazardous and bold, especially because the bridge would be closer to the [anticipated] attacks of Wellington. I tried to demonstrate the contrary to him by [mentioning] both the excellent position at Santarém, which under such circumstances would risk nothing by a movement on its right flank, and the good selection and quantity of troops that were to defend it. The marines and Beaufort returned from their reconnaissance, which had not been made beyond Alviela because of the flooding Tagus. They were to complete it as soon as the water returned to its bed. The reconnaissance had been made by going up the river, and it was quite difficult because of the extensive flooding. Two days later I met Captain Parmentier at Golegã, where he was engaged in completing it. He assured me that with the present level of the Tagus, we could go down the river in perfect safety because the sandbars were completely covered and it was quite easy to sail continuously along our bank. He strongly insisted that we take advantage of this moment. I objected because of the moonlight and the advantage of waiting a few more days in order to cover ourselves with the obscurity of darkness and conceal most of the knowledge of our operation from the enemy, at least while we were crossing the gorges of Tancos to reach the main basin before the moon rose. Afterward this officer descended the Tagus twice from Punhete to Santarém, and the second time he executed the operation in eight hours with a flotilla of six boats and forty-five men. I still have the report on those two expeditions.[9] Captain Parmentier merited being appointed [commander] by Major Reynaud. I would have chosen him myself because I knew that he had made most of the expeditions to the Island of Lobau under my orders and under those of the brave General Baste, who was later killed beside me during the attack of Brienne, at the same time as the good General Decouz, who commanded a division of the Young Guard.[10]

9. At 9:30 P.M. on February 19, Parmentier drifted out into the Tagus from the Zezere and downstream. Although the Portuguese sentries on the southern bank of the Tagus opened fire, Parmentier's little flotilla continued down the river. Delayed by sandbars and drifting logs, it reached the estuary of the Alviela at 5:30 A.M. One boat went as far as Santarém. See Koch, *Mémoires de Masséna,* VII, 327; D'Urban, *Peninsular Journal,* p. 183.

10. Count Pierre Baste (1768–1814) went to sea in 1781 and in 1790 became a lieutenant aboard the *David.* In 1811 he was promoted to the rank of rear admiral. He served abroad various French vessels, fought at Aboukir, and in 1804 was given a flotilla of barges at Boulogne. Baste was attached to the Grand Army in 1807 and the next year was with Dupont at Baylen. Following his exchange, Baste was given a unit of the Guard and sent to Valladolid with Dorsenne. In 1813 he commanded a brigade of the Young Guard in Decouz's division and was killed at Brienne on January 29, 1814.

Baron Pierre Decouz (1775–1814) enlisted in a volunteer battalion in 1793. He served with the Army of Italy until 1798, when he sailed with Napoleon to Egypt. Attached to Lannes's staff, he fought at Austerlitz and Pultusk. Decouz was reassigned to the Army of Germany in 1808 and then to the Armies of Italy and Naples until 1811. In 1813 he was given command of a division of the Young Guard under Ney, and at Brienne he was mortally wounded.

General Reynier also found my operation noble and brilliant. After that, every time he was questioned about crossing, either by letter or verbally, he defended and sustained my opinion as if it had been his own. Since he wrote almost everyday, he liked to return to the same subject, and he had many occasions to speak out in favor of it. Nevertheless, he did not completely renounce his diversionary plan for two crossings and specifically his favorite idea of Boa Vista. But there the least flooding would have detached his bridge from the left bank; in addition, when we attacked to occupy that bank, the enemy would have a large circular canal in front of them which was a good defense and would be impassable if they excavated the smallest trench there.

It was very important for us to receive news of the 5th Corps, since its movements were generally to regulate ours. The Prince was not able to obtain trustworthy information from the spies we employed; therefore, he sent a strong reconnaissance with orders [dated January 28] to reach Vila Flor on the Tagus. This point had been designated by the Major General as our rendezvous point with the 5th Corps, as announced in the dispatches. His Excellency continued to send frequent messengers. A needless care, since at that time Marshal Soult had not yet crossed the Portuguese frontier and he was busy taking the deplorable fortress of Badajoz—quite useless for his advantage. All the help that he brought to the army, all the diversions mentioned in his report, were limited to clearing the banks of the Tagus of a few wretched Spanish cadres. During the battle at Gebora, he defeated and threw them back with a few French infantry regiments;[11] those cadres were recruited from all the bands marauding in the neighborhood. It was certainly not those miserable troops which stopped him from advancing. At least he was entirely free after February 19, when he had completely destroyed them. According to the Prince, Marshal Soult was afraid that the 5th Corps would be taken away from him. We shall see a little later what consequences Soult's decisions were to have on the results of this war.

11. In the action referred to as Gebora, Spanish General Mendizabal collected 9,000 infantry and 3,000 calvary on the heights of San Cristobal, beyond the outworks of Badajoz. The Spanish failed to take the most elementary precautions against surprise and were attacked by Soult on February 19, 1811. In the ensuing action, half the Spanish infantry were killed or taken and the remainder fled into Badajoz or beyond the Portuguese frontier. See *Wellington's Dispatches,* Wellington to Liverpool, February 23, 1811, VII, 288–90; John W. Fortescue, *A History of the British Army* (London, 1910–30), VIII, 24.

A man arrived from Montemor-o-Velho and said he was one of ours. He came to fetch the Marquis d'Alorna's proclamations and spread them within his region. The Prince asked me to interrogate him. I was able to extract only very little news and we got rid of him with a few proclamations. He announced that a French unit (Claparède's division),[12] marching to collect food, had encountered Silveira. Attacking him about January 8 or 9, Claparède had pushed Silveira back up to Lamego. Wilson and Miller had hurried to his aid. The French force, we were told, retired to Trancoso. The inhabitants of Coimbra still expected to see us and had orders to leave the country. They were very tired of these annoyances and also very unhappy about the disorders of our marauders. There were only two gunboats at Figueira; Trant's militia was at Coimbra, but they were busy destroying or carrying away all the provisions remaining between the Mondego and the Vouga rivers. Wilson and Miller also had only militia. They were still under the command of General Bacelar, situated at Pedro do Sul. A report from General Gardanne also announced a band of militia near Tonda.

The flooding Zezere had broken the bridge at Punhete. We feared more extensive destruction. I went there, and the bridge was already reestablished. By chance I met Marshal Ney with Generals Marchand and Ferey. We talked about the passage, about its preparations, while still asking ourselves if we should do it. The Marshal guaranteed that he could seize the post and clear away the cannon with his veteran regiments but he wanted many men. We discussed the question of coming out of the Zezere or of transporting the boats, as well as gathering or dividing the resources for the passage. We talked a great deal without reaching any conclusion or decision. The Marshal dwelt on the necessity of minutely calculating all details regarding the localities, the weather, and the execution. As I accompanied him at his departure, he started to tell me that it would be better if he were not in the army, that he was troubled by the operations, that he was not

12. Count Michel Marie Claparède (1770–1842) joined a volunteer unit in 1793 and served in various armies defending the coast of France. In 1798 he was transferred to the Army of Italy, and he served at Genoa in 1799. With Moreau at Hohenlinden and LeClerc in Santo Domingo, Claparède did not return to France until 1802. After Austerlitz, Jena, and Pultusk, he was promoted to general of division and sent to Spain as governor of Valladolid in 1809. In 1810 Claparède was given a division of D'Erlon's 9th Corps, and he served in Portugal and Spain, fighting at Fuentes de Oñoro.

made to serve as a shadow, that the crossing should not be made at Punhete, and that we should maneuver on several points, designating Santarém as one of them. The Marshal continued to talk and I wanted to accompany him farther, but I could not find my horse.

General Éblé told me we had forty wagons nearly finished and a machine for launching the boats. He still thought that the passage could be made above Punhete but that it would be easier and more brilliant below. He asked for three days to prepare the latter; he would have liked the crossing made immediately because of the flooding waters. He did not want to divide the boats nor make a diversion. He thought the crossing could be effected during the daylight; but then the most glorious part—the isolation of Hill—would be lost. The waters were higher on the Tagus and the Zezere than we had seen them up to then. The former was carrying some of the water of the latter.

I found the Prince worried about all kinds of new problems. There were so many different opinions, unworthy of being listened to, and so much opposition, unworthy of being considered. Everywhere individuals were still working on the minds of the soldiers, to arouse and agitate them. We examined the various proposed plans. It was easy to recognize that they were generally without any foundation. We then considered the crossing on the basis of various points of view; the instinct of the army, the execution of the government's order—its instructions and its actual benefits—the interests of the Prince himself, his glory and responsibility, and all the diverse reports from the direction of the enemy. Everywhere I saw reasons to cross the Tagus and none to retrace our steps. We spoke unreservedly and with absolute confidence. I persisted in my opinion, especially my idea of a crossing at Santarém, which seemed to be as beautiful as it was easy. If there had been any apprehension of mishap or important fighting, I would have renounced it for fear of expending munitions and becoming encumbered by the wounded. But why, I asked, should we not try, in any case, to cross and live in Alentejo? We could wait for new orders from Paris, and when the impossibility of maintaining ourselves and living there became obvious and acknowledged, then we could finish by returning toward the north. However, in leaving the Tagus, we would expose ourselves. We would be unable to operate any longer, since it would be necessary to sacrifice the pontoons and wait at least five or six months until harvesttime came or until we could take advantage of the fords on the Tagus—an expedient always dangerous for an army. If we returned to the Mondego, the actual campaign would be unsuccessfully concluded. It would have to be started again. The government might object very strongly and its arrangements might be upset; still, its orders had been executed by holding the positions during December and January.

Among the remarks that the Prince was willing to listen to was the ridiculous complaint that we had not besieged and captured Abrantes, although we had no siege guns or munitions for that, and that we had not crossed the Tagus earlier, although preparations for the bridge had just been finished and the enemy batteries had made it necessary to construct wagons for transporting the boats. Who could have reasonably proposed crossing the Tagus by throwing an army corps on its other bank with one weak bridge, exposed to so many accidents? We needed two bridges and at least eighty pontoons, not counting the barges, launches, etc., which were just completed.

Nevertheless General Fririon, the army's chief of staff, who carefully concerned himself with our situation, wished to see our inaction ended. He hoped to communicate his legitimate worries to me on the frequent occasions when I had to see him. He had complimented me numerous times about my last project, and he indicated to me how much he wanted to see it executed. His commendation, so creditable because of his talents and personal merit, acquired new weight because of his intimate ties to, and frequent communications with, General Éblé, general director and supreme judge of the operations. Later on we tried together to use all possible resources to execute the maneuver at Santarém. On the other hand, Marshal Ney, who had learned about this project, although I did not know how, wrote a very long and rather passionate letter to the Prince. He praised and approved of everything but he added one obvious little measure of having the departure of the convoys preceded by a trial boat. He also proposed to relieve Loison's division at Punhete with the 9th Corps. Taking everything into consideration, he added, the 2nd Corps had received more than 165,000 rations of meat from him. Moreover, herds were sent in great quantity; the Marshal announced that he had found more than 8,000 hundredweight of corn on the Zezere near Castanheira.[13]

13. On February 11 forage columns of the 6th Corps discovered several large

It is correct to say that this new project, circulated among the principal commanders of the army, had started some kind of revolution in their thinking and even in their wills. Thus we were nearly at the point of effecting the great maneuver on the Tagus with every hope of complete success. If we had opposed the movement, it seemed that we would have found ourselves carried by the strength of events. So our many preparations were finished: the results of our reconnaissances and our experiences had been assessed; general agreement for the project had been received in succession by the Prince, the Marshal, Generals Reynier, Éblé, Fririon, etc.; there was evidence of a great success; everything had been determined. After the recent departure of Casabianca, we did not expect any news from France for some time. We were accustomed to the necessity of acting without receiving it. Suddenly we saw General Foy arrive with Colonel Lamour on December 25 [*sic*].[14] They brought a detachment of several hundred men gathered at Ciudad Rodrigo that belonged to various regiments. Rumor magnified the number at first; we thought it was another reinforcement. The arrival of a general of the army who had just received a fine promotion further increased the effect produced by the rumors. All this stirred up a ferment almost as strong as that produced by the arrival of General Drouet.

Here is what General Foy said—at least this is what I thought I overheard, and what the Prince told me. I say "I thought," for later everyone spoke with less assurance. "The Emperor was very satisfied with the operation of the army; its perseverance on the Tagus had served him admirably in maintaining a very vigorous opposition party in England, in retaining the determination of the courts of Europe which were uncertain of the results of this struggle, and in holding around Lisbon an English army which might have moved on other points

grain depots at Castanheira, Alveres, and Pampilhosa totaling 1,760,000 pounds. In addition to these welcome supplies, Ney also informed Masséna, "the detachment I directed on both banks of the Zezere has returned tonight. They have only collected 40 cattle and 1,500 sheep for the first and second division; the third division has 45 cattle and 2,000 sheep. Another detachment of the 2nd Corps collected 1,300 sheep, pigs, and cattle which form about 25,000 rations of meat on the hoof. Thus the 2nd Corps has received in six days . . . a total of 165,000 rations of meat; that is fifteen days' meat." See Bonnal, *Ney*, Ney to Masséna, February 11, 1811, III, 459–60; Ney to Reynier, February 11, 1811, Correspondance: Armée de Portugal, Carton C^{7}11.

14. Foy actually reached the French positions on February 5, with 1,862 men. See Fririon, *Journal historique*, pp. 131–32; Girod de l'Ain, *Foy*, p. 128.

more dangerous for the interests of France. Paris had not expected us to remain in our position until now. There was strong opposition to the march on the Mondego. They desired us to cross the Tagus, occupy both banks, and retain Santarém as long as possible. The siege of Tortosa must be ended now. The Emperor was more certain than ever of a Continental peace, and he even hoped for a general peace. It was almost certain that the Prince of Wales would remove his troops from Portugal or make peace at his accession to the throne or to the regency. Napoleon had been personally assured by Emperor Alexander, but he knew that the Russian court hated him. If Alexander let himself be pushed into war, he had five hundred thousand men ready and he would attack immediately. Two principal objects occupied him—war with Portugal and negotiations with Turkey. Then the Emperor had spoken about the different generals and added, 'I well know that the Prince is not supported, but I can rely only on him for such operations. He thought he could climb these mountains as he had those of Italy in the past. I know that the English army is respectable, commanded by officers full of honor, etc.' "[15]

As usual, the letter from the Major General dated December 22 was not precise in anything and only said that "the Emperor attaches much importance to your holding the enemy in check and to your having bridges on the Zezere and the Tagus." He added that the 9th Corps was assigned to disperse the militia in northern Portugal, that twenty thousand men of the Imperial Guard were to occupy Ciudad Rodrigo and Almeida, and that the 5th Corps would implement the expected diversion and communicate with us.[16] But Marshal Soult, in a letter full of compliments, politeness, devotion, and combined plans, limited himself to the announcement that on January 10 he would be in front

15. During Foy's interview in Paris Napoleon commented on Masséna's relations with his corps commanders: "This insubordination of Ney and Junot is singular. What folly! Junot was a captain and Ney general of brigade when Masséna was commanding the armies." With regard to the Allies, Napoleon observed, "The English are full of courage and honor; they defend themselves well. Masséna and Ney do not know them but Reynier, whom they have beaten two or three times, knows them well. Wellington is admittedly a clever man. This total devastation of a country is cleverly conceived. I would not be able to do that with all my power." Girod de l'Ain, *Foy*, pp. 106–113.

16. Although some of the information in this letter also appeared in Berthier's letter to Masséna dated December 4, 1810, the specific letter Pelet refers to could not be found in any of the published correspondence of Napoleon, Berthier, Masséna, etc., the Correspondance: Armée de Portugal, or the Archives de Masséna.

of Badajoz with a considerable siege train (which only prevented him from going any farther). According to a letter from General Belliard this siege would commence on the 12th.[17] Therefore we had to make up our minds to wait until it pleased God to allow the siege to end. As for the announced reinforcements, they were kept so far away from us that if they ever arrived, we could consider them as being absolutely extraneous to our operations. There was another letter from the Prince de Neufchâtel to General Drouet in which His Highness complained of the inaction of the 9th Corps, which was supposed to disperse the militia, scour the country, assure our communications and provisions, and give news of the army.

On the previous day I had had orders to go to the 2nd Corps. I took all this news and the Major General's letter to communicate to General Reynier. Then we took care of his provisions. They complained of terrible misery—first he and then his generals. It was good to know that the Prince had given the Marshal orders to relieve the 2nd Corps. The Marshal had replied that he was ready, but he wrote to General Reynier requesting him to waive his request. In order to please him, the General wrote an evasive and dilatory letter to His Excellency. The Marshal then proposed a reserve of two regiments of his army corps.[18] In addition, the Prince asked him to form a depot of 330,000 pounds of corn, and he himself would add a few hundredweight. The Marshal accepted. I carried this proposed arrangement to

17. Count Auguste Daniel Belliard (1769–1832) was attached to a national guard unit in 1791 and the following year fought at Valmy and Jemappes. He served as Sérurier's chief of staff in 1796 and fought at Castiglone, Caldiero, and Arcola. After service with Joubert's division in Italy and Desaix's division in Egypt, Belliard was promoted to general of division. As Murat's chief of staff, he was at Austerlitz, Jena, Eylau, and Friedland. In 1808 Belliard went to Spain as Murat's chief of staff and served in this capacity for Joseph's Army of the Center.

18. On January 31 Masséna requested Ney to begin preparations to replace the 2nd Corps at Santarém. In response Ney pointed out, "This measure, especially if carried out in bad weather, will be sufficient to destroy the supplies of the regiments and place us in misery greater than that of the 2nd Corps." Ney suggested that Reynier's foragers be sent into the fertile area of Ourém. Ney also wrote to Reynier, "It seems infinitely more suitable to me to establish detachments of your corps at Ourém, Pombal . . . where they can send all the supplies they procure to Santarém while I, for my part, will place one or two infantry regiments in reserve and at your disposition. . . . I hope that you believe as I do, that it is in the interest of both our corps not to change our position at this moment." Reynier responded, "I am extremely grateful for the aid that you have given me in order to aid the 2nd Corps. . . . It would be unfortunate to prolong our position much longer." See Bonnal, *Ney,* Masséna to Ney, January 31; Ney to Masséna and Reynier, February 1; Reynier to Ney, February 1, 1811, III, 449–53.

General Reynier; it was not agreeable to him. He complained in the presence of his generals and colonels. Then I said in front of him and everyone else that he had not wanted to be relieved. There was a very vigorous altercation, and they were after me like a swarm of hornets. There was another discussion about his passage to the island of Boa Vista, now separated by a large branch of the Tagus; the enemy could garrison it completely with infantry and artillery in a single night, deployed for a distance of twelve to fourteen hundred yards. The General defended his opinion with stubbornness and inflexibility. I attacked it in the same mode. I showed him my plan, but because of his attitude he found it poor.

The next day I returned to the General's quarters in a much better mood, for bad humor damaged everything. I listened to his miseries. With the prospect of future operations in which he could play some part, I was able to induce him quietly to decide that if we acted immediately, it would be better if he stayed in position with some help; however, if we wanted to hold Santarém for an extended period, he would have to be relieved—a reasonable proposition that he had not wanted to hear about the day before. Then he returned to his project for Boa Vista. I explained my plan completely and ended by reading it to him. He strongly approved of all its dispositions. We selected the arsenal as a favorable location for the bridge site and the establishment of the artillery, since some batteries had already been there, and finally we noted troop positions on the heights toward the Rio Maior. We agreed on the fortifications to be made to reinforce this position. These works were limited to a few things on the left and abatis on the plain—the most dangerous point. He considered the heights to be unassailable if defended by four divisions with a detachment established near Ponte Calhariz, but by this bridge, or by a nearby ford, the enemy could easily march from Rio Maior to Santarém. What is more, three to four divisions and all the cavalry remained to be directed against Hill. The General agreed that Lord Wellington, threatened on the left, would extend himself on this side, that he would not be able to defend the bank of the Tagus opposite Santarém, that he would not attack, and finally that Hill would be outflanked and withdraw as fast as possible. Moreover, Wellington would be forced to withdraw at least to Vilafranca in fear of an operation on his rear, similar to the first one, if he remained in Cartaxo. I looked at his maps again. General Clauzel had given him a drawing of the area between Leiria and Rio Maior; it was found in the countryside and it confirmed our plans.

I went and looked at the Tagus. The waters were very high, the canal at Alpiarça was flooded, and the English posts on the bank no longer had any communication with Almeirim. Thus, if we made the crossing now, we would not have a hundred Englishmen in front of us, but the operation against Hill would be lost and the magazines of Almeirim, Chamusca, etc., would be burned. I saw Colonels Donnadieu and Desgraviers of the 47th Line and 4th Léger. One had one-fourth ration of corn and one-fourth of a pound of meat per day for his men, and the other had full rations for fifteen days. Talking about various things, we settled everything between us. I returned leisurely through Pernes. I found the Duc completely recovered from his wound. The roads and especially the field of Golegã were impassable because of the mud. General Reynier, writing to the Prince, added by postscript that my project was very good. The day before, when he sent me to Santarém, the Prince had told me, "I am going to send one of my horses to your stable. You use you horses enough for me." He added, "I wish I could give you enough." I was amazed with admiration and satisfaction; so was everyone else about the affair and the moment he had chosen. He immediately sent me the beautiful mare he rode at the battle of Essling.

When I returned from Santarém, I found General Foy repeating nearly the same details [of his instructions from Paris] which I wrote down in my Journal; I believe I transcribed them literally. But as the days went by it seemed to the Prince that the instructions were losing their tenor and positivity. Finally, they appeared very different to His Excellency when he asked to have them written out two days later.[19] Moreover, any of us might have altered these very important reports somewhat by our preoccupation with our own projects and positions. The officers coming from Paris might have neglected to record them immediately. There was also the influence that was always exercised by strongly pronounced opinions, questions, and decisions of important people. Finally, as a result of the vagueness that was necessarily introduced into ideas by a considerable lapse of time spent during a perilous journey, new ideas were naturally introduced. I myself ex-

19. Foy's letter to Masséna dated February 7, 1811, reiterated what Berthier's letters had already stated. See Correspondance: Armée de Portugal, Carton C[7]11.

perienced all the difficulties of this position a few weeks later. Did General Foy exercise his influence on the spirit of the army and most of the *état major,* whom he visited as soon as he arrived, especially those whom he found imbued with the difficulties of the crossing and so opposed in reality to the operations on the Tagus? It is also necessary to mention that vagueness always existed in the orders of the government (this could not be otherwise at such distances in time as well as in miles) and that it was even greater in conversations and verbal instructions, which created immense difficulties of precise and positive wording. Finally, the Prince seemed to want to cloak his responsibility with that of General Foy by obtaining precise orders or formal instructions from him. It was possible for the general to avoid this extremity by relying completely on the sense of the written instruction of the Major General.

Whatever the case may have been, the rumor that the passage had been ordered, or at least desired, by the government circulated so quickly and acquired such credit that the opposition was silenced for a while. At first even they felt compelled to announce themselves ostentatiously in favor of the project they had opposed so strongly. The most recalcitrant now wanted to have always been for the crossing, but the fervor soon declined. As soon as they recognized the vagueness and uncertainty that existed in the instructions, and saw that nothing was changed in their position or in ours, the same feelings and interests resumed all their influence. They even gained new vigor, as always happened. Soon they no longer refrained from saying that it was necessary to withdraw the army to Spain and reestablish ourselves there. They acquired a new protagonist, for General Foy ended up by declaring against the crossing, and he even bragged that he had changed General Reynier's opinion.

When I arrived at Torres Novas, I found the Prince very irritated by the uncertainty of the written orders, the vagueness of the verbal instructions, the delay of the promised reinforcements and announced cooperation, the dangers resulting from any operation whatever, the responsibilities that seemed to cling to and weigh on him as he showed greater zeal and devotion, and finally the violation of those promises on whose faith he had come to Portugal. All these considerations, together with those [opinions] that had been repeated continually for so long on the difficulties, the inconveniences, and the dangers of the crossing, on the facilities and advantages of a march on the Mondego, seemed to justify his turning to the easiest and most generally approved operation. Thus the Prince appeared to be quite far from the first and quite disposed toward the other. Even before the first overture he made to me, I argued vigorously. I proved to him that his reputation, that of the army, and that of France were involved in his decision. I insisted. I pressed forward.

The Prince proceeded from two plans which I tried to prove were inexact—the extreme difficulty of the crossing and the impossibility of holding, by means of two bridgeheads, both banks of the Tagus with our strength. I opposed the plans, the reasoning, and the fears. I pointed out that Europe had its eyes glued on the two armies. The first army had left its position, reputedly vanquished; the enemy proclaimed our retreat. I observed clearly that soon after we marched to the Mondego we would be forced to move to Oporto or Spain. The only objection against Alentejo was the lack of communication with Spain, blocked by the fortresses, but now it seemed that they were definitely coming to seize them for us and open the gates. If we waited for the arrival of the 5th Corps, the impression would be given it was rescuing us, while we could make a brilliant operation and thus crown it by a campaign which would be inglorious without it. If we could not reach Hill, we could still execute a great and spirited battle with the flight of the English from the right flank, the certain capture of a few men, a few cannon, wagons, sick, etc.

Nevertheless, the Prince complained angrily; he had not heard of the arrival of any troops after it had been announced that the 9th Corps, the Young Guard, the 3rd Corps, the Army of Interior, and finally the 5th Corps would come, and more specifically, he had seen the army which was expected to approach the Tagus starting a siege far away. Instead of being posted either at Espinhel or Castelo Branco to assure our communications by either route and to help the army if needed, Claparède's division had been sent quite uselessly to the Douro. His Excellency wanted this division to be placed at Castelo Branco and Sarzedas to support the bridgehead on the right bank of the Tagus while the Young Guard, cantoned near Almeida and Rodrigo, would have been sufficient to assure Beira Alta. In this matter, the Prince was unquestionably correct in complaining about the orders that had been given, and there was nothing to say to him in reply. Yet these orders were secret, while his conduct would be public and the only thing known of this campaign. Thus I said everything my enthusiasm and devotion could inspire, even more than they seemed to permit. But I could see the good and the evil, and I could not keep silent. The Prince told me that one should not get impassioned about the project. I answered that one must be very devoted to his person to dare to argue so much with him and to oppose so vigorously the opinion of everyone surrounding him and, in some way, assume all the responsibility of it. He came back at me with the uncertain answers to the precise questions that he had asked General Foy. Finally, he ended by saying he wanted to have the reports of the marines and the artillery and see the generals before making up his mind. Then I exclaimed, "You will cross." As he returned, I held him back and said, "As a last resort, if the marines, the artillery, and the troops find the passage possible, it must be executed; otherwise, we cannot do it!" In the evening all this led us to discuss plans for a movement on the Mondego.

The Prince was being pushed toward Oporto. I opposed this with all my strength. In everything, I was concerned only about the good of the campaign and not about myself at all. I did not forget that one of the principal leaders of the opposition would give me a great sum of money if we went to Oporto. My fortune was very limited, but I was a thousand leagues above such temptation.

I presented the difficulties involved in crossing the Mondego River. I proposed that Coimbra be invested in advance and that the region beyond be invaded by the cavalry. In regard to the positions to be taken, the principal corps would be at Coimbra, one near Murcella, and one toward the Côa in Beira. Later on there would be the possibility of moving on Alcántara and the Tagus. Then the morning's conversation was resumed, as vigorously on my part and less eagerly on his. I spoke about the ease of making the crossing now, risking only the boats, and the impossibility of the enemy opposing it in front of Santarém because of the flooding of Almeirim. This truncated project was not without inconvenience, but it was better than nothing. I had received a favorable report from Major Reynaud on the subject of the embarkation, the departure, and the conduct of the boats. I gave it to the Prince.

We talked of movements on the enemy line and the burning of the magazines beyond the Tagus, which made us hope that there were a few detachments ahead of the 5th Corps. A spy told us that Lord Wellington had ordered the inhabitants of the unoccupied regions, under the most severe penalties, to destroy and burn everything,[20] and the others to prepare to return to the districts we then occupied. These first orders, executed rigorously by soldiers, disaffected the inhabitants very much. We ran to look at those enemy fires, and we saw nothing. I wished to God that they would make a movement, for the Prince was ready to attack them on either side of the Tagus, and everything was prepared for that. But they kept on working carelessly across from Punhete. They erected new epaulements and some kind of a battery there. The Prince gave orders to General Loison to reconnoiter beyond Abrantes on the bank of the Tagus.

General Foy returned from Marshal Ney's quarters. After all possible pledges were given to the Prince at Punhete, the Marshal told Foy in these very terms, "I have guaranteed that I will cross the Tagus, but not that I will maintain myself on the other side." The Prince asked the general for a written report on his mission to Paris. The general, thinking of everything he might forget to put down, got out of it with much cleverness, writing in vague generalities; he delivered reports which only paraphrased the instructions of the Major General. The latter seemed bound to have rendered them even more vaguely than usual. Meanwhile, all the inferences of General Foy were against the crossing of the Tagus. The same day General Éblé and the marines came to give their report. The indifference of the Prince discouraged them a little. Major Reynaud said to me, "I can see quite clearly that he does not care." However, the report was very favorable to the feasibility of the operation.

20. With regard to the defense of Alentejo, Wellington wrote to Stuart on January 16, "I propose to keep Beresford's corps, or at all events a part of it, on the left of the Tagus as long as possible, in order, if I can, to save the Alentejo, though I shall not be surprised if the French were to make a great attempt to pass the Tagus before, or at the same time that they should attack us on the right of the river. The Government, therefore, should still persevere in their endeavors to prevail upon the inhabitants of the Alentejo to remove their property within the lines, and out of the enemy's reach." See *Wellington's Dispatches,* VII, 147–49.

Chapter Eleven

THE RETREAT IS DETERMINED

Among the causes that contributed to the ruin of our venture in Spain, the most important was the lack of centralization in military operations, which often furnished excellent details but were usually counterproductive. In the absence of this basic problem, the gold, the intrigues, and the help of England would have been insufficient [to ruin us]. The diversion from the north would have been too late and the resistance of the Spaniards terminated as soon as Joseph's army began to form. Aragon and Andalusia were tranquil, and the *civicos* carried on the services in the cities, escorting couriers and sometimes defending the countryside against the guerrillas. If there had been a joint center of action, which alone could have combined movements and produced considerable results, our operations would have been reduced to a limited number of points—the two extremities of the Ebro, Lisbon, and Cadiz, which would have been linked to France by a telegraph line. Operations would have been conducted successively, beginning with the expulsion of the English. Then the end of 1810 would have seen the end of the Spanish war or at least its final effort at the siege of Cadiz. Napoleon alone had sufficient strength and genius to undertake this vast scheme, restrain the differences among his marshals, and force them to work toward coordinated results. If, despite the affection of the Italian people and all the good he accomplished for them, Prince Eugène had been moved to Spain, or if, in his absence,

Jérôme[1] had been sent instead of Joseph; if only Marshal Jourdan had been given the necessary authority as major general and if his efforts had not been constantly thwarted by the King's weakness, events in Spain would have taken a completely different course. Marshal Jourdan had enjoyed brilliant glory during our earlier triumphs.[2] I do not know what intrigues have since minimized them. I had worked for several months as an engineer in the administration of His Excellency, and I doubt if any of our marshals understood the science of war as well as he.

Napoleon realized quite well that he could not direct the war from four hundred leagues away. He found himself continually deceived by inexact reports, whether by statements initially untrue or ultimately by unpredictable changes of events and the armies. Thus his orders reflected this distance and were often contradictory. Eventually instructions were almost impossible because of the multitude of diverse possibilities. General orders were necessarily vague in order to provide enough leeway and freedom for the various armies and prevent them from impeding each other. If there had been too many orders, the armies would have ceased to complement and assist each other. As a result, latitude was given to the commanders. In the same way, there

1. Prince Eugène Rose de Beauharnais (1781–1824) joined the French army in 1796 and served on Napoleon's staff in Italy and Egypt. With the establishment of the Empire he was made general of brigade; in 1805 he was proclaimed Viceroy of Italy. In 1809 Eugène was given command of the Army of Italy, and he won the battle of Raab. He served at Wagram and went through the Russian campaign, but in 1813 he returned to Italy to assume command of the Army of Italy. He signed a truce with the Austrians in the following year and relinquished his title of Viceroy of Italy.

Prince Jérôme Bonaparte (1784–1860) went to sea in 1800 and two years later was given command of the *Epervier*. He served in the Prussian campaign and in 1807 was made King of Westphalia. Jérôme commanded the right wing of the Grand Army in 1812; however, he quit his post when he was placed under the command of Davout in June 1812. Jérôme served at Waterloo and was made a marshal in 1850.

Pelet comments in a footnote, "General opinion was not very favorable to these two individuals. I have had the honor to serve with both and knew them quite well. Prince Jérôme showed much activity and had very sound ideas at the beginning of the Russian campaign. He left the army only for honorable reasons."

2. Count Jean Baptiste Jourdan (1762–1833) enlisted in 1778 and served in America until 1782. He became a captain in a national guard unit in 1789 and four years later was general of division. Jourdan became a marshal in 1804 and ended his career in the foreign affairs ministry in 1830. He commanded in the Low Countries and Germany during the war of the First Coalition. He was elected to the Council of Five Hundred, served as ambassador to the Cisalpine Republic, and was King Joseph's "major general" at the battles of Talavera and Vitoria.

was no liaison between the major and minor operations, and each was directed according to its purposes and special interests. Thus there were a few partial successes everywhere but no sustained progress toward the invasion of Portugal. Moreover, there was a vast area of uncertainty and divagation in the verbal communications carried by officers on mission; their communications lost all positivity and tenor during the journeys. It was impossible for these officers to state precisely what they had missed during a conversation and which sometimes contradicted the written instructions. This had already happened to Casabianca and to General Foy. It was to happen to me a little later because my notions of the army's position were entirely opposite to what was believed in Paris.

The defect of centralization was felt even more in our area than in the south of Spain, where our attacks were more determined and the enemy's means of defense much less considerable. It had already resulted in failure during the maneuvers at Talavera and in the expedition of Marshals Soult and Victor against Portugal, if Victor's maneuver ever took place.[3] Now the digressions of the corps [5th Corps, etc.] which were to have supported us ended by draining the final resolution of the Prince and resulted in our withdrawal from Portugal. Using all the latitude the Prince had given me, but strictly fulfilling my responsibilities, I fought [for the Tagus crossing] as long as the last ray of hope remained, until the time of the great conference at Golegã. Each day brought new discussions about the passage between His Excellency and myself, but the following one is the last I will report, because they are heartrending for me and their multiplicity would make them tiring for the reader.

General Reynier requested boats to forage the island of Boa Vista and search for food there. He returned to the project of [crossing at] Santarém, praising it in all its aspects and saying that it conformed more closely than all the others to the instructions of the Major General because it would hold the enemy in check. He also talked about

3. After the expulsion of John Moore's army in January 1809, Napoleon ordered Soult to invade Portugal from the north, seize Oporto, and advance on Lisbon. Simultaneously, Victor was to march his corps from Mérida into Portugal in support of Soult. Pelet was skeptical about this plan and comments in a footnote, "It is difficult to believe that we seriously wanted to conquer Portugal by attacking it from its two extremes—the Minho and Alentejo. If this were true, we made a great mistake unless we wanted to profit by the first confusion."

the probability of overtaking Hill. The Prince decided to send him six boats. I could not refrain from telling him that this would alert the enemy and that as a result it would be necessary to renounce everything. Finally I said that for such a mission we should send fifteen boats and make a great forage by means of a flying bridge opposite Santarém between the Tagus and the flooded stream of Alpiarça, since the enemy could not cross it. Our discussion of the crossing began again as usual, because I could not resign myself to the idea of returning to Spain. I still maintained that we could not leave Portugal; we must retain at least one well-established foothold there. Anything appeared preferable to a retrograde movement.

The Prince spoke to me more vigorously about his disgust, the vexations of his command, and the bad organization of the army. From what he told me of the situation, there were not then more than twenty-eight thousand infantry in the 2nd, 6th, and 8th Corps, from which a thousand men had to be deducted because they were sick, disabled, and wounded. They had been collected at Tomar to be returned to France. General Fririon asserted that at least one-sixth to one-eighth of the infantry were noncombatants attached to the equipment train or were without arms. This reduced the available infantry to twenty-four thousand men. The cavalry was not numerous. Its horses had been eating green forage for a long time and were weakened from hauling grain. The horses of the artillery were in the most miserable state.

I continued to tell the Prince that it was better to leave the command rather than to be left by it. If he was so tired, he should withdraw the army from its poor position and then present his requirements to the government. But the only proper way to get out of the position was to cross the Tagus. Finally, as my last response, I repeated the proposition of throwing a bridge behind the flooding Alpiarça and then at least waiting in our positions for answers to Casabianca's dispatches, since he had already been gone for a long time. The Prince was also inclined toward this last opinion. Moreover, he claimed, as did a few of our people, that the enemy were interested in allowing us to cross in order to have a river between them and us. "Yes, but at Coimbra there would also be the Mondego River [between the two armies], and you would not be able to live there very long," [I responded]. "The government will send convoys," [the Prince said]. "It would be even easier through Alentejo and I would rather go to the

Guadiana than to the Mondego." "How can we straddle the Tagus?" [asked the Prince]. "It is possible with a good system of bridgeheads at Punhete." "But then we cannot hold the enemy in check and advance toward them in case of a movement on their part." "We can do so by keeping the bridgeheads if they deliver battle, but we have no indication they would do so there or anywhere else; moreover, a withdrawal behind the works and the river is always assured." The Prince finally became angry and said that making a plan was nothing—the execution was everything! (Alas! If I were able to execute mine and then give up everything.) Finally, since the government had announced that the 5th Corps would arrive, he would cross if they came; otherwise he would not. He added that the future would tell us who was right. The quartermaster general arrived as the Prince was shouting like a demon and pounding heavily on the table. When the quartermaster left, the Prince took my hand and said, "Believe me, my dear friend, I do have very strong reasons to sacrifice this bridge which has cost me so much and for which I have waited so long." "Monsieur le maréchal, these reasons must be quite strong because the sacrifice is very great." As for General Reynier's expedition, it was giving up a kingdom for a few oxen. The Prince called me back and told me, "I will not have time to prepare the order of march for Coimbra because General Junot is coming. You must do it yourself." He knew that after this very brisk discussion, everything was ended and I would work with the same devotion and complete sacrifice for the new project, although I had vigorously opposed it.

The Prince did not talk about this topic any longer, but his decision had been made only after the most thoughtful and deep reflection. For a few days he looked troubled and anxious, but he escaped various distractions by working on his business continually. He was not worried about his position but about his reputation and that of his army. Moreover, it was not difficult to guess what the important reasons were that stopped him; they were to be found in the morale of the troops, which he judged as a deeply experienced man, rather than in the operation itself. First of all, there were whatever ideas he had on the intrinsic value of the various army corps, the merit of most of his generals, and the spirit and particular character of each of his corps commanders. In the next place, there was the memory of what had happened during the earlier battles at the Côa, Celorico, and Bussaco; the just fears which he could conceive and which unfortunately materialized later; the genuine difficulties of the operation, which at several separate points demanded the bravest troops, the talent and devotion of all the commanders, and the most perfect harmony; and the universal opinion raised against the passage since its inception. Lastly, I also believed that his disgust at this type of war influenced him, as well as a degree of rancor against our government.

After casting him into the middle of a sea of danger and misery, the government allowed him to fight there without assistance; they had the audacity to point out that he should push his forbearance and the sufferings of his army to the last extreme, while they were far away. Now that I think about this more calmly and with a few more years of cruel experience and very harsh lessons, I no longer dare to decide myself which was right—this high and consummate experience, or a firm but perhaps too ardent zeal. Nevertheless, I persisted in believing that the operation [crossing the Tagus] was feasible and even easy at either point. With excellent troops, well commanded or with perfect cooperation, it would have had the most brilliant results. But if Marshal Ney attacked as poorly as he had at Bussaco, if he abandoned the position ordered, either ahead or behind, as at Freixedas, Condeixa, and Celorico, if General Reynier allowed his comrades and allies to be killed quietly as on the Alva, at Fuentes de Oñoro, etc., if Junot did even worse than that, as he threatened, then this operation could have produced the most fatal results for the army and perhaps for our affairs in Spain. For often the most noble projects have had the most fatal consequences. It would have been necessary for the Prince to conduct his divisions himself, but could he do so?

General Éblé started to protest immediately about the boats that the Prince wished to send to the 2nd Corps. He was given orders to organize all the preparations to throw up the bridge or burn the boats at a moment's notice.[4] The general had the artillery *chef d'état major*, Colonel Fontenay, reconnoiter the ways to cross at Santarém; they were easy and excellent. General Drouet continued asking to leave because of provisions. The Prince induced him to remain until February 25. Cavailher and Richoux gave the Prince a survey of the vicinity of

4. Masséna wrote to Éblé on February 19, "Do not waste a minute in making all your preparations for the passage of the Tagus or for the destruction of the bridge equipment." See Girod de l'Ain, *Grands Artilleurs*, p. 454.

Punhete on a scale of 1 to 20,000th. It was one of the most excellent pieces of topography that could have been done, and they deserved His Excellency's sound compliments. Cavailher then went to reconnoiter the region of Chão de Macãs and Richoux went toward Leiria. General Ferey had orders to make another reconnaissance on Vila Velha, between Vila Flor and Montalvão, to obtain news of the 5th Corps. This reconnaissance furnished no information. Later Ferey was told to invest Abrantes in such a way that the garrison could not advance in our direction.

Meanwhile the Prince ordered one of the bridge boats to go down the Tagus from Punhete to Santarém to determine if navigation was possible. After the decision he had made, this useless experiment might have become a subject of reproach. I opposed it in vain. Parmentier descended as I have already mentioned, and no one opened fire on him. The trip to Santarém took him twelve hours, from eight o'clock in the evening until eight o'clock in the morning, for he did not know the river. He was forced to land six times, but he promised to pilot the following expeditions and to conduct them in much less time. As a matter of duty, I opposed the trip. Yet I hoped for its success with all my heart. Unable to accompany our argonaut on his trip, my dear friend Beaufort and I went a rather long distance during the evening to hear if there were any shots as he passed.

On orders from the Prince, I busied myself with the dispositions for our retrograde maneuver on Pombal and the Mondego. Its execution was very delicate at the right end of our line, which was extended considerably in a direction parallel to the line; after all, the maneuver was in the midst of very difficult and mountainous terrain. First, it was necessary to implement a ninety-degree pivot along the entire front, with the left wing behind, in order to place the army in a direction nearly perpendicular to the line of retreat. This move, already quite complicated in itself and executed in front of an enemy greatly superior in number and warned in advance by our preparations, became more dangerous because an attack on the middle of our columns, especially through Leiria, would occasion the most grave difficulties. To throw us back on the Zezere, or at least on the road to Espinhal and consequently on Spain, Lord Wellington would only have had to unite the troops on his left near Leiria, which was the closest point to us, and occupy the axis of our pivot. This strategic point, on which all the maneuvers of our army necessarily revolved, was not as close as we were to Pombal and Coimbra. Therefore it was necessary to establish, before anything else, a force of resistance at Leiria to prepare a defense for the center during its maneuver. Above all, it was necessary to paralyze the movements of the enemy and check them in the center of their position by keeping them in complete uncertainty regarding the goal of our maneuver or by menacing them on various points. To do so, we had to threaten the enemy simultaneously on both wings of their long broken line by taking advantage of our interior lines of operation. The preparations made at Punhete either to erect or to burn the bridge were to be continued openly in a way to threaten an immediate crossing. Those pieces of wood kept one-third of the English army there until the last moment.

People who were not able to see the details of the maneuver claimed that the pontoons were burned two days before our departure. They were very wrong. The movement was started on March 5, but the pontoons were burned only on the 7th.[5] At the other end an attack was prepared on the weakest segment of the enemy line; their left was necessarily weakened because they would have moved troops to the right and the center. Such an attack could have driven in the entire position of the Rio Maior and forced their left behind Moinho Novo. The movements in our center would take place around the Serra de Midé [Aire], which occupied the middle and a good part of the terrain between Leiria and Punhete. Subordinated first to one and then to the other of the two demonstrations, they would be directed in such a way that when the enemy discovered our retreat, he would not know immediately whether it was executed on either bank of the Zezere or on Coimbra. Everything was foreseen and calculated gradually, everything would be measured step by step, and the well-balanced plan would be ready for any eventuality. By the third day the maneuver would be unmasked and ended and the bridge burned. The army would be concentrated between Tomar and Leiria in a manner to sustain an enemy attack or to commence its regular retrograde march in front of the enemy.

5. According to Pelet's order of march, Loison's infantry and Lamotte's cavalry would only withdraw from Punhete on March 7, after Éblé's bridge equipment and boats were fired. For details of the French withdrawal see "Ordre de marche sur Pombal, Ancião, et Espinhal," March 1, 1811, Correspondance; Armée de Portugal, Carton C[7]12.

These dispositions were prepared and executed as I have indicated. However, before starting this movement it was first necessary to assure ourselves of the bridge at Coimbra. I continued to say that the Mondego, which was almost dry when we saw it in September, would now be a violent river. This second part of my retrograde project received some alterations. I proposed to direct the 9th Corps with four regiments of cavalry, commanded by General Montbrun, from Pombal toward Espinhal and the Mondego; they would cross that river at the ford of Penacova or at the bridge of São João de Rei, then move on the mountain of Bussaco and send the cavalry on the plain of Coimbra to open the passage. The 2nd Corps would repair to Espinhal, the 8th Corps would go to form a reserve near Condeixa, and the 6th Corps would be at Redinha, with its right at Soure, its left near Penela, and its advance guard at Pombal. The 6th Corps would maintain itself as long as possible in this position and later concentrate at Redinha and Condeixa. Then the 8th Corps, crossing the Mondego, would establish itself to the right and left of Coimbra. The 2nd Corps would be on the Alva, with its right on the Mondego and its left toward the mountains. The 9th Corps would move near Viseu; the cavalry would extend to the Vouga. In retaining Pombal or at least Redinha, the 6th Corps would support the 2nd Corps, placed in such a way that the enemy could not move on the frontier of Spain by the left bank of the Mondego nor on the rear of the army.

Such were the dispositions with which I developed the plan that we had agreed upon. The first part of the strategic work was most beautiful and difficult and could not be contested. Like most of the schemes set up and planned, when it was finished this one was later found completely developed in the dispatch of the Major General, made on February 26 [*sic*] and given to General Foy on March 5 [*sic*].[6] For the second part, each page of my Journal and every conversation with the Prince presented the same question—how would we cross the Mondego? The Prince recalled the picture of this river as it had looked during our passage, and he could not imagine that it would have changed appearance so much. He was much more concerned about the difficulties of our maneuver. The Prince believed that he would need all his forces to execute it and was convinced that a single regiment of

6. Apparently Pelet is referring to Berthier's letter of March 29, 1811. See Jones, *Journals of Sieges*, III, 206–8.

the 9th Corps would be sufficient for the expedition to Coimbra. But this regiment was refused him at a crucial moment, as we shall see later on.

Another subject no less important, which was discussed for a long time, was a meeting of the corps commanders. The Prince had had this kind of conference in mind for several days. Again I had the misfortune not to share his point of view on this matter. At first I was afraid that those gentlemen would gather, as they already had at Bussaco, in order to force the hand of the commander in chief. I knew that most of them supported my project, but I opposed the meeting nevertheless. I also remembered that according to Eugène and the great Frederick,[7] a general had only to hold a council of war to accomplish nothing. This idea has always set me against that kind of ceremony. I have never been able to understand how anything that should be directed and conducted by a single head could be combined and discussed by many. The Prince resolved it himself only with much trouble. Nevertheless, the gravity of the circumstances in which we found ourselves decided it. He had them convene at Golegã to propose three possibilities: to remain, to cross, or to withdraw. The date was fixed for February 18. I again permitted myself some observations on the place of the meeting, which should have been only at His Excellency's quarters or at Punhete, and on the fact that General Drouet had not been invited. The Prince had a good answer for everything, but General Drouet remembered the omission quite well and proved it by his conduct afterwards. It was one more deficiency in consideration and politeness which was to cost the Prince a great deal later on.

We reached the most critical moment at this conference; it was to decide our fate. The Prince sent me to Punhete [on February 17] to examine in great detail the actual condition of our works, those of the enemy, and what we could learn or judge of the forces they held there,

7. Prince Eugène of Savoy (1663–1736) entered the military under the Hapsburgs in 1683 and took part in the defense of Vienna and the capture of Belgrade. He destroyed a Turkish army at Zenta and during the War of Spanish Succession won the battle of Turin. Sharing command with Marlborough, Eugène participated in the battles of Blenheim, Oudenarde, and Malplaquet and became one of the most brilliant soldiers in Austrian history.

Frederick II, King in Prussia (1712–86), violated the Pragmatic Sanction and went to war against Maria Teresa in the War of Austrian Succession (1740–48). In 1756 fighting was renewed in the Seven Years War. In this protracted struggle Frederick retained Silesia. His numerous successful battles in these wars earned him the sobriquet "Frederick the Great."

with orders to come and join him at Golegã the next day and to make my report in front of the assembled generals. He told me in the morning, "If they are truly for the crossing with all their hearts, we shall cross and I will give my orders for the 24th." I could not ask for anything better than this. Besides, I would talk, discuss, consult, and probably not make my true resolution known. In the morning the Prince sent a messenger, which he believed fairly safe, with a note to Marshal Mortier, pressing him to execute his movement before the first days of March.

Our post at Punhete appeared weaker along the line of the Tagus. Many night and day signals had been established by the enemy, and they were frequently used. There were a few workers at the new battery. We could count eight embrasures that had been staked out. The enemy were constructing the fourth battery; it swept the Zezere and its bridge of boats perfectly. The three others were also on the slope of the mountain along the Tagus, and all were directed toward the mouth of the Zezere. They had [eight], two, four, and seven, or a total of twenty-one embrasures; we could see only gabions and a few epaulements along the bank, but not a single cannon. Moreover, there were few sentries and even fewer [soldiers] walking around. Colonel Jean Pierre Bechaud wrote from the advance post that he had seen two red columns of 1,000 to 1,200 men each, coming up the bank opposite Montalvão. The next day we thought we saw some kind of review at Chamusca to which those troops might have been going. The enemy placed a few workers in the cove where the first debarkation was going to take place. At first we thought they were making an entrenchment; later we recognized that it was probably some repairs on the road.

On the night of February 15–16 two marines with a boat deserted from Punhete without our being able to learn the reason for their action. They did not know how to read or write. One was an old sailor and the other a glib talker from Paris. They probably furnished the enemy with some vital details about our bridge equipment, about the wagons that had been constructed, four of which were already loaded with their boats, and about the newly repaired road from which the enemy could quite easily infer the new dispositions for the bridges. The deserters might have talked about the departure of Captain Parmentier in the trial boat, but they were ignorant of the goal of his expedition, and Parmentier had not yet reappeared at Punhete. A few days earlier the most trustworthy of our guides, named Ignacio, who had constantly followed us on our missions around Punhete and during the survey at the confluence [of the Zezere], had likewise deserted.[8] With such men it was easy for the enemy to get precise information about our work and even something about our plans. The two marines must have confirmed their ideas about the establishment of the bridge above Punhete. In that case, if we had made the expedition from Santarém, it was a safe wager of a thousand to one that we would have obtained complete success against such preoccupied people. However, what happened to these men, embarked in one of our boats at ten o'clock in the evening, when they threw themselves on the other bank? Only two shots were fired [at them], and one so high that the bullet struck the highest part of Punhete.

General Éblé received me with his usual coolness when I arrived at his works, but it was soon replaced by the most affectionate cordiality. He was preparing for either possibility—to put up or burn his bridge in twenty-four hours. His artillery horses were dying like flies. We could not even move the wagons, the number of which had been reduced by the latest task; it was necessary to reduce them even further. We had been forced to destroy one of our guns; the gun carriage had been burned and the gun was spiked and, I believe, buried; it was the only artillery piece that remained in Portugal. The Prince had the dragoon horses collected for Éblé, but they were of little help because of their deterioration and inability to pull. He then put at Éblé's disposition the horses of the *cantinières* or others who exceeded the number fixed by regulation.

During supper a story about an unfortunate Portuguese peasant was told. The man wanted to join a conversation between the English and French posts, who were bragging about the good wine of the country,

8. On February 24 Wellington wrote to Beresford about a deserter, perhaps the guide referred to as Ignacio: "A deserter came in yesterday from Santarem, a Spanish creole, belonging to the marine, who has been attached to the 2d corps, which he joined about two months ago with Gardanne. He says that the enemy have in a wood, just above Santarem, two bridges, as he calls them; and another at Santarem, at which he says he had been employed at work." Reynier's aide-de-camp, who had occasion to talk with Wellington, told him "that the man who deserted lately in a boat is a robber and a murderer. He is the Spanish creole whom I sent to you. He is at all events, a liar of the first magnitude." See *Wellington's Dispatches,* Wellington to Beresford, February 24, 28, 1811, VII, 313–14, 321–22.

and he said to our soldiers, "If you drink good wine, you have plundered it from us." The English started beating him black and blue. The English were never wanting in politeness when it came to thrashing those who insulted us. A terrible lesson for those people who depended on others for their arms and defense. They saw themselves pillaged and beaten by their friends and by their enemies. I had again encountered those unfortunate bands of Portuguese. Orderlies took them to search for their miserable food in the woods; they ate wild fruits, acorns, grass, and blackberries as a last resort. They were crowded into a few poor huts in each village and died there from sickness and hunger.

I went to Golegã with General Éblé. The posts on the Tagus seemed to him to be entirely empty. In general, everyone agreed that there were fewer troops. The plain of Golegã had sufficient grass, and all the army horses, at least those for several leagues around, were eating it, although we were quite afraid of the effects. When the Prince had gathered the commanders, he called on me for the report he had ordered. General Foy arrived. He said, in résumé, "The Emperor is too far away to be able to direct this war himself. He can only indicate what he desires, and it is that we remain as close as possible to the English, that we separate as little as feasible when it becomes necessary to withdraw, and that we hold them in check." The Emperor had asked if the army could cross the Tagus. The general had responded that it would be very difficult, even impossible, without enormous effort. The luncheon of these gentlemen was very gay. Ours was very mediocre; to compensate we went to watch the maneuvers of some English and Portuguese battalions with an excellent *état major* on the plain of Chamusca.

The conference was rather long. Finally, the gentlemen left each other in a rather good mood. The Prince spoke to me briefly and sent me to Generals Fririon and Solignac to obtain the details. According to everyone, the Prince started the conversation.[9] General Reynier pro-

9. According to Koch, Masséna first addressed his officers by declaring, "You all know the miserable state of the army. All the resources in the territory that we occupy are exhausted. . . . The cavalry and artillery horses can no longer find food." After describing the increasing strength of the Allies, Masséna pointed out, "The allies, immovable in their positions, seem to be waiting until famine forces us to retire and all this leads me to believe that they will always leave the initial movement to us." See Koch, *Mémoires de Masséna,* VII, 314.

posed and explained my project at Santarém, which he had always supported and fought for. Marshal Ney supported it strongly, while the Duc d'Abrantès said nothing. After General Foy had spoken on the intentions of the Emperor, he said that it would be better to go on to the Mondego than to throw ourselves entirely on the left bank of the Tagus, and that this appeared to conform more to the interest and the purpose of the Emperor. Next General Reynier persisted in his opinion, all the same; the Marshal wavered and the Duc spoke strongly and resolutely against the crossing. The Marshal concluded by saying that either solution was of little importance to him. General Reynier repeated frequently, "It is for you [to decide], Prince." "No, it is for you, General, who can expect something from it." The Marshal claimed that His Excellency did not want to cross in order to avoid joining Soult. The Prince answered, "Whenever the Emperor is absent and his Major General is not sent expressly by him, the command belongs to me above anyone else." General Reynier asserted that we should move toward the 5th Corps, an erroneous notion, and that Soult was expected to have taken Elvas, also false. The General obtained his boats for Boa Vista and wanted to build some [more] at Santarém.

Finally, the Prince concluded in the following way: "The circumstances and I—we will decide whether it is necessary to cross. [If so] you, Marshal, will cross and General Reynier will contain the enemy." General Fririon assured me that we were no longer thinking about [retiring into] Spain. Apparently Loison was the principal plotter of this agitation so that he could leave the army and withdraw. Nevertheless, the question had not been discussed nor thoroughly examined and nothing could be decided—the usual result of conferences. But we saw generally that we could not rely on the men who were there. If the 5th Corps or news about it arrived, that is, if the enemy retired, we would cross; otherwise we would not. Yet they all praised each other, and the Prince, enthusiastically. I was not able to restrain myself any longer when the sad Lazowski said, "We would much prefer to go to Alentejo in order to approach Spain." I ran away. Everything was green and the flowers were blooming around me, but everything was quite dark in the depths of my heart.[10]

10. For details of the conference at Golegã on February 18, the divergent views of the generals, and the various eyewitness reports that conflict with Pelet's account, see Horward, "Invasion of Portugal," pp. 530–35.

That evening the Prince called me. He talked about the secret intentions he had discerned in his three corps commanders, about the limited confidence he could place in them to command their army corps, about the particular organization of the divisions that prevented him from conducting maneuvers himself, about the justifiable distress that all this caused him and that entirely estranged him, not only from a difficult operation, but from one that was not imperative. He finally announced to me that he found himself forced, with the greatest regret, to renounce completely the plan for bridges on the Tagus.[11] What could one respond to such weighty reasons? His Excellency than talked about the possibility of bringing the boats up the Zezere. I had had this idea earlier, but in order to move all our bridge equipment up to the great bend parallel to Espinhal, and to maintain it there, we would have had to hold the position at Espinhal. The difficulties of the river had stopped me. I thought such a move was impossible because of everything that had been said about the river. If it was necessary to communicate from one bank of the Zezere to the other, I suggested the bridge of Pedrógão to His Excellency, but it was impracticable for artillery. I called his attention particularly to the need for organizing equipment for a light bridge on the Mondego, fearing that since we had decided not to cross the Tagus we would be stopped by the Mondego. A fatal prophecy that I did not stop repeating during those final days! At Torres Novas we talked only about the council of war, the decisions made, and the retreat. The quartermaster general came and complained that he had not been summoned to the council and that Lagarde* performed the function of secretary since he was not there. The Prince answered him, "I did not call you there as proof that it was not a council of war, which I could not and did not want to hold."

The seven boats requested by General Reynier descended the Tagus during the night. In seven hours they reached the mouth of the Alviela, where they were to stop, and one boat went down to Santarém, arriving there in eight hours. They had come out of the Zezere without being noticed. There were a few random shots against them and (it was claimed) a few cannon shots opposite Tancos. Of the forty-five

11. On the basis of the reports of the conference at Golegã, it is obvious that Masséna's lieutenants were not in favor of a withdrawal to the Mondego at that time. See "Résumé de la conférence de Gollegan [*sic*]," February 21, 1811, Correspondance: Armée de Portugal, Carton C⁷11; Girod de l'Ain, *Foy*, pp. 129–32.

men, only two were very slightly wounded and they continued to maneuver. When General Reynier made his expedition against Boa Vista, a landing on the left bank of the Tagus took place in ten minutes. Our troops remained [on Boa Vista] six to seven hours without encountering anything from the enemy, yet we had seen signal fires all the way from Abrantes down to below Santarém during the night. Thus before the enemy appeared the bridges could have been finished and our infantry would have been across to the other side using barges or the flying bridges. General Hill finally appeared very late with three or four thousand English and Portuguese soldiers. If he had encountered Ney's infantry and Montbrun's cavalry halfway, what would have happened to him and all those who were following his column? At first only 150 men of the 47th Line landed and later a much larger number because none of those who had arrived wanted to return without firing his gun. Nevertheless, the expedition produced almost nothing. The channel was fordable at that time and most of the herd grazing there was able to escape.[12]

We received contradictory reports from the line, from spies or emissaries, and from deserters. Some reports indicated the arrival of new reinforcements for the English army which, in addition to those coming from Sicily and Malta, would total more than twenty thousand men, of an extraordinary ten-day distribution of biscuits for the enemy, of the concentration of fifteen thousand English at Cartaxo, of much food at Valada, of new English and Portuguese troops at Alcoentre and in front of the 8th Corps, and of the enemy's previously announced intention to act about February 20 and to resolve the campaign by an attack. It was also the time when Lord Wellington ordered the Portuguese peasants to return into the Line under penalty of death. It was said that Wellington, having received carte blanche, had assembled a council where it was believed an attack was decided upon, that he had

12. Parmentier, with 300 men of the 47th Line, seized the island of Boa Vista and found 66,000 to 88,000 pounds of grain and a number of swine, cattle, and sheep which he ordered taken to the French bank of the Tagus. Beresford, who happened to be in the vicinity, realized the implications of the French success immediately; he ordered the English 39th Foot, mounted on horses of a defunct dragoon regiment, and a Portuguese cavalry brigade to cross the narrow channel separating the island from the English bank of the Tagus. Parmentier's men, after making three trips back to their base, were surprised and driven off. See *Wellington's Dispatches,* Wellington to Beresford, February 24, 1811, VII, 313–14; D'Urban, *Peninsular Journal,* pp. 183–84; Koch, *Mémoires de Masséna,* VII, 326–29.

come himself to reconnoiter the bridge site on the Rio Maior at Alfores,* and that his troops had worked there and also on a road from that point to Marmeleira, where ovens were being built. There the numerous excellent roads from Cartaxo, Alcoentre, and Rio Maior ended. Two English regiments were on the other side of the stream of Valle at São João da Ribeira, Azambujeira, and Marmeleira, where General Houston was posted.[13] The enemy still occupied the bridge of Calhariz in strength. Finally, we arrested a Portuguese officer who had been taken prisoner previously; he had broken his parole and deserted. He declared that one of these mornings the general headquarters would be attacked and all the generals killed.

All these reports were probably nothing but rumors, but prudence demanded that we neglect nothing since everything seemed to indicate extensive movements in the Allied army. Nevertheless, since they had waited so long, I could not believe they would resolve to attack us when they saw that we were ready to maneuver in some way and probably to evacuate a country where we could no longer find food, unless they were apprehensive about the arrival of the 5th Corps and wanted to attack before the arrival of those reinforcements to prevent operations they feared might follow. Other reports announced, on the contrary, that the enemy had orders to withdraw in case of attack. Captain Théodore Nicolas Joseph Desmarets of the 9th Corps marched from Caldas [da Rainha] to Rio Maior and found very few people there. He said that the rumors of a concentration of troops at Rio Maior and Alcoentre were at the least exaggerated. General Clauzel had seen nothing new at the posts before him. It was the same with the 2nd Corps. The work at the Ponte de Alfores might have had no other object than to sustain the post of Calhariz more directly during the new floods of the Rio Maior. An officer near Punhete said he had seen ten pieces of English light artillery maneuvering. After Parmentier's first expedition, an extensive reconnaissance of enemy generals had come to examine the condition of our works. We were about to see if those batteries at Punhete were going to be armed. In fact, they were not then. Were they ever going to be?

13. Sir William Houston (1766–1842) entered the army as an ensign in 1781 and reached the rank of major general by 1811, when he was sent to the Peninsula. He commanded a brigade in the Egyptian campaign and again during the Walcheren expedition; he was given command of Wellington's 7th Division from January until August 1811, when he was sent home in poor health.

Amid these contradictory rumors, General Solignac arrived from Pernes; he had left the Duc d'Abrantès extremely worried about his position and about some of the new movements on his advance posts, one of which had been seized. The Duc had given him orders to reconnoiter a position on the Almonda as if he were ready to retire to it; this movement would have exposed the entire army. The Prince ordered me to visit the line of the 8th Corps the next day to search for a central position and a reserve site for Solignac's division. This recalled the disposition to be taken in case of attack and to the necessity of tightening and protecting the line. A general order took care of all these dangers. However, if the enemy attacked, it would become difficult, perhaps even impossible, to maneuver in front of them, for they would probably reinforce themselves between Alcoentre and the stream of Valle, where they already occupied a position near its confluence with the Rio Maior. Then they would push toward our right. Thus we would lose our line of retreat on the Mondego and be thrown back on the Zezere.

The great advantage the enemy would derive from such a maneuver was the only thing that persuaded us to believe in an impending attack. In such a case, four possibilities remained to be chosen. First, to withdraw through Tomar and Espinhal, a difficult movement with the enemy on our flanks and with our right exposed to a fierce battle, in order to give the left time to draw itself parallel [with the other French forces]. Second, to throw ourselves behind the Zezere and withdraw on Guarda—bad roads, poor region, where our prospect was Spain and the loss of Portugal. The third was the Prince's old plan to await the enemy in the positions at Atalaia, throw all our bridges across the Zezere, and give battle; but, if forced to withdraw, we would find ourselves forced to march on Guarda or the Erjas through Castelo Branco. Furthermore, to use this plan was to deliver battle out of sheer wantonness, where we had little to hope and everything to fear because of the lack of munitions and the condition of the army. Finally, the fourth plan was to unite behind the Zezere and cross the Tagus under the cover of this river. This avoided a useless battle and maintained us in Portugal. These various possibilities were discussed in succession. We felt that the last was admittedly the best. The Prince and I were in sufficient agreement on the third, and we were completely against the first two. Nevertheless, we decided it was better to start the movement ourselves rather than wait for such a maneuver, but first of all it was necessary to replace the Prussian and Irish troops at headquarters with French regiments.

The Duc d'Abrantès told me on his word of honor that if he were vigorously attacked he would not be able to maintain his very extended position because he did not have all his troops and the corps was weak. He would resist if we wished, but he would be wiped out. He dwelt at length on the need to withdraw before being attacked, and the sooner the better. He had everything to fear because some men were not armed, some were sick, and the state of the artillery and cavalry [was deplorable]; moreover, he would demonstrate the futility and impossibility of a bridge on the Tagus whenever we wished. He protested his devotion to the Prince and [insisted] that the commanders had never agreed among themselves to oppose his wishes. I promised to relate in detail his position, to urge His Excellency to concentrate all his detachments, and to send a regiment of the 6th Corps in reserve toward the center of the gap between the 2nd Corps.

I went to visit the advance posts and the line of the 8th Corps with Beaufort. General Taupin was quite willing to take the trouble to accompany us. We arrived above Escariz[?] and reconnoitered the streams of Valle, Outeiro, and Fráguas; each was outflanked and cut by the Ponte de Calhariz below their junction. The bridge was found to be not only on the right but almost behind Santarém, facing the gap between the 8th and 2nd Corps. The 2nd Corps reached almost to Romeiros. The 8th Corps occupied about three leagues of ground from Azoia de Cima to Tremês, Alcanede, and Mosteiros with Clauzel's division and a few reserves at [Alqueidão ?] and Abraã. Solignac's division was at Pernes with a regiment at Torres Novas. At this very moment the Prince sent Solignac's entire division to Pernes at the disposal of the Duc. This disposition was becoming very necessary for although the right was supported by the almost impassable mountains, its vast deployment was alarming; it was also necessary to preserve the army's line and that of the 2nd Corps instead of the 8th Corps, which only had good defense posts, as a matter of fact, at Azoia, Tremês, Alcanede; thus its actual line of concentration was truly on the Alviela and not on the Almonda. Moreover, the 2nd Corps left the entire right flank at Santarém unmasked. The Ponte de Calhariz was a very delicate point, which Generals Clauzel and Taupin watched rather carefully.

However, it was up to the English General to give some serious alert to the whole army with the smallest disposition of troops beyond this bridge.

We spent the night at General Clauzel's quarters in Alcanede. We had eaten very good cornbread at the table of the Duc. The general still had some wheat bread and his division had eaten corn for only the last few days. He had enough to last until the end of the month. The dragoons of Grandseigne's brigade had nothing but beans for nourishment and the horses had grass. Several of his officers had prisoners who endured their fate with great happiness and showed much more resignation than was proper. The general complained very much about the espionage of Portuguese peasants. They came into the middle of the posts, sliding through the grass on their stomachs. We were supposed to visit the posts beyond Alcanede; the weather was very bad. General Clauzel showed them to us from the top of an old castle. At Mosteiros, beyond the height, there was a regiment of dragoons. The advance cavalry posts were a short league ahead of Alcanede. Ahead of this division the terrain was deeply cut, full of valleys, and a number of roads ran from Rio Maior, Marmeleira, the Ponte de Calhariz, etc., but there did not appear to be many troops in front of them for the time being. According to a deserter of that day, the largest force was at Cartaxo and extended through Alcoentre toward Cercal and Tagarro. There were only a few companies at Rio Maior and Portuguese regiments at Marmeleira, where the left of the corps placed at Cartaxo was to be supported. The advance posts on the Rio Maior were obliged to depend on the corps at Alcoentre, and General Houston's advance guard was lying between the valley and the Rio Maior.

In the event of an attack, General Clauzel expected to unite the troops at Alcanede on the heights and move from there by the hills of Abraã to reach Pernes. The troops observing the bridges of Calhariz and São João would concentrate at Tremês and those on the left would be at Azoia de Cima. Once the two villages had been defended, these detachments would retreat successively on Pernes. These arrangements left open the direct road from Torres Novas through Quinta de Alviela. The general was quite willing to correct this oversight. We spoke at length about the plan for the bridge at Santarém and the operations on the Tagus. He supported this view strongly and I record his opinion here because it deserves to be noted.

We returned along the road of Abraã, which was rather difficult for carriages. At the bridge of Alviela there was a tannery, El Quinta, in a delightful position (where the Alviela seemed to emerge from the middle of rocks), as well as excellent defenses. From there we passed Alcanede, a very pretty village, and Zibreira and reached Torres Novas. The roads were bad and the mud rendered them almost impassable.

The 8th Corps found itself protected from any danger after the concentration of Solignac's division. The Prince ordered me to make a report with a general defensive deployment for this corps. He then showed me what he called "the diatribe of General Reynier," with whom he was very irritated. In effect, the General wrote that when he returned to his quarters he had concerned himself with what had occurred at Golegã, and he sent a report entitled "Résumé de la conférence de Golgau" [*sic*] in which he set forth the condition and position of the army.[14] He examined four possibilities that had been proposed. First, to withdraw on the Mondego, a project he considered fatal for the army while Tomar was still intact. Second, to cross the Tagus at Punhete, a rather difficult operation. Third, to cross at Santarém with the whole army united (this was my project), and he went deeply into this. He proposed it, he insisted on it, but the plan was not very well developed and the main characteristic of the attack against General Hill was forgotten. Fourth, to remain in our position—an inconvenience because of the ruinous condition of the horses. In general, he maintained that retreat was not necessary, that it was better to cross at Punhete than not to cross at all, that it was better to remain than to retire, and finally that it was necessary to wait from March 10 to 15 for the return of the dispatches sent to Paris. The Prince was furious about this—its title, the rather inexact assertions, the contents, the approach, the impropriety, and finally the results this kind of protestation might have. The General still claimed that it was necessary to relieve his suffering army corps—at the very moment when he was making private arrangements with the 6th Corps and had written to the Prince that the 2nd Corps had just been concentrated.

His Excellency immediately sent this report to the corps commanders so that they could put their opinions at the bottom of it. The Duc d'Abrantès wrote that it did not entirely conform to the truth. The

14. Eight pages of the "Résumé de la conférence de Gollegan [*sic*]," February 21, 1811, are in the Correspondance: Armée de Portugal, Carton C^{7}11.

Prince received the same declaration from several of the general officers. All this uproar could have been halted with a counter résumé which would have been signed by the Marshal, the Duc, and Reynier himself. The latter was one of the corps commanders who treated me poorly. Yet we were in considerable agreement, or rather complete unanimity, in our opinions. The Prince had never let me know that he complained about this concord. Moreover, I did not hide anything and if I sacrificed my opinion to all of theirs for the good of our expedition, I wished it to be known that it was done in spite of me. I would have done better to keep my ideas to myself, but when I made them known to General Reynier and others, it was either by order of the Prince or for the good of the service.

The Prince himself wrote a very bitter letter to General Reynier.[15] The General apologized for his habit of reporting on everything, that he was wrong about the title since there had not been any conference, and that the questions had not been posed as he had stated them. He protested his devotion. A little later the Marshal responded that it would be desirable to try to remain until March 20, but the third division was suffering a great deal. He refused to provide any kind of help in the form of grain for the other army corps or for the sick and wounded that he left in the greatest need in the environs of Tomar, although he had plenty of grain. Meanwhile, as the colonel of the 39th Line withdrew, he said that his regiment had enough food for fifteen days and the colonel of the 27th Line said that his removal from Martinchel cost him twelve days' food. The latter arrived at Torres Novas and relieved the 86th Line. In general, the entire 6th Corps was very well [provisioned] with regard to food.

I had trouble making the deployment for the 8th Corps because the ground was difficult. I did not know it well enough, and all our topographies differed a little from one another. For the withdrawal on

15. Masséna wrote to Reynier on February 22, "I am surprised that you have called a simple conversation we had during dinner at General Loison's headquarters on the 18th of this month 'Résumé de la conférence de Golgau [*sic*].' But my astonishment increased when I read the reflections about which we said nothing, the facts altered from those that actually occurred." Correspondance: Armée de Portugal, Carton C^{7}11. Masséna also wrote to Ney on February 23 about Reynier's "Résumé": "I was extremely surprised that the gist corresponded so little with the title, because some of the observations made at the lunch at Golgan [*sic*] were altered and others included which we did not discuss, while some actual points were omitted." See Bonnal, *Ney*, pp. 477–78.

Pernes, I concentrated the first division at Alcanede, with a defense on the height, the reserve at Abraã, and posts opposite Romeira to protect that village and to communicate with Pêro Filho, where the light cavalry of the 2nd Corps was posted, and with Azoia, where there was a detachment of its infantry. In the second general position for the 2nd and 8th Corps, the right was on the bridge of El Quinta de Alviela behind Alcanede, the flanks were in the mountains on the right, the center was at Pernes with many cannon, and the left was on the bridge of Alviela behind Santarém. These two corps were supported by the 6th Corps. This work gave me much difficulty. When I took it to the Prince, he said, "The position is too long and too detached," and he dictated a letter to me to which I summarily added the details of the position. He then asked me for the plan for the march to the Mondego, but I had hardly started reading before he found himself dictating. He had me write his private plan in the margin and ordered me to add, as I often did, the distances and the most important observations. Finally he had me read a rough draft of the letter I had prepared for the Major General before the conference, and he added several notes because of the changes that had occurred in our situation.

Colonel Valazé announced that the enemy battery of eight guns was completed, but we did not see any trace of armament. We discussed the change to be made in their fortifications under various circumstances. We agreed that, as far as possible, we should prepare in advance the reconnaissance and even some fortifications for crossing the Mondego, which could be done later only with the greatest difficulty. Meanwhile *chef d'escadron* Jean Joseph Salel, in charge of the 2nd Corps' marauders, returned from a raid in the neighborhood of Góis, Arganil, and beyond Ponte de Murcella, announcing the evacuation of Coimbra by the enemy troops. They had withdrawn on February 20 to Oporto when a French force arrived between the Mondego and Douro. The marauders had gathered a great quantity of livestock. The Prince divided it among the various army corps. Salel had encountered three thousand of our pillagers near Miranda do Corvo. They scoured the country in small isolated bands of six to seven men without hindrance. Few of the peasants were armed and they fled at their approach, leaving the villages nearly intact. This region abounded in corn. According to him, we would find more than a thousand bags; we could expect that the army would have enough food for more than two months in its new position. Another detachment of the 27th Line advanced on February 17 to Coimbra and established a post of thirty men before the city, very near the first houses. No enemy detachments had been seen. We could only hear drums and some confusion across the bridge. In these ways we found wheat, wine, and a great deal of corn.

The unfortunate news that had been gathered announcing the evacuation of Coimbra at that time greatly influenced the decisions the Prince made in arranging for the movement toward the Mondego, which we discussed every morning. No one was able to give us exact information on the state of the river; moreover, it would have been almost useless because of the frequent and sudden changes that occurred during that season. With some reason, the Prince believed that the evacuation of Coimbra was a result of the movement in northern Portugal by the 9th Corps, about which the Major General had written. He assumed it was Claparède's division, since other reports had announced its arrival near Lamego and it was now occupying that region. Thus His Excellency refused to reduce his force before such a strong enemy at the moment when he was about to make such a delicate movement; he also insisted that in his dispositions for the march he would ignore the Mondego, which we had crossed when it was almost dry. He changed what I had proposed for the 9th Corps, believing that a single regiment from that division would be enough to form a junction with General Claparède's division and outflank Coimbra above the Mondego. After some discussion and slight changes, the Prince adopted the first part of the operation for the ninety-degree pivot backward with the hinge of resistance at Leiria menacing Alcoentre, and the obvious preparations for the passage at Punhete to disengage our maneuver.

We again sent an officer to Paris. At this moment, when the Prince was taking a definite stand, it was extremely important to make a good choice, for everything depended on the way his decision was presented and supported. Even now there were many views and rapidly changing opinions at court. It was necessary that the messenger should be quite restrained. We discussed the choice for a long time. The Prince told me that even his son would not dare fight for him against Napoleon. Later he was able to see that such a thing was not impossible.

For a long time I insisted that the retrograde maneuver be delayed until March 10 or 15 in order to have answers from France about the reports of Casabianca; then the government would have nothing to complain about since, in the postscript to the dispatch to the Major General, the Prince held out to him [the possibility of] a withdrawal on the Mondego. His Excellency had willingly agreed to this delay and had written to Generals Reynier and Junot to know whether they could hold until then and to urge them vigorously to do so. General Reynier answered that he eagerly desired to do so, but without food it was absolutely necessary that he be relieved. The Duc responded that holding was absolutely impossible. This convinced the Prince and forced him to begin his movement at an earlier date than expected, since there was nothing but danger to face without any possible hope of orders or aid. In addition, a report from the commander of the fortress, later confirmed, announced that a detachment of five hundred men, coming from Rodrigo through Castelo Branco, had been forced to withdraw before the Portuguese regiment of Braga, assisted by a large force of militia. We thought that this detachment, escorting an officer, was carrying orders. For the past few days we had no longer heard the cannon from the direction of Badajoz.[16] The rumor spread that the siege had been raised and that Marshal Soult had lost his artillery. On the other side of the Tagus, opposite *chef de bataillon* Alban Martinel of the 32nd Léger, we had seen at a distance French prisoners captured over there in an action said to be disastrous. Finally, we had been told that the siege was set for January 10 to 12, and it seemed that Badajoz would have been captured or abandoned by the end of February.

All the reports claimed that General Picton had crossed the Tagus with part of his division; that the enemy had sent troops on to Abrantes, where the Regiment of Estremadura had already arrived in order to move on our rear; that the Portuguese were reinforcing themselves on the lines and relieving the English posts; and that General Beresford had gone to Abrantes a few days earlier and that it was already in a formidable state of defense.

16. As a result of an acoustical phenomenon in the atmosphere, the siege guns at Badajoz could be heard almost 90 miles away by the men of the Army of Portugal during the first two weeks of February. However, on February 15 the sound diminished, giving rise to the theory that the city had fallen or the siege had been raised.

Until the very last moment all my wishes revolved around the Tagus. However, when I saw that no hope remained that we would cross it and that the maneuver on the Mondego was entirely decided, I felt that it was my duty to search for all the means, not only to improve the maneuver but to give it, in the true interest of France and the army, every possible improvement and even a bright aspect to hide from the eyes of Europe all the unfortunate aspects of a retrograde movement during war. Thus, despite my repugnance, I found myself forced to return to the plan for a march on Oporto that I had opposed so strongly. This was the second city of Portugal, one of the most important commercial cities of Europe, and a principal English trading port. Considering all this, it seemed evident to me that, in occupying it, we could serve our government by causing much harm in this nation of shopkeepers and by all the profits that would result from it; finally, we could share the domination of Portugal with the English by opposing regency to regency, army to army, and ultimately by installing ourselves in the kingdom. By means of this fixed establishment and by the evident exhaustion on both sides, we could hope to detach from the British party some of the militia leaders, whom we had already approached, and to attempt to form some new Portuguese units. On the other hand, the riches of Oporto, wisely employed to sustain the army, would provide everything for us (thanks to the greed of the Spaniards, which we had already experienced in the frontier provinces) through the occupation of a vast bridgehead from the left bank of the Mondego opposite Coimbra and a few points on the same bank along both flanks. We would also hold the enemy completely in check, for we would still be free to present ourselves before the Lines of Lisbon in five or six marches.

There was certainly no intention in my project to bury the army between the Minho and the Douro. Nevertheless, I expected to occupy the country from the Douro to the Mondego and to hold Coimbra and Oporto at both extremities like two bridgeheads. The strength of the army would be near Coimbra, the cavalry would be on the Vouga, and the 9th Corps would be at Viseu and on the Alva with fortified bridges on the Mondego to ensure our communication with the fortresses and Spain. In order to conserve all the resources Oporto could furnish and to eliminate all plans for illicit gain and all types of calumny, I thought we should choose a governor who would be respected by everyone.

For example, General Éblé was the personification of integrity, refinement, and honor, whose firmness and rigor could almost become rudeness. The general could have the government of Oporto and preserve all its utility for the artillery by uniting the *grand parc* of the army; thanks to his care, it would soon be regenerated beneath the city walls. Two chosen brigades put at his disposal would occupy the city and a certain radius of terrain around it.

On all occasions the Prince had indicated his repugnance for such a plan, either because of the memory of the disaster of Soult's army or because of the memory of the motives for occupying the city, or perhaps because of the influence it would exert on the avidity of some people and on the discipline of the army. He always repeated to me, "Let no one talk to me about Oporto and the Minho." Nevertheless, I talked to him about it at the end. I could even insist, because he knew my devotion and the obvious innocence of my conduct during the six years that I had been with him. Finally, unable to obtain anything from him, I proposed that we burn the English magazines on the left bank [of the Tagus] and intercept their navigation. He did not even want to go near there.

It was a day of rejoicing everywhere, even at Torres Novas, for almost everyone, but it was a day of great affliction and bitterness for me. The Prince had ordered me to make copies of the report to the Major General and the plan for the march on the Mondego. There were so many incongruities in both, caused by the various changes in what the Prince had projected, that I found it easier and absolutely necessary to recast the two original plans completely, and the day was devoted to this sad task. They were rather long and consequently had to be done very fast. However imperfect the report was, I feel obliged to append all of it to this work, because it was an official and authentic document that presented a picture of a great part of the campaign and threw some light on little-known or misrepresented events.[17] I gave it

17. Although a copy of this report to Berthier was not found in Pelet's manuscript, it is available in published works as well as the Correspondance: Armée de Portugal, Carton C⁷12, Masséna to Berthier, March 6, 1811. Masséna wrote, "I have constructed works on both banks of the estuary of the Zezere in order to prepare a triple bridgehead at Punhete. I have fabricated 120 boats and pontoons for the construction of three bridges: one on the Zezere and the two others on the Tagus above and below the confluence [of the Zezere]. Since the enemy has some kind of obstruction at the mouth of the Zezere with formidable batteries and works opposite our positions, I have built 50 wagons to transport a part of

to the Prince the very same day, and he wanted to have it copied immediately. General Foy carried it; he probably learned of it a few days before leaving. (It should be remembered that I was only the editor of this report and at the time my duty forced me to forget and even sacrifice my private opinions.) I then drew up the general orders for the retrograde movements according to the plan that had been fixed by the Prince or that was based on some parts of my project which he was willing to retain. These arrangements were the very ones that were executed. The deployment of the first part has been given earlier; it was approved by the Prince in totality and was copied down immediately. His Excellency was kind enough to show it to General Loison. Rather than looking for errors in the strategy, the general was only able to find some mistakes in the language. I gave in to him without pretension, but not without smiling about this grammarian who, in this terrible catastrophe of certain tragedy, noticed only a grammatical mistake.[18]

A rather curious thing, showing the fickleness of the human spirit, was that as we neared the decisive moment, and when affairs took such a turn that it became harder to resist the pull of circumstances, the league in opposition became almost reconciled to the operations on the Tagus. Those who had most ardently opposed the passage at first became its most fervent partisans. Without doubt this was based on a great change of views and on the effect that the idea of a retreat produced on every French soul, especially when they could visualize it

my bridge equipment below Punhete in the only favorable place to establish a bridge. . . . But these movements have not been concealed from the enemy . . . and he has constructed other works opposite the point chosen for the new position. . . . The passage of the Tagus has become more difficult with each passing day and it was even judged very hazardous by a part of the general officers of the army. . . . This was the situation when General Foy arrived February 5, bringing Your Highness's dispatch of December 22. After his report and what General Foy said . . . I have counted on the prompt cooperation of the 5th Corps that you announced would arrive on the left bank of the Tagus at Villa Flor. . . . Having received no direct orders to cross this river . . . I have judged it necessary to suspend this operation so as not to expose the army uselessly. . . . I now believe that it conforms . . . to the intentions of His Majesty and to the interests of the army to march on Pombal and to take a position there and to maintain the troops as long as possible on the banks of the Mondego. This is the decision I have taken because it is impossible to remain here any longer in our position."

18. It is rather odd that Loison considered himself a grammarian since he did not learn to read or write until the age of twenty-one, when he was recuperating from wounds received during the storming of the Tuileries on August 10, 1792.

more closely. In effect, preparations were starting everywhere. We requested the last of the grain in order to distribute it. All the horses were gathered for the artillery. General Éblé destroyed or threw into the Zezere lead, iron, and useless objects, which in any case could not be taken away. These sad preparations threw gloom on every soul and spread general distress. If in those moments there were persons vile enough to rejoice, they must have hidden such shameful feeling quite deeply.

The rumors of retreat also spread among the troops. For a long time part of the army had longed for a change in position. The old soldiers said that "the Prince would not leave until the last blade of grass and the last saddle of the army had been eaten." Once more they saw repeated the cruel extremes of the siege and [the suffering] on the Riviera of Genoa, but this time without utility and glory. At least there they fought daily in defense of a city almost French; the hope of aid and even the prospect of glorious conquest remained, while here we found ourselves surrounded on every side by misery and misfortune at the end of the world. Nevertheless, they craved only food and their soldierly speeches always ended with, "If we had vegetables they could not chase us out of here in ten years, and if we had a few more men they would soon be dislodged from their rocks at Sobral." Yet those who suffered the most saw the approach of the retreat only with feelings of bitterness, although it was to change their fate. The men who had complained the most against Alentejo and the dangers of the Tagus loudly demanded they be taken there rather than retreat. Those sentiments were noble and praiseworthy for the army, and the general in chief himself felt proud of it. Yet we had to consider them thereafter as useless and belated. What could have been done with success and glory at the beginning or even in the middle of the month, was becoming more dangerous and even impossible at the end, because of the arrival of reinforcements for the enemy army from everywhere.

General Reynier, finding great difficulty in withdrawing his artillery in front of the enemy, asked that his maneuver be masked by an order to change positions as if he were to be relieved by the 6th Corps; this would conceal the goal of his maneuver from his troops and the English. The Prince proved to him that he would not be pursued, according to the measures set up by the general order, but he nevertheless sent him instructions ostensibly announcing the arrival of the 6th

Corps.[19] On the English side of the advance post it was asked when Marshal Mortier would arrive, and on the French side when the landing of those twenty thousand reinforcements would occur, as threatened for such a long time. The English said the reinforcements had already arrived.

Copies of the general order were addressed to the commanders of the army corps, and the day for the commencement of the movement was indicated as March 5, although this date was not entirely decided upon. Each army corps was to reconnoiter its roads and its positions, and the bridges were to be destroyed.[20] The 8th Corps most forcefully urged departure, announcing that everything was ready there. But the 2nd Corps still had some men on forage duty who would not return for four days. Orders were given to General Montbrun to send some cavalry detachments on the rear to gather all the foragers and isolated men. Marshal Ney received special instructions about the position entrusted to him at Leiria and about the importance of his maneuver. He was to leave a strong detachment at Ourém to be linked with the rest of the army. The Marshal had ten good infantry regiments, four of cavalry, and all his artillery for this operation. If the Allies followed the 2nd and 8th Corps too closely, Marshal Ney was to make thorough preparations for an attack on the left and rear of the enemy line to stop their pursuit.[21] This type of movement was not dangerous for us; however, if the enemy marched on Leiria, then the Marshal was to hold them back stubbornly. The 8th Corps and Loison's division were to move to Pombal, and Reynier toward Ancião while we concentrated near or above Pombal to receive the enemy army. Moreover, all the maneuvers, even the preparatory ones, were not to be started until the last moment.

19. As Masséna promised, he wrote to Reynier on March 1, "I announce to you that I have given the order to the 6th Corps to go and relieve you in your position; make your dispositions to march on March 5 or 6. Prepare all your detachments to leave." Correspondance: Armée de Portugal, Carton C[7]12.

20. For details of the withdrawal, see "Ordre de marche sur Pombal, Ancião, et Espinhal," March 1, 1811, in Correspondance: Armée de Portugal, Carton C[7]12.

21. The details governing Ney's movements can be found in Masséna's letter to him dated March 1, which concluded, "Leiria is absolutely the pivot on which the army will maneuver. If the enemy wants to threaten us in our change of position, it will only be by the main road that he will be able to act, debouching in force. But with ten regiments of infantry and four of cavalry, with all your artillery, you will have sufficient force to halt him." See Correspondance: Armée de Portugal, Carton C[7]12.

The orders were repeated and sent only in succession, as they became necessary, to elaborate the general instructions. In spite of these precautions, the Marshal and the Duc committed two indiscretions which could have given the enemy a warning of our dispositions. The Marshal set up his headquarters at Leiria immediately and the Duc sent his equipment workers to Chão de Macãs. The Prince finally decided to send General Foy to Paris again. The general received his orders for departure, his instructions, and his dispatches immediately, but he was not to leave the army until the line had been closed and the maneuver nearly completed. He was to send a courier from Ciudad Rodrigo to the 5th Corps to inform them of our movement.

The rumors of our departure were quickly communicated to the enemy army. Their reconnaissance patrols, which usually went out in the middle of the day, advanced at dawn to learn if our advance post had started moving. More than ever, they sent peasants to prowl around our cantonment and they finally said, "Well, gentlemen, since you are sending your baggage away, you will follow it soon!" The Portuguese peasants would shout this to us from one side of the Tagus to the other, but in a less polite manner. Our detachments again intercepted a few packets of letters. They described the mood of the Portuguese. There was much misery and discontent among the inhabitants as well as the military, and there was no desire to fight. They were astonished that the French army could live in such a country. They claimed that we had multiplied like flies, that the lack of food would force us to retire into Spain, that Santarém had been evacuated, and that we had strangled eight thousand of our sick soldiers. The Portuguese received only a half ration, often delayed for several days.

The Prince, writing to General Drouet, had asked him for one regiment. I believed that it was to take Coimbra from the rear and assure us of its possession in advance, without indicating the 9th Corps' intended destination. Nevertheless, the general responded, "We will try to do our best," and then, "I regret that I cannot send the regiment requested to Cabaços. Send one from your army." The Prince was quite piqued, but the general had the right to act in this way, remembering the conference at Golegã. His Excellency supposed he would insist on his order. Drouet responded in the same way the next day, March 4, but in a more terse and bold manner, to say the least.[22]

22. In a letter to Drouet dated March 3, Masséna requested him "to send a

We saw the artillery *parc* of the 2nd and 8th Corps passing; they commenced the retrograde movement. They were succeeded and preceded by a great amount of baggage because the orders had not been executed, and some corps commanders committed personal indiscretions which we could not refrain from denouncing vigorously. We found much of this trouble with the 8th Corps. There was a great multitude of escort soldiers, perhaps one-fourth of the army. We were then able to learn how little truth there was in the continual complaints about provisions. Certain regiments carried great quantities of grain and the *état major* of the 2nd Corps pulled a large supply of forage behind. I was then certain, just as I had been at Sobral, that the army could have remained in its last position for many more days if everybody had been willing to do his duty.[23]

During the night the Prince received information from Punhete that the enemy seemed to want to attack. He immediately sent two battalions of the 70th Line and General Lamotte's cavalry on to Martinchel, which had been evacuated. Nevertheless, we thought it was only a simple English reconnaissance; before dawn they were removing the abatis from the Ponte de Asseca, believing we had already left Santarém. The Prince sent officers to all the army corps to instruct them about the progress and details of the maneuvers. He sent me to Punhete with orders for General Loison to hold the approaches of that village firmly in case of serious attack, with the particular injunction to prolong this essential defense to the last extreme. I arrived there quickly but found nothing serious. The enemy had the same troops on the

regiment of Conroux's division to Cabaços to hold it while the army makes its combined maneuver." Drouet responded, "I will do my best in regard to the general movement," but refused to move his regiments to Cabaços "because Conroux's division was already too weak to form this detachment, since it had to furnish a large guard for the hospital. 'In any case, I do not doubt that Your Highness will be able to send a regiment of his army if he judges it indispensable.' " Indignantly, Masséna responded, "Your refusal disarranges my dispositions and if we encounter failure, the blame will fall on you. . . . Your position, for the moment, places you under the Army of Portugal, and you are forced in consequence to cooperate with its change of position." See Masséna to Drouet, March 3, Correspondance: Armée de Portugal, Carton C[7]12; Koch, *Mémoires de Masséna,* Drouet to Masséna, March 5, Masséna to Drouet, March 5, 1811, VII, 332–33.

23. Pelet's assertion is substantiated by the information Wellington received; he wrote to Beresford on February 24, 1811, that a deserter "says that they have not been badly off for meat, but that the bread is very bad, and that they do not get a quarter of a pound a day, but that they have plently of vegetables." See *Wellington's Dispatches,* VII, 313–14.

line of the Tagus—four hundred men at Arripiado. Signals had been going the entire night and they continued during the day. Yet it seemed to me that I saw a few more fires on the plain of Chamusca.

This is what happened during the affair at Punhete. On March 3 an ambush had been set up for scouts from the Abrantes garrison, and they had fallen into it. To protect them the garrison had occupied the village of Rio de Moinhos with some two or three thousand troops, all of them Portuguese. When I went there only eight or nine hundred men were left. There had been some anxiety at Punhete, but they were now reassured. I talked to everyone about the strength of this position, by itself and with its works, of its importance for the general movement of the army, and also of the need to keep some boats intact until the last moment. The preparations were agreed upon and settled. The chain of posts was tightened and carefully surveyed to stop deserters or spies. A battalion of the 70th Line was situated on each bank at Martinchel, the 82nd Line was at Montalvo beyond the gap from Punhete to Martinchel. The cavalry was to be displayed and deployed in front of the enemy the next morning, and the fires were to be multiplied extensively so that the enemy would believe new troops had arrived. Most of the boats were already on their wagons, filled with flammable material. A few preparations were ostensibly made for crossing.

At length, everything had been disposed so that the enemy would fear the establishment of the bridge above Punhete at any moment. But inside the village other preparations filled my soul with a sad bitterness. Tears came to my eyes at seeing those boats and the bridge equipment ready to be burned; we had done many great and noble things with such equipment on the Danube in 1809. In a remote place, hidden from the enemy, we sawed the planks, split the beams with axes, and burned the rigging little by little. General Éblé and I stayed for two hours, sitting on the hills, talking with great friendship and consoling each other.[24] He shared my opinion about Oporto and many other things. We saw a group of English officers of the *état major*, who

24. The destruction of the bridge was ordered on March 3 in a sympathetic letter from Masséna to Éblé: "Circumstances force us to make the sacrifice of the bridge equipment that has cost us so much in pain and has been constructed completely under your care. . . . Prepare everything so that none of this equipment exists at dawn on the 7th. You will begin to burn or destroy it by other means only on the night of the 6–7th and as late as possible. Take precautions to leave nothing for the enemy." See Correspondance: Armée de Portugal, Carton $C^{7}12$.

followed out operations attentively. A hut had been erected for those observers.

It was very difficult to hide our actual work completely, but during war demonstrations often resemble operations and appearances are authentic. We could attempt either to attract them to this point or draw then away. General Éblé was upset by the departure of two hundred sailors who had been taken away from him at a very inopportune moment. With them, he could have carried everything off at one time; however, he did not leave the enemy enough to make even a toothpick. Two days later, taking my hand, he told me with tears in his eyes, "I wish you had been there, everything was well executed." The saltpeter mill and the tar-covered fascines had been prepared and all the pontoons were to be burned. The anchors and grappling hooks were to be thrown to the bottom of the Zezere, the barges were to be destroyed with bombs, and the bridge on the Zezere was to be pulled back during the night of March 6–7 and burned on the right bank. I talked to the general about the necessity of completing the preparations to burn the bridge as fast as possible, in case General Reynier was pushed too vigorously on Golegã and so that he could withdraw on Tomar by either bank of the Zezere. The fortifications of Punhete began to go well and to take form suitable to the terrain. When I returned, there seemed to be fewer fires on the plain of Chamusca.

The Prince had received no news of enemy maneuvers on the other points of the line. I proposed to him to have General Reynier communicate with Loison and Éblé for their reciprocal arrangements, and to order the Duc d'Abrantès to occupy the Ponte Nova,* near Torres Novas, with his leading troops and to destroy the other bridges. These orders were given in announcing to the army corps that His Excellency would remain at Torres Novas until noon on March 6. General Reynier hoped to be beyond the Alviela by dawn.

Chapter Twelve

THE RETREAT: FIRST PHASE

Now that our offensive operations have terminated, let us pause at one of those critical moments when great matters and the fate of men as well as the fortune of empires are decided. If we are irrevocably subordinated to the inflexible decrees of destiny, at least we can allow ourselves to glance at the apparent causes of those events and to search for the possible consequences that various combinations might have produced. So without casting ourselves on a vast ocean of conjecture, we can ask ourselves what might naturally and immediately have resulted from the following suppositions.

Marshal Soult had certainly received the orders which the Major General had communicated to us on December 4 and 22 for cooperation between the 5th Corps and the Army of Portugal.[1] What would have happened if Marshal Soult had sent the 5th Corps to the Tagus

1. In addition to the letters sent by Berthier to Soult, Foy dispatched two letters to Soult dated January 24 and 27, 1811, appealing for aid. He wrote, "Famine will soon drive the French army from its hold on the English army. . . . In this situation, the appearance of a French corps on the left bank four or five leagues below Abrantes would have extremely important consequences for the glory and interests of our armies." Three days later Foy wrote again, "I implore you in the name of the patriotism which exists in all French hearts and the sentiments that inflame us all for the interest of our august master, to present a corps of troops on the left bank of the Tagus opposite the mouth of the Zezere. . . . It is scarcely four days from Badajoz to Brito opposite Punhete. . . . The fate of Portugal and the fulfillment of the Emperor's will are in your hands." See Girod de l'Ain, *Foy,* pp. 125–26, 354–57.

between Vila Flor and Montalvão during the first days of January? In only four marches from Badajoz to Abrantes, those troops would have found our bridge equipment sufficiently prepared for a crossing, which could no longer have been prevented. Then the French army would have established itself on both banks of the Tagus. If the 5th Corps had been strong enough and wanted to advance farther, the English Lines could have been attacked with some hope of success. Lisbon would probably have been occupied and Portugal conquered. If this were not possible, the army could have established double bridges, a triple bridgehead, and threatened Lisbon from both banks, while it covered the siege on the Guadiana and extended itself in Alentejo to live in ease awaiting orders from the government.

If Marshal Soult had wanted to advance with all the troops he employed for the sieges and the operations in Estremadura, success would no longer have been uncertain. This maneuver could have taken place before he began the siege of Badajoz, and it could still have been made after the battle of Gebora if a few forces were left to protect the siege artillery in Olivenza. The 5th Corps would have arrived before the end of February, and then it would have been entirely possible for us to throw up two bridges on the Tagus. If Marshal Mortier had succeeded in notifying us that he would combine his movement with ours, the maneuver at Santarém could have taken place. The bridge would have been set up to link our two armies, Hill would have been abandoned, and we would have fallen upon Lord Wellington and pushed the enemy vigorously into the Lisbon harbor. After attacking Wellington from the directions of Santarém, Rio Maior, and Alcoentre with the 6th and 9th Corps, and from the Ponte de Calhariz with the 8th and 2nd Corps, we could have rendezvoused with the southern corps along both banks of the Tagus at Lisbon. The forces of the two English generals would have been in the harbor and perhaps even farther if we could only have effected our crossing unceremoniously at Punhete near the end of January. (It is not for me to judge, especially at this time, the motives that governed the conduct of Marshal Soult.) With our establishment in Portugal thus insured, we could have kept our bridges, communicated by force with Marshal Soult who, after covering the sieges which would not have lasted as long, would have been forced to cooperate with our operation.

However, if we had executed only the maneuver on the Tagus at

Santarém against Hill and Wellington at the beginning of February as I had proposed, we would have obtained by ourselves all the success the cooperation of Marshal Soult's army could have guaranteed us. There was no possible danger; we could have obtained the greatest results of the entire war with an army half as strong as the one opposed to us. Thus one way or the other, with the crossing of the Tagus and the cooperation of the 5th Corps in the south, we could have chased the English from the Peninsula, or at the least covered the sieges of the fortresses in front of them in order to establish a better line of operation against Portugal. With Badajoz taken, the 5th Corps could still have besieged Elvas without delaying operations at Cadiz, where Marshal Soult would have returned. Then there would have been no combat at Barrosa, no battles of Gebora and Albuera,[2] and if the Abbé de Pradt,[3] who has not flattered the god of war during the past four years, is to be believed, the submission of Spain would have followed.

Finally, if Napoleon had suddenly appeared in Spain at the end of 1810, as he had in 1808 (an arrival which was continually announced at the advance posts of the English army and rumored throughout Spain, and it seemed they wanted those in Bayonne to believe it), if he had marched forward with the second division of the 9th Corps, Seras's 5th Division, the reserve of the Young Guard, with everything that later composed the Army of the North, and with all that he found available near the frontier and in Portugal, at the same time temporarily directing the attention of the other armies toward his goal, he would then have been able to explode a thunderbolt quite easily on the walls of Lisbon as he had announced, fulfilling his prediction of ending the Spanish war there. He would certainly have scaled those formidable Lines or, rather, they would have fallen before so many

2. On March 5, 1811, the battle of Barrosa was fought near Cadiz by Major General Thomas Graham and Marshal Victor. The French were repulsed in this bloody battle and the safety of Cadiz was assured. The battle between Soult and Beresford at Albuera took place on May 16, 1811; both generals claimed victory, but Soult was unable to relieve Badajoz.

3. Abbé Dominique Gorges Frédéric Dufour de Pradt (1759–1837) was a clergyman who emigrated during the Revolution. Through the intervention of Duroc, he returned to France where he found favor with Napoleon. He was invested with the bishopric of Poitiers by Pius VII in 1805 and four years later was made archbishop of Malines. He served as the French ambassador to Warsaw in 1812. Pelet observes in a footnote that the Abbé claimed the Cortes of Cadiz was preparing to recognize Joseph as king when the news of Albuera was announced. See de Pradt, *Mémoires historiques sur la révolution d'Espagne* (3rd ed., Paris, 1817), p. 243.

troops, and England, embarking its army, would probably have renounced a major part of Portugal.

Portugal and Spain, exhausted by the war, would have needed only an honorable pretext, a master blow, or the disappearance of their claimed defenders, to surrender. All this could have been accomplished in less than a month, and the clamor of the triumph would have been a warning to every corner of Europe almost at the same time as news of Napoleon's arrival in Spain. In that case there probably would have been no war in Russia, the Continental System would have been consolidated, the Prince Regent would perhaps have prevailed over his ministry, and the peace of Europe would not have been disturbed for a long time. If Napoleon had been able to withdraw one hundred thousand of his veteran soldiers from a pacified Spain, who would have attacked him again? I allowed myself to talk to him about it a month later, but by then a great many of these advantages no longer existed. His attention had been attracted in some other direction and he only responded to me, "The north, my dear friend, the north."

Napoleon left Moore[4] and Spain in order to go to Eckmühl and Wagram, but it was expected that he would return to finish his task. Whatever can be said of his two-month campaign, the Spanish armies had been dispersed, the English army thrown into the sea, and Burgos and Madrid captured. He could not have become disgusted with the Spanish war. Did he then become less adventurous and less a conqueror after his marriage to an Austrian Archduchess. He at least appeared so to those who observed him carefully. Even in the middle of his Russian campaign his secret was obvious—he was a husband and father. Then he could occupy himself only with the most important interests and follow his career where the defense of his system, his destiny, and that of France, as well as the intrigues of England (the evil genius in all European affairs for so many centuries) dragged him in spite of himself.

The presence of Napoleon in Spain, restoring the centralization that

4. Sir John Moore (1761–1809) enlisted in the 51st Foot as an ensign in 1776; he served in the American Revolution, during the defense of Gibraltar in 1792–93, and in the conquest of Corsica in 1794. Between 1794 and 1808 he commanded troops in the West Indies, Ireland, Holland, Egypt, Sicily, and Sweden. Sent to the Peninsula in 1808, Moore and his army were pursued across Spain by Napoleon's forces. Although most of his army escaped after the battle of Corunna in January 1809, Moore died in a counterattack against the French.

we saw lacking in the affairs of this country, would have ensured its prompt pacification. However, the English ministry could see that it would be lost if the invasion of Spain in 1810 had been as successful as the one in the reign of Louis XIV in 1701; it had first to save the English army and its establishments in Portugal as quickly as possible and then to save itself. The ministry carefully watched everything that might attract Napoleon away from the Peninsula and aroused new enemies against him; to this end it made the most enormous sacrifices. For a long time the ministry kept up this tumult in the north, on which Napoleon had fixed his eyes, and thereby prevented the execution of his plans in Spain. Later the ministry thwarted his dispositions and forced him to change given orders, which had two great advantages for the enemy. The English oligarchy achieved everything by gaining time and prolonging the war while struggling against a single man, because institutions last while men pass rapidly away. In the slow and circumspect conduct of Wellington, it was possible to see that they had set up a system and expected everything from the delay. On the other hand, Napoleon hurried through his short human life-span, forming a new system from the debris of each one of the powers, following the successive and unprovoked attacks by Europe. Napoleon felt the necessity to restrain immediately the continually aggressive strength of his sole and true enemy in order to have time to consolidate and strengthen his creation. Yet could he think of raising the edifice before assuring and clearing away its foundation?

However, let us put aside this vast field of conjecture and political scheming which is irrelevant to our subject, if anything that touches the glory of France can be irrelevant to a true Frenchman. At this very moment it can be justly evaluated by us, but feelings are too strong for complete impartiality; they will be judged by history; however, it is necessary to furnish history with the documents of our great operations.

Let us return to Spain, to the sad spectacle of our retrograde maneuver. At the beginning it was not entirely without glory, having as much as any retreat could merit. The movements were effected by the troops in echelon during the night of March 5–6. Clauzel's division of the 8th Corps, occupying Tremês and Alcanede, started marching at nine o'clock in the evening and took its position on the left bank of the Alviela; then Solignac's division went to Torres Novas. General Reynier also pulled his troops back successively on Santarém and the Alviela. These two army corps left their advance posts occupying their positions on the line until dawn. Their maneuvers were neither bothered nor even followed by the enemy. The soldiers of the 2nd Corps left at the advance posts a straw dummy on which they had written "God damn! What a victory!"[5] Everything was rather peaceful at Punhete. Simultaneously, Marshal Ney sent a division on Molianos to make a demonstration while he reconnoitered his right very carefully toward the sea. General Loison moved with one brigade on Asseiceira. The troops at Punhete were deployed in order to make maneuvers and dispositions that would tax the enemy; during the night a great number of fires were lit at various points.

During the morning we saw the first troops of the 2nd and 8th Corps arriving. The 17th and 22nd Line crossed Torres Novas with their band playing. Music at such a time broke our hearts. My friends and I were extremely moved. Everything in the city had been evacuated and everything was well disposed to receive the English if they followed our retreat. Did anybody want this? Fortunately no one appeared, for a battle would have been a useless sacrifice for us. About eleven o'clock the two army corps were united. The 2nd Corps had left its rear guard near the bridge of Almonda, which was only barricaded. The 8th Corps was on the road to Pernes. As soon as the Prince was assured they were in position and the enemy had not stirred, he left for Chão de Macãs. He approached the 6th and 9th Corps and placed himself at the center of the maneuver. We went through Argea to Paialvo and Carregueiros. As far as Paialvo the road was wretched to cross, but beyond it was passable although a little difficult for the artillery. The country was stony and barren with exposed limestone. We learned at Calvo or Chão de Macãs that there was nothing new in the direction of Leiria. At that point we hoped we would be able to complete our maneuver without difficulties. We could already consider it as being well advanced, since half of our pivot was finished. If the enemy marched to the right on our axis, it would be sufficient to hold them a whole day between Molianos and Leiria while the rest of the army set itself back in line.

5. Lemonnier-Delafosse of the 31st Léger also recounted the story of the stuffed figures at the French outposts. See his *Souvenirs,* p. 118.

The last troops left Torres Novas at six o'clock in the morning. A few English dragoons appeared, and all the bells were rung as a sign of rejoicing because the city had changed masters.[6] During the march there were only a few gunshots. Three or four English squadrons followed the rear guard and stopped at the junction of the Tomar road. The 2nd Corps had noticed an enemy column coming from Almeirim, ascending toward Chamusca on the left bank of the Tagus, although they were never able to learn its exact strength or even the composition of the troops. Some said there were twenty battalions and others much less, but according to everyone there was some artillery following it. Was this column going to reinforce the passage point or cross the Tagus at Abrantes to follow us? In any case its direction was incorrect. *Chef d'escadron* Marbot, who had followed the 2nd Corps, brought us news that worried us a little. During the first moments, rumors spread that Marshal Soult was seven or eight leagues from the Tagus on the other bank. At first this made us wish to see the enemy pursue us.

General Éblé and Colonel Valazé told us what had happened at Punhete at two or three o'clock. The 66th Line and the light cavalry recrossed the Zezere, the bridge was withdrawn at two o'clock, and the boats were quickly pulled onto the bank and set on fire immediately. In an hour the boats were all burning and enveloped in flames. The Légion du Midi, remaining on the left bank until the last moment, crossed over in a barge that was destroyed by shells. The other boats had been similarly burned above Punhete and Martinchel. Nothing of value remained for the Allies, not even the beams and wood. Ultimately we withdrew without any news of the enemy, although they lit their signals when they heard the first footsteps of the troops on the bridge and extended them across their entire line.

On the evening of the 7th the army found itself in a line perpendicular to its direction of retreat. The 6th Corps was at Leiria and Ourém, and the 2nd Corps formed our left at Tomar, flanking the march of

6. As the Allied pickets followed the French withdrawal, they found death and destruction in their path. An English officer recalled, "The unfortunate inhabitants that have remained in their villages have the appearance of people who have been kicked out of their graves and reanimated. . . . The houses were nearly all unroofed, and the people in a starving condition. Two young ladies had been brutally violated in a house that I entered, and were unable to rise from a mattress of straw." See George Simmons, *A British Rifleman: The Journals and Correspondence of Major George Simmons, Rifle Brigade, during the Peninsular War and the Campaign of Waterloo,* ed. Willoughby Verner (London, 1899), pp. 137–38.

the army and covering the Espinhal road to Ponte de Murcella in case of accident. The 8th Corps, in the center, bivouacked around Chão de Macãs on the left bank of the Bezelga. The first division was in front of and along the bank of that stream and the second behind the village on the roads to Leiria and Pombal. The left slope of the valley formed a small rideau and made a rather good position. However, the position on the opposite slope was about twelve hundred yards away and more lofty; the escarpment was rather steep and the Bezelga was closer to it. This very fertile valley had several small hamlets in it.

General Foy left from there with a detachment of three hundred men by the Espinhal road.[7] When he departed, the Prince told him, in reference to me, "I have often requested the rank of colonel for him. I ask you to renew this request to the Major General and the Emperor with ardent persistence. You will tell him that he is the officer who made the expedition on the Island of Lobau, and particularly that on the Island of Moulin, which we have since talked about so often."[8] General Foy had had his orders and dispatches for several days and the time of his departure was fixed.

According to the general order, the army was to place itself as follows: the 6th and 9th Corps at Casal dos Ovos in a good position on the Rio Madalena* which we had reconnoitered the preceding year. The 8th Corps was at Branco, where the headquarters were to be halted, though they were later moved to Pombal. The 2nd Corps was at Ocaril and Pereiro and Loison's division at Arneiro. We left Chão de Macãs with the last troops of the 8th Corps at eight or nine o'clock in the morning. Some thirty English dragoons entered the village as we left. The Prince, marching with the 65th Line, which formed the extreme rear guard, stopped on the crest of the hills to see the enemy's movements. Nothing could be seen yet behind us or in the direction of Ourém. We then crossed the range that linked the wretched moun-

7. Foy left Chão de Macãs on March 8 and reached Paris on March 26; however, he did not return to the army until May 10.

8. In a footnote, Pelet recalls his role in the capture of the Island of Moulin, beyond Lobau: "I told Napoleon, who arrived there, about this operation that actually had been regarded as impossible. It proved to me that nothing was impossible in war. Then he called me the officer of the reconnaissance. Everyone asked my name, but nobody remembered it because I was more worried about my duty than making court. I was named Monsieur N—— in the Bulletin [of the Army]." However, after Pelet published his *Mémoires sur la guerre de 1809, en Allemagne* in 1824–26, he received credit from historians for his role there.

tains of Montachique with those of Serra da Estrêla. It was necessary to know and study the terrain to determine where we were. The elevation was not considerable—hardly any rocks, some gravel, a little limestone, and the remainder covered with woods. We found this last range diminishing as we had expected because it was so far away from the principal range. In general the road there was good and easy with few ascents and descents. Beyond we followed the winding but rather flat crest of an abutment that opened on the Liz and the Soure. Passing through Memoria and Branco, we arrived on the main road from Leiria. The weather was very bad and the Prince stopped for a time at General Montbrun's quarters in the village of Branco near the main highway; then he went with the headquarters to Pombal.

Marshal Ney, who had not seen the enemy during those two days, sent Delabassée's brigade, which was part of his advance guard, to the junction of the route from Leiria and Chão de Macãs, and the 9th Corps to Travaços near Pombal. Rather belatedly, General Solignac had been followed by the enemy, who debouched from Ourém with seven or eight squadrons attached to the ones who were behind the 8th Corps. In all, this made twelve squadrons with two cannon and one howitzer which the enemy had sent after us up to that time. Their cavalry pushed the dragoons of Adjutant Commander Grandseigne a little, but the 65th Line contained them, killing a few of their men. The Prince, warned of this maneuver, ordered Marshal Ney to send his cavalry to support the 8th Corps before he started his retrograde movement on the next day, to take a position at the junction, and to wait there for the corps, whose march he was to cover.

On March 6 I proposed in my Journal a question that interested me very much. What was Lord Wellington doing now? He had known for several days that our army was making preparations to move. He had a great number of spies among the residents of Torres Novas and Santarém—peasants, deserters, foreigners, etc. He knew that the baggage had been on its way since March 4 and that we would certainly march on the 5th. He was so sure of this that his officers talked to us about it at the advance posts along the entire line. At Punhete he saw troop reinforcements and preparations as if to throw up a bridge. Boats were navigating on the Tagus which threatened them with a crossing even farther down. He probably knew the exact number of boats we had constructed; he saw the 2nd and 8th Corps marching and approaching Punhete on the left and center of the line simultaneously. At the other end of the line, near Leiria, a division was marching offensively against his left and rear, menacing his entrenchments by the direct road to Lisbon. Yet the English General could not expect an actual attack by an army like ours against forces which were so superior and entrenched to the hilt, especially after five months of waiting for help which he knew quite well had not arrived. But this army was composed of Frenchmen commanded by Masséna. If Wellington's left remained unprotected, a flank march could easily be made and then it would not be absolutely impossible for us to reach Sobral ahead of him.

Nevertheless, Wellington seemed to be more anxious about a passage on the Tagus after we evacuated the left bank [of the Zezere?] for the movement on Leiria. Although a long time had slipped by without our trying to cross the river, he knew quite well what was happening every day near Badajoz, and he was certain that nothing was joining us from that direction. Moreover, the works at Punhete must have reassured him. Would we not attempt these demonstrations to cover a retrograde movement? In that case, we could only march on Coimbra; in order for us to withdraw on one of the banks of the Zezere, we would have had to refrain from engaging any of our advanced troops that were at Leiria in the middle of these diverse movements. Either a crossing of the Tagus or a march on the Mondego were the most probable moves, and at the same time they seemed to be the most contrary to the interests of the English army, because both of them increased the sojourn of the French in Portugal and consolidated our establishment there; yet these two maneuvers were very delicate and even dangerous. Although it was not very difficult to determine from the indications which maneuvers we were obliged to choose, suppose the uncertainty were prolonged further. Would the English General have allowed these movements to take place quietly when they were made by an army of less than twenty-eight thousand combatants before a force three times [*sic*] as numerous and rendered even more formidable by the advantages of its position?[9] Would he allow our army to take so

9. In fact, Wellington was completing plans to attack Masséna's army. The main attack was to be made against Junot's position, with a secondary effort directed against Reynier at Santarém. Arrangements were made for Beresford to cross the Tagus at Abrantes and attack Loison, but Wellington decided to delay

many cannon, sick and wounded, and even our pontoons if we wished?

In the midst of such uncertainties, what would a great general do? First, if his superiority were so immense, he could make no mistake. He could march from every direction on Leiria, Torres Novas, and Golegã, quite assured of superiority everywhere. If, with many fewer troops, he had wanted to overrun the most vital point and simultaneously maneuver according to the rules of strategy, it seemed to me that he would have to throw his left on Leiria and then advance it and move his center progressively toward Torres Novas; the latter would have been repulsed [?]. Thus the enemy held themselves ready either to approach the Tagus and reinforce the troops defending the left bank in case of a crossing, or to attack us during the operation. In addition, by this maneuver the fronts of their columns would anticipate us at Leiria, and as soon as our movement was unmasked they could extend themselves on the Pombal road and throw us back on the Alva. But without entering into all these calculations, he who knows only the sword in war must cut knots that cannot be unraveled, and everything may be reduced to a single maneuver—an attack by the center when one has superiority in valor or number. In any case, Lord Wellington had two corps of the French army and a part of the 6th Corps in front of him, that is, more than two-thirds of our troops. Since he had been ready to march with his whole army for a long time, and especially after March 4, why did he not move on the plains of Torres Novas with his main force and bring all the boats and resources up along the left bank of the Tagus for the passage? If he left two divisions at Alcoentre, Wellington would then have been ready for anything and he would have been able to oppose us very closely, bridge to bridge, sword to sword, maneuver to maneuver; but it appears that doubts and calculations delayed the English General up to the last minute during the three days our maneuver lasted. The march of the columns on the left bank of the Tagus, the small number of troops pursuing us on Branco, the delay of those arriving at Leiria—all this

his attack until additional reinforcements arrived from England. Wellington visited Rio Maior on March 5, noting the French positions. He wrote to Beresford the same day, "I should think the movement of the troops [French] has not yet been made, at least generally. . . . The reinforcements have arrived, and we shall be able in a few days to attack the enemy if he retains this position, or possibly to attack him in any other which he may take." See D'Urban, *Peninsular Journal,* p. 185; *Wellington's Dispatches,* VII, 338–40.

proves it sufficiently. In the end the question would be resolved in favor of the English General's insight, but not his activity—so cannon were fired at Lisbon on the 6th to celebrate the deliverance of Portugal (the distance from Cartaxo to the capital was not great and it was possible to correspond in a few minutes by telegraph). These maneuvers were not rearranged after the event as so often occurs in military reports. The dispositions of our movement were recorded in the army correspondence and in the dispatches of the Major General on February 26, while those of the enemy general were made only as he maneuvered.

Let us carry our observations a little further. Lord Wellington's attention was not confined to our army. At the other end of his line a weak corps had taken Badajoz from him, thus opening the most accessible part of Portugal. Consequently, Wellington had to choose between two lines of operation—against the 5th Corps or against us; or, rather, he was obliged to profit by his strength and pursue both of them, since he would again have the advantage of interior lines against our exterior ones. In four marches he could have moved to Badajoz. Since the 5th Corps was not very large, a detachment of eight to ten thousand Englishmen would have been sufficient when united with the Portuguese forces scattered on the frontier or in the fortresses and the stragglers from the battle of Gebora. These troops could have forced Marshal Soult to raise the siege of a fortress that contained a garrison of nine thousand men, who until the last moment had undertaken some excellent sorties. The very announcement of the English approach and our withdrawal could have forced the 5th Corps to withdraw from its daring enterprise; thus, the English would have punished the mistakes of those who rushed this operation. If Lord Wellington had foreseen our maneuver and marched his detachment as soon as March 5, General Hill could have arrived before the breach was practicable and saved that very important fortress.[10] Wellington would have been able

10. With regard to Badajoz, Wellington wrote on March 5 to Beresford, who was commanding the Allied force on the left bank of the Tagus, "We cannot rely upon Badajoz holding out, or that the besieging army will not receive another reinforcement; and I am therefore inclined to be of [the] opinion that we ought to take advantage of the enemy's quitting the Tagus to relieve that place, and set up again the army of the left." On March 8 he wrote to Stuart, "I detach a large force, under Sir William Beresford, for the assistance of Badajoz, which I propose to join as soon as I shall have settled matters on this side." See *Wellington's Dispatches,* VII, 338–40, 348–49.

to accomplish this by marching in force as soon as our bridge equipment had been burned and by sending considerable cavalry ahead of him as soon as the goal of our operations had been sufficiently unmasked. This was fresh proof that Wellington only realized what we were doing after he received the report announcing the formation of a line from Leiria to Tomar—and then it was too late.

Thus good fortune gave our maneuver the merit of contributing to the success at Badajoz. If we had withdrawn from the Zezere and simply marched backward on March 5 with a rather strong rear guard, Lord Wellington would have been the master of all his maneuvers, for even with Hill's unit detached he had enough troops left to maneuver against us with superior forces along the whole line. In this way, he could have mastered our movements, still reinforced the forces at Badajoz, and maintained some advantage in number against our army.

Finally, if it had been necessary to send half his English divisions to save Badajoz, it seemed that duty, politics, and gratitude should have impelled him to do so. With excellent information on everything that was happening as far away as Almeida, and even in northern Spain, and consequently aware that no reinforcements were marching toward us, what did he have to fear from our army once it had started its retreat? Could not an able and active general have achieved all these results and struck us at every point by means of the central maneuver that I have already mentioned? Certainly now was the time to have this very important battle in order to try to rout our army somewhat and hasten our retreat. If Lord Wellington had marched on the Rio Maior on March 5 or on Golegã and Torres Novas at dawn on the 6th, if he had pushed the 2nd and 8th Corps as he could have hoped to do because of his great superiority in numbers, we would have been forced to withdraw to the other side of the Zezere, which we could no longer have defended with the batteries of Punhete on our flanks and Abrantes at our rear. We were entirely outflanked by that fortress and as a result would have been pushed away from the Tagus and thrown back toward the Serra da Estrêla. On the same day [March 6] he could have sent the troops on the left bank of the Tagus to Badajoz and the other forces would have supported this advance guard by the bridge at Abrantes. The English General could have sought to treat the Army of the South like the Army of Portugal and even to seize Badajoz through the breach we had [used to] enter.

Thus by a single vigorous action, Portugal could have been delivered and the affairs of Spain well advanced. Then Badajoz could have been repaired and a minor detachment would have been sufficient between this fortress, Campo Maior, and Elvas. The remainder of the detachment could have rejoined the English army by way of Alfaiates, leaving a garrison on the Tagus at Alcántara or elsewhere to link the operations of the Douro and those of the Guadiana. [If] Lord Wellington had another fifteen to twenty thousand men at Fuentes de Oñoro, he could have been as far ahead by the month of May as he had been at the end of the year. But after March 8 it was a mistake to detach any units from the English army and until March 14 or 15, the farther away we were in time and distance, the greater was this mistake. I must also say that the battle of Gebora was another mistake, for a general should look into the future. By then Lord Wellington saw the time approaching when we would have to leave this wholly devastated country or we would be forced to maneuver one way or the other, but in any case he had to sustain the army of La Romana [which had been engaged in this battle].

We found Pombal in a terrible state of devastation. A great number of the houses had been ruined or burned by our marauders. It was said that Tomar and Leiria were in ashes. We saw an immense column of smoke rising in the direction of the latter. These last misfortunes were the work of our stragglers, for we then began to experience this plague of the army.[11] The devastation was caused especially by the abandoned state in which the soldiers left the houses. Here we must complain about a rumor that may have been spread by those who might themselves have been negligent in this regard and whose principles, obvious for a long time, made them suspect of at least a lack of supervision. It was claimed the Prince had given orders to burn everything in retreat.[12] In fact he himself always prescribed, recommended, and

11. According to a pamphlet published in 1811 in Lisbon and entitled "Relacão da victoria dos excercitos combinados em Ega e Miranda do Corvo, Condeixa e Redinha" (located in the Biblioteca Nacional at Lisbon), "There are a number of stragglers wandering through the hills; they are surrendering themselves or falling into the hands of the *ordenanza*. The *ordenanza* deliver them to the troop commanders or kill them according to the treatment they or their families have received from the French during the period of the invasion. Those who were violently insulted did not give quarter and ran them through with the sword."

12. In a letter from Picton to Colonel Pleydel dated March 24, 1811, Picton complained of the destruction left by Masséna: "The country through which we

observed every measure which could mitigate the horrors of war when it did not necessitate imperiling the rigorous needs of the service. Torres Novas was proof and example of the care the Prince had taken and of the policy he maintained there. We were assured that orders had been effective until the last moment. This province had known so many calamities that it was doubtful whether any help could bring its unfortunate inhabitants back to life even if all those who had created so much mischief bothered to remedy it. We found the peasants crammed into a few houses in each village. Fifty were in a miserable hut at Branco, and in a few hours we had removed six dead.

The movement of the 8th Corps was executed perfectly the next day [March 7], thanks to the dispositions ordered. Sometimes its rear guard was pressed slightly, and without the excellent reserve of the 6th Corps it might have found itself in difficulty at the junction of the two roads. The cavalry preceded it. It was claimed they did marvelously; their splendid actions were minimized by the Duc who, as a matter of fact, received the credit for them. On the contrary the Marshal and even General Montbrun himself said that the cavalry did not do well; but they could not have done any better, for their horses, weakened and encumbered with food as though they were dromedaries, moved only with great pain, while those of the enemy jumped and ran around, and their hussars came up to us with impunity. In general, we held and nothing had to be abandoned. The 6th Corps, in perfect order, received the 8th Corps, which marched past its support rather well. Then everyone praised the foresight of the old general who had prepared the whole march. The enemy himself complimented and praised our withdrawal, its plan, and the manner in which it was executed.[13]

The army took up positions. The 6th Corps had Mermet's division ahead of the crossroads [of Leiria and Casal dos Ovos] with the cav-

advanced affording no [*sic*] one article of human subsistence, the enemy having destroyed everything with fire and sword." Again in the same letter, "Nothing can exceed the devastation and cruelties committed by the enemy during the whole course of his retreat; setting fire to all the villages and murdering all the peasantry for leagues on each flank of his columns. Their atrocities have been such and so numerous, that the name of a Frenchman must be execrated here for ages." See Thomas Picton, *Memoirs of Lieutenant General Sir Thomas Picton*, ed. Heaton B. Robinson (2nd ed., London, 1836), I, 381–88.

13. Pelet himself must receive credit for planning a large part of the French withdrawal.

alry at its head, Marchand's division in reserve, and Marcognet's brigade at Pombal; its artillery and baggage were all perfectly placed and well echeloned. The 8th Corps was at Venda da Cruz, one league beyond Pombal; the 9th at Travaços, half a league before Pombal; the 2nd at Venda Nova on the road to Espinhal; and General Loison occupied Ancião.

My friends and I went sadly through the streets of Pombal. We wished to see the tomb of the renowned marquis again, but everything was ruined and devastated. Of the remains of this great man, who had served this country with his power and good deeds for such a long time, there was left only a chalk inscription where a French hand had vainly written, "Respect this tomb." In the evening we went to forget our miseries by walking all through the bivouacs. The stroll was superb and the Pombal road magnificent. This view looked like a military celebration in the middle of a beautiful promenade illuminated by fires shining among the thickness of the olive trees, amidst the trophies of our arms.

The Prince occupied himself with a method for crossing the Mondego, and, wishing to approach it, he gave the following orders for the next day, March 10. General Montbrun and Colonel Valazé, with the 15th and 25th Dragoons and the sappers, were to reconnoiter the Mondego. Marcognet's brigade would move to Condeixa to support them, the 9th Corps would be at Redinha, and the 8th Corps at Soure near the lower part of the Mondego. Marshal Ney would be at Pombal with three regiments of General Trelliard's dragoons, and General Loison would be between Ancião and Redinha.[14] These dispositions were the result of a plan agreed upon and communicated to the Major General for the purpose of occupying a position before Coimbra, between the sea and the Zezere, and remaining as long as possible in the region on the left bank of the Mondego. The arrangements were urgent, but unfortunately they were completely suspended upon the arrival of the Marshal, who came to His Excellency's quarters to tell him that the English were reinforcing themselves ahead of him, that some infantry had arrived, and that four thousand men could be seen. He asked that we remain in position to halt the enemy movement, as he wanted, and

14. The extraordinary accuracy of Pelet's details is shown by a comparison with Masséna's letter to Ney of March 9, 1811, in Correspondance: Armée de Portugal, Carton C[7]12.

to learn what forces were following us. This pause would also prove to the enemy that they were not pushing us and that our retreat was made in great order. The Prince made an error in believing the Marshal's repeated request and indeed his pleas, but how could a French general resist? I witnessed this noble and touching conversation. They agreed that the Marshal would return to the advance post early the next day, that the Prince would be there at six or seven o'clock, and that all movement would be suspended. The enemy infantry had come through Branco, along with a good part of the cavalry which had joined them at Chão de Macãs; this therefore was the force sent to follow us.

The Marshal wrote during the night to report that the entire enemy army was there and that the fires were increasing considerably. At dawn [on March 10] the Prince mounted his horse and went to the advance posts.[15] As he passed, he ordered General Drouet not to make any movement, but this did not please the general. At first we found the second brigade of General Marchand and then that of General Mermet, echeloned with their artillery and cavalry in front, and the line of the advance post beyond the junction of the two roads. The enemy's vedettes were on the plateau, their great fires and their infantry near the Branco road on the right of the Soure, and some posts were ahead on both banks. Their position, located on the two hills of Branco and covered by the river, was only defensive at that time. Nothing appeared on the road from Leiria. Thus Wellington had certainly been deceived by our maneuvers and had remained uncertain about the goal of our operation until the last moment, since he had not marched on Leiria nor sent a strong force behind us.[16] It was probable,

15. Ney, apparently alarmed by the concentration of the Allied army, wrote to Masséna early on March 10, "The Portuguese deserters assure me that the English army, 40,000 strong, is in full march against us, that the right of the army has passed Caldas, that the center is by Leiria, and that the left comes from Abrantes." Ney concluded, "Your Excellency will sense the critical situation in which I find myself if I am attacked by a force so superior that my only safety remains in a precipitant retreat. The only way to avoid this disaster is to retire before daybreak so that I am behind Pombal before the enemy can follow me in great force." See Bonnal, *Ney,* III, 485.

16. On the contrary, Wellington's army was on the move on March 6. The Light Division and Pack's Portuguese brigade were following Junot, Spencer's First Division pursued Reynier, and the remainder of the army was marching toward Leiria. Wellington wrote confidently to Stuart, "The French retired from their position . . . and they literally march day and night. . . . We are close at their heels, and have taken some prisoners; and I mean to continue to press them

however, that he would receive reinforcements by that road. Whatever the case may have been, the English did not seem to be ready to abandon Lisbon completely, but we could not believe that their whole army was there. Moreover, they should have extended themselves more, at least up to the Leiria road. A Portuguese officer, a deserter or spy, assured us that only Craufurd's weakly supported division was in front of us.

Shortly after we reached the line, General Drouet arrived and started discussing his departure and his autonomy with the Prince, who showed too much patience and kindness, especially in the presence of the other commanders. The general told him that he would leave and alone answer for his army corps and government; he could not entertain orders contrary to those of the Major General. In vain the Prince and the Marshal pressed him to remain. The general backed all of us into a corner, asking whether we were going to fight or not; since there was no reason for a battle, he insisted on withdrawal. It was finally agreed that he would leave in the evening but would move only in very short stages of two leagues so that he could reinforce the army in case of need.

We remained for a long time to examine and discuss the plans and maneuvers of the enemy; Wellington had two approaches on Pombal, one by the road and another along the right bank of the Soure. I vainly recommended that we occupy them.[17] There was even less agreement on the size of the enemy forces; this was very important for us to know since their number would determine our operations. The day was lost in discussion. This was a monumental mistake, even twofold, because we were not yet assured of the bridge on the Mondego in this

so hard that they will not have time to do much harm." See *Wellington's Dispatches,* Wellington to Beresford, March 6, 1811, VII, 344–45; Wellington to Stuart, March 8, 1811, VII, 348–49.

17. While Masséna and Ney were reconnoitering the position at Pombal, Masséna declared, "The honor of the army is entrusted to you; come what may, it is necessary to hold." Ney suggested a position behind Pombal, but Masséna responded, "It is necessary to remain before [Pombal]: that position is good. Moreover, is it not necessary to gain time until our baggage and headquarters have marched off?" In a letter that evening, Ney complained to Masséna, "Is it with three brigades rather than the entire 6th Corps that I am obliged to hold the position before or behind Pombal?" Ney concluded his letter by indicating that he would withdraw from in front of Pombal at 2:00 A.M., March 11, and retreat on Venda da Cruz, leaving only a post at Pombal. See Koch, *Mémoires de Masséna,* VII, 353–54; Masséna to Ney, 8:00 P.M., March 11, 1811, Archives de Masséna, LI.

operation. It was necessary to do quickly what was most pressing in order to approach the river and effect the passage; to halt only at Redinha on the other side of the Anços; to cover the operations against Coimbra and then reconnoiter the forces and intentions of the enemy. It was also necessary to choose a defensive position where the army could establish a line and force the English to deploy themselves, whereas the line we then occupied was completely to our disadvantage. At the least we should have marched at noon, since the enemy did not make any movement. We had showed them we did not fear their attacks. At that time we had General Montbrun leave with the troops destined for the expedition on the Mondego. Nothing indicated that we could cross it at that time, but the passage became more and more improbable the longer we delayed it.

In the evening the Prince sent me with orders for Marshal Ney to withdraw at one o'clock in the morning. General Drouet was to leave at midnight for Redinha, and the Duc d'Abrantès was to place himself between that village and Soure very early. The Marshal asked me what the 2nd Corps was going to do. I answered that it was to cover and guarantee the defile of the Alva and Ponte de Murcella in case we could not cross the Mondego. He strongly approved of this, insisting on the necessity of hurrying the movement—he who had made us lose the whole day. He also insisted that we cross the Mondego if we had to. He did not appear very convinced that it would be necessary.

General Montbrun finally received orders to leave with the 15th and the 25th Dragoons. Colonel Valazé and *chef de bataillon* Beaufort accompanied him with three companies of sappers to set up some kind of a passage on the Mondego. Montbrun insisted on going toward the lower part of the river, which was only a vast plain of water as a result of extensive flooding. The Marshal pointed out a ford three thousand yards below Coimbra, but how could we hope to find fords during the rainy spring season? I talked with Valazé about the necessity of approaching Coimbra as soon as possible either for the establishment of the bridge or for a strategic operation. The colonel was obliged to induce the general to go toward Pereira, or at least to send him there. A formal order was given before their departure the next day. The peasants started to take up arms again and open fire on the foragers. We were forced to communicate with General Loison at Ancião by way of Redinha. The rain and the unfavorable weather continued.

The Prince, learning that the Marshal had waited until five o'clock in the morning to start his maneuver, gave me orders to go to him. It was not long before the Prince himself went after him. The 9th Corps had left and the 6th Corps had moved to occupy its position momentarily. The 69th Line relieved the 76th Line at Pombal; the latter set off for Condeixa where the 39th Line and 3rd Dragoons were already posted. I found the Marshal at the head of the cavalry. His army corps was deployed as follows: the 6th Léger was in a position not far from Pombal with the 11th Dragoons and four pieces of artillery. Then the 59th, 50th, and 27th Line and the 25th Léger of Mermet's division were echeloned by regiment on the flanks of the road with two guns each. The rest of the artillery was in a double column on the road. Everything was in the most beautiful order. The pickets were recalled with the sound of the drums and the trumpets. The cavalry filed by. The 6th Dragoons, echeloned by squadrons to form the rear guard on the plain, were forbidden to go on the road where they would encounter gunfire. I asked the Marshal for permission to stay with him and receive a fine lesson in war maneuvers. It would have been difficult to find a better teacher.

The enemy were still in the same positions, but the remainder of their infantry must have been closer behind the heights. They had taken up arms at the dawn [?], thinking we had left, because they put them down without any other movement. Leaving behind the 6th Dragoons and a battalion of the 25th Léger with two guns, the Marshal put the division in movement, each regiment in column by platoon at the distance of a platoon and, it seemed to me, marching by the third rank. After the Marshal had crossed the plain and arrived at a small grove of olive trees, he himself posted a company of voltigeurs from a battalion of the 25th Léger, and they became the rear guard for the cavalry. Thus he watched all the movements of his regiments, ordering the divisions to lengthen or shorten their steps to separate those that had first formed. Perhaps he halted too frequently and became too involved in minute details. Arriving parallel with the 6th Léger, Mermet's division overtook it, and Mermet was charged with the rear guard, supported by the 69th Line in a column, close to the entrance of Pombal.

As we returned, we met the Prince, who left in a short time for Redinha. The Marshal had talked with me at length about our situation and I continued this conversation with the Prince.[18] We concerned ourselves with the difficulties of our position if the enemy followed us with all their forces, but we still did not know or really expect the difficulties that would result in crossing the Mondego with all the rivers flooded. I boldly reminded him of the nature of the river and the big bend it formed near Montemor; of the rumors circulating that the reinforcement recently arrived by sea and not yet disembarked would be sent to Figueira; of the possibility of an enemy march on that point by their left flank; and finally of the ravages Trant had committed beyond Coimbra when he destroyed all the food that remained.[19] All these obstacles would probably have forced us to give up the Mondego, sooner or later, in order to retain firmly the exits of the Alva, since they were more practicable and nearer to our fortresses. Nevertheless, a flank maneuver which should in that case have been made in a direction perpendicular to the one we were following was already very difficult in itself; it would have been more dangerous for an army burdened with numerous artillery (sixty-four pieces) and forced to drag its sick and wounded, its food, and its baggage while pressed between an enemy superior in force and a swollen river. Thus, we had arrived at a position where we considered ourselves fortunate to be established along the Dueça or the Ceira in an oblique position between the Mondego and the Zezere. At that moment our question was reduced to knowing the exact defenses of Coimbra, the state of its bridge, and the number of troops the enemy had behind us. Thus, when Adjutant Commander Béchet de Léocourt asked me that evening at Redinha, "Well, what are we doing? Are we crossing, or are we going into Spain?" I answered him, "It is up to you gentlemen of the

18. Pelet here apologizes in a footnote, "I am forced to write down many of these conversations when they describe our situation as well as the way important people thought of it. They are legitimate and reinforce my opinions partially; from them we can judge everyone. Some malicious people will say it is better to speak less and act more, but they will only be repeating what has been said much earlier."

19. An *Edital* signed by Trant on February 5, 1811, declared, "It is becoming more and more urgent for the enemy to find food. It cannot be doubted that they will try to cross the Mondego River on the first occasion to seize the cattle and wheat that were transported north of this river. . . . Inside of an eight-day period starting now, all the cattle, goats, sheep, etc., and all the wheat and stores of corn must be moved north of the Vouga River under the punishment of having all the food confiscated for the benefit of the troops and immediate arrest." See Colleção da Academia das Sciências de Lisboa.

rear guard to decide the question. Do you have the whole enemy army in front of you? If so, we probably could not think of crossing. If you have only part of it, we can work at it."

When we arrived at Redinha about three o'clock [on March 11], we heard cannon and musket fire. The enemy had attacked the 6th Léger, which had remained a little too isolated. A force more than three times ours with numerous artillery had been directed against that brave regiment, which suffered considerably but sustained its efforts vigorously. As the regiment passed through the city, it was attacked on its flanks by some troops that had followed the right of the Soure, spreading some disorder. The English occupied Pombal and its old Moorish castle for a moment, but the 69th Line, another excellent regiment of the same brigade placed in reserve at the exit of the city, charged the enemy with bayonets and chased them out of Pombal. The English, wanting to fight for the city, lost many soldiers in the houses and on the streets, but they reinforced themselves continuously. In order to end this useless fight, the Marshal set fire to what was left of the city, and the armies kept their respective positions on the two banks of the Soure, with the enemy extended on our flank along the heights of the left bank.[20]

Our rear guard reached Pombal. The divisions of Mermet and Marchand were echeloned to the rear, and the Marshal moved his headquarters to Venda da Cruz. The 8th Corps and the cavalry had been halted at Redinha; Loison's division was near Rabaçal, and the 2nd Corps was around Espinhal. General Montbrun, who was to reach the Mondego that day, was content to send a reconnaissance while he stopped at Condeixa. We knew from reports and prisoners that Lord Wellington was present; it was said that the enemy had shown many men at Pombal. Adjutant Commander Béchet de Léocourt, chief of staff of the 6th Corps, limited their attack to four thousand men. The countryside was horribly devastated. The rain had caused a considerable loss of biscuit. Destitution was beginning to overtake some of the

20. At 4:00 A.M. two companies of the 95th Rifles and 3rd Caçadores, supported by the remainder of the Light Division, Ross's artillery, and the 1st German Hussars, attacked Colonel Fririon's 6th Léger. Wellington's attack was rather limited since the divisions of Picton and Cole had not yet arrived. Ney had 63 casualties and Wellington 37. See Simmons, *British Rifleman*, pp. 139–40; *Wellington's Dispatches*, Wellington to Liverpool, March 14, 1811, VII, 354–61; Delagrave, *Mémoires*, pp. 192–93n; Oman, *Peninsular War*, IV, 614.

soldiers, especially the sick who, under the command of a superior officer, were detached from their corps and far from all assistance.

The passage between the Serra da Estrêla and the Mondego, the most direct communication with Spain and the one where we might be forced to retire at any moment, became more and more important to us. The Prince sent Captain Cavailher, one of his aides-de-camp and an excellent engineer, to reconnoiter the various roads to Ponte de Murcella. The enemy had descended the valley of the Soure during the evening and outflanked the right of the 6th Corps from far away. The 6th Corps received orders to march on Redinha. We soon learned that the enemy was following it. With General Fririon I went to see the Marshal. As we arrived at Venda da Cruz, we saw the front of our column leaving the village. Redinha was three leagues away from Pombal, and Venda da Cruz was halfway between them. The road made a rather pronounced angle, open at the east, and the Soure ran beside the road to the hamlet; the ground there was advantageous for the enemy, who could outflank our position by the other bank of the river. Beyond Venda da Cruz, the terrain still continued to ascend along a series of abutments which dominated each other in the direction of Redinha. The road was very good, presenting stretches which were directly enfiladed by the heights. All this terrain formed excellent defensive positions for us, even better since it was buttressed on the left by a chain of mountains very near Redinha. The summits of all the hills, immediately above the village, offered the best of these positions. However, for withdrawal this site had a long defile in the rear formed by the village of Redinha and a very narrow bridge across the Anços, which had rather steep banks and was fifty-one feet wide; the reverse of this same summit offered an excellent position to the enemy. The crest, opposite the other side of the Anços, was less favorable for us. The two armies knew this ground well since they had crossed it a short time earlier and were able to derive every possible advantage.

We found the 6th Corps marching perfectly during the retreat with the first division at its head and the second restraining the enemy, who still showed no disposition to attack. In the rear we saw that everything was perfectly placed. The artillery was well echeloned on the various enfilading heights and the terrain was well reconnoitered. Marchand's division and the cavalry moved to crown the hill above

Redinha, Mermet's division established itself on a berm immediately below, and the 3rd Hussars were to the right of the road between the two divisions. I ran as fast as possible to a small hill to look at the left, where the Anços made a very pronounced hook and ran parallel to the Pombal road in a valley some eight hundred yards wide. The foot of the mountain was crossed by several roads and another one came from Pombal through the valley; some cavalry with one cannon scouted this area, but the position was too extensive for two infantry divisions.

The Prince soon arrived on the line and remained there for a short time; seeing nothing new that would induce us to anticipate an attack, he left for Condeixa to be near the Mondego. *Chef de bataillon* Couche, commander of the engineers of the 6th Corps, followed him to reconnoiter the region and indicate to the Marshal the positions the Prince wanted to have occupied between Condeixa and Redinha, since there were three short leagues between the two villages. Beyond the Anços the road neared the mountain, circling the bed of the valley, and crossed a rough and difficult country with very limited foothills, many ravines, defiles, and finally perplexing terrain, but there we could not establish a line of two or three regiments. Midway was a wide valley opening onto a cultivated ridge; we probably could find some road there to climb to its summit more easily and descend toward Rabaçal and Fonte Coberta; right behind the ridge the terrain was regular. We came across a slope that the road ascended. On the right there were rocks and woods and on the left a steep escarpment; all in all, a good position for a division. I designated the position there as "number one." Half a league behind, there was another abutment, shorter but just as steep and covered with rocks and stones near the summit; it dominated and effectively swept the route. At the least it could halt the enemy for a few hours and force them to outflank or bypass it to the west; furthermore it formed a reserve for the preceding abutment. I designated this as "number two."

Finally, a quarter of a league in front of Condeixa rose a lofty and dominant hill. Its slope was divided in two by a berm, and the road crossed it in a single straight line, embanked by the slopes and enfiladed from one end to the other. In front of this position was a stream about forty feet wide, running through difficult and cultivated ground. The left of the hill rested firmly on the chain of mountains and the right dropped down two thousand yards; beyond, it was extended by a small rideau to a bend in the stream about four thousand yards away. In total this formed a large and superb position for the army, and behind it was Condeixa, rather poorly entrenched by the enemy. All this region was easy to defend and occupy. The Portuguese had constructed some epaulements and barricades across the road at the embanked areas. We passed through Condeixa, which was obstructed by a great number of wagons from the *parc* or the food train, herds, and baggage. Our uncertainty about the direction we were going had halted the march.

When the Prince arrived, he received reports of the reconnaissance on Coimbra and the Mondego. General Montbrun, having received orders to move on the Mondego, first announced his intention of going toward Pereira and then ascending the river near Coimbra on March 11. Nevertheless, he stopped at Condeixa, which Marcognet's brigade had not yet reached. From there he ordered Treussart to go to Pereira, and Captain Armand François Claude de Briqueville to Vila Nova to observe the Mondego. He gave sixty dragoons to Valazé and Beaufort for reconnoitering the approaches to Coimbra. These officers, forced to echelon along the road, arrived in front of the city with eight men and established themselves as vedettes. They saw that the Mondego was extremely high and even touched the keystone of the bridge arches. The second arch nearest the city was broken and open for some forty feet; the preceding arch was half damaged. Planks placed across both of the arches served for the passage of a rather large number of people who went to the other side when they saw our troops. The Mondego then appeared to be almost four hundred yards wide near the bridge. On that day they saw very few troops and no cannon. The reports of these officers, which I still have before me, along with an outline of the bridge, allowed us to believe that with some infantry we could have entered the city immediately behind the fugitives. However, the planks over the arches could have been very quickly seized and thrown into the water, and perhaps the enemy had not wanted to fire their cannon and take up weapons against eight men, whereas the next day their cannonade would have been rather heavy when they saw a large number of our troops.

There was no possibility that the flooded river was fordable anywhere or that any boats remained on our bank. The officers found the road barricaded at several points and only a small number of Portuguese on foot or horses. On their return they were followed for half an hour by these Portuguese, and the next day they saw a considerable number of troops. According to Treussart's report, which I have kept, the Mondego was very high. They found it divided from Pereira to Tentúgal by a very low island partially covered with water and more than a league in width. At Pereira the branch had three feet of water and at Tentúgal it was much deeper; it could not be crossed without boats. According to the inhabitants, there was no ford below Coimbra, and the city was defended by twelve to thirteen thousand Portuguese, not counting several regiments scattered as far as Figueira. Treussart had seen three hundred men at Tentúgal in a position very advantageous for the enemy. Regarding General Montbrun's operations, the general decided to approach Coimbra the next day; he wanted to establish, without much reason, a few men near the bridge abutment on the left bank and protect them with barriers. At that time he was vigorously cannonaded with artillery established on the ramps of the slopes of Coimbra.

As a result of these reconnaissances, we could no longer consider either the bridge at Coimbra or the fords on the Mondego. We could not find boats or any other means whatever for crossing. Reports announced the arrival of some boats at Figueira and some landings which might have carried the reinforcements announced for Coimbra. The reconnaissance sent toward our right had encountered enemy detachments, and it was said that one of their columns, marching in our direction, had passed the Soure and reached a point almost parallel to Condeixa and was in consequence quite close to the Mondego. Thus the river, impassable for us at this time, was defended by Portuguese forces that appeared rather considerable. The English could occupy the opposite bank at any moment. Even if we had had the means to set up a bridge, we could not have risked such an operation at this time.[21] Wellington's army was very close to Coimbra and could have attacked us during the middle of our river passage or engaged in a violent and frightful battle with the rear guard, and even crushed the army if it were cut in two by an accident at the bridge.

Accordingly, on the arrival of these reports, it was quickly decided

21. Eight miles below Coimbra, Montbrun's scouts discovered a point where a trestle bridge could be erected. Apparently a bridge was started, but it was abandoned because they lacked adequate time.

to renounce the Mondego and move as little as possible toward the Ceira or the Alva, and to take up a position on one of these two rivers which, descending from the Serra da Estrêla and flowing into the Mondego, blocked that great passage to Spain. Very fortunately, the disposition of the columns of march assured us of the possibility of such a movement. What would have occurred if our army had marched along a single road, as armies often did, rather than taking those parallel roads through Ancião and Espinhal? If the enemy had been able to turn us rather uselessly by this flank, our left was perfectly safe, firmly supported by the mountains whose reverse was occupied by General Loison and parallel to the 6th Corps' position before Condeixa. Nevertheless, we did not have much time to lose in beginning our movement, and the daily consumption of food forced us to accelerate it.

At about three or four o'clock [on March 12] Lieutenant Saint Charles, an aide-de-camp of General Fririon, arrived in great haste to inform the Prince that Marshal Ney was being attacked by the entire English army at Redinha. The Prince mounted his horse to gather the troops of the 8th Corps and march to aid the 6th Corps. Meanwhile, he sent me as fast as possible to the Marshal. I found the engagement over; thus it had lasted a very short time. The Marshal was very near to the burning village of Redinha. He told me that soon after our departure, and while his two divisions were established in line on the position, the enemy advanced their English infantry columns which included from twenty to twenty-five thousand men. They had been deployed in front of a small woods where Mermet's division was first posted. After maneuvering rather a long time under the fire of all our artillery, they suffered terribly although they did not advance the six guns they had shown when their troops had been in line. Then the Marshal decided to commence his retrograde movement by echelon and move beyond the gorge. When Marchand's division got beyond it, they found themselves situated on the other side of the valley while the enemy had directed one column by our left toward Redinha and the bridge.

We still had six pieces in front of the village, and they were in a rather awkward position. With two battalions of the 27th and 50th Line, the Marshal attacked the enemy, who were very near. Our battalions threw themselves on several English battalions, under a murderous fire, and pushed them back in great disorder. During this time our guns were withdrawn, Redinha was set afire, and the enemy was contained. The Marshal complained that he had lost many men. His losses have since been exaggerated. In my presence he praised the colonel of the 27th Line, who referred him to his *chef de bataillon*, Colette. We acknowledged that this battalion lost two hundred men, but the 50th Line, who shared the success and glory, lost only sixty. It was claimed that the 3rd Hussars, who performed perfectly, lost thirty men, but only three were killed and twice that number wounded. Colonel Louis Marie Levesque, Comte de Laferrière, had been wounded leading a charge. In general, the battle was brilliant and very glorious, even for the 6th Corps. It was rather lively, but we had many who wished to exaggerate it. The enemy must have lost a great many men to our artillery. A single horse, superbly harnessed and with four or five wounds, had come to us; his rider, whom we assumed to have been some type of English officer, had probably been killed. The prisoners placed the number of troops deployed by the English at thirty thousand men, without counting those in the rear.[22]

I returned with the Marshal, and he told me that he was going to form a rear guard composed of the 25th Léger, 27th and 39th Line, and four cannon for the brave General Ferey. The Marshal expected to move to Condeixa. I urged him [not to], I implored him in the name of the Prince, but he did not appear to be affected very much. Finally, he yielded and requested some positions. I reminded him of the positions that *chef de bataillon* Couche had pointed out to him: "number one" for Marchand's first division, "number two" for the second, and then the superb position of Condeixa for his whole army corps. He

22. At 5:30 A.M., March 12, Wellington dispatched three columns against Ney's position at Redinha; the Light Division advanced before the village, Picton marched on Ney's right but was repulsed by Mermet's bayonet charge, and Pack's brigade marched between these two divisions. Wellington paused in his attack to await Cole's Fourth Division, and Ney impatiently observed, "It was an imposing spectacle in which an army of 25,000 English and a great number of Portuguese were repelled at each instance by a force of 6,000 men that I maneuvered without having recourse to my reserves, who occupied my line of retreat." By 3:00 P.M. Cole had arrived and the Allied army began to advance. After contesting the village, Wellington started to outflank the 6th Corps, forcing Ney to retire. Ney concluded his description of the battle by declaring, "I think that Lord Wellington will agree and render justice to the valiant conduct of the troops of His Imperial Majesty." See Bonnal, *Ney*, Ney to Masséna, March 12, 1811, III, 488–92. The French lost 227 men and the English 206. See Delagrave, *Mémoires*, p. 198n; Oman, *Peninsular War*, IV, 614–15.

adopted them after some difficulty. It was still necessary to confer about how long he would hold. I beseeched him again. Finally, the Marshal anticipated the time himself and promised me forty-eight hours before evacuating Condeixa: twenty-four hours holding in the two positions, numbers one and two, and twenty-four hours at the position in front of Condeixa. This was agreed upon and thereafter we could calculate and act. It was almost night; thus the Marshal had promised to hold for the two days of March 13 and 14.[23] We looked at the positions together and he concurred. I rejected the necessity of going all the way into Spain, at least immediately. He asked me whether we were crossing or not. I gave the same response as I had to his chief of staff, Béchet de Léocourt, "Is the English army there or not?" "Certainly it is all there, with Lord Wellington." "Then all our doubt ends, for we cannot attempt to cross the river without boats or other means with such an army on our rear." In fact, the prisoners declared that Lord Wellington was following us with the entire Allied army, since Cole's division had rejoined it and given up pursuit of the 2nd Corps.[24]

The Marshal feared the enemy would make some maneuver on his flank in order to go through Fonte Coberta, which was along our line of communication with Ponte de Murcella. I agreed with him completely. In short, I was very pleased by his promises and dispositions. We soon met the Prince, who hurried to the 6th Corps, on the way back to Condeixa. I proposed to the Prince a move on Fonte Coberta with the entire 8th Corps, or rather on the junction of the routes of Ponte de Murcella and Rabaçal where Loison's division would arrive. We did not know whether Fonte Coberta was at this junction or not. I had always thought it was half a league away, in accordance with my new information. The Prince put off a decision, without reason, until

23. At 8:00 P.M. on the night of March 12, after the battle of Redinha, Masséna wrote to Ney, "It is essential that we hold before Condeixa all day tomorrow [March 13] in order to give our baggage time to file on the route to Miranda do Corvo." See Archives de Masséna, LI.

24. Sir Galbraith Lowry Cole (1772–1842) entered the army in 1787 and became a major in the 86th Foot in 1793. He served as a staff officer until 1797 when he was elected to the Irish House of Commons. Cole was in command at Malta in 1805 and the next year he was in charge of a brigade in the battle against Reynier at Maida; he was promoted to major general and in 1809 sent to the Peninsula where he commanded the Fourth Division throughout Masséna's invasion. During the French retreat Colonel Miles Nightingale's brigade rather than Cole's division followed Reynier's corps.

the next day; meanwhile he sent orders to Clauzel's division to support General Loison's division. Solignac's division was to move in the direction of Soure. Both of them should have been sent to and established at the actual crossroad to Casal Novo, but great things are often decided with little reason. General Montbrun was still near Coimbra, making useless warnings of his presence with the 15th and 25th Dragoons and some companies of voltigeurs. The Prince wrote to the 9th Corps not to leave Miranda do Corvo, and to the 2nd Corps to occupy Espinhal in order to hold the army in line and protect all the communications up to the defiles beyond Espinhal. General Drouet replied that he would stay. Nevertheless, I believed he finally abandoned this point, which was, it is true, very close to Corvo and the route of the 2nd Corps, though we did not know it. Lopez's map showed a distance of three leagues between Miranda do Corvo and Corvo when in fact it was only half a league. Marshal Ney came to the Prince's quarters very early. He claimed they had heared and even seen the entire English army, or at least a great part of it, during the night, marching on our left. I expected some such movement. I feared it but I thought his report was somewhat exaggerated. The Marshal believed he saw very few campfires ahead of him, and he uttered this superb phrase for a military man, "I am afraid of the enemy as long as I do not see him."

Meanwhile all Condeixa was full of artillery, baggage, herds, commissariat, sick, and the regiments. There was terrible confusion, but no remedy at first because of our uncertainty about the direction to follow, the perilous roads, and then because of the nature of the terrain surrounding Condeixa. The terrain there was cut by a multitude of small irrigation canals and gardens which prevented the regular establishment of bivouacs and the *parc* and limited the number of passages, all of which were very narrow. By dawn the officers had chosen various exits for the wagons, the troops, and the baggage. We started to evacuate, though slowly and with difficulty; I likewise hurried, listening for anything in the direction of Loison's division, for in war it is always necessary to have one's ear cocked toward a sensitive spot, that is, where one most fears an attack.

Meanwhile the Marshal was still with the Prince, and he continued to harass him. He told me boldly in the presence of Adjutant Commander Béchet de Léocourt that it was absolutely necessary to destroy and burn all the wagons and baggage. This was of little importance to me, for I had nothing but an overcoat, but I protested vigorously that he should at least wait until we were attacked and pressed before proposing this measure, since unfortunately the equipment is an army's last resource in the final extremity, and it was a matter of honor to keep it. The Marshal continued to shout at the Prince that he had never seen himself in such a difficult position, that never had a general or an army found itself in such trouble, and that we would be very fortunate to escape by any means at all. Then some officers and other well-intentioned men made comparisons with the mountains of Guimarães, with Vimeiro, Baylen, etc. I was enraged. At any other time and with other people, I would have burst into laughter, so little did I believe all this nonsense. The Marshal often expressed his feeling to me as follows: "It is necessary for me to endure it." Never have I been so still, especially as I watched the hours slip by and the baggage pass without hearing anything from our left, but never have I seen men appear so afraid, although they certainly should have been no more fearful than we were; meanwhile the Marshal urged the Prince to leave for Fonte Coberta. Solignac's division and the dragoons of Montbrun were put under his command; he gave orders and acted like the general in chief; he walked around and only ceased when he saw us. On the road he still promised to hold on to the various positions, as he had agreed the day before. Nevertheless, his soldiers were starting their preparations at Condeixa and were throwing doors, windows, and furniture inside the houses. We thought this to be preparations in case of attack. Almost immediately after our departure [from Condeixa], the village was set on fire, and the 6th Corps was in movement by two o'clock in the morning.[25]

The road to Murcella, emerging on the east of Condeixa, soon began to ascend [the hill]; it was not very good. One league away was Casal Novo, three-quarters of a league beyond was the junction with the Rabaçal road, which passed through Fonte Coberta, and half a league farther on was the road leading directly to that village. We were al-

25. On the night of March 12, Ney ordered his troops to retire and take up positions before Cartaxo [?] to cover Condeixa. Ferey was ordered to march at 5:00 or 6:00 A.M. and act as the rear guard for the entire army. See Bonnal, *Ney*, "Ordre de mouvement du 6th Corps," March 12, 1811, III, 495–96.

ready in the low mountains, our forces separated by great hills. We took this last road, turning along the cliff of a gorge. Soon we met General Clauzel, who had only left [Condeixa] that morning. I urged him to hurry to reach Loison's division as soon as possible. We could hear a cannonade in the vicinity of Coimbra against General Montbrun's dragoons, who had showed themselves near the bridge. The sound of the cannon made us think our army might still be expected to be on the Mondego, and perhaps the enemy continued to believe it; hence they would throw their left toward the river. As a result, the Marshal found the English line unoccupied before him. If such a move had been made, it would be very favorable for us and indeed inopportune on their part. They could have pushed us by the center with much greater advantage. It would have been desirable to place Solignac's division between Condeixa and General Loison. The Marshal placed it on the right; therefore he was anxious about his right and not about his left. It seemed that from that time on he engineered the movements daily. I watched these developments with great sorrow for I expected some kind of attack from the English army on our center, that is, on Loison's division.

We soon arrived at Fonte Coberta, and we posted ourselves rather poorly in that awful hole. General Loison, who had arrived the day before by the road from Rabaçal and Ancião, was near the village of Póvoa da Pega. His division and artillery, camped on the heights forward, had seen nothing during the entire morning. Soon Clauzel's division arrived without its artillery; the guns had been entrusted to the 8th Corps because those of Loison's division were sufficient for this area. This division was placed before Loison on the Rabaçal road. Our flanks were not protected. We had reason to be suspicious of the gorges through which we passed. A few battalions were sent onto the summits. From the heights we could see everything around us very clearly. We were near an open valley midway between Redinha and Condeixa. During the entire day we saw only a few posts, a few cavalry patrols, and only one column of fifteen hundred men at most on the opposite reverse that was moving toward Condeixa along the foot of the mountain and across our two abandoned positions. This could not be considered as a maneuver to outflank the left of the 6th Corps. Thus it is clear that there was no flanking maneuver against these various positions, and there could not have been any because of the terrain and the dispositions we had taken.[26]

We were without news or reports from the Marshal. At three o'clock the Prince learned by chance that he had evacuated positions number one and two and the superb position of Condeixa, that he had set the village on fire without receiving a single shot from the enemy, and that later on the 6th Corps had retired along the route to Ponte de Murcella.[27] The junction with the [Rabaçal] road behind us was not occupied by our troops. At the first news, the Prince wrote to the Marshal to express his astonishment and great anger about such a maneuver and the useless burning of the village.[28] He then gave the Marshal orders to occupy the junction, which was the only passage by which General Loison's artillery [could rejoin the army].[29] He sent his own son to carry this important dispatch. I urged the young duke to gallop across the gorge and to be careful when he recrossed it on his return. I do not know where he found the Marshal, but the latter had him run about very indiscreetly to the right and left, keeping him nearby. In

26. Underestimating Wellington's tactics, Pelet did not believe he would attempt to outflank the 6th Corps. However, while Ney was deploying his force before Condeixa, Wellington began his grand flanking maneuver. The Light Division and Cole's division advanced directly on Condeixa, the Sixth Division initiated a sweeping movement on Ney's right flank, while Picton's division moved east of the 6th Corps to cut Ney's retreat route and link with the remainder of the French army. See *Wellington's Dispatches,* Wellington to Liverpool, March 14, 1811, VII, 354–61.

27. Ney wrote on March 13 announcing his unanticipated withdrawal from Condeixa, but his letter did not reach Masséna until approximately 3:00 P.M. Ney wrote, "I evacuated Condeixa. The enemy maneuvered on my left and directed a strong column on Fuente Cuberta [*sic*]. I sent a detachment to Montbrun to effect his withdrawal to Miranda do Corvo." See Koch, *Mémoires de Masséna,* VII, 373.

28. Masséna responded to Ney's announcement of withdrawal at 3:45 P.M.: "I received your letter by which you inform me that you have evacuated Condeixa. I am very angry. I do not know if our equipment will have time to move to Miranda do Corvo. And still more inopportune is the fact that Montbrun, retiring from Coimbra, will permit Trant and Silveira to move to Ponte de Murcella. The burning of Condeixa is unfortunate. The system that we appear to have adopted necessarily reflects great disfavor on the French army." Masséna concluded, "I want you to remain two leagues before Miranda do Corvo. . . . In remaining there all day tomorrow, our equipment will have time to file through Foz de Arouce." See Correspondance: Armée de Portugal, Carton C[7]12.

29. Both Masséna and Pelet felt that the crossroads west of Casal Novo were vital for the safe withdrawal of the army and more specifically for Loison's artillery. Unaware of Wellington's movements behind Ney, they both assumed that Ney had evacuated the junction to embarrass Masséna. However, if he had not retired from this position, his two divisions would have been outflanked, encircled, and overwhelmed.

the evening the junction was completely abandoned, and the 6th Corps bivouacked at Casal Novo. The Prince sent several officers to reconnoiter roads practicable for wagons that led directly to this village.

As we ate our supper we saw some men on one of the summits. At first we did not know what was happening, but we could easily see that our position was now bad, not only for the general headquarters but also for Clauzel's division. Captain Girbault went to reconnoiter toward the gorge with four dragoons. He was pushed back very quickly by fifty English horsemen who rode into the center of the headquarters, and the guard placed at the Prince's door fired on them. The alarm was spread very swiftly. There were shouts everywhere to mount the horses. It was a moment of terrible confusion. The enemy cavalry, seeing themselves so well received, retired at a gallop.[30] We lost nothing in this skirmish and even seized an English horse that continued charging all by itself.

Now we were hurled toward Spain. The misfortunes that I had feared and predicted for so long were now at hand. I was broken-hearted—dishonored. What a distinguished retreat! The perfidy was horrible, for it was clear and incontestable. Where now would we be able to stop? On whom could we depend, I shouted. Now that I can judge events with some perspective and less passion, I am obliged to report everything that seems to justify the conduct of the Marshal. Lopez's map was very faulty, especially in the region of the Mondego. We were forced to make some kind of maps on the basis of our information and itineraries. In the one I have before me, Fonte Coberta is placed at the junction of the roads of Condeixa and Rabaçal while in fact it was half a league behind [west] the latter road. It was said that we had sent a copy of this map to the 6th Corps. During those two days [March 13–14] the location of Fonte Coberta was the only issue between the Prince and the Marshal. Perhaps the Marshal thought that as he withdrew from Condeixa he would find the Prince with Loison's division on his route. Nevertheless, if he had commited this error [of leaving the junction unprotected], he should have corrected it after

30. After this incident, Masséna said to Fririon, "The unannounced retrograde movement of these two divisions [Ney's] is an act that cannot be justified. I have not placed Marshal Ney under my orders, the Emperor has." See Fririon, *Journal historique*, pp. 150–51.

his arrival at Casal Novo. To rectify this mistake he could have chosen between retracing his steps and occupying the junction himself, which would have been a courteous thing to do, or sending troops there, which was consistent with his duty. The circumstances of the road should have been much better known, since the enemy baggage and artillery had passed by Fonte Coberta [recently]. I must add that the junction was on the bank of a stream opposite the position occupied by the Marshal when he stopped at Casal Novo, according to his usual tactics. Finally, justice demands that I mention the Marshal's letter to the Prince, which was a kind of report on the affair [at Condeixa]. It said that he was certain the enemy had at least twelve thousand infantry on the heights to the left of Condeixa in the direction of Fonte Coberta ready to move down, that he had been feebly followed into Casal Novo, and that he had occupied the junction with posts. He proposed to remain in these positions the next day. This letter, dated March 13 at Casal Novo, is in my hands. I do not believe its contents, but I have reported it.[31]

At this time everything compelled us to avoid an engagement with a weak part of our army, surrounded by such terrain and during such dispositions. Now the great problem was the escape of all of General Loison's artillery, since the junction of the one road practicable for wagons was abandoned to the enemy. To increase our difficulties further, shots were being fired in that direction. Night had come and it was quite dark; there was a proposal to bring Clauzel's division closer, which was done, and to advance to open the way as soon as the moon rose. The Prince sent General Fririon to the Marshal's quarters, but he could not be located; he finally sent me there too. Loison claimed that he was only a few steps away and I went on foot with Girbault and Richoux.

After following the main road, we went to the right to avoid the enemy posts. We fell into a multitude of small valleys, vineyards, and olive trees, and it took us more than two hours to find our way. At length we reached the bivouacs of General Mermet and Colonel Piquet* and finally the quarters of the Marshal. He was sleeping in the first room and arose immediately. He started speaking in front of everyone. I kept silent, but when we were alone I complained about

31. For Ney's defense, see footnote 27 above.

the evacuation of the two positions and Condeixa, and particularly about abandoning the junction of the road. He claimed the enemy were on all sides. I answered him that we were ahead of his left and had seen nothing, and that his left was so secure that the enemy had turned quietly around us. As for his right, he had nothing to fear and everything to gain if the enemy moved there. He was much amused by the Prince's troubles. I responded quite seriously and added that the artillery of the 6th Corps was now endangered. His main justification was that he preferred to take the chance of losing his baggage and cannon rather than his soldiers, and he was to repeat this same statement a thousand times during the retreat. I always replied that the preservation of the cannon assured the honor of the army. He complained candidly that it was General Loison's fault if his artillery was jeopardized at Fonte Coberta, since he had given him orders to send it to Condeixa. I pointed out that this was inexact and told him that the order had not been given in that manner, but if Loison had returned with his division to Condeixa, the center would have been evacuated and the army divided.

The Prince had changed this disposition and he informed the Marshal immediately; moreover the Marshal's order was given in a very odd manner while Loison was at Ancião and we were at Pombal. The Marshal had written him, "If you remain three days without receiving any orders from me, you will go to Condeixa with your artillery." He also complained of the reproach included in the [Prince's] letter about the conflagrations. We talked for a long time, seated beside an old table on which he had the kindness to place a bottle of excellent wine of which I was in great need since I was extremely tired. I proposed to attack the next day at dawn in order to clear the junction and then to advance some infantry battalions immediately. He wanted to have work done on a wretched road leading from Lamas to Fonte Coberta in order to withdraw the artillery by that route, and he had even given orders to *chef de bataillon* Couche to move there the next day with nine hundred workers. He continued to jest, saying that the next day we would see that he could extract us from our adverse position.

It has remained my conviction that the Marshal was not displeased about our troubles, nor entirely innocent of the trick played on the Prince and especially on General Loison, whom he did not like, and that he might even have wished to see the artillery compromised somewhat so that he could show himself as the vindicator and liberator of the army. Meanwhile I had left the Prince ready to maneuver as soon as the moon appeared. I awaited the effect of his dispositions. Before long I heard the artillery pass. Then I asked the Marshal jokingly if he had left some in the rear, and on his negative reply I told him, "Ah well, this is ours arriving, it is safe." The Marshal laughed grudgingly. I went and threw myself on some hay to try to rest and sleep.

The Prince pushed the enemy's advance post and covered the junctions with two divisions formed in line in a body. He had the artillery pass behind them. They were now marching on the road. The Prince had remained behind; he soon passed through Casal Novo, where he did not want to halt. I had sprained my ankle while going to the Marshal's quarters. Our horses were not there, so the Prince had me mount a mare that was being led for him. We continued marching on Miranda do Corvo. The moon was bright, and the 6th Corps was placed on some excellent heights to the right at Casal Novo.[32] The left was a little to the rear in the direction of Lamas, where Solignac's division was posted. These two villages were on the two ends of a range of heights interspersed with hills, and we climbed a considerable slope. The road meandered across those various summits, and toward Lamas it was very muddy; no doubt the village got its name from the mud (*lama*). We climbed still higher to cross a mountain covered with pines, after which a cliff road descended with the Dueça on its left. We crossed this road before arriving at Miranda; it was situated on a rather high plateau, encircled by the river. The 9th Corps had left Miranda without remaining there as had been requested. The 2nd Corps was at Corvo, half a league southward.

The enemy, maneuvering in front of the 6th Corps as usual, sought to extend its right into the valley of Casal Novo. After they had deployed their columns on the other [west] bank of the river, the Marshal started to march, retiring the first line from the village and moving it behind the second line on the height. In this way he continued his withdrawal, echeloned by brigades, stopping the enemy at each posi-

32. Marbot recalled, "During this long and toilsome march, Masséna's attention was much occupied with the danger to which Mme. N——[Leberton] was exposed. Several times her horse fell over fragments of rock invisible in the darkness, but although cruelly bruised, the brave woman picked herself up. After several of these falls, however, she could neither remount her horse nor walk on foot and had to be carried by grenadiers." See Marbot, *Mémoires,* II, 435.

tion. He made them pay dearly for every rash or desultory movement. This affair was designed for Marshal Ney's talents. He displayed his brilliant boldness and ability in maneuvering. The army cited it for a long time and designated it under the title of "*combat des positions*."[33] Thus the 6th Corps reached the foot of the mountain of pines; the Prince hurried there when he heard gunfire. Lamas was disputed for a long time by the two armies. My friend Marbot and I were engaged there, and as he crossed sabers with the English hussars he received some minor wounds.[34] The 6th Corps surrounded the village. Clauzel's division occupied Miranda and joined with the 2nd Corps, sending some posts on the other side of the Dueça to cover our right and the road to Coimbra. Solignac's division was in position and in reserve on one of the abutments of the mountain before Miranda. The right was supported on the Dueça with a company placed at the bottom of the valley to lead the way. The left was moved up to the ravines which were likewise protected. From there we could see the post of the 2nd Corps, rather near in the direction of Corvo. Between these two divisions of the 8th Corps was another abutment, a very good position for a brigade.

The Prince and the Marshal met near the village and argued with each other. I heard very strong and distressing words. The Marshal said to him, "You want to break the back of my army corps," and then on the subject of the artillery which he wanted to retain, "Ah well, send someone to parley." At that, the Prince flew into a passion. The

33. Ney's rearguard actions from Pombal, Redinha, and Condeixa to Casal Novo, Casal de Azan, Vila Seca, Chão de Lamas, Miranda do Corvo, etc. were indeed brilliant. Captain William Napier of the 43rd Foot observed, "Ney commenced his retreat, covering his rear with guns and light troops, and retiring from ridge to ridge with admirable precision, and, for a long time, without confusion and with very little loss." See Napier, *War in the Peninsula,* III, 55. Picton recalled, "The enemy's rearguard, during the whole course of the retreat, was commanded by Marshal Ney in person; and all his movements afforded a perfect lesson in that kind of warfare. Moving at all times upon his flank, I had an opportunity of seeing everything he did; and I must be dull in the extreme if I have not derived some practically useful knowledge from such an example." See Picton, *Memoirs,* Picton to Pleydel, March 24–29, 1811, I, 381–88.

34. Marbot regarded his wound as more than "minor": "I flew upon the English officer; we met; he gave me a slash across the face, I ran my sword into his throat. His blood spurted all over me, and the wretch fell. . . . Meanwhile, the two hussars were hitting me all over, chiefly on my head. . . . At length, however, the elder of the two hussars . . . let me have more than an inch of his point in my right side. I replied with a vigorous backhander; my blade struck his teeth and passed between his jaws . . . slitting his mouth to the ears. He made off promptly." See Marbot, *Mémoires,* II, 438–39.

Duc, who was there, attempted to make peace. This sad scene drove French hearts to despair and even inspired deadly fears. The Marshal retired, all alone as usual, before the conversation became too inflamed. He asked me for positions. I indicated to him General Solignac's position, the one in the rear for a brigade, and finally Miranda as an excellent reserve. I also pointed out some English skirmishers who were gaining on our right. The firing still continued steadily in the village below; it was feared that the enemy, in extending themselves among the pines up to the Dueça and to the Coimbra road, would reach our rear. Fortunately, we did not have to worry. In such a case the Marshal did not want to listen to anything, and he showed himself indifferent to everything. Briqueville was behind and was pushing me, saying, "Courage, hold, good." Soon the firing dwindled, the fighting stopped, and the troops were withdrawn to their respective positions.

At last the army was united despite many obstacles and erroneous maneuvers. Thanks to the disposition of the general in chief, all the columns had been directed in such a manner that the enemy always found the army in line and the approaches occupied, and they were thus unable to implement any dangerous flanking movement against us. Meanwhile General Montbrun's dragoons had not appeared, and we had no news of them. The Marshal only said that the general would probably retire to Miranda because he had not given him any orders, or at least rather poorly conceived ones.[35] At length General Montbrun appeared, guided by the fires, the noise of the cannon, and especially by his experience in war. His march contributed a great deal in preventing the enemy from outflanking us by the Dueça. Loison's division came to unite with its army corps by occupying the position of General Solignac. The latter crossed to the other bank of the Dueça at Miranda. I indicated these various positions to the 6th Corps' engineer commander, who did not seem to approve of them very much because each day they appeared more difficult to the corps.

We should have destroyed some segments of the cliff road before Miranda. This would have sufficed to halt the march of the enemy artillery for a few hours. The position the army occupied was difficult to seize but good. It would have become much better if the 6th Corps

35. In fact, Ney did send Montbrun instructions to retire on Miranda do Corvo on March 13. See footnote 27 above.

had been withdrawn on Miranda, the 8th Corps had occupied Corvo, and the 2nd Corps had been in reserve on the Miranda do Corvo road, half a league away. Both these villages were on the right bank of the meandering Dueça, but the road that joined them and the junction with the Espinhal road was on the left bank. Without much difficulty we could probably establish direct communication along the left bank. This crossroads of the Mondego and the Zezere was as important for attacking Portugal as for defending it. Nevertheless, it appeared that the junction could be turned on the west by the road from Foz de Arouce to Coimbra and on the east by that of Pêrna and Pedrógão.

The Marshal had burned a few miserable carriages with great commotion and without necessity, and as a result the remaining wagons were not to be seen any more. He came to the Prince's quarters at Miranda and told him flippantly, "I am going to burn my carriages and those of the generals." The Prince responded, "Mine is burning at this moment." It was a beautiful berlin, and I was heartsick. Instead of all this ostentatious zealousness, it would have been better to put our wounded and sick in the carriages than to uselessly destroy them, and make those who were accustomed to riding walk on foot. At least these instruments of softness and luxury would have served a good function for once in their lives. General Reynier and the Duc were at the Prince's quarters, and we concluded by concerning ourselves with very grave matters. Although nothing was pressing, since the massed army certainly could not be turned during the night and it would even have been very easy to move the 6th Corps behind the 8th and 2nd Corps in a few minutes, it was summarily decided to begin moving again with a second night march. We hoped to establish ourselves in a position on the Ceira beyond Foz de Arouce, with the 2nd Corps on the left, the 6th in the center, and the 8th on the right. Leaving the Prince's quarters, the Marshal admitted to the Duc his offense against His Excellency, but he was to begin again at the first opportunity.

When I write in the interest of truth and for the advancement of my profession, after being more than impartial or perhaps even too severe toward my general and commanders, let no one expect greater discretion toward the foreigner, for this would be cowardly. The English General, after remaining in doubt too long, then wanted to overtake us everywhere; he failed in everything because he lost Badajoz and was unable to break up our rear guard. If the Mondego had not been crossed, it was everyone's fault and not because of the merit of his maneuvers. Lord Wellington neglected to send his large detached force [toward Badajoz] between March 5 and 7 and put all his available troops in pursuit of us. He should have persisted in his first decision and profited by his great concentration of strength. What might then have been the goal of his operations? No one could misconstrue it, especially in a war with the English. It was to hurt us as much as possible by risking only a few of his troops, by opposing our projects, and by pursuing the thread of his plan. His principal goal was thus the deliverance of Portugal, so precious to the English. Then his task was to prevent our army from halting on the left bank of the Mondego and occupying a bridge near Coimbra, and then to obstruct us from crossing this river. Finally, he wanted to use his resources to injure and harass us so that our withdrawal would be disastrous, and he even attempted to rout us so we could not stop at the fortresses of Almeida and Ciudad Rodrigo where we could live only by extending ourselves.

The English General could not have had more propitious terrain or more favorable opportunities than in the area between Pombal and the Mondego. He should have attacked on March 10 at Pombal when our army was imprudently and even a little thoughtlessly united on flat terrain and in a very bad position. The English General should have charged vigorously at Redinha instead of parading, and even more strongly at Condeixa where nothing [*sic*] was done to give battle at a time when we had our backs to Coimbra and the Mondego, and when he held us in two equally difficult situations—passage of a river and a gorge on a narrow bridge, or full march by the flank. Moreover, it was necessary for him to push the attack through the center on the main highway while advancing the right flank slightly. I concluded [my observations] by reducing everything to a single maneuver, and without that, what was the use of having large armies? In case there was a battle or during maneuvers, the English General should have acted on his right against our left, constantly gaining terrain toward the flank and along the route to the Alva. After a successful battle, our army would have found itself severely compromised and pressed severely with much loss. If the maneuver on the right had had some success, if we had been attacked at the time when we feared it so much at Fonte Coberta, Condeixa, Corvo, and Casal Novo, we would have had to fight dreadful battles and suffer great losses. But for all these operations there was not one soldier too many in the English army. All their divisions would have had to remain united until we had changed our direction. Once we had our baggage behind us, our flanks more secure, and had taken the main road, then everything was over.

Thus I can only consider the following as mistakes: first, the march of the entire English army behind us; second, the sizable unit later detached at Pombal when Badajoz had already been taken (according to the usual calculations for sieges, they should have known that it could not defend itself any longer); third, the departure of Cole's division or the one which followed General Reynier. It was a prime necessity to have a small corps equal in strength to half or one-third of the 2nd Corps behind it; this force would have been able to harass and attack the 2nd Corps continually, because Reynier covered a very important pass, and to detain and prevent it from arriving on time. Perhaps it would have been even better to send a rather substantial detachment to push General Reynier and arrive at Corvo before the main body of our army. Finally, it should be noted that from Pombal to Condeixa there should have been vigorous actions or even a battle instead of endless maneuvers, useless deployments, groping on the flanks, and vain offensive demonstrations made from Pombal to the Alva. At Casal Novo and thereafter maneuvers alone were necessary, unaccompanied by the ill-timed shedding of human blood. Then after providing for the safety of Coimbra, it would have been necessary to press constantly on our left while maneuvering continuously toward the opposite flank in order to drive us back quite slowly toward our fortresses, our depots, our reinforcements, etc. On [March 13], when we were not attacked at Condeixa and when we had renounced hope of an offensive, the enemy could have sent all kinds of detachments to the Guadiana—no longer to watch us take Campo Maior or to be satisfied with reoccupying this fortress—but to press Badajoz vigorously and reattack it through the breaches before it was supplied and repaired. Then twelve thousand men and the militia corps would have been sufficient to follow us toward Spain or between the Tagus and the Guadiana where the operations of the English army were soon to draw us.

The foregoing calculations are not those of a second lieutenant, like the anonymous schemes and observations of Captain Guingret.[36] I obviously cannot accept the contrary reasons he gave, especially those plans which were only presented after the event. These plans were known well enough to us. Why were they not made at the same time in the enemy camp? We must not lose sight of the fact that the French army had perhaps no more than twenty thousand actives in its ranks, if we deduct the escort detachments, the crippled, the sick, the wounded, and the men who were unarmed or dismounted, while the enemy had three times this number at their disposal.[37] Further the [limited] strength of the 5th Corps could perfectly assure Wellington against a siege of Elvas and above all an invasion of the Alentejo.

These calculations would be pointless and ridiculous if the Allied army had not been much stronger than the French army. While the operations that I have proposed could have been undertaken with a slightly inferior army because of the positions forced on the French army, perhaps these calculations would be indiscreet in any other circumstances. Nevertheless, all we have left is to collect the debris of our past glory, to fight against the powerful prestige of success and strength, the treachery and slander of satirist in every country, and even to correct the errors of some of our friends. It is a sad duty and Europe should no longer be offended. Thus let the reader's imagination return to the past, let it pass back many years and ask itself who would have condemned the brilliant tactics of the French armies at that period and in those circumstances?

36. For Guingret's comments see *Relation historique,* pp. 176–79.

37. There were 2,218 officers and 38,533 men, in addition to 6,295 sick or non-combatants on March 15. See "Situation au 15 mars, 1811," Correspondance: Armée de Portugal, Carton C[7]12.

Chapter Thirteen

THE RETREAT: SECOND PHASE

Up to the Mondego, our operation had been solely one of maneuvers. Now it was to change its nature. It was no longer a frontal or positional change. We were leaving and beating a retreat. What a word! *Retreat* should have been scratched from the military dictionary, as an Austrian field marshal, a royal prince, said more than twenty-five years ago. I cite this willingly, for although I can do without any authorities myself I search for them as far as I am able to support what I advocate.

Now, what can we say about the retreat, we Frenchmen who have gone through twenty years of triumph and glory! Yet it is necessary that our soldiers hear the science of retreat highly praised, particularly at a time when even the art of battle, certainly the most significant element of warfare because the field commander cannot be aided by anyone else, is being belittled. And if a retreat is thus extolled, we may expect that some day we will hear praise for defeats or even routs. This unprecedented opinion [about a retreat] has spread because we have too often confused this type of movement with the art of the defensive. However, an active defense is not entirely inert; by its boldness, maneuvers, and vigor, it balances the superiority of numbers and resources and is in the end more glorious perhaps than an ordinary offensive. Nevertheless, there is great and genuine merit in directing a retreat if one has been reduced to this extreme after doing everything humanly possible to avoid it. The attainment is even greater in a French army; such a movement is most contrary to the character and spirit of our soldiers since all the negative passions become more acutely developed. But it must be recognized that a retreat can very seldom be executed by an army which has been truly engaged either in a battle or on a campaign. Thus the system of retreat seems to be incompatible with the firm confidence and audacity so necessary in war, and it pushes calculations of excessive caution much too far. What I am attacking now are those reputations founded solely on titles [awarded for retreats] and my reproaches are made against the inability of certain men to conduct such movements. It is the prominence that we give these movements over the more brilliant and much more difficult parts of our noble profession which I am attacking. Finally I am denouncing the division and classification that has been made, not only in recent times but also during antiquity, of an art which is truly indivisible, which must embrace the total of all the parts, and which is part of the character and talent of a general. This has happened not only in our time but in all ages, for there is nothing that is not abused and for which a justification cannot be made.

Thus since the time of Xenophon, that eternal protector of retreat makers, all the vanquished and ill-fated generals have lined up to put themselves under his protection and steal a beam from his halo. But how far they are from the one whom they have invoked; he marched and fought for eight months with ten thousand Greeks against the Persian armies, crossing a great part of Asia and covering himself with immortal glory.[1] There is another warrior, no less familiar to all ages, who has become the shield of those who spend their time doing nothing; it is Fabius, the patron of those who temporize.[2] Everything seems to have been said when his illustrious name has been mentioned, along with the famous verse of Eunice borrowed from Vergil. But why, by temporizing, should one not invoke Timothy,[3] who is represented as

1. Xenophon (ca. 430–ca. 355 B.C.) was a Greek who served Cyrus the Younger of Persia. After Cyrus's death, Xenophon was chosen as one of the leaders of the Ten Thousand Greeks who were forced to fight their way through hostile and unknown country pursued by Tissaphernes. He described this escape in the *Anabasis.*

2. Fabius Maximus Verrucosus (d. 203 B.C.) was a Roman general who opposed Hannibal in the Second Punic War. He harassed the Carthaginian army but refused to confront it in battle, choosing instead to protect the city of Rome with his army.

3. Eunice was the Christian mother of Timothy.

sleeping while Fortune, taking cities in a net, was at his feet? In effect, why should one torment oneself so much and run after that capricious goddess? "She is found seated at the door of a friend who is fast asleep." Still the art of war comprises all movements; there is no single maneuver, neither backward nor forward. A retreat needs a wise, slow pace without being allowed to lapse into what an author has so pleasantly called "the expectant war," but these are the misfortunes of the profession and we must not make glorious titles for them.

After expressing such opinions on retreats, one cannot expect me to praise our withdrawal from Portugal unquestioningly. However, if any retreat is worthy of eulogy, I believe ours should be accorded that honor. Aside from mentioning the difficulty of crossing a hundred leagues of entirely ruined and devastated country, in the midst of an armed population aroused by the most horrible misery, with terrain full of obstacles for us and advantages for the enemy, we faced an army superior in number in front of us. Without boasting about the perilous maneuvers which forced us to change direction in front of the Allies several times, of the success which accompanied all our movements, of the glorious fights which took place, of our return with so much artillery and equipment, of the considerable opposition in our army, we could not want more commendation than we received from the English military. Yet at first we succeeded in frustrating their vigilance and calculations, repulsing their attacks, and containing their efforts.

We made our first night march without real necessity, but not without the usual inconveniences that follow this type of movement. We started at seven o'clock [March 14] under the leadership of Captain Cavailher, who had just reconnoitered and mapped all the ground to the Alva. We crossed a large pine forest by a rather good, sandy, and level road. The dragoons were at the head of the column. Behind them marched the 2nd Corps, then the 8th Corps, and finally the 6th Corps, which did not begin its movement until the middle of the night.

From what I could see of the positions, the one on the right bank [of the Ceira] was very fine and excellent for the defense that we wished to establish temporarily for the army. However, because the Ceira turned toward the west to empty into the Dueça, running parallel to the Mondego, it was very easy to turn the right of this position. Likewise, some roads existed between Foz de Arouce and the mountains which turned our left toward the south. The greatest disadvantage of this position was its proximity to the Alva, whose bridge was cut, though the passage of the valley was extremely difficult in itself.

The Ceira, sixteen to twenty yards wide, was deeply embanked and its bottom was full of rocks, resulting in some difficult fords. The bridge [over the Ceira] had a large arch in the middle and two smaller ones on each side; the one toward the right bank was damaged a little. There was a ford above the bridge, and a quarter of a league above and below it we found two others so poor that many men were drowned there. The hills on the right bank were abrupt and the slopes very uniform with few cuts. Toward our right, some two hundred yards away to the north, was a difficult ravine which turned a little behind the position. Immediately beyond the position, the ground was rather practicable and the road leading to Ponte de Murcella was generally favorable. Above the bridge and halfway up the slope was a rather rounded berm, suitable for the establishment of a few small pieces that would advantageously overlook the river and the bridge, while the heavy artillery could be placed on the crest of the height. The first needed to be covered with a breastwork because the berm was dominated somewhat by the left bank. Some two hundred yards away on the left bank was Foz de Arouce. On the north of this village, toward the Ceira, was a hill covered with woods which ended on a plateau dominating the berm. However, this hill was dominated by those on the other bank, on which some works had once been constructed to defend the crossing at the bridge. These heights extended toward the west and cut the road on which we had come. To the south of the village, the plains and terrain stretched out, inundated by a river which must have been the Arouce (Foz de Arouce means "mouth of the Arouce"). All these factors covered and limited the approaches for a position on the right bank.

Leaving Foz de Arouce, I saw one of the most horrible spectacles of my life, one which produced on me a terrible impression not yet expunged—a miserable eighty-year-old woman, almost naked, under the hoofs of our horses. I had her picked up and put in a house not far from the village. Thus surrounded by war, at every step we found something to break our hearts. But it must be understood that if some men in the military were stupid or cruel enough to speak coldly about the horrors with which they themselves had been contaminated or which they had seen committed, the great majority of men in the ranks maintained all their sensitivity; they would not have regarded themselves as guilty of evils they had not committed, nor of horrors they could not prevent, nor of all the good they neglected to do.

As the Prince crossed the bridge, we went to reconnoiter the position in detail. The 6th Corps had arrived. Afterward Loison's division crossed and established itself at the center, and the other divisions of the 6th Corps prepared to follow him. The 2nd Corps was already posted to the left and the 8th Corps to the right. Many artillery wagons and baggage belonging to all the army corps, but especially to the 6th Corps, still remained on the left bank. Since we had shown rather poor arrangements in this regard, the Prince sent me at nine o'clock in the morning to tell the Marshal to leave his rear guard on the heights covering the village until everything had crossed the bridge, and then to have the sappers destroy the breastwork directed against us on the plateau north of Foz de Arouce; finally, in case of an attack, he was to burn the village, which formed a rather long, narrow, and twisted passage. This was the only village for which such an order was given that the Marshal did not set afire.

I had much difficulty extricating myself from the swamps that I was then crossing on the left. Beyond the village I found the Marshal and his rear guard on the road at the end of the heights. I gave him the Prince's orders. The enemy was following him only at a distance. I saw him post the 25th Line and then the 39th Line. We followed the ridges, which were very good for defense and would have [extended] some fourteen to sixteen hundred yards up to the plateau above the Ceira. Arriving there, I told him that this point had been recommended by the Prince. He ordered Marchand's division to go there; then correcting himself, "No, it is a post for a corporal and four men," he sent two companies there. At first I told him they were too many and then that they were too few. "Take a howitzer also." I pointed out that it could be imperiled; it was like a signal. We approached the village and the bridge. He became angry because he had been lodged in Foz de Arouce, but then added, "No, my place is with the advance guard." In approaching the position along the right bank, he recognized that it was good and advantageous. But when he realized that he was near the Prince, he told me, "I have seen enough. The position on this side is much better. I will leave my army corps here and even have the other troops that have crossed return. It will be better for their cooking and their bivouac." Vainly, I repeated the orders of the Prince, which were for the rear guard only, but the Marshal galloped off.

He rode for a long time. We kept on arguing rather vigorously during the whole time. At first the Marshal spoke sharply about the necessity of replacing the rear guard of his corps, which was overburdened; about the necessity of going to Spain as quickly as possible; about sacrificing the baggage and even the artillery if necessary; and about the forced retreat to which we were reduced. I argued, denying all these points. On the contrary I spoke about the necessity of finally halting and about the difficulties in going into Spain. He then said impertinently, "Ha, ha, we sing differently." I answered him very curtly, "I do not sing; it is well known that when I speak it is on my own account. I have always spoken this way." He longed for the time when he would be separated and able to go his own way. He spoke especially of what he would have done if we had crossed to the other bank of the Tagus—an indiscreet confidence and fatal predictions. He complained that we had remained at Pombal for two days. [I replied,] "You yourself requested it in my presence, and you would have stayed one day more if General Drouet had not shown a firm will to leave." He disapproved, strangely, because the lines of retreat we had chosen were diagonal instead of perpendicular to the Zezere and in the direction of Alcántara. I pointed out to him there was no road in that direction. He cited former campaigns; with the same examples I proved the contrary. I mentioned the difficulties that the Duc d'Abrantès had experienced near Joaninho. Then he said that I did not believe anything that he said or did. He complained that French troops had not seized Coimbra by storm a few days before our [anticipated] arrival and that we were not assured of our communication route. Finally he complained about all the maneuvers; he was always complaining that we marched too much or that we did not march enough. I discussed the beginning of the operation, up to Pombal. He had nothing to say about it. This was the only operation for which I was responsible, because in my plan the 9th Corps was to precede us and seize Coimbra. This plan was not carried out. Woe is he who has predicted, foreseen, and detailed everything; he only earns more torment than anyone else because he also has the pain of foresight. My Journal proves this. The

Marshal spoke about the position at Condeixa as if it did not exist, although it was one of the most beautiful that could have been imagined. He claimed that he was outflanked by the whole enemy army. I told him again that at the most two entire divisions of fifteen thousand men marched toward his left, but not to turn it.[4] Now the conversation became more spirited. At this moment as at so many others, he forced me to say to him, "Everyone belongs to the same *patrie*, to the same flag; are we not all French?"

I met the Prince again on the other side of the Ceira. I was obliged to tell him most of what had occurred and the dispositions that had been taken. Someone came from the 6th Corps to examine the bridge. Moreover, it was necessary to argue in order to assure them that it was not completely mined.

There was nothing more picturesque than the Ceira crossing. Some of the men found the occasion to cheer themselves up by making drawings which would have given great pleasure to Callot and in any other circumstance would have been quite amusing.[5] The bridge had been reserved for the army corps and the artillery wagons. Crowds of isolated men moved toward it and were pushed back by the guards. The Marshal had renewed his orders to inspect the wagons of the 6th Corps and to collect [and hamstring] all the donkeys. These unfortunate beasts deserved all our gratitude for carrying our sick and wounded and our food for such a long time. We called this "the massacre of the innocent."[6] This indiscreet measure had as its first result the drowning of some men who ventured to save the companions of their hardship; they were carried away by the rapid waters of the Ceira, although we attempted vainly to save them. The men fled in all directions with their donkeys and threw themselves into the water to shield them from their murderers. Since the poor beasts were of a very small species in general, they could not cross the fords themselves as their

4. See above, footnote 26 of Chapter 12, for Ney's defense.

5. Jacques Callot (1592–1635) was a French etcher and engraver who achieved renown under the patronage of Cosmos de Medici. Among his most famous works was a series of scenes entitled *Les Misères de la guerre*.

6. In order to eliminate excessive baggage, guards were stationed at the approaches to the bridge and each wagon was examined; if any vehicle was carrying nonessentials, it was destroyed and its draft animals were hamstrung. In all some 500 animals were hamstrung so they would be useless to the Allies. For various accounts of this incident, see Lemonnier-Delafosse, *Souvenirs*, p. 121; Noel, *Souvenirs*, p. 144; Hulot, *Souvenirs*, p. 343; Guingret, *Relation historique*, p. 157; Simmons, *British Rifleman*, p. 146.

drivers did; two soldiers would get together and carry them by the head and tail. The *cantinières* fought to defend their donkeys and several of them, their heads covered with feathers, gathered their silk or velvet dresses above their hips and carried their mounts across the river. On these donkeys were beautiful parrots, infants, monkeys, and Japanese liquor services used as bottle cases. Beside them were mules with parade horse-cloths, grotesquely loaded with baggage.

Herds of cattle and sheep were pushed into the middle of the current and we often saw sheep (like snowballs) rolling about in the current. Driven by premature fears, some spectators following the army, laborers, and commissioners mounted horses or caissons to cross as fast as possible. Here and there broken carriages, pillaged by the soldiers, showed shameful rapine in broad daylight. Some of those who should have punished the thefts and pillaging found themselves publicly accused of receiving stolen goods and taking advantage of it. Around the bridge there were other scenes. Detachments made up of all flags and of all nations—for we had Prussian, Irish, Swiss, Hanoverian, and Portuguese troops with us—were pushing each other, shouting and swearing in every language. The unfortunate wounded grenadiers, mounted on donkeys with their feet dragging on the ground and caps on their heads, waited sadly for their turn to cross. The poor sick men dragged themselves along on their guns and asked for a piece of biscuit. Meanwhile, perched on the cannon and some of the wagons, we saw the Andromaches and Portuguese Cassandras, voluntary captives, who were now wrapped in the coats of the soldiers and the mantles of prelates and monks. Is it necessary to say anything more? They were still exchanged, not according to their rank, but according to their intrinsic value; for a few *duras* or several ounces of gold they acquiesced quietly to all this.

This varied spectacle allayed the boredom of a rather prolonged wait. We remained in position until three o'clock. Then, seeing that nothing new had happened, the Prince retired to his headquarters. At five or six he heard some heavy cannon fire and rather vigorous musketry toward the Ceira. The firing on the city continued until night. As usual the Marshal did not send a report nor any information. The Duc wrote that three or four Portuguese battalions were seen in front of him toward his right, but on the other side of the Ceira, and that they had fired a little and withdrawn. He said that they were fighting in the center. On the left there was nothing new. Later the Marshal claimed that General Reynier had cantoned his troops and left only posts on the line and had therefore been of no help to him. As a matter of fact, he had been unable to help because of their respective positions. Some officers left immediately [for the Ceira], and we soon learned what had happened.

This is what Marshal Ney himself told me the next day about the affair at Foz de Arouce. At nearly four o'clock the enemy appeared; they always timed their attacks so that they could end their engagement at will; besides, they never maneuvered until they had gathered all their forces against our rear guard, and they usually moved on the flanks of a position to force us to withdraw by overrunning us. The enemy appeared, deployed, and presented frontal attacks against the left of the heights in the direction of the road. Around five o'clock, while they were placing troops beyond the swampy plain and extending themselves on our right, the fight started. After a few moments of fine resistance as usual, alarm spread among our troops for some unknown reason. Some said that it was because Colonel Lamour had been killed in front of the 39th Line (he was only wounded and taken prisoner); others because the soldiers who were withdrawing the artillery were ordered to run. Perhaps it was because the soldiers felt that this was a bad disposition, since they were excellent judges of such matters and had been able to see all the defiles behind them. The fact was that the 25th Léger, a very brave regiment, was thrown back on the 39th Line and the latter on the 50th or 59th Line. Everything was extremely confused—all mixed up. The disorder was carried to the divisions of Marchand and Mermet. The cannon were abandoned in the village and everybody ran toward the bridge, which was crowded with troops. Instead of containing the enemy or at least crossing by the ford, the light cavalry came through the middle of the infantry and trampled them. Many of the infantry threw themselves into the water and were drowned, while others were crushed on the bridge or swept away by the crowd and knocked down. In the affray the eagle-bearer of the 39th Line was drowned and the eagle was left on the bottom of the river. We feared that it was in the hands of the enemy. The Marshal assured me that this had not happened.[7]

7. Wellington mentioned this eagle in a letter to Liverpool of July 4, 1811, after it was found by a Portuguese peasant. "I send to England . . . the eagle of the

Nevertheless, the Marshal was unable to remedy the disorder; he said to me that in such a case one must not try to halt it. Fortunately, he rushed to the plateau (where at first he had wanted to post the corporal), where the 6th Léger and 69th Line were very opportunely posted. The 76th Line, which had crossed just before the attack, deployed itself on the right bank of the Ceira, firing against the plateau in the belief that they already saw the enemy there. The error was soon realized, but the embarrassment to the Marshal was great. He always showed more strength of mind when the danger was greatest. Seeing the English advancing in force onto the heights through the pines and upon the village by the road, he directed a battalion of the 69th Line in tight column and a few companies of the 6th Léger to attack with bayonet. The other battalion was deploying with its left near Foz de Arouce. He had them execute a frontal change with the right wing in front and then open ranks to fire point-blank on the English entering the village.[8] These movements stopped the enemy flatly. Twelve cannon fired vigorously on them from the right bank, while their own pieces were very far away. Three companies of voltigeurs of the 39th Line, running ahead of our right, shooting and trumpeting continuously, continued their forward movement and found themselves behind the enemy columns. At length hideous shouts came from the bridge; perhaps the English believed that they were calls for an attack. All or some of these factors affected their columns; they were soon pushed back and started fleeing on their side while we fled on ours. The terror and panic spread along their whole line, which immediately broke into a run.[9] The village was not occupied by any

39th regiment, which was thrown into the river Ceira, near Foz d'Arouce, on the night of the 15th March last, when the 6th corps of the army of Portugal, which formed the rear guard of the army . . . were driven across the river by the 3rd and Light divisions of the British army." See *Wellington's Dispatches*, VIII, 78.

8. When Erskine, following the French guard, observed their fires before Foz de Arouce at approximately 3:00 P.M., he issued orders for his men to bivouac. See Simmons, *British Rifleman*, pp. 144–46. However, when Wellington arrived and reconnoitered the French position, he ordered an immediate attack. The Light Division, supported by the 6th Division, approached Ferey's rear guard while Picton, seconded by Spencer, advanced on Mermet. See *Wellington's Dispatches*, Wellington to Liverpool, March 16, 1811, VII, 369–72.

9. Pelet's account of the action at Foz de Arouce corresponds closely with Ney's letters to Masséna of March 16 and 17. "If General Lamotte [of the light cavalry], instead of taking flight, had held the plain parallel with infantry, fighting with advantage and attempting several charges, in order to give the reserve time to come up, it is presumable that the enemy would never have overrun the 25th Léger. . . . The 39th Line which served as a reserve for the 25th Léger was on

troops and our pieces of artillery remained there, abandoned for more than an hour. One cannon collided with a wall and had a broken wheel. The signal howitzer on the plateau had remained at half elevation.

During the night we occupied the village and all the artillery was recovered. We noticed preparations to blow up the bridge. There was a mine with a fuse in one of the piers. We loaded it with two hundred pounds of powder at three o'clock in the morning. The bridge was blown up after all the troops had withdrawn.

The enemy did not use more than five guns in this affair. Our losses were greatly exaggerated. The Marshal estimated them to be only 220 men, since only part of Mermet's and Marchand's divisions had been engaged.[10] At the time of attack I think the Marshal wanted to withdraw his troops, but with the gorges at his back he no longer had the time and everything started. The crossing of the 76th Line to the right bank seemed to prove this. Perhaps the retrograde movement had dragged those brave troops along. Initially the Marshal remained on the left bank and was one of the last to return. When fighting first began, his soldiers, who idolized him, were very concerned about him and accused themselves of having already abandoned him. Nevertheless, it was later said that many people complained of the way the engagement was undertaken against the formal order of the Prince. It was certain that these orders existed, that I carried them myself, and that I made a written report to the Prince. The outcome of this combat could have been disastrous if the attacks of the 69th Line had been repulsed or even contained. The action was only the result of an act of disobedience, because the enemy certainly would not have attacked our formidable position on the right bank of the Ceira, and we had found everything prepared to blow up the bridge.

For some time I had proposed putting the whole army in battle formation in an excellent position so the enemy would be forced to show all their troops and thus find out exactly what to expect from them. At

the point of marching to support it when Colonel Lamour . . . was unfortunately killed. The loss of this officer . . . threw the 39th Line into disorder and it retreated in confusion. At this moment, the light artillery effected its retreat in great haste and it resulted in panic." See Bonnal, *Ney*, III, 507–14.

10. Ney reported 220 casualties at Foz de Arouce in a letter to Masséna on March 16. See Bonnal, *Ney*, III, 507–8. Fortescue, however, placed the French losses at 400. See his *British Army*, VIII, 86. The Allies lost a total of 71 men. See Oman, *Peninsular War*, IV, 615–16.

first I believed the position of Condeixa to be very favorable for this project, and then Redinha up to Miranda, and even Foz de Arouce. We entertained the hope of stopping the enemy by such a demonstration and even of reestablishing actual contact with the English by a battle or at least a good combat. But every day we lost more hope, since we lacked absolutely all the elements required for a battle. The Prince often said, "They will make me unfurl the red flag." But he too gradually discarded the ideas as the commanders of the corps manifested greater ill will. He saw clearly that he could no longer remain in the same army with Marshal Ney and that it was necessary for one or the other to leave. In this state of affairs, he wanted to find himself a peaceful place where he could make a decision and put it into execution. The worthy General Éblé shared all his chagrin, anxieties, and opinions; like us, he no longer saw the elements for a battle in the army, although he too eagerly desired one.

Everything seemed to combine to prevent us from halting the army on any position. It must also be admitted that, as we knew the situation better and especially as the spirit [of dissension] developed in a more frightful manner each day, we felt the necessity of establishing ourselves only in well-assured positions and, above all, the need to approach our depot and the fortresses of Almeida and Ciudad Rodrigo in order to hold there for a while. In halting for a day or two, the enemy would have time to await the arrival of the rear of their troop columns, their artillery, and the corps that had been detached to Coimbra or were in movement to form their line and maneuver on our flanks. Flanking movements on our left would have been especially dangerous for us since all our lines were very extended and inclined on the rear along the road to Celorico; and since their maneuvers would take place through the upper valleys, from the top to the bottom, against our flanks, we would have difficulty opposing any resistance there. The enemy corps marching to our right, on the other side of the Mondego, would be able to imperil our rear and even precede us to the fortresses of Almeida and Ciudad Rodrigo or hurl the militia of northern Portugal there. All these considerations became even more important as long as we still had to overcome difficult obstacles in the rear. The gorge of the Alva was one of the most rugged, with the usual difficulties. Its bridge was completely cut and very difficult to repair, while the general position of the river was extremely unfavorable for us. From that time, all eyes were turned toward these fortresses and the need to advise the governors to take suitable measures for their immediate safety and to gather food for themselves as well as for us. General Foy should have carried such orders, just in case of an emergency. The only thing we could do now was to approach the fortresses slowly to collect men and the effects belonging to the corps as well as the supplies which had been prepared there, so we could start campaigning again in any direction as soon as the army was reorganized.

The Prince had asked General Drouet to stop at Murcella to cover that major communication point. We found him still there [on March 16], working to repair the bridge. Colonel Valazé was there with Beaufort and all the companies of sappers.[11] At first it was said the bridge would not be ready until the next day, but they hurried and made so much progress on the vital work that the army was able to cross around four or five o'clock. While the army waited, it was necessary [to find] a position to place the troops. The Prince, scouring a part of the terrain with the Duc d'Abrantès, sent me onto the crest of the Serra Igreja Nova [?], which was above Murcella. I made the reconnaissance with Cavailher. The left of the position was supported by a rather high hill with a kind of ravine beyond, then by the plateau of Santa Quitéria, and finally by a pass and road which descended toward Arganil. On the right was a series of rather round and accessible plateaus, and beyond a few roads descended toward the Alva. In the center the crest was somewhat inclined in the form of a gutter or pass, and the slopes were very rocky and difficult because of their steepness. Moreover, on this crest we found no woods or grass. At that moment it was almost completely covered with fog. There we met General Boyer, chief of staff of the 8th Corps, who was also reconnoitering on his own. Together we examined the terrain whenever there was a break in the fog; then we looked at the sketch that Cavailher had already made.

The crest was to be occupied by the army corps. The flanks were reconnoitered far ahead and secured with cavalry at the bottom of the rather wide Alva valley. Orders were given to the 6th and 8th Corps

11. Drouet had been laboring for two days to repair the bridge over the Alva. See Masséna to Ney, March 15, 1811, Correspondance: Armée de Portugal, Carton $C^7$12.

to place themselves in this position and to the 2nd Corps to move on Arganil and cross the Alva two leagues above Murcella in order to ensure the left and the bend behind the river. General Reynier came along rather poor roads, but he crossed through good country. This disposition was not suitable. The army should have remained on the Ceira and established itself for the day while the bridge on the Alva was repaired and the carriages crossed. The enemy could not have attacked from the front and they needed time to maneuver around our flanks. For greater safety we should have placed one or two divisions intermediately at Venda Nova.

Headquarters were with Lorcet's brigade at Venda Nova, the center of the crossroads of the Serra da Estrêla, the Mondego, and Coimbra; this junction had to be watched. We heard some gunfire near the Mondego; a patrol was sent there. As the Prince returned to headquarters, he learned that part of the 6th Corps had remained in position on the Ceira, despite his formal orders. I had to leave again to go and see the Marshal and notify him of the condition of the bridge and the position on the Alva, to urge him in a friendly manner to fall back and not expose himself by remaining in such an isolated position, and finally to see what was going on; this was the kind of order I was usually given. I left as Mermet's and Loison's divisions arrived at Venda Nova. Those of the 8th Corps were there, protecting that important point. Then Clauzel's division moved up to the position of Igreja Nova, which should not have been left abandoned. I expected to see Marshal Ney on the road at any moment. I went two leagues without seeing anyone except Captain Sprünglin, one of his officers; the Marshal had sent him to carry orders for the divisions of the 6th Corps to halt and support him.

Finally I found the Marshal on the crest of the heights overlooking the Ceira with Marchand's single division exposed along the entire line; this position should have been occupied by an entire army. The weather was terrible. The Marshal seemed a little subdued after the affair of the previous day.[12] He told me in an affected manner, "I feel that I

12. On March 16 one of Ney's aides-de-camp recalled, "Never have I seen Marshal Ney in such bad humor as on this day. He was angry with the 39th Line for the disorders of the previous night and the loss of its eagle and colonel. He was furious with General Lamotte, whose inconceivable conduct had caused the congestion on the bridge and the disaster that resulted. He refused a company of the 39th Line who came to form the guard for his quarters, he removed General La-

must devote myself to saving the army, its artillery, and its baggage. I am remaining here with my division. I will be attacked, but I will cross. I will form the columns en masse. I will make squares." I responded very coldly that there was no question of that: the bridge would be ready at four o'clock, and most of the wagons had already crossed by the ford. I urged him to withdraw at nightfall. I proposed that he echelon with the other divisions, but he refused despite the order he had given to Captain Sprünglin. Together we traveled over the position. He told me about the affair of the previous day and seemed to be very touched. He complained considerably about the personal conduct of the Duc d'Abrantès. With regard to General Reynier, he said that he would march his army corps in order to support him as soon as the first cannon shots were heard. His battalions were widely scattered and only two or three were united in reserve. None of his artillery on the crest was able to see the bridge or the river. On each of his flanks was a gun with two posts of five men to give warning. I expressed some astonishment at all this. He told me that his cannon went as fast as the horses. He had only a piece of bread and water, and only one servant with him. I offered him some of my brandy and he honored me by accepting it. Then alone I went along the bank of the Ceira near the ruined bridge. We could only see the enemy vedettes; there were no infantry posts on the bank of the river, but a great number of campfires beyond the heights of Foz de Arouce. They told me at the advance posts that from a distance they had seen Lord Wellington on the line. Moreover, in the morning a man with a decoration had been killed as he came to reconnoiter the bridge; it was thought that he was a general officer. I was touched at seeing that division in such a position and so unsupported in front of forces ten times more numerous—it had an adventurous and romantic air and enchanted me. I paid the Marshal a very sincere compliment despite what I had told him about the dangers of his position.

The road to Ponte de Murcella passed through slightly undulating terrain and I crossed several valleys. Two-thirds of the way to Murcella was a position with some rocks. The Prince sent Mermet's divi-

motte from command of the light cavalry, he sent him to the Prince d'Essling's headquarters . . . and he was carried to the point of seizing a pistol from his holster and threatening to blow his [Lamotte's] brains out if he did not retire at that instant." See Sprünglin, *Souvenirs*, p. 473.

sion there; it was to push the rear guard of General Ferey farther back [to establish] the Marshal in echelon. Loison's division took a position at Venda Nova, and General Solignac straddled the heights of Igreja with a detachment at Murcella. A brigade of General Clauzel was moved onto the other bank of the Alva to cover the bridge from that side.

We left for Murcella, where headquarters had been established; it was a miserable hamlet on the reverse of the mountain and in the midst of rather well-cultivated terrain. I hurried quickly to the bridge. It was not repaired yet, and we crossed by the ford as well as we could. Some people, always easily frightened, were in a hurry to reach the other side. There was an unending procession, descending on one side and climbing on the other. Between four and five o'clock the bridge was finished. The herds and the sappers' equipment crossed first, and then a large and heavy forge was sent to test its strength. After that each file passed, and a proper guard maintained very exact order.

The Prince made dispositions for occupying the right bank of the Alva. The 2nd Corps was to descend by Arganil and start marching at seven o'clock to establish itself on the left of the position. The 8th Corps moved on the right, and the 6th Corps placed itself in the center, opposite Murcella. Marchand's division was to start its movement at four o'clock in the morning. General Montbrun went to the rear with his cavalry; he was obliged to send some patrols on to Galizes, at the mouth of the Alva [*sic*], and to reascend the river. Ségur returned very late from the banks of the Ceira. He had left the banks at four o'clock in the afternoon without seeing anything new there. Marshal Ney had the great temerity to confront all the forces of Lord Wellington although he was more than two leagues away from the French army, with a single division, but what regiments—the 6th Léger, the 69th, 39th, and 76th Line—and how can we describe the conduct of those who were in front of him?

The Alva seemed to emerge from the Serra da Estrêla parallel to Maceira, and it descended along the rocks which were called "the Cântaros"; they were the highest points and often covered with snow. As it flowed from the mountains, the Alva turned toward the west and ran almost parallel to the Almeida road and the Mondego. It flowed into the Mondego one league from Ponte de Murcella. Below that point, the valley appeared difficult, narrow, and rocky, and above it was wide, well cultivated, and crossed by several roads and bridges which the peasants had cut. Their effort was rather useless because fords were situated next to two of the bridges. This route, so inclined on our line of retreat, and the great number of communications roads would be extremely disadvantageous for us, even to the point that we could not establish ourselves on this line for any length of time. On the contrary, the position of Murcella was in general much more favorable for the enemy, who could ensure the flank of their defense more immediately through one of the ravines which opened onto the Alva, especially to cover the approaches of Coimbra and the banks of the Mondego.

At Ponte de Murcella, the Alva had a double bend formed like a bastioned front, with a rather recessed curtain on the left bank. From this side it was easy, at the same time, to flank the other segments of the line by both banks, to take the lower terrain by reverse in this kind of loop, and to seize the troops who would want to cross the bridge. This made the defense of this bank and the berm of Murcella more favorable; the position was very dominant, with the extremely steep mountain slopes like a kind of wall. All this formed a very formidable position on the left bank. It was said to be covered with fortifications and even completely inaccessible. Yet we saw hardly any traces of entrenchments and only some trivial works of no significance which could not contain six hundred men; but behind it the slope fell rapidly. Beware—troops that would be pushed back there! This mountain extended so closely onto that of Bussaco that it seemed to be of the same system and nature, and I hardly saw the outlet from the Mondego. We profited by these advantageous dispositions by combining the defense of both banks of the Alva. It appeared that the enemy had prepared a road through Penacova to communicate from one side [of the river?] to the other.

The counterposition we occupied was, then, not as strong nor as steep, but it was still very good. The front, slightly advanced, rested within a vast circumference on both banks at the Alva. The slope was more gradual and less steep, but it was also more favorable for artillery fire. The loop before the bridge was dominated, but the line that crossed it was in turn strongly dominated. And from a small woods situated on the left, we saw the bridge perfectly. However, nobody wanted to reconnoiter this position. As far as I was concerned, I saw an excellent and advantageous one there. In the center, the 6th Corps occupied the line of the loop with its front ranks; its second line was behind on the crest; and its skirmishers were on the banks of the Alva, defending the first crossing. The other two corps, flanking the center to the right and the left, furnished it with reserves. At the top of his voice the Duc d'Abrantès demanded support on his flanks and it was given to him. M. Delachasse-Verigny marked the positions of the 6th Corps and the Duc strongly approved of them. The 2nd Corps did not appear. We searched for it everywhere. It was supposed to descend the Alva, but it had had to lodge in some village named Sortelha, which was very far behind us, although on the banks of the river.

It is necessary to point out that the Mondego was a very small river above the estuaries of the Alva and the Dão, which were, with the Dueça and the Ceira, its principal sources. Its basin narrowed considerably and its bed became a little wider and deeper. Under any other circumstances, the army would have crossed to the right bank of the Mondego, established itself there, and returned to Coimbra. However, at this time the force of circumstances and the irrevocable attitude of the mind were dragging the army in the opposite direction, far from our former plans, which we had had to abandon.

The 6th Corps crossed to the right bank of the Alva.[13] It started by leaving the rear guard on the crest, then it moved down to Murcella and completed its crossing with hardly anyone left on the other side. The wagons were crossing the bridge night and day, and there was no one left to destroy our works. I would have preferred their destruction. A few of the enemy showed themselves on the crest. The cavalry saw nothing new in either direction, except for a few armed peasants and militia on the other side of the Mondego. They also had a few boats which they were guarding. Beaufort left Sobreira with some dragoons to go and reconnoiter near Guarda.

The misery became more acute. The biscuit was exhausted, and our unfortunate sick had to beg to sustain themselves! Moreover, the weather and the climate were cold, but we began to find some food in the villages.[14] This misery was the only difficulty, and our retreat took

13. The crossing of the Alva took place on March 17.
14. The French found supplies only at the expense of the Portuguese villagers.

place in the greatest order. Except for a very small number of wagons and some luggage that had been left behind, nothing had been destroyed or abandoned and the enemy had gathered nothing behind us.

If the Prince had nurtured some desire of starting a battle with the enemy to halt them and thereby repair the disorders of the last marches, or if he had insisted on his earlier project of establishing himself in one of the positions conceived before we knew the terrain adequately, the conduct of the Marshal very quickly forced him to renounce both these ideas. The Marshal, giving way to his passions, had openly announced plans that were too obvious during the past few days. He wrote without ceremony on March 18 that if he did not receive orders to march that day he would leave the next day with his army corps.[15] The Prince responded by simply giving *chef d'escadron* Laboissière, first aide-de-camp of the Marshal who had brought his letter, the next day's schedule for the march of the army.

A very important issue had arisen. The question was to determine the direction the army was going to take, since there was no way to

Foraging gave way to pillaging, which degenerated into horrible excesses among some elements in the army. This is illustrated by a proclamation of March 25, 1811, from the Bishop of Coimbra to the priests in the 290 parishes of his dioceses, requesting information on the destruction caused during the French invasion. The responses are in a carton entitled "Papéis da Diocese de Coimbra relativos as Invasoes Francesas," deposited in the Arquivo da Universidade de Coimbra. Father Antonio Inacio Coelho of Arganil reported that 191 people—131 men, 56 women, and 4 clergy—died in his parish as a result of the French occupation. The priest wrote: "Isabela Cardoza, over sixty, who was sick in bed, was taken and put in a chair, and they took her blood as if she were an animal and beat her a great deal. Antonio Madeira was a mute, and he was murdered in the field. Because he could not speak they tore his mouth, broke his jawbone, and stabbed him six times with a sword." The priest of Foz de Arouce reported that 10 men and 4 women died in December 1810 at the hands of the French and that 16 men and 20 women were killed in March 1811.

15. Pelet's statement is rather misleading. Ney did write to Masséna on March 18: "With great impatience, I await orders of movement because each moment of delay can ruin the army which we have miraculously saved. I inform His Excellency that if the general order of movement for me to fall back on Galizes does not come today, I will leave tomorrow morning with the entire 6th Corps to occupy this position." However, Pelet does not mention Ney's reason for wanting to withdraw: "My left is completely uncovered. General Reynier is too far from me. . . . The enemy will be able to deceive me by a light frontal attack and move in force to turn my left and cut off my retreat on Galizes." See Correspondance: Armée de Portugal, Carton $C^7$12. Ney was correct, for on March 18 Erskine's Light Division and the Sixth Division advanced on Ney at Ponte de Murcella, while the First, Third, and Fifth divisions marched eastward through Forcado to outflank the French at Pombeiro. See *Wellington's Dispatches*, Wellington to Liverpool, March 21, 1811, VII, 383–86.

halt it between the Mondego, which became a small stream near its source, and the Serra da Estrêla. The preceding year we had learned at our expense that it was practicable enough for an entire corps to go through the Serra. First, should the army go on to Salamanca and gather food, clothing, and reinforcements in order to rebuild and reorganize itself? This was everyone's desire, and the favorite idea of Marshal Ney, and everyone seemed to support it. Second, should we remain around the fortresses of Almeida and Ciudad Rodrigo, where we could neither canton nor live, since the garrison and the troops passing through had consumed the last harvest? Third, should we move toward Estremadura and the Tagus? Or would we regard our return in the direction of Salamanca, our original starting point, as shameful and the end of the campaign and the complete abandonment of Portugal? Finally, was the English General to be left in complete freedom to concentrate his operations on the Tagus or to detach units to act against Badajoz, Madrid, and Galicia? To this very important consideration should be added the failure to fulfill the government's orders as well as its dissatisfaction with its endangered interest and with the opinion of Europe, and finally everything that was to follow.

As far as I was concerned, and as I had said when we left Torres Novas, "Here is my route schedule for ———." On the other hand the third choice seemed to offer a means of arranging and satisfying everything. First, as I had said then and even before, it would have been expedient to send orders to bring provisions to Condeixa or Miranda and to move closer to Ciudad Rodrigo, because everything that arrived from France belonged to our army. Since this had not been done, it was now necessary for the army to take a position at Celorico; this town and Almeida were well-known and established defense positions and at the same time were near our supplies. Then we would quickly extract for ourselves all the replacement material in the vicinity or send detachments to hunt for it. As soon as those indispensable [items] were collected and the remainder had been sent along the road to Baños, the army would move on the Erjas and Puerto de Perales by flank marches. Then the army would send an advance guard toward Idanha or Castelo Branco, occupy Alcántara with a bridgehead on the Tagus, and maintain the posts at Penamacor and Monsanto to communicate by its right with the 9th Corps and the troops of the government charged to defend the fortresses of Almeida and Ciudad Rodrigo; the army would be in a position to move three or four marches to aid these fortresses if the English menaced them seriously, but this would be impossible for a long time.

Simultaneously the army would communicate through Badajoz with the Army of the South (if it had not been taken by then, it never would be) and Talavera with Madrid. The military cantonments would be set up at Coria or Plasencia. We would endeavor to rest and reorganize the army. If there was no food at these points, we would collect it from the rear by every possible means. If this became absolutely impracticable, then the army would concentrate on the Alagón near Coria, with a way of crossing the Tagus at Alcántara. This disposition would establish a general center of attack against the heart of Portugal by both banks of the Tagus while defending the western frontier of Spain. It would join the Armies of the North and the South; protect both the fortresses and the provinces, since the army could move together with the other armies toward Rodrigo and Almeida or Badajoz by means of short marches; and finally cover Madrid perfectly. Besides, this disposition forced Lord Wellington to advance and set himself before us, while depriving him of the advantages of interior operations against the Douro or the Guadiana. No thinking man could imagine that Wellington would come and throw himself in the narrow corridor between the Serra da Estrêla or the Sierra de Gata and the difficult banks of the Douro when we were on his flanks. This was, however, the judgment of the antagonists of this plan.

There were still other ideas which agitated us. We worried not only about what we should do, but what the enemy would do; some saw them everywhere and reported them continually—on the left of the Mondego, on the right, toward the Douro, toward the Tagus, and at the foot of the mountain. They saw not only the army jeopardized, but also the fortresses and Spain. On the other hand, some maintained that the English pursuit would stop at the Alva;[16] that they would take a position behind that river with a detachment in front of us if we still retired; that their actual system of defense in northern Portugal was at

16. Even before Wellington reached the Alva, Cole's Fourth Division and de Gray's cavalry were detached and sent to join Beresford on the Tagus. Thus Wellington had approximately 38,000 men as he continued the pursuit beyond the Alva. See *Wellington's Dispatches*, Wellington to Liverpool, March 16, 1811, VII, 368.

Murcella and Bussaco; that they lost more and more of their advantages by going farther away, while we gained as we neared our base; and finally that in this arid and completely devastated country their subsistence would become rather difficult and halt them for some time, or at least prevent them from acting en masse. As for broad operations on their flank, the terrain and circumstances now rendered this very difficult, if not almost impossible. Yet at this moment we recognized the urgent necessity to march rapidly to take advantage of the time we gained as a result of the disrupted bridges and the increasing difficulties of the English army; to gather reinforcements and materials and to prepare the new flank march and change directions, a rather difficult movement to execute near the Tagus.

I had presented these diverse opinions in a summary report to the Prince after Fonte Coberta. I thought for a long time about them because they were pointed out in the extensive report to the Major General.[17] As soon as we had abandoned the project of the Tagus, our thoughts turned to the future. We could foresee where we would end, and from that time on it was necessary to find remedies for these misfortunes. A sad situation, anticipating these disasters without being able to prevent them, but at least we continued to fight them. The plan mentioned above to march on the Tagus became the cause of the striking rupture between the Prince and the Marshal. The plan had been bothering His Excellency for a long time, especially after he renounced the hope of a battle. The Prince accepted the plan completely. He even wanted to hasten its execution, and yet he decided to continue our retrograde movements though with very deep regrets and bitter sorrow. Nevertheless, the retreat was necessary for various reasons. Therefore the Prince decided to remain for one day in our excellent position on the Alva in order to unite the army, to allow the artillery and baggage a little time to take the advance, and also to follow the system we had adopted without appearing to flee before the English army. He had given orders to start marching the next day, one hour before daybreak, to take the following positions: the 6th Corps at Venda do Porto, the 8th at Lourosa, the 2nd at Avô and Sandomil in

17. Apparently Pelet refers to a letter dated March 29 from Berthier to Masséna: "The very explicit intention of the Emperor is to plan a movement with the Army of the South, a corps of the Army of the Center, and your army in the month of September after the harvest to overthrow the English." See *Wellington's Dispatches* (1852 ed.), IV, 844.

the valley of the Alva, and finally the headquarters at Galizes in the center of the army. No preparations had been made to destroy the bridge [on the Alva]; it was feared it would not be burned or blown up when we left our position. Colonel Valazé went and gave orders; before long it was completely ruined.

Officious reports intensified the bitterness between the Prince and the Marshal even more. General Loison never missed an occasion to pay assiduous and very self-seeking court to both of them. He came to tell us that the Marshal claimed that I had halted the movement. The Prince flew into a rage and told him to his face that indeed he was very much attached to me and regarded me as his son, but that I would not permit myself to give advice, especially of such a nature. From that morning, the Marshal complained that his left was completely unsupported and that the bridge of Obispo was neither guarded nor reconnoitered.[18] The Prince sent me to give him some information on Reynier's position. The General had written he was one league [away] in a straight line, but he vigorously recommended that we watch the passages of Santa Quitéria, through which he had passed to Arganil. The Marshal claimed that this information was not exact; that the 2nd Corps was extended and cantoned in good villages where they lived well, while his own 6th Corps lacked everything; that his soldiers were now cleaning and preparing their arms to fight while the others ate and rested; and finally that it was urgent to replace them with other corps which had done nothing.[19] I pointed out to him that he had rested for five months while the others were on the line at Sobral and at Santarém. He asserted the enemy was maneuvering on us, although we saw nothing anywhere. Finally, he was extremely anxious and moody.

Meanwhile the crests were covered by a thick fog that completely enveloped them. Suddenly it dissipated. I looked and saw a mass of English infantry and cavalry on the heights of Santa Quitéria, and col-

18. See note 15 above for Ney's concern about his left.

19. Pelet undoubtedly bases this statement on a paragraph of Ney's letter of March 18 to Masséna which stated, "I repeat to Your Excellency, it is urgent that the three army corps of the Army of Portugal are alternately employed to contain the enemy and bring up the march of the army during the retreat. The 6th Corps has been employed in this duty since the 7th of this month when I left Leiria. Since then, the troops have been constantly camped and reassembled without being able to go and maraud and without taking even a moment to rest." See Correspondance: Armée de Portugal, Carton $C^7 12$.

umns of infantry, cannon, and mules descending by a winding road. We could follow the columns as they crossed through the glades in some woods, but we did not see their fronts. The order was quickly sent to prepare arms, and to the 8th Corps to march immediately to Moita, a junction of the Murcella and Arganil roads, in reserve for the 6th and 2nd Corps. General Reynier soon wrote that he was going to be attacked immediately and needed support. This had already been provided. The Marshal arrived; he said that everything should be put in movement and that the enemy were going to attack us. The Prince coldly bade him return to his army corps at once. The Duc arrived out of breath and asked me how many men I saw. I said eight to ten thousand men. A much larger number was reported. He pressed the march of his 8th Corps. Opposite us there was nothing on the crest of Murcella, and there never would be anything, but our center, if not already outflanked, soon would be because of the slope of the valley.

The Prince remained at the head of some cavalry to examine the unfolding of the enemy's plans and dispatched me to the Marshal again to remain with him until the end of his movement. I found him still in a very bad mood, protesting strongly against the departure of the 8th Corps, claiming that it should support him immediately and that he was going to be attacked. I demonstrated the contrary and maintained that the enemy were marching on our left and that this was the point to be reinforced; moreover, nothing was seen in front of him. He asserted that at least one hour was necessary to unite and put his army corps in march. I assured him that he had ample time. He urged me to go and halt the 8th Corps. I seized this pretext to leave and rid myself of these worries, convinced that the only thing the Marshal wanted was to overtake the 8th Corps and take the position at the front of the column in order to execute the escapade he had announced to me three days earlier. I left quite slowly, looking behind me on the crest without seeing much there. At last I reached the Prince just ahead of his escort at Moita, where he found himself face to face with some English dragoons. Without doubt they had arrived by the ford on the Alva. The 8th Corps set itself in position. I came on the left beyond the advance post to see the bridge of Obispo and its surroundings. The valley of the Alva was quite wide and the slopes were very gentle. I saw only thirty enemy horsemen and some infantry who fired on ten of our dragoons. Moreover, the enemy were setting up camp for we saw their bivouac fires sparkling and perceived many more behind the mountains. I ran to tell the Prince that there would certainly not be an attack that evening. At Murcella the enemy fired a dozen cannon rounds to bid us farewell. Thus their great flank maneuver was reduced to the occupation of the left bank of the Alva.[20] Furthermore, this movement was no less dangerous. I talked about it to the Prince at Murcella in the presence of Lagarde, when everyone was proposing his own plans. The Prince bawled me out as one bawls out a young boy who insists that he is right. At Lobeira* I did not agree with him on the subject of a report on these last events. I had prepared it to be sent to Paris, and I read it to him in front of his secretary. He made a few observations that did not please me very much. The secretary became involved and then I displayed some irritation. The report remained as it was. It seems to me that the project of marching on the Erjas was announced and detailed in that report. I have nothing remaining of it.

It would have been desirable to spend the night in the vicinity of Moita to wait for the large number of soldiers that the corps had sent out for food without orders and for the many men who had been foraging; the delay would also avoid the losses of stragglers and men who remained in the villages during each night march. Each of these factors cost us as many men as a small battle, but who could control an army corps? Accordingly, the Prince gave orders to march slowly with frequent halts at the various positions indicated in his order for the day's march. [By the night of March 18] the 2nd Corps was near Avô and Sandomil, the 8th at Lourosa, the 6th at Venda do Porto, and the headquarters at Galizes. These marches were very short and rear guards were left; since the time of our departure coincided with the return of the marauders at dusk, the loss was less considerable than we had feared. We arrived at Galizes by a passable road and we lodged as well as we could in that miserable hole, where the Prince was kind

20. In a footnote Pelet turns on critics of the campaign who claimed the French had been beaten and outmaneuvered. Referring to the positions on the left bank of the Alva, Pelet comments, "These were the impregnable positions, according to unnamed people, that had been forced on our left. But what troops were overthrown? Where did the enemy present their columns to attack the front of our positions? Where was the boldness and rapidity of the enemy movements? What equipment did we sacrifice except for a few luxurious carriages of no use? Where were the great losses in men and horses? How and where was the army in danger of being destroyed?"

enough to give me a morsel to eat from his own ration because nothing had been prepared for anyone.

Meanwhile the army found itself echeloned on a kind of abutment, very accessible, and with a gentle slope toward the Mondego and the Alva. We could not stop in such a position, however improbable an attack from the enemy, who were always toward our left. The Prince sent me early to the Marshal and to the Duc to consult with them about how far their corps could march during the day, according to what they had done the previous night. The Marshal had announced that he would stop the 6th Corps only after it had passed beyond Galizes, and it was proper for the Duc to be apprised of this. I found the Duc at Lourosa, a rather large and very ancient village built on granite. He told me that he would arrive at Maceira and that his troops could start marching immediately, having had four hours of rest. Beyond Lourosa, I followed the old road and met Captain Despenoux, who had returned from the rear guard without encountering the Marshal. I then learned that he had moved forward and I returned, chasing in all directions the marauders who rushed into the houses.

We found the road that the English had laid out from Galizes to Maceira. They had repaired the road wherever it was necessary, turning through the most rocky or narrowest part of the land. Bypassing the villages, the route twisted around the tops of the valleys and followed the crests. The result of all this was an undulating road that was very good almost everywhere except where it unavoidably passed through some of the villages. The old road, on the contrary, was narrow, full of rocks, and very difficult.

The Prince left after sending an order to the 8th Corps to go to Maceira, the 6th Corps to Chamusca, the 2nd Corps to Santo Romão, and the cavalry toward Vinhó. We followed a rather good road without great ascents and descents across a relatively desolate country sprinkled with pines; since the Alva we had begun to see the granite peaks which abound around Almeida. On the right, the Serra da Estrêla was very close and crowned by "the Cântaros," the granite peaks covered with snow. The rest of the range seemed to be rounded, with gentle slopes covered with bushes. The bottom of the valley appeared to be cultivated and the intermediate slopes were covered with woods. All this indicated the possibility of communicating from one slope to the other and crossing the range without many of the difficulties which we [considered] as insurmountable. The valley of the Alva seemed to be narrower, but the various bottoms were full of ravines and rocks, ascending to "the Cântaros" in a vast funnel. Thus, after traveling through the miserable villages of Chamusca and Caragozela we arrived by a very gentle slope at the height where the Alva had its source. From there we descended along some slopes to reach Maceira.[21] The English had made some kind of ditches on these slopes in the form of entrenchments; this made a rather respectable position defended by a stream that ran along the bottom, almost perpendicularly to the bed of the Alva, and flowed into the Mondego. Maceira was a rather large village, where everything was granite; its neighborhood was very populous. Half a league away was Cea, a pretty town, and slightly farther toward the east was Santo Romão. A quarter of a league to the north was a large village where the 8th Corps had its headquarters; it must have been Torrozelo. We no longer found food near the road and the marauders were forced to go on the flanks, where the peasants received them with gunfire. Yet they brought back a rather great quantity of wine, ham, and chicken. We enjoyed ourselves walking through the bivouacs. Happiness had returned to the voices of the men and we began to hear *La Mère Godichon* sung again. At Maceira, Captain Porcher de Richebourg left to carry reports to the government and the report I have already mentioned.[22]

In this country each army corps was forced to march in a single column. It was fortunate that we had gained the respect of the enemy so they let us march peacefully and that we had sent the baggage far ahead so its march was not delayed. Yet when the country opened up, the various columns marched along different roads. The orders of

21. By the night of March 19, Drouet had reached Santo Romão, Reynier was at Avô and São João, Junot occupied Maceira, and Ney bivouacked at Chamusca. See Masséna to Ney, March 19, 1811, Correspondance: Armée de Portugal, Carton C⁷12.

22. Richebourg carried Masséna's letter to Berthier dated March 19, describing the events which had forced him to withdraw from central Portugal: "I think that in the actual state of things . . . it is in the interest of His Majesty to withdraw the army to our base of operation . . . to recover a little from fatigue and long privations, and to reorganize and replace the things we lack completely. Moreover, it appears impossible to feed our troops in the restricted and mountainous country that has been exhausted by the two armies and recently ravaged with great barbarity by the English. . . . We find everything destroyed: factories, mills, homes, and many villages burned. . . . I will march as slowly as possible, disputing every foot of terrain with the enemy but avoiding . . . combats that kill our brave soldiers." See Correspondance: Armée de Portugal, Carton C⁷12.

march made this an exact order. General Reynier always marched on our right flank, but he was sometimes forced to send his artillery along the main road. In reference to this subject he complained about the Marshal, who had not always protected his cannon well. He left a detachment of his troops especially to follow the stragglers, whose number increased because of the wine.

We were going to Sampayo, where the headquarters and the 8th Corps were; the 6th Corps was at Vinhó, the 2nd at Gouveia, and the *parc* and baggage at Cortiçô. The terrain gradually became smoother and contrasted strongly with the mountainous country we had crossed. The mountains were very near, now extremely rocky, and their streams ran directly into the Mondego; they offered some temporary defenses along their valleys because the Mondego had become easily fordable and the mountains were not always impassable, despite their rocks. I had continued [to record] the topography on our marches of the roads and the neighboring terrain. My unexpected departure from the army resulted in the dispersion of most of these rather precious materials.

Before coming to the final decision on the direction of the army, which kept us very busy, an absolute decision had to be made according to our plans. The Prince, reassured by the agreement of the generals in the *état major,* decided to get the opinion of General Reynier, who was the most able of the commanders of the army corps in understanding strategic movements. Moreover, he knew perfectly the country where we were going to maneuver. The Prince sent me to him at Gouveia to talk about our operation. He found the plan acceptable and the only one we could execute at that time. He strongly approved of the flank march through the Puerto de Perales. He was only afraid that we would have great difficulties in finding food in that area, where he himself had extracted many provisions the previous year, and that we would soon find ourselves forced to go up the Tagus toward Almaraz or have grain brought in from Navalmoral and Talavera; this would be easy. He thought that we would not find much food between the Tagus and the Guadiana. I invited him to write all this out in a memorandum and more particularly to consult his notes and recollections. At the same time he promised me to send some very exact manuscripts on his reconnaissances. He sent all this the next day with a rather extensive and fairly good map of the country between Ciudad Rodrigo and the Tagus extending toward Coria and Plasencia. When he left Gouveia, I accompanied him in order to continue our conversation. He was going directly on to Guarda along a road that crossed the mountain. When the General started to go a little higher up the mountain, I left him to rejoin the Prince. The General took only his mountain artillery with him and sent the remainder of his *parc* through Celorico and Freixedas, because the roads were practicable only for the wagons made locally.

After crossing a fully cultivated country with many villages, houses, and much food everywhere, I found the headquarters at Vila Cortez but not a single inhabitant. The positive opinion of General Reynier was sufficient to determine that of the Prince, if he had not yet made up his own mind. Thus he decided to stay at Celorico on March 22 and 23, to give suitable orders for the fortresses and their depots, and to march on the 24th for Guarda, Sabugal, and Alfaiates in the regions he wanted to occupy. On arriving at Celorico, the Prince wrote immediately to Marshal Ney to inform him that the army would stop for two days in the positions they were taking in order to refit and prepare for new movements. The 6th Corps was at Càrrapichana, the Marshal at Cortiçô, the 8th Corps was around Celorico, the 2nd Corps at Guarda occupying Belmonte, the cavalry at Baraçal, and Claparède's division of the 9th Corps near Alfaiates. Conroux's division of the same corps,[23] which had left Celorico, was at Freixedas with General Drouet. Moving by forced marches from Miranda, General Drouet did not stop until he was within reach of the frontier. Thus the army was concentrated and in a very advantageous position with regard to food and in a rather respectable one for the army or its flanks, assured that the enemy would not disturb them. If the enemy wanted to test our army, we could be out of reach in a single march, beyond the Mondego in the positions of Freixedas. The *parc* and equipment of all the army corps had been directed on that village to avoid the defiles of Guarda.

The Marshal had not been followed beyond the position at Maceira,

23. Nicholas François Conroux, Baron de Pépinville (1779–1813), enlisted in an artillery regiment in 1786; he became an aide-de-camp to General Morlot in 1793 and served in Germany until joining the Army of Italy. He served with Bernadotte and Davout and was promoted to general of division after Wagram. In 1810 Conroux was assigned a division in Drouet's corps when it marched into Spain.

where the enemy showed only a few cavalry with one or two light pieces. He replied to the Prince by exaggerating the forces and maneuvers of the Allies;[24] he claimed that Lord Wellington was marching along the right bank of the Mondego and that there were two thousand English at Fornos. At the same time he sent a letter from General Marchand, with whom he had corresponded very little on such matters. The general asserted that to stop the army in this position was to destroy it; that he would no longer answer for his soldiers, who would disband in order to search for food; and that the enemy was behind us. As though we had not been in a similar position for eight months and now had considerable food on hand.

At Celorico we learned of a rumor that had been spread on the subject of the army (I did not know by whom) that it was beaten, annihilated, and scattered, and that we were not bringing back a single gun or even a horse. My anger made me ill. I was extremely thin and felt exhausted because of considerable grief and fatigue. I had not stopped working and despairing. I had to remain in bed. The Prince had the kindness to concern himself about me. I hastened to tell him that I was resting to be ready to begin anew. My poor friend Cavailher was also sick, but in a much worse way. He endured the symptoms of a deadly illness during my absence and was carried by grenadiers on a stretcher during the march of the army.

The Marshal started this deplorable day [March 22] by writing to the Prince a letter that was rather well organized but which did not appear correctly based and reasoned. I believe that it was dated at noon. He said that according to what he saw and heard, it seemed that the Prince wanted to move the army in the direction of Coria and execute a flank march in the presence of a formidable enemy, and that it was his duty to point out the difficulties of the present position and the dangers of this maneuver. The Marshal claimed that Madrid would be unmasked, that the enemy could march on Salamanca and Valladolid, and that they would be able to seize the Puerto de Baños to maneuver

24. Wellington was forced to halt momentarily at the Ceira until the bridge could be repaired and after March 19 he lost contact with all but the rear guard of the French army. Without adequate logistical support, only the Light, Third, and Sixth divisions continued the pursuit. On March 20, 600 French soldiers and 3 officers were taken by Wellington's advanced guard. See *Wellington's Dispatches*, Wellington to Liverpool, March 16, 1811, VII, 369–72; Wellington to Beresford, March 20, 1811, VII, 374–76.

by the Guadarrama. He ended by concluding that the loss of Spain would inevitably follow.[25]

At the same time the Prince wrote to him, as well as to the other corps commanders, to let them know of his intentions and the measures that had been taken for the march of the army on Coria and for the delay the next day. This dispatch crossed the first letter of the Marshal.[26] The latter responded at four or six o'clock that after the Prince had officially made the project known to him, which he had written against in the morning, it was his duty to protest against its execution, since it would have grave results for the army and for Spain. He declared that he would execute the orders only if the Prince had received them from the Emperor. He complained in the body of the letter that he had the enemy around him and that he was going to be attacked. He said, "Since you always wait for the moment of the greatest danger to make up your mind, I am obliged to prevent the total ruin of the army." Finally, he added, "I feel that by my disobedience I am taking great responsibility on myself, but even if I were to be dismissed or lose my head on a scaffold, I will not obey."[27] The *post*

25. Pelet's account here is quite similar to Ney's letter to Masséna dated 2:00 P.M. on March 22. Ney wrote, "It seems that Your Highness is disposed to march to your left to approach the Tagus through Alcántara. This maneuver, which will expose the communications with Castile and abandon the fortresses of Almeida and Ciudad Rodrigo to their meager resources, appears very extraordinary to me at this moment since we do not know if Wellington will continue his offensive march toward the Spanish frontier. All these observations, Prince, are suggested by me in the desire to contribute all my efforts to the good of the service of the Emperor." See Correspondance: Armée de Portugal, Carton C[7]12.

26. Masséna responded at about 3:00 P.M. to Ney's letter of 2:00 P.M.: "I have received your letter, which . . . I find very improper. The army needs to remain in these actual positions three or four days to give the wounded time to file to Almeida. . . . It is not a question at all of going to Salamanca, but to Coria, Plasencia, and that vicinity to find food." See Correspondance: Armée de Portugal, Carton C[7]12.

27. Pelet's account of Ney's response is again accurate. Ney wrote, "I received this instant the letter that Your Excellency wrote me, by which I am made part of a plan that he has ordered to march the Army of Portugal to Coria and Plasencia. . . . I was . . . against this maneuver in my preceding [letter] of some hours ago. . . . I formally protest against it and declare to Your Excellency that unless the Emperor has given you new instructions relative to a movement to operate toward the Tagus, which I do not believe is the actual case, the 6th Corps will not execute the movement that you mentioned to me in your letter today. . . . Your Excellency is mistaken in thinking that food can be obtained in abundance in this region of Coria and Plasencia. . . . I am aware that my responsibility is great in making formal opposition to your intentions, but even if I were destined to be cashiered or lose my head, I certainly could not follow the movement Your Excellency ordered." See Ney to Masséna, 4:00 P.M., March 22, 1811, Correspondance: Armée de Portugal, Carton C[7]12.

scriptum added that he was giving orders to his army corps to leave for Freixedas the next day and that he would go to Almeida on the following day. These statements were copied into my Journal several days later, and I do not affirm the exact words of this quotation, for my extracts were sometimes made on the documents immediately after they were read. As far as the real sense is concerned, the remainder of my Journal can be relied on; I guarantee it.

The Prince called me immediately. I found him determined to use all his authority against the Marshal. Nothing stopped him, not the courage and the violence of this warrior, the devotion of the unmanageable army corps that he had commanded for more than six years, the considerable influence he had in the army, the fears of discord which seemed necessarily to follow in the presence of a formidable enemy and amidst a rebellious population, nor the degree of responsibility that rested on him. The Prince did not hesitate an instant, and it was then that I recognized his great strength of character. I confess I found myself struck by the chain of circumstances that unfolded before me, and I first sought every means to avert the turmoil. I had always done my best to maintain peace and harmony between these two great men. I repeated to the Prince what I had told him so often, that his great name and authority permitted him to do many things, and what would be weakness in others became moderation in him. I portrayed to him the separation and destruction of the army, the danger of his orders being scorned, and the still more dangerous dissension. After much insistence, he finally decided to write the Marshal in an attempt to bring him to his senses. He dictated an impressive letter in a tone of moderation and dignity, exhortation and firmness. What a scandal and what an example for the French armies! What consequences for the Empire! What affliction for the *patrie*! What a triumph for the enemy! Let the Marshal reflect seriously! Let him regain the worthy sentiments of his glory and past conduct! As the commander in chief of the army, the Prince owed to the sovereign he represented the authority that had been invested in him; he had to deal severely with this explicit disobedience after overlooking many others. Only the Prince could have dictated such a letter. It was short and even his first thoughts were great and noble.[28] However, he knew the Marshal and prepared all his orders as the circumstances required.

28. Masséna's reply was forceful and left no doubt of his intentions: "I have

It appeared that the letter of the Prince was a subject of much reflection for the Marshal. He responded immediately that "he persists with all his resolution until he is shown a formal letter of the Emperor for the operation."[29] Captain Despenoux, aide-de-camp of the Prince, took his letter to the Marshal. He returned with an answer after one hour, yet there was a good league between the two headquarters.

The Prince had made up his mind. This matter seemed so important to me; yet of all his decisions this was the only one in which I took no part. Generals Fririon and Éblé went to visit the Prince. He had the following orders prepared: the one to the Marshal stated that because of formal disobedience, the authority the Prince held from the Emperor forced him to relieve the Marshal from command of the 6th Corps and to give it to the oldest general of division of the army corps. He enjoined the Marshal to return to Spain to await orders from the Major General. The command of the 6th Corps passed to General Loison, and General Ferey took his division. Orders were communicated to Generals Marchand and Mermet, prohibiting them from obeying the Marshal and executing orders other than those of the Prince transmitted by General Loison.[30] The latter had been notified and arrived without delay. It was further decided that I would go to Paris immediately to give an account of the situation, the disobedience of the Marshal, and in general all the operations of the campaign. Since my mission had been announced for the end of the retreat [campaign], I had declared that I would not accept, considering that it was too late and

received your three letters. You cannot doubt my surprise. Their contents force me to come to an extreme that I had sought to avoid until this day. Your disobedience is too definite for me not to invoke the authority the Emperor has given me over the Army of Portugal. . . . Will you please inform me if you are going to persist in your disobedience by rejecting the authority the Emperor has confided in me." See Masséna to Ney, 8:00 P.M., March 22, 1811, Correspondance: Armée de Portugal, Carton C⁷12; Archives de Masséna, LI.

29. Ney's response was as firm as the Prince's letter: "I persist in not permitting the 6th Corps to march on Coria and Plasencia unless Your Excellency . . . makes the Emperor's orders known in this regard." Ney concluded by indicating that he would "march on Almeida tomorrow." See Ney to Masséna, 9:30 P.M., March 22, 1811, Correspondance: Armée de Portugal, Carton C⁷12.

30. Masséna's final letter of the day settled the issue: "It is with regret that I see you continue to formally disobey my orders. . . . In order to maintain the authority His Majesty gave me . . . [and] for the good of the service and the interests of the Emperor, I have ordered the divisional generals, Loison, Mermet, and Marchand, to ignore your orders from the present . . . and I order you to go to Spain and await the orders of His Majesty." See Masséna to Ney, 10:30 P.M., March 22, 1811, Correspondance: Armée de Portugal, Carton C⁷12. For slight variations in wording, see Bonnal, *Ney,* III, 533–34, and Archives de Masséna, LI.

useless. At that moment the Prince's interest prevailed even over the various dangers that influenced me, and most certainly over my bad state of health, as well as the dissatisfaction that I could expect from the court. I had devoted myself with the greatest sacrifice to the confidence and kindness that the Prince had shown to me. He said to me, "You do not need any instructions. You will see the Emperor and tell him everything that you judge proper." At the same time he gave me a very concise letter for the Major General and copies of the various letters of the Prince and the Marshal, prepared in advance.

Without commotion, I began my journey to Paris, my heart full of bitterness, very worried about the sickness of my old friend Cavailher and tormented by anxieties of what would happen in the future to this army I was leaving, either because of the extremities to which it had been carried by the Marshal or because of an attack by the enemy. It must not be overlooked that Lord Wellington was readily informed about what occurred among us. Not very much time had passed since several Portuguese officers of superior rank and grade who had been with us had gone over to the enemy. From them and many others, everything was probably known. If Lord Wellington had taken advantage of the moral disorder that these events had occasioned in our army, a strong attack through the center might have had terrible results, but this was not his favorite kind of attack.

EPILOGUE

Pelet left Masséna's headquarters at Celorico on March 23, 1811, carrying all the pertinent information regarding Ney's insubordination, as well as a dispatch for Berthier setting out his own responsibilities.[1] The Prince had written, "My first aide-de-camp . . . will discuss [the correspondence] in great detail with you. He will give Your Excellency an account on the retrograde movement and the position of the army. . . . He is thoroughly familiar with the country through which we marched in Portugal and will give Your Highness all the information you desire."[2]

With a small escort, Pelet started his long journey across Spain. He passed through Almeida, Ciudad Rodrigo, and Salamanca, and at Valladolid he met Marshal Bessières, now in command of the Army of the North. They discussed the exhausted condition of Masséna's cavalry and Bessières's newly formed army. Traveling up to forty miles a day, Pelet reached Irun on the Spanish frontier at dawn on March 29.

1. Pelet originally planned to include the account of his mission to Paris as Chapter 14 of his manuscript, but it was inadvertently separated from the main body of the "Campagne de Portugal" and mixed in with his rough draft (917^2). Chapter 14 was published in 1895 as "Une mission auprès de I'Empereur Napoléon en 1811 pendant la campagne de Portugal" in Vol. XI, *Mémoires de la société Bourguignonne de géographie et d'histoire,* ed. A. d'Avout (Dijon). A narrative version of Pelet's mission rather than a direct translation has seemed more appropriate here; my account, however, is based on the original manuscript.

2. Masséna to Berthier, March 22, 1811, Correspondance: Armée de Portugal, Carton $C^7$12.

"From there," Pelet recalled, "I hurried toward my beloved France." Despite his weakened physical condition, he had journeyed more than four hundred miles in less than six days, an extraordinary pace even for someone in good health.

After Pelet entered France, he was given a calash to continue his journey toward Paris. He spent most of the trip reviewing his Journal and examining the dossier given him by Masséna. Between Poitiers and Tours, he encountered Colonel Casabianca, who had been dispatched to Paris by Masséna on January 22 and was now on his way south to rejoin the army. Casabianca, Pelet recalled, "appeared very embarrassed and even displeased to see me. Finally he told me that Napoleon was furious, that he fretted and fumed against the Prince, that he said we had dishonored ourselves, that we should have attacked the enemy and been killed, that he would not excuse the retreat beyond the Mondego . . . that the Prince was lost, and that the Emperor was terribly angry with me." Casabianca also hinted that Pelet would not be given a hearing at the Tuileries and would be badly treated because the Emperor was particularly dissatisfied with him.

When Pelet arrived in Paris, his friends, as well as those of Masséna, confirmed Casabianca's comment "that the Emperor did not want to listen to talk about" him. Nevertheless, Pelet had made up his mind to carry out his orders. "I have my entire campaign in mind and have anticipated many arguments and responses," he wrote, "and the entire case is very detailed. I am sure of success if I see the Emperor."

A few hours after he reached Paris, Pelet presented himself at Berthier's headquarters. Berthier requested news of the army and of Masséna; he read the dispatches carried by Pelet. When Pelet indicated that he wished to talk with Napoleon, he was ushered into the pages' chamber, where he remained for three hours. Berthier finally returned and declared in a discourteous manner that Pelet could not see the Emperor. At Pelet's insistence on an audience, Berthier told him to appear the next day but warned him, "I have not spoken to the Emperor about the dispute between the Prince and the Marshal; he knows nothing. Therefore it is not necessary to speak to him about it if you see him. The Prince was right to dismiss him, but the Emperor knows nothing about it."

Later the same day Pelet saw General Maximilien Foy, who had been sent to Paris by Masséna on March 8. Foy told Pelet he would not be permitted to see the Emperor. He also warned Pelet against criticizing Ney and mentioned that he had been described by Napoleon as "this young topographic engineer who dreams only of redoubts."

The next morning Pelet went to the Major General's headquarters. Berthier, grumbling, wanted to know what Pelet intended to tell the Emperor. "*I have orders to see the Emperor* and *I will see him*," Pelet responded. When Berthier inquired whether Masséna gave orders in Paris, Pelet answered, "No, but he gave them to the army and to me and I will execute them at the Chateau, on the parade ground, or anywhere." Pelet again waited in the pages' chamber. Before Berthier left, he revealed that Napoleon knew Pelet was there and would call him.

Pelet waited and watched hour after hour while a long line of dignitaries filed into the Emperor's study. Luncheon was served to Napoleon, and the procession of distinguished personages continued to enter his chambers for the next six hours. General Henri Bertrand finally tried to announce Pelet, but Napoleon refused to see him. When dinner was carried into Napoleon's suite at 8:30 P.M., Pelet decided to leave. Shortly after reaching his own quarters, however, he received a letter from the chamberlain saying that the Emperor had asked for him and that he would be received the following day.

Pelet arrived early in the morning to find that Napoleon had gone hunting and could not see him; nevertheless, Pelet insisted on waiting. His persistence was at length rewarded and he was ushered into the Emperor's study. Napoleon, still dressed in riding clothes, approached Pelet in an irritable manner, inquiring, "Are you the first aide-de-camp or is it Casabianca, whom I have just made a colonel?" "It is I who am and who should be," Pelet answered. The Emperor told him that he had "done good things in Portugal" and then he burst out with criticisms of Masséna's conduct in the Portuguese campaign. He exclaimed, "You have lost everything that you can lose in war; you have lost the honor of arms. It would have been better if you had lost the army! Damn it! Sixty thousand Frenchmen retreat before thirty thousand English! Is my army to be as [ineffective as] my navy? Poor nation! Poor nation!" With tears in his eyes he added, "You have compromised the honor of the finest infantry in the world."

Hoping to refute these charges, Pelet repeated again and again that Masséna did not have sixty thousand men, but Napoleon "did not wish to listen to anything." After making charges of ignorance and incompetency, he cried out, "Must I say it to you, Monsieur? The Prince was very poorly advised . . . and in difficult moments it is good to have someone who will aid and support you. On all critical occasions, I hope that one of the men to whom I give my confidence will help me to carry this heavy burden [of war]. But the Prince is too poorly advised for that."

Pelet was at first stunned by Napoleon's onslaught, but he soon collected himself and answered, "Permit me to accept this criticism myself. I alone was close to the Prince and I advised him. He had only me to work with, and I possessed his military confidence entirely. I acquired it by six years of good service, and he could not give any stronger proof of it than by sending me to Your Majesty under these circumstances. I came to inform you about all the events of the campaign and the private motives . . . that determined his decisions. Until then you cannot judge the Prince, nor me, nor the campaign in Portugal." Napoleon was apparently impressed with Pelet's forthright statement; his anger slowly subsided as he entered into serious conversation.

Napoleon began his discussion by criticizing the withdrawal to the Mondego and the movement eastward to the Alva. He called the failure to secure the passage of the Mondego an "unpardonable fault." Pelet acknowledged that he had planned the retreat to the Mondego, but he also described his proposal that the 9th Corps should secure the crossing and mentioned Drouet's refusal to send even a regiment, as Masséna had requested. Pelet noted that the 9th Corps was not under the orders of Masséna at the time and that instructions had not arrived from Paris. "Why did he not use other troops," asked the Emperor. Pelet replied that the army was too small and the area to be protected too extensive; moreover, he said, the "enemy army was too large and too close, and the movement was too difficult if units were detached." Pelet also pointed out that although the Mondego had been easily fordable in the autumn, the unpredictable rains later rendered it impassable. In addition, because of the dearth of draft animals the bridge equipment had to be burned and the Mondego could not be crossed.

Napoleon then asked, "Why turn toward the Alva?" Pelet explained Masséna's reasons. To the next query, "Why direct the large corps along the route to Pombal?" Pelet replied tersely that it was done "with the intention of moving them on the banks of the Mondego and beyond." Napoleon attacked Masséna's system of retreat and Pelet defended it as his own work as far as the Mondego. Pelet's description of various details of the retreat, he recalled, included "some comments on the conduct of the Marshal which passed lightly and the Emperor made no reply. He asked for many details of the combats: 'Where was the Prince, the Marshal, the troops? Where was I?' I described these details with precision."

After some discussion of the Tagus, the Emperor inquired, "Why did he [Masséna] not cross?" Pelet retorted, "Because the Prince was told that it was then or appeared to be contrary to your intentions, plans, desires, and interests." Obviously surprised, Napoleon asked, "Who said that?" Pelet repeated Foy's comments and mentioned the orders from Paris which indicated this policy. Turning to the withdrawal to Santarém, Napoleon credited that maneuver to Reynier. "No, Sire," said Pelet, "it was my favorite idea and I was the first and only one to conceive it."

The Emperor then asked about the battle of Bussaco. "Why march on Lisbon after having been beaten so badly at Bussaco?" Pelet objected that the French "were not defeated at Bussaco; neither general nor army was beaten." The conversation soon turned to the commanders at Bussaco and more specifically to Marshal Ney's conduct. Pelet recalled, "I gave some details of his conduct. Not being able to give complete information, I spoke of the letter he had written to General Reynier,[3] of his proposal for the attack, etc." Napoleon intimated it was necessary to rise above these petty problems. "The Prince has done well," he admitted. "I recognize only one man in an army; the one who commands it, and when it disobeys him, he has only to take the recalcitrants and dispose of them."

Again the Emperor wanted to know why Masséna had marched on Lisbon. Pelet told him that this goal "had been designated, if not ordered, and that if we had not marched forward, he would have been the first to complain. . . . Moreover, we were ignorant of the exact state of the enemy forces, and the existence and possibility of their Lines. We hoped that the English would be obliged to embark after

3. Pelet was referring to Ney's letter to Reynier at 10:30 A.M. on September 26, 1810, at Bussaco. See footnote 20 of Chapter 5.

a battle that we did not fear and desired." Again and again Pelet reiterated the errors of the campaign—the French ignorance of the Lines of Torres Vedras, of the British system of defense, and of Portuguese topography. Pelet "stressed and returned frequently to this major error, which resulted in all our other errors when we established the campaign strategy and the direction of the operations."

Apparently hoping to undermine Pelet's argument, Napoleon claimed that he had not given formal orders to march on Lisbon, but Pelet retorted with details of Berthier's dispatches. The conversation again digressed to the various phases of the campaign, the disobedience of Ney, and Drouet's uncooperative attitude. Pelet maintained that "written proof of everything I have asserted is in the Prince's portfolio and Your Majesty may see it whenever he wishes." Napoleon continued his questions. " 'Why did the Prince not take command of the divisions [Ney's] and give them orders himself?' I replied that he could not do so without destroying the authority of the corps commanders." Pelet explained the roles of the commanders while the Emperor listened attentively. "I thought Masséna was much stronger and more mature," he observed. "When I returned from Egypt, he had completed his campaign in Switzerland; there he demonstrated great competence, prudence, and reserve. He is still the same, just as I observed him in Italy; he cannot make war by great maneuvers. The movement on Leiria was good; it was within his capabilities; the other one escaped him—the movement at Coimbra."

Perhaps irritated by what he regarded as Pelet's efforts to defend Masséna, Napoleon declared, "Masséna needs no excuses with me. I am attached to him; he is an old friend. If I considered only the interests of the moment, I would recall him, but I wish to maintain the greatest military name of my Empire . . . untarnished. He can still be useful to the state and my family, although he is now at an age when one makes war only on great occasions and when everyone takes up arms in defense of the *patrie*. Obviously, this is his last campaign. I wish to give him the means to take revenge on the enemy and to retire with his glory intact."

Pelet complained of Soult's cavalier attitude toward supporting Masséna's operations and Napoleon agreed; he then turned to Masséna's personal well-being, his health, morale, and intentions. Pelet pointedly described the "uncertainty in which the Prince found himself because of the vague orders that had been given to him and because of Napoleon's complete silence; and of the necessity for Napoleon to write a few words himself." Perhaps embarrassed, the Emperor promised to send Masséna everything "that he requests and desires; he will be content." In reference to outdated and vague orders, Pelet suggested that general instructions and policy statements should be sent to the commanders permitting the flexibility they needed to respond to unanticipated contingencies. Napoleon agreed: "I am too good and experienced a soldier to wish to direct the war five hundred leagues away myself. I send orders and instructions to my ambassadors, but I choose my generals and give them my confidence."

As their conversation continued, Napoleon expressed concern about the reports in English newspapers that equipment and even cannon had been abandoned at Santarém. Pelet reassured him several times that nothing had been left in the hands of the enemy. When Napoleon expressed grave disappointment about the capture of the hospitals at Coimbra, Pelet explained Masséna's decision to leave the wounded behind. Napoleon could not accept this loss. He was also critical of Masséna for not attacking the Allied positions beyond Santarém along the Rio Maior before retiring. Pelet rejected this criticism as unworthy of serious discussion. Napoleon then returned to the subject of the retreat. "Why did you not attack when you reached the Ceira or the Alva with your rear covered and assured?" Pelet pointed out that the army would have had to abandon its wounded and much of the baggage. Furthermore, he said, the terrain in both positions favored a defensive operation rather than an offensive one. "Why attack," he asked, "when we had to retreat to find food and supplies?" He concluded by declaring firmly: "If the Prince had thought only of his glory and interests, he would have given the enemy battle; however, he was too good a Frenchman and too attached to your interests and person to do this."

As time passed, the discussion turned to the various divisional and corps commanders and the need to reorganize the Army of Portugal; Pelet strongly recommended that the corps be replaced with divisions under the direct command of Masséna.[4] Pelet also complained about the promotions and decorations withheld from the army. Describing

4. Apparently Pelet's comments on the reorganization of the army had some effect, for on April 27 Napoleon instructed Berthier, "Write to the Duc de Raguse

the efforts and suffering of the various branches of the army, he gradually returned to Napoleon's outburst at the beginning of the interview and insisted that "we had lost nothing in the honor of our arms, we had been forced to retire after six months of cruel famine and inconceivable waiting, the enemy had never forced us to take a step but on the contrary had always been repulsed, and finally they had [taken] neither prisoners nor cannon."

The Emperor's attitude gradually changed during the discussion. "At the beginning," Pelet recalled, "Napoleon was somber, severe, and irritated. He flew into a passion, but feebly; his eyes were fixed, cold, and sometimes irritated, but always penetrating. Toward the middle, he was calm, more and more reasonable. At the end, he became pleasant, taking an amiable tone, and at some moments with a gracious smile." Napoleon finally concluded the three-hour interview by requesting that Pelet return in two days with a memorandum on the operations in Portugal. Before leaving, Pelet reminded the Emperor of the six requests for his promotion that had been made during the campaign. Napoleon smiled and said, " 'It is good,' as though it were agreed upon."

The following day Berthier called Pelet to his headquarters. The two men conferred about the reorganization of the Army of Portugal and Berthier indicated that Ney would be disciplined. "We are unable to try a Marshal of France. The Emperor is supposed to be unaware of what has taken place, but the Prince has done well. The Emperor vigorously approves of it and the Marshal will receive a grave reprimand." When Pelet mentioned the 5th Corps, Berthier "was a little embarrassed, as if the orders were not very clear or precise or contrary to the others." The same was true of "the orders of the 9th Corps that had not arrived or were not executed." After two hours of conversation, Berthier dismissed Pelet. As Pelet left Berthier's study, he noticed the arrival of Marshal Auguste Marmont but thought little of it until the next day.

When Pelet returned to Napoleon's quarters, he took a seat in the waiting room but was soon called into the Emperor's presence. Pelet recalled that the Emperor received him "with an engaging look." He

. . . that it is necessary that he take all suitable measures to organize his army, that I leave him master to organize it in six divisions, without making army corps." See *Correspondance de Napoléon Ier*, No. 17660, Napoleon to Berthier, April 27, 1811, XXII, 136.

declared, "I want to show you the report on your campaign which I will put in *Le Moniteur* tomorrow.[5] Give me your advice; it is not yet complete—the wording is not finished, but I will straighten it out." Pelet read the article over Napoleon's shoulder. "Well, do you find it accurate and well presented?" he was asked. "I found it very complimentary for us and . . . I said so. I made some observations on dates, names of places, on some facts, and on the suppression of the combat of Miranda do Corvo where, I recalled, Marbot had been wounded."

The interview then proceeded on a pessimistic note. Napoleon was still concerned about the cannon and baggage which the British claimed to have captured. Pelet vowed that nothing had been abandoned in the rear. After further discussion about the reorganization of the army, the Emperor asked Pelet's opinion of Marmont as a replacement for Ney. "I do not know Monsieur le Maréchal," Pelet replied, "but there will be the same conflict of authority and difficulties as with Marshal Ney." "No, my dear friend," Napoleon assured him, "Masséna and Marmont are from the same family; they are of the Army of Italy while Ney is from a foreign army [the Army of the Rhine]. . . . Masséna commanded my great divisions while the other [Marmont] was my aide-de-camp; in one way or another he has long been accustomed to authority and subordination, while Ney took part in the great wars of the north [Germany]; he commanded armies there and made a great name for himself." There was no question in Napoleon's mind that

5. The *Moniteur* of April 8, 1811, announced: "An aide-de-camp of Marshal Prince d'Essling has arrived at Paris. He left the headquarters at Celorico on March 23. All the magazines that the Army had formed were completely exhausted by February 28. The foragers, sent as far as twenty leagues from headquarters, have brought back nothing. By March 1, the army was reduced to using the biscuit reserve that could only furnish fifteen days' food; moreover, there was no possibility of awaiting the harvest nor hoping for any resources before June. Then only three choices remained to the Prince. [He could] attack the English in the lines of Lisbon, but military principles thwarted him as long as his heavy artillery had not arrived. [He could] cross the Tagus to form a junction with the Army of Andalusia, and from there form communications . . . with Seville and Madrid, to find artillery resources in Badajoz, to extract his food in Alentejo, to change his line of operations and to hold a double bridgehead that the army had constructed on the right and left bank of the Zezere at Punhete. . . . The third choice was to recross the Mondego, retire to Guarda, and establish communications with Ciudad Rodrigo where there were shoes, clothing, munitions, resources for the artillery, magazines, and the treasury of the army that had not been paid for six months. On March 3, the Prince d'Essling decided on the last choice." The article then proceeded to describe in glowing terms the French withdrawal, often day by day, from March 4 to 22.

Marmont's presence was required in Portugal. He concluded, "It is quite necessary that I have a man there representing me in case of accident."

Pelet then read the memorandum he had prepared and they discussed it line by line. Pelet described the composition and organization of both the French and the Allied armies, noting their logistical support. The two men pored over the great maps in Napoleon's cartographic room; Pelet described maneuvers and plans for the coming campaign. When they returned to the study, Napoleon thoughtfully observed, "We must wait. We can decide nothing here since events have long passed by the time we receive the first news. We must wait and see. I cannot wage war five hundred leagues away nor predict the movements made by the enemy armies from such a distance."

Before concluding the interview, Napoleon asked about Pelet's previous service in the army. Pelet described his six years with Masséna, his role on the Island of Lobau, his strategy for the Portuguese campaign, and Masséna's confidence in him. However, Pelet added, "The Prince regards me as his student and a young officer; this makes it easy for me to propose, insist, and if need be debate anything, even ideas that the Prince regards as his own." When the interview ended, the Emperor ordered Pelet to report to Berthier and said "'Adieu, Colonel,' twice with a graceful nod." Pelet thus received his long-awaited promotion; two days later he was wearing his epaulets.

Pelet visited Berthier's headquarters several times while he was in Paris. On April 11 Berthier received a copy of an English newspaper with an account of Masséna's retreat from Portugal.[6] Napoleon asked for comments on the article and Pelet wrote candidly, "This report is true, authoritative, and honorable for those who sent it; it exaggerated

6. Pelet was probably referring to the London *Times* of April 8, 1811, No. 8264, which included extracts of Wellington's letters to Liverpool dated March 14 and 16. In the first dispatch, Wellington wrote, "The whole country, however, affords many advantageous positions to a retreating [enemy] army, of which the enemy have shown that they know how to avail themselves. They are retreating from the country . . . covering their rear on every march by the operations of either one or two corps d'armée in the strong positions which the country affords. . . . Before they quitted their position they destroyed a part of their cannon and ammunition, and they have since blown up whatever the horses were unable to draw away. . . . I am concerned to be obliged to add to this account, that their conduct throughout this retreat has been marked by a barbarity seldom equalled and never surpassed . . . and they have since burnt every town and village through which they have passed." See *Wellington's Dispatches*, VII, 354–61, 369–72.

only slightly our losses in men and the advantages derived. It has some condemnation against our pillaging, the burning of villages, and the horrors of war, but the English were involved in at least three-fourths of it."

On April 13 Colonel Pelet received instructions to prepare for his return to Portugal. Berthier warned him, "The Prince should now limit himself to occupying the right bank of the Tagus, to resting and establishing his army there, and to holding the enemy in check as far as possible without engaging in anything or compromising himself." Before Pelet left Paris he met Ney, who had just returned from Spain. Ney greeted him cordially and they talked about the Portuguese campaign and the events of March 23, when the Marshal was relieved of his command. Ney complained about what Pelet had said to the Emperor concerning his conduct and his wish to see the Prince removed. To the latter charge Pelet responded, "'I did not say that, only that you had done everything to make it possible.' Then [Ney claimed] that I had bothered his officers. I gave him my word of honor to the contrary and added, 'You know I am too frank to employ such methods and too proud to believe that I have need of them.'" As Pelet recalled their parting, "We left each other very good friends and after that time and in every country (particularly in Russia) he gave me proof of his goodwill toward me."

Pelet began his long journey southward through Tours and Poitiers; he left Bayonne on April 16 and pushed on to Burgos, where he learned that Bessières had marched to Salamanca with cavalry and infantry to reinforce Masséna for an anticipated battle with Wellington. Pelet raced on behind Bessières, but when he reached Salamanca he was dismayed to learn that Bessières had only a cavalry unit and six cannon with him; the other detachments of his command had been sent to Soult. Bessières promised to march with his troops the following morning, but he confided his fears that a battle had already been fought because Masséna had only eight days' rations which must by then have been consumed.

Finally on April 26, five weeks after leaving the army, Pelet reached Masséna's quarters at Ciudad Rodrigo. "I rejoined the Prince, who embraced me warmly and showered me with affection," he recollected. "We passed long hours talking of the Emperor, Paris, and the army. The Prince was not always satisfied, although I attempted to soften anything which might have displeased him. He appeared to me to have decided to quit the army. But I doubted it a little because there was a difference between leaving and saying that he wanted to leave his command. His disgust had been increased by recent events." However, as the conversation continued, Pelet suggested that if he truly wished to quit the army and "to end his command with a blow worthy of him, he must crush the enemy, save the fortress, assure the safety of the army, and then go."

Apparently many of the officers thought Pelet had drowned or been murdered on his trip to Paris. Solignac did not believe that he was back and promoted until he saw him. "These two epaulets produced an excellent effect on everyone as a shining example of the satisfaction with the course of events in which I had taken part," recalled Pelet. After visiting all the officers whom Napoleon had mentioned, flattering "their desires, feelings, and passions," he wrote confidently, "I believe I succeeded in restoring a little spirit in the army."

Soon after Pelet arrived, Masséna and the other officers of the *état major* briefed him on the condition of the army and the events that had occurred during his absence. It was obvious that Ney had been correct in his objection to the march on the Tagus. Masséna's army had been overtaken by Wellington at Sabugal on March 28 and had suffered almost eight hundred casualties. Thus, as Ney had insisted, Masséna could only withdraw to the fortresses. As a result Wellington's army had blockaded Almeida and taken up positions along the Portuguese frontier. Masséna now decided to advance against the Allied army as soon as possible in order to relieve the French garrison; Pelet therefore assumed his old duties and began drawing up plans for the new operation.[7] On May 3–5 the armies of Masséna and Wellington were again locked in battle around the little village of Fuentes de Oñoro. Despite the valiant efforts of the French soldiers, they failed to wrest the village from the determined Anglo-Portuguese army and were forced to fall back on Ciudad Rodrigo. Moreover, the French sustained 2,665 casualties while Wellington's losses totaled 1,804 men.[8]

7. For details of the advance into Portugal and the orders for the battle of Fuentes de Oñoro, see "Ordres généraux," May 2, 3, and "Dispositions générales," May 4, drawn up by Pelet, both in Correspondance: Armée de Portugal, Carton C[7] 12.

8. The French lost 2,665 men and the Allies 1,871, according to Koch. Oman maintained that the French losses were 2,844 and the Allied losses were 1,804 men. See Koch, *Mémoires de Masséna,* VII, 545; Oman, *Peninsular War,* IV, 622–24,

Meanwhile General Foy returned to the army from Paris with "important dispatches" for Masséna, Bessières, and Marmont. Reaching the French headquarters at Ciudad Rodrigo on May 10, he found Masséna's exhausted army recovering from their exertions at Fuentes de Oñoro.[9] Foy reported to the Prince and delivered his dispatches. Masséna was not surprised at the contents of Berthier's letter, which announced, "The Emperor, Monsieur le maréchal Prince d'Essling, has judged it proper to give the command of his army to M. le maréchal Duc de Raguse [Marmont]. The intention of His Majesty is that immediately after you have relinquished your command, you should return to Paris." Berthier added, "The Emperor expressly ordered that you should bring your son home and one of your aides-de-camp. Colonel Pelet, all your other aides-de-camp, and all the officers of the *état major* are obliged to remain with M. le Duc de Raguse."[10] Pelet nevertheless resolved to accompany Masséna and his son back to Paris despite the Emperor's specific orders.[11] Although Pelet ran the risk of incurring the Emperor's disfavor because of his willful disobedience, Napoleon must have admired his loyalty, for in July 1811 he made him a Chevalier of the Empire.

Masséna was not so fortunate. Napoleon refused to receive him for several months after his return to France. He did not assume a new command until 1813, when he was appointed governor of the eighth military district at Toulon, and the Marshal never again commanded a French army. During the Hundred Days, Masséna finally cast his lot with Napoleon, a decision which earned him the enmity of the Bourbons. He was relieved of his military duties in 1816 and died the following year from complication of those maladies which had been aggravated by the rigors of the Portuguese campaign.

Although the French campaign in Portugal led to the demise of Masséna's illustrious military reputation and had a disastrous effect upon the Napoleonic Empire, it nevertheless achieved notable success during its early stages. Obviously, the campaign as a whole gave neither Masséna nor his army an opportunity to demonstrate their

630. For details of the battle, see Jean Sarramon, "Campagne de Fuentes de Oñoro 15 avril–11 mai 1811," in *Carnet de la Sabretache,* CDXXV (1962), 1–88.

9. Girod de l'Ain, *Foy,* 142–44.

10. Koch, *Mémoires de Masséna,* Berthier to Masséna, n.d., VII, 558.

11. Bessières to Berthier, May 12, 1811, Correspondance: Armée de Portugal, Carton $C^7$12.

abilities, but it cannot be denied that the Army of Portugal captured two fortresses, marched more than 250 miles through an abandoned and devastated country, and in less than four weeks had fought Wellington at Bussaco and pursued him to within 19 miles of Lisbon. At this point Masséna was on the threshold of success; only reinforcements and supplies were needed to complete the conquest of Portugal. Unfortunately, Napoleon seemed to lose interest in and perspective on the campaign when Masséna did not achieve the lightning success he had expected. With its requests disregarded by an apparently indifferent government, Masséna's army then languished month after month, waiting for the promised men and arms.

It is a tribute to the army that, as preparations were being completed for the retreat, one of its number could write, "In the middle of this suffering and privation, far from France, facing an enemy that refused to fight, the army remained calm and patient. It was great in its courage, it was sublime in its resignation, and finally it acquired an incontestable right to the admiration of its fellow citizens. The morale of our soldiers, the elite of which France is so proud, was not dampened."[12] Nevertheless, the ramifications of the French failure in Portugal were monumental. If Wellington's army had been driven into the sea in 1810, Spanish resistance would have diminished and the history of the Empire would probably have been vastly different. It was only after Masséna's reverse in Portugal that Wellington mounted his sustained drive to expel the French from the Peninsula. This was accomplished in October 1813 when the triumphant Allied army crossed the Bidassoa River and invaded France, while Napoleon sought to defend his capital from the invading armies of the Sixth Coalition.

In the meantime Pelet, back in Paris, soon became involved in preparations for the campaign in Russia. Three months before the invasion actually began, General Marchand, the chief of staff for the right wing of the Grand Army, requested that Pelet be attached to his staff. No doubt he recalled Pelet's role in the Portuguese campaign.[13] Napoleon's army crossed the Niemen River on June 24, 1812, and less than two months later Pelet was fighting in the suburbs of Smolensk. With Davout's corps at Borodino he took an active part in the bloody

12. Fririon, *Journal historique*, p. 134.

13. On Pelet's appointment, see Dossier 1096 (Baron Pelet, général de division), located at the Service historique de l'armée at Vincennes.

battle for that village. As a result of his efforts during the invasion, especially at Borodino, Pelet was given command of the 48th Line in General Étienne Ricard's division of Davout's corps. It was only a week later, on October 18, that the French began their retreat and Pelet marched out of Moscow along the Moscow-Kaluga road. Ricard's division was left before Smolensk to serve as a link with the rear guard of the Grand Army, commanded by Ney, while the rest of the French corps hurried toward Orsha.

Ney's rear guard joined Ricard's division and the two forces advanced toward Krasnoi. Pelet was walking on foot at the head of his regiment when he became aware of the presence of troops ahead of him. "I thought we would find the French army at Krasnoi," he recalled.[14] However, as the fog lifted, "I was hit by some bullets that whizzed around my ears, followed by some shell." It was not Davout's corps but General Mikhail Miloradovich with the advance guard of the Russian army, twenty-four guns, and considerable cavalry which confronted the French rear guard. Pelet and the other regimental commanders formed their infantry and waited for Ney's troops to come up. When the Marshal arrived, the advance was sounded and 650 men of Pelet's 48th Line and the other troops of Ricard's division attacked. As the Russian artillery poured grape into the French lines, Pelet recollected, "the front of my column was riddled; my arm was shattered . . . I was hit on the right foot and a short time later I was hit by a third bullet in the left leg." Unable to break through the Russian army, the French fell back; Pelet's 48th Line lost 23 officers and 527 men. At this point Ney and Pelet again met. The Marshal asked Pelet to join him at his headquarters, where they discussed their critical predicament at length. Pelet proposed crossing the Dnieper River on the ice at night, but Ney wanted to March toward Mohilew. After some debate Ney finally agreed to adopt Pelet's plan. Pelet recalled this as "the most beautiful moment of my life, wounded as I was in body and soul."[15] Accordingly, the remnants of the French column retired along

14. For Pelet's own account of the retreat from Russia and the battle of Krasnoi, see "Le combat de Krasnoë et la retraite de Ney sur le Dnieper," ed. A. d'Avout, *Carnet de la Sabretache*, XV (1906), 519–52, 626–40, 683–702.

15. Pelet was disappointed that he did not receive any recognition for his plan which made possible the escape of the rear guard from Krasnoi. He wrote bitterly in his notebook, "He [Ney] received the title of Prince de la Moskowa, certainly for this maneuver in the retreat which was his finest action; I remained a colonel. I

the Smolensk road and followed the bank of the Dnieper to Shirokorenyay. At dawn on the morning of November 19 Ney's battered column filed across the frozen Dnieper. Two days later Napoleon was gratified to learn of Ney's extraordinary escape, although only 900 men remained of the rear guard.

After Pelet had returned to France and recovered from his wounds, he was promoted to general of brigade. During 1813 he served with Marmont's 6th Corps, in General François Rouget's 4th division of the Young Guard, and finally as commander of the second brigade in General Pierre Decouz's division of the Young Guard.[16] Pelet took part in the fighting at Dresden and Leipzig, and when Decouz was killed at Brienne on January 29, 1814, he assumed provisional command of the division. Three days later he led it into battle at Rothière. During the first ten days of February, Pelet commanded his division at the bridge of Lesmont, at Champaubert, and at Montmirial. Reassigned to a brigade of *Chasseurs à pied* in General Louis Friant's division, Pelet served at Vauchamps on February 14 and four days later at Montereau. He survived the battles of Cambronne, Craonne, Laon, Rheims, and Arcis-sur-Aube in March. However, after Napoleon's abdication the following month he found himself in the Royal Chasseurs and a Chevalier of the Order of Saint Louis.[17]

When Napoleon returned from Elba in February 1815, Pelet rallied to the imperial eagles. He was appointed a major of the *Chasseurs à pied* in the most illustrious unit of the army—the Old Guard—and was given command of some 1,100 men of the 2nd Chasseurs in General Charles Morand's division. By June 8 Pelet and his chasseurs were marching northward through Compiègne toward the Belgian frontier. On June 15 the French army crossed the Sambre, and at Ligny the following day the bayonets of Pelet's chasseurs helped to turn back the Prussian attacks of Marshal Gebhard Blücher.

On June 18, while French artillery and infantry assaulted the Allied position before Waterloo at Mont Sainte Jean, Pelet's chasseurs were held in reserve. But with the arrival of the Prussians at Plancenoit,

then wrote and told him that I would not forget *the honor that I had in cooperating there.*" See Pelet's "Combat de Krasnoë," XV, 627, 636.

16. Pelet wrote twelve articles on this campaign. Entitled "Des Principales opérations de la campagne de 1813," they were published in the first three volumes of *Le Spectateur militaire*, 1826–1827.

17. Dossier 1096 (Baron Pelet, général de division).

Pelet was ordered by Morand to "take your first battalion to Plancenoit, where the Young Guard is in disorder. Support it, sustain that position."[18] "After a terrible but rather short struggle, the village, gardens, and orchards were recaptured" by Pelet's chasseurs.[19] As the Prussians attacked and counterattacked to regain Plancenoit, Pelet recalled, "I came, I went, I had the 'charge' beat, then the 'rally' and the 'rotation.' " Finally, "at the moment I was most threatened, most pressed, and even destitute, a platoon of grenadiers arrived. . . . I halted it in order to rally some chasseurs. Then I ordered a bayonet charge without firing a single gunshot; they went as a wall and overthrew everything." When the Prussians reinforced their skirmishers, Pelet recounted, "I maintained myself amid the hail of shells, the fires that began to burn in the various houses, the terrible and continuous fusillade, and the multitude of skirmishers with which they surrounded us. . . . I was no longer able to unite my men but they were all under cover pouring a constant and murderous fire on the enemy."[20] With the arrival of the main Prussian army, the French army collapsed. Pelet collected some 250 of his chasseurs and began to retire, pursued by eager Prussian cavalrymen who sought to capture their eagle.[21] Although the Prussians called up artillery, Pelet and his men successfully reached the main line of retreat, saving "the Eagle and the honor of the Regiment."[22]

When Louis XVIII returned to Paris in July 1815 with the baggage of the Allied army, Pelet, at thirty-seven, found himself on half pay. After three years of inactivity, he was appointed to a commission for the Defense of the Kingdom and attached to the *Corps royal d'état major* through the efforts of Marshal Gouvion Saint-Cyr. Pelet reverted to inactive status again in 1821 and was not restored to the active list until 1830. During the reactionary years of Charles X's reign, he

18. For Pelet's account of Waterloo, see "L'infantrie de la garde à Waterloo," ed. A. d'Avout, *Carnet de la Sabretache,* XIV (1905), 33–54, 107–28.

19. Jean B. Charras, *Histoire de la Campagne de 1815: Waterloo* (5th ed., Basel, 1863), I, 318.

20. Pelet, "L'infantrie de la garde à Waterloo," XIV, pp. 42–43.

21. Pelet's two battalions of the 2nd *Chasseurs à Pied* included 32 officers and 1,131 men at Waterloo. See Hippolyte de Mauduit, *Les derniers jours de la grande armée ou souvenirs, documens et correspondance inédite de Napoléon en 1814 et 1815* (Paris, 1847), "Table général de l'armée du Nord," pp. 476–494.

22. William Siborne, *The Waterloo Campaign, 1815* (4th ed., Birmingham, 1894), p. 579.

worked diligently in the archives at the *Dépôt de la guerre.* By 1826 his four-volume *Mémoires sur la guerre de 1809, en Allemagne* had been published in Paris, and in the next two years he wrote a series of twelve articles entitled "Des Principales operations de la campagne de 1813" which appeared in the *Le Spectateur militaire.* In 1827 an article entitled "Coup-d'oeil militaire sur le Portugal" was published in the same journal.

With the overthrow of the Bourbons in July 1830, Pelet, like many others who had served in the armies of Napoleon, found favor with the new government of Louis Philippe. Soult, now minister of war, appointed Pelet as director of the *Dépôt de la guerre* as well as director of the *École d'état major.* In addition he was promoted to the rank of lieutenant general and elected to the French Assembly.

Although Pelet participated in the French expedition to Belgium in 1832 and was later given command of the 2nd infantry division on the Meuse, he was anxious to return to his research and studies. In 1835 he began the publication of the maps of the *état major.* In the same year his voluminous eleven-volume work on the War of Spanish Succession was begun; this series, *Mémoires militaires relatifs à la succession d'Espagne sous Louis XIV,* was to consume the next fifteen years of his life. Indeed, the year 1835 was an eventful one, for in July Pelet was gravely wounded during an assassination attempt on the life of the king by Giuseppi Fieschi. He became a peer of France in 1837 and four years later assumed the presidency of the Consultative Committee of the *état major.* In 1849, the year after Louis Napoleon's election as president of the Second Republic, Pelet was sent to Sardinia on a secret mission to advise King Charles Albert in his war against Austria. Pelet was elected to the Legislative Assembly in 1850, and after Louis Napoleon's coup d'état of December 1851 he was appointed to the Senate and later to the French *Académie des Science morales et politiques.* During and after the Crimean War, Napoleon III continued to consult Pelet, whose intellectual and physical faculties remained active until his death. On December 20, 1858, at the age of eighty-two, Jean Jacques Pelet died with his greatest ambition—to receive a marshal's baton—unfulfilled despite his effective and faithful service to his country.

The life of Jean Jacques Pelet spanned the political upheavals of France during one of its most critical periods; he lived under two republics, two empires, and the reigns of four monarchs. As a soldier, he served France effectively and loyally for more than half a century. He marched with several of the most illustrious marshals of the Empire, including Masséna, Marmont, Davout, and Ney, as well as Napoleon himself; he took part in many of the most memorable campaigns fought by Frenchmen, and fortunately he lived to record those campaigns for posterity. By the end of his life, he was a living chronicle of France's greatest times; he had become a link between the great age of Napoleon and the bourgeois-minded France of the 1850s. As director of the *Dépôt de la guerre* and the *École d'état major* after 1830, he exerted an extensive influence on the French military. But perhaps his most important role was in 1810, when he marched into Portugal as a lowly *chef de bataillon* and Masséna's first aide-de-camp.

Appendix

APPENDIX

COMPLEMENT OF THE ARMY OF PORTUGAL[1]

September 15, 1810

Commander in Chief, Marshal André Masséna,
Duc de Rivoli, Prince d'Essling
Commander of Artillery, General Jean Baptiste Éblé
Commander of Engineers, General Joseph Félix Lazowski
Chief of Staff, General François Nicolas Fririon
Quartermaster General, Jean François Lambert

THE 2nd CORPS

Commander in Chief, General Jean Louis Reynier
Commander of Artillery, General Louis Tirlet
Commander of Engineers, *Chef de bataillon* Brulley
Chief of Staff, Adjutant Commander Bardot

	OFFICERS	MEN	HORSES
FIRST INFANTRY DIVISION.			
General Pierre Hugues Merle			
First Brigade.			
General Jacques Thomas Sarrut			
2nd Léger. Colonel Merle			
(1st, 2nd, 3rd, 4th battalions)	77	2,281	18
36th Line. Colonel Berlier			
(1st, 2nd, 3rd, 4th battalions)	82	1,994	35

1. The complement of the French army is based primarily upon the documents in the Archives Nationales cited in Oman, *Peninsular War*, III, 540–43; Fririon, *Journal historique*, pp. 59–69; and Koch, *Mémoires de Masséna*, VII, 568–71.

	OFFICERS	MEN	HORSES
Second Brigade.			
General Jean François Graindorge			
4th Léger. Colonel Desgraviers-Berthelot			
(1st, 2nd, 3rd, 4th battalions)	77	2,078	29
Division total	236	6,353	82
SECOND INFANTRY DIVISION.			
General Étienne Heudelet de Bierre			
First Brigade.			
General Maximilien Foy			
17th Léger. Colonel Beuret			
(1st, 2nd, 3rd battalions)	57	1,341	18
70th Line. Colonel Lavigne			
(1st, 2nd, 3rd, 4th battalions)	71	2,387	34
Second Brigade.			
General Pierre Louis Arnauld			
31st Léger. Colonel Meunier			
(1st, 2nd, 3rd, 4th battalions)	57	1,711	23
47th Line. Colonel Donnadieu			
(1st, 2nd, 3rd, 4th battalions)	76	2,387	39
Division total	261	7,826	114
LIGHT CAVALRY DIVISION.			
General Pierre Soult			
First Brigade			
1st Hussar. Major Chigny			
(1st, 2nd squadrons)	30	318	338
22nd Chasseurs. Colonel Desfossés			
(1st, 2nd, 4th squadrons)	28	276	341
Second Brigade			
Hanoverian Chasseurs. Major Siguye			
(1st, 2nd, 3rd, 4th squadrons)	21	324	312
8th Dragoons. Colonel Devaux			
(1st, 2nd squadrons)	23	274	287
Division total	102	1,192	1,269
ARTILLERY, ENGINEERS, TRAIN.			
Colonel Fontenay	25	1,554	1,225
ÉTAT MAJOR	66		
Corps total	690	16,925	2,690

THE 6th CORPS

Commander in Chief, Marshal Michel Ney, Duc d'Elchingen
Commander of Artillery, General Joseph Claude Charbonnel
Commander of Engineers, *Chef de bataillon* Couche
Chief of Staff, Adjutant Commander Bechet de Léocourt

	OFFICERS	MEN	HORSES
FIRST INFANTRY DIVISION.			
General Jean Gabriel Marchand			
First Brigade.			
General Antoine Louis Maucune			
6th Léger. Colonel Amy (1st, 2nd battalions)	42	1,436	
69th Line. Colonel Fririon (1st, 2nd, 3rd battalions)	56	1,661	
Second Brigade.			
General Pierre Louis Marcognet			
39th Line. Colonel Soyer (1st, 2nd, 3rd battalions)	58	1,628	
76th Line. Colonel Chemineau (1st, 2nd, 3rd battalions)	58	1,732	
Division total	214	6,457	
SECOND INFANTRY DIVISION.			
General Julien Augustin Mermet			
First Brigade.			
General Martial Bardet de Maison-Rouge			
25th Léger. Colonel De Conchy (1st, 2nd battalions)	37	1,678	
27th Line. Colonel Menne (1st, 2nd, 3rd battalions)	59	1,827	
Second Brigade.			
General Mathieu Delabassée			
50th Line. Colonel Frappard (1st, 2nd, 3rd battalions)	65	2,056	
59th Line. Colonel Coste (1st, 2nd, 3rd battalions)	60	1,834	
Division total	221	7,395	
THIRD INFANTRY DIVISION.			
General Louis Henri Loison			
First Brigade.			
General Édouard François Simon			
Légion du Medi. *Chef de bataillon* Spring (1st battalion)	18	546	9
Hanoverian Legion. Colonel Hermann (1st, 2nd battalions)	29	1,129	22
26th Line. Colonel Barrère (5th, 6th, 7th battalions)	64	1,561	24
Second Brigade.			
General Claude François Ferey			
32nd Léger. Colonel Martinel (2nd battalion)	20	393	10

	OFFICERS	MEN	HORSES
66th Line. Colonel Béchaud			
(4th, 5th, 6th battalions)	68	1,762	22
82nd Line. Colonel Rocheron			
(4th, 6th battalions)	40	1,196	24
Division total	239	6,587	111
LIGHT CAVALRY BRIGADE.			
General Auguste Étienne Lamotte			
3rd Hussars. Colonel Laferrière-Levesque			
(1st, 2nd, 3rd squadrons)			
15th Chasseurs. Colonel Mourier			
(1st, 2nd, 3rd squadrons)			
Brigade total	74	1,606	980
ARTILLERY, ENGINEERS, TRAIN.			
General Joseph Claude Charbonnel	28	1,403	1,723
ÉTAT MAJOR	82		
Corps total	858	23,448	2,814

THE 8th CORPS

Commander in Chief, General Jean Andoche Junot, Duc d'Abrantès
Commander of Artillery, General Louis François Foucher de Careil
Commander of Engineers, Colonel Valazé
Chief of Staff, General Pierre François Boyer

	OFFICERS	MEN	HORSES
FIRST INFANTRY DIVISION.			
General Bertrand Clauzel			
First Brigade.			
General Jean François Ménard			
19th Line. Colonel Fabry			
(4th battalion)	19	634	14
25th Line. *Chef de bataillon* Aberjoux			
(4th battalion)	16	571	12
28th Line. *Chef de bataillon* Bragairat			
(4th battalion)	17	442	12
34th Line. *Chef de bataillon* Gruet			
(4th battalion)	15	624	13
Second Brigade.			
General Eloi Taupin			
15th Léger. Colonel Saint-Faux			
(4th battalion)	21	813	11
46th Line. *Chef de bataillon* Vegier			
(4th battalion)	18	546	7

	OFFICERS	MEN	HORSES
75th Line. *Chef de bataillon* Servant			
(4th battalion)	19	532	9
Third Brigade.			
General Roch Godart			
22nd Line. *Chef de bataillon* Armand			
(1st, 2nd, 3rd, 4th battalions)	80	2,427	47
Division total	205	6,589	125
SECOND INFANTRY DIVISION.			
General Jean Baptiste Solignac			
First Brigade.			
General Pierre Guillaume Gratien			
15th Line. *Chef de bataillon* Fabre			
(1st, 2nd, 3rd battalions)	63	1,262	17
86th Line. *Chef de bataillon* Jounau			
(1st, 2nd, 3rd battalions)	55	1,090	13
Second Brigade.			
General Jean Guillaume Thomières			
65th Line. Colonel Coutard			
(1st, 2nd, 3rd, 4th battalions)	82	2,680	52
Irish Regiment. *Chef de bataillon* O'Meara			
(2nd, 3rd battalions)	37	971	14
Prussian Regiment. Colonel Aubier	29	957	18
Division total	266	6,960	114
CAVALRY BRIGADE.			
General Charles Marie Escorches de Saint Croix			
1st and 2nd Dragoons. *Chef d'escadron* Dubessy			
(3rd, 4th squadrons)			
4th and 9th Dragoons. *Chef d'escadron* Ludot			
(3rd, 4th squadrons)			
14th and 26th Dragoons. *Chef d'escadron* Mermet			
(3rd, 4th squadrons)			
Brigade total	92	1,771	1,663
ARTILLERY, ENGINEERS, TRAIN.			
General Louis François Foucher de Careil	17	964	1,409
ÉTAT MAJOR	75	0	168
Corps total	655	16,284	3,479

RESERVE CAVALRY CORPS

Commander, General Louis Pierre Montbrun
Chief of Staff, *Chef d'escadron* Martin

	OFFICERS	MEN	HORSES
First Brigade.			
General Jean Baptiste Lorcet			
3rd Dragoons. *Chef d'escadron* Labarbée (1st, 2nd, 3rd squadrons)			
6th Dragoons. Colonel Picquet (1st, 2nd, 3rd, 4th squadrons)			
Brigade total	52	1,040	1,249
Second Brigade.			
General Louis Joseph Cavrois			
11th Dragoons. Colonel Dejean (1st, 2nd, 3rd, 4th squadrons)	27	643	497
Third Brigade.			
General Charles Mathieu Gardanne (Ornano)			
15th Dragoons. Colonel Boudinhou (1st, 2nd, 3rd, 4th squadrons)			
25th Dragoons. Colonel Ornano (1st, 2nd, 3rd, 4th squadrons)			
Brigade total	57	1,369	1,304
Horse Artillery	6	294	237
Corps total	142	3,337	3,287

SPECIALIZED UNITS OF THE ARMY

	OFFICERS	MEN	HORSES
ARTILLERY, ENGINEERS, TRAIN.	54	2,311	668
GENDARMERIE.			
Chef de bataillon Beaudisson	6	171	200
ÉTAT MAJOR GÉNÉRAL	66	0	0
Army total	2,471	62,476	13,127

COMPLEMENT OF THE ANGLO-PORTUGUESE ARMY[2]

September 1810

Commander in Chief, Arthur Wellesley, Viscount Wellington

2. The complement of the Allied army is derived from Oman, *Peninsular War,* III, 544–48, and Fortescue, *History of the British Army,* VII, 508–10.

Commander of Artillery, Brigadier General Edward Howorth
Commander of Engineers, Lieutenant Colonel Richard Fletcher
Quartermaster General, Colonel George Murray

INFANTRY

	OFFICERS	MEN
FIRST INFANTRY DIVISION.		
Lieutenant General Brent Spencer		
Stopford's Brigade		
1st Coldstream Guards	24	790
1st Scots Fusilier Guards	26	791
60th Foot, 1 company of 5th battalion	2	51
Brigade total	52	1,632
Lord Blantyre's Brigade		
24th Foot, 2nd battalion	30	338
42nd Foot, 2nd battalion	23	391
61st Foot, 1st, 2nd battalions	36	648
60th Foot, 1 company of 5th battalion	3	47
Brigade total	92	1,424
Lowe's Brigade		
1st Line battalion, King's German Legion	28	510
2nd Line battalion, King's German Legion	31	453
5th Line battalion, King's German Legion	30	460
7th Line battalion, King's German Legion	24	429
Light battalions, King's German Legion (Detach.)	6	90
Brigade total	119	1,942
Pakenham's Brigade		
7th Foot, 1st battalion	26	843
79th Foot, 1st battalion	38	885
Brigade total	64	1,728
Division total	327	6,726
SECOND INFANTRY DIVISION.		
Major General Rowland Hill		
W. Stewart's Brigade		
3rd Foot, 1st battalion	32	826
31st Foot, 2nd battalion	27	384
48th Foot, 2nd battalion	27	454
66th Foot, 2nd battalion	30	433
60th Foot, 1 company of 5th battalion	1	33
Brigade total	117	2,130

	OFFICERS	MEN
Inglis's Brigade		
29th Foot	31	430
48th Foot, 1st battalion	32	519
57th Foot, 1st battalion	28	727
60th Foot, 1 company of 5th battalion	1	50
Brigade total	92	1,726
Catlin Crawfurd's (Wilson's) Brigade		
28th Foot, 2nd battalion	32	522
34th Foot, 2nd battalion	36	617
39th Foot, 2nd battalion	27	394
60th Foot, 1 company of 5th battalion	2	42
Brigade total	97	1,575
HAMILTON'S PORTUGUESE DIVISION attached to the Second Division:		
Archibald Campbell's Brigade		
4th Line Regiment (2 battalions)		1,164[3]
10th Line Regiment (2 battalions)		1,086
Brigade total		2,250
Fonseca's Brigade		
2nd Line Regiment (2 battalions)		1,317
14th Line Regiment (2 battalions)		1,373
Brigade total		2,690
Division total	306	10,371
THIRD INFANTRY DIVISION.		
Major General Thomas Picton		
Mackinnon's Brigade		
45th Foot, 1st battalion	35	560
74th Foot, 1st battalion	38	456
88th Foot, 1st battalion	40	679
Brigade total	113	1,695
Lightburne's Brigade		
5th Foot, 2nd battalion	31	464
83rd Foot, 2nd battalion	43	461
90th Foot, 5th battalion (3 companies)	16	145
Brigade total	90	1,070
Champlemond's (Harvey's) Portuguese Brigade		
9th Line Regiment (2 battalions)		1,234
21st Line Regiment (1 battalion)		541
Brigade total		1,775
Division total	203	4,540

3. The regimental rolls of the Portuguese army do not differentiate between officers and men; thus here and below separate figures cannot be given.

	OFFICERS	MEN
FOURTH INFANTRY DIVISION.		
Major General Lowry Cole		
Alexander Campbell's Brigade		
7th Foot, 2nd battalion	29	585
11th Foot, 1st battalion	42	920
53rd Foot, 2nd battalion	25	448
60th Foot, 1 company of 5th battalion	2	58
Brigade total	98	2,011
Kemmis's Brigade		
27th Foot, 3rd battalion	34	785
40th Foot, 1st battalion	48	1,007
97th Foot	27	493
60th Foot, 1 company of 5th battalion	4	50
Brigade total	113	2,335
Collins's Portuguese Brigade		
11th Line (2 battalions)		1,438
23rd Line (2 battalions)		1,405
Brigade total		2,843
Division total	211	7,189
FIFTH INFANTRY DIVISION.		
Major General James Leith		
Barnes's Brigade		
1st Foot, 3rd battalion	35	733
9th Foot, 1st battalion	30	585
38th Foot, 2nd battalion	29	467
Brigade total	94	1,785
Spry's Portuguese Brigade		
3rd Line (2 battalions)		1,134
15th Line (2 battalions)		905
Thomar Militia (attached)		580
Brigade total		2,619
Lusitanian Legion (3 battalions). Baron Eben		1,646
8th Line (2 battalions). Colonel Douglas		1,161
Total		2,807
Division total	94	7,211
LIGHT INFANTRY DIVISION.		
Brigadier General Robert Craufurd (Major General William Erskine)		
Beckwith's Brigade		
43rd Foot, 1st battalion	40	804
95th Foot, 1st battalion (4 companies)	12	384

	OFFICERS	MEN
3rd Portuguese Caçadores		656
Brigade total	52	1,844
Barclay's Brigade		
52nd Foot, 1st battalion	29	946
95th Foot, 1st battalion (4 companies)	12	358
1st Portuguese Caçadores		546
Brigade total	41	1,850
Division total	93	3,694
INDEPENDENT BRIGADES OF PORTUGUESE INFANTRY		
First Brigade.		
Brigadier General Denis Pack		
1st Line Regiment (2 battalions)		1,089
16th Line Regiment (2 battalions)		1,130
4th battalion Caçadores		550
Brigade total		2,769
Fifth Brigade.		
Brigadier General A. Campbell		
6th Line Regiment (2 battalions)		1,317
18th Line Regiment (2 battalions)		1,386
6th battalion Caçadores		546
Brigade total		3,249
Sixth Brigade.		
Brigadier General Coleman		
7th Line Regiment (2 battalions)		815
19th Line Regiment (2 battalions)		1,124
2nd battalion Caçadores		406
Brigade total		2,345
Independent Brigades total		8,363
LECOR'S PORTUGUESE DIVISION		
Bradford's Brigade		
12th Line Regiment (2 battalions)		1,277
13th Line Regiment (2 battalions)		1,078
5th battalion Caçadores		456
Division total		2,811

CAVALRY

BRITISH CAVALRY		
De Grey's Brigade		
3rd Dragoon Guards	18	392

	OFFICERS	MEN
4th Dragoons (4 squadrons)	29	391
Brigade total	47	783
Slade's Brigade		
1st Dragoons	20	513
14th Light Dragoons	17	417
Brigade total	37	930
Anson's Brigade		
16th Light Dragoons	23	440
1st Hussars, King's German Legion	19	420
Brigade total	42	860
Fane's Brigade		
13th Light Dragoons	29	401
British cavalry total	155	2,974
PORTUGUESE CAVALRY.		
Brigadier General Harry Fane		
1st Regiment		422
4th Regiment		451
7th Regiment		223
10th Regiment		354
Portuguese cavalry total		1,450

ARTILLERY

	GUNS	OFFICERS	MEN
BRITISH ARTILLERY			
Royal Horse Artillery		18	314
A Troop. Captain H. Ross	6		
I Troop. Captain R. Bull	6		
Royal Foot Artillery		37	663
6th Company, 7th battalion.			
Captain G. Thompson	6		
7th Company, 8th battalion.			
Captain R. Lawson	6		
GERMAN ARTILLERY			
King's German Legion Artillery		19	299
2nd Company.			
Captain C. von Rettberg	6		
4th Company.			
Captain A. Cleeves	6		
PORTUGUESE ARTILLERY			
1st Regiment. Major A. Dickson	12		330

	GUNS	OFFICERS	MEN
2nd Regiment. Major von Arentschildt ..	12		440
4th Regiment. Captain Antonio de Sousa	6		110
UNDETERMINED ARTILLERY			
? Regiment serving with Leith's 5th Division[4]	12		...
Artillery total	78	74	2,156

SPECIALIZED UNITS OF THE ARMY

	OFFICERS	MEN
ENGINEERS	24	19
TRAIN	25	397
STAFF CORPS	1	40
Total	50	456
Army total	1,513	57,941

4. It has been impossible to determine the identity of the artillery batteries serving with Leith's Fifth Division, but it is known that 4 pieces of six were sent from his division to guard the road from Gondolem to Carvalho. In addition several more of his guns were dispatched to reinforce Arendschildt's exhausted batteries at San Antonio de Cantaro. Thus the total complement of Wellington's army must have included several hundred additional men.

Glossary and Bibliography

GLOSSARY

Abatis. A military obstacle constructed a short distance from a fieldwork and made of large tree limbs or entire small trees placed side by side with the branches pointing toward the enemy.

Approaches. Trenches extending from the parallels and leading toward the point of attack. Because of the appearance of their construction, they are often referred to as zigzags, *cheminements,* or *boyaux.*

Artillery parc. Encampment for the artillery train, accouterments, and munitions not in immediate use. The term also refers to an artillery train attached to an army on campaign.

Balustrade. A parapet or low screen consisting of a coping rail supported on balusters.

Banquette. A small, raised bank of earth three or four feet wide, running along the inside of and four or five feet below the top of a parapet, on which men were posted to fire at the enemy.

Bastion. A projecting part of a fortification, consisting of two faces meeting at an angle; it was prolonged by two flanks set at angles to the faces. The flanks of two adjacent bastions of a parapet were connected by a straight section of wall called a curtain. The bastion was formed so that it could be well seen and defended everywhere by the flanking fire of other parts of the fortification.

Berm. A narrow ledge or path; specifically, in fortifications a shelf two or three feet wide constructed along the exterior slope of a parapet and designed to prevent the material of which it was composed from falling into the ditch below.

Breastwork. A parapet, perhaps four feet high, thrown up to protect soldiers from enemy fire.

Bridgehead. A fortification formed by a circle of closed works, houses, villages, etc., above and below a point where a bridge was to be established. Its function was to protect and defend the approaches to the bridge in the event of enemy attack.

Caponiere. A protected passage from the main fortress to an outwork, frequently ten to twelve feet wide and five feet deep, covered on each side by a parapet; it extended from a fortress curtain to the gorge of a detached work.

Casemate. A bombproof vault built under a parapet and usually designed to quarter cannoneers or the garrison.

Cavalier. A work, often horseshoe in shape; constructed within a bastion and raised ten or twelve feet above it to command a specific point.

Chasseurs à cheval. French light cavalry. *Chasseurs à pied* are light infantry.

Chef de bataillon. The commander of a battalion (up to 840 men). The English equivalent was roughly a major; however, in duties this rank corresponded more closely to that of a lieutenant colonel (nonexistent in Napoleon's army). Three battalions constituted a regiment (up to 2,520 men), commanded by a colonel. Each French regiment had a major but he was a staff officer and his duties centered on headquarters and the administration of the regiment.

Cornet. The third-ranking commissioned officer in a troop of horse or dragoons, subordinate to the captain and lieutenant and equivalent to an ensign in the infantry. His duty was to carry the standard in the front ranks of the squadron.

Counterscarp. The outer slope or side of a ditch or moat, usually faced (reveted) with masonry to make the besiegers' descent into the ditch difficult.

Covered way or *road.* An area up to thirty feet in width, between the counterscarp and the crest of the glacis, completely surrounding the fortress and its outworks.

Crenel. A narrow opening or embrasure in a parapet; crenels were interspersed with solid sections of parapet called merlons.

Curtain. The portion of a fortress wall between two adjacent bastions.

Demilune. A work, usually triangular in form, constructed to cover a curtain and the flanks of a bastion.

Detached work. A fortification so far beyond the main works that it could receive no direct support from the latter and needed to have a considerable degree of independence.

Ditch or *moat.* An excavation encircling the rampart of a fort. The term *moat* usually applied to a ditch filled with water. The two slopes or sides of the ditch were called the *escarp* and the *counterscarp.*

Earthwork. A temporary field fortification of various forms. The essential part consisted of sheltered trenches covered by a parapet and protected against enfilade fire.

Echelon. A formation of troops in which each unit was placed slightly to the left or right of the unit ahead of it.

Embrasure. An opening in a fortress parapet or an artillery emplacement through which the guns were fired.

Enceinte. The principal encircling wall of a fortified place, consisting of bastions, curtains, and the main ditch.

Enfilade. Fire directed from the flanks of a position so as to sweep the length of any line of works or troops.

Epaulement. A barricade of earth thrown up beside a battery to cover the troops behind it from the enfilade fire of an enemy.

Escarp. The slope or side of the ditch next to the rampart; faced with stones or bricks in permanent fortifications.

Esplanade. An uncluttered area of a fortified place set apart for drill and exercise.

Fascine. A bundle of twigs, small branches, or brushwood, tied together with rope; used in field fortifications as facing on the interior of a parapet or on the sides of embrasures.

Faussebraie. A lower wall erected several yards outside the main fortress wall; it provided shelter for firing against besiegers before they entered the ditch; however, once seized it provided cover for the enemy and afforded a ready means of scaling the walls.

Field fortifications or *fieldworks.* Temporary fortifications of various forms and styles, including open, closed, or half-closed earthenworks for the protection of more important works.

Flèche. A simple temporary fieldwork consisting of two faces forming a projecting angle and easily constructed for the defense of a position.

Flying column. A detachment of considerable strength, organized for rapidity of movement and usually composed of all arms, complete in equipment and supplies, independent of a fixed base.

Fourth battalion. Initially a unit that remained at the regimental depots, it provided reinforcements for the first three battalions serving in the field. Later these inexperienced battalions were indiscriminately collected into provisional brigades and sent to reinforce weakened divisions irrespective of where their first three battalions were serving.

Fraise. Rows of stakes ranged in an inclined position at chest height and directed toward the attackers.

Gabion. Hollow, cylindrical, bottomless baskets made of wickerwork or twigs and used in the construction of earthworks. When filled with earth, gabions formed a convenient facing in fieldworks, in the construction of batteries, and in the formation of trenches.

Gallery. A covered passage, sunk or cut into the earth and used for simple communication; also utilized to place a mine and blow up the counterscarp.

Gazonnement. Wedge-shaped pieces of fresh sod about a foot long and half a foot thick; used to cover ramparts, parapets, banquettes, etc.

Glacis. The downward slope of earth beyond a ditch or moat, gradually blending into the natural ground within a distance of 200 feet or less.

Grapeshot. A combination of small shot, from 1½ ounces to 4 pounds, tightly tied in a thick canvas bag to form a kind of cylinder adaptable to a cannon barrel.

Grenade. Hollow balls or shells of iron about 2½ inches in diameter charged with white powder. With a small fuse they were set afire by soldiers and thrown 20 or 30 yards.

Grenadiers. The tallest and strongest soldiers of the infantry regiment, formed into companies to serve on the right of a battalion or to lead an attack.

Honors of war. Any unusual privilege granted to an army that capitulated: retention of arms or standards, permission to march in military formation, etc.

Howitzer. A short mobile cannon used for indirect or high-angle fire at enemy positions behind cover. It differed from a mortar in that its trunnions were pivoted at the middle rather than at the base.

Léger. Light infantry regiment designed for inclusion in each infantry division.

Lunette. A fieldwork consisting of a simple salient with flanks; usually constructed to strengthen a ravelin or the wall of a fortress.

Merlon. See *Crenel.*

Mine. A subterranean passage carried forward from the lines of the besiegers to a point under the rampart of a fortification in order to blow it up.

Mortar. A short cannon with large bore made of cast iron or brass and mounted for high-angle fire, usually 45 to 70 degrees' elevation; particularly useful in throwing hollow shells containing combustible material.

Palisades. Rows of strong stakes, six or seven inches wide and eight or ten feet long, sharpened at the top. They were set vertically in the ground at a depth of three feet and intervals of three inches, parallel to the crest of the glacis, to secure it from surprise.

Parallel. Deep, wide trench roughly parallel to the front to be attacked. Generally two or three in number, they connected the several lines of attack.

Parapet. Usually a mound or walls of earth eighteen or twenty feet wide and raised six or seven feet above the crest of the rampart; it served to protect the troops from enemy fire.

Pavilion. A military construction forming the extremities of a battlement; also officers' quarters in a barracks or the location where the fortress colors were flying.

Picket. A small detachment of infantry or cavalry sent to form outposts. Pickets in turn sent out vedettes; they were expected to protect their forces from surprise.

Platform. A floor, usually of timber, on which cannon were placed; constructed behind an embrasure.

Pontoniers. Officers and soldiers attached to a unit responsible for the construction of temporary floating bridges over rivers.

Rampart. A broad embankment or wall of earth, generally faced with stone or brick, surrounding a fortified place and forming its main defense.

Ravelin. A detached work composed of two faces forming a salient angle and raised in front of the counterscarp.

Redans. A series of indentations in the wall of a fortress, flanking each other, and generally constructed in front of bastions.

Redoubt. A small work without bastions placed at some distance from a fortification to guard a vital position or obstruct the progress of the enemy. Redoubts usually had ditches, some means of giving flanking fire, and a significant garrison of soldiers.

Reverse. Literally, the back side or part of a trench, abutment, position, etc.

Revetment. An exterior wall or facing of stone or brick, supporting the front of a rampart on the side next to the ditch.

Ricochet. The trajectory of a projectile after striking, especially at a low angle. The smaller the angle of fall and the harder the surface struck, the greater the likelihood that a ricochet will occur.

Salient. The segment of a fortification, trench, etc., that protruded farthest toward the enemy.

Sap. A trench or an approach, ten or twelve feet broad, made under cover when the besiegers reached the fortress and the garrison's fire was heavily concentrated on the sappers.

Sapper. A soldier trained to work in the saps and given extra pay for this duty. A brigade of sappers included eight men working alternately in teams of four.

Talus. Similar to a berm; a ledge formed on the inside or outside of any slope to prevent the earth from falling into a ditch or other structure below.

Telegraph. A structure situated on a high hill and composed of a mast and yardarms from which balls were suspended. Varying arrangements of the balls indicated different letters or phrases to the next telegraph post.

Terreplein. The upper or horizontal surface of a rampart behind the parapet where the guns were located.

Tirailleur. Originally, a "bad shot"; later, a soldier who fired as he pleased, hence, a skirmisher or marksman. Utilized to distract the enemy or delay his advance.

Traverse. Generally, a parapet of earth built to cover a part of a fort against enfilade or reverse fire.

Vedette. A cavalry outpost; they were established on rising ground and along all avenues of approach to insure the safety of an encamped force.

Voltigeurs. Units composed of men of small stature formed into companies of infantry who served as skirmishers or marksmen; voltigeurs were also expected to ride behind the cavalrymen on their horses when necessary.

BIBLIOGRAPHY

Manuscripts

The most important and useful of the manuscript sources were the collections of the Service historique de l'armée at the Archives de la Guerre in the Chateau de Vincennes. More specifically, the writings of Pelet are scattered through the vast collection entitled "Mémoires historiques." In addition to the drafts of his "Campagne de Portugal" (917^{1-2}, 920^{1-2}, 921^{1-2}), the cartons entitled "Histoire de la campagne de Portugal, 1810–1812" (918^{2}), "Armée de Portugal" (919), and "Campagnes de 1689 à 1813" (901^{2}) include a limited number of Pelet's papers relative to the campaign. Another carton, "Guerre d'Espagne, 1808–1812" (916), contains his "Correspondance relative à la publication dans *Spectateur militaire* du Journal historique de la campagne de Portugal, par M. le Commandant Fririon, 1841."

A very valuable collection at Vincennes was the extensive "Correspondance: Armée de Portugal," which included five cartons (C^{7}8–12) of army, corps, and divisional correspondence. Other helpful documents included Pelet's service dossier, "Baron Pelet, général de division" (1096), and the service records of the various officers serving in the Army of Portugal. A source of primary material that became available to the author in the later stages of writing was the Archives de Masséna now located at the home of the 6th Prince d'Essling in Paris. Fourteen volumes of this collection (LI–LXIV) contain Masséna's extremely valuable letter registry and all the original correspondence from his generals during the Portuguese campaign.

In Portugal the holdings of the Academia de Ciências, especially the "Colleção da Academia das Sciências de Lisboa," and the "Papéis da diocese de Coimbra relativos as Invasoes Francesas" at the Arquivo da Universadide de Coimbra reflect the impact of the invasion upon the Portuguese government and people. In England, the Hill Papers in the British Museum (Add. MSS 35093) and the Stuart de Rothesay Papers in the Public Record Office (342/19–21) were helpful in determining aspects of the English involvement in Portugal.

Published Correspondence, Memoirs, Diaries

Abrantès, Laure Permon Junot, Duchesse d'. *Mémoires de Madame la Duchesse d'Abrantes ou souvenirs historique sur Napoleon, la Révolution, le Directoire, le Consulat, l'Empire et la Restauration.* 18 vols. Paris: Mame-Delauney, 1831–33.

Belmas, Jacques Vital. *Journaux des siéges faits ou soutenus par les français dans la péninsule, de 1807 à 1814.* 4 vols. Paris: Firmin Didot, 1836–37.

Bonaparte, Joseph. *Mémoires et Correspondance politique et militaire du Roi Joseph.* 10 vols. Ed. A. Du Casse. Paris: Perrotin, 1855.

Bonaparte, Napoleon. *The Confidential Correspondence of Napoleon Bonaparte with his Brother Joseph, sometime King of Spain.* 2 vols. London: John Murray, 1855.

———. *Correspondance de Napoléon 1er publiée par ordre de l'Empereur Napoléon III.* 32 vols. Paris: Imprimerie Impériale, 1858–69.

———. *Lettres inédites de Napoléon 1er (An VIII–1815).* Ed. Léon Lecestre. 2 vols. Paris: E. Plon, Nourrit, 1897.

Bonnal, Henri. *La vie militaire du maréchal Ney, duc d'Elchingen, prince de la Moskowa.* 3 vols. Paris: Chapelot, 1910–14.

Burgoyne, John. *Life and Correspondence of Field Marshal Sir John Burgoyne.* Ed. George Wrottesley. 2 vols. London: Richard Bentley, 1873.

Colomb, André. "Journal of André Colomb: Chevalier de la Legion d'Honneur (1809–1815). Ed. and trans. Donald D. Horward. *Journal of the Society for Army Historical Research,* XLVI, No. 185 (Spring 1968), 6–27.

Delagrave, Colonel André. *Mémoires du colonel Delagrave, Campagne du Portugal (1810–1811).* Ed. Édouard Gachot. Paris: Ch. Delagrave, 1902.

Dumouriez, Charles François. *État présent du royaume de Portugal en l'année 1766.* Lausanne: F. Grassett, 1775.

D'Urban, Benjamin. *The Peninsular Journal of Major General Sir Benjamin D'Urban, 1808–1817.* Ed. I. J. Rousseau. London: Longmans, Green, 1930.

Fririon, François Nicolas. *Journal historique de la campagne de Portugal, entreprise par les français, sous les ordre du maréchal Masséna, prince d'Essling, du 15 septembre 1810 au 2 mai 1811.* Paris: Leneveu, 1841.

Fusil-Fleury, Madame Louise. *L'Incendie de Moscou, la petite orpheline de Wilna, passage de la Bérésina, et retraite de Napoléon jusqu'à Wilna.* London: Schulze and Dean, 1817.

Godart, Roch. *Mémoires du général baron Roch Godart (1792–1815).* Paris: Ernest Flammarion, 1895.

Guingret, Captain. *Relation historique et militaire de la campagne de Portugal, sous le maréchal Masséna, prince d'Essling.* Limoges: Bargeas, 1817.

Halliday, Andrew. *Observations on the Present State of the Portuguese Army, as Organised by Lieutenant-General Sir William Carr Beresford.* London: John Murray, 1811.

Hulot, Jacques Louis. *Souvenirs militaires du baron Hulot, général d'artillerie, 1773–1843.* Paris: Spectateur militaire, 1886.

Jones, John T. *Journals of Sieges carried on by the Army under the Duke of Wellington, in Spain, during the years 1811 to 1814; with notes and additions; also Memoranda Relative to the Lines Thrown up to Cover Lisbon in 1810.* 3rd ed. London: John Weale, 1846.

———. *Memoranda Relative to the Lines Thrown up to Cover Lisbon in 1810.* London: C. Roworth, 1829.

———. *Mémoire sur les Lignes de Torrès Védras, élevées pour couvrir Lisbonne en 1810.* Paris: Anselin, 1832.

"Journal of a Soldier of the Seventy-first regiment from 1806 to 1815." In *Memorials of the Late War.* 2 vols. Edinburgh: Constable, 1828.

Kincaid, John. *Adventures in the Rifle Brigade and Random Shots of a Rifleman.* London: Macaren and Company, n.d.

———. *Random Shots from a Rifleman.* London: T. and W. Boone, 1847.

Koch, Jean Baptiste. *Mémoires de Masséna rédigés d'après les documents qu'il a*

laissés et sur ceux du dépot de la guerre et du dépot des fortifications. 7 vols. Paris: Paulin and Lechevalier, 1848–50.
Leach, Jonathan. *Rough Sketches of the Life of an Old Soldier* . . . London: Longman, Rees, Orme, Brown, and Green, 1831.
Leith-Hay, Andrew. *A Narrative of the Peninsular War.* 4th ed. London: John Hearns, 1850.
Lemonnier-Delafosse, Jean Baptiste. *Campagnes de 1810 à 1815 ou souvenirs militaires.* Le Havre: Alph. Lemale, 1850.
Londonderry, Charles William Vane, Marquess of. *Narrative of the Peninsular War from 1808 to 1813.* 2 vols. 3rd ed. London: Henry Colburn, 1829.
Marbot, Jean-Baptiste. *Mémoires du général baron de Marbot.* 3 vols. 5th ed. Paris: E. Plon, Nourrit, 1891.
———. *The Memoirs of Baron de Marbot.* Trans. A. J. Butler. 2 vols. London: Longmans, Green, 1892.
Moyle Sherer, G. *Recollections of the Peninsula.* London: Longman, Hurst, Rees, Orme, and Brown, 1823.
Napier, George T. *Passages in the Early Military Life of General Sir George T. Napier.* Ed. W. C. E. Napier. 2nd ed. London: John Murray, 1886.
Napier, William F. P. *History of the War in the Peninsula and in the South of France from A.D. 1807 to A.D. 1814.* 5 vols. New York: W. J. Widdleton, 1864.
Noel, Jean Nicolas Auguste. *Souvenirs militaires d'un officier du premier empire, 1795–1832.* Paris: Berger-Levrault, 1895.
Pelet, Jean Jacques. "Coup-D'Oeil Militaire sur le Portugal." *Le Spectateur militaire,* II (1827), 413–45.
———. "Des Principales operations de la campagne de 1813." *Le Spectateur militaire,* I–III, 1826–27.
———. "Le combat de Krasnoë et la retreate de Ney sur le Dnieper." Ed. A. d'Avout. *Carnet de la Sabretache,* XV (1906), 519ff.
———. "L'infantrie de la garde à Waterloo. Ed. A. d'Avout. *Carnet de la Sabretache,* XIV (1905), 33ff.
———. *Mémoires sur la guerre de 1809, en Allemagne.* 4 vols. Paris: Roret, 1824–26.
———. "Une mission auprès de l'Empereur Napoléon en 1811 pendant la campagne de Portugal." Ed. A. d'Avout. *Mémoires de la Société bourguignonne de géographie et d'histoire* (Dijon), XI (1895), 282–349.
Pérez de Herrasti, Andrés. *Relacion histórica y circunstanciada de los sucesos del sitio de la plaza de Ciudad Rodrigo en el año de 1810.* Madrid: Repullés, 1814.
Picton, Thomas. *Memoirs of Lieutenant General Sir Thomas Picton.* 2 vols. Ed. Heaton B. Robinson. London: Richard Bentley, 1836.
Pradt, Dominique Gorges Frédéric Dufour de. *Mémoires historiques sur la révolution d'Espagne.* 3rd ed. Paris: Rosa, 1817.
Rocca, Albert Jean de. *Mémoires sur la guerre des français en Espagne.* 2nd ed. Geneva: Jules-Guillaume Fick, 1887.
Santocildes, D. José Maria de. *Resumen histórico de los ataques, sitio y rendición de Astorga; de su reconquista y del segundo sitio puesto á la ciudad* . . . Madrid: Imprenta Real, 1815.
Simmons, George. *A British Rifleman: The Journals and Correspondence of Major George Simmons, Rifle Brigade, during the Peninsular War and the Campaign of Waterloo.* Ed. Willoughby Verner. London: A. C. Black, 1899.
Sprünglin, Emmanuel-Frédéric. "Souvenirs." *Revue Hispanique.* Paris: Klincksieck, 1904.
Thiébault, Paul Charles. *Mémoires du général Baron Thiébault.* 5 vols. 4th ed. Paris: E. Plon, Nourrit, 1895.

———. *The Memoirs of Baron Thiébault.* Trans. A. J. Butler. 2 vols. London: Smith, Elder, 1896.

———. *Relation de l'expédition du Portugal, faite en 1807 et 1808, par le Ier corps d'observation de la Gironde, devenu armée de Portugal.* Paris: Margimel, Anselin, and Pochard, 1817.

Tomkinson, William. *The Diary of a Cavalry Officer in the Peninsular and Waterloo Campaigns, 1809–1815.* Ed. James Tomkinson. London: Swan Sonnenschein, 1894.

Wellington, Arthur Wellesley, Duke of. *The Dispatches of Field Marshal the Duke of Wellington, during His Various Campaigns in India, Denmark, Portugal, Spain, the Low Countries, and France, from 1799 to 1818.* Ed. John Gurwood. 13 vols. London: John Murray, 1835–38. 8 vols. London: John Murray, 1852.

Wilson, Robert. *A Narrative of the Campaigns of the Loyal Lusitanian Legion, under Brigadier General Sir Robert Wilson . . . during the years 1809, 1810, and 1811.* London: T. Egerton, 1812.

Newspapers

The Times (London), April 8, 1811, No. 8264.

Le Moniteur (Paris), April 8, 1811, p. 352.

Secondary Sources

Atteridge, Andrew Hilliard. *The Bravest of the Brave, Michel Ney, Marshal of France, Duke of Elchingen, Prince of the Moskowa, 1769–1815.* New York: Brentano, 1912.

Chambers, George L. *Bussaco: Wellington's Battlefields Illustrated.* London: Swan Sonnenschein, 1910.

Charras, Jean B. *Histoire de la Campagne de 1815: Waterloo.* 5th ed. 2 vols. Basel: H. Georg, 1863.

Fletcher, Joseph Smith. *The History of the St. Leger Stakes, 1776–1901.* London: Hutchinson, 1902.

Fortescue, John W. *A History of the British Army.* 20 vols. London: Macmillan, 1910–30.

Gachot, Édouard. "Masséna en Portugal, 1810–1811." *Revue de la société des amis du musée de l'armée,* LXI (1958), 19–22.

Girod de l'Ain, Maurice. *Grands Artilleurs: Drouot, Senarmont, Éblé.* Paris: Berger-Levrault, 1895.

———. *Vie militaire du général Foy.* Paris: E. Plon, Nourrit, 1900.

Gómez de Arteche y Moro, D. José. *Guerra de la independencia: Historia Militar de España de 1808 à 1814.* 14 vols. Madrid: Credito Commercial, 1868–1903.

Guia de Portugal, "Beira Litoral." 3 vols. Lisbon: Fundação Calouste Gulbenkian, 1945.

Horward, Donald D. *The Battle of Bussaco: Masséna vs. Wellington.* Tallahassee: Florida State University, 1965.

———. "The French Invasion of Portugal, 1810–1811." Ann Arbor, Mich.: University Microfilms, 1962.

Luz Soriano, Simão José da. *Historia da guerra civil e do estabelecimento do governo parlamentar em Portugal, 1777–1834.* 19 vols. Lisbon: Imprensa Nacional, 1866–90.

Martinien, Aristide. *Tableaux par corps et par batailles des officiers tués et blessés pendant les guerres de l'empire (1805–1815).* Paris: Charles-Lavauzelle, 1899.

Marshall-Cornwall, James. *Marshal Massena.* London: Oxford University Press, 1965.

Mauduit, Hippolyte de. *Les dernier jours de la grande armée ou souvenirs, documens et correspondance inédite de Napoléon en 1814 et 1815.* Paris: Auteur, 1847.

Oman, Charles. *A History of the Peninsular War.* 7 vols. Oxford: Clarendon Press, 1902–30.

Parisot, Jacques T., *et al. Victoires, conquêtes, désastres, revers et guerres civiles des français, de 1792 à 1815.* 27 vols. Paris: Panchouke, 1817–22.

Sarramon, Jean. "Campagne de Fuentes de Oñoro 15 avril–11 mai 1811." *Carnet de la Sabretache,* CDXXV (1962), 1–88.

Siborne, William. *The Waterloo Campaign, 1815.* 4th ed. Birmingham: Edward Arber, 1894.

Thiers, Louis Adolphe. *History of the Consulate and the Empire of France under Napoleon.* Trans. D. F. Campbell and J. Stebbing. 12 vols. London: Chatto and Windus, 1894.

Tuetey, Louis. *Catalogue général des manuscrits des bibliothèques publiques de France: archives de la guerre.* 3 vols. Paris: E. Plon, Nourrit, 1912.

United States Board on Geographic Names. *Portugal and the Cape Verde Islands: Gazetteer No. 50.* Washington: U.S. Government Printing Office, 1961.

———. *Spain and Andorra. Gazetteer No. 51.* Washington: U.S. Government Printing Office, 1961.

Wyld, James, ed. *Maps and Plans of the Principal Movements, Battles, and Sieges in which the British Army was engaged during the War from 1808 to 1814 in the Spanish Peninsula and the South of France.* London: James Wyld, [1841].

Index

INDEX